CONTEMPORARY ISSUES IN CURRICULUM

FOURTH EDITION

ALLAN C. ORNSTEIN

St. John's University

EDWARD F. PAJAK

Johns Hopkins University

STACEY B. ORNSTEIN

New York University

PEARSON

Boston ■ New York ■ San Francisco
Mexico City ■ Montreal ■ Toronto ■ London ■ Madrid ■ Munich ■ Paris
Hong Kong ■ Singapore ■ Tokyo ■ Cape Town ■ Sydney

Series Editor: Kelly Villella Canton
Editorial Assistant: Angela Pickard
Executive Marketing Manager: Krista Clark
Production Editor: Gregory Erb
Editorial Production Service: Lifland et al., Bookmakers
Composition Buyer: Linda Cox
Manufacturing Buyer: Linda Morris
Electronic Composition: Omegatype Typography, Inc.
Interior Design: Omegatype Typography, Inc.
Cover Administrator: Linda Knowles

For related titles and support materials, visit our online catalog at www.ablongman.com.

Between the time website information is gathered and then published, it is not unusual for some sites to have closed. Also, the transcription of URLs can result in unintended typographical errors. The publisher would appreciate notification where these occur so that they may be corrected in subsequent editions.

Library of Congress Cataloging-in-Publication Data

Contemporary issues in curriculum / [edited by] Allan C. Ornstein, Edward F. Pajak,
   Stacey B. Ornstein. — 4th ed.
      p.   cm.
   Rev. ed. of: Contemporary issues in curriculum. 2003.
   Includes bibliographical references and index.
   ISBN 0-205-48925-7
   1. Education—United States—Curricula.   2. Curriculum planning—United States.   I.
Ornstein, Allan C.   II. Pajak, Edward, 1947–   III. Ornstein, Stacey B.

LB1570.C813   2007
375.001—dc22   2006044535

Printed in the United States of America

10   9   8   7   6   5   4   3   RRD-VA   10   09   08   07

CONTRIBUTORS

Benjamin S. Bloom, Emeritus, University of Chicago
Ronald S. Brandt, Association for Supervision and Curriculum Development
Ted Britton, WestEd's National Center for Improving Science Education
Evans Clinchy, Northeastern University
Linda Darling-Hammond, Stanford University
Tom Ganser, University of Wisconsin, Whitewater
Geneva Gay, University of Washington
Andrew Gitlin, University of Georgia
William Glasser, William Glasser Institute, California
Carl D. Glickman, Emeritus, University of Georgia
John Goodlad, Institute for Educational Inquiry
Maxine Greene, Emeritus, Teachers College, Columbia University
Thomas R. Guskey, University of Kentucky
Frederick M. Hess, American Enterprise Institute
Harold Hodgkinson, Center for Demographic Policy, Washington, D.C.
Lawrence Kohlberg, Emeritus, Harvard University
Alfie Kohn, Author and Lecturer on Education and Human Behavior
Frank Levy, Massachusetts Institute of Technology
Matthew Lipman, Montclair State College, New Jersey
Susan Loucks-Horsley, WestEd, Arizona
Todd I. Lubart, Yale University
Jane Roland Martin, Emeritus, University of Massachusetts
Frank Masci, Johns Hopkins University
Peter McLaren, University of California, Los Angeles
Richard J. Murnane, Harvard Graduate School of Education
Nel Noddings, Stanford University
Jeannie S. Oakes, University of California at Los Angeles
Allan Odden, University of Wisconsin, Madison
Allan C. Ornstein, St. John's University
Stacey B. Ornstein, New York University
Edward F. Pajak, Johns Hopkins University
Parker J. Palmer, American Association for Higher Education
David Perkins, Harvard Graduate School of Education
Richard Rothstein, Economic Policy Institute
James T. Sears, Author and Lecturer on Gay Studies and Curriculum
Thomas J. Sergiovanni, Trinity University
Lee S. Shulman, Stanford University
Nancy Faust Sizer, Francis W. Parker Charter School, Massachusetts
Theodore R. Sizer, Coalition of Essential Schools, California
Robert E. Slavin, Johns Hopkins University

Dennis Sparks, National Staff Development Council
Robert J. Sternberg, Yale University
Elaine Stotko, Johns Hopkins University
Don Tapscott, New Paradigm Learning Corporation, Ontario
Ralph W. Tyler, Center for Advanced Study in the Behavioral Sciences, California
Herbert J. Walberg, Emeritus, University of Illinois, Chicago
Harry K. Wong, Author and Lecturer on Teacher Success and Retention

Contents

PREFACE

This fourth edition of *Contemporary Issues in Curriculum* is a book for students study-ing curriculum, instruction, supervision, administration, and teacher education. It is a text written for those who are exploring the issues that have the potential to influence the implementation, planning, and evaluation of curriculum at all levels of learning. The articles reflect the emergent trends in the field of curriculum.

The book is divided into six parts: philosophy, teaching, learning, instruction, su-pervision, and policy. Each part consists of six or seven chapters and is preceded by an introduction that provides a brief overview of the articles and focuses the reader's atten-tion on the issues to be discussed. The introduction is immediately followed by a new feature—a professional profile of a prominent curriculum theorist. Each chapter begins with a set of focusing questions and ends with several discussion questions. A pro-con chart that explores views on both sides of a current controversial curricular concern and a case study problem appear at the end of each part. These instructional features help the reader integrate the content and issues of the book.

Most authors focus primarily on issues affecting the theoretical or practical applica-tions of curriculum and present the popularly accepted views in the field. Most authors focus on curriculum and teaching as they relate to the individual, society, and groups, or they emphasize philosophy, teaching, and trends found at various educational levels. We have tried to balance our discussion by focusing on six major areas that influence the field: philosophy, teaching, learning, instruction, supervision, and policy. To ensure that the breadth and depth of viewpoints in the field are represented, we have included articles that portray current trends and illustrate the dynamism within the field of curriculum. The readings present views that reflect traditionally held beliefs as well as other perspectives that might be considered more controversial in nature. Students and practitioners should have an opportunity to investigate the breadth of issues that are affecting curriculum and be able to access such information in a single source. Readers are encouraged to examine and debate these issues, formulate their own ideas regarding the issues affecting the field of curriculum, and decide what direction that field should take.

We acknowledge, with gratitude, the many authors who granted us permission to reprint their work. Allan Ornstein expresses love for Esther, his wife, and especially his children, Joel, Stacey, and Jason, and advises them to always take the high road in life. Edward Pajak thanks Diane, his wife, and their children, Alexandra and Zachary, for their encouragement and support. Stacey Ornstein dedicates this book to her family and thanks them for their continuous support in all her endeavors.

We thank the following reviewers for their helpful suggestions: Tim Duggan, Univer-sity of South Dakota, and Robert W. Seney, Mississippi University for Women.

PART ONE

Curriculum and Philosophy

How does philosophy influence the curriculum? To what extent does the curriculum reflect personal beliefs and societal ways? How do different conceptions of curriculum affect schooling and student achievement? In what way has curriculum been a catalyst in empowering certain segments of society while disenfranchising others?

In Chapter 1, Allan Ornstein considers how philosophy guides the organization of the curriculum. He explores how beliefs about the purposes of education are reflected in the subject matter and the process of teaching and learning. In the second chapter, Ronald Brandt and Ralph Tyler present a rationale for establishing educational goals. They identify the sources that they believe should be considered before articulating goals, as well as how goals should be used in planning learning activities.

In Chapter 3, Peter McLaren pays tribute to the memory of Paulo Freire, who was one of the first philosophers to write about education in terms of politics, globalism, and liberation. McLaren outlines Freire's life and teachings, his influence on North American critical theory, and his unique emphasis on the power of love. Next, Maxine Greene reminds us of the essential role that arts experiences play in helping students develop esthetic awareness. She explains why encounters with the arts are likely to enrich students' learning experiences. She also discusses why experience with the arts is critical to combating the delivery of prescriptive curricula and developing students' metacognitive strategies. In Chapter 5, Jane Roland Martin argues for a broad definition of cultural wealth and against equating education with schooling. She suggests that an artificially narrow conception of the purposes and functions of school has resulted in a false sense of security. Martin proposes a radical reconceptualization in which schools share the responsibility for passing on our rich cultural wealth with an array of institutions. In the last chapter in Part One, John Goodlad not only questions the effectiveness of attempts at educational reforms, but suggests that their introduction may be detrimental to school effectiveness. He compares the effect of reforms to the well-intentioned introduction of kudzu and rabbits into fragile ecosystems, where their out-of-control growth caused devastation.

PROFESSIONAL PROFILE: PHILOSOPHY

Name:
Henry A. Giroux

Email:
girouxh@mcmaster.ca

Latest degree/university:
Doctor of Arts, Carnegie-Mellon University,
College of Humanities and Social Sciences

Position:
Global TV Network Chair Professorship,
McMaster University, Hamilton, Ontario, Canada

Previous positions:
Assistant Professor, Boston University

Distinguished Professor of Education, Miami
University

Waterbury Chair Professor of Education, Penn State University

Person most influential in your career:
Paulo Freire. He brilliantly theorized the connection between critical education and social change and developed a comprehensive understanding of teaching as a political and
moral practice.

Number-one achievement:
Through my books and articles, I have consistently developed a theory of critical
pedagogy and the role it plays within educational theory as well as a range of other
disciplines.

Number-one regret:
Not having had the opportunity to meet Herbert Marcuse and Pierre Boudieu before
they died.

Favorite educational journal:
The *Boston University Journal of Education* between 1977 and 1995. It was a model
for rigorous scholarship and engaged commitment to crucial social issues. But more
importantly, it was courageous in addressing crucial educational and social issues, and it
spoke directly to teachers.

Favorite educational book:
Pedagogy of Freedom by Paulo Freire. In my estimation, this is the best book that Paulo
ever wrote, clearly elucidating his previous work and exhibiting the various directions
his scholarship took over the next twenty-five years. This is a book that should be read
by every student of education, as well as every student in any other discipline concerned
with the promise of an inclusive global democracy.

Best book/chapter you wrote:
My books have always been the product of different historical contexts and hence address different issues. On the question of youth, *The Abandoned Generation* is my best book. Regarding educational theory and practice, *Schooling and the Struggle for Public Life* is another important book. I also have to mention *Teachers as Intellectuals,* which dignifies teachers by suggesting that what they bring to the teaching act is a measure of insight and intelligence, as well as expertise in content.

Additional interests:
Music, films, and exercising, among others.

Curriculum/philosophy relationship:
Curriculum should always emerge out of a philosophical project and should be weighed against the principles that inform it. What is crucial to understand is that curriculum is not merely about the acquisition of skills, but is also a political and ethical project deeply concerned about matters of power, knowledge, values, and agency. For me, curriculum matters when it empowers students to become critical agents capable of understanding and engaging those forces that bear down on their lives as citizens and members of a larger global community.

Professional vision:
Schools should provide students with possibilities for linking knowledge and social responsibility to the imperatives of a substantive democracy. Education is not training. Learning at its best is connected to the imperatives of social responsibility and political agency. Public and higher education are vital democratic spheres necessary to develop and nourish the proper balance between public values and commercial power, between identities founded on democratic principles and identities steeped in forms of competitive, self-interested individualism. In part, this suggests that as educators we must begin to organize against the corporate takeover of schools, fight to protect the power of unions, expand the rights and benefits of staff personnel, and put more power into the hands of faculty and students. This points to the necessity for developing school practices that recognize how issues related to gender, class, race, and sexual orientation can be used as a resource for learning rather than being contained in schools through a systemic pattern of exclusion, punishment, and failure. Similarly, if curricular justice suggests that school knowledge be organized around the needs of the least advantaged, then school and classroom authority should rest in the hands of teachers and communities and not be under the control of "experts," imported from the business community or the world of for-profit schools.

Public schools don't need standardized curriculum and testing. On the contrary, they need curricular justice—forms of teaching that are inclusive, caring, respectful, and economically equitable and whose aim, in part, is to undermine those repressive modes of education that produce social hierarchies and legitimate inequality while simultaneously providing students with the knowledge and skills needed to become well-rounded critical actors and social agents.

Implicit in this argument is the assumption that the responsibilities of educators cannot be separated from the consequences of the knowledge they produce, the social relations they legitimate, and the ideologies they disseminate to students. Teaching in this sense highlights considerations of power, politics, and ethics fundamental to any form of teacher–student interaction. A *critical pedagogy* honors students' experiences by connecting what goes on in classrooms to their everyday lives. Within such an approach, knowledge is subjected to critical scrutiny and engagement, and pedagogy is seen as a moral and political practice crucial to the production of capacities and skills necessary for students to both shape and participate in public life. In this case, the school can be used as a strategic site for addressing social problems and helping students understand what it means to exercise rights and responsibilities as critical citizens actively engaged in forms of social learning that expand human capacities for compassion, empathy, and solidarity.

Professional advice to teacher or curriculum specialist:
Never separate learning from the precepts of social justice; recognize that schooling must be understood within a broader social and political context; never allow yourself to be reduced to simply a technician implementing educational recipes; always take seriously the knowledge and experience that students bring to school; heed John Dewey's advice about connecting the meaning of curriculum and schooling to the imperatives of a substantive democracy; and never lose sight of how crucial education is for sustaining democracy and keeping justice alive.

Philosophy as a Basis for Curriculum Decisions

ALLAN C. ORNSTEIN

FOCUSING QUESTIONS

1. How does philosophy guide the organization and implementation of curriculum?
2. What are the sources of knowledge that shape a person's philosophy of curriculum?
3. What are the sources of knowledge that shape your philosophical view of curriculum?
4. How do the aims, means, and ends of education differ?
5. What is the major philosophical issue that must be determined before we can define a philosophy of curriculum?
6. What are the four major educational philosophies that have influenced curriculum in the United States?
7. What is your philosophy of curriculum?

Philosophic issues always have had and still do have an impact on schools and society. Contemporary society and its schools are changing fundamentally and rapidly, much more so than in the past. There is a special urgency that dictates continuous appraisal and reappraisal of the role of schools, and calls for a philosophy of education. Without philosophy, educators are directionless in the whats and hows of organizing and implementing what we are trying to achieve. In short, our philosophy of education influences, and to a large extent determines, our educational decisions, choices, and alternatives.

PHILOSOPHY AND CURRICULUM

Philosophy provides educators, especially curriculum specialists, with a framework for organizing schools and classrooms. It helps them answer questions about what the school's purpose is, what subjects are of value, how students learn, and what methods and materials to use. Philosophy provides them with a framework for broad issues and tasks, such as determining the goals of education, subject content and its organization, the process of teaching and learning, and, in general, what experiences and activities to stress in schools and classrooms. It also provides educators with a basis for making such decisions as what workbooks, textbooks, or other cognitive and noncognitive activities to utilize and how to utilize them, what and how much homework to assign, how to test students and how to use the test results, and what courses or subject matter to emphasize.

The importance of philosophy in determining curriculum decisions is expressed well by the classic statement of Thomas Hopkins (1941): "Philosophy has entered into every important decision that has ever been made about curriculum and teaching in the past and will continue to be the basis of every important decision in the future. . . . There is rarely a moment in a school day when a teacher is not confronted with occasions where philosophy is a vital part of action."

Hopkins' statement reminds us of how important philosophy is to all aspects of curriculum decisions, whether it operates overtly or covertly. Indeed, almost all elements of curriculum are based on philosophy. As John Goodlad (1979b) points out, philosophy is the beginning point in curriculum decision making and is the basis for all subsequent decisions regarding curriculum. Philosophy becomes the criterion for determining the aims, means, and ends of curriculum. The aims are statements of value, based on philosophical beliefs; the means represent processes and methods, which reflect philosophical choices; and the ends connote the facts, concepts, and principles of the knowledge or behavior learned—what is felt to be important to learning.

Smith, Stanley, and Shores (1957) also put great emphasis on the role of philosophy in developing curriculum, asserting it is essential when formulating and justifying educational purposes, selecting and organizing knowledge, formulating basic procedures and activities, and dealing with verbal traps (what we see versus what is read). Curriculum theorists, they point out, often fail to recognize both how important philosophy is to developing curriculum and how it influences aspects of curriculum.

Philosophy and the Curriculum Specialist

The philosophy of curriculum specialists reflects their life experiences, common sense, social and economic background, education, and general beliefs about people. An individual's philosophy evolves and continues to evolve as long as there is personal growth, development, and learning from experience. Philosophy is a description, explanation, and evaluation of the world as seen from personal perspective, or through what some social scientists call "social lenses."

Curriculum specialists can turn to many sources of knowledge, but no matter how many sources they draw on or how many authorities they listen to, their decisions are shaped by all the experiences that have affected them and the social groups with which they identify. These decisions are based on values, attitudes, and beliefs that they have developed, involving their knowledge and interpretation of causes, events, and their consequences. Philosophy determines principles for guiding action.

No one can be totally objective in a cultural or social setting, but curriculum specialists can broaden their base of knowledge and experiences by trying to understand other people's sense of values and by analyzing problems from various perspectives. They can also try to modify their own critical analyses and points of view by learning from their experiences and those of others. Curriculum specialists who are unwilling to modify their points of view, or compromise philosophical positions when school officials or their colleagues espouse another philosophy, are at risk of causing conflict and disrupting the school. Ronald Doll (1986) puts it this way: "Conflict among curriculum planners occurs when persons . . . hold positions along a continuum of [different] beliefs and . . . persuasions." The conflict may become so intense that "curriculum study grinds to a halt." Most of the time, the differences can be reconciled "temporarily in deference to the demands of a temporary, immediate task." However, Doll further explains that "teachers and administrators who are clearly divided in philosophy can seldom work together in close proximity for long periods of time."

The more mature and understanding and the less personally threatened and ego-involved individuals are, the more capable they are of reexamining or modifying their philosophy, or at least of being willing to appreciate other points of view. It is important for curriculum specialists to regard their attitudes and beliefs as tentative—as subject to reexamination whenever facts or trends challenge them. Equally dangerous for curriculum specialists is the opposite—indecision or lack of any philosophy, which can be reflected in attempts to avoid commitment to a set of values. A measure of positive conviction is essential to prudent action. Having a personal philosophy that is tentative or subject to modification does not lead to lack of conviction or disorganized behavior. Curriculum specialists can arrive at their conclusions on the best evidence available, and they then can change when better evidence surfaces.

Philosophy as a Curriculum Source

The function of philosophy can be conceived as either the base for the starting point in curriculum development or an interdependent function of other functions in curriculum development. John Dewey (1916) represents the first school of thought by contending that "philosophy may . . . be defined as the general theory of education," and that "the business of philosophy is to provide [the framework] for the aims and methods" of schools. For Dewey, philosophy provides a generalized meaning to our lives and a way of thinking, "an explicit formulation of the . . . mental and moral attitudes in respect to the difficulties of contemporary social life." Philosophy is not only a starting point for schools; it is also crucial for all curriculum activities. For as Dewey adds, "Education is the laboratory in which philosophic distinctions become concrete and are tested."

Highly influenced by Dewey, Ralph Tyler's (1949) framework of curriculum includes philosophy as only one of five criteria commonly used for selecting educational purposes. The relationship between philosophy and the other criteria—studies of learners, studies of contemporary life, suggestions from subject specialists, and the psychology of learning—is the basis for determining the school's purposes. Although philosophy is not the starting point in Tyler's curriculum, but rather interacts on an equal basis with the other criteria, he does seem to place more importance on philosophy for developing educational purposes. Tyler (1949) writes, "The educational and social philosophy to which the school is committed can serve as the first screen for developing the social program." He concludes that "philosophy attempts to define the nature of the good life and a good society," and that the "educational philosophies in a democratic society are likely to emphasize strongly democratic values in schools."

There can be no serious discussion about philosophy until we embrace the question of what is education. When we agree on what education is, we can ask what the school's purpose is. We can then pursue philosophy, aims, and goals of curriculum. According to Goodlad (1979b), the school's first responsibility is to the social order, what he calls the "nation-state," but in our society the sense of individual growth and potential is paramount. This duality—society versus the individual—has been a major philosophical issue in Western society for centuries and was a very important issue

in Dewey's works. As Dewey (1916) claimed, we not only wish "to make [good] citizens and workers" but also ultimately want "to make human beings who will live life to the fullest."

The compromise of the duality between national allegiance and individual fulfillment is a noble aim that should guide all curriculum specialists—from the means to the ends. When many individuals grow and prosper, then society flourishes. The original question set forth by Goodlad can be answered: Education is growth and the focal point for the individual as well as society; it is a never-ending process of life, and the more refined the guiding philosophy the better the quality of the educational process.

In considering the influence of philosophic thought on curriculum, several classification schemes are possible; therefore, no superiority is claimed for the categories used in the tables here. The clusters of ideas are those that often evolve openly or unwittingly during curriculum planning.

Four major educational philosophies have influenced curriculum in the United States: Perennialism, Essentialism, Progressivism, and Reconstructionism. Table 1.1 provides an overview of these education philosophies and how they affect curriculum, instruction, and teaching. Teachers and administrators should compare the content of the categories with their own philosophical "lens" in terms of how they view curriculum and how other views of curriculum and related instructional and teaching issues may disagree.

Another way of interpreting philosophy and its effect on curriculum is to analyze philosophy in terms of polarity. The danger of this method is to simplify it in terms of a dichotomy, not to recognize that there are overlaps and shifts. Table 1.2 illustrates philosophy in terms of traditional and contemporary categories. The traditional philosophy, as shown, tends to overlap with Perennialism and Essentialism. Contemporary philosophy tends to coincide with Progressivism and Reconstructionism.

Table 1.2 shows that traditional philosophy focuses on the past, emphasizes fixed and absolute values, and glorifies our cultural heritage. Contemporary philosophy emphasizes the present and future and views events as changeable and relative; for the latter, nothing can be preserved

TABLE 1.1   Overview of Educational Philosophies

	Philosophical Base	Instructional Objective	Knowledge	Role of Teacher	Curriculum Focus	Related Curriculum Trends
Perennialism	Realism	To educate the rational person; to cultivate the intellect	Focus on past and permanent studies; mastery of facts and timeless knowledge	Teacher helps students think rationally; based on Socratic method and oral exposition; explicit teaching of traditional values	Classical subjects; literary analysis; constant curriculum	Great books; *Paideia* proposal
Essentialism	Idealism, Realism	To promote the intellectual growth of the individual; to educate the competent person	Essential skills and academic subjects; mastery of concepts and principles of subject matter	Teacher is authority in his or her field; explicit teaching of traditional values	Essential skills (three Rs) and essential subjects (English, arithmetic, science, history, and foreign language)	Back to basics; excellence in education
Progressivism	Pragmatism	To promote democratic, social living	Knowledge leads to growth and development; a living-learning process; focus on active and interesting learning	Teacher is a guide for problem solving and scientific inquiry	Based on students' interests; involves the application of human problems and affairs; interdisciplinary subject matter; activities and projects	Relevant curriculum; humanistic education; alternative and free schooling
Reconstructionism	Pragmatism	To improve and reconstruct society; education for change and social reform	Skills and subjects needed to identify and ameliorate problems of society; learning is active and concerned with contemporary and future society	Teacher serves as an agent of change and reform; acts as a project director and research leader; helps students become aware of problems confronting humankind	Emphasis on social sciences and social research methods; examination of social, economic, and political problems; focus on present and future trends as well as national and international issues	Equality of education; cultural pluralism; international education; futurism

Source: Allan C. Ornstein and Francis P. Hunkins, *Curriculum: Foundations, Principles, and Theory,* 3rd ed. (Boston: Allyn and Bacon, 1998), p. 56.

TABLE 1.2   Overview of Traditional and Contemporary Philosophies

Philosophical Consideration	Traditional Philosophy	Contemporary Philosophy
Educational philosophy	Perennialism, Essentialism	Progressivism, Reconstructionism
Direction in time	Superiority of past; education for preserving past	Education is growth; reconstruction of present experiences; changing society; concern for future and shaping it
Values	Fixed, absolute, objective, and/or universal	Changeable, subjective, and/or relative
Educational process	Education is viewed as instruction; mind is disciplined and filled with knowledge	Education is viewed as creative self-learning; active process in which learner reconstructs knowledge
Intellectual emphasis	To train or discipline the mind; emphasis on subject matter	To engage in problem-solving activities and social activities; emphasis on student interests and needs
Worth of subject matter	Subject matter for its own importance; certain subjects are better than others for training the mind	Subject matter is a medium for teaching skills, attitudes, and intellectual processes; all subjects have similar value for problem-solving activities
Curriculum content	Curriculum is composed of three Rs, as well as liberal studies or essential academic subjects	Curriculum is composed of three Rs, as well as skills and concepts in arts, sciences, and vocational studies
Learning	Emphasis on cognitive learning; learning is acquiring knowledge and/or competency in disciplines	Emphasis on whole child; learning is giving meaning to experiences and/or active involvement in reform
Grouping	Homogeneous grouping and teaching of students by ability	Heterogeneous grouping and integration of students by ability (as well as race, sex, and class)
Teacher	Teacher is an authority on subject matter; teacher plans activities; teacher supplies knowledge to student; teacher talks, dominates lesson; Socratic method	Teacher is a guide for inquiry and change agent; teacher and students plan activities; students learn on their own independent of the teacher; teacher-student dialogue; student initiates much of the discussion and activities
Social roles	Education involves direction, control, and restraint; group (family, community, church, nation, etc.) always comes first	Education involves individual expression; individual comes first
Citizenship	Cognitive and moral development leads to good citizenship	Personal and social development leads to good citizenship
Freedom and democracy	Acceptance of one's fate, conformity, and compliance with authority; knowledge and discipline prepare students for freedom	Emphasis on creativeness, nonconformity, and self-actualization; direct experiences in democratic living and political/social action prepare students for freedom
Excellence vs. equality	Excellence in education; education as far as human potential permits; academic rewards and jobs based on merit	Equality of education; education which permits more than one chance and more than an equal chance to disadvantaged groups; education and employment sectors consider unequal abilities of individuals and put some restraints on achieving individuals so that different outcomes and group scores, if any, are reduced
Society	Emphasis on group values; acceptance of norms of and roles in society; cooperative and conforming behavior; importance of society; individual restricted by custom and tradition of society	Emphasis on individual growth and development; belief in individual with ability to modify, even reconstruct, the social environment; independent and self-realizing, fully functioning behavior; importance of person; full opportunity to develop one's own potential

forever, for despite any attempt, change is inevitable. The traditionalists wish to train the mind, emphasize subject matter, and fill the learner with knowledge and information. Those who ascribe to contemporary philosophies are more concerned with problem solving and emphasize student interests and needs. Whereas subject matter is considered important for its own sake, according to traditionalists, certain subjects are more important than others. For contemporary educators, subject matter is considered a medium for teaching skills and attitudes, and most subjects have similar value. According to the traditionalists, the teacher is an authority in subject matter, who dominates the lesson with explanations and lectures. For the contemporary proponent, the teacher is a guide for learning, as well as an agent for change; students and teachers often are engaged in dialogue.

In terms of social issues and society, traditionalists view education as a means of providing direction, control, and restraint, while their counterparts focus on individual expression and freedom from authority. Citizenship is linked to cognitive development for the traditional educator, and it is linked to moral and social development for the contemporary educator. Knowledge and the disciplines prepare students for freedom, according to the traditional view, but it is direct experience in democratic living and political/social action which prepares students for freedom, according to the contemporary ideal. Traditionalists believe in excellence, and contemporary educators favor equality. The traditional view of education maintains that group values come first, where cooperative and conforming behaviors are important for the good of society. Contemporary educators assert that what is good for the individual should come first, and they believe in the individual modifying and perhaps reconstructing society.

The Curriculum Specialist at Work

Philosophy gives meaning to our decisions and actions. In the absence of a philosophy, educators are vulnerable to externally imposed prescriptions, to fads and frills, to authoritarian schemes, and to other "isms." Dewey (1916) was so convinced of the importance of philosophy that he viewed it as the all-encompassing aspect of the educational process—as necessary for "forming fundamental dispositions, intellectual and emotional, toward nature and fellow man." If this conclusion is accepted, it becomes evident that many aspects of a curriculum, if not most of the educational processes in school, are developed from a philosophy. Even if it is believed that Dewey's point is an overstatement, the pervasiveness of philosophy in determining views of reality, the values and knowledge that are worthwhile, and the decisions to be made about education and curriculum should still be recognized.

Very few schools adopt a single philosophy; in practice, most schools combine various philosophies. Moreover, the author's position is that no single philosophy, old or new, should serve as the exclusive guide for making decisions about schools or about the curriculum. All philosophical groups want the same things of education—that is, they wish to improve the educational process, to enhance the achievement of the learner, to produce better and more productive citizens, and to improve society. Because of their different views of reality, values, and knowledge, however, they find it difficult to agree on how to achieve these ends.

What we need to do, as curricularists, is to search for the middle ground, a highly elusive and abstract concept, in which there is no extreme emphasis on subject matter or student, cognitive development or sociopsychological development, excellence or equality. What we need is a prudent school philosophy, one that is politically and economically feasible, that serves the needs of students and society. Implicit in this view of education is that too much emphasis on any one philosophy may do harm and cause conflict. How much one philosophy is emphasized, under the guise of reform (or for whatever reason), is critical because no one society can give itself over to extreme "isms" or political views and still remain a democracy. The kind of society that evolves is in part reflected in the education system, which is influenced by the philosophy that is eventually defined and developed.

CONCLUSION

In the final analysis, curriculum specialists must understand that they are continuously faced with curriculum decisions, and that philosophy is important in determining these decisions. Unfortunately, few school people test their notions of curriculum against their school's statement of philosophy. According to Brandt and Tyler (1983), it is not uncommon to find teachers and administrators developing elaborate lists of behavioral objectives with little or no consideration to the overall philosophy of the school. Curriculum workers need to provide assistance in developing and designing school practices that coincide with the philosophy of the school and community. Teaching, learning, and curriculum are all interwoven in school practices and should reflect a school's and a community's philosophy.

REFERENCES

Brandt, R. S., & Tyler, R. W. (1983). "Goals and Objectives." In F. W. English, ed., *Fundamental Curriculum Decisions.* Alexandria, VA: Association for Supervision and Curriculum Development.

Dewey, J. (1916). *Democracy and Education.* New York: Macmillan, pp. 383–384.

Doll, R. C. (1986). *Curriculum Improvement: Decision-making and Process,* 6th ed. Boston: Allyn and Bacon, p. 30.

Goodlad, J. I. (1979a). *Curriculum Inquiry.* New York: McGraw-Hill.

Goodlad, J. I. (1979b). *What Schools Are For.* Bloomington, IN: Phi Delta Kappa Educational Foundation.

Goodlad, J. I. (1984). *A Place Called School.* New York: McGraw-Hill.

Hopkins, L. T. (1941). *Interaction: The Democratic Process.* Boston: D.C. Heath, pp. 198–200.

Smith, B. O., Stanley, W. O., & Shores, J. H. (1957). *Fundamentals of Curriculum Development,* rev. ed. New York: Worldbook.

Tyler, R. W. (1949). *Basic Principles of Curriculum and Instruction.* Chicago: University of Chicago Press, pp. 33–34.

DISCUSSION QUESTIONS

1. Which philosophical approach reflects your beliefs about (a) the school's purpose, (b) what subjects are of value, (c) how students learn, and (d) the process of teaching and learning?
2. What curriculum focus would the perennialists and essentialists recommend for our increasingly diverse school-age population?
3. What curriculum would the progressivists and reconstructionists select for a multicultural student population?
4. Should curriculum workers adopt a single philosophy to guide their practices? Why? Why not?
5. Which philosophy is most relevant to contemporary education? Why?

2

Goals and Objectives

RONALD S. BRANDT
RALPH W. TYLER

FOCUSING QUESTIONS

1. Why is it important to establish goals for student learning?
2. How do goals and objectives differ?
3. What are three types of goals?
4. What are the factors that should be considered in developing educational goals?
5. What is the relationship between goals and learning activities?
6. In what ways are curriculum goals integral to the process of evaluation?
7. What types of goals should be addressed by schools?

Whether planning for one classroom or many, curriculum developers must have a clear idea of what they expect students to learn. Establishing goals is an important and necessary step because there are many desirable things students could learn—more than schools have time to teach them—so schools should spend valuable instructional time only on high-priority learnings.

Another reason for clarifying goals is that schools must be able to resist pressures from various sources. Some of the things schools are asked to teach are untrue, would hinder students' development, or would help make them narrow, bigoted persons. Some would focus students' learning so narrowly it would reduce, rather than increase, their life options.

FORMS OF GOALS AND OBJECTIVES

Statements of intent appear in different forms, and words such as goals, objectives, aims, ends, outcomes, and purposes are often used interchangeably. Some people find it useful to think of goals as long-term aims to be achieved eventually and objectives as specific learning students are to acquire as a result of current instruction.

Planners in the Portland, Oregon, area schools say these distinctions are not clear enough to meet organizational planning requirements. They use "goal" to mean any desired outcome of a program, regardless of its specificity, and "objective" only in connection with *program change objectives,* which are defined as statements of intent to change program elements in specified ways. Doherty and Peters (1981) say this distinction avoids confusion and is consistent with the philosophy of "management by objectives."

They refer to three types of goals: instructional, support, and management. Educational goals are defined as learnings to be acquired; support goals as services to be rendered; and management goals as functions of management, such as planning, operating, and evaluating. Such a goal structure permits evaluation to focus on measures of learning acquired (educational outcomes), measures of quantity and quality of service delivery (support outcomes), and measures of quality and effectiveness of management functions (management outcomes).

The Tri-County Goal Development Project, which has published 14 volumes containing over 25,000 goal statements,[1] is concerned only with *educational goals*. For these collections, the following distinctions are made within the general category of "goals":

> *System level goals* (set for the school district by the board of education)
> *Program level goals* (set by curriculum personnel in each subject field)
> *Course level goals* (set by groups of teachers for each subject or unit of instruction)
> *Instructional level goals* (set by individual teachers for daily planning)

Examples of this outcome hierarchy are shown in Figure 2.1.

What distinguishes this system of terminology from others is its recognition that a learning outcome has the same essential character at all levels of planning (hence the appropriateness of a single term, goal, to describe it) and that the level of generality used to represent learning varies with the planning requirements at each level of school organization. The degree of generality chosen for planning at each level is, of course, a matter of judgment; there is no "correct" level but only a sense of appropriateness to purpose.

Teachers, curriculum specialists, and university consultants who write and review course goals use the following guidelines (Doherty & Peters, 1980, pp. 26–27):

1. Is the stated educational outcome potentially significant?
2. Does the goal begin with "The student knows . . ." if it is a knowledge goal and "The student is able to . . ." if it is a process goal?
3. Is the goal stated in language that is sufficiently clear, concise, and appropriate? (Can it be stated in simpler language and/or fewer words?)
4. Can learning experiences be thought of that would lead to the goal's achievement?
5. Do curricular options exist for the goal's achievement? (Methodology should not be a part of the learning outcome statement.)
6. Does the goal clearly contribute to the attainment of one or more of the program goals in its subject area?
7. Can the goal be identified with the approximate level of student development?
8. Can criteria for evaluating the goal be identified?

Curriculum developers need to decide the types and definitions of goals most useful to them and to users of their materials. Some authors advise avoiding vagueness by using highly specific language.[2] Mager (1962) and other writers insist that words denoting observable behaviors, such as "construct" and "identify," should be used in place of words like "understand" and "appreciate." Others reject this approach, claiming that behavioral objectives "are in no way adequate for conceptualizing most of our most cherished educational aspirations" (Eisner, 1979, p. 101). Unfortunately

---

System Goal: The student knows and is able to apply basic scientific and technological processes.

Program Goal: The student is able to use the conventional language, instruments, and operations of science.

Course Goal: The student is able to classify organisms according to their conventional taxonomic categories.

Instructional Goal: The student is able to correctly classify cuttings from the following trees as needle-leaf, hemlock, pine, spruce, fir, larch, cypress, redwood, and cedar.

FIGURE 2.1   Examples of Goals at Each Level of Planning

this dispute has developed into a debate about behavioral objectives rather than dialogue over the kinds of behavior appropriate for a humane and civilized person.

The debate is partly semantic and partly conceptual. To some persons the word "behavior" carries the meaning of an observable act, like the movement of the fingers in typing. To them, behavioral objectives refer only to overt behavior. Others use the term "behavior" to emphasize the active nature of the learner. They want to emphasize that learners are not passive receptacles but living, reasoning persons. In this sense behavior refers to all kinds of human reactions.

For example, a detailed set of "behavioral goals" was prepared by French and others (1957). Organized under the major headings of "self-realization," "face-to-face relationships," and "membership in large organizations," *Behavioral Goals of General Education in High School* includes aims such as "Shows growing ability to appreciate and apply good standards of performance and artistic principles." These are expanded by illustrative behaviors such as "Appreciates good workmanship and design in commercial products."

The other aspect of the debate over behavioral objectives arises from focusing on limited kinds of learning, such as training factory workers to perform specific tasks. The term "conditioning" is commonly used for the learning of behaviors initiated by clear stimuli and calling for automatic, fixed responses. Most driving behavior, for example, consists of conditioned responses to traffic lights, to the approach of other cars and pedestrians, and to the sensations a driver receives from the car's movements. Conditioning is a necessary and important type of learning.

In some situations, though, an automatic response is inappropriate. A more complex model of learning compatible with development of responsible persons in a changing society conceives of the learner as actively seeking meaning. This implies understanding and conscious pursuit of one's goals. The rewards of such learning include the satisfaction of coping with problems successfully.

Planning curriculum for self-directed learning requires goals that are not directly observable:

ways of thinking, understanding of concepts and principles, broadening and deepening of interests, changing of attitudes, developing satisfying emotional responses to aesthetic experiences, and the like.

Even these goals, however, should use terms with clearly defined meanings. Saying that a student should "understand the concept of freedom" is far too broad and ambiguous, both because the meaning of the term "concept" is not sufficiently agreed on among educators and because concept words such as "freedom" have too great a range of possible informational loadings to ensure similar interpretation from teacher to teacher. If used at all, such a statement would be at the program level and would require increasingly specific elaboration at the course and lesson plan levels.

Some educators find it useful to refer to a particular type of goal as a *competency*. Used in the early 1970s in connection with Oregon's effort to relate high school instruction to daily life (Oregon State Board, 1972), the term "minimum competency" has become identified with state and district testing programs designed to ensure that students have a minimum level of basic skills before being promoted or graduated. Spady (1978) and other advocates of performance-based education point out that competency involves more than "capacities" such as the ability to read and calculate; it should refer to *application* of school-learned skills in situations outside of school.

One definition of competency is the ability to perform a set of related tasks with a high degree of skill. The concept is especially useful in vocational education, where a particular competency can be broken down through task analysis into its component skills so that teachers and curriculum planners have both a broad statement of expected performance and an array of skills specific enough to be taught and measured (Chalupsky & others, 1981).

CONSIDERATIONS IN CHOOSING GOALS

Educational goals should reflect three important factors: the nature of organized knowledge, the nature of society, and the nature of learners (Tyler, 1949). An obvious source is the nature of organized fields of study. Schools teach music, chemistry, and algebra because these fields have been developed through centuries of painstaking inquiry. Each academic discipline has its own concepts, principles, and processes. It would be unthinkable to neglect passing on to future generations this priceless heritage and these tools for continued learning.

Another factor affecting school goals is the nature of society. For example, the goals of education in the United States are quite different from those in Russia. In the United States we stress individuality, competition, creativity, and freedom to choose government officials. Russian schools teach loyalty to the state and subordination of one's individuality to the welfare of the collective. One result is that most U.S. schools offer a great many electives, while the curriculum in Russian schools consists mostly of required subjects. For example, all students in Russia must study advanced mathematics and science to serve their technologically advanced nation (Wirszup, 1981).

U.S. schools have assumed, explicitly or implicitly, many goals related to the nature of society. For example, schools offer drug education, sex education, driver education, and other programs because of concerns about the values and behavior of youth and adults. Schools teach visual literacy because of the influence of television, consumer education because our economic system offers so many choices, and energy education because of the shortage of natural resources.

A goal statement by Ehrenberg and Ehrenberg (1978) specifically recognizes the expectations of society. Their model for curriculum development begins with a statement of "ends sought": "It is intended that as a result of participating in the K–12 educational program students will consistently and effectively take *intelligent, ethical action:* (1) to accomplish the tasks society legitimately expects of all its members, and (2) to establish and pursue worthwhile goals of their own choosing."

The curriculum development process outlined by the Ehrenbergs involves preparing a complete rationale for the ends-sought statement and then defining, for example, areas of societal expectations. The work of the curriculum developer consists of defining a framework of "criterion tasks," all either derived from expectations of society or necessary to pursue individual goals. These tasks, at various levels of pupil development, become the focus of day-to-day instruction. In this way, all curriculum is directly related to school system goals.

A third consideration in choosing goals, sometimes overlooked, is the nature of learners. For example, because Lawrence Kohlberg (1980) found that children pass through a series of stages in their moral development, he believes schools should adopt the goal of raising students' levels of moral reasoning. Sternberg (1981) and other "information processing" psychologists believe that intelligence is, partly at least, a set of strategies and skills that can be learned. Their research suggests, according to Sternberg, that schools can and should set a goal of improving students' intellectual performance.

Recognizing that students often have little interest in knowledge for its own sake or in adult applications of that knowledge, some educators believe goals not only should be based on what we know about students, but should come from students themselves. Many alternative schools emphasize this source of goals more than conventional schools typically do (Raywid, 1981).

While knowledge, society, and learners are all legitimate considerations, the three are sometimes in conflict. For example, many of the products of the curriculum reform movement of the 1960s had goals based almost exclusively on the nature of knowledge. The emphasis of curriculum developers was on the "structure of the disciplines" (Bruner, 1960). Goals of some curriculums failed to fully reflect the nature of society and students, so teachers either refused to use them or gave up after trying them for a year or two (Stake & Easley, 1978).

In the 1970s, educators and the general public reacted against this discipline-centered emphasis by stressing practical activities drawn from daily life. Schools were urged to teach students how to balance a checkbook, how to choose economical purchases, how to complete a job application, and how to read a traffic ticket. Career education enthusiasts, not content with the reasonable idea that

education should help prepare students for satisfying careers, claimed that *all* education should be
career-related in some way.

Conflicts of this sort between the academic
and the practical are persistent and unavoidable,
but curriculum developers err if they emphasize
only one source of goals and ignore the others. If
noneducators are preoccupied with only one factor, educational leaders have a responsibility to
stress the importance of the others and to insist
on balance.

SCOPE OF THE SCHOOL'S RESPONSIBILITY

There have been many attempts to define the general aims of schools and school programs, including the well-known Cardinal Principles listed by a
national commission in 1918. The seven goals in
that report—health, fundamental processes, worthy home membership, vocation, civic education,
worthy use of leisure, and ethical character—
encompass nearly every aspect of human existence, and most goal statements written since that
time have been equally comprehensive.

Some authors contend that schools are mistaken to assume such broad aims. Martin (1980)
argued that intellectual development and citizenship are the only goals for which schools should
have primary responsibility and that other institutions should be mainly responsible for such goals
as worthy home membership. He proposed that
schools undertake a new role of coordinating educational efforts of all community agencies.

Paul (1982) reported that in three different
communities large numbers of teachers, students,
and parents agreed on a limited set of goals confined mostly to basic skills. Paul contended that
schools often confuse the issue when involving
citizens in setting goals because they ask what students should learn rather than what schools should
teach. Goal surveys conducted by her organization
showed, she said, that adults want young people
to develop many qualities for which they do not
expect schools to be responsible.

Undeniably, the aims and activities of U.S.
schools are multiple and diverse. They not only
teach toothbrushing, crafts, religion, care of animals, advertising, cooking, automobile repair,
philosophy, hunting, and chess; they also provide

health and food services to children, conduct parent education classes, and offer a variety of programs for the elderly. Periodic review of these
obligations is clearly in order. However, in trying
to delimit their mission, schools must not minimize concern for qualities that, though hard to
define and develop, distinguish educated persons
from the less educated.

A carefully refined statement of goals of
schooling in the United States was developed by
Goodlad (1979) and his colleagues in connection
with their Study of Schooling. Deliberately derived
from an analysis of hundreds of goal statements
adopted by school districts and state departments
of education so as to reflect accurately the currently declared aims of U.S. education, the list
comprises 65 goals in 12 categories, including
"intellectual development," "self-concept," and
"moral and ethical character."

An equally broad set of goals is used in
Pennsylvania's Educational Quality Assessment,
which includes questions intended to measure
such elusive aims as "understanding others" and
"self-esteem." School districts must give the tests
at least once every five years as part of a plan to
make schools accountable for the 12 state-adopted
goals (Seiverling, 1980). An adaptation of the
Pennsylvania goals was used by the ASCD Committee on Research and Theory (1980) in connection with their plan for *Measuring and Attaining
the Goals of Education.*

In many cases, schools contribute modestly
or not at all to helping students become loving
parents and considerate neighbors. In other cases,
school experiences may have lasting effects on
values, attitudes, and behavior. We believe school
goals should include such aims as "interpersonal
relations" and "autonomy," as well as "intellectual
development" and "basic skills" (Goodlad, 1979),
although the goal statement should specifically
recognize that most goals are not the exclusive
domain of schools but are a shared responsibility
with other institutions.

ESTABLISHING LOCAL GOALS

It is usually helpful to begin identification of goals
by listing all the promising possibilities from various sources. Consider contemporary *society.* What

things could one's students learn that would help them meet current demands and take advantage of future opportunities? General data about modern society may be found in studies of economic, political, and social conditions. Data directly relevant to the lives of one's students will usually require local studies, which can be made by older students, parents, and other local people.

Consider the *background of the students:* their previous experiences, things they have already learned, their interests and needs—that is, the gaps between desired ways of thinking, feeling, and acting and their present ways. This information should be specific to one's own students, although generalized studies of the development of children and youth in our culture will suggest what to look for.

Consider the potential of the various *subject fields.* What things could one's students learn about their world and themselves from the sciences, history, literature, and so on? What can mathematics provide as a resource for their lives? Visual arts? Music? Each new generation is likely to find new possibilities in these growing fields of knowledge and human expression.

In the effort to identify possible goals, don't be unduly concerned about the form in which you state these "things to be learned." For example, you may find a possibility in "Learn new ways of expressing emotions through various experiences provided in literature," and another in "Understand how animal ecologies are disturbed and the consequences of the disturbance." These are in different forms and at different levels of generality, but at this stage the purpose is only to consider carefully all the promising possibilities. Later, those selected as most important and appropriate for one's students can be refined and restated in common form so as to guide curriculum developers in designing learning experiences. At that point, it will probably be helpful to standardize terms and definitions. At early stages, however, curriculum developers should use terminology familiar and understandable to teachers, principals, parents, and citizens rather than insisting on distinctions that others may have difficulty remembering and using.

The comprehensive list of possible outcomes should be carefully scrutinized to sift out those that appear to be of minor importance or in conflict with the school's educational philosophy. The list should also be examined in the light of the apparent prospects for one's students being able to learn these things in school. For example, we know that things once learned are usually forgotten unless there are continuing opportunities to use them. So one criterion for retaining a goal is that students will have opportunities in and out of school to think, feel, and act as expected. We also know that learning of habits requires continuous practice with few errors, so work and study habits should be selected as goals only if they are to be emphasized consistently in school work.

This procedure for identifying what students are to be helped to learn is designed to prevent a common weakness in curriculum development: selection of goals that are obsolete or irrelevant, inappropriate for students' current levels of development, not in keeping with sound scholarship, not in harmony with America's democratic philosophy, or for which the school cannot provide the necessary learning conditions.

A common practice when planning curriculum is to refer to published taxonomies (Bloom & others, 1956; Krathwohl & others, 1964). Taxonomies can be useful for their original purpose—classifying goals already formulated—but they do not resolve the issue of the relevance of any particular goal to contemporary society or to one's own students. The Bloom and Krathwohl taxonomies are organized in terms of what the authors conceive to be higher or lower levels, but higher ones are not always more important or even necessary. In typewriting, for example, so-called higher mental processes interfere with the speed and accuracy of typing.

A similar caution applies to uncritically taking goals from curriculum materials of other school systems. The fact that educators in Scarsdale or some other district chose certain goals is not in itself evidence that they are appropriate for your students.

Development of general goals for a school system should be a lengthy process with opportunities for students, parents, and others to participate. This can be done, for example, by sponsoring "town meetings," by publishing draft statements of goals in local newspapers with an invitation to respond, and by holding and publicizing hearings on goals sponsored by the board of education.

A factor that complicates the matter is that some sources of goals are simply not subject to a majority vote. Knowledge—whether about physics, poetry, or welding—is the province of specialists. Educators sometimes know more about the nature of children and the learning process than many other adults in the community. Nevertheless, in a democracy there is no higher authority than the people, so the people must be involved in deciding what public schools are to teach.

Most general goals, because they are so broad and because they deal with major categories of human experience, are acceptable to most people. Few will quarrel with a goal such as "Know about human beings, their environments and their achievements, past and present." The problem in developing a general goal statement is usually not to decide which goals are proper and which are not, but to select among many possibilities those which are most important, are at the proper level of generality, and are at least partially the responsibility of schools.

While general goals are not usually controversial, more specific ones can be. For example, parents might not quarrel with "Understand and follow practices associated with good health," but some would reject "Describe two effective and two ineffective methods of birth control." Thus, parents and other citizens should be involved in formulating course and program goals as well as general system goals.

USING GOALS TO PLAN LEARNING ACTIVITIES

To some extent, well-stated goals imply the kinds of learning activities that would be appropriate for achieving them. For example, if an instructional goal is "Solve word problems requiring estimation involving use of simple fractions such as $1/2$, $1/4$, $2/3$," students would have to practice estimating solutions to practical problems as well as learning to calculate using fractions. In many instances, however, knowing the goal does not automatically help an educator know how to teach it. For example, to enable students to "understand and appreciate significant human achievements," one

teacher might have students read about outstanding scientists of the 19th century, supplement the readings with several lectures, and give a multiple-choice examination. Another teacher might decide to divide students into groups and have each group prepare a presentation to the class about a great scientist using demonstrations, dramatic skits, and so on. Forging the link between goals and other steps in curriculum development requires professional knowledge, experience, and imagination.

A factor that distorts what might appear to be a straightforward relationship between goals and activities is that every instructional activity has multiple goals. The goal-setting process is sometimes seen as a one-to-one relationship between various levels of goals and levels of school activity. For example, the mission of a local school system might be to "Offer all students equitable opportunities for a basic education plus some opportunities to develop individual talents and interests." "Basic education" would be defined to include "Communicate effectively by reading, writing, speaking, observing, and listening." A middle school in that district might have a goal such as "Read and understand nonfiction at a level of the average article in *Reader's Digest*" or, more specifically, "Students will be able to distinguish between expressions of fact and opinion in writing."

While similar chains of related goals are basic to sound curriculum planning, developers should never assume that such simplicity fully represents the reality of schools. When a teacher is engaged in teaching reading, he or she must also be conscious of and teach toward other goals: thinking ability, knowledge of human achievements, relationships with others, positive self-concept, and so on.

Not only must teachers address several officially adopted "outside" goals all at once; they must cope with "inside" goals as well. Although Goodlad (1979) uses declared goals to remind educators and the public what schools are said to be for, he cautions that the ends-means model doesn't do justice to the educational process and offers, as an alternative, an ecological perspective. Insisting that school activities should "be viewed for their intrinsic value, quite apart from their linkage or lack of linkage to stated ends" (p. 76), he points out that in addition to "goals that have been set outside of the system for the system" there are also goals inside the system—"students' goals, teachers' goals, principals' goals, and so on—and . . . these goals are not necessarily compatible" (p. 77).

The message to curriculum developers is that although "outside" goals and objectives are fundamental to educational planning, the relationship between purposes and practices is more complex than it may seem.

USING GOALS IN CURRICULUM EVALUATION

Some writers argue that specific objectives are essential in order to design suitable evaluation plans and write valid test items. The work of the National Assessment of Educational Progress shows, however, that even evaluators may not require objectives written in highly technical language.[3] National Assessment objectives do not contain stipulations of conditions or performance standards; in fact, they are expected to meet just two criteria: clarity and importance. The educators, citizens, and subject matter experts who review the objectives are asked, "Do you understand what this objective means? How important is it that students learn this in school?" Objectives are often considered clear and important even though they are stated briefly and simply. When the objectives have been identified, National Assessment staff members or consultants develop exercises designed to be operational definitions of the intended outcomes. Conditions, standards of performance, and so on are specified for the exercises, not for the objectives.

Setting goals is difficult because it requires assembling and weighing all the factors to be considered in selecting the relatively few but important goals that can be attained with the limited time and resources available to schools. The demands and opportunities of society, the needs of students, the resources of scholarship, the values of democracy, and the conditions needed for effective learning must all be considered.

A common error is the failure to distinguish purposes appropriate for the school from those attainable largely through experiences in the home and community. The school can reinforce the family in helping children develop punctuality, dependability, self-discipline, and other important habits. The school can be and usually is a community in which children and adults respect each other, treat each other fairly, and cooperate. But the primary task for which public schools were established is to enlarge students' vision and experience by helping them learn to draw upon the resources of scholarship, thus overcoming the limitations of direct experience and the narrow confines of a local environment. Students can learn to use sources of knowledge that are more accurate and reliable than folklore and superstition. They can participate vicariously through literature and the arts with peoples whose lives are both similar to and different from those they have known. The school is the only institution whose primary purpose is enabling students to explore these scholarly fields and to learn to use them as resources in their own lives. Great emphasis should be given to goals of this sort.

Goals are frequently not stated at the appropriate degree of generality–specificity for each level of educational responsibility. Goals promulgated by state education authorities should not be too specific because of the wide variation in conditions among districts in the state. State goals should furnish general guidance for the kinds and areas of learning for which schools are responsible in that state. The school district should furnish more detailed guidance by identifying goals that fall between the general aims listed by the state and those appropriate to the local school. School goals should be adapted to the background of students and the needs and resources of the neighborhood, especially the educational role the parents can assume. The goals of each teacher should be designed to attain the goals of the school. The test of whether a goal is stated at the appropriate degree of generality–specificity is its clarity and helpfulness in guiding the educational activities necessary at that level of responsibility.

CONCLUSION

When states list specific skills as goals and develop statewide testing programs to measure them, they may overlook a significant part of what schools should teach: understanding, analysis, and problem solving. If students are taught only to follow prescribed rules, they will be unable to deal with varied situations. Another common limitation of such lists is their neglect of affective components, such as finding satisfaction in reading and developing the habit of reading to learn.

The form and wording of goals and objectives should be appropriate for the way they are to be used. For clarity, we have generally used the term "goal" for all statements of intended learning outcomes regardless of their degree of specificity, but we recognize that no one formula is best for all situations. The criteria for judging goals and objectives are their usefulness in communicating educational purposes and their helpfulness to teachers in planning educational activities.

ENDNOTES

1. Available from Commercial-Educational Distributing Service, P.O. Box 4791, Portland, OR 97208.
2. Collections of "measurable objectives" may be purchased from Instructional Objectives Exchange, Box 24095-M, Los Angeles, CA 90024-0095.
3. National Assessment has developed objectives for a number of subject areas, including art, citizenship, career and occupational development, literature, mathematics, music, reading, science, social studies, and writing. Because they have been carefully written and thoroughly reviewed, the objectives and accompanying exercises are a helpful resource for local curriculum developers, although they are designed only for assessment, not for curriculum planning.

REFERENCES

ASCD Committee on Research and Theory, Wilbur B. Brookover, Chairman. (1980). *Measuring and Attaining the Goals of Education.* Alexandria, VA: Association for Supervision and Curriculum Development.

Bloom, Benjamin S. (Ed.). (1956). *Taxonomy of Educational Objectives: The Classification of Educational Goals. Handbook I: Cognitive Domain.* New York: David McKay.

Bruner, Jerome. (1960). *The Process of Education.* Cambridge, MA: Harvard University.

Chalupsky, Albert B., Phillips-Jones, Linda, & Danoff, Malcolm N. (1981). "Competency Measure-

ment in Vocational Education: A Review of the State of the Art." Prepared by American Institute for Research. Washington, DC: Office of Vocational and Adult Education, U.S. Department of Education.

Commission on the Reorganization of Secondary Education, U.S. Office of Education. (1918). *Cardinal Principles of Secondary Education.* Washington, DC: Government Printing Office.

Doherty, Victor W., & Peters, Linda B. (1980). *Introduction to K–12 Course Goals for Educational Planning and Evaluation,* 3rd ed. Portland, OR: Commercial-Educational Distributing Services.

Doherty, Victor W., & Peters, Linda B. (1981, May). "Goals and Objectives in Educational Planning and Evaluation." *Educational Leadership* 38: 606.

Ehrenberg, Sydelle D., & Ehrenberg, Lyle, M. (1978). *A Strategy for Curriculum Design—The ICI Model.* Miami: Institute for Curriculum and Instruction.

Eisner, Eliot W. (1979). *The Educational Imagination.* New York: Macmillan.

French, Will. (1957). *Behavioral Goals of General Education in High School.* New York: Russell Sage Foundation.

Goodlad, John I. (1979). *What Schools Are For?* Bloomington, IN: Phi Delta Kappa.

Kohlberg, Lawrence. (1980, October). "Moral Education: A Response to Thomas Sobol." *Educational Leadership* 38: 19–23.

Krathwohl, David R., & others. (1964). *Taxonomy of Educational Objectives: The Classification of Educational Goals, Handbook II: Affective Domain.* New York: David McKay Company, Inc.

Mager, R. F. (1962). *Preparing Instructional Objectives.* Palo Alto, CA: Fearon Publishers.

Martin, John Henry. (1980, January). "Reconsidering the Goals of High School Education." *Educational Leadership* 37: 278–285.

Oregon State Board of Education. (1972). "Minimum State Requirements Standards for Graduation from High School." Salem, Oregon.

Paul, Regina. (1982, January). "Are You Out on a Limb?" *Educational Leadership* 39: 260–264.

Raywid, Mary Anne. (1981, April). "The First Decade of Public School Alternatives." *Phi Delta Kappan* 62: 551–554.

Seiverling, Richard F. (Ed.). (1980). *Educational Quality Assessment: Getting Out the EQA Results.* Harrisburg, PA: Pennsylvania Department of Education.

Spady, William G. (1978, October). "The Concept and Implications of Competency-Based Education." *Educational Leadership* 36: 16–22.

Stake, R. E., & Easley, J. A., Jr. (1978). *Case Studies in Science Education.* 2 vols. Washington, DC: U.S. Government Printing Office.

Sternberg, Robert J. (1981, October). "Intelligence as Thinking and Learning Skills." *Educational Leadership* 39: 18–20.

Tyler, Ralph W. (1949). *Basic Principles of Curriculum and Instruction.* 1974 ed. Chicago: University of Chicago Press.

Wirszup, Izaak. (1981, February). "The Soviet Challenge." *Educational Leadership* 38: 358–360.

DISCUSSION QUESTIONS

1. What should the goals of contemporary education be?
2. Should the goals of education be the same for all students?
3. What is the best method for defining goals: by behavioral objectives or by competencies?
4. Who should assume responsibility for determining educational goals: the federal government, the state board of education, local school districts, building principals, or the faculty at each school? Why?
5. What is the best criterion for judging goals and objectives?

A Pedagogy of Possibility

PETER McLAREN

FOCUSING QUESTIONS

1. What is critical pedagogy?
2. Are teaching and curriculum guided by political ideology?
3. How are literacy and freedom related?
4. Does education always liberate?
5. Does love have a place in education?

[W]hat I have been proposing from my political convictions, my philosophical convictions, is a profound respect for the total autonomy of the educator. What I have been proposing is a profound respect for the cultural identity of students—a cultural identity that implies respect for the language of the other, the color of the other, the gender of the other, the class of the other, the sexual orientation of the other, the intellectual capacity of the other; that implies the ability to stimulate the creativity of the other. But these things take place in a social and historical context and not in pure air. These things take place in history and I, Paulo Freire, am not the owner of history.

—Paulo Freire, 1997a, pp. 307–308

Paulo Freire was one of the first internationally recognized educational thinkers who fully appreciated the relationship among education, politics, imperialism, and liberation. Generally considered the inaugural philosopher of critical pedagogy, Freire was able to effectively recast pedagogy on a global basis in the direction of a radical politics of historical struggle, a direction that he expanded into a lifetime project. Long before his death on May 2, 1997, Freire had acquired a mythic stature among progressive educators, social workers, and theologians as well as scholars and researchers from numerous disciplinary traditions, for fomenting interest in the ways that education can serve as a vehicle for social and economic transformation. What is now termed "a politics of liberation" is a topic of pivotal significance among educational activists throughout the globe and one to which Freire had made important and pioneering contributions.

FREIRE'S PHILOSOPHY OF PEDAGOGY: A PREFERENTIAL OPTION FOR THE POOR

Freire's life vehemently unveils the imprints of a life lived within the margins of power and prestige. Because his work was centered around the issue of social and political change, Freire has always been considered controversial, especially by educational establishments in Europe and North America. While he is recognized as one of the most significant philosophers of liberation and a pioneer in critical literacy and critical pedagogy, his work continues to be taken up mostly by educators working outside of the educational mainstream. The marginal status of Freire's followers is undoubtedly due to the fact that Freire believed educational change must be accompanied by significant changes in the social and political structure in which education takes place. It is a position most educators would find politically untenable or hopelessly utopian. It is certainly a position that threatens the interests of those already well served by the dominant culture.

Freire believed that the ongoing production of the social world through dialogue occurs in dialectical interplay with the structural features of society such as its social relations of production, cultural formations, and institutional arrangements. In the process of becoming literate—a process Freire referred to as "praxis"—meaning circulates, is acted upon, and is revised, resulting in political interpretation, sense-making, and will formation. The outcome of this intersubjectivity produced through praxis is never fully predetermined.

A staunch critic of neo-liberalism, Freire perceived a major ideological tension to be situated in the ability of people to retain a concept of the political beyond a consumer identity constructed from the panoply of market logics. Further, the sociality and the discourses of daily life cannot be a priori defined as excluding the realm of politics.

Freire's personal contact with Brazilian peasants early in his life profoundly shaped his assent to popular revolts against economic exploitation in Latin America, Africa, and elsewhere. Given the basic contradictions facing a social order encapsulated in the exploitation of the vast majority of Brazilian society, the task or mission of Freire centered on the transformation of the relations of the production of social wealth (together with the ideological-political levels). Yet such an attempt to establish a new social order underwritten by a just system of appropriation and distribution of social wealth was to relegate Freire to the ranks of educators considered to be subversive to the state. For Freire, the very protocols of literacy and the act of "coming to know" must themselves be transformed in order to make a prominent place for issues of social justice and the struggle for emancipation. Freire taught that in order for the oppressed to materialize their self-activity as a revolutionary force, they must develop a collective consciousness of their own constitution or formation as a subaltern class, as well as an ethos of solidarity and interdependence. For Freire, a pedagogy of critical literacy becomes the primary vehicle for the development of "critical consciousness" among the poor, leading to a process of exploration and creative effort that conjoins deep personal meaning and common purpose. Literacy, for Freire, becomes the common "process" of participation open to all individuals. The problem of "critical consciousness" cannot be posed in abstraction from the significant historical contexts in which knowledge is produced, engaged, and appropriated.

Freire lamented the brute reality that witnessed the oppressed always living as the detachable appendages of other people's dreams and desires. It seemed to Freire that the dreams of the poor were always dreamt for them by distant others who were removed from the daily struggles of the working class and were either unable or unwilling to recognize the dreams that burned in the habitats of their hearts. Based on a recognition of the cultural underpinnings of folk traditions and the importance of the collective construction of knowledge, Freire's pedagogical project created a vivid new vocabulary of concern for the oppressed, and uncoiled a new and powerful political terminology that enabled the oppressed to analyze their location within the privileging hierarchy of capitalist society and engage in attempts to dislocate themselves from existing cycles of social reproduction. Literacy programs developed by Freire and his colleagues for disempowered peasants are now employed in countries all over the world. By linking the categories of history, politics, economics, and class to the concepts of culture and power, Freire managed to develop both a language of critique and a language of hope that work conjointly and dialectically and which have proven successful in helping generations of disenfranchised peoples to liberate themselves.

Freire recognized that there is no way of representing the consciousness of the oppressed that escapes the founding assumptions of the culture and society in which the teacher of a cultural worker is implicated (Freire, 1973, 1978, 1985, 1993a, 1993b, 1998a; Freire & Macedo, 1987). Long before postmodernists brought us their version of "identity politics," Freire understood that the subjectivities of the oppressed are to be considered heterogeneous and ideologically pertuse and cannot be represented extratextually—that is, outside of the discursive embeddedness of the educator's own founding value and epistemological assumptions (McLaren & Leonard, 1993).

Freire understood that as the oppressed take more control of their own history, they assimilate more rapidly into society, but on their own terms. He warrants the reputation as a preeminent critical educationalist in the way that he was able to foreground the means by which *the pedagogical* (the localized pedagogical encounter between teacher and student) is implicated in *the political* (the social relations of production within the global capitalist economy). Whereas mainstream educators often decapitate the social context from the self and thereby cauterize the dialectical movement between them, Freire stresses the dialectical motion between the subject and object, the self and the social, and human agency and social structure.

Educators who work within a Freirean-inspired critical pedagogy are indebted to Freire's philosophical insights more than to his commentaries on teaching methodologies (Taylor, 1993). Freire's working vocabulary of philosophical concepts enables the world of the oppressed to become visible, to inscribe itself as a text to be engaged and understood by the oppressed and non-oppressed alike. Freire's work does not reduce the world to a text but rather stipulates the conditions for the possibility of various competing and conflicting discourses, or ways of making sense out of lived experiences. Freire interrogates the catachresis of value by urging educators to identify the aporias within their own philosophies of teaching and daily life (1998a, 1998b).

In all of Freire's teachings, the concept of truth becomes vitiatingly unwound as the truth becomes linked to one's emplacement in the reigning narratives *about* truth. Of course, Freire's own work can be used against itself in this regard, and interpreted as an epiphenomenon of the narratives that create the textual effects of his own work. Freire would have encouraged readers to scrutinize and critique the ideology of his work in the same manner that he encouraged them to interrogate other texts.

FREIRE'S INFLUENCE ON NORTH AMERICAN CRITICAL PEDAGOGY

Discovering that pedagogy existed largely in pathological conditions, Freire sought to advance new approaches to teaching and learning, carefully avoiding those "banking" varieties that separated mind from body, thought from action, and social critique from transformative praxis. Often accompanied by Dewey's (1916) approaches to teaching and learning as well as those, like Habermas (1979, 1987), that stress communicative competency and non-distorted forms of communication, critical pedagogy constitutes a set of practices that uncovers the ways in which the process of schooling represses the contingency of its own selection of values and the means through which educational goals are subtended by macrostructures of power and privilege. For Freire, pedagogy has as much to do with the teachable heart as the teachable mind, and as much to do with efforts to change the world as it does with rethinking the categories that we use to analyze our current condition within history. In this way, Freire has pushed the debate over pedagogy out of familiar well-worn grooves. In essence, Freire's work is about hope. He writes: "Hope is a natural, possible, and necessary impetus in the context of our unfinishedness . . . without it, instead of history we would have pure determinism" (1998b, p. 69).

Freire's work has unarguably been the driving force behind North American efforts at developing critical pedagogy. Critical pedagogy is a way of thinking about, negotiating, and transforming the relationship among classroom teaching, the production of knowledge, the institutional structures of the school, and the social and material relations of the wider community, society, and nation-state (McLaren, 1993, 1997a; McLaren & Lankshear, 1994). Developed by progressive teachers attempting to eliminate inequalities on the basis of social class, it has also sparked a wide array of anti-sexist, anti-racist, and anti-homophobic classroom-based curricula and policy initiatives. Freirean-inspired critical pedagogies in North America have grown out of a number of theoretical developments such as Latin American philosophies of liberation (McLaren, 1993); critical literacy (Macedo, 1994; Lankshear & McLaren, 1993); the sociology of knowledge (Giroux & McLaren, 1989; McLaren, 1995; Fine, 1991); the Frankfurt school of critical theory (Giroux, 1983; McLaren & Giarelli, 1995); adult education (Hall, 1998); feminist theory (Weiler, 1988; Gore, 1993; Lather, 1991; Ellsworth, 1989); bilingual and bicultural education (Moraes, 1996; Darder, 1991; Wink, 1997; Cummins, 1989); teacher education (McLaren, 1993) and neo-Marxist cultural criticism (McLaren, 1997b). In more recent years it has been taken up by educators influenced by debates over postmodernism and poststructuralism (Kincheloe, 1993; Kanpol, 1992; Aronowitz & Giroux, 1991; Giroux & McLaren, 1989; McLaren, 1995); cultural studies (Giroux & McLaren, 1994; Kincheloe, 1993; Giroux, Lankshear, McLaren, & Peters, 1996); and multiculturalism (Sleeter & McLaren, 1995; McLaren, 1997c; Kincheloe & Steinberg, 1997; Sleeter & Grant, 1988; Leistyna, 1999; McCarthy, 1988). For Freire, schools are places where, as part of civil society, spaces of uncoerced interaction can be created.

Yet even with such a divergent array of influences, at the level of classroom life, Freirean pedagogy is often erroneously perceived as synonymous with whole language instruction, adult literacy programs, and new "constructivist" approaches to teaching and learning based on Vygotsky's work. Not all such programs are necessarily Freirean, but they need to be judged in relation to the contextual specificity of their philosophy, their praxis, and their ethos of critical responsiveness with respect to bringing about a more just and humane social order. Lankshear and McLaren (1993, pp. 43–44) have summarized six learning principles from Freire's work which are intended to provide teachers with pivotal points of reference in the development of their pedagogical practices:

1. The world must be approached as an object to be understood and known by the efforts of learners themselves. Moreover, their acts of knowing are to be stimulated and grounded in their own being, experiences, needs, circumstances, and destinies.
2. The historical and cultural world must be approached as a created, transformable reality which, like humans themselves, is constantly in the process of being shaped and made by human deed in accordance with ideological representations of reality.
3. Learners must learn how to actively make connections between their own lived conditions and being and the making of reality that has occurred to date.

4. They must consider the possibility for "new makings" of reality, the new possibilities for *being* that emerge from new makings, and become committed to shaping a new enabling and regenerative history. New makings are a collective, shared, social enterprise in which the voices of all participants must be heard.
5. In the literacy phase, learners come to see the importance of print for this shared project. By achieving print competence within the process of bringing their experience and meanings to bear on the world in active construction and reconstruction (of lived relations and practice), learners will actually *experience* their own potency in the very act of understanding what it means to be a human subject. In the post-literacy phase, the basis for action is print-assisted exploration of generative *themes*. Addressing the theme of "Western culture" as conceived by people like Hirsh and reified in prevailing curricula and pedagogies, and seeking to transcend this conception . . . involves exactly the kind of praxis Freire intends.
6. Learners must come to understand how the myths of dominant discourses are, precisely, myths which oppress and marginalize them—but which can be transcended through transformative action.

While critics often decry Freire's educational approach for its idealist vision of social transformation, its supporters, including Freire, have complained that critical pedagogy has often been domesticated and reduced to student-directed learning approaches devoid of social critique.

Once considered by the faint-hearted guardians of the American dream as a term of opprobrium, critical pedagogy has become so completely psychologized, so liberally humanized, so technologized, and so conceptually postmodernized that its current relationship to broader liberation struggles and to Freire's stress on revolutionary class struggle seems severely attenuated if not fatally terminated. Because Freire believed that the challenge of transforming schools should be directed at overcoming socioeconomic injustice linked to the political and economic structures of society, any attempt at school reform that claims to be inspired by Freire—but that is only concerned with social patterns of representation, interpretation, or communication, and that does not connect these patterns to redistributive measures and structures that reinforce such patterns— exempts itself from the most important insights of Freire's work. Freire's approach stipulates a trenchant understanding of patterns of distribution and redistribution in order to transform—and not just interpret—the underlying economic structures that produce relations of exploitation. Freire was also concerned with practicing a politics of diversity and self-affirmation—in short, a cultural politics—not as a mere end-in-itself but in relation to a larger politics of liberation and social justice. Consequently, a Freirean pedagogy of liberation is totalizing without being dominating in that it always attends dialectically to the specific or local "act of knowing" as a political process that takes place in the larger conflictual arena of capitalist relations of exploitation, an arena where large groups of people palpably and undeniably suffer needless privations and pain due to alienation and poverty. Thus, a pedagogy of the oppressed involves not only a redistribution of material resources, but also a struggle over cultural meanings in relation to the multiple social locations of students and teachers and their position within the global division of labor.

Has Freire's name become a floating signifier to be attached adventitiously to any chosen referent within the multi-stranded terrain of progressive education? To a certain extent this has already happened. Liberal progressives are drawn to Freire's humanism; Marxists and neo-Marxists are drawn to his revolutionary praxis and his history of working with revolutionary political regimes; left liberals are drawn to his critical utopianism; and even conservatives begrudgingly respect his stress on ethics. No doubt his work will be domesticated by his followers—as selected aspects of his corpus are appropriated uncritically and decontextualized from his larger political project of struggling for the realization of a truly socialist democracy—in order to make a more comfortable fit with various conflicting political agendas. Consequently, it is important to read Freire in the context of his entire corpus of works, from *Pedagogy of the Oppressed* (1993b) to his reflection on this early work, *Pedagogy of Hope* (1994), and to his *Pedagogy of Freedom* (1998b).

FREIREAN PEDAGOGY: ITS SHORTCOMINGS

Those who have an important stake in the meaning of Freire's life and work will continue to disagree over how his politics and pedagogy should be interpreted. The assertive generality of Freire's formulations of and pronouncements on pedagogy can be highly frustrating, in that they index important concerns but do not fully provide the necessary theoretical basis for positing more progressive and programmatic alternatives to the theories and perspectives that he is criticizing. For instance, few accounts are provided as to how teachers are to move from critical thought to critical practice. Yet Freire's weakness is also a source of his strength and marks the durability of his thought. It is precisely his refusal to spell out alternative solutions that enables his work to be "reinvented" in the contexts in which his readers find themselves, thereby enjoying a contextually specific "translation" across geographic, geopolitical, and cultural borders. It also grants to Freire's corpus of works a universal character, as they are able to retain their heuristic potency (much like the works of Marx) such that they can be conscripted by educators to criticize and to counterpoint pedagogical practices worldwide. In fact, Freire urged his readers to reinvent him in the context of their local struggles. What could be retained in every instance of this reinvention process is Freire's constant and unstoppable ethics of solidarity and an unrepentant utopianism. Freire writes that "the progressive educator must always be moving out on his or her own, continually reinventing me and reinventing what it means to be democratic in his or her own specific cultural and historical context" (1997a, p. 308).

Some have assigned to Freire's work the Archimedian conceit of the idealist utopian view of society. But such a criticism risks overlooking the practical utility of Freirean pedagogy, especially when one considers the success of the literacy campaigns that relied heavily on his work. Freire seizes on the occult presence of seeds of redemption at the center of a world gone mad. Yet his politics of liberation resists subsumption under a codified set of universal principles; rather it animates a set of ethical imperatives that together serve as a precipitate of our answering the call of the other who is suffering from a heavy heart and an empty stomach. Such imperatives do not mark a naive utopian faith in the future; rather, they presage a form of active, irreverent, and uncompromising hope in the possibilities of the present.

The legacy of racism left by the New World European oppressor—that Blacks and Latino/as are simply a species of inferior invertebrates—was harshly condemned but never systematically analyzed by Freire. And while Freire was a vociferous critic of racism and sexism, he did not, as Kathleen Weiler (1996) points out, sufficiently problematize his conceptualization of liberation and the oppressed in terms of his own male experience.

From the perspective of North American critical pedagogy, Freire's politics of liberation partakes of its own political inertia consequent in the limited range of narratives out of which he constructs his praxis of hope and transformation. For instance, Freire failed to articulate fully his position on Christianity (Elias, 1994) and the male bias in his literacy method (Taylor, 1993). Freire rarely addressed the ways in which oppression on the bases of ethnicity, class, and sexual orientation are intermingled. As a number of North American critics have pointed out, Freire failed to fully engage the issue of white male privilege (Ladson-Billings, 1997) or the interest and agency of African Americans apart from a wider movement of emancipatory practices (Murrell, 1997). When Freire did address this issue, he often retreated into mystical abstractions, thereby discounting the deep significance of patriarchy as a practice of oppression (Weiler, 1996). Yet these lacunae should in no way diminish the genius, courage, and compassion of Freire's work.

The modality of theoretical envisioning deployed by Freire is decidedly modernist but, as I have argued elsewhere (McLaren, 1997c), some trappings of postmodernist discourses are immanent—yet barely registered—in Freire's peripatetic articulation of human agency. Social theory identified as "postmodern" runs the serious risk of ignoring the brute reality that working people the world over share a common subjection to a capitalist exploitation. The violent realities of the global economy are often dissipated within postmodern social theories. On the other hand, pedagogies of liberation such as Freire's, underwritten by modernist Marxian discourses, often seriously ignore issues of race, gender, and sexual orientation. Freire was aware of these omissions (Freire, 1997b, 1998a, 1998b) and had begun to address them with a passionate conviction in his most recent work. Despite the fact that deconstructionists such as Stuart Parker (1997) have revealed much of the work of the critical educational tradition—exemplified by the work of Freire—to be located within modernist assumptions of teacher autonomy, assumptions that essentially serve as "devices of enchantment" which can be deconstructed as discursive fictions, Freire's work holds vital importance. Freire's contribution remains signal not for its methodology of literacy alone but in the final instance for its ability to create a pedagogy of practical consciousness that presages critical action (Taylor, 1993). Freire's primary achievement remains that of his role as the "Vagabond of the Obvious," a term which he often used to describe his pedagogical role. The shortcomings of Freire's work constitute more than minor rhetorical fallout to be sure, but as Freire's aforementioned critics also acknowledge, they should not detract from Freire's central importance as a foundational educational thinker, a philosopher who ranks among the most important educators of this century or any other.

Bearing witness to enduring imbalances of power on a global level—the worldwide problem of overcapacity, the random destruction by unregulated markets accompanying the new bargain-basement capitalism, the imposition of exchange values upon all productions of value, the creation of a uniform culture of pure consumption, or Wal-Martization of global culture, the vampirism of Western carpetbaggers sucking the lifeblood from the open veins of South America, opportunistic politicians, assaults on diasporic cultures, and a new wave of xenophobia—have brought about a serious political inertia within the United States left in general and the educational left in particular. The logic of privatization and free trade—where social labor is the means and measure of value and surplus social labor lies at the heart of profit—now shapes the very fabric of our lifeworld. The logic of transnational capitalism now flagrantly guides educational policy and practice to such an extent that one could say without exaggeration that education has been reduced to a subsector of the economy. To the extent that the future of education is intimately connected to the ability of teachers to become more critically self-reflective in analyzing ways in which their own lives and those of their students have been inscribed by enchaining discursive practices and material social relations supporting powerful elite groups at the expense of the majority of the population, Freire's work is indispensable to the progressive evolution of educational thought. Of course, the continuing advancement of critical pedagogy and Freirean praxis cannot be divorced from the crisis of the late bourgeois world whose greatest symptom includes the logic of consumption as a regulating democratic ideal. Freire was always a revolutionary and as such never abandoned the dream of a radical transformation of the world. Freire writes:

> My rebellion against every kind of discrimination, from the most explicit and crying to the most covert and hypocritical, which is no less offensive and immoral, has been with me from my childhood. Since as far back as I can remember, I have reacted almost instinctively against any word, deed, or sign of racial discrimination, or, for that matter, discrimination against the poor, which quite a bit later, I came to define as class discrimination. (1994, p. 144)

As Freire's future hagiographers wrestle in the educational arena over what represents the "real" Freire and his legacy, Freire's work will continue to be felt in the lives of those who knew him and who loved him. Just as importantly, his work will continue to influence generations of educators, scholars, and activists around the world.

Freire acknowledged that decolonization was a project that knows no endpoint, no final closure. It is a lifetime struggle that requires counterintuitive insight, honesty, compassion, and a willingness to brush one's personal history against the grain of "naive consciousness" or common-sense understanding. After engaging the legacy of revolutionary struggles of the oppressed that has been bequeathed to us by Freire, it remains impossible to conceive of pedagogical practice evacuated of

social critique. Freire has left stratified deposits of pedagogical insight upon which future developments of progressive education can be built. There is still reason to hope for a cooperative pedagogical venture among those who support a Freirean class-based pedagogical struggle, feminist pedagogy, or a pedagogy informed by queer theory and politics, that may lead to a revival of serious educational thinking in which the category of liberation may continue to have and to make meaning. The internationalization of the market and its border-crossing dimensions strongly suggests that in order to halt the continuing assaults of the market on human subjectivity, cultural workers must create alliances across national borders.

THE POWER OF LOVE

What sets Freire apart from most other leftist educators in this era of cynical reason is his unashamed stress on the importance and power of love. Love, he claims, is the most crucial characteristic of dialogue and the constitutive force animating all pedagogies of liberation:

> Dialogue cannot exist, however, in the absence of a profound love for the world and for people. The naming of the world, which is an act of creation and re-creation, is not possible if it is not infused with love. Love is at the same time the foundation of dialogue and dialogue itself. It is thus necessarily the task of responsible Subjects and cannot exist in a relation of domination. Domination reveals the pathology of love: sadism in the dominator and masochism in the dominated. Because love is an act of courage, not of fear, love is commitment to others. No matter where the oppressed are found, the act of love is commitment to their cause—the cause of liberation. And this commitment, because it is loving, is dialogical. As an act of bravery, love cannot be sentimental: as an act of freedom, it must not serve as a pretext for manipulation. It must generate other acts of freedom; otherwise, it is not love. Only by abolishing the situation of oppression is it possible to restore the love which that situation made impossible. If I do not love the world—if I do not love life—if I do not love people—I cannot enter into dialogue. (1993b, pp. 70–71)

For Freire, love always stipulates a political project since a love for humankind that remains disconnected from politics does a profound disservice to its object. It is possible to love only by virtue of the presence of others. A love that does not liberate feeds off its object like worms on a corpse. Its narcissism destroys the other by turning the other into itself; it transforms the other into inert matter that it uses to fertilize its own image. Here the act of love becomes the act of self-love, as the subject becomes its own object, consuming itself in an orgy of necrophilia. Whereas authentic love opens up the self to the Other, narcissistic love culminates in a self-dissolving spiral by refusing the Other who stands at the door of self-understanding. Only when the Other is encountered behind the door can the self find its authentic eyes, ears, and voice in the art of dialogic, reciprocal understanding.

Love both embodies struggle and pushes it beyond its source. In Freirean terms, revolutionary love is always pointed in the direction of commitment and fidelity to a global project of emancipation. This commitment is sustained by preventing nihilism and despair from imposing their own life-denying inevitability in times of social strife and cultural turmoil. Anchored in narratives of transgression and dissent, love becomes the foundation of hope. In this way love can never be reduced to personal declarations or pronouncements but exists always in asymmetrical relations of anxiety and resolve, interdependence and singularity. Love, in this Freirean sense, becomes the oxygen of revolution, nourishing the blood of historical memory. It is through reciprocal dialogue that love is able to serve as a form of testimony to those who have struggled and suffered before us, and whose spirit of struggle had survived efforts to extinguish it and remove it from the archives of human achievement. Refusing to embrace the Orphic lyre or the crown of thorns, Freirean pedagogy faces the intractable forces of capitalist domination with a bittersweet optimism. Freire understood that while we often abandon hope, we are never abandoned by hope. This is because hope is forever engraved in the human heart and inspires us to reach beyond the carnal limits of our species being.

The Freirean agent works silently but steadfastly in the margins of culture and the interstices of collapsing public sectors, away from the power-charged arenas of public spectacles of accusation and blame regarding what is wrong with our schools. Freirean educators do not conceive of their work as an antidote to today's sociocultural ills and the declining level of ambition with respect to contemporary society's commitment to democracy. Rather, their efforts are patiently directed at creating counter-hegemonic sites of political struggle, radically alternative epistemological frameworks, and adversarial interpretations and cultural practices, as well as advocacy domains for disenfranchised groups.

Freirean pedagogy is vitally important for contemporary educators to revisit, to build upon, and to reinvent in the contextual specificity of today's sociopolitical context with its traumatizing inequalities. Like Freire, we need to restore to liberation its rightful place as the central project of education.

ENDNOTES

Peter McLaren is a professor of education at the Graduate School of Education and Information Studies, University of California, Los Angeles. He specializes in critical pedagogy, critical theory, and critical ethnography. He is an Associate of the Paulo Freire Institute, São Paulo, Brazil.

This paper is part of a larger text delivered at the Annual Convention of the American Educational Research Association, San Diego, April, 1998.

REFERENCES

Aronowitz, S., & Giroux, H. A. (1991). *Postmodern Education.* Minneapolis, MN: University of Minnesota Press.

Cummins, J. (1989). *Empowering Minority Students.* Sacramento, CA: California Association for Bilingual Education.

Darder, A. (1991). *Culture and Power in the Classroom: A Critical Foundation for Bicultural Education.* Westport, CT: Bergin and Garvey.

Dewey, J. (1916). *Democracy and Education.* New York: Macmillan Company.

Elias, J. (1994). *Paulo Freire: Pedagogue of Revolution.* Melbourne, FL: Krieger Publishing Company.

Ellsworth, E. (1989). "Why Doesn't This Feel Empowering? Working through the Repressive Myths of Critical Pedagogy." *Harvard Educational Review,* 59(5): 297–324.

Fine, M. (1991). *Framing Dropouts.* Albany, NY: State University of New York Press.

Freire, P. (1973). *Education for Critical Consciousness.* New York: Seabury Press.

Freire, P. (1978). *Pedagogy in Process. The Letters to Guinea Bissau.* New York: Seabury Press.

Freire, P. (1985). *The Politics of Education: Culture, Power, and Liberation.* South Hadley, MA: Bergin & Garvey.

Freire, P. (1993a). *Pedagogy of the City.* New York: Continuum.

Freire, P. (1993b). *Pedagogy of the Oppressed.* New York: Continuum.

Freire, P. (1994). *Pedagogy of Hope: Reliving Pedagogy of the Oppressed.* New York: Continuum.

Freire, P. (1997a). "A Response." In P. Freire, J. W. Fraser, D. Macedo, T. McKinnon, & W. T. Stokes (Eds.), *Mentoring the Member: A Critical Dialogue with Paulo Freire* (pp. 303–329). New York: Peter Lang Publishers.

Freire, P. (1997b). *Teachers as Cultural Workers: Letters to Those Who Dare to Teach.* (D. Macedo, K. Koike, & A. Oliviera, Trans.). Boulder, CO: Westview Press.

Freire, P. (1998a). *Pedagogy of the Heart.* New York: Continuum.

Freire, P. (1998b). *Pedagogy of Freedom: Ethics, Democracy, and Civic Courage.* Boulder, CO: Rowman and Littlefield Publishers, Inc.

Freire, P., & Macedo, D. (1987). *Literacy: Reading the Word and the World.* South Hadley, MA: Bergin & Garvey.

Giroux, H. A. (1983). *Theory and Resistance in Education: A Pedagogy for the Opposition.* South Hadley, MA: Bergin & Garvey.

Giroux, H. A., Lankshear, C., McLaren, P., & Peters, M. (1996). *Counternarratives: Cultural Studies and Critical Pedagogies in the Postmodern Spaces.* London and New York: Routledge.

Giroux, H., & McLaren, P. (Eds.). (1989). *Critical Pedagogy, the State, and Cultural Struggle.* Albany, NY: State University of New York Press.

Giroux, H., & McLaren, P. (Eds.). (1994). *Between Borders: Pedagogy and the Politics of Cultural Studies.* New York and London: Routledge.

Gore, J. (1993). *The Struggle for Pedagogies: Critical and Feminist Discourses as Regimes of Truth.* New York: Routledge.

Habermas, J. (1979). *Communication and the Evolution of Society.* (T. McCarthy, Trans.) Boston: Beacon Press.

Habermas, J. (1987). *The Theory of Communicative Action: Vol. 2, Lifeworld and System: A Critique of Functionalist Reason.* (T. McCarthy, Trans.) Boston: Beacon Press.

Hall, B. (1998). " 'Please Don't Bother the Canaries': Paulo Freire and the International Council for Adult Education." *Convergence, xxxi*(1–2): 95–103.

Kanpol, B. (1992). *Towards a Theory and Practice of Teacher Cultural Politics: Continuing the Postmodern Debate.* Norwood, NJ: Ablex Publications.

Kincheloe, J. (1993). *Toward a Critical Politics of Teacher Thinking: Mapping the Postmodern.* South Hadley, MA: Bergin and Garvey.

Kincheloe, J., & Steinberg, S. (1997). *Changing Multiculturalism.* Buckingham/Philadelphia: Open University Press.

Ladson-Billings, G. (1997). "I Know Why This Doesn't Feel Empowering: A Critical *Race* Analysis of Critical Pedagogy." In P. Freire, J. W. Fraser, D. Macedo, T. McKinnon, & W. T. Stokes (Eds.), *Mentoring the Mentor* (pp. 127–141). New York: Peter Lang Publishers.

Lankshear, C., & McLaren, P. (Eds.). (1993). Introduction. In C. Lankshear & P. McLaren (Eds.), *Critical Literacy: Politics, Praxis, and the Postmodern* (pp. 1–56). Albany, NY: State University of New York Press.

Lather, P. (1991). *Getting Smart: Feminist Research and Pedagogy within the Postmodern.* New York and London: Routledge.

Leistyna, P. (1999). *Presence of Mind: Education and the Politics of Deception.* Boulder, CO: Westview Press.

Macedo, D. (1994). *Literacies of Power.* Boulder, CO: Westview Press.

McCarthy, C. (1988). "Rethinking Liberal and Radical Perspectives on Racial Inequality in Schooling: Making the Case for Nonsynchrony." *Harvard Educational Review, 58*(3): 265–279.

McLaren, P. (1993). *Life in Schools: An Introduction to Critical Pedagogy in the Social Foundations of Education.* White Plains, NY: Longman, Inc.

McLaren, P. (1995). *Critical Pedagogy and Predatory Culture.* New York and London: Routledge.

McLaren, P. (1997a). "La Lucha Continua: Freire, Boal and the Challenge of History. To My Brothers and Sisters in Struggle." *Researcher, 1*(2): 5–10.

McLaren, P. (1997b). "Freirean Pedagogy: The Challenge of Postmodernism and the Politics of Race." In P. Freire, J. W. Fraser, D. Macedo, T. McKinnon, & W. T. Stokes (Eds.), *Mentoring the Mentor* (pp. 99–125). New York: Peter Lang Publishers.

McLaren, P. (1997c). *Revolutionary Multiculturalism: Pedagogies of Dissent for the New Millenium.* Boulder, CO: Westview Press.

McLaren, P., & Giarelli, J. (Eds.). (1995). *Critical Theory and Educational Research.* Albany, NY: State University of New York Press.

McLaren, P., & Lankshear, C. (Eds.). (1994). *Politics of Liberation: Paths from Freire.* New York and London: Routledge.

McLaren, P., & Leonard, P. (Eds.). (1993). *Paulo Freire: A Critical Encounter.* New York and London: Routledge.

Moraes, M. (1996). *Bilingual Education: A Dialogue with the Bahktin Circle.* Albany, NY: State University of New York Press.

Murrell, P., Jr. (1997). "Digging Again the Family Wells: A Freirean Literacy Framework as Emancipatory Pedagogy for African-American Children." In P. Freire, J. W. Fraser, D. Macedo, T. McKinnon, & W. T. Stokes (Eds.), *Mentoring the Mentor* (pp. 19–58). New York: Peter Lang Publishers.

Parker, S. (1997). *Reflective Teaching in the Postmodern World: A Manifesto for Education in Postmodernity.* Buckingham and Philadelphia: Open University Press.

Sleeter, C., & Grant, C. (1988). *Making Choices for Multicultural Education: Five Approaches to Race, Class, and Gender.* Columbus, OH: Merrill Publishing.

Sleeter, C., & McLaren, P. (Eds.). (1995). *Multicultural Education, Critical Pedagogy, and the Politics of Difference.* Albany, NY: State University of New York Press.

Taylor, P. (1993). *The Texts of Paulo Freire.* Buckingham and Philadelphia: Open University Press.

Weiler, K. (1988). *Women Teaching for Change: Gender, Class and Power.* South Hadley, MA: Bergin & Garvey.

Weiler, K. (1996). "Myths of Paulo Freire." *Educational Theory 46*(3): 353–371.

Wink, J. (1997). *Critical Pedagogy: Notes from the Real World.* White Plains, NY: Longman Publishers.

DISCUSSION QUESTIONS

1. How does critical pedagogy differ from ordinary teaching?
2. Should teaching and curriculum be guided by political ideology? Must they be?
3. How is literacy the cornerstone of freedom?
4. What would an emancipatory curriculum look like? How would it be taught?
5. What should be the place of love in education?

4

Art and Imagination:
Overcoming a Desperate Stasis

MAXINE GREENE

FOCUSING QUESTIONS

1. What are the existential contexts of education?
2. How do encounters with the arts influence student engagement in learning?
3. How might experience with the arts affect student (a) imagination, (b) construction of reality, and (c) depth of perspective?
4. What is the relationship between individual freedom and learning?
5. What are the contradictory goals of education?
6. What is the relationship between encounters with the arts and the goals of education?

The existential contexts of education reach far beyond what is conceived of in Goals 2000. They have to do with the human condition in these often desolate days, and in some ways they make the notions of world-class achievement, benchmarks, and the rest seem superficial and limited, if not absurd. They extend beyond the appalling actualities of family breakdown, homelessness, violence, and the "savage inequalities" described by Jonathan Kozol, although social injustice has an existential dimension.

Like their elders, children and young persons inhabit a world of fearful moral uncertainty—a world in which it appears that almost nothing can be done to reduce suffering, contain massacres, and protect human rights. The faces of refugee children in search of their mothers, of teenage girls repeatedly raped by soldiers, of rootless people staring at the charred remains of churches and libraries may strike some of us as little more than a "virtual reality." Those who persist in looking feel numbed and, reminded over and over of helplessness, are persuaded to look away.

It has been said that Pablo Picasso's paintings of "weeping women" have become the icons of our time.[1] They have replaced the statues of men on horseback and men in battle; they overshadow the emblems of what once seemed worth fighting for, perhaps dying for. When even the young confront images of loss and death, as most of us are bound to do today, "it is important that everything we love be summed up into something unforgettably beautiful."[2] This suggests one of the roles of the arts. To see sketch after sketch of women holding dead babies, as Picasso has forced us to do, is to become aware of a tragic deficiency in the fabric of life. If we know enough to make those paintings the objects of our experience, to encounter them against the background of our lives, we are likely to strain toward conceptions of a better order of things, in which there will be no more wars that make women weep like that, no more bombs to murder innocent children. We are likely, in rebelling against such horror, to summon up images of smiling mothers and lovely children, metaphors for what *ought* to be.

Clearly, this is not the only role of the arts, although encounters with them frequently do move us to want to restore some kind of order, to repair, and to heal. Participatory involvement with the many forms of art does enable us, at the very least, to *see* more in our experience, to *hear* more on normally unheard frequencies, to *become conscious* of what daily routines, habits, and conventions have obscured.

We might think of what Pecola Breedlove in *The Bluest Eye* has made us realize about the metanarrative implicit in the Dick and Jane basal readers or in the cultural artifact called Shirley Temple, who made so many invisible children yearn desperately to have blue eyes.[3] We might recall the revelations discovered by so many through an involvement with *Schindler's List.* We might try to retrieve the physical consciousness of unutterable grief aroused in us by Martha Graham's dance "Lamentation," with only feet and hands visible outside draped fabric—and agony expressed through stress lines on the cloth. To see more, to hear more. By such experiences we are not only lurched out of the familiar and the taken for granted, but we may also discover new avenues for action. We may experience a sudden sense of new possibilities and thus new beginnings.

The prevailing cynicism with regard to values and the feelings of resignation it breeds cannot help but create an atmosphere in the schools that is at odds with the unpredictability associated with the experience of art. The neglect of the arts by those who identified the goals of Goals 2000 was consistent with the focus on the manageable, the predictable, and the measurable. There have been efforts to include the arts in the official statements of goals, but the arguments mustered in their favor are of a piece with the arguments for education geared toward economic competitiveness, technological mastery, and the rest. They have also helped support the dominant arguments for the development of "higher-level skills," academic achievement, standards, and preparation for the workplace.

The danger afflicting both teachers and students because of such emphases is, in part, the danger of feeling locked into existing circumstances defined by others. Young people find themselves described as "human resources," rather than as persons who are centers of choice and evaluation. It is suggested that young people are to be molded in the service of technology and the market, no matter who they are. Yet, as many are now realizing, great numbers of our young people will find themselves unable to locate satisfying jobs, and the very notion of "all the children" and even of human resources carries with it deceptions of all kinds. Perhaps it is no wonder that the dominant mood in many classrooms is one of passive reception.

Umberto Eco, the Italian critic of popular culture, writes about the desperate need to introduce a critical dimension into such reception. Where media and messages are concerned, it is far more important, he says, to focus on the point of reception than on the point of transmission. Finding a threat in "the universal of technological communication" and in situations where "the medium is the message," he calls seriously for a return to individual resistance. "To the anonymous divinity of Technological Communication, our answer could be: 'Not thy, but *our* will be done.'"[4]

The kind of resistance Eco has in mind can best be evoked when imagination is released. But, as we well know, the bombardment of images identified with "Technological Communication" frequently has the effect of freezing imaginative thinking. Instead of freeing audiences to look at things as if they could be otherwise, present-day media impose predigested frameworks on their audiences. Dreams are caught in the meshes of the salable; the alternative to gloom or feelings of pointlessness is consumerist acquisition. For Mary Warnock, imagination is identified with the belief that "there is more in our experience of the world than can possibly meet the unreflecting eye."[5] It tells us that experience always holds more than we can predict. But Warnock knows that acknowledging the existence of undiscovered vistas and perspectives requires reflectiveness. The passive, apathetic person is all too likely to be unresponsive to ideas of the unreal, the as if, the merely possible. He or she becomes the one who bars the arts as frivolous, mere frills, irrelevant to learning in the postindustrial world.

It is my conviction that informed engagements with the several arts would be the most likely way to release the imaginative capacity and give it play. However, this does not happen automatically or "naturally." We have all witnessed the surface contacts with paintings when groups of tourists hasten through museums. Without time spent, without tutoring, and without dialogue regarding the arts, people merely seek the right labels. They look for the artists' names. There are those who watch a ballet for the story, not for the movement or the music; they wait for Giselle to go mad or for Sleeping Beauty to be awakened or for the white swan to return.

Mere exposure to a work of art is not sufficient to occasion an aesthetic experience. There must be conscious participation in a work, a going out of energy, an ability to notice what is there to be noticed in the play, the poem, the quartet. "Knowing about," even in the most formal, academic manner, is entirely different from creating an unreal world imaginatively and entering it perceptually, affectively, and cognitively. To introduce people to such engagement is to strike a delicate balance between helping learners to pay heed—to attend to shapes, patterns, sounds, rhythms, figures of speech, contours, lines, and so on—and freeing them to perceive particular works as meaningful. Indeed, the inability to control what is discovered as meaningful makes many traditional educators uneasy and strikes them as being at odds with conceptions of a norm, even with notions of appropriate "cultural literacy." This uneasiness may well be at the root of certain administrators' current preoccupation with national standards.

However, if we are to provide occasions for significant encounters with works of art, we have to combat standardization and what Hannah Arendt called "thoughtlessness" on the part of all those involved. What she meant by thoughtlessness was "the heedless recklessness or hopeless confusion or complacent repetition of 'truths' which have become trivial and empty."[6] There is something in that statement that recalls what John Dewey described as a "social pathology"—a condition that still seems to afflict us today. Dewey wrote that it manifests itself "in querulousness, in impotent drifting, in uneasy snatching at distractions, in idealization of the long established, in a facile optimism assumed as a cloak."[7] Concerned about "sloppiness, superficiality, and recourse to sensations as a substitute for ideas," Dewey made the point that "thinking deprived of its normal course takes refuge in academic specialism."[8]

For Arendt, the remedy for this condition is "to think what we are doing." She had in mind developing a self-reflectiveness that originates in situated life, the life of persons open to one another in their distinctive locations and engaging one another in dialogue. Provoked by the spectacle of the Nazi Adolf Eichmann, Arendt warned against "clichés, stock phrases, adherence to conventional, standardized codes of expression and conduct," which have, she said, "the socially recognized function of protecting us against reality, that is, against the claim on our thinking attention that all events and facts make by virtue of their existence."[9] She was not calling for a new intellectualism or for a new concentration on "higher-order skills." She was asking for a way of seeking clarity and authenticity in the face of thoughtlessness, and it seems to me that we might ask much the same thing if we are committed to the release of the imagination and truly wish to open the young to the arts.

Thoughtfulness in this sense is necessary if we are to resist the messages of the media in the fashion Eco suggests, and it is difficult to think of young imaginations being freed without learners finding out how to take a critical and thoughtful approach to the illusory or fabricated "realities" presented to them by the media. To be thoughtful about what we are doing is to be conscious of ourselves struggling to make meanings, to make critical sense of what authoritative others are offering as objectively "real."

I find a metaphor for the reification of experience in the plague as it is confronted in Albert Camus' novel. The pestilence that struck the town of Oran (submerged as it was in habit and "doing business") thrust most of the inhabitants into resignation, isolation, or despair. Gradually revealing itself as inexorable and incurable, the plague froze people in place; it was simply *there*. At first Dr. Rieux fights the plague for the most abstract of reasons: because it is his job. Only later, when the unspeakable tragedies he witnesses make him actually think about what he is doing, does he reconceive his practice and his struggle and talk about not wanting to be complicit with the pestilence. By then he has met Tarrou, who is trying to be a "saint without God" and who has the wit and, yes, the imagination to organize people into sanitary squads to fight the plague and make it the moral concern of all.

Tarrou has the imagination too to find in the plague a metaphor for indifference or distancing or (we might say) thoughtlessness. Everyone carries the microbe, he tells his friend; it is only natural. He means what Hannah Arendt meant—and Dewey and Eco and all the others who resist a lack of concern. He has in mind evasions of complex problems, the embrace of facile formulations of the human predicament, the reliance on conventional solutions—all those factors I would say stand in the way of imaginative thinking and engagement with the arts. "All the rest," says Tarrou, "health, integrity, purity (if you like)—is a product of the human will, of a vigilance that must never falter." He means, of course, that we (and those who are our students) must be given opportunities to choose to be persons of integrity, persons who care.

Tarrou has a deep suspicion of turgid language that obscures the actualities of things, that too often substitutes abstract constructions for concrete particulars. This is one of the modes of the thoughtlessness Arendt was urging us to fight. She, too, wanted to use "plain, clear-cut language." She wanted to urge people, as does Tarrou, to attend to what is around them, "to stop and think." I am trying to affirm that this kind of awareness, this openness to the world, is what allows for the consciousness of alternative possibilities and thus for a willingness to risk encounters with the "weeping women," with Euripides' *Medea,* with *Moby Dick,* with Balanchine's (and, yes, the Scripture's) *Prodigal Son,* with Mahler's *Songs of the Earth.*

Another novel that enables its readers to envisage what stands in the way of imagination is Christa Wolf's *Accident: A Day's News.* It moves me to clarify my own response to the technical and the abstract. I turn to it not in order to add to my knowledge or to find some buried truth, but because it makes me see, over the course of time, what I might never have seen in my own lived world.

The power the book holds for me may be because it has to do with the accident at Chernobyl, as experienced by a woman writer, who is also a mother and grandmother. She is preoccupied by her brother's brain surgery, taking place on the same day, and by the consequences of the nuclear accident for her grandchildren and for children around the world. She spends no time wondering about her own response to such a crisis; her preoccupation is with others—those she loves and the unknown ones whom she cannot for a moment forget. It is particularly interesting, within the context of an ethic of care, to contain for a moment within our own experience the thoughts of a frightened young mother, the narrator's daughter, picturing what it means to pour away thousands of liters of milk for fear of poisoning children while "children on the other side of the earth are perishing for lack of those foods."

The narrator wants to change the conversation and asks her daughter to "tell me something else, preferably about the children." Whereupon she hears that "the little one had pranced about the kitchen, a wing nut on his thumb, his hand held high. Me Punch. Me Punch. I was thrilled by the image."[10] Only a moment before, another sequence of pictures had come into her mind and caused her to

admire the way in which everything fits together with a sleepwalker's precision: the desire of most people for a comfortable life, their tendency to believe the speakers on raised platforms and the men in white coats; the addiction to harmony and the fear of contradiction of the many seem to correspond to the arrogance and hunger for power, the dedication to profit, unscrupulous inquisitiveness, and self-infatuation of the few. So what was it that didn't add up in this equation?[11]

This passage seems to me to suggest the kind of questioning and, yes, the kind of picturing that may well be barred by the preoccupation with "world-class achievement" and by the focus on human resources that permeate Goals 2000.

But it does not have to be so. Cognitive adventuring and inquiry are much more likely to be provoked by the narrator's question about "this equation" than by the best of curriculum frameworks or by the most responsible and "authentic" assessment. To set the imagination moving in response to a text such as Wolf's may well be to confront learners with a demand to choose in a fundamental way between a desire for harmony with its easy answers and a commitment to the risky search for alternative possibilities.

Wolf's narrator, almost as if she were one of Picasso's weeping women, looks at the blue sky and, quoting some nameless source, says, "Aghast, the mothers search the sky for the inventions of learned men."[12] Like others to whom I have referred, she begins pondering the language and the difficulty of breaking through such terms as "half-life," "cesium," and "cloud" when "polluted rain" is so much more direct. Once again, the experience of the literary work may help us to feel the need to break through the mystification of technology and the language to which it has given rise.

The narrator feels the need to battle the disengagement that often goes with knowing and speaking. When she ponders the motives of those who thought up the procedures for the "peaceful utilization of nuclear energy," she recalls a youthful protest against a power plant and the rebukes and reprimands directed at the protesters for their skepticism with regard to a scientific utopia. And then she lists the activities that the men of science and technology presumably do not pursue and would probably consider a waste of time if they were forced to:

> Changing a baby's diapers. Cooking, shopping with a child on one's arm or in the baby carriage. Doing the laundry, hanging it up to dry, taking it down, folding it, ironing it, darning it. Sweeping the floor, mopping it, polishing it, vacuuming it. Dusting. Sewing. Knitting. Crocheting. Embroidering. Doing the dishes. Doing the dishes. Taking care of a sick child. Thinking up stories to tell.

Singing songs. And how many of these activities do I myself consider a waste of time?[13]

Reading this passage and posing a new set of questions, we cannot but consider the role of such concrete images in classroom conversation and in our efforts to awaken persons to talk about what ought to be. The narrator believes that the "expanding monstrous technological creation" may be a substitute for life for many people. She is quite aware of the benevolent aspects of technology: her brother, after all, is having advanced neurosurgery (which he does survive). But she is thinking, as we might well do in the schools, about the consequences of technological expansion for the ones we love. Her thinking may remind us of how important it is to keep alive images of "everything we love." I want to believe that by doing so we may be able to create classroom atmospheres that once again encourage individuals to have hope.

This brings me back to my argument for the arts, so unconscionably neglected in the talk swirling around Goals 2000. It is important to make the point that the events that make up aesthetic experiences are events that occur within and by means of the transactions with our environment that situate us in time and space. Some say that participatory encounters with paintings, dances, stories, and the rest enable us to recapture a lost spontaneity. By breaking through the frames of presuppositions and conventions, we may be enabled to reconnect ourselves with the processes of becoming who we are. By reflecting on our life histories, we may be able to gain some perspective on the men in white coats, even on our own desires to withdraw from complexity and to embrace a predictable harmony. By becoming aware of ourselves as questioners, as makers of meaning, as persons engaged in constructing and reconstructing realities with those around us, we may be able to communicate to students the notion that reality depends on perspective, that its construction is never complete, and that there is always more. I am reminded of Paul Cézanne's several renderings of Mont St. Victoire and of his way of suggesting that it must be viewed from several angles if its reality is to be apprehended.

Cézanne made much of the insertion of the body into his landscapes, and that itself may suggest a dimension of experience with which to ground our thinking and the thinking of those we teach. There are some who suggest that, of all the arts, dance confronts most directly the question of what it means to be human. Arnold Berleant writes that

> in establishing a human realm through movement, the dancer, with the participating audience, engages in the basic act out of which arise both all experience and our human constructions of the world. . . . [That basic act] stands as the direct denial of that most pernicious of all dualisms, the division of body and consciousness. In dance, thought is primed at the point of action. This is not the reflection of the contemplative mind but rather intellect poised in the body, not the deliberate consideration of alternative courses but thought in process, intimately responding to and guiding the actively engaged body.[14]

The focus is on process and practice; the skill in the making is embodied in the object made. In addition, dance provides occasions for the emergence of the integrated self. Surely, this ought to be taken into account in our peculiarly technical and academic time.

Some of what Berleant says relates as well to painting, if painting is viewed as an orientation in time and space of the physical body—of both perceiver and creator. If we take a participatory stance, we may enter a landscape or a room or an open street. Different modes of perception are asked of us, of course, by different artists, but that ought to mean a widening of sensitivity with regard to perceived form, color, and space. Jean-Paul Sartre, writing about painting, made a point that is significant for anyone concerned about the role of art and the awakening of imagination:

> The work is never limited to the painted, sculpted or narrated object. Just as one perceives things only against the background of the world, so the objects represented by art appear against the background of the universe. . . . [T]he creative act aims at a total renewal of the world. Each painting, each book, is a recovery of the totality of being. Each of them presents this totality to the freedom of the spectator. For this is quite the final goal of art: to

recover this world by giving it to be seen as it is, but as if it had its source in human freedom.[15]

In this passage Sartre suggests the many ways in which classroom encounters with the arts can move the young to imagine, to extend, and to renew. And surely nothing can be more important than finding the source of learning not in extrinsic demands, but in human freedom.

All this is directly related to developing what is today described as the active learner, here conceived as one awakened to pursue meaning. There are, of course, two contradictory tendencies in education today: one has to do with shaping malleable young people to serve the needs of technology in a postindustrial society; the other has to do with educating young people to grow and to become different, to find their individual voices, and to participate in a community in the making. Encounters with the arts nurture and sometimes provoke the growth of individuals who reach out to one another as they seek clearings in their experience and try to live more ardently in the world. If the significance of the arts for growth, inventiveness, and problem solving is recognized at last, a desperate stasis may be overcome, and people may come to recognize the need for new raids on what T. S. Eliot called the "inarticulate."

I choose to end this extended reflection on art and imagination with some words from "Elegy in Joy," by Muriel Rukeyser:

> Out of our life the living eyes
> See peace in our own image made,
> Able to give only what we can give:
> Bearing two days like midnight. "Live,"
> The moment offers: the night requires
> Promise effort love and praise.
>
> Now there are no maps and no magicians.
> No prophets but the young prophet, the sense of
>   the world.
> The gift of our time, the world to be discovered.
> All the continents giving off their several lights,
> the one sea, and the air. And all things glow.[16]

These words offer life; they offer hope; they offer the prospect of discovery; they offer light. By resisting the tyranny of the technical, we may yet make them our pedagogic creed.

ENDNOTES

1. Judi Freeman, *Picasso and the Weeping Women* (Los Angeles: Los Angeles Museum of Art, 1994).
2. Michel Leiris. "Faire-part," in E. C. Oppler, ed., *Picasso's Guernica* (New York: Norton, 1988), p. 201.
3. Toni Morrison, *The Bluest Eye* (New York: Washington Square Press, 1970), p. 19.
4. Richard Kearney, *The Wake of Imagination* (Minneapolis: University of Minnesota Press, 1988), p. 382.
5. Mary Warnock, *Imagination* (Berkeley: University of California Press, 1978), p. 202.
6. Hannah Arendt, *The Human Condition* (Chicago: University of Chicago Press, 1958), p. 5.
7. John Dewey, *The Public and Its Problems* (Athens, OH: Swallow Press, 1954), p. 170.
8. Ibid., p. 168.
9. Hannah Arendt, *Thinking: Vol. II, The Life of the Mind* (New York: Harcourt Brace Jovanovich, 1978), p. 4.
10. Christa Wolf, *Accident: A Day's News* (New York: Farrar, Straus & Giroux, 1989), p. 17.
11. Ibid.
12. Ibid., p. 27.
13. Ibid., p. 31.
14. Arnold Berleant, *Art and Engagement* (Philadelphia: Temple University Press, 1991), p. 167.
15. Jean-Paul Sartre, *Literature and Existentialism* (New York: Citadel Press, 1949), p. 57.
16. Muriel Rukeyser, "Tenth Elegy: An Elegy in Joy," in idem. *Out in Silence: Selected Poems* (Evanston, IL: TriQuarterly Books, 1992), p. 104.

DISCUSSION QUESTIONS

1. What are the implications of understanding the existential contexts of education and educational goals?
2. Why does inclusion of the arts in the school curriculum continue to be a topic of debate among many educators?
3. Why is mere exposure to a work of art insufficient for stimulating an aesthetic experience?
4. How does a neglect of the arts in school experiences affect students?
5. How might repeated significant encounters with the arts be used to combat standardization?

5

There's Too Much to Teach

JANE ROLAND MARTIN

FOCUSING QUESTIONS

1. Is there more content to teach today than schools can cover in the time available?
2. Who should decide what content gets taught?
3. Should schools share responsibility for teaching with other institutions?
4. Where else, besides school, do students learn about culture?
5. Should other institutions be held accountable for what students learn?

A colleague to whom I was explaining my current research project on culture and curriculum expressed surprise that an unregenerate feminist philosopher of education like me would concern herself with the cultural heritage. "Isn't that an item on the conservative agenda?" she asked. Conservatives have indeed appropriated this subject, but it is a huge mistake to allow the issue of transmitting the cultural heritage to become the property of any single group on the political spectrum. Surely, the disposal of a culture's wealth is—or should be—everyone's business.

A culture's stock is passed down to its new members whether one likes it or not—by education, socialization, acculturation, exposure, what have you. In view of the superabundance of cultural stock, the question is not *whether* to transmit but *which* accomplishments, practices, skills, techniques, values, attitudes, fields of knowledge, world views of the past to hand down, in *what* form to transmit them, and to whom. One who cedes these problems to a specific party, whatever its political coloration, must be prepared to settle for its choices: ones that have ultimately to do with the kind of people we hope our young will become and the kind of society we want ours and theirs to be.

The question of what is included in this culture's heritage has been hotly contested in recent years. Oddly enough, however, the explosion of new scholarship on gender, race, class, ethnicity, and sexual orientation that occasioned the debates has elicited little, if any, discussion of the deeper problems—problems of, for instance, defining the wealth, justifying decisions of which portions to preserve and transmit, deciding who or what is responsible for its preservation—to which the brute fact of cultural abundance gives rise. That the abundance question is not on every educator's mind is a result, I submit, of this culture's tacit assent to a set of interrelated assumptions about culture and education. In what follows I will examine several of these presuppositions. In particular, I will argue that a reductive definition of cultural wealth, the unwarranted equation of education and schooling, and an unduly narrow conception of the aims and functions of school have conspired to give us a false sense of security. In the concluding section I will then sketch what I take to be one part of the problem's solution.

CULTURAL ABUNDANCE

At a conference on excellence in education I attended in the mid 1980s, a member of the audience interrupted the speaker to ask what he should stop teaching the kids in his classes. "We can't do everything we're supposed to, and you're telling us to do more," this distraught man shouted. When the speaker was slow to respond, someone else jumped up and said, "I can answer your question. We've got to cut out the trivia and just teach what's important." As it happened, he thought that philosophy was important whereas the speaker leaned toward history. Much to the disappointment of a group of listeners whose wandering attention had become riveted by the unfolding drama, the relative merits of history and philosophy were not debated. Nor was the original question joined.

Surely I was not alone in regretting the speaker's decision to get on with her lecture that afternoon instead of taking time out to comment on the brute fact of cultural abundance. I cannot have been the only person to wish that she had seen fit to explore, however briefly, its accompanying problem of curriculum selection. Almost every school teacher, college instructor, and professor of education has at one time or another been driven to the brink by the thought of how much there is to teach and how impossible it is to do it all. Just about everyone who has received an education has at least once or twice wondered why he or she was being told to learn this rather than that.

The speaker's unwillingness to engage the question made me realize just how ephemeral is the discomfort that caused the junior high teacher to leap to his feet, and for good reason. One who forgets about cultural abundance and the attendant problem of curriculum selection does not feel guilty about exposing the next generation to only a small portion of our cultural heritage. Indeed, one will never know how little of the cultural inheritance one has oneself acquired.

Memory loss concerning what has sometimes been called "the" problem of curriculum is expedited by the fact that we are accustomed today to adopting a framework of thought whose fundamental premise is scarcity. In the case of culture and curriculum, however, the issue is abundance. We are used to there being too little wealth to distribute, but in this instance there is too much. Our vast cultural resources are what makes the question of what to teach so pressing; indeed, this is why content selection is a problem in the first place. The question "What should be taught?" is appallingly difficult to answer precisely because

the pool of potential subject matter is so large that no one can hope to teach or learn everything in it. Even if we discount information thought to be false and exclude skills considered to be useless and attitudes held to be undesirable, a single individual cannot master it all.

How paradoxical that even as so many of the world's resources have been shrinking, the inheritance from which curriculum's content is drawn has been growing! The problem of curriculum selection is becoming ever more pressing not just because information has accumulated over the years. As one commentator has said, there are now "dozens and dozens of disciplines, each one nearly a separate nation with its own governance, psychology, entelechy" (Ozick, 1987). Within each discipline there are also now dozens and dozens of perspectives. In addition, researchers have begun to find out about the works, experiences, practices, and achievements of people who have always been part of society but have never quite been acknowledged as members of culture.

It is unlikely that my intrepid junior high school teacher had in mind the burgeoning scholarship on women, African Americans, Native Americans, gays and lesbians, poor people, the differently abled, and Hispanic and Asian Americans when he protested that there was too much to teach. Nevertheless, since 1970 an enormous amount of work has been done in these areas with often astonishing results. Indeed, it is precisely because this work has been so fruitful that it has been perceived as a threat to the Western canon.

Although I count myself one of the canon's critics (cf. Martin, 1992, 1994), I part company with those who speak and act as if new cultural wealth can indefinitely be added to the school and university curriculum without removing some of the old. When all is said and done, curriculum space is finite. True, if we cut out the trivia—supposing agreement can be reached on what is and is not trivial—there may be room for Virginia Woolf, Zora Neal Hurston, and Langston Hughes as well as *Hamlet.* Nevertheless, there will still be much more to teach than fits into existing curriculum space.[1]

But now a puzzle arises. Although today's new scholarship increases our cultural stock, insofar as this work has looked back in anger, it has managed to diminish the value of much of the old. On balance, are we not perhaps well-advised to pretend that this new work does not exist? I would say that we are much better off knowing and acknowledging the limitations of those earlier achievements, if only because theories that falsely generalize—for instance, from data on the psychological development of White middle-class males to human development in general—can dangerously mislead; and narratives that trade in stereotypes—of, for instance, American Indians—can cruelly deceive. Besides, the new scholarship is doubly valuable. Even as it constitutes new stock, it recovers cultural assets that have over time been lost to us—the activities of 17th-century midwives and the diaries of slaves, for instance.

It would be a terrible mistake, however, to suppose that in the United States today we have forgotten or mislaid or allowed to decay only those portions of our cultural stock that relate to women and minorities. When, for instance, I read Wendell Berry's essays on farming—in particular, his description of the activities and attitudes of a good farmer of "the old school" (1987, pp. 152–161)—I thought mainly about the old agricultural knowledge and skill, attitudes, and perspectives that are now at risk. I also wondered how much has already been forgotten and how much of that is perhaps irretrievable.

Yet, what difference does it make if the know-how to construct a wrought-iron field gate or to lay a hedge (Berry, 1987, pp. 21–48) is lost to us? What difference if a 105-year-old medicine man with extensive knowledge of the healing properties of Amazon rain forest plants dies and leaves no apprentices (McFarling, 1994, p. 29)? Or, to sound a quite different note, what difference if cuts in funding to the National Endowment for the Humanities wreak havoc on this country's libraries and archives? Is it not to be expected that knowledge, skills, and art forms handed down from artisan to apprentice, farmer to son, midwife to daughter, and choreographer to dancer will finally be forgotten? Surely, what counts as vital knowledge in one historical period is quite irrelevant to another. Surely, one of the main virtues of an advanced civilization is that it liberates us from the techniques of the past.

The truth is that one never knows enough about the old knowledge, traditions, and practices

to be sure that there is nothing more to be learned from them. Furthermore, one never knows what the future will bring. Although a once precious skill or practice may now be unusable and an idea or concept developed at an earlier time seems irrelevant to our present plight, who can say that, 50 years hence, we will not be able to adapt it to good advantage?

"You sound just like a child of the Depression," a young friend said when I told her why cultural stock is worth preserving. "My grandmother even had a box on her shelf labeled 'String Too Short to Use.'" I agree that thrift can be carried too far, but I also know that new ways of doing things can have such devastating effects that our estimates of the value of the old ways undergo revision. Moreover, I do not mean to suggest that every bit of cultural stock should be preserved. Racism, child abuse, lynching, wife beating, and physical and psychological torture are cultural practices that ought not under any circumstances be handed down as living legacies to future generations—which is not to say that we should not pass down knowledge *about* them so that past mistakes are not repeated. My point is, rather, that just as it is a mistake to turn one's back on the wealth generated by the new scholarship, it is unwise to dismiss old, indigenous practices and know-how out of hand. Indeed, even as I was writing my reasons for preserving this wealth, an international news service announced a new study by anthropologists and ecologists recommending a return to the tilling methods used by pre-Columbian farmers in the Andes.

DEFINING THE WEALTH

"I have the solution to your problem," a literary scholar said when I told her about my research: "Whatever I can't fit into my lectures I put on the reading list." Her manifest surprise when I tried to explain what to me was so obvious—that our culture's wealth does not fit on even the most extensive reading list—informed me that she was implicitly operating under a neat but narrow definition.

When, in 1776, Adam Smith inquired into the wealth of nations, he was as concerned with its nature as its causes. "That wealth consists in money, or in gold and silver, is a popular notion which naturally arises from the double function of money, as the instrument of commerce and as a measure of value," he said in Volume I of his treatise on the topic (1976, p. 450). Indeed, the definition of wealth as money was such a commonplace in his day that, in Smith's view, even David Hume had not sufficiently questioned it when studying mercantilism, Europe's then dominant economic system. "It would be too ridiculous to go about seriously to prove, that wealth does not consist in money, or in gold and silver; but in what money purchases, and is valuable for purchasing," Smith wrote in *An Inquiry into the Nature and Causes of the Wealth of Nations* (1976, p. 459). And he added: "Money, no doubt, makes always a part of the national capital; but it has already been shown that it generally makes but a small part, and always the most unprofitable part of it" (p. 459).

That cultural wealth consists entirely of "high" culture—or perhaps more accurately of the "higher" learning—is as popular a notion in end of 20th-century United States as the confusion of money, or gold and silver, with wealth was in 18th-century England. If that earlier false equation was due to money's double role, possibly ours arises from a similar duality. Granted, one cannot say that the attainment of the knowledge of art, literature, history, philosophy, and the behavioral and the natural sciences is a measure of an individual's value in the United States today. Anti-intellectualism is too strong a current in the society. Yet it is fair to call the acquisition of the higher learning the main measure of value within the educational sphere. And, similarly, as money was the instrument of the commerce of Smith's day, the higher learning is the instrument of the education of our own.

It has rightly been said that Smith democratized the concept of a nation's wealth by broadening the definition to include not just the wealth of kings, or even the wealth of the merchant class, but the goods that *all* people in a society consume (Heilbroner, 1953, p. 45). In rejecting the narrow definition of cultural wealth as high culture or the higher learning, I take similar action. Of course, high culture is a part of our cultural wealth. But there is far more to a culture's wealth than the ac-

knowledged classics of art, music, and literature; more even than philosophy and economics, history, science, and psychology.

Culture in the broadest sense of the term includes not just artistic and scholarly products. It encompasses the institutions and practices, rites and rituals, beliefs and skills, attitudes and values, and world views and localized modes of thinking and acting of *all* members of society over the *whole* range of contexts. Not everything in a culture's stock counts as wealth, of course, for the term "wealth" carries with it a positive assessment. But it is a far cry from acknowledging that a culture's stock consists in liabilities as well as assets to the assumption that high culture or the higher learning exhausts its riches.

The sense of culture—and by extension cultural wealth—that I have in mind is akin to the anthropologist's. When anthropologists study cultures, they do not dream of limiting their sights to some small esoteric subset of practices and accomplishments. Anthropological definitions of culture as "all learned behavior"—or, alternatively, as "the whole range of human activities which are learned and not instinctive" (Beattie, 1964, p. 20; Herskovits, 1952, p. 21)—encompass whatever might correspond to our own conceptions of high, popular, and material culture, and they embrace countless other items as well. An old farmer's know-how, an artisan's craft, a mother's daily lessons to her offspring in the 3Cs of care, concern, and connection are all, therefore, grist for an anthropologist's mill. As cultural assets, these also fall squarely in the category of cultural wealth.

The price of an arbitrary reduction of cultural wealth to high culture is enormous, for it effectively cuts off future generations from huge portions of cultural wealth. But now suppose that the definition of cultural wealth is every bit as broad as it needs to be.[2] Another puzzle immediately arises. Slavery, war, child abuse, wife beating, and the torture of political prisoners are not natural phenomena; they are learned, not innate. But, then, according to a broad definition of culture, they are cultural practices. Must we therefore consider these a part of a culture's *wealth?* Not at all. *Representations* of immoral achievements and evil practices—whether historical, psychological, sociological, or philosophical studies or fictional, artistic, photographic, or theatrical portrayals—can all belong to the wealth of cultures, although whether or not they do must be determined on a case-to-case basis. This wealth does not include the human atrocities themselves, however.

Think of the Nazi concentration camps and the uses to which they were put. They were creations of culture, not nature—of that there can be no doubt. Yet by no stretch of the imagination do they constitute part of the wealth of cultures. In contrast to the concentration camps themselves, however, the artifacts of the camps, the photographs of victims and perpetrators, and the scale models in the Holocaust Memorial Museum in Washington, DC, can certainly be said to increase cultural wealth. Providing the underpinnings for a coherent narrative about a culture's depravities, they enable visitors to connect to the victims of the story.

One is tempted to say that instead of adding to humankind's cultural riches, the concentration camps so depleted its coffers as to place all of us in debt. But the metaphor of cultural wealth breaks down at just this juncture. Debts can be repaid, but there is no way to undo what the Nazis did. Coffers can be filled again, but new cultural riches do not cancel out inhuman acts. True, cultural assets such as the Unified Nations Declaration of Human Rights could be viewed as partial repayment of the debt incurred. Yet one takes the measure of a metaphor not just by the illumination it provides, but also by what it casts in shadow. My object in importing Adam Smith's language into the cultural domain is to make plain the fact of cultural abundance. The last thing I wish to do, however, is to hide the very existence of human evil or to trivialize its significance.

The good and the bad, assets and liabilities alike, constitute a culture's *stock* from which source its cultural wealth is drawn. A culture's wealth, in other words, is only that portion of cultural stock which is deemed valuable. Arbitrarily designating high culture our only valuable stock, we make the process of forgetting the problem of what to teach our children that much easier. Define cultural wealth narrowly and the mandate to transmit the cultural heritage to the next genera-

tion is of course greatly simplified. Selection will still be necessary because even high culture is so abundant that one cannot map all of it onto any given person's curriculum. But the twin problems of cultural abundance and curricular selection will at least appear manageable. Granted, with a non-reductive definition of cultural wealth, one might still end up deciding to transmit only high culture. However, the choice would have been made in full recognition that a single portion of wealth was being passed down.

PRESERVING THE WEALTH

It is a measure of how deeply ingrained in our collective consciousness is the equation between culture and high culture that no one considers absurd a definition of culture that mistakes a part for the whole. Yet it verges on the ridiculous that we take pride in being a literate culture, worry that literacy rates may have declined, yet do not count the 3Rs themselves as items of cultural wealth. It is equally inconsistent that we call the existence of moral codes one of the marks of civilization, yet define cultural wealth so that the 3Cs of care, concern, and connection do not belong to it. And it makes little sense that religious doctrines, political practices, medical treatments, and engineering skills—indeed the whole range of human occupations—are excluded from this category.

The problem with our own or any reductive definition of cultural wealth is that this culture's stock, like any culture's, is broadly based. No single type of thing can possibly exhaust its wealth because so many types constitute its stock. Were cultural wealth a purely theoretical construct having no practical application, an exclusionary rendering of it would be of little consequence. Education's mandate to transmit the cultural heritage anchors this concept in everyday affairs, however. After all, what is a culture's heritage if it is not its wealth? Of course, in the name of transmitting that heritage, a culture may, in spite of its good intentions, hand down cultural liabilities to its young—for instance, the practices of child abuse and war—as well as assets. Yet surely the object is to pass on to them whatever cultural stock is perceived to be of value. And just as certainly, insofar as cultural wealth is identified with high culture, a nation or society will be ignoring the greater part of its wealth.

Still and all, a broad definition of cultural wealth appears to have one fatal flaw, namely that of assigning high value to trivial pursuits. In actuality, however, rather than commit this cardinal sin, a democratic definition leaves open the question of the relative value of the various items of wealth, just as it is neutral on the issue of which parts of the wealth should be handed down. In excluding apparently trivial pursuits from the category of cultural wealth *by definition,* we deny ourselves the opportunity to discover their educational possibilities. We also run the risk that the know-how someone might some day be able to adapt to new purposes will become extinct.

A reductive definition of cultural wealth does more damage than this, however. It is a dangerous policy to restrict the wealth of cultures to high culture because no single institution of a society is the conservator of a culture's whole wealth. Suppose a portion of the whole were being squandered by one of the custodians; or, less melodramatically, that for reasons beyond anyone's control, its guardian could no longer preserve and nurture it. If the assets were not considered to belong to the culture's wealth, their loss would not even be noticed. If noticed, their disappearance would cause no alarm. On the other hand, if the items appeared on an inventory of cultural wealth, they would sooner or later be missed, whereupon decisions could be made about whether a new form of guardianship was required.

The supposition is not purely hypothetical. The guardianship of the old farmer's know-how was once a family matter but, for complex economic, technological, and sociological reasons quite beyond the control of any one individual or family grouping, the self-appointed caretaker of this portion of our wealth has for some time been unable to carry out its responsibilities. The fact that we are only dimly aware of this historic trend and quite unmoved by it is an alarming confirmation of the desperate need for a panoramic view of the contents of cultural wealth.

To cite another case in point, at the time I write it is no longer possible to ignore how violent America's youth—in particular its boys and young men—have become. Some have blamed the movement of women into the workforce for this condition. Almost no one who discusses the changes in home and family has thought to ask if these institutions have become ineffectual transmitters of the 3Cs and an ethics of care (Gilligan, 1982; Noddings, 1984). Because we do not count such virtues as belonging to our cultural wealth, it does not occur to most of us that home and family have traditionally been considered their custodians. Nor do we stop to think that if these assets are no longer being adequately conserved or successfully handed down, new guardians may have to be appointed.

Now, I do not want to paint too grim a picture of cultural loss. There are many wonderful instances of good conduct toward America's past—some as prosaic as cookbooks, others as uncommon as the living museums at Williamsburg, Virginia, and Sturbridge, Massachusetts. Museums and libraries, opera companies and ballet corps, recording companies and publishing houses, historical societies and book clubs—these and countless other institutional forms have been created to recover, protect, and nurture cultural assets. Some of the custodial arrangements serve simply as warehouses for keeping old stock. Others put tools, diaries, household goods, musical scores, and other artifacts on display. Some treat practices and artifacts alike as rusty relics. Transmitting as they preserve, others put the relics into a form in which they can be studied and understood. On occasion they even provide opportunities for something more.

In addition to institutions like museums that have been specifically designed to protect and preserve the wealth, ones like school, home, church, neighborhood, and workplace do so in the course of transmitting it to the next generation. Preservation and transmission may be theoretically distinct processes, the one directed to the protection of assets for the next generation and the other to handing the stock over, passing it down to them, yet these two functions are often so intimately connected in practical life as to be virtually indistinguishable. Keep a set of documents in an archive long enough for the next generation to take physical possession of it and it will, in effect, have been transmitted to them. Teach your skills to your sons and daughters and your know-how will be preserved.

Despite the number and variety of custodians, however, our assets are not secure. Smith wrote, "It can seldom happen that the circumstances of a great nation can be much affected either by the prodigality or misconduct of individuals; the profusion or imprudence of some, being always more than compensated by the frugality and good conduct of others" (1976, p. 362). A nation's cultural wealth may not be threatened by the prodigality of a few individuals so long as their imprudence is compensated for by the frugality of the majority. But the prospect of such compensation scarcely seems warranted when the greater part of a people have no knowledge of what cultural assets they possess and, in any case, exhibit a devil-may-care attitude toward that inheritance.

John Stuart Mill, whose *Principles of Political Economy* caused him to be compared "not unfavorably with Adam Smith himself" (Heilbroner, 1953, p. 125), believed that people by nature act so as to maximize their own pleasure or happiness. Where Smith seemed to think that capitalism was innate, Mill took men and women, one and all, to be hedonists by birth. Yet Mill was also the person who said that every individual should act so as to maximize the happiness of the greatest number. Having no faith in miracles and finding no evidence whatsoever that an invisible hand would make things right, he looked to education to bring private pleasure into line with the public good. Education and opinion, he wrote in *Utilitarianism,* should so use their power over human character "as to establish in the mind of each individual an indissoluble association between his own happiness and the good of the whole" (Mill, 1962, p. 269). Mill made it clear, moreover, that it was not enough simply to rule out the possibility in people's minds of happiness to oneself being consistent with conduct opposed to the general good. Education and opinion should also make sure that "a direct impulse to promote the general good may be in every individual one of the habitual motives of action, and the sentiments connected therewith may fill a large and prominent

place in every human being's sentient existence" (Mill, 1962, p. 269).

Discovering no signs of an invisible hand that brings private intentions regarding cultural wealth into line with the general welfare, I in turn look to education and opinion to put a halt to our collective squandering. Mill knew from his own experience that education does not only take place in schools. Like him, I use the term *education* in its broadest sense. Wherever it is housed, education should so employ its power as to establish in girls and boys, men and women, builders and buyers, and citizens and governors a direct impulse to preserve the wealth of cultures, along with the sentiments connected therewith. And education must also help public opinion reach this same conclusion.

EDUCATIONAL AGENCY

Try now to imagine Adam Smith proposing his broad definition of the wealth of nations and at the same time giving tacit consent to the old mercantile system. The discrepancy between the traditional ways of thinking and acting and his new, enlarged vision of a nation's wealth would have been painfully apparent. A similarly jarring experience is in store for those who adopt a broad definition of cultural wealth while leaving intact the present false equation between education and schooling and the antiquated narrow definition of the latter's function.

In the United States, at least, the reduction of education to schooling is a relatively recent phenomenon. According to Bernard Bailyn (1960, p. 16ff), the family was the main agency of education in the forming of U.S. society, and whatever it did not accomplish, the local community and the church undertook. Thus, the extended colonial family shaped the attitudes, patterns of behavior, manners, and morals of all the young in its care and also gave instruction in the agricultural or trade skills they would need as adults. The external community then reinforced the instruction young people received at home while introducing them to the outside world and, in particular, to governmentally imposed discipline. Finally, the church gave formal instruction in Christian doctrine while initiating children into the conceptual framework and the imagery underlying their culture's way of understanding and interpreting human existence.

Schools existed in the early colonial period, but they played a relatively small role. Indeed, even when, in the mid-19th century, a system of free, universal, public schooling was under construction in the United States, most people took school to be a minor part of education. Lawrence Cremin tells us that the generation that instituted "the common school" is also the one that established public libraries, lyceums, mechanics' institutes, agricultural societies, penny newspapers (Cremin, 1965, pp. 6–7). And the next generation introduced still more educative agencies, among them the social settlement.

It was only in the 20th century that school came to be seen as the sum total of education. And it is still so perceived. True, religious leaders present themselves as educators, museums house education departments, and television networks label some programs "educational." Nevertheless, the conflation of education and schooling to which Ivan Illich so dramatically drew attention (Illich, 1970) continues to govern this culture's educational thought. You open a newspaper or magazine to its education section expecting to read about schools and universities. The government appoints a new commissioner of education and everyone assumes that his or her domain is the nation's schools. And, perhaps most telling of all, those people who describe themselves as education's critics and reformers and are labeled as such by others are, from first to last, school's critics and reformers.

Education is not the sole medium for transmitting cultural wealth, yet it is so central to the preservation and transmission of cultural assets that it is quite imprudent to reduce it to one of its institutional forms. A broad definition of cultural wealth requires a broad conception of *educational agency* so that large quantities of stock are not lost to posterity. When school is considered to be "the" educating agent, it is only natural to see it as "the" one true or legitimate transmitter of the heritage. But then, even if the assets in school's custody are assured safe passage, whatever is in the keep of other custodians is all too easily overlooked.

As it happens—indeed, as befits school's history—the assets that our culture has placed in school's keep represent one small portion of the wealth. When as a result of the Industrial Revolution occupations left the household, school eventually took on the task of preparing young people to enter the workplace—something home gave up doing with work's exodus (Cremin, 1968, ch. 2; Lazerson & Grubb, 1974). School also shouldered what had once been the local community's job of initiating children into the larger society (Cremin, 1965, 1968). With home continuing to be held responsible through its domestic curriculum for educating members of the next generation for life in the world of the transformed private home, school's duty became that of educating them to take their places in the world of politics, work, and the professions.

Serving a different but equally important educational function from that of home, school quite naturally confined itself to transmitting a different but equally important portion of our cultural wealth. Needless to say, this division of responsibilities had gendered implications. For with the world of the private home culturally identified as women's realm and the world of work, politics, and the professions as men's, it stands to reason that school would not be expected to bother with wealth that, having been accumulated by women, was marked by the imprints of femininity; that, indeed, school would have its hands full trying to pass down to future generations the wealth that had been amassed by men and carried the imprints of masculinity.

The historic division between school and home of responsibilities for transmitting our culture's heritage effectively made school the guardian of a fraction of the wealth. That portion has been considerably reduced, moreover, by the assimilationist policies to which our nation has subscribed. Full-fledged members of the world of work, politics, and the professions were—and to a great extent still are—expected to shed whatever minority religious, ethnic, and racial identities their families might have and to take on those of the dominant White, Protestant, middle-class, male tribe. As the institution charged with preparing young people for membership in that world, school's role was thus further circumscribed. The wealth placed in its keep was, in turn, limited to those assets that, when handed down, would meet the dominant group's needs and perpetuate its interests.

SHARING RESPONSIBILITY

It is downright irrational to persist in assigning school a function that is defined in relation to and relies on home's educational agency while denying the existence of that very agency. It is also the height of folly to assign what we take to be our one and only educational agent the single task of preparing children for life in the public sphere, although even as adults they will continue to dwell in private homes. Besides, given the great changes home has undergone in recent decades and the importance to both the development of children and the life of society of the cultural wealth that home has been charged with transmitting, to equate education with schooling, yet continue to endorse a function for school that is premised on home's carrying out an opposite but equally important function, is short-sighted in the extreme.

The breakdown in the latter part of this century of this culture's gender-based division of labor renders that old gendered definition of school's function obsolete. The system that denied women entry into the world of work, politics, and professions had numerous problems, not the least of which was the subordination of women. Nonetheless, if one accepted its premises, it provided a plausible rationale for the way home and school divided up their educational responsibilities. Except in the very poorest families, mothers stayed home to do, and to teach their daughters to stay home and do, the domestic work that boys in school relied on as they mastered the knowledge, skills, attitudes, and values required by society's economic and political work, work whose execution the fathers and uncles who actually engaged in these occupations counted on. Now things have changed. Briefly put, the people culturally assigned responsibility for preserving and transmitting the domestic portion of our cultural wealth are too busy to do this job well. Today, girls accompany boys to school and women from all walks of life enter the public world.[3]

If society's domestic work were limited to what goes by the name of "housework," it might not matter that the cultural wealth in home's keep is now at risk. But the domestic work to which I refer consists not just of housekeeping but also of the emotional and educational labor that in this culture have been major constituents of domesticity. Were there a third sex that could be prevailed upon to fill the domestic arena with its presence and hand down domestic assets such as the 3Cs and the ethics of care to the next generation, it might not be so misguided of us to allow school to persist in serving its old function. But unless one wants to count the electronic media as such—and we all know how much attention it pays to preserving and transmitting the virtues of care, concern, and connection—there is none in the offing.

In view of the disruption of the old gendered division of labor and the fact that school is now generally thought to be the predominant—nay, the one and only—educational agent in the United States, the gendered division of educational functions makes no sense. In consequence, the present division of responsibilities for transmitting our culture's wealth loses whatever plausibility it once had. As if this were not enough to demonstrate how imperative it is to redefine both school's function and its custodial duties, one need only consider the great shifts in the composition of this nation's population. Casting doubt on the assimilationist model of schooling that has for so long been held up as an ideal, they too throw into question the limited conception of what wealth belongs in school's hands.

To avoid misunderstanding, let me stress that to say that school's function needs to be redefined in light of the historic social transformations of the last few decades is not to say that school should shoulder all of education's tasks. To say that this nation needs to give school responsibility for wealth it once disdained is not to say that school should try to transmit all our culture's wealth by itself. School cannot possibly do it all. Nor, once the false equation with education is rejected, is there any reason for school to attempt the impossible. On the other hand, that school is already an overburdened institution does not justify those who would cling to outmoded conceptions of its mission.

Yet will school still *be* school if it takes on new functions, and with them shoulders responsibility for transmitting different portions of our cultural wealth? If one learns nothing else from the writings of historians like Bailyn and Cremin, one discovers that education in general and schooling in particular are as subject to change, as much a part of the societal flux, as everything else. Thus, to suppose that school has some immutable task or function that it and only it must carry out, or that it can have in its custody one and only one small portion of our heritage, is to attribute to school an essential nature it does not possess. Yes, school can add new functions and become guardian to different forms of cultural wealth. It can also shed or share old functions and time-honored custodial duties without losing its identity. After all, those old roles and responsibilities were themselves once brand new.

School clearly stands in need of radical reconceptualization. With the rejection of the false equation between education and schooling, one can see, however, that the process of rethinking must be part of a new theory of educational agency, one in which the whole range of custodians of cultural wealth are considered bona fide educational agents with practices and policies of their own.

In Bailyn's narrative, the community cooperated with home and family by elaborating on their teachings. Now the tables have been turned and home tends to be regarded simply as school's helper in the educational process, and a very minor one at that.[4] I do not for a moment mean to suggest that with a redefined function and a new list of custodial responsibilities, school will need no more help. My point is, rather, that when school itself is seen as one among many educational agents, it will no longer be in a position to treat the aims and procedures of other institutions as automatically subordinate to its own.

If, when the whole range of cultural custodians are acknowledged to be educational agents, school will not be able to reduce home's educative function to that of proctoring children's homework—or, for that matter, reduce industry's educational function to that of providing expensive equipment—school nevertheless stands to gain from the reconceptualization I am proposing. For it will then be able to count on the collaboration and cooperation of genuine partners in the educational process.

I have recently argued at some length that school should begin to share responsibility with home for transmitting our culture's domestic curriculum (Martin, 1992). Let me now add to that conception of shared educational agency by saying that I also firmly believe that school needs to start sharing some of its present functions and custodial responsibilities with other educational agents: for instance, vocational education with industry; science, social studies, and art education with museums; music education with symphony orchestras and opera companies; and physical education with health professions.[5] San Francisco's Exploratorium, as described by Hilde Hein (1990), is a good example of the kind of sharing I envision. To be sure, Frank Oppenheimer, its founder, never did convince the state to consider the Exploratorium part of its official educational system (Hein, 1990, p. 145). Yet as Hein points out, the museum has never had a separate education department, for it "as a whole is dedicated to teaching and learning, and that is what everyone at the museum does" (p. 125). Oppenheimer always insisted "that museums are educational institutions and . . . that there is no essential difference between the preservation of culture by museums and its transmission by education" (p. 146).

CONCLUSION

The overabundance problem that so tormented the teacher who rose to his feet that day in Albany, New York, is not easily solved. In proposing a new era of cooperation among the whole range of cultural custodians, I approach it from a particular perspective—that of transmitting the wealth—and in so doing offer what I know to be just one part of the problem's solution.[6] I am fully aware that it is not easy to shed old habits of thought. I am not so naive as to be suggesting that no material conditions are implicated in this culture's educational assumptions. Still and all, I believe that if we can envision an array of institutions, all of which share the tasks of preserving our vast cultural assets, see themselves and are seen by others as legitimate educational agents, and work together to transmit the wealth, we will at least have gained insight into our problem and may even have a better idea of what to strive for.

One vital step in ushering in an era of cooperation across the whole range of cultural custodians is the acknowledgment that school has much to gain from treating other educational agents as partners rather than as humble assistants or else dangerous rivals. Another step is the acceptance of the principle of accountability by the whole range of educational agents. One of the worst by-products of the false equation of education and schooling is that no unacknowledged educational agent can, in good logic, be charged with *mis*educating our youth. Yet in bombarding young people with unwholesome, antisocial models of living and in making these appear fatally attractive, the print and electronic media are guilty of doing precisely this. A beginning to holding them accountable for the damage they are doing in preserving and transmitting our culture's liabilities rather than its wealth is to make public their actual status as educational agents.

In conclusion, let me return briefly to Mill. Mill wanted education and opinion to ensure that a direct impulse to promote the general good was a habitual motive of action of each individual. My partial solution to the problem posed by cultural superabundance requires that the actions of the whole range of cultural custodians/educational agents be similarly inspired. Would that it were enough to democratize the definition of cultural wealth and broaden our conception of what counts as an educational agent! Would that we could redefine school's function and leave it at that! These measures enable one to see just how pressing the problem of abundance is and to breathe a sigh of relief that the tasks of preservation and transmission are not school's alone. But more is required, and that more involves the education of the whole range of cultural custodians themselves in accepting their educational responsibilities, in working together with other educational agents, and above all in bringing private gain into line with the public good.

ENDNOTES

This article was delivered as the 20th De Garmo Lecture sponsored annually by the Society of Professors of Education and delivered in April 1995 at the AERA Meeting in San Francisco.

1. As there will be if we follow the more general dictum "Be more efficient," of which "Cut the trivia" is a special case. Another common response to the problem of superabundance, namely "Teach students how to learn and then they can go on and learn whatever they want or need to know," is also deficient. Among other things, it begs the question of whether the acquisition of all cultural wealth should be optional, it presupposes that all the wealth will be preserved and will be out there waiting to be acquired even if no one transmits it, and it assumes that all forms of wealth are equally easy to recognize and are equally accessible.

2. I should point out that it needs to be broad enough to encompass even those domestic processes and practices that transform human infants into creatures of culture and are often perceived, therefore, as standing closer to nature than to culture (cf. Ortner, 1974).

3. Which is not to say that the two sexes are treated equally when they get to school or that women are always treated well when they enter the public world.

4. Viz. the silent treatment accorded home in the reports of the 1980s on the condition of American education.

5. Such sharing already occurs, but the parties to it are usually perceived as school's helpers rather than as educational agents in their own right.

6. For an outline of my ideas on another part, see Martin (1993).

REFERENCES

Bailyn, B. (1960). *Education in the Forming of American Society.* New York: Vintage.

Beattie, J. (1964). *Other Cultures.* New York: The Free Press.

Berry, W. (1987). *Home Economics.* San Francisco: North Point Press.

Cremin, L. (1965). *The Genius of American Education.* New York: Vintage.

Cremin, L. (1968). *The Transformation of the School.* New York: Knopf.

Gilligan, C. (1982). *In a Different Voice.* Cambridge, MA: Harvard University Press.

Heilbroner, R. L. (1953). *The Worldly Philosophers.* New York: Simon and Schuster.

Hein, H. (1990). *The Exploratorium: The Museum as Laboratory.* Washington, DC: Smithsonian Institution Press.

Herskovits, M. J. (1952). *Economic Anthropology.* New York: Alfred A. Knopf.

Illich, I. (1970). *Deschooling Society.* New York: Harper & Row.

Lazerson, M., & Grugg, W. N. (Eds.). (1974). Introduction. In *American Education and Vocationalism* (pp. 1–50). New York: Teachers College Press.

Martin, J. R. (1992). *The Schoolhome.* Cambridge, MA: Harvard University Press.

Martin, J. R. (1993). "The New Problem of Curriculum." *Synthese 94:* 85–104.

Martin, J. R. (1994). *Changing the Educational Landscape.* New York: Routledge.

McFarling, U. L. (1994, October 3). "Nature's Vanishing Pharmacy." *The Boston Globe,* pp. 25, 28–29.

Mill, J. S. (1962). *Utilitarianism, on Liberty, Essay on Bentham.* New York: New American Library.

Noddings, N. (1984). *Caring.* Berkeley: University of California Press.

Ortner, S. B. (1974). "Is Female to Male as Nature Is to Culture?" In M. Z. Rosaldo & L. Lamphere (Eds.), *Women, Culture & Society* (pp. 67–87). Stanford, CA: University of Stanford Press.

Ozick, C. (1987, January 18). "The Muse, Postmodern and Homeless." *New York Times Book Review,* 9.

Smith, A. (1976). *An Inquiry into the Nature and Causes of the Wealth of Nations.* Chicago: University of Chicago Press.

DISCUSSION QUESTIONS

1. What does Martin mean by the term *cultural wealth?*
2. Could a process be developed to fairly decide which knowledge is of most value for students to learn? What would that process be like?
3. What is the difference between education and schooling?
4. How might schools enter into partnerships with other institutions, as Martin suggests?
5. Should producers of television shows, movies, video games, and music videos play a part in the partnership? Should they be held responsible for what students learn?

6

Kudzu, Rabbits, and School Reform

JOHN I. GOODLAD

FOCUSING QUESTIONS

1. What are schools for?
2. What guidelines or recommendations can you make for modifying or improving school purposes?
3. How would you describe the relationship between schools and society?
4. What standards would you recommend to improve schooling?
5. In what way can we hold teachers accountable? Parents? Students?
6. Why is the publication *A Nation at Risk* considered a major turning point in school reform?
7. How would you improve high-stakes testing to conform to the purposes of schooling?

Recently, colleagues and I were more than a little startled by a letter to the editor of one of our local newspapers. It had been wryly captioned "Civic Spirit," and it read as follows:

> Our son recently finished 90 hours of community service. The crime to fit this punishment? He just happens to be a graduating senior.
>
> We believe community service is a wonderful way for drunk drivers, juvenile delinquents—any member of society who has cost the community pain, money, etc.—to pay back a little of what they owe. Is it appropriate for productive, high-achieving high school students to be required to do more "punishment" than the average teenage burglar? In our opinion, any teenager who stays out of trouble is contributing to their community.

Presumably, the couple writing this letter assumed that they had performed their civic duty by bringing a high-achieving student into the world. Their son, in turn, had taken care of his community responsibilities through academic achievement.

I am reminded of a quite different letter to a newspaper editor reporting the behavior of an aging woman at an open meeting of a state's budget committee.

> Exasperated by the repeated cuts in allocations for schools, she stood up and spoke out in protest. The committee's chairman interrupted her.
>
> "You are a schoolteacher, I assume."
>
> "No, I am not," she replied.
>
> "Then you must have a daughter or son who is."
>
> "No, I do not."
>
> "Surely, grandchildren in school?"
>
> "I have no children," she replied, "but I have to live with everyone else's children."

THE HARD AND TOUGH AND THE SOFT AND TENDER

These two letters illustrate a long-standing tension regarding the purposes of our schools. At the turn of the 19th century into the 20th, William James referred to the "hard and tough" and the "soft and tender" as the warp and woof in the fabric of U.S. social and political ideology. He saw the need for balancing the two. But they have tended to be out of balance, with one rising and the other falling in cycles of two to three decades, and schooling following several years behind.

The rhetoric of school purpose has been relatively stable, however. The dozen or so goals that surface again and again in commissioned reports and district guidelines for schools have consistently embraced personal, social, vocational, and academic attributes. In 1987, Mortimer Adler wove the rhetorical fabric this way: "Preparation for duties of citizenship is one of three objectives for any sound system of public schooling in our society. Preparation for earning a living is another, and the third is preparation for discharging everyone's moral obligation to lead a good life and make as much of one's self as possible."[1] Poll after poll and study after study have revealed that we want all three.

Nonetheless, reform era after reform era— each politically driven—puts policy and practice out of balance. Adults with quite ordinary academic records invent the past in exhorting schools to be hard and tough, as schools supposedly were for them. "Educating the whole child" is frequently viewed as the dangerous notion of woolly-headed progressive educators. Indeed, it is not so much the substance of reform cycles but more the side effects that do harm. Whether soft and tender or hard and tough, school reforms fade and die, frequently from their own excesses. But their side effects live on as "eduviruses" that add cost to the system and create roadblocks to the serious redesign and sustained improvement we need.

The School Reform Enterprise

More than in most European countries, U.S. education policy has tied schooling directly to the nation's economic health. In addition, we have lagged behind most developed nations in ensuring that young people receive the human services that ready them for school and buttress their educational experiences once they are enrolled. The landmark report of the National Commission on Excellence in Education, *A Nation at Risk,* employed military language and metaphor in tying the schools to our declining competitiveness in the global economy.[2] Had the charges been well founded, our schools would have been declared triumphant when the economy soared in the 1990s. But there was not a word of tribute. Instead, the current hard-and-tough era of school reform has overrun local schools like kudzu, threatening to squeeze out all else.

School reform has taken on social, political, and economic capital in its own right. Candidates Bush and Gore cloaked their presidential campaigns in it. I shudder each time another elected state chief executive declares herself or himself to be an "education governor." President Reagan was monumentally bored with the prospect of a report from his National Commission on Excellence in Education—at least until his handlers convinced him of the political mileage to be gained from promoting school reform. Since then, the rituals have served politicians admirably. The trick is to keep alive and well the message that our schools are failing. Even though most parents rate their local schools quite high, particularly at the elementary level, they are told that there are bad schools out there and that the ills of those schools are contagious. We pay careful attention to these messages, and perhaps we don't notice that it is school reform itself that spreads these infections.

Should we relax, then, in the belief that our schools are just fine and need no change? Of course not. Is the need for improvement only in our urban centers, frequently cited as overwhelmed by viruses? Of course not, even though the needs in our cities are great and the challenges daunting.

No, the harsh reality is that, should school reform outrun its political usefulness and victory be declared, our schools would no more be engines propelling the nation's economy than they were in 1983. Worse, they would be less connected to their long-standing social, personal, and intellectual purposes, even if the test scores were demonstrably improved beyond the rhetorical expectations of school reform, which is unlikely.

The trouble is that the school reform enterprise has been prescribing the wrong medicines for quite some time. It has ignored the broad purposes of schooling in a democratic society, ignored the huge body of research that would be eagerly examined if the field of interest were something other than schooling, and ignored the implications for school policy and practice of the relevant knowledge accumulating in such fields as anthropology, linguistics, psychology, sociology, and more. Some serious historical and philosophical inquiry might well have given weight to the opinions of political leaders. Moreover, the marginalized advice of critics was coming not just from self-serving "educationists," as charged, but from some of our most thoughtful analysts, scholars, and respected public figures. Of course, school reform has stirred one sector of the economy—the testing industry and that growing panoply of companies seeking profit from the public's investment in schooling.

With the health needs of our schools scarcely examined, the choice of medicines could reflect only ill-informed opinion. The random coupling of ends and means leads to unintended, unexamined consequences. In the realm of human health, these are called side effects and are so labeled. In school reform, the side effects go unheralded and become viruses in the education system. When the next era of school reform comes around, the targets of blame are once more the students, their teachers, teacher educators, and the schools—the perennial victims of what Rona Wilensky refers to as the mythology of school reform.[3] Those who should be held accountable are by then out to lunch.

Standards and Testing

The hard and tough has had a long run in schooling this time around. In the 1990s, it appeared that the usual excesses would be self-correcting. The idea of academic standards in subject matter, methods of inquiry, and even pedagogy surfaced and was advanced by such scholarly bodies as the National Academy of Sciences. National commissions did excellent work in developing standards in the major subjects of school curricula. "Standards" became the key word in promoting the cause of school reform nationwide. There were soon sets of national, state, and local district standards competing for attention, with accompanying tension over which should triumph.

The warnings of critics were quickly confirmed, however, when issues of what student attainment to measure and how to measure it arose,

right on schedule. The central issue had to do, of course, with aligning standards, tests, and classroom teaching. Who can be held accountable when the tests are prepared to measure the standards but teachers do not teach to the standards because they are ill prepared or because they disagree with them, and the test items are thus selected from content unfamiliar to the students?

This is familiar school reform terrain, visited and revisited in various forms and to little avail throughout the 20th century. A few decades ago, many states sought to harness teacher competencies to student proficiencies. Or was it teacher proficiencies to student competencies? Then pressure was brought to bear on higher education to prepare teachers in the required competencies. Or was it proficiencies? It was a costly undertaking in time and dollars, and it was extremely repugnant to people educated to be thoughtful decision makers. For several years after the whole enterprise collapsed, some state departments went on collecting data regarding institutional compliance. Were school reform not almost completely ahistorical, we might have something to show for each new era of reform, beginning with a critical appraisal of boondoggles about to be repeated. Since education is intended, in part, to keep us from repeating our mistakes, the conduct of education should be exemplary in avoiding repeated failures.

There is nothing wrong with standards. They guide and drive the whole of individual and collective behavior. And tests of many kinds provide useful feedback. Self-imposed standards and tests drive most of us, for better or for worse. Both guided my daily teaching and assessment of 34 pupils spread over eight grades in the one-room school for which I was steward many years ago. The results of standardized tests received months after their administration in my classroom would have helped me not at all. To plan each day's schedule, I had to know how well each child was reading, spelling, and figuring. And so it was for many subsequent years of teaching children, youths, and adults. And so it is with teachers generally. They need and want help, of course, but they deeply resent both totalitarian intrusion into decisions for which they will be held responsible and the side effects that invariably accompany such reform mandates.

There is plenty in the standards and testing elements of the current school reform era that warrants careful scrutiny. The necessary analyses abound, and they are rich in thoughtful recommendations. Were the school reform enterprise not so isolated from and suspicious of the robust scholarly inquiry that now exists and the lessons to be learned from it, there could be useful residue from which constructive school change might be built.

However, it is characteristic of school reforms—whether of the soft and tender or hard and tough variety—not to fade gracefully away but to expire from their own excesses, leaving little residue. The problem with the present, long-lasting era lies not in its leaving too little residue, but too much. This baggage is made up partly of dangerous assumptions and partly of damage to specific human beings, to teaching as a career, to our educational institutions, and to the high level of intelligence the infrastructure of our democracy requires.

BETTER TEACHERS, BETTER SCHOOLS?

Now that the narrative of economic utility is driving our schools, the influence of the business community on school reform should come as no surprise. Not just high school or college graduation rates but also grades and test scores rank high in the selection of workers in many sectors of the marketplace. When high test scores fail to deliver the desired qualities, employers beat the drum for tougher standards and tests. What these employers do not understand is that high test scores predict high test scores, but not much else: not problem-solving skills, not good work habits, not honesty, not dependability, not loyalty, and not the dispositions and virtues embedded in our expectations for schooling.

Research on cognition reveals that the transfer of learning from one domain of human behavior to another is low. Each domain must be taught directly. The challenge to educators is illustrated by the fact that even students doing well in school-based mathematics commonly fail to recognize the same operations in daily life outside of school. Of course, there is little assurance that teachers, especially in elementary schools, will have had more than skimpy preparation in either

the necessary mathematics or pedagogy. Nonetheless, serious attention to the education of educators ranked low in school reform eras throughout the 20th century.

Over the past year, I have been asking members of groups to which I speak to select from four items the one they believe to have most promise for improving our schools. Three of the four are politically popular:

- standards and tests mandated by all states;
- a qualified, competent teacher in every classroom;
- nonpromotion and grade repetition for all students who fail to reach grade-level standards on the tests; and
- schools of choice for all parents.

From an audience of about a thousand people at the 2001 National School Boards Association conference, one person chose the first. All the rest chose the second, which usually is the unanimous choice, whatever the group.

As part of a comprehensive study of teacher education in the United States conducted in the late 1980s,[4] a colleague found no mention of teacher education in commissioned reports on school improvement and no mention of schools in commissioned reports on the improvement of teacher education between 1892 and 1986.[5] The National Commission on Teaching and America's Future connected the relationship between good teachers and good schools in its 1996 report and detailed the steps we must take in order to have competent, caring, and qualified teachers in every classroom by 2006. The media and the school reform industry yawned. School reform has a life of its own. It has little to do with what our schools are for or what most people want in the way of improving them.

Yet we find raising the scores on mandated tests, ending "social promotion," offering vouchers, and creating charter schools on the front burners of politically driven school reform. None of these—or even more promising alternatives—will go anywhere without competent, caring, qualified teachers. Laura Bush's presumably well-intentioned appeal to retiring military personnel to consider a second career in teaching only obscures the critical issues. If teaching our young in schools became a lifelong professional career—adequately rewarded and supported, with decision-making authority commensurate with responsibility—teacher shortages would fade away. The Flexner Report of 1910 propelled medical education from an apprenticeship model to a professional model, driven by scientific inquiry. But the process took several decades.[6] We could do the same for teacher education, teaching, and the schools if it were not for our beguilement with the mythology of school reform.

KUDZU, RABBITS, AND EDUVIRUSES

The ongoing debate over school policy and practice has narrowed almost exclusively to how to make standards and testing better. As I said above, there could be some positive residue. But this should not and must not continue to take our attention away from the baggage that almost invariably accompanies school reform—a rather nasty concept—and is passed along from reform era to reform era. It is not what is currently central to the debate in education but what is largely ignored that will ultimately bite back.

In 1876, the kudzu vine was introduced into the United States to shade the porches of southern mansions. In the 1940s, it was widely planted to control erosion. Capable of growing luxuriously up to one foot per day, kudzu kills forests by entirely covering trees and shrubs. Today, it covers between two and four million acres in the southern U.S. and costs an estimated $50 million yearly in lost farm and timber production. Its initial appeal and use have long been forgotten.

At about the same time—and also to satisfy the desires of the privileged—wild rabbits were introduced into Australia. In 1859, Thomas Austin brought 24 rabbits from England and released them on his property in southern Victoria. Expected to expand in number and provide a hunting mecca for Austin and his guests, the rabbits quickly outran both these expectations and the exterminating capabilities of the hunters. During the seventh year following their importation, the successful shooting of over 14,000 scarcely dented the wild rabbit population. More than a century later, the introduction of rabbit calicivirus disease—intended to reduce the rabbit population—created a plague so deadly that it is now the target of one of the world's biggest biological control programs. Currently, the Australian government reports that, all told, rabbits cost the nation's agricultural industries hundreds of millions of dollars each year in loss of crops and land degradation.

The direct and indirect costs of the "eduvirus" school reform disease are much more difficult to calculate. As with the introduction of kudzu and rabbits, the explanations offered for proposed school reforms are virtuous: "It's all for the children." When *A Nation at Risk* sounded the alarm bell for school improvement, a variety of innovative initiatives, largely supported by private philanthropy, sprang into existence in most parts of the country. As with cottage industries, which schools largely are, those who plowed the fields and ground the wheat were doing what they believed in, and they were held responsible for that work. They put their careers on the line. As experienced educators, they understood the terrain and the dangers of introducing kudzu and wild rabbits into it. Limited resources and the deep structures of schooling had the dual effect of restraining both progress (unfortunately) and foolishness (fortunately). Such conditions are unfavorable to the incubation and spread of eduviruses.

But then "McSchool" took over, and test scores became the bottom line. With some school districts, notably in Texas, tying administrators' salary adjustments to test scores, pressures on teachers and students to produce quickly followed. After the initial round of testing in Houston, outsourcing the schooling of some low achievers to a private firm bumped up scores the next time around in the schools from which they had departed. This and other maneuvers of dubious virtue and little educational value raised scores and attracted attention, but the curricular and pedagogical changes supposedly responsible remain obscure.

The speed with which school reform eduviruses have spread has far outpaced that of the side effects of introducing kudzu into the southern United States and rabbits into Australia. Rod Paige, then superintendent of the Houston schools, soon had a bully pulpit as secretary of education from which to tout a model of reform that aligned nicely with the education plank in

President Bush's school reform platform: "Leave no child behind."

Meanwhile, far to the northwest of Houston, the teachers of a one-school rural district turned down the pro bono offer of a biologist-turned-science-educator to help the children understand the front-burner environmental issues of their community. They did not see how this would help raise test scores. On Long Island, hundreds of parents, many attracted initially to the long-standing high reputation of Scarsdale's schools, anticipated the arrival of the eduvirus. With school district support, they agreed to keep their children out of school on test day. Testing, they said, was destroying what had made their schools good.

IT'S ALL FOR THE CHILDREN

We readily identify with instances such as these even as we fail to connect with aggregated data. We read about the need for millions of new teachers over the next few years, and old proposals for getting more teachers more quickly are resurfacing. Yet career teachers and administrators in droves are taking early retirement or new jobs, and about one-third of new teachers leave the field during their first three years. Most states are putting pressure on colleges and universities to graduate their students, including future teachers, in four years. They also put pressure on schools to get the test scores up. But the overloaded preparation programs of primary teachers average just a course and a half in the teaching of reading, very little preparation in mathematics, and just one course in teaching math. But up with the test scores and leave no child behind!

Late in his presidency, Bill Clinton took to the bully pulpit to advocate the abolition of so-called social promotion. The Bush Administration picked up the baton, and conservative school reformers blamed the practice on the soft-headed products of that liberal scheme, professional teacher education. Actually, the idea is a very hard-headed economic one. In the late 1890s, Charles William Eliot, president of Harvard University, and William Rainey Harper, president of the University of Chicago, expressed concern over the negative impact of nonpromotion on the educational and personal well-being of high school students, many of whom dropped out of school when they failed a grade. Their words affected practice not at all. But a study by Leonard Ayers in the next decade brought down the order to ease up on grade retention practices in many districts. He found that flunking large numbers of children in elementary schools increased the number of years they would have to spend in school and so increased the costs of their schooling. "It's all for the children" is often the language of school reform—but very little of it really is.

Several decades passed before educational research supported the concerns of Eliot and Harper regarding the negative effects of nonpromotion on the personal and social adjustment of children. While this research showed that children who struggled and were promoted to the next grade fared a little better, even in the academic domain, than comparable children who were retained, it also showed that slow progress takes its toll, whatever the grade placement. Children know when they are not doing well, and they are troubled by it. They don't need to be punished again by being branded failures. Subsequently, educators (when school reformers were not telling them what they had to do) figured out some ways to motivate, challenge, and assist even the slowest learners. But no reform era made their ideas politically correct. Today's conventional wisdom has it that the innovations of these educators were tried and found wanting. So much for innovation.

Arguments for children's well-being, no matter how well grounded, rarely win the day in eras of school reform. The current testing crusade has now become politically correct. Counterarguments commonly receive the "you're against change" response. The data on the low correlation between test scores and honesty, civility, and civic responsibility are brushed aside. The impact of failure on children's psyches is declared an illusion. There is scant debate over what to do or how to do it. The charge to school principals and teachers is to just do it.

But the spread of the eduviruses is slowly arousing concern. School board members, educators, and parents are more and more listening to the speeches and reading the writing of thoughtful critics. Once again, the expectations created by the rhetoric of reform have not been fulfilled. And, once again, it will be awareness of the economic implications that will accelerate the demise of still another failed school reform era.

To date, the counter movement has primarily addressed problems with *how* testing is used, not the shortcomings of testing as a vehicle for school improvement. The expressed concern of educators has been primarily with the narrow focus of the tests, the accompanying impact on teaching and the curriculum, and the high-stakes accountability attached to administrator, teacher, and student performance. At the time of this writing, five major education organizations were joining in an effort to provide guidelines for companies and organizations seeking to develop tests for the Bush plan to test all pupils in grades 3 through 8 yearly.

What these organizations seek are assessments that are appropriate to a broad range of students, the results of which will help teachers teach. Such a noble effort is more likely to slow, rather than accelerate, the testing frenzy. Indeed, should their intent be heeded, they might even derail the testing express altogether. Already the major lesson being learned in the current reform era is that enormous costs are associated with developing, printing, administering, scoring, and aggregating the results of even the present, much-less-sophisticated tests for millions of children. What the five groups are calling for—and what many others regard as desirable as well—would cost many times more, so long as the assumption prevails that determining school quality requires testing all or almost all students.

Once it becomes clear to states and local school districts that valid and useful testing, mandated on a broad scale, will not only cut into their own budgets but also consume much of the 7 percent contributed to public schooling by the federal government, the well-meant proposals of these organizations will be dead on arrival. And several new boards will be nailed into the coffin being readied for the corpse of still another failed school reform effort. The most vocal leaders of that failed reform, if they are still around, will be first in line with their shovels as the casket disappears into the ground. Ironically, the cause of death will have been economic reality, not educational reasoning and moral principle.

WHAT OUR SCHOOLS ARE FOR

The most dismayingly scary characteristic of the current school reform era is the preoccupation with simplistic prescription devoid of diagnosis and purpose. Whether or not he actually said so, Alexander Hamilton considered the people, collectively, to be "a great beast." Thomas Jefferson wrote about the incompatibility of ignorance and freedom and viewed education as the route to civilizing the beast. Roughly half a century later, reflecting on his long visit to America, Alexis de Tocqueville wrote that "there is nothing more arduous than the apprenticeship of liberty." Writing in 1997, political scientist Benjamin Barber claimed, "There is only one road to democracy: education. And in a democracy where freedom comes first—educators and politicians alike take notice—the first priority of education must be the apprenticeship of liberty. Tie every educational reform to this principle, and not only education but democracy itself will flourish."[7]

Is not an apprenticeship in democracy the primary mission of schooling? Given that this apprenticeship is arduous, dare we assume that our schools and the cacophony of "teaching" that occurs outside schools are providing it? I think not. Such is clearly not the intent of the education young people now receive during the time they are not in school. And the function of schools today appears to be more to sort the young for their place in society than to educate them for productive, responsible, satisfying participation in it.

No political leader has emerged to champion the relationship between education and democracy and the role of our schools in it. The presidential debates preceding the elections of 1992, 1996, and 2000 exemplify the void. What stands out instead are empty homilies: all children ready for school, all children can learn, leave no child behind, post the Ten Commandments on classroom walls, and so on.

Perhaps the cataclysmic events of September 11, 2001, will provide the needed wake-up call. Understandably, as Kevin Sack pointed out in the

New York Times shortly after that day, school colors nationwide quickly changed to red, white, and blue. But will the schools be directed to provide the educational apprenticeship necessary to eradicate the misunderstandings that set people against people worldwide?

It appears that the writers of the Constitution were incredibly prescient. Even though the need for an educated citizenry is implicit, there is no mention of a federal responsibility for schooling. Still, Hamilton's beast did a pretty good job of democratizing itself, even as immigrants from all over the world added to its size and diversity. Observers came from far and wide to view the great American experiment of a democracy committed to schooling for all.

The American people have looked to their schools not only for the teaching of reading, writing, and figuring but also for the civilizing of their offspring. They have said over and over that they want it all from their schools: the development of personal, social, vocational, and academic attributes. The woman who protested the budget cuts, with whose story I began this chapter, had it right: We must live with all our children. It takes a nation to ensure the necessary apprenticeship in democracy for all of us. And we, the people, appear to understand that the linchpin of this apprenticeship is a qualified, caring, competent teacher in every classroom. The role of presidents and governors is to cheer us on, not to mislead us with the mythology of school reform.

ENDNOTES

1. Mortimer J. Adler, *We Hold These Truths* (New York: Macmillan, 1987), p. 20.
2. National Commission on Excellence in Education, *A Nation at Risk* (Washington, D.C.: U.S. Government Printing Office, 1983).
3. Rona Wilensky, "Wrong, Wrong, Wrong," *Education Week,* 9 May 2001, pp. 48, 32.
4. John I. Goodlad, *Teachers for Our Nation's Schools* (San Francisco: Jossey-Bass, 1990).
5. Zhixin Su, "Teacher Education Reform in the United States, 1890–1986," Center for Educational Renewal, Occasional Paper No. 3, College of Education, University of Washington, Seattle, 1986.
6. Abraham Flexner, *Medical Education in the United States and Canada* (New York: Carnegie Foundation for the Advancement of Teaching, 1910).
7. Benjamin R. Barber, "Public Schooling: Education for Democracy," in John I. Goodlad & Timothy J. McMannon (Eds.), *The Public Purpose of Education and Schooling* (San Francisco: Jossey-Bass, 1997), p. 31.

DISCUSSION QUESTIONS

1. Why does the author compare education reform to a virus?
2. Does requiring high school students to perform community service promote the ideal of democracy?
3. What would be an example of a "soft and tender" school reform and why might it be desirable?
4. How would schools be different than they are today if policy makers were really concerned about children's well-being?
5. How has what you do as a teacher changed in recent years?

PRO-CON CHART 1

Should the schools introduce a values-centered curriculum for all students?

PRO	CON
1. There are certain basic core values that educators involved in curriculum development should be able to agree on.	1. Values are not objective or neutral. Therefore, educators involved in curriculum development cannot easily agree on them.
2. The classroom is a place in which students can define what values are and share a diversity of viewpoints.	2. Engaging students in discussion will lead to peer pressure and indoctrination.
3. Students should be able to explore their values in a classroom setting.	3. Unstated teacher attitudes may impinge upon students' ability to identify their own preferences.
4. Valuing is part of citizenship education, and therefore schools have a responsibility to teach valuing.	4. Values are not part of civic education. Moreover, values education is the responsibility of the home, not the school.
5. Students need to learn to express themselves forthrightly and to make choices without fear of condemnation.	5. There is no assurance that the teacher can model values, much less provide appropriate instructional activities that will promote these behaviors.

CASE STUDY 1

A Clash Concerning the Arts Curriculum

Andrea Brown had recently been hired as the assistant principal in charge of curriculum at the Newberry Elementary School. Brown, an advocate for arts education, had a humanistic orientation to curriculum. The principal, Al Sigel, had an essentialist view of the curriculum. Adhering to a back to basics focus, Sigel felt that math, science, and computer education should be emphasized and that arts courses were frivolous.

The state code and the school's educational manuals indicated that all students were required to receive 40 minutes of music, art, and dance per week. Without discussing his intentions with Brown or eliciting faculty reactions, Sigel distributed a memo to the staff at the first faculty meeting of the school year indicating that music, art, and dance courses were to be eliminated from the academic schedule as specific courses and that teachers should integrate these subjects into social studies and English. The extra class time was to be equally distributed to provide additional math, science, and computer education classes.

Upon learning about this decision, several parents approached Brown and asked that she assist them in getting the arts classes placed back into the schedule. Brown felt an ethical and educational obligation to address the parents' concern. While cognizant of the legal implications, she also believed the arts were an essential curriculum component. She pondered how she might approach this situation.

Assume that you are the assistant principal. Consider the circumstances described in the case. How would you propose to handle the parents' concerns?

Consider also the implications of taking one of the following actions in response to the parents' request:

1. Confront the principal and cite the state- and school-mandated requirements concerning course time allocations.

2. Resign from the position and state that she and Sigel had irresolvable differences regarding their philosophical orientation to curriculum.

3. Take the curriculum-related concerns to the district superintendent in charge of instruction.

4. Present an inservice workshop to the teaching staff about the intrinsic and utilitarian values of an arts education.

5. Lead a coalition of concerned parents and ask for a meeting with the principal.

PART TWO

Curriculum and Teaching

What are the trends that influence student success and teachers' selection of instructional approaches? What methods are most appropriate for teaching a diverse population of learners? How do teachers' identities, teacher thinking, practical knowledge, and teacher effectiveness affect the ways in which teachers deliver the curriculum?

In Chapter 7, Nel Noddings explains why caring for oneself and others is an important outcome of education and how curriculum can be chosen to develop the inner growth of students. She proposes that schools should become communities of caring, where care becomes a major purpose that guides school policy, as well as the individual and collective practices of teachers. Next, Parker Palmer describes three origins of difficulties that teachers face: the enormous scope and ever-changing nature of subject matter, the complexity of students as real human beings, and the fact that the best teaching emerges from who the teacher is as a person. Taking time to listen to the teacher who resides within oneself, he proposes, is a better guide to practice than the latest instructional techniques.

In Chapter 9, Allan Ornstein raises the question of whether teaching should be considered an art or a science. His discussion of this issue provides a framework for a proposal to reconceptualize teaching and its study in a way that would place greater emphasis on matters of moral and humanistic importance. Next, Herbert Walberg provides a comprehensive review of research on the effects of various methods of teaching. He summarizes what is known about the psychological elements of teaching, the various patterns that individual teachers can implement in their classrooms, the more complex systems of instruction that require special planning and resources, and effective instructional methods for specific content areas and populations of students.

In Chapter 11, Lee Shulman argues that the results of teacher effectiveness research should not constitute the sole basis for defining the knowledge base of teaching. He suggests that teaching involves understanding, reasoning, transformation, and reflection. Shulman presents a six-step model that illustrates his conception of pedagogy. This model delineates the processes involved in pedagogical reasoning and action. In Chapter 12, Edward Pajak, Elaine Stotko, and Frank Masci suggest that support for new teachers should respect and nurture and build on their preferred styles of teaching. Four styles are identified—knowing, caring, inspiring, and inventing—and suggestions for a new and powerful way to differentiate support for beginning teachers are offered. In the last chapter in Part Two, Linda Darling-Hammond documents the importance of qualified teachers for student achievement and describes four factors that research has shown help to reduce teacher attrition. A number of practical steps that leaders can take to retain good teachers are described.

PROFESSIONAL PROFILE: TEACHING

Name:
Jere Brophy

Email:
jereb@msu.edu

Latest degree/university:
Ph.D., Clinical Psychology and Human
Development, University of Chicago

Position:
University Distinguished Professor of Teacher
Education and of Counseling, Educational
Psychology, and Special Education, College
of Education, Michigan State University,
1976–present

Previous positions:
Research Associate (Assistant Professor),
University of Chicago; Assistant/Associate Professor of Educational Psychology,
University of Texas at Austin

Person most influential in your career:
During graduate school, Robert D. Hess recruited me to play a key research assistant
role in his groundbreaking work (with Virginia C. Shipman) on social class differences
in childbearing beliefs, attitudes, and behavior. Involvement in this study helped me
appreciate that scientific research can often have significant practical as well as theoretical implications, and can involve raising new questions and developing new research
methods. This led me to shift from clinical practice to research as a career choice. Then,
in my early years at Texas, personal friendship and shared interests with Tom Good led
to our collaborative research on teacher expectation phenomena, and subsequently to
teacher effects research. This shifted my research focus from child development to education (and in particular, classroom teaching).

Number-one achievement:
I have made both empirical and research synthesis contributions in several areas
(teacher expectations, teacher effects, the dynamics of teacher–student relationships,
coping with problem students, motivating students to learn, curriculum and instruction
in elementary social studies). I value them all in different ways and cannot pick one
above the rest. However, I am probably best known for my writings on teacher effects,
teacher praise, and teacher expectations.

Number-one regret:
I haven't found time to do research that I would like to do on motivation, especially on
helping students appreciate the potential applications of school learning to life outside
of school.

Favorite educational journal:
The *Journal of Educational Psychology* because it is the major source for new empirical contributions to this field, and the *Educational Psychologist* because it is the major
source for synthesis and position papers in psychology and in education.

Favorite educational book:
The Struggle for the American Curriculum, 1893–1958, by Herbert Kliebard (New York: Routledge, 1986), a clear and well-written synthesis of major positions on the nature and purposes of schooling that have influenced debates about education in this country over the years. This book gave me a historically grounded grasp of the big picture that helps me assimilate emerging developments and recognize that most aspects of supposedly new ideas are repackaged and renamed versions of old assumptions and rationales.

Best book/chapter you wrote:
I value all of my books in different ways, but I would look to textbooks because they are more challenging to write than research monographs that address a narrow set of topics for a narrow audience. Among the texts, I am most proud of *Looking in Classrooms,* now in its ninth edition, and *Motivating Students to Learn,* now in its second edition. Each of these books is based primarily on scholarly research literature, but each synthesizes the findings in the form of concepts and principles, explained with minimal jargon and with emphasis on applications.

Additional interests:
Sports, music, and reading, particularly suspense, psychological fiction, and social and political nonfiction

Curriculum/teaching relationship:
I emphasize teaching for understanding (of basic concepts and principles), appreciation (of why material is worth learning), and application (to life outside of school). This requires a close alignment of curriculum and instruction that features networks of connected content structured around big ideas, developed with emphasis on their connections and application (via authentic activities). Unless the curriculum is structured and taught in this fashion, it is likely to feature parades of minutia or disconnected facts memorized for tests and soon forgotten, along with parades of monotonous worksheets and other inauthentic activities. Without powerful ideas to provide a basis for authentic applications, there is little alternative to rote memorizing and skills practice activities.

Professional vision:
Teachers as informed decision makers knowledgeable about the major sources for curriculum (knowledge of enduring value including but not limited to disciplinary knowledge; the needs and interests of the students they teach; and the knowledge, skills, and values that our society wants to develop in its young people). Successfully planning and adapting lessons requires not only knowing one's subjects but knowing which aspects of them to develop in which ways with one's students (pedagogical content knowledge), as well as how to connect the curriculum to the personal lives and family and cultural backgrounds of the students.

Professional advice to teacher or curriculum specialist:
Spend less time on abstract and ideological writings and more time on close analysis and critique of the textbook series and other instructional resources that teachers are actually likely to work with in schools (with an eye toward adapting and supplementing them to address their weaknesses).

7

Teaching Themes of Care

NEL NODDINGS

FOCUSING QUESTIONS

1. How is caring an essential part of teaching?
2. Why is it important to teach children to care?
3. How can caring be incorporated into the curriculum?
4. Are some subject areas more suited for teaching themes of care?
5. What might a curriculum that included themes of caring look like and how would it be implemented?

Some educators today—and I include myself among them—would like to see a complete re-organization of the school curriculum. We would like to give a central place to the questions and issues that lie at the core of human existence. One possibility would be to organize the curriculum around themes of care—caring for self, for intimate others, for strangers and global others, for the natural world and its nonhuman creatures, for the human-made world, and for ideas.[1]

A realistic assessment of schooling in the present political climate makes it clear that such a plan is not likely to be implemented. However, we can use the rich vocabulary of care in educational planning and introduce themes of care into regular subject-matter classes. Here, I will first give a brief rationale for teaching themes of care; second, I will suggest ways of choosing and organizing such themes; and, finally, I'll say a bit about the structures required to support such teaching.

WHY TEACH CARING?

In an age when violence among schoolchildren is at an unprecedented level, when children are bearing children with little knowledge of how to care for them, when the society and even the schools often concentrate on materialistic messages, it may be unnecessary to argue that we should care more genuinely for our children and teach them to care. However, many otherwise reasonable people seem to believe that our educational problems consist largely of low scores on achievement tests. My contention is, first, that we should want more from our educational efforts than adequate academic achievement and, second, that we will not achieve even that meager success unless our children believe that they themselves are cared for and learn to care for others.

There is much to be gained, both academically and humanly, by including themes of care in our curriculum. First, such inclusion may well expand our students' cultural literacy. For example, as we discuss in math classes the attempts of great mathematicians to prove the existence of God or to reconcile a God who is all good with the reality of evil in the world, students will hear names, ideas, and words that are not part of the standard curriculum. Although such incidental learning cannot replace the systematic and sequential learning required by those who plan careers in mathematically oriented fields, it can be powerful in expanding students' cultural horizons and in inspiring further study.

Second, themes of care help us to connect the standard subjects. The use of literature in mathematics classes, of history in science classes, and of art and music in all classes can give students a feeling of the wholeness in their education. After all, why should they seriously study five different subjects if their teachers, who are educated people, only seem to know and appreciate one?

Third, themes of care connect our students and our subjects to great existential questions. What is the meaning of life? Are there gods? How should I live?

Fourth, sharing such themes can connect us person-to-person. When teachers discuss themes of care, they may become real persons to their students and so enable them to construct new knowledge. Martin Buber put it this way:

> Trust, trust in the world, because this human being exists—that is the most inward achievement of the relation in education. Because this human being exists, meaninglessness, however hard pressed you are by it, cannot be the real truth. Because this human being exists, in the darkness the light lies hidden, in fear salvation, and in the callousness of one's fellowman the great love.[2]

Finally, I should emphasize that caring is not just a warm, fuzzy feeling that makes people kind and likable. Caring implies a continuous search for competence. When we care, we want to do our very best for the objects of our care. To have as our educational goal the production of caring, competent, loving, and lovable people is not anti-intellectual. Rather, it demonstrates respect for the full range of human talents. Not all human beings are good at or interested in mathematics, science, or British literature. But all humans can be helped to lead lives of deep concern for others, for the natural world and its creatures, and for the preservation of the human-made world. They can be led to develop the skills and knowledge necessary to make positive contributions, regardless of the occupation they may choose.

CHOOSING AND ORGANIZING THEMES OF CARE

Care is conveyed in many ways. At the institutional level, schools can be organized to provide continuity and support for relationships of care and trust.[3] At the individual level, parents and teachers show their caring through characteristic forms of attention: by cooperating in children's activities, by sharing their own dreams and doubts, and by providing carefully for the steady growth of the children in their charge. Personal manifestations of care are probably more important in children's lives than any particular curriculum or pattern of pedagogy.

However, curriculum can be selected with caring in mind. That is, educators can manifest their care in the choice of curriculum, and appropriately chosen curriculum can contribute to the growth of children as carers. Within each large domain of care, many topics are suitable for thematic units: in the domain of "caring for self," for example, we might consider life stages, spiritual growth, and what it means to develop an admirable character; in exploring the topic of caring for intimate others, we might include units on love, friendship, and parenting; under the theme of caring for strangers and global others, we might study war, poverty, and tolerance; in addressing the idea of caring for the human-made world, we might encourage competence with the machines that surround us and a real appreciation for the marvels of technology. Many other examples exist. Furthermore, there are at least two different ways to approach the development of such themes: units can be constructed by interdisciplinary teams, or themes can be identified by individual teachers and addressed periodically throughout a year's or semester's work.

The interdisciplinary approach is familiar in core programs, and such programs are becoming more and more popular at the middle school level. One key to a successful interdisciplinary unit is the degree of genuinely enthusiastic support it receives from the teachers involved. Too often, arbitrary or artificial groupings are formed, and teachers are forced to make contributions that they themselves do not value highly. For example, math and science teachers are sometimes automatically lumped together, and rich humanistic possibilities may be lost. If I, as a math teacher, want to include historical, biographical, and literary topics in my math lessons, I might prefer to work with English and social studies teachers. Thus it is important to involve teachers in the initial selection of broad areas for themes, as well as in their implementation.

Such interdisciplinary arrangements also work well at the college level. I recently received a copy of the syllabus for a college course titled

"The Search for Meaning," which was co-taught by an economist, a university chaplain, and a psychiatrist.[4] The course is interdisciplinary, intellectually rich, and aimed squarely at the central questions of life.

At the high school level, where students desperately need to engage in the study and practice of caring, it is harder to form interdisciplinary teams. A conflict arises as teachers acknowledge the intensity of the subject-matter preparation their students need for further education. Good teachers often wish there were time in the day to co-teach unconventional topics of great importance, and they even admit that their students are not getting what they need for full personal development. But they feel constrained by the requirements of a highly competitive world and the structures of schooling established by that world.

Is there a way out of this conflict? Imaginative, like-minded teachers might agree to emphasize a particular theme in their separate classes. Such themes as war, poverty, crime, racism, or sexism can be addressed in almost every subject area. The teachers should agree on some core ideas related to caring that will be discussed in all classes, but beyond the central commitment to address themes of care, the topics can be handled in whatever way seems suitable in a given subject.

Consider, for example, what a mathematics class might contribute to a unit on crime. Statistical information might be gathered on the location and number of crimes, on rates for various kinds of crime, on the ages of offenders, and on the cost to society; graphs and charts could be constructed. Data on changes in crime rates could be assembled. Intriguing questions could be asked: Were property crime rates lower when penalties were more severe—when, for example, even children were hanged as thieves? What does an average criminal case cost by way of lawyers' fees, police investigation, and court processing? Does it cost more to house a youth in a detention center or in an elite private school?

None of this would have to occupy a full period every day. The regular sequential work of the math class could go on at a slightly reduced rate (e.g., fewer textbook exercises as homework), and the work on crime could proceed in the form of interdisciplinary projects over a considerable period of time. Most important would be the continual reminder in all classes that the topic is part of a larger theme of caring for strangers and fellow citizens. It takes only a few minutes to talk about what it means to live in safety, to trust one's neighbors, to feel secure in greeting strangers. Students should be told that metal detectors and security guards were not part of their parents' school lives, and they should be encouraged to hope for a safer and more open future. Notice the words I've used in this paragraph: caring, trust, safety, strangers, hope. Each could be used as an organizing theme for another unit of study.

English and social studies teachers would obviously have much to contribute to a unit on crime. For example, students might read *Oliver Twist,* and they might also study and discuss the social conditions that seemed to promote crime in 19th-century England. Do similar conditions exist in our country today? The selection of materials could include both classic works and modern stories and films. Students might even be introduced to some of the mystery stories that adults read so avidly on airplanes and beaches, and teachers should be engaged in lively discussion about the comparative value of the various stories.

Science teachers might find that a unit on crime would enrich their teaching of evolution. They could bring up the topic of social Darwinism, which played such a strong role in social policy during the late 19th and early 20th centuries. To what degree are criminal tendencies inherited? Should children be tested for the genetic defects that are suspected of predisposing some people to crime? Are females less competent than males in moral reasoning? (Why did some scientists and philosophers think this was true?) Why do males commit so many more violent acts than females?

Teachers of the arts can also be involved. A unit on crime might provide a wonderful opportunity to critique "gangsta rap" and other currently popular forms of music. Students might profitably learn how the control of art contributed to national criminality during the Nazi era. These are ideas that pop into my mind. Far more various and far richer ideas will come from teachers who specialize in these subjects.

There are risks, of course, in undertaking any unit of study that focuses on matters of controversy or deep existential concern, and teachers should anticipate these risks. What if students want to compare the incomes of teachers and cocaine dealers? What if they point to contemporary personalities from politics, entertainment, business, or sports who seem to escape the law and profit from what seems to be criminal behavior? My own inclination would be to allow free discussion of these cases and to be prepared to counteract them with powerful stories of honesty, compassion, moderation, and charity.

An even more difficult problem may arise. Suppose a student discloses his or her own criminal activities? Fear of this sort of occurrence may send teachers scurrying for safer topics. But, in fact, any instructional method that uses narrative forms or encourages personal expression runs this risk. For example, students of English as a second language who write proudly about their own hard lives and new hopes may disclose that their parents are illegal immigrants. A girl may write passages that lead her teacher to suspect sexual abuse. A boy may brag about objects he has "ripped off." Clearly, as we use these powerful methods that encourage students to initiate discussion and share their experiences, we must reflect on the ethical issues involved, consider appropriate responses to such issues, and prepare teachers to handle them responsibly.

Caring teachers must help students make wise decisions about what information they will share about themselves. On the one hand, teachers want their students to express themselves, and they want their students to trust in and consult them. On the other hand, teachers have an obligation to protect immature students from making disclosures that they might later regret. There is a deep ethical problem here. Too often educators assume that only religious fundamentalists and right-wing extremists object to the discussion of emotionally and morally charged issues. In reality, there is a real danger of intrusiveness and lack of respect in methods that fail to recognize the vulnerability of students. Therefore, as teachers plan units and lessons on moral issues, they should anticipate the tough problems that may arise. I am arguing here that it is morally irresponsible to simply ignore existential questions and themes of care; we must attend to them. But it is equally irresponsible to approach these deep concerns without caution and careful preparation.

So far I have discussed two ways of organizing interdisciplinary units on themes of care. In one, teachers actually teach together in teams; in the other, teachers agree on a theme and a central focus on care, but they do what they can, when they can, in their own classrooms. A variation on this second way—which is also open to teachers who have to work alone—is to choose several themes and weave them into regular course material over an entire semester or year. The particular themes will depend on the interests and preparation of each teacher.

For example, if I were teaching high school mathematics today, I would use religious/existential questions as a pervasive theme because the biographies of mathematicians are filled with accounts of their speculations on matters of God, other dimensions, and the infinite—and because these topics fascinate me. There are so many wonderful stories to be told: Descartes' proof of the existence of God, Pascal's famous wager, Plato's world of forms, Newton's attempt to verify biblical chronology, Leibniz's detailed theodicy, current attempts to describe a divine domain in terms of metasystems, and mystical speculations on the infinite.[5] Some of these stories can be told as rich "asides" in five minutes or less. Others might occupy the better part of several class periods.

Other mathematics teachers might use an interest in architecture and design, art, music, or machinery as continuing themes in the domain of "caring for the human-made world." Still others might introduce the mathematics of living things. The possibilities are endless. In choosing and pursuing these themes, teachers should be aware that they are both helping their students learn to care and demonstrating their own caring by sharing interests that go well beyond the demands of textbook pedagogy.

Still another way to introduce themes of care into regular classrooms is to be prepared to respond spontaneously to events that occur in the school or in the neighborhood. Older teachers have one advantage in this area: they probably have a greater store of experience and stories on which to draw. However, younger teachers have the advantage of being closer to their students' lives and experiences; they are more likely to be familiar with the music, films, and sports figures that interest their students. All teachers should be prepared to respond to the needs of students who are suffering from the death of friends, conflicts between groups of students, pressure to use drugs or to engage in sex, and other troubles so rampant in the lives of today's children. Too often schools rely on experts—"grief counselors" and the like—when what children really need is the continuing compassion and presence of adults who represent constancy and care in their lives. Artificially separating the emotional, academic, and moral care of children into tasks for specially designated experts contributes to the fragmentation of life in schools.

Of course, I do not mean to imply that experts are unnecessary, nor do I mean to suggest that some matters should not be reserved for parents or psychologists. But our society has gone too far in compartmentalizing the care of its children. When we ask whose job it is to teach children how to care, an appropriate initial response is "Everyone's." Having accepted universal responsibility, we can then ask about the special contributions and limitations of various individuals and groups.

SUPPORTING STRUCTURES

What kind of schools and teacher preparation are required, if themes of care are to be taught effectively? First, and most important, care must be taken seriously as a major purpose of schools; that is, educators must recognize that caring for students is fundamental in teaching and that developing people with a strong capacity for care is a major objective of responsible education. Schools properly pursue many other objectives—developing artistic talent, promoting multicultural understanding, diversifying curriculum to meet the academic and vocational needs of all students, forging connections with community agencies and parents, and so on. Schools cannot be single-purpose institutions. Indeed, many of us would

argue that it is logically and practically impossible to achieve that single academic purpose if other purposes are not recognized and accepted. This contention is confirmed in the success stories of several inner-city schools.[6]

Once it is recognized that school is a place in which students are cared for and learn to care, that recognition should be powerful in guiding policy. In the late 1950s, schools in the United States, under the guidance of James Conant and others, placed the curriculum at the top of the educational priority list. Because the nation's leaders wanted schools to provide high-powered courses in mathematics and science, it was recommended that small high schools be replaced by efficient larger structures complete with sophisticated laboratories and specialist teachers. Economies of scale were anticipated, but the main argument for consolidation and regionalization centered on the curriculum. All over the country, small schools were closed, and students were herded into larger facilities with "more offerings." We did not think carefully about schools as communities and about what might be lost as we pursued a curriculum-driven ideal.

Today many educators are calling for smaller schools and more family-like groupings. These are good proposals, but teachers, parents, and students should be engaged in continuing discussion about what they are trying to achieve through the new arrangements. For example, if test scores do not immediately rise, participants should be courageous in explaining that test scores were not the main object of the changes. Most of us who argue for caring in schools are intuitively quite sure that children in such settings will in fact become more competent learners. But, if they cannot prove their academic competence in a prescribed period of time, should we give up on caring and on teaching them to care? That would be foolish. There is more to life and learning than the academic proficiency demonstrated by test scores.

In addition to steadfastness of purpose, schools must consider continuity of people and place. If we are concerned with caring and community, then we must make it possible for students and teachers to stay together for several years so that mutual trust can develop and students can feel a sense of belonging in their "schoolhome."[7]

More than one scheme of organization can satisfy the need for continuity. Elementary school children can stay with the same teacher for several years, or they can work with a stable team of specialist teachers for several years. In the latter arrangement, there may be program advantages; that is, children taught by subject-matter experts who get to know them well over an extended period of time may learn more about the particular subjects. At the high school level, the same specialist teachers might work with students throughout their years in high school. Or, as Theodore Sizer has suggested, one teacher might teach two subjects to a group of 30 students rather than one subject to 60 students, thereby reducing the number of different adults with whom students interact each day.[8] In all the suggested arrangements, placements should be made by mutual consent whenever possible. Teachers and students who hate or distrust one another should not be forced to stay together.

A policy of keeping students and teachers together for several years supports caring in two essential ways: it provides time for the development of caring relations, and it makes teaching themes of care more feasible. When trust has been established, teacher and students can discuss matters that would be hard for a group of strangers to approach, and classmates learn to support one another in sensitive situations.

The structural changes suggested here are not expensive. If a high school teacher must teach five classes a day, it costs no more for three of these classes to be composed of continuing students than for all five classes to comprise new students—i.e., strangers. The recommended changes come directly out of a clear-headed assessment of our major aims and purposes. We failed to suggest them earlier because we had other, too limited, goals in mind.

I have made one set of structural changes sound easy, and I do believe that they are easily made. But the curricular and pedagogical changes that are required may be more difficult. High school textbooks rarely contain the kinds of supplementary material I have described, and teachers are not formally prepared to incorporate such material. Too often, even the people we regard as strongly prepared in a liberal arts major are unprepared to discuss the history of their subject, its relation to other subjects, the biographies of its great figures, its connections to the great existential questions, and the ethical responsibilities of those who work in that discipline. To teach themes of care in an academically effective way, teachers will have to engage in projects of self-education.

At present, neither liberal arts departments nor schools of education pay much attention to connecting academic subjects with themes of care. For example, biology students may learn something of the anatomy and physiology of mammals but nothing at all about the care of living animals; they may never be asked to consider the moral issues involved in the annual euthanasia of millions of pets. Mathematics students may learn to solve quadratic equations but never study what it means to live in a mathematicized world. In enlightened history classes, students may learn something about the problems of racism and colonialism but never hear anything about the evolution of childhood, the contributions of women in both domestic and public caregiving, or the connection between the feminization of caregiving and public policy. A liberal education that neglects matters that are central to a fully human life hardly warrants the name,[9] and a professional education that confines itself to technique does nothing to close the gaps in liberal education.

The greatest structural obstacle, however, may simply be legitimizing the inclusion of themes of care in the curriculum. Teachers in the early grades have long included such themes as a regular part of their work, and middle school educators are becoming more sensitive to developmental needs involving care. But secondary schools, where violence, apathy, and alienation are most evident, do little to develop the capacity to care. Today, even elementary teachers complain that the pressure to produce high test scores inhibits the work they regard as central to their mission: the development of caring and competent people. Therefore, it would seem that the most fundamental change required is one of attitude. Teachers can be very special people in the lives of children, and it should be legitimate for them to spend time developing relations of trust, talking with students about problems that are central to their lives, and guiding them toward greater sensitivity and competence across all the domains of care.

ENDNOTES

1. For the theoretical argument, see Nel Noddings, *The Challenge to Care in Schools* (New York: Teachers College Press, 1992); for a practical example and rich documentation, see Sharon Quint, *Schooling Homeless Children* (New York: Teachers College Press, 1994).

2. Martin Buber, *Between Man and Man* (New York: Macmillan, 1965), p. 98.

3. Noddings, *The Challenge to Care in Schools.*

4. See Thomas H. Naylor, William H. Willimon, and Magdalena R. Naylor, *The Search for Meaning* (Nashville, TN: Abingdon Press, 1994).

5. Nel Noddings, *Educating for Intelligent Belief and Unbelief* (New York: Teachers College Press, 1993).

6. See Deborah Meier, "How Our Schools Could Be," *Phi Delta Kappan,* January 1995, pp. 369–373; Quint, *Schooling Homeless Children.*

7. See Jane Roland Martin, *The Schoolhome: Rethinking Schools for Changing Families* (Cambridge, MA: Harvard University Press, 1992).

8. Theodore Sizer, *Horace's Compromise: The Dilemma of the American High School* (Boston: Houghton Mifflin, 1984).

9. See Bruce Wilshire, *The Moral Collapse of the University* (Albany: State University of New York Press, 1990).

DISCUSSION QUESTIONS

1. Is teaching themes of care a legitimate responsibility for schools?
2. What are some advantages of an interdisciplinary unit on caring?
3. What might be some obstacles to implementing a curriculum that included themes of care?
4. What arguments would be useful for convincing a school board that themes of caring should be included in the curriculum?
5. What steps would you take as curriculum director to implement themes of caring in classrooms districtwide?

8

The Heart of a Teacher

PARKER J. PALMER

FOCUSING QUESTIONS

1. Is teaching an occupation or is it a vocation?
2. Does it matter who a teacher is as a person? Why?
3. What are the qualities of a great teacher?
4. Why do some teachers eventually become disillusioned and cynical?
5. How might teacher colleagues support each other's efforts to become great teachers?

WE TEACH WHO WE ARE

I am a teacher at heart, and there are moments in the classroom when I can hardly hold the joy. When my students and I discover uncharted territory to explore, when the pathway out of a thicket opens up before us, when our experience is illumined by the lightning-life of the mind—then teaching is the finest work I know.

But at other moments, the classroom is so lifeless or painful or confused—and I am so powerless to do anything about it—that my claim to be a teacher seems a transparent sham. Then the enemy is everywhere: in those students from some alien planet, in that subject I thought I knew, and in the personal pathology that keeps me earning my living this way. What a fool I was to imagine that I had mastered this occult art—harder to divine than tea leaves and impossible for mortals to do even passably well!

The tangles of teaching have three important sources. The first two are commonplace, but the third, and most fundamental, is rarely given its due. First, the subjects we teach are as large and complex as life, so our knowledge of them is always flawed and partial. No matter how we devote ourselves to reading and research, teaching requires a command of content that always eludes our grasp. Second, the students we teach are larger than life and even more complex. To see them clearly and see them whole, and respond to them wisely in the moment, requires a fusion of Freud and Solomon that few of us achieve.

If students and subjects accounted for all the complexities of teaching, our standard ways of coping would do—keep up with our fields as best we can, and learn enough techniques to stay ahead of the student psyche. But there is another reason for these complexities: we teach who we are.

Teaching, like any truly human activity, emerges from one's inwardness, for better or worse. As I teach, I project the condition of my soul onto my students, my subject, and our way of being together. The entanglements I experience in the classroom are often no more or less than the convolutions of my inner life. Viewed from this angle, teaching holds a mirror to the soul. If I am willing to look in that mirror, and not run from what I see, I have a chance to gain self-knowledge—and knowing myself is as crucial to good teaching as knowing my students and my subject.

In fact, knowing my students and my subject depends heavily on self-knowledge. When I do not know myself, I cannot know who my students are.

I will see them through a glass darkly, in the shadows of my unexamined life—and when I cannot see them clearly, I cannot teach them well. When I do not know myself, I cannot know my subject—not at the deepest levels of embodied, personal meaning. I will know it only abstractly, from a distance, a congeries of concepts as far removed from the world as I am from personal truth.

We need to open a new frontier in our exploration of good teaching: the inner landscape of a teacher's life. To chart that landscape fully, three important paths must be taken—intellectual, emotional, and spiritual—and none can be ignored. Reduce teaching to intellect and it becomes a cold abstraction; reduce it to emotions and it becomes narcissistic; reduce it to the spiritual and it loses its anchor to the world. Intellect, emotion, and spirit depend on each other for wholeness. They are interwoven in the human self and in education at its best, and we need to interweave them in our pedagogical discourse as well.

By intellectual I mean the way we think about teaching and learning—the form and content of our concepts of how people know and learn, of the nature of our students and our subjects. By emotional I mean the way we and our students feel as we teach and learn—feelings that can either enlarge or diminish the exchange between us. By spiritual I mean the diverse ways we answer the heart's longing to be connected with the largeness of life—a longing that animates love and work, especially the work called teaching.

TEACHING BEYOND TECHNIQUE

After three decades of trying to learn my craft, every class comes down to this: my students and I, face to face, engaged in an ancient and exacting exchange called education. The techniques I have mastered do not disappear, but neither do they suffice. Face to face with my students, only one resource is at my immediate command: my identity, my selfhood, my sense of this "I" who teaches—without which I have no sense of the "Thou" who learns.

Here is a secret hidden in plain sight: good teaching cannot be reduced to technique; good teaching comes from the identity and integrity of the teacher. In every class I teach, my ability to connect with my students, and to connect them with the subject, depends less on the methods I use than on the degree to which I know and trust my selfhood—and am willing to make it available and vulnerable in the service of learning.

My evidence for this claim comes, in part, from years of asking students to tell me about their good teachers. As I listen to those stories, it becomes impossible to claim that all good teachers use similar techniques: some lecture non-stop and others speak very little, some stay close to their material and others loose the imagination, some teach with the carrot and others with the stick.

But in every story I have heard, good teachers share one trait: a strong sense of personal identity infuses their work. "Dr. A is really there when she teaches," a student tells me, or "Mr. B has such enthusiasm for his subject," or "You can tell that this is really Prof. C's life."

One student I heard about said she could not describe her good teachers because they were so different from each other. But she could describe her bad teachers because they were all the same: "Their words float somewhere in front of their faces, like the balloon speech in cartoons." With one remarkable image she said it all. Bad teachers distance themselves from the subject they are teaching—and, in the process, from their students.

Good teachers join self, subject, and students in the fabric of life because they teach from an integral and undivided self; they manifest in their own lives, and evoke in their students, a "capacity for connectedness." They are able to weave a complex web of connections between themselves, their subjects, and their students, so that students can learn to weave a world for themselves. The methods used by these weavers vary widely: lectures, Socratic dialogues, laboratory experiments, collaborative problem-solving, creative chaos. The connections made by good teachers are held not in their methods but in their hearts—meaning heart in its ancient sense, the place where intellect and emotion and spirit and will converge in the human self.

If good teaching cannot be reduced to technique, I no longer need suffer the pain of having my peculiar gift as a teacher crammed into the Procrustean bed of someone else's method and the standards prescribed by it. That pain is felt throughout education today as we insist upon the method *du jour*—leaving people who teach differently feeling devalued, forcing them to measure up to norms not their own.

I will never forget one professor who, moments before I was to start a workshop on teaching, unloaded years of pent-up workshop animus on me: "I am an organic chemist. Are you going to spend the next two days telling me that I am supposed to teach organic chemistry through role-playing?" His wry question was not only related to his distinctive discipline but also to his distinctive self: we must find an approach to teaching that respects the diversity of teachers as well as disciplines, which methodological reductionism fails to do.

The capacity for connectedness manifests itself in diverse and wondrous ways—as many ways as there are forms of personal identity. Two great teachers stand out from my own undergraduate experience. They differed radically from each other in technique, but both were gifted at connecting students, teacher, and subject in a community of learning.

One of those teachers assigned a lot of reading in her course on methods of social research and, when we gathered around the seminar table on the first day, said, "Any comments or questions?" She had the courage to wait out our stupefied (and stupefying) silence, minute after minute after minute, gazing around the table with a benign look on her face—and then, after the passage of a small eternity, to rise, pick up her books, and say, as she walked toward the door, "Class dismissed."

This scenario more or less repeated itself a second time, but by the third time we met, our high SAT scores had kicked in, and we realized that the big dollars we were paying for this education would be wasted if we did not get with the program. So we started doing the reading, making comments, asking questions—and our teacher proved herself to be a brilliant interlocutor, co-researcher, and guide in the midst of confusions, a "weaver" of connectedness in her own interactive and inimitable way.

My other great mentor taught the history of social thought. He did not know the meaning of silence and he was awkward at interaction; he lectured incessantly while we sat in rows and took notes. Indeed, he became so engaged with his material that he was often impatient with our questions. But his classes were nonetheless permeated with a sense of connectedness and community.

How did he manage this alchemy? Partly by giving lectures that went far beyond presenting the data of social theory into staging the drama of social thought. He told stories from the lives of great thinkers as well as explaining their ideas; we could almost see Karl Marx, sitting alone in the British Museum Library, writing *Das Kapital.* Through active imagination we were brought into community with the thinker himself, and with the personal and social conditions that stimulated his thought.

But the drama of my mentor's lectures went farther still. He would make a strong Marxist statement, and we would transcribe it in our notebooks as if it were holy writ. Then a puzzled look would pass over his face. He would pause, step to one side, turn, and look back at the space he had just exited—and argue with his own statement from an Hegelian point of view! This was not an artificial device but a genuine expression of the intellectual drama that continually occupied this teacher's mind and heart.

"Drama" does not mean histrionics, of course, and remembering that fact can help us name a form of connectedness that is palpable and powerful without being overtly interactive, or even face to face. When I go to the theater, I sometimes feel strongly connected to the action, as if my own life were being portrayed on stage. But I have no desire to raise my hand and respond to the line just spoken, or run up the aisle, jump onto the stage, and join in the action. Sitting in the audience, I am already on stage "in person," connected in an inward and invisible way that we rarely credit as the powerful form of community that it is. With a good drama, I do not need overt interaction to be "in community" with those characters and their lives.

I used to wonder how my mentor, who was so awkward in his face-to-face relations with students, managed to simulate community so well.

Now I understand: he was in community without us! Who needs 20-year-olds from the suburbs when you are hanging out constantly with the likes of Marx and Hegel, Durkheim, Weber and Troeltsch? This is "community" of the highest sort—this capacity for connectedness that allows one to converse with the dead, to speak and listen in an invisible network of relationships that enlarges one's world and enriches one's life. (We should praise, not deride, First Ladies who "talk" with Eleanor Roosevelt; the ability to learn from wise but long-gone souls is nothing less than a classic mark of a liberal education!)

Yet my great professor, though he communed more intimately with the great figures of social thought than with the people close at hand, cared deeply about his students. The passion with which he lectured was not only for his subject, but for us to know his subject. He wanted us to meet and learn from the constant companions of his intellect and imagination, and he made those introductions in a way that was deeply integral to his own nature. He brought us into a form of community that did not require small numbers of students sitting in a circle and learning through dialogue.

These two great teachers were polar opposites in substance and in style. But both created the connectedness, the community, that is essential to teaching and learning. They did so by trusting and teaching from true self, from the identity and integrity that is the source of all good work—and by employing quite different techniques that allowed them to reveal rather than conceal who they were.

Their genius as teachers, and their profound gifts to me, would have been diminished and destroyed had their practice been forced into the Procrustean bed of the method of the moment. The proper place for technique is not to subdue subjectivity, not to mask and distance the self from the work, but—as one grows in self-knowledge—to help bring forth and amplify the gifts of self on which good work depends.

TEACHING AND TRUE SELF

The claim that good teaching comes from the identity and integrity of the teacher might sound like a truism, and a pious one at that: good teaching comes from good people. But by "identity" and "integrity" I do not mean only our noble features, or the good deeds we do, or the brave faces we wear to conceal our confusions and complexities. Identity and integrity have as much to do with our shadows and limits, our wounds and fears, as with our strengths and potentials.

By identity I mean an evolving nexus where all the forces that constitute my life converge in the mystery of self: my genetic makeup, the nature of the man and woman who gave me life, the culture in which I was raised, people who have sustained me and people who have done me harm, the good and ill I have done to others and to myself, the experience of love and suffering—and much, much more. In the midst of that complex field, identity is a moving intersection of the inner and outer forces that make me who I am, converging in the irreducible mystery of being human.

By integrity I mean whatever wholeness I am able to find within that nexus as its vectors form and re-form the pattern of my life. Integrity requires that I discern what is integral to my selfhood, what fits and what does not—and that I choose life-giving ways of relating to the forces that converge within me: do I welcome them or fear them, embrace them or reject them, move with them or against them? By choosing integrity, I become more whole, but wholeness does not mean perfection. It means becoming more real by acknowledging the whole of who I am.

Identity and integrity are not the granite from which fictional heroes are hewn. They are subtle dimensions of the complex, demanding, and life-long process of self-discovery. Identity lies in the intersection of the diverse forces that make up my life, and integrity lies in relating to those forces in ways that bring me wholeness and life rather than fragmentation and death.

Those are my definitions—but try as I may to refine them, they always come out too pat. Identity and integrity can never be fully named or known by anyone, including the person who bears them. They constitute that familiar strangeness we take with us to the grave, elusive realities that can be caught only occasionally out of the corner of the eye.

Stories are the best way to portray realities of this sort, so here is a tale of two teachers—a tale based on people I have known, whose lives tell me more about the subtleties of identity and integrity than any theory could.

Alan and Eric were born into two different families of skilled craftspeople, rural folk with little formal schooling but gifted in the manual arts. Both boys evinced this gift from childhood onward, and as each grew in skill at working with his hands, each developed a sense of self in which the pride of craft was key.

The two shared another gift as well: both excelled in school and became the first in their working-class families to go to college. Both did well as undergraduates, both were admitted to graduate school, both earned doctorates, and both chose academic careers.

But here their paths diverged. Though the gift of craft was central in both men's sense of self, Alan was able to weave that gift into his academic vocation, while the fabric of Eric's life unraveled early on.

Catapulted from his rural community into an elite private college at age 18, Eric suffered severe culture shock—and never overcame it. He was insecure with fellow students and, later, with academic colleagues who came from backgrounds he saw as more "cultured" than his own. He learned to speak and act like an intellectual, but he always felt fraudulent among people who were, in his eyes, to the manor born.

But insecurity neither altered Eric's course nor drew him into self-reflection. Instead, he bullied his way into professional life on the theory that the best defense is a good offense. He made pronouncements rather than probes. He listened for weaknesses rather than strengths in what other people said. He argued with anyone about anything—and responded with veiled contempt to whatever was said in return.

In the classroom, Eric was critical and judgmental, quick to put down the "stupid question," adept at trapping students with trick questions of his own, then merciless in mocking wrong answers. He seemed driven by a need to inflict upon his students the same wound that academic life had inflicted upon him—the wound of being embarrassed by some essential part of one's self.

But when Eric went home to his workbench and lost himself in craft, he found himself as well.

He became warm and welcoming, at home in the world and glad to extend hospitality to others. Reconnected with his roots, centered in his true self, he was able to reclaim a quiet and confident core—which he quickly lost as soon as he returned to campus.

Alan's is a different story. His leap from countryside to campus did not induce culture shock, in part because he attended a land-grant university where many students had backgrounds much like his own. He was not driven to hide his gift, but was able to honor and transform it by turning it toward things academic: he brought to his study, and later to his teaching and research, the same sense of craft that his ancestors had brought to their work with metal and wood.

Watching Alan teach, you felt that you were watching a craftsman at work—and if you knew his history, you understood that this feeling was more than metaphor. In his lectures, every move Alan made was informed by attention to detail and respect for the materials at hand; he connected ideas with the precision of dovetail joinery and finished the job with a polished summary.

But the power of Alan's teaching went well beyond crafted performance. His students knew that Alan would extend himself with great generosity to any of them who wanted to become an apprentice in his field, just as the elders in his own family had extended themselves to help young Alan grow in his original craft.

Alan taught from an undivided self—the integral state of being that is central to good teaching. In the undivided self, every major thread of one's life experience is honored, creating a weave of such coherence and strength that it can hold students and subject as well as self. Such a self, inwardly integrated, is able to make the outward connections on which good teaching depends.

But Eric failed to weave the central strand of his identity into his academic vocation. His was a self divided, engaged in a civil war. He projected that inner warfare onto the outer world, and his teaching devolved into combat instead of craft. The divided self will always distance itself from others, and may even try to destroy them, to defend its fragile identity.

If Eric had not been alienated as an undergraduate—or if his alienation had led to self-reflection instead of self-defense—it is possible that he, like Alan, could have found integrity in his academic vocation, could have woven the major strands of his identity into his work. But part of the mystery of selfhood is the fact that one size does not fit all: what is integral to one person lacks integrity for another. Throughout his life, there were persistent clues that academia was not a life-giving choice for Eric, not a context in which his true self could emerge healthy and whole, not a vocation integral to his unique nature.

The self is not infinitely elastic—it has potentials and it has limits. If the work we do lacks integrity for us, then we, the work, and the people we do it with will suffer. Alan's self was enlarged by his academic vocation, and the work he did was a joy to behold. Eric's self was diminished by his encounter with academia, and choosing a different vocation might have been his only way to recover integrity lost.

WHEN TEACHERS LOSE HEART

As good teachers weave the fabric that joins them with students and subjects, the heart is the loom on which the threads are tied: the tension is held, the shuttle flies, and the fabric is stretched tight. Small wonder, then, that teaching tugs at the heart, opens the heart, even breaks the heart—and the more one loves teaching, the more heartbreaking it can be.

We became teachers for reasons of the heart, animated by a passion for some subject and for helping people to learn. But many of us lose heart as the years of teaching go by. How can we take heart in teaching once more, so we can do what good teachers always do—give heart to our students? The courage to teach is the courage to keep one's heart open in those very moments when the heart is asked to hold more than it is able, so that teacher and students and subject can be woven into the fabric of community that learning and living require.

There are no techniques for reclaiming our hearts, for keeping our hearts open. Indeed, the heart does not seek "fixes" but insight and understanding. When we lose heart, we need an understanding of our condition that will liberate us from that condition, a diagnosis that will lead us toward new ways of being in the classroom simply by telling the truth about who, and how, we are. Truth, not technique, is what heals and empowers the heart.

We lose heart, in part, because teaching is a daily exercise in vulnerability. I need not reveal personal secrets to feel naked in front of a class. I need only parse a sentence or work a proof on the board while my students doze off or pass notes. No matter how technical or abstract my subject may be, the things I teach are things I care about—and what I care about helps define my selfhood.

Unlike many professions, teaching is always done at the dangerous intersection of personal and public life. A good therapist must work in a personal way, but never publicly: the therapist who reveals as much as a client's name is derelict. A good trial lawyer must work in a public forum, but unswayed by personal opinion: the lawyer who allows his or her feelings about a client's guilt to weaken the client's defense is guilty of malpractice.

But a good teacher must stand where personal and public meet, dealing with the thundering flow of traffic at an intersection where "weaving a web of connectedness" feels more like crossing a freeway on foot. As we try to connect ourselves and our subjects with our students, we make ourselves, as well as our subjects, vulnerable to indifference, judgment, ridicule.

To reduce our vulnerability, we disconnect from students, from subjects, and even from ourselves. We build a wall between inner truth and outer performance, and we play-act the teacher's part. Our words, spoken at remove from our hearts, become "the balloon speech in cartoons," and we become caricatures of ourselves. We distance ourselves from students and subject to minimize the danger—forgetting that distance makes life more dangerous still by isolating the self.

This self-protective split of personhood from practice is encouraged by an academic culture that distrusts personal truth. Though the academy claims to value multiple modes of knowing, it honors only one—an "objective" way of knowing that takes us into the "real" world by taking us "out of ourselves."

In this culture, objective facts are regarded as pure while subjective feelings are suspect and sullied. In this culture, the self is not a source to be tapped but a danger to be suppressed, not a potential to be fulfilled but an obstacle to be overcome. In this culture, the pathology of speech disconnected from self is regarded, and rewarded, as a virtue.

If my sketch of the academic bias against selfhood seems overdone, here is a story from my own teaching experience. I assigned my students a series of brief analytical essays involving themes in the texts we were going to be reading. Then I assigned a parallel series of autobiographical sketches, related to those themes, so my students could see connections between the textbook concepts and their own lives.

After the first class, a student spoke to me: "In those autobiographical essays you asked us to write, is it okay to use the word 'I'?"

I did not know whether to laugh or cry—but I knew that my response would have considerable impact on a young man who had just opened himself to ridicule. I told him that not only could he use the word "I," but I hoped he would use it freely and often. Then I asked what had led to his question.

"I'm a history major," he said, "and each time I use 'I' in a paper, they knock off half a grade."

The academic bias against subjectivity not only forces our students to write poorly ("It is believed . . ." instead of "I believe . . . "); it deforms their thinking about themselves and their world. In a single stroke, we delude our students into believing that bad prose turns opinions into facts and we alienate them from their own inner lives.

Faculty often complain that students have no regard for the gifts of insight and understanding that are the true payoff of education—they care only about short-term outcomes in the "real" world: "Will this major get me a job?" "How will this assignment be useful in 'real' life?"

But those are not the questions deep in our students' hearts. They are merely the questions they have been taught to ask, not only by tuition-paying parents who want their children to be employable, but by an academic culture that distrusts and devalues inner reality. Of course our students are cynical about the inner outcomes of education: we teach them that the subjective self is irrelevant and even unreal.

The foundation of any culture lies in the way it answers the question "Where do reality and power reside?" For some cultures the answer is the gods; for some it is nature; for some it is tradition. In our culture, the answer is clear: reality and power reside in the external world of objects and events, and in the sciences that study that world, while the inner realm of "heart" is a romantic fantasy—an escape from harsh realities perhaps, but surely not a source of leverage over "the real world."

We are obsessed with manipulating externals because we believe that they will give us some power over reality and win us some freedom from its constraints. Mesmerized by a technology that seems to do just that, we dismiss the inward world. We turn every question we face into an objective problem to be solved—and we believe that for every objective problem there is some sort of technical fix.

That is why we train doctors to repair the body but not to honor the spirit; clergy to be CEOs but not spiritual guides; teachers to master techniques but not to engage their students' hearts—or their own. That is why our students are cynical about the efficacy of an education that transforms the inner landscape of their lives: when academic culture dismisses inner truth and pays homage only to the objective world, students as well as teachers lose heart.

LISTENING TO THE TEACHER WITHIN

Recovering the heart to teach requires us to reclaim our relationship with the teacher within. This teacher is one whom we knew when we were children but lost touch with as we grew into adulthood, a teacher who continually invites me to honor my true self—not my ego or expectations or image or role, but the self I am when all the externals are stripped away.

By inner teacher, I do not mean "conscience" or "superego," moral arbiter or internalized judge. In fact, conscience, as it is commonly understood, can get us into deep vocational trouble. When we listen primarily for what we "ought" to be doing with our lives, we may find ourselves hounded by external expectations that can distort our identity and integrity. There is much that I "ought" to be doing by some abstract moral calculus. But is it my vocation? Am I gifted and called to do it? Is this particular "ought" a place of intersection between my inner self and the outer world, or is it someone else's image of how my life should look?

When I follow only the oughts, I may find myself doing work that is ethically laudable but that is not mine to do. A vocation that is not mine, no matter how externally valued, does violence to the self—in the precise sense that it violates my identity and integrity on behalf of some abstract norm. When I violate myself, I invariably end up violating the people I work with. How many teachers inflict their own pain on their students— the pain that comes from doing a work that never was, or no longer is, their true work?

The teacher within is not the voice of conscience but of identity and integrity. It speaks not of what ought to be, but of what is real for us, of what is true. It says things like, "This is what fits you and this is what doesn't." "This is who you are and this is who you are not." "This is what gives you life and this is what kills your spirit— or makes you wish you were dead." The teacher within stands guard at the gate of selfhood, warding off whatever insults our integrity and welcoming whatever affirms it. The voice of the inward teacher reminds me of my potentials and limits as I negotiate the force field of my life.

I realize that the idea of a "teacher within" strikes some academics as a romantic fantasy, but I cannot fathom why. If there is no such reality in our lives, centuries of Western discourse about the aims of education become so much lip-flapping. In classical understanding, education is the attempt to "lead out" from within the self a core of wisdom that has the power to resist falsehood and live in the light of truth, not by external norms but by reasoned and reflective self-determination. The inward teacher is the living core of our lives that is addressed and evoked by any education worthy of the name.

Perhaps the idea is unpopular because it compels us to look at two of the most difficult truths about teaching. The first is that what we teach will never "take" unless it connects with the inward, living core of our students' lives, with our students' inward teachers.

We can, and do, make education an exclusively outward enterprise, forcing students to memorize and repeat facts without ever appealing to their inner truth—and we get predictable results: many students never want to read a challenging book or think a creative thought once they get out of school. The kind of teaching that transforms people does not happen if the student's inward teacher is ignored.

The second truth is even more daunting: we can speak to the teacher within our students only when we are on speaking terms with the teacher within ourselves.

The student who said that her bad teachers spoke like cartoon characters was describing teachers who have grown deaf to their inner guide, who have so thoroughly separated inner truth from outer actions that they have lost touch with a sense of self. Deep speaks to deep, and when we have not sounded our own depths, we cannot sound the depths of our students' lives.

How does one attend to the voice of the teacher within? I have no particular methods to suggest, other than the familiar ones: solitude and silence, meditative reading and walking in the woods, keeping a journal, finding a friend who will simply listen. I merely propose that we need to learn as many ways as we can of "talking to ourselves."

That phrase, of course, is one we normally use to name a symptom of mental imbalance—a clear sign of how our culture regards the idea of an inner voice! But people who learn to talk to themselves may soon delight in the discovery that the teacher within is the sanest conversation partner they have ever had.

We need to find every possible way to listen to that voice and take its counsel seriously, not only for the sake of our work, but for the sake of our own health. If someone in the outer world is trying to tell us something important and we ignore his or her presence, that person either gives up and stops speaking or becomes more and more violent in attempting to get our attention.

Similarly, if we do not respond to the voice of the inward teacher, it will either stop speaking or become violent: I am convinced that some forms of depression, of which I have personal experience, are induced by a long-ignored inner teacher trying desperately to get us to listen by threatening to destroy us. When we honor that voice with simple attention, it responds by speaking more gently and engaging us in a life-giving conversation of the soul.

That conversation does not have to reach conclusions in order to be of value: we do not need to emerge from "talking to ourselves" with clear goals, objectives, and plans. Measuring the value of inner dialogue by its practical outcomes is like measuring the value of a friendship by the number of problems that are solved when friends get together.

Conversation among friends has its own rewards: in the presence of our friends we have the simple joy of feeling at ease, at home, trusted and able to trust. We attend to the inner teacher not to get fixed but to befriend the deeper self, to cultivate a sense of identity and integrity that allows us to feel at home wherever we are.

Listening to the inner teacher also offers an answer to one of the most basic questions teachers face: how can I develop the authority to teach, the capacity to stand my ground in the midst of the complex forces of both the classroom and my own life?

In a culture of objectification and technique we often confuse authority with power, but the two are not the same. Power works from the outside in, but authority works from the inside out. We are mistaken when we seek "authority" outside ourselves, in sources ranging from the subtle skills of group process to that less-than-subtle method of social control called grading. This view of teaching turns the teacher into the cop on the corner, trying to keep things moving amicably and by consent, but always having recourse to the coercive power of the law.

External tools of power have occasional utility in teaching, but they are no substitute for authority, the authority that comes from the teacher's inner life. The clue is in the word itself, which has "author" at its core. Authority is granted to people who are perceived as "authoring" their own words, their own actions, their own lives, rather than playing a scripted role at great remove from their own hearts. When teachers depend on the coercive powers of law or technique, they have no authority at all.

I am painfully aware of the times in my own teaching when I lose touch with my inner teacher, and therefore with my own authority. In those times I try to gain power by barricading myself behind the podium and my status while wielding the threat of grades. But when my teaching is authorized by the teacher within me, I need neither weapons nor armor to teach.

Authority comes as I reclaim my identity and integrity, remembering my selfhood and my sense of vocation. Then teaching can come from the depths of my own truth—and the truth that is within my students has a chance to respond in kind.

INSTITUTIONS AND THE HUMAN HEART

My concern for the "inner landscape" of teaching may seem indulgent, even irrelevant, at a time when many teachers are struggling simply to survive. Wouldn't it be more practical, I am sometimes asked, to offer tips, tricks, and techniques for staying alive in the classroom, things that ordinary teachers can use in everyday life?

I have worked with countless teachers, and many of them have confirmed my own experience: as important as methods may be, the most practical thing we can achieve in any kind of work is insight into what is happening inside us as we do it. The more familiar we are with our inner terrain, the more surefooted our teaching—and living—becomes.

I have heard that in the training of therapists, which involves much practical technique, there is a saying: "Technique is what you use until the therapist arrives." Good methods can help a therapist find a way into the client's dilemma, but good therapy does not begin until the real-life therapist joins with the real life of the client.

Technique is what teachers use until the real teacher arrives, and we need to find as many ways as possible to help that teacher show up. But if we want to develop the identity and integrity that good teaching requires, we must do something alien to academic culture: we must talk to each other about our inner lives—risky stuff in a profession that fears the personal and seeks safety in the technical, the distant, the abstract.

I was reminded of that fear recently as I listened to a group of faculty argue about what to do when students share personal experiences in class—experiences that are related to the themes of the course, but that some professors regard as "more suited to a therapy session than to a college classroom."

The house soon divided along predictable lines. On one side were the scholars, insisting that the subject is primary and must never be compromised for the sake of the students' lives. On the other side were the student-centered folks, insisting that the lives of students must always come first even if it means that the subject gets shortchanged. The more vigorously these camps promoted their polarized ideas, the more antagonistic they became—and the less they learned about pedagogy or about themselves.

The gap between these views seems unbridgeable—until we understand what creates it. At bottom, these professors were not debating teaching techniques. They were revealing the diversity of identity and integrity among themselves, saying, in various ways, "Here are my own limits and potentials when it comes to dealing with the relation between the subject and my students' lives."

If we stopped lobbing pedagogical points at each other and spoke about who we are as teachers, a remarkable thing might happen: identity and integrity might grow within us and among us, instead of hardening as they do when we defend our fixed positions from the foxholes of the pedagogy wars.

But telling the truth about ourselves with colleagues in the workplace is an enterprise fraught with danger, against which we have erected formidable taboos. We fear making ourselves vulnerable in the midst of competitive people and politics that could easily turn against us, and we claim the inalienable right to separate the "personal" and the "professional" into airtight compartments (even though everyone knows the two are inseparably

intertwined). So we keep the workplace conversation objective and external, finding it safer to talk about technique than about selfhood.

Indeed, the story I most often hear from faculty (and other professionals) is that the institutions in which they work are the heart's worst enemy. In this story, institutions continually try to diminish the human heart in order to consolidate their own power, and the individual is left with a discouraging choice: to distance one's self from the institution and its mission and sink into deepening cynicism (an occupational hazard of academic life) or to maintain eternal vigilance against institutional invasion and fight for one's life when it comes.

Taking the conversation of colleagues into the deep places where we might grow in self-knowledge for the sake of our professional practice will not be an easy, or popular, task. But it is a task that leaders of every educational institution must take up if they wish to strengthen their institution's capacity to pursue the educational mission. How can schools educate students if they fail to support the teacher's inner life? To educate is to guide students on an inner journey toward more truthful ways of seeing and being in the world. How can schools perform their mission without encouraging the guides to scout out that inner terrain?

Now that this century of objectification and manipulation by technique has drawn to a close, we are experiencing an exhaustion of institutional resourcefulness at the very time when the problems that our institutions must address grow deeper and more demanding. Just as 20th-century medicine, famous for its externalized fixes for disease, has found itself required to reach deeper for the psychological and spiritual dimensions of healing, so 20th-century education must open up a new frontier in teaching and learning—the frontier of the teacher's inner life.

How this might be done is a subject I have explored in earlier essays,[1,2] so I will not repeat myself here. In "Good Talk about Good Teaching," I examined some of the key elements necessary for an institution to host noncompulsory, non-invasive opportunities for faculty to help themselves and each other grow inwardly as teachers. In "Divided No More," I explored things we can do on our own when institutions are resistant or hostile to the inner agenda.

Our task is to create enough safe spaces and trusting relationships within the academic workplace—hedged about by appropriate structural protections—that more of us will be able to tell the truth about our own struggles and joys as teachers in ways that befriend the soul and give it room to grow. Not all spaces can be safe, not all relationships trustworthy, but we can surely develop more of them than we now have so that an increase of honesty and healing can happen within us and among us—for our own sake, the sake of our teaching, and the sake of our students.

Honesty and healing sometimes happen quite simply, thanks to the alchemical powers of the human soul. When I, with 30 years of teaching experience, speak openly about the fact that I still approach each new class with trepidation, younger faculty tell me that this makes their own fears seem more natural—and thus easier to transcend—and a rich dialogue about the teacher's selfhood often ensues. We do not discuss techniques for "fear management," if such exist. Instead, we meet as fellow travelers and offer encouragement to each other in this demanding but deeply rewarding journey across the inner landscape of education—calling each other back to the identity and integrity that animate all good work, not least the work called teaching.

ENDNOTES

1. Parker J. Palmer, "Good Talk about Good Teaching: Improving Teaching Through Conversation and Community," *Change Magazine*, November/December, 1993, pp. 8–13. A revised version appears as Chapter VI in *The Courage to Teach.*

2. Parker J. Palmer, "Divided No More: A Movement Approach to Educational Reform," *Change Magazine*, March/April, 1992, pp. 10–17. A revised version appears as Chapter VII in *The Courage to Teach.*

REFERENCE

Palmer, P. J. (1998). *The Courage to Teach: Exploring the Inner Landscape of a Teacher's Life.* San Francisco: Jossey-Bass.

DISCUSSION QUESTIONS

1. Have you ever personally known any great teachers? What made them great teachers?
2. In what ways have you been profoundly influenced by teachers you have encountered?
3. Do all great teachers have certain qualities in common?
4. What does Palmer mean when he talks about listening to the "inner teacher"?
5. What are some implications of Palmer's ideas for curriculum? For professional development?

9

Critical Issues in Teaching

ALLAN C. ORNSTEIN

FOCUSING QUESTIONS

1. In what ways may teaching be considered to be a science?
2. In what ways may teaching be considered to be an art?
3. How are teachers portrayed in the popular media?
4. How much influence do teachers have in making the world a better place?
5. How should schools and teachers address the horrors of 20th-century violence?

This chapter will briefly examine the issue of whether teaching is a science or an art; it is an issue that has gained attention among teachers of teachers and their students. This issue is also used as a springboard to introduce the second part of the piece: how we can improve teaching by emphasizing humanistic and moral issues, as well as the need for reconceptualizing the nature of teaching. In the second part of the chapter, the discussion will extend beyond the traditional themes of teaching. The content will most likely upset some readers, and still others may find it far too emotional or argumentative. I do believe, however, that when a critic or commentator attempts to rethink, reevaluate, or reconceptualize a field of study, a subject, or a domain that is rooted in tradition, a certain amount of resistance and criticism will surface and reflect the reader's thoughts.

THE SCIENCE VERSUS THE ART OF TEACHING

We cannot agree on whether teaching is a science or an art. Some readers may say that this is a hopeless dichotomy, similar to that of theory versus practice, because the real world rarely consists of neat packages and either–or situations. N. L. Gage uses this distinction between *teaching as a science* and *as an art* to describe the elements of predictability in teaching and what constitutes good teaching. A science of teaching, he contends, "implies that good teaching will some day be attainable by closely following vigorous laws that yield high predictability and control." Teaching is more than a science, he observes, because it also involves "artistic judgment about the best ways to teach." When teaching leaves the laboratory or textbook and goes face to face with students, "the opportunity for artistry expands enormously."[1] No science can prescribe successfully at all the twists and turns as teaching unfolds or as teachers respond with judgment, insight, or sensitivity to promote learning. These are expressions of art that depart from the rules and principles of science.

Is such a limited scientific basis of teaching even worthwhile to consider? Yes, but the practitioner must learn as a teacher to draw not only from his or her professional knowledge (which is

This chapter is based on portions of the author's book *Teaching and Schooling in America: Prior and Post 9-11* (Boston: Allyn and Bacon, 2003). The book is concerned with life and death, good and evil, peace and war, education and miseducation, traditional and progressive education, equality and inequality. It starts with the ancient Greeks and Romans and ends with post 9-11 society, including American, Chinese, Indian, and Arabic cultures.

grounded in *scientific principles*), but also from a set of personal experiences and resources (sometimes called *craft knowledge*) that is uniquely defined and exhibited by the teacher's own personality and "gut" reaction to classroom events that unfold (which form the basis for the *art of teaching*). For Philip Jackson, the hunches, judgments, and insights of the teacher, as he or she responds spontaneously to events in the classroom, are as important as, and perhaps even more important than, the science of teaching.[2] The routine activities of the classroom, the social patterns and dynamics among students, and the accommodations and compromises between students and teachers are much more important than any theory about teaching, because it is the everyday routines and relationships that determine the processes and outcomes of teaching.

To some extent, the act of teaching must be considered intuitive and interactive, not prescriptive or predictable. According to Elliot Eisner, teaching is based primarily on feelings and artistry, not scientific rules. In an age of science and technology, there is a special need to consider teaching as an art and craft. Eisner condemns the scientific movement in psychology, especially behaviorism, and the scientific movement in education, especially school management, as reducing the teaching act to trivial specifications. He regards teaching as a "poetic metaphor" more suited to satisfying the soul than to informing the head, more concerned with the whole than with a set of discrete skills or stimuli. Our role as teachers, he claims, should not be that of a "puppeteer," an "engineer," or a manager; rather, it is "to orchestrate the dialogue [as the conductor of a symphony] moving from one side of the room to the other."[3]

The idea is to perceive patterns in motion, to improvise within the classroom, and to avoid the mechanical or prescribed rules. The need is to act human, to display feelings to affirm and value our students. The idea is to be able to smile, clap, and laugh with your students while you teach them. Sadly, many teachers lack the self-confidence to openly express their emotions, feelings, or real personality.

Louis Rubin has a similar view of teaching: that effectiveness and artistry go hand in hand. The interplay of students and teacher is crucial

and cannot be predetermined with carefully devised strategies. Confronted with everyday problems that cannot be easily predicted, the teacher must rely on intuition and on "insight acquired through long experience."[4] Rubin refers to such terms as "with-it-ness," "instructional judgments," "quick cognitive leaps," and "informal guesses" to explain the difference between the effective teacher and the ineffective teacher. Recognizing the limits to rationality, he claims that for the artistic teacher a "feel for what is right often is more productive than prolonged analysis." In the final analysis, Rubin compares the teacher's pedagogy with the "artist's colors, poet's words, sculptor's clay, and musician's notes,"[5] in my view all of which need a certain amount of artistic judgment to get the right mix, medium, or blend.

Other researchers are more extreme in their analysis of teaching solely as an art, providing romantic accounts and tales of successful teaching and teaching strategies, described in language that could hardly be taken for social science research. They consider the act of teaching akin to drama, an esthetic and kinesthetic endeavor, and feel that those who wish to teach should audition in a teaching studio and be trained as performing artists. Good teaching is likened to good theater, and a good teacher is likened to a good actor.[6]

Seymour Sarason describes the teacher as a performing artist. Like an actor, conductor, or artist, the teacher attempts to *instruct* and *move* the audience.[7] More significantly, this author maintains that the actor, artist, or teacher attempts to *transform* the audience in terms of thinking and instilling new ideas. By transforming the audience, we alter the person's outlook toward objects or ideas. Revolutionary thought, I maintain, is built on poetry, music, art, movies, and speeches. And, ultimately, it is the esthetics, ideas, and values (the art, music, food, customs, laws, and thoughts) that define who we are. Hence, it is teachers in the broadest sense, including actors, artists, poets, writers, and of course parents, who make the difference for society.

Given the metaphor of the *performing artist,* a certain amount of talent or innate ability is needed to be effective, along with sufficient rehearsal and caring behavior. But knowledge or understanding of the audience is also needed. *Mr. Holland's Opus* makes the point. The teacher was unsuccessful in the beginning of the movie, despite his knowledge of music, compassion, and desire to give the students his "all." In the remaining part of the movie, however, through some "magical" awakening, he redefined his methods (science of teaching) and acting (art of teaching), with the result that the audience (students) became interested and learned to appreciate good music. Mr. Holland originally thought the problem was in the minds of the audience. Not until he realized that it was the other way around, that it was his attitude that needed to be improved, was he successful.[8]

In *The King and I,* the British teacher, Anna, was successful from the outset, despite cultural differences and the gender inequalities of the society (Siam). Not only was she caring and compassionate, but she also understood her students. She was able to adapt to their needs, interests, and abilities—and affirm their individuality. The song "Getting to Know You" makes the point. She reminded some of us of the school teachers we knew when we were kids—the loving and joyful teacher in Sylvia Ashton-Warner's *Teacher,* written some 40 years ago, or a combination of the author's two favorite elementary school teachers whom he remembers fondly and dedicated one of his books to: Mrs. Katz, "a warm, friendly, and understanding teacher," and Mrs. Schwartz, "a tough, nurturing school marm who drilled the facts and enforced the rules."[9]

Both movies underscore the need for teachers to understand students and for good teachers to connect with the audience. Through either previous learning (*pedagogical knowledge*) or practical experience (*craft knowledge*), the teacher must know how students think and feel. A certain amount of training helps one to understand students, but it is only a starting point. A successful teacher first understands and accepts himself or herself, then understands and accepts others. Arthur Jersild summed it up some 50 years ago: "self understanding requires something quite different from the methods . . . and skills of know-how . . . emphasized in education [courses]." Planning, role playing, and all the other methods and techniques—what we call scientific principles—are helpful, but what is also needed

"is a more personal kind of searching, which will enable the teacher to identify his own concerns and to share the concerns of his students."[10] Thus, teaching is not just an academic or cognitive enterprise; it involves people and an affective (feelings, attitudes, and emotions) or artistic component that has little to do with pedagogical or scientific knowledge.

The more we consider teaching as an art, packed with emotions, feelings, and excitement, the more difficult it is to derive rules or generalizations. If teaching is more an art than a science, then principles and practices cannot be easily codified or developed in the classroom or easily learned by others. Hence, there is little reason to offer instructional method courses in education. If, however, teaching is more of a science, or at least partly a science, then pedagogy is predictable to that extent; it can be observed and measured with some accuracy, and the research can be applied to the practice of teaching (as a physician applies scientific knowledge to the practice of medicine) and also learned in a college classroom or on the job.

But a word of caution is needed. The more we rely on artistic interpretations or on old stories and accounts about teachers, the more we fall victim to fantasy, wit, and romantic rhetoric, and the more we depend on hearsay and conjecture, rather than on social science or objective data, in evaluating teacher competency. On the other hand, the more we rely on the scientific interpretations of teaching, the more we overlook those common-sense and spontaneous processes of teaching, and the sounds, smells, and visual flavor of the classroom. The more scientific we are in our approach to teaching, the more we ignore what we cannot accommodate to our empirical assumptions or principles. What sometimes occurs, according to Eisner, is that the educationally significant but difficult to measure or observe is replaced by what is insignificant but comparatively easy to measure or observe.[11]

It is necessary to blend artistic impressions and relevant stories about teaching, because good teaching involves emotions and feeling, with the objectivity of observations and measurements and the precision of language. There is nothing wrong with considering good teaching to be an art, but we must also consider it to lend itself to a prescriptive science or practice. If it does not, then there is little assurance that prospective teachers can be trained to be teachers—told what to do, how to instruct students, how to manage students, and so forth—and educators will be extremely vulnerable to public criticism and to people outside the profession telling them how and what to teach.

True knowledge of teaching is achieved by practice and experience in the classroom. According to some observers, the beliefs, values, and norms—that is, the knowledge—that teachers come to have the most faith in and use most frequently to guide their teaching are those consistent with traditions that have "worked" in the classroom. Although it seems to be more everyday and common sense–based than highly specialized and theoretical, the process still includes the receiving and using of data that can be partially planned and scientifically analyzed. But we assume that there are still professional and technical skills that can be taught to teachers and designed and developed in advance with underlying scientific principles and research-based data. Some of us would refer to this as *pedagogical knowledge* or *craft knowledge* as opposed to subject-matter or content-based knowledge.

Indeed, the real value of scientific procedures may not be realized in terms of research or theoretical generalizations that can be translated into practice. Research may have limited potential for teachers, but it can help them to become aware of the problems and needs of students. Scientific generalizations and theories may not always be applicable to specific teaching situations, but such propositions can help in the formulation of a reliable and valid base for teaching in classrooms. Scientific ideas can serve as a starting point for the discussion and analysis of the art of teaching.

RECONCEPTUALIZING TEACHING

To argue that good teaching boils down to a set of prescriptive behaviors, methods, or proficiency levels, that teachers must follow a "new" research-based teaching plan or evaluation system, or that decisions about teacher accountability can be assessed in terms of students passing a multiple-choice test is to miss the human aspect of teaching, the real *stuff* of what teaching is all about.

Stress on assessment and evaluation systems illustrates that behaviorism has won at the expense of humanistic psychology. Put in different terms, the ideas of Thorndike and Watson have prevailed over the ideas of Dewey and Kilpatrick. It also suggests that school administrators, policy makers, and researchers would rather focus on the *science* of teaching—behaviors and outcomes that can be observed, counted, or measured—than on the *art* of teaching with its humanistic and hard-to-measure variables.

Robert Linn contends that assessment of teachers and students can be easily mandated, implemented, and reported and thus have wide appeal under the guise of "reform." Although these assessment systems are supposed to improve education, they don't necessarily do so.[12] Real reform is complex and costly (for example, reducing class size, raising teacher salaries, introducing special reading programs, extending the school day and year), and it takes time before the results are evident. People such as politicians and business leaders, who seem to be leading this latest wave of reform, want a quick, easy, and cheap fix. Thus, they will always opt for assessment because it is simple and inexpensive to implement. It creates heightened media visibility, the feeling that something is being done, and the Hawthorne effect or novelty tends to elevate short-term gains. This assessment focus (which is a form of behaviorism) also provides a rationale for teacher education programs, because it suggests that we can identify good teaching. Yet it is questionable, given our current knowledge of teaching and teacher education and the importance of personality, whether new teachers can be properly prepared in terms of both academic rigor and practical reality.

For those in the business of preparing teachers, there is the need to provide a research base and rationale showing that teachers who enroll and complete a teacher education program are more likely to be effective teachers than those who lack such training. The fact that there are several alternative certification programs for teachers in more than 40 states, through which nearly 5 percent (as high as 16 percent in Texas and 22 percent in New Jersey) of the nationwide teaching force entered teaching,[13] makes teachers of teachers (professors of education) take notice and try to demonstrate that their teacher preparation programs work and that they can prepare effective teachers. Indeed, there is a need to identify teacher behaviors and methods that work under certain conditions, leading many educators to favor behaviorism (or prescriptive ideas and specific tasks) and assessment systems (closed-ended, tiny, measurable variables) that correlate teaching and learning.

Being able to describe detailed methods of teaching and how and why teachers do what they do should improve the performance of teachers. But all the new research hardly tells the whole story of teaching—what leads to teacher effectiveness and student learning. Being able to describe teachers' thinking or decision making and analyzing their stories and reflective practices suggest that we understand and can improve teaching. The new research on teaching, with its stories, biographies, reflective practices, and qualitative methods, provides a platform and publication outlet for researchers. It promotes their expertise (which in turn continues to separate them from practitioners) and permits them to continue to subordinate teaching to research. It also provides a new paradigm for analyzing teaching, because the old models (teacher styles, teacher characteristics, teacher effectiveness, etc.) have become exhausted and repetitive. The issues and questions related to the new paradigm create new educational wars and controversy between traditional and nontraditional researchers, between quantitative and qualitative advocates. It is questionable, however, whether this new knowledge base about teaching really improves teaching and learning or leads to substantial and sustained improvement.

The Need for Humanistic Teaching

The focus of teacher research should be on the learner, not on the teacher; on the feelings and attitudes of the student, not on knowledge and information (because feelings and attitudes will eventually determine what knowledge and information are sought after and acquired); and on the long-term development and growth of the students, not on short-term objectives or specific teacher tasks. But if teachers spend more time with the learners' feelings and attitudes, as well as on social and personal growth, teachers may be penalized when cognitive student outcomes (little pieces of information) on high-stake tests are correlated with their behaviors and methods in class.

Students need to be encouraged and nurtured by their teachers, especially when they are young. They are too dependent on approval from significant adults—first their parents, then their teachers. Parents and teachers need to help young children and adolescents to establish a source for self-esteem by focusing on their strengths, supporting them, discouraging negative self-talk, and helping them to take control of their lives with their own culture and values.

People (including young people) with high self-esteem achieve at high levels, and the more one achieves, the better one feels about oneself. The opposite is also true: Students who fail to master the subject matter get down on themselves and eventually give up. Students with low self-esteem give up quickly. In short, student self-esteem and achievement are directly related. If we can nurture students' self-esteem, almost everything else will fall into place, including achievement scores and academic outcomes. Regardless of how smart or talented a child, if he or she has personal problems, cognition will be detrimentally affected.

This builds a strong argument for creating successful experiences for students to help them to feel good about themselves. The long-term benefits are obvious: The more students learn to like themselves, the more they will achieve; and the more they achieve, the more they will like themselves. But this takes time, involves a lot of nurturing, and does not show up on a standardized test within a semester or school year; moreover, it does not help the teacher who is being evaluated by a content- or test-driven school administrator who is looking for results now. It certainly does not benefit the teacher who is being evaluated for how many times he or she attended departmental meetings, whether the shades in the classroom were even, or whether his or her instructional objectives were clearly stated.

It is obvious that certain behaviors contribute to good teaching. The trouble is that there is little agreement on exactly what behaviors or methods are most important. There are some teachers who gain theoretical knowledge of "what works," but are unable to put the ideas into practice. Some teachers with similar preparation act effortlessly in the classroom and others consider teaching a chore. All this suggests that teaching cannot be described in terms of a checklist or a precise model. It also suggests that teaching is a humanistic activity that deals with people (not tiny behaviors or competencies) and how people (teachers and students) develop and behave in a variety of classroom and school settings.

Although the research on teacher effectiveness provides a vocabulary and system for improving our insight into good teaching, there is a danger that this research may lead to some of us becoming too rigid in our view of teaching. Following only one teacher model or evaluation system can lead to too much emphasis on specific behaviors that can be easily measured or prescribed in advance, at the expense of ignoring humanistic behaviors, such as esthetic appreciation, emotions, values, and moral responsibility, that cannot be easily measured or prescribed in advance.

Although some educators recognize that humanistic factors influence teaching, we continue to define most teacher behaviors in terms of behaviorist and cognitive factors. Most teacher evaluation instruments tend to de-emphasize the human side of teaching because it is difficult to measure. In an attempt to be scientific, to predict and control behavior and to assess group patterns, we sometimes lose sight of the attitudes of teachers and their relations with students.

In providing feedback and evaluation for teachers, many factors need to be considered so that the advice or information does not fall on deaf ears. Teachers appreciate feedback processes whereby they can improve their teaching as long as the processes are honest and professionally planned and administered, as long as teachers are permitted to make mistakes, and as long as more than one model of effectiveness is considered so that they can adapt recommended behaviors and methods to fit their own personality and philosophy of teaching.

Teachers must be permitted to incorporate specific teacher behaviors and methods according to their own unique personalities and philosophies, to pick and choose from a wide range of research and theory, and to discard other teacher behaviors that conflict with their own style without the fear of being considered ineffective. Many school districts, and even state departments of education, have developed evaluation instruments and salary plans based exclusively on prescriptive and product-oriented behaviors. Even worse, teachers who do not exhibit these behaviors are often penalized or labeled as "marginal" or "incompetent."[14] There is danger that many more school districts and states will continue to jump on this bandwagon and make decisions based on prescriptive teacher research, without recognizing or giving credibility to other teacher behaviors or methods that might be humanistic because they deal with feelings, emotions, and personal connections with people—what some educators label as fuzzy or vague criteria.

Humanistic Teaching

In the early 20th century, humanistic principles of teaching and learning were envisioned in the theories of progressive education: in the *child-centered* lab school directed by John Dewey at the University of Chicago from 1896 to 1904; the *play-centered* methods and materials introduced by Maria Montessori, which were designed to develop the practical, sensor, and formal skills of prekindergarten and kindergarten slum children of Italy starting in 1908; and the *activity-centered* practices of William Kilpatrick, who in the 1920s and 1930s urged that elementary teachers organize classrooms around social activities, group enterprises, and group projects and allow children to say what they think.

All these progressive theories were highly humanistic and stressed the child's interests, individuality, and creativity—in short, the child's freedom to develop naturally, free from teacher domination and the weight of rote learning. But progressivism failed because, in the view of Lawrence Cremin, there were not enough good teachers to implement progressive thought in classrooms and schools.[15] To be sure, it is much easier to stress knowledge, rote learning, and right answers than it is to teach about ideas, to consider the interests and needs of students, and to give them freedom to explore and interact with each other without teacher constraints.

By the end of the 20th century, the humanistic teacher was depicted by William Glasser's "positive" and "supportive" teacher who could manage students without coercion and teach without failure.[16] It was also illustrated by Robert Fried's "passionate" teacher and Vito Perrone's "teacher with a heart"—teachers who live to teach young children and refuse to submit to apathy or criticism that may infect the school in which they work.[17] These teachers are dedicated and caring, they actively engage students in their classrooms, and they affirm their identities. The students do not have to ask whether their teacher is interested in them, thinks of them, or knows their interests or concerns. The answer is definitely yes.

The humanistic teacher is also portrayed by Theodore Sizer's mythical teacher called "Horace," who is dedicated and enjoys teaching, treats learning as a humane enterprise, inspires his students to learn, and encourages them to develop their powers of thought, taste, and character.[18] Yet the system forces Horace to make a number of compromises in planning, teaching, and grading, which he knows that, if we lived in an ideal world (with more than 24 hours in a day), he would not make. Horace is a trooper; he hides his frustration. Critics of teachers don't really want to hear him or face facts; they don't even know what it is like to teach. Sizer simply states, "Most jobs in the real world have a gap between what would be nice and what is possible. One adjusts."[19] Hence, most caring, dedicated teachers are forced to make some compromises, take some shortcuts, and make some accommodations. As long as no one gets upset and no one complains, the system permits a chasm between rhetoric (the rosy picture) and reality (slow burnout).

There is also the humanistic element in Nel Noddings' ideal teacher, who focuses on the nur-

turing of "competent, caring, loving, and lovable persons." To that end, she describes teaching as a caring profession in which teachers should convey to students the caring way of thinking about one's self, siblings, strangers, animals, plants, and the physical environment. She stresses the affective aspect of teaching: the need to focus on the child's strengths and interests, the need for an individualized curriculum built around the child's abilities and needs.[20] Caring, according to Noddings, cannot be achieved by a formula or checklist. It calls for different behaviors for different situations, from tenderness to tough love. Good teaching, like good parenting, requires continuous effort, trusting relationships, and continuity of purpose—the purpose of caring, appreciating human connections, and respecting people and ideas from a historical, multicultural, and diverse perspective.[21]

Actually, the humanistic teacher is someone who highlights the personal and social dimension in teaching and learning, as opposed to the behavioral, scientific, or technological aspects. We might argue that everything that the teacher does is "human" and the expression "humanistic teaching" is a cliché. However, I would use the term in a loose sense to describe the teacher who emphasizes the arts as opposed to the sciences and people instead of numbers. Although the teacher understands the value of many subjects, including the sciences and social sciences, he or she feels that there is the need for students to understand certain *ideas* and *values,* some rooted in 3,000 years or more of philosophy, literature, art, music, theater, and the like. Without certain agreed-on content, our heritage would crumble and we would be at the mercy of chance and ignorance; moreover, our education enterprise would be subject to the whim and fancy of local fringe groups.

Humanistic education, according to Jacques Barzun, the elegant and eloquent writer on history and humanism, leads to a form of knowledge that helps us to deal with the nature of life, but it does not guarantee a more gracious or noble life:

> The humanities will not sort out the world's evils and were never meant to cure [our] troubles. . . . They will not heal diseased minds or broken hearts any more than they will foster political democracy or settle international disputes.

The humanities (and, if I may add, the humanistic teacher) "have meaning," according to Barzun, "because of the inhumanity of life; what they depict is strife and disaster"[22]; and, if I may add, by example, they help us to deal with the human condition and provide guidelines for moral behavior, good taste, and the improvement of civilization.

On a schoolwide level, the author would argue that humanism (what Fried calls "passion," Perrone calls "heart," Sizer calls "dedication," Noddings calls "caring," and Barzun calls "the well-rounded person") means eliminating homogeneous grouping and the labeling and tracking of students and reducing competitive grading. It means that we eliminate the notion that everyone should go to college since it creates frustration, anger, and unrealistic expectations among large numbers of children and youth. According to Paul Goodman, it requires that society find viable occupational options for noncollege graduates and jobs that have decent salaries, respect, and social status.[23] It suggests, according to John Gardner, that we recognize various forms of excellence—the excellent teacher, the excellent artist, the excellent plumber, and the excellent bus driver; otherwise, we create a myopic view of talent and a subsequent tension that will threaten a democratic society.[24] It also means that we appreciate and nurture different student abilities, aptitudes, and skills, what Howard Gardner calls "multiple intelligences."[25]

Humanistic versus Nonhumanistic Thought

If we fail to adapt a more caring and compassionate view of teaching and schooling, then we fall victim to excessive competiveness and materialism—and eventually to class differences that will divide society into dominant and subordinate groups. Pursuant to neo-Marxist and radical postmodern thinking, we create a permanent underclass who live in "squalid" (Kozol's word), "dehumanizing" (Freire's word), and "colonialized" (Giroux's and McClain's word) conditions. The outcome is a society in which a disproportionate number of low-achieving students and poor, minority, and special needs children are locked into future low-end jobs, unemployment, or what Oscar Lewis, some 40 years ago, referred to as the "culture of poverty," whereby poverty is transferred from generation to generation.[26] In short, a new subordinate group, the have-nots, is construed as dumb, lazy, and de-skilled by a school system and society that encourage competitiveness and judge people on different characteristics and different outcomes.

This human situation is tolerated by the majority of the populace because egalitarianism, social justice, and human dignity are wrongly conceived or ignored. Our prejudices become ingrained in our thinking because they become institutionalized by society. Moreover, we come to rely on "scientific objectivity" to excuse or defend educational and social practices that generate and then perpetuate these dominant–subordinate conditions. There should be no room in this country, or in any society that claims to be civilized, for second-class citizenship, or even for people who think of themselves as second-class citizens. There have been enough second-class citizens in the world.

Down through the ages, the vast majority of humans have been barbarians, slaves, serfs, peasants, and extremely poor and uneducated. Almost one half to one percent of the population—the monarchs and nobility, popes and cardinals, military leaders and generals, czars, capitalists, and the like—have possessed more than 50 percent of the wealth and resources existing within their particular period of history. Even today, 1.2 billion people (or 20 percent of the world's population) live on less than one dollar a day, and 50 percent of the developing countries' 4.5 billion population live on less than two dollars a day, the greatest percentages being in South Asia, sub-Saharan Africa, and Latin America.[27] These poor people live under squalid conditions that very few of us, except for a few scholars and human rights workers, fully comprehend or care to know about. But it is this poverty and hopelessness in developing countries, and the resulting difference in quality of life and culture, that leads to deep and lasting hatred toward the more prosperous Western World and a form of madness in which people don't care if they die or are blown to pieces.

Too many people in this country and other countries have been forced to give up their identities, to move from their world to another world, to assimilate: to pass for white, Christian, or "straight." No one should have to pretend her or his whole life; to live in a closet; to disown her or his family, ethnic group, or religion—never to return to her or his people. Of course, we can argue that ethnocentrism and religious zeal are also sources of the worst atrocities. True believers come in all shapes, stripes, and ideologies, and there has been a steady oversupply of lawless opportunists and willing executioners, no matter how low their position in the chain of command may be, who take pleasure in the destruction and annihilation of other people.

Some readers may consider the above interpretation as an attempt to instill neo-Marxist, postmodern, or illusory rhetoric in the discussion, but the author contends that lack of humanism and moral teaching has resulted in lack of conscience and caring throughout the ages and throughout the globe. The outcomes are similar for all time: human suffering, oppression, fanaticism, and wholesale slaughter of human life under a political or religious ideology that mocks the individual and is suffused with hatred, brute force, and terrorism. It represents the exploitive and dark side of the human psyche, inflicted on humans by humans for centuries, from the treatment of Roman gladiators, African slaves, and European peasantry to the burning of witches and hanging of blacks and gays in the United States. Of course, the Japanese atrocities in Nanking, the Holocaust in Europe, the purges of Stalin and Mao, and the killing fields of Pol Pot are the darkest pages of history, totally irrational and extreme forms of evil that cannot be fully understood with only words. Narratives from victims, photographs, and films must become part of the discourse for us to fully comprehend the extent of this rampant barbarism and blasphemy. Blaming today's generation for another generation's sins is not the answer, but learning from old injustices and immorality is valuable so that we do not repeat history, so that we become a more civil and compassionate society.

Remembering the Dead

All of us have lived most of our lives in the 20th century, and all the lost souls who no longer exist because of mankind's cruelty and hatred must be remembered. Most of the voices and faces we never knew; therefore, it is easy to become detached from their demise and to treat them as an abstract statistic. In fact, the larger the number of dead, thousands or millions, the easier it is to become detached by adding zeros (because the mind is unable to fathom the reality and enormity of the deed) unless the individual or his or her loved ones were part of the cruel nature of history. Among the dead, some were famous for something and are in our encyclopedias, but the vast majority have been forgotten and funneled into anonymity and nothingness. All they can hope is for the poet, painter, or musician to make use of them through pen, canvas, or lyrics in order for the living to gain understanding. In this connection, it is for the teacher to educate the next generation—to make use of these forgotten and transitory people, to help them to return among the living just for a brief moment, to explain the order of magnitude of lost lives and a counting system that involves five, six, or seven zeros.

As educators who grew up in the 20th century, we must now educate students of the 21st century that the most cruel and vile acts against humanity were committed in the 20th century, much worse than the attacks on the World Trade Center, which I mention because some of us have lost loved ones or known people who died. Despite its educated populace, the most heinous deeds were committed in the last century, which produced the most efficient machines to kill the most people. And, after being surrounded by mass murder, rape, and pillage, we become detached from these violent and deathward-leaning acts; we deal with these encounters by abstracting and anatomizing them through a variety of academic subjects and topics. We keep them under lock and key so that our young children and students have almost no real knowledge of Nanking, the Holocaust, Stalin's or Mao's purges, the killing fields, or more recently Kosovo and Rwanda. Even at home—Antietam (4,000+ dead), Gettysburg (50,000+), Pearl Harbor (2,300), and now the World Trade Center (2,900)—the dead are forgotten, as if they never existed, except by some individual who buried a loved one.

As teachers, we must make sense of our past through our philosophy, history, literature, art, poetry, and music. We are required to ask our students to think about the true believers and zealots and the willing oppressors and opportunists who have ravaged the earth. We must pay homage to the millions who perished in the wars and witch hunts, the purges and extermination camps of the 20th century. We must hear their voices, see their faces, and understand their final thoughts of life in the midst of background screams, muzzled groans, and sad goodbyes—and then the stench of death—to fully comprehend the barbaric deeds of humanity, and how many more times throughout all time that evil has prevailed over good.

Indeed, I am reminded of an old soldier, a World War II veteran, discussing the Battle of the Bulge (275,000 dead). He could not remember how he celebrated his last birthday or why he just opened the refrigerator, but he could vividly recount the conditions of the battlefield as if it had been yesterday: gray foreboding clouds, the snow-covered grass, the cold nipping at his toes and fingers, the rubble of the dead around him, the eyes of the enemy and the tatter of machine guns in front, the smell of fuel oil and ashes of annihilation mixed in the countryside air.

In detail, he could still recall the names of the fallen dead on his left side and right side, the last words and groans of his doomed comrades; but soon the old soldier would die along with his memories. For that moment, there was nothing impersonal or abstract about the slaughter—the excruciating combat, the lost voices and faces, the sense of madness around him.

We must try to provide, as part of the teaching role, some reassurance to our students that good can prevail over evil, that morality can topple immorality. Although we should not be weighed down by the past, we must remember all the nameless and voiceless people who suffered and died a senseless or terrible death before their time and keep the specter and memory of the nations, tribes, and political and religious zealots that committed the acts of violence against these victims. We must fight off fading memories and amnesia so that we have a chance to prevent, or at least reduce, the worst natures in us, the resulting blasphemy and evil that have characterized so many of the inhabitants of the last century.

As teachers, we should inspire our students and help them to deal with the nature of life and society; this is one of our most important professional roles. Yet it ought to come as no surprise that we rarely connect with our students in this way. Is it because we lack passion, a sense of history or loyalty to an ideal, or merely shy from moral messages? I think that it is all these, and thus we fail the memory of the people of the last century and previous centuries who died unjustly.

As teachers, we often fail in our role to elaborate on the agony of our history, that the need to reduce the ruthlessness and atrocities of humans rests with us. All the people who are alive today are connected to the past like a cloud that sweeps through the constellations and eventually disappears. Among the thinkers of society, and especially among our writers, poets, and artists, as well as our teachers, there should be a thirst for knowledge that remembers the dead and then goes beyond the borders of the dead to elaborate on life and improve society.

Students' Learning Opportunities

Edward Pajak questions whether teaching children about evil is likely to make them virtuous. Introducing students to this kind of "content" before they are emotionally mature and intellectually sophisticated may have exactly the opposite effect of what is intended.[28] There is a human tendency to identify with the aggressor and those in power, to laugh at or ridicule the victim. Like many adults, young children may not have the intellectual or emotional capacity to process horrifying information in a clear and sophisticated manner. Premature and excessive emphasis on the dark side of history and society informs unsophisticated students about which groups represent "legitimate" targets for hate.

But we cannot protect the new generation from the chambers of horrors that have characterized most of our history. We cannot continue to allow only a little darkness to spill out in our classrooms, to keep the horrors hemmed in by limiting the dark side of human behavior to a few sentences or paragraphs in a textbook or a few comments in class. However, I would rely on Piaget's principles of cognition, that the child's formal mental operations (or advanced stage of cognition) develop between ages 11 and 15, whereby the adolescent is capable of analyzing ideas, engaging in abstract operations, and clarifying values. Even before the age of 11, the concepts of right and wrong, fairness, and basic democratic laws and principles are understood. Similarly, Piaget's theory of moral development, along with Kohlberg's notion of moral reasoning and moral ideology, suggests that teens can understand the principles of ethics, contractual obligations, conscience, and justice. There is some variation, of course, which has to do with the student's family, religion, and cultural background, due to biases and prejudices that develop outside the school. But this is exactly what the teacher has to overcome; it is part of the teacher's role.

Let me put it in a different way: Blind hatred, erroneous claims of superiority, and ideological fanaticism, by which the individual is drowned out by the mass, made impotent, then dehumanized and/or slaughtered, represent the ugly side of humanity. They can be depicted as the opposite of the music of Bach; the art of Michelangelo; the stories of Cervantes and Shakespeare; the philosophy of Kant, Locke, and Rousseau; the poems of Robert Frost, Emily Dickinson, and Lao-Tzu; and the spiritual messages of Muhammad, Buddha, and Gandhi. Teachers, in the past, have emphasized the good side of humanity. I urge that both sides need to be explored. By ignoring the ugly side of civilization, teachers unwittingly create a void among future generations—a lack of humanity, compassion, and moral constraint.

The ideals of right and wrong, justice and goodness are rooted in Western morality, Greek and Judeo-Christian ideas, as well as Eastern philosophy and religious thought, and should be incorporated into the curriculum. Education without concern for certain universal and humanistic truths, values, and ways of behaving hinders the moral fiber of society. Taken to the next step, it leads to man's natural aggression, based on biological and animal instincts. Freud would say this means that the *id* has gained the upper hand over the *super ego* (personal and social conscience). In the worst case scenario, it suggests the rise of Nieztche's "superman" complex and the subsequent rationale for racism, imperialism, colonialism, religious fanaticism, and militarism, accompanied by the death of hundreds of millions of people (50 million people alone in World War II) and the destruction of hundreds of nation-states and racial, ethnic, or religious groups, since Rome was built and Christ preached the gospel. With moral constraints, man's aggressive instincts are played out in board rooms and on Wall Street, as well as on high school, college, and professional football fields and wrestling arenas; on Saturday and Sunday mornings on suburban pee-wee soccer fields and on big-city asphalt basketball courts; and daily among us older "folks" (Bush's term) who commit road rage on American highways and byways—what most of us would call socially acceptable behavior or wink at and write off as a little extreme.

But the teaching of knowledge without morality leads to extreme competitiveness, human stratification, and survival of the fittest. Put in different words, unchecked emphasis on performance through which the same students always "win" and another group always "loses"; or the elitist notion that the right of a student to an education persists only as far as his or her intellectual capabilities; or the labeling, categorizing, and tracking of students and noting of differences among people (smart, dumb; superior, inferior) suggest a school system and a society that encourage, and even foster, all the wrong "isms"—colonialism, imperialism, fascism, and racism. In fact, almost all militant and imperialist societies stress their own efficiency and superiority over other societies—nothing more than excuses and theories for explaining man's inhumanity to man. Even worse, this type of thinking and behavior is often derived from and supported by "scientific explanations," laws, religious theology, or political ideology—doctrines created by people to suppress other people.

Moral and Civic Virtues

Teaching and schooling should be committed to a higher purpose, a humanistic–moral purpose designed not only to enhance academic grades but also for personal and social responsibility. It should be built around people and community, around respecting, caring for, and having compassion toward others. It means that teachers in the classroom deal with social and moral issues, with the human condition and good and evil. It means that students be encouraged to ask "why," as opposed to being encouraged to give the "right" answer. The question should start with family conversation, but must be nurtured in school during the formative years of learning so that a sense of social and moral consciousness is developed. But precisely on this score, our teachers and schools register a disturbing deficit, originally because it was thought to tread on the spiritual domain and now because there is little time to inquire about and discuss important ideas and issues, because the curriculum is test driven by trivia items of knowledge and short-answer outcomes.

According to one social critic, "why?" is the existential question that every individual must be permitted to ask and must receive an appropriate and meaningful answer to from those in power or who mete out justice. If the question is denied, then the individual has no basic rights.[29] It is the purest form of totalitarianism in which the individual is trivialized, as in the Roman empire, where the ruling classes' main amusement was watching humans being eaten by animals or fighting each other to the death; in the cattle cars to the concentration camps of Auschwitz and Maidenek, where the individual was reduced to a serial number and human remains were often retrofitted into soap products, lamp shades, and gold rings; and in the Serbian ethnic cleansing and rape of Bosnia and Kosovo and the cleansing and rape of Rwanda.

How many of us can locate Rwanda on the map? Does anyone among us know where Auschwitz and Maidenek are located? How many among us, except for a few elderly statesmen, scholars, and descendants of the victims, care? Given the "luxury of late birth" and "geographical distance," who among us are expected to do more than cite a few numbers or statements to put the horrors of humanity into some context or understanding? Who cares about the sufferings of all the folk groups, tribes, and nations since we came out of the caves? How many of us know the names of one or two people who died in Nanking, at Pearl Harbor, in the Holocaust, at Juno or Utah beach, in the killing fields of Cambodia, or in Croatia or Kosovo? Can we cite one name that appears on the Arch of Triumph or the Vietnam Memorial? Who can recall or ever knew the name of the pilot (Paul Tibbots) who dropped the A-bomb on Hiroshima—what his thoughts were as he approached the target or after the carnage and cloud of dust? Who among us care to know or can explain what happened or why it happened that more than 100 million soldiers and civilians died in war (or related civilian activities) in the last century in what I would call the most ruthless century—consisting of the most vile deeds and crimes against people? How do we weigh the smug claims of Western technology and industry with the millions who died beside railroad tracks and in battle trenches?

Well, we all die—no kidding—but many of us die when we are not ready to die, without any maps or charts of the journey. Modern philosophy, history, and literature have sanitized these deaths. We have more details (dates, names, and places) than we can process, so those who were murdered, raped, gassed, and executed have been generalized into nonindividuals. The lucky ones were cared for by people who rarely knew anything about their history, knew nothing about who they were, and sometimes did not even know their names. It is an old story, repeated several times in different places and periods of history, yet it must be examined by teachers and students so that there is a better chance of preventing, or at least reducing, this common madness in society.

And Americans are not innocent, given our inhuman and criminal treatment of Native Americans and black Americans—that is, the near extermination and remaining dismemberment of an entire Indian civilization over a 50-year period under the banner of westward expansion and the subhuman treatment of blacks during 100 years of slavery, followed by the exclusion of blacks from American society during the Post-Reconstruction and Jim Crow era (keenly illustrated by white and black toilets and segregated schools and housing and other public facilities).

We all know when injustices are being perpetrated, but we often do not act or want to deal with them. Throughout the ages, man has deceived himself by remaining indifferent or looking the other way in the midst of the worst atrocities and crimes, connoting a human flaw or moral fault in our character. Periodically, a nation or ethnic group has to pay a heavy price and be held accountable for its actions or inactions. Although the past has taught us how not to act, we periodically fall from civilized to uncivilized practices because our dark side checkmates our good side (the music of Bach, the plays of Shakespeare), because of our aggressive and competitive nature to beat the next person. As long as we have bread on our table and sufficient clothes on our back, we often remain silent, look the other way, or become true believers—in effect, blinded by our own inaction to the vile deeds of others.

Moral practices start with the family and continue with the church and community, but teachers must play an active role if ours is to be a more compassionate, caring, and just society. As teachers, we need to encourage open debate concerning the thorniest issues of the present and past, welcome discussions without ad hominem attacks or stereotypes, and build a sense of community (what the French call *civisme*) and character. We are forced to flee from our comfortable classroom niches, go beyond facts, raise thoughtful questions that stem from meaningful readings, and transcend the cognitive domain into the moral universe. We must promote this type of teaching for all grade levels.

Our readings in school should have a moral flavor to encourage discussion, thinking, and ultimately the transformation of the learner. Even at the primary grade level, reading must not be wasted by assigning "See Spot Run" or "A Sunday Trip to Granny"; rather the emphasis should be on folktales and stories, such as "Jack and the Beanstalk," "Rumpelstiltskin," "Seasons," and "The Mouse and the Wizard," from all parts of the world.

The relationships among history, literary criticism, and philosophy raise many questions about human conditions and civilizations. These ideas express the nature of humanity and society, considered by some to be part of the Great Books, Junior Great Books, or Great Ideas programs. Call it what you want, these readings deal with moral conscience and historical consciousness, and this is what students should be reading.

The idea is for the teacher to capture the students' imaginations, to have them explore ideas and issues, support arguments, and draw conclusions—what some of us might call *critical thinking*. At the same time, students need to examine, analyze, and interpret morally laden books to help them understand the evil or dark side of humans—what happens when morality is dethroned for greed, hatred, or some god or ideology; when excellence or efficiency is pushed to an extreme in which *all* trains are expected to run on time and all soldiers are expected to follow orders and die for the glory of some god, the nation, or the ego of old politicians.

There is need to balance the scales of justice and face the truth when history is rewritten for religious or nationalistic reasons or for apologies and excuses that what happened was historically inevitable or historically justifiable; or when "those people" were different from us, backward and uneducated; or when "they" had too much power and money—whatever hocus-pocus rationale is used to distort the truth and alter beliefs. Teachers must decide what is important in the curriculum, what has been omitted and what has been included for discussion. Often big-city teachers are rendered impotent in this professional role, and the curriculum is imposed on them from the central office by a few bureaucrats (former teachers and principals) who eventually lose touch with the community, classroom reality, and the needs of students. Regardless of our politics and idiosyncratic judgments, as professionals we need to become more involved in curriculum development and decide how the content in class achieves a balanced portrait of the past and present, of other people and nations. We need to take positions— moral positions appropriate for a changing society and diverse society, a society that is willing to face and deal with its problems. Students must be encouraged by their teachers to raise questions, take positions, and act morally responsible. To some extent, it is a position set forth by old reconstructionists such as John Dewey, George Counts, and Ted Brameld.

The writer, poet, musician, and teacher need to summon the shades of the past to fight off anonymity and amnesia. Through selected readings or even through film (for students who are unable to read fluently), we need to restore our fading and faltering memories, to show that the dead who were taken before it was their time to die did not die in vain. A war memorial is not the answer. It may serve political or nationalistic interests and raise the specter (genre) of jingoism, but it cannot convey the moral lessons of the past. It can evoke tears and stimulate pride, but it cannot lead to critical and analytical thought to clarify arguments, to explain and defend concepts and ideas, and to maintain purposeful and critical discussion.

The writer, poet, musician, and teacher must remember the people who lived and died. As teachers, we must capture the agony and lessons of history as well as the goodness of humanity through our philosophy, history, literature, music, and art. We must retain the vestiges of the lost world, where people died a terrible death as victims of war, poverty, nationalism, racism, or religious fanaticism, and try to make sense of all the senseless crimes that people are capable of committing.

The people who shaped my world and your world, for the greater part, no longer exist. We have twenty-five or thirty years as teachers to make an imprint on the next generation, to remember the millions who are not in the encyclopedias and who no longer exist, to pass on their thoughts and deeds to the next generations. As teachers, the necessity of our work requires that we understand what is at stake: improving and enriching society by making the next generation care about what is morally right and motivating students to accomplish great things that exhibit the good side of what is human.

Moving from literature and philosophy to active teaching and learning means that students be encouraged and rewarded for moral and community action, for helping others and volunteering their time and service. It means that character development and civic service receive the same attention and recognition that we give to A students and star quarterbacks. It calls for special assemblies, special scholarships, and special staff

development programs that promote character development, the desire to help others, and the expectation of social and civic involvement. It means that we give character development—helping and caring for others, contributing and giving back to the school and community—as much attention as we give academics and sports in school.

I am not talking about a special course or program to meet some "service-learning" requirement, but rather a school ethos or a common philosophy that teachers and administrators support. The idea must permeate the entire school and be expected and required for all students. One or two teachers attempting to teach moral responsibility or civic participation cannot effect long-term change; it takes a team effort and schoolwide policy. It demands nothing less than a reconceptualization of the roles, expectations, and activities of students and teachers involved in the life of schools and communities. The idea flows back to the early philosophy and cardinal principles of progressive education of the 1910s and 1920s and the old core curriculum of the 1930s and 1940s, which promoted the study of moral and social issues, social responsibility, and civic education and youth service for the community and nation.

It also means that we consider the basic elementary school, conceived by Ernest Boyer and the Carnegie Foundation, that focuses on the child and community, where schools are kept small so that people work together and feel connected and empowered; it means that the school provides emotional and social support for children, beyond academics, to focus on the whole child and to teach the importance of values, ethics, and moral responsibility.[30] It suggests that a moral and civil society is a requirement for democracy to work, as so keenly described 150 years ago in Alex de Tocqueville's classic treatise *Democracy in America;* it means that we teach the importance of connecting with nature and the ecology of our planet, to preserve our resources and ensure our future. It requires that we bring competitiveness and social cohesion, excellence and equality, as well as material wealth and poverty, into harmony—not an easy task, like squaring a circle. Finally, we need to look into the future: The bomb is an eclipse, but the products of technology and the biological sciences—from medicines and foods to better babies (altering the DNA of generations to come) and extending life (by eliminating or adding genes or inserting computer chips)—offer new ways to play god and leave us with many moral issues to ponder.

FINAL WORDS

A few final and personal notes to the reader. We have shared some reflective moments together, maybe as long as an hour, and perhaps some of these thoughts will last. All of us are filled with memories of people who lived and died, and all of us can personally identify with our own racial, ethnic, or religious group that has suffered from the ruthless behavior of others. All of us who perceive ourselves as members of a minority group understand the notions of subordination and suffering. We experience our own transitoriness and mortality every day as we read in the news or see on television the acts of violence committed by people toward other people.

The wisdom of the Bible and the virtues of religious leaders provide me with little comfort or hope, because the people who should know better and preach hope are often burdened by their own biases, prejudices, and ill-feelings toward other people who summon up different interpretations of the past and present. Although the clergy can be construed as teachers, their mission and agenda center around ideology, and their methods historically have been used to promote this way of thinking. The sword and fire, or worse, are the same methods adopted by modern-day totalitarian nations.

As I take hold of my pen and describe a cruel and sad world—flawed by its own stupidity, hatred, and crimes, a host of isms—I provide the idea for teachers to speculate about their own roles and what education is all about or should be about. I hope that a deep sense of human guilt and teacher triumph of consciousness of humanity will help future citizens of the world be more responsible in terms of character and compassion. Indeed, it is the teacher's role to keep revisiting history, to fight off amnesia and to become a spokesperson for the dead, and thus to improve the human condition. It is a professional role rarely, if ever, described

in the education literature in such a blunt way; it is an idea worth considering, in a world where the United States is at the zenith of its power, but would rather hide from the evils of the world.

Finally, I am reminded of an old saying that was popular when, in the words of Billy Joel, "I wore a younger man's clothes" (in my case, cutoff shorts and roman sandals): "We don't know what World War III will be fought with, but World War IV will be fought with rocks."[31] I am reminded of the mundane words of last goodbyes—"I love you," "I will wait for you in heaven," "Tell her I will forever miss her." I am reminded of Carl Sandburg's *Grass*—all the wars, all the dead, and all the grass that keeps growing; then I think of James Joyce's *The Dead,* describing the demise of the ordinary people, "falling faintly through the universe."

On a more personal level, I am reminded of Yevgeni Yevtushenko, who saw himself and his ancestors "persecuted, spat on, and slandered" for centuries in Europe. It culminated in his homeland, Mother Russia, with the death of tens of thousands in Belostok (the most violent pogrom) and hundreds of thousands at Babi Yar (a mass murder, mass grave). "Like one long soundless scream . . . I'm every old man executed here/ As I am every child murdered./ Rest the victims' bones." So few people seem to care, so few seem to remember. Yet, because of the long roads and caravans traveled by my ancestors, I recall that so many people in so many lands, since ancient Egypt and Rome, have been thrown back by the boot, the sword, and the law—by a soldier, crusader, king, or despot. I have no need to hear false excuses or false proclamations in the name of hatred, stupidity, or herd behavior. I have no patience or pity for fools, zealots, and tyrants who strip people of their dignity and then put them to death. Even worse, I fear those in power who are given to genocidal impulses and are bent on reducing whole villages to rubble and destroying whole cultures and civilizations to nothing more than a line or two in some morally toned poems like "The Waste Land" or "Babi Yar." I can only take some limited comfort in John Donne's holy sonnet "Death, be not proud": "we wake eternally, and Death shall be no more."

I am reminded of all the English teachers trying to teach these poems, and also trying to teach the *Iliad, King Lear, Gulliver's Travels,* and *The Death of Ivan Illych,* the best that has been thought and said in our culture. Then I am reminded of all the bored students, squirming and sweating in their seats, dozing and doodling, watching the clock tick by tick, and missing the bittersweet phrases and opportunity to reflect on ways ordinary and tragic.

I long for a simpler day: *Little House on the Prairie, Leave It to Beaver, Gilligan's Island,* and *Ozzie and Harriet.* But the clock cannot be turned back. In another instant, I recall Mickey and Minnie and Uncle Miltie; Huey, Louie, and Dewey; Captain Video, Captain Kangaroo, and Howdy Doody; "Here's to You, Mrs. Robinson"; Marilyn and Jolt'n Joe. Has anyone seen my childhood heroes—Jackie, Pee Wee, and Duke? Can you tell me where? They're all gone, especially John, Bobby, and Martin, but remembered in history books.

I can also recall playing catch with Dad and stickball in the schoolyard with Jack and Larry. Then there were Mrs. Katz, Mrs. Schwartz, and Miss Hess from P.S. 42 Queens; Mr. Faulkner, Mr. Tietz, and Miss Gussow from Far Rockaway High School. All my favorite teachers are gone, too, but I thought it would be the right thing to do, in the dearness of remembering a simpler period and vanishing era, to recall the names of teachers, largely forgotten, who taught for 25 to 30 years and made a difference to thousands of kids from my generation. All of you can cherish the names of other teachers who made a difference in your lives—and all of you can ponder the larger role of teaching in the changing world that we live in.

ENDNOTES

1. N. L. Gage, *The Scientific Basis of the Art of Teaching* (New York: Teachers College Press, Columbia University, 1978), pp. 15, 17.

2. Philip Jackson, *Life in Classrooms,* 2nd ed. (New York: Teachers College Press, 1990).

3. Elliot W. Eisner, "The Art and Craft of Teachers," *Educational Researcher* (April 1983), p. 8. Also see Elliot W. Eisner, *The Kind of Schools We Need* (Portsmouth, NH: Heinemann, 1998).

4. Louis J. Rubin, *Artistry of Teaching* (New York: Random House, 1985), p. 61.

5. Ibid., pp. 60, 69.

6. Jonathan Cohen, *Educating Minds and Hearts* (New York: Teachers College Press, Columbia University, 1999); Robert Fried, *The Passionate Teacher* (Boston: Beacon Press, 1995).

7. Seymore B. Sarason, *Teaching as a Performing Art* (New York: Teachers College Press, Columbia University, 1999).

8. Ibid.

9. Sylvia Ashton-Warner, *Teacher* (New York: Simon and Schuster, 1964); Allan C. Ornstein, *Strategies for Effective Teaching,* 2nd ed. (Dubuque, IA: Brown and Benchmark, 1995), dedication page.

10. Arthur Jersild, *When Teachers Face Themselves* (New York: Teachers College Press, Columbia University, 1955), p. 3.

11. Elliot W. Eisner, "The Promise and Perils of Alternative Forms of Data Representation," *Educational Researcher* (August—September 1997), pp. 4–11.

12. Robert L. Linn, "Assessment and Accountability," *Educational Researcher* (March 2000), pp. 4–15.

13. Abbey Goodnough, "Regents Create a New Path to Teaching," *New York Times,* July 15, 2000, pp. B4, B7.

14. Allan C. Ornstein, "Beyond Effective Teaching," in A. C. Ornstein, ed., *Teaching: Theory into Practice* (Boston: Allyn and Bacon, 1995), pp. 273–291.

15. Lawrence A. Cremin, *The Transformation of the School* (New York: Random House, 1961).

16. William Glasser, *Schools Without Failure* (New York: Harper & Row, 1969); Glasser, *The Quality School* (New York: HarperCollins, 1990).

17. Robert Fried, *The Passionate Teacher;* Vito Perrone, *Teacher with a Heart* (New York: Teachers College Press, 1998).

18. Theodore R. Sizer, *Horace's Compromise* (Boston: Houghton Mifflin, 1985).

19. Ibid., p. 20.

20. Nel Noddings, *The Challenge to Care in Schools* (New York: Teachers College Press, Columbia University, 1992).

21. Ibid.

22. Jacques Barzun, *Teachers in America,* rev. ed. (Lanham, MD: University Press of America, 1972).

23. Paul Goodman, *Compulsory Mis-Education* (New York: Horizon Press, 1964).

24. John Gardner, *Excellence: Can We Be Equal Too?* (New York: Harper & Row, 1962).

25. Howard Gardner, *Frames of Mind: The Theory of Multiple Intelligences* (New York: Basic Books, 1983).

26. Oscar Lewis, "The Culture of Poverty," *Scientific American* (October 1996), pp. 19–25.

27. "Poverty and Globalization," Center for Global Studies Conference, St. John's University, April 26, 2001. Based on 1998 World Bank Data.

28. Comments made by Edward Pajak to the author, September 6, 2001.

29. Fritz Stern, "The Importance of 'Why'," *World Policy Journal* (Spring 2000), pp. 1–8.

30. Ernest L. Boyer, "The Basic School: Focusing on the Child," *Elementary Principal* (January 1994), pp. 29–32.

31. Francis X. Clines, "A New Form of Grieving," *New York Times,* September 16, 2001, Sect. 4, p. 3.

DISCUSSION QUESTIONS

1. How would you defend the claim that teaching should be considered an art?
2. How would you defend the claim that teaching should be considered a science?
3. What qualities does the author think are most important for a teacher to possess?
4. What are the benefits of having teachers focus their instruction on the dark side of human nature? What are the drawbacks?
5. Who should decide which topics are legitimate for students to learn about? How should such decisions be made?

10

Productive Teachers:
Assessing the Knowledge Base

HERBERT J. WALBERG

FOCUSING QUESTIONS

1. What are the components of teaching that emphasize what teachers do?
2. What does the behavioral model emphasize concerning cues, engagement, correctives, and reinforcement?
3. How do explicit teaching and comprehension teaching differ?
4. What is open education?
5. How do programmed instruction, mastery learning, adaptive instruction, and computer-assisted instruction differ in terms of planning and instructional components?
6. How do the aims of accelerated programs, ability grouping, whole-group instruction, and cooperative learning programs differ?
7. What approaches and goals are emphasized by microteaching and inservice education?

Some teaching techniques have remarkable effects on learning, while others confer only trivial advantages or even hinder the learning process. Over the past decade, there has been an explosion of research activity centering on the question of what constitutes effective teaching. Ten years ago, several psychologists observed signs of a "quiet revolution" in educational research. Five years later, nearly 3,000 studies of effective teaching techniques existed. By 1987, an Australian/U.S. team was able to assess 134 reviews of 7,827 field studies and several large-scale U.S. and international surveys of learning.[1]

Here, I will give an overview of the findings to date on elementary and secondary school students and will evaluate the more recent and definitive reviews of research on teaching and instruction. Surveying the vast literature on the effects of various instructional methods allows us to consider the advantages and disadvantages of different techniques—including some effective ones that are no longer popular.

I will begin by considering the effects of the psychological elements of teaching, and I will discuss methods and patterns of teaching that a single teacher can accomplish without unusual arrangements or equipment. Then I will turn to systems of instruction that require special planning, student grouping, and materials. Next I will describe effects that are unique to particular methods of teaching reading, writing, science, and mathematics. Finally, I will discuss special students and techniques for dealing with them and the effects of particular types of training on teachers. It is important to bear in mind that, when we try to apply in our own classrooms the methods we have read about, we may attain results that are half—or twice—as good as the average estimates reported below. Our success will depend not only on careful implementation but also on our purposes. The best saw swung as a hammer does little good.

PSYCHOLOGICAL ELEMENTS

A little history will help us to understand the evolution of psychological research on teaching. Even though educators require balance, psychologists have often emphasized thought, feeling, or behavior at the expense of the other two components of the psyche. Today, thinking or cognition is sovereign in psychology, but half a century ago behaviorists insisted on specific operational definitions (and they continue to do so). In particular, Yale psychologists John Dollard and Neal Miller, stimulated by E. L. Thorndike and B. F. Skinner, wrote about cues, responses, and positive reinforcement, especially in psychotherapy. Later Miller and Dollard isolated three components of teaching—cues, engagement, and reinforcement—that are similar to the elements of input, process, and output in physiology.[2] Their influential work led researchers to consider what teachers *do* instead of focusing on their age, experience, certification, college degrees, or other factors not directly connected to what their students learn.[3]

The behavioral model emphasized (1) the quality of the instructional cues impinging on the learner, (2) the learner's active engagement, and (3) the reinforcements or rewards that encourage continuing effort over time. Benjamin Bloom recognized, however, that in cycles of cues and effort learners may fail the first time or even repeatedly. Thus they may practice incorrect behavior, and so they cannot be reinforced. Therefore, he emphasized feedback to correct errors and frequent testing to check progress. Inspired by John Carroll's model of school learning, Bloom also emphasized engaged learning time and stressed that some learners require much more time than others.[4]

The effects of cues, engagement, reinforcement, and corrective feedback on student learning are enormous.[5] The research demonstrating these effects has been unusually rigorous and well-controlled. Even though the research was conducted in school classes, the investigators helped to ensure precise timing and deployment of the elements and relied on short-term studies, which usually lasted less than a month. Similar effects are difficult to sustain for long time periods.

Cues

As operationalized, cues show students what is to be learned and explain how to learn it. Their quality depends on the clarity, salience, and meaningfulness of explanations and directions provided by the teacher, the instructional materials, or both. Ideally, as the learners gain confidence, the salience and number of cues can be reduced.

Engagement

The extent to which students actively and persistently participate in learning until appropriate responses are firmly entrenched in their repertoires is known as engagement. Such participation can be indexed by the extent to which the teacher engages students in overt or covert activity. A high degree of engagement is indicated by an absence of irrelevant behavior and by concentration on tasks, enthusiastic contributions to group discussion, and lengthy study.

Corrective Feedback

Corrective feedback remedies errors in oral or written responses. Ideally, students should waste little time on incorrect responses, and teachers should detect difficulties rapidly and then remedy them by reteaching or using alternative methods. When necessary, teachers should also provide students with additional time for practice.

Reinforcement

The immense effort elicited by athletics, games, and other cooperative and competitive activities illustrates the power of immediate and direct reinforcement and shows that some endeavors are intrinsically rewarding. By comparison, classroom reinforcement may seem crass or jejune. The usual classroom reinforcers are acknowledgment of correctness and social approval, typically expressed by praise or a smile. More unusual reinforcers include providing contingent activity—for example, initiating a music lesson or other enjoyable activity as a reward for 90 percent correctness on a math test. Other reinforcers are tokens or check marks that are accumulated for discrete accomplishments and that can be exchanged for tangible reinforcers such as cookies, trinkets, or toys.

In special education programs, students have been reinforced not only for academic achievement but also for minutes spent on reading, for attempts to learn, and for the accuracy with which they perform tasks. Margo Mastropieri and Thomas Scruggs have shown that results can be impressive when the environment can be rigorously controlled and when teachers can accurately gear reinforcement to performance, as in programs for unruly or emotionally disturbed students. Improved behavior and achievement, however, may fail to extend past the period of reinforcement or beyond the special environment.[6]

Educators ordinarily confine reinforcement to marks, grades, and awards because they must assume that students work for such intangible, long-term goals as pleasing parents, furthering their education, achieving success in later life, and the intrinsic satisfaction of learning itself. Even so, when corrective feedback and reinforcement are clear, rapid, and appropriate, they can powerfully affect learning by efficiently signaling students what to do next. In ordinary classrooms, then, the chief value of reinforcement is informational rather than motivational.

METHODS OF TEACHING

The psychological elements just discussed undergird many teaching methods and the design of most instructional media. Techniques to improve the affective or informational content of cues, engagement, correctives, and reinforcement have shown a wide range of effects.

Cues

Advance organizers are brief overviews that relate new concepts or terms to previous learning. They are effective if they connect new learning and old. Those delivered by the teacher or graphically illustrated in texts work best.

Adjunct questions alert students to key questions that should be answered—particularly in texts. They work best when questions are repeated on posttests, and they work moderately well when posttest questions are similar or related to the adjuncts. As we might expect, however, adjunct questions divert attention from incidental material that might otherwise be learned.

Goal setting suggests specific objectives, guidelines, methods, or standards for learning that can be spelled out explicitly. Like the use of adjunct questions, goal setting sacrifices incidental for intended learning.

Learning hierarchies assume that instruction can be made more efficient if the facts, skills, or ideas that logically or psychologically precede others are presented first. Teaching and instructional media sequenced in this way appear to be slightly more effective. However, learners may adapt themselves to apparently ill-sequenced material, and it may even be advantageous to learn to do so, since human life, as Franz Kafka showed, may depart from logic.

Pretests are benchmarks for determining how much students learn under various methods of teaching. Psychologists have found, however, that pretests can have positive cuing effects if they show students what will be emphasized in instruction and on posttests.

Several principles follow from surveying the effects of these methods. To concentrate learning on essential points and to save time (as would be appropriate in training), remove elaborations and extraneous oral and written prose. To focus learners on selected questions or to teach them to find answers in elaborated prose, use adjunct questions and goal setting. To encourage the acquisition of as much undifferentiated material as possible, as in college lecture courses, assign big blocks of text and test students on randomly selected points.

Although the means of producing certain results may seem clear, reaching a consensus on educational purposes may be difficult. Clarity at the start saves time and helps learners to see things the teacher's way, but it limits individual autonomy and deep personal insights. Zen masters ask novices about the sound of one hand clapping and wait a decade or two for an answer. Hiroshi Azuma and

Robert Hess find that Japanese mothers use more indirection and vagueness in teaching their young children than do assertive American mothers, and I have observed Japanese science teachers asking questions and leaving them long unresolved. Do the Japanese cultivate initiative and perseverance by these methods?

Engagement

High expectations transmit teachers' standards of learning and performance. They may function both as cues and as incentives for students to put extended effort and perseverance into learning.

Frequent tests increase learning by stimulating greater effort and providing intermittent feedback. However, the effects of tests on performance are larger for quizzes than for final examinations.

Questioning also appears to work by promoting engagement and may encourage deeper thinking—as in Plato's accounts of Socrates. Questioning has bigger effects in science than in other subjects. Mary Budd Rowe and Kenneth Tobin have shown that *wait time*—allowing students several seconds to reflect rather than the usual .9 of a second—leads to longer and better answers.

Correctives and Reinforcement

Corrective feedback remedies errors by reteaching, either with the same or with a different method. This practice has moderate effects that are somewhat higher in science—perhaps because learning science often involves more conceptualizing while learning other subjects may allow more memorizing.

Homework by itself constructively extends engaged learning time. Correctives and reinforcement in the form of grades and comments on homework raise its effects dramatically.

Praise has a small positive effect. For young or disturbed children, praise may lack the power of the tangible reinforcers used in psychological experiments. For students who are able to see ahead, grades and personal standards may be more powerful reinforcers than momentary encouragement. Moreover, praise may be under- or oversupplied; it may appear demeaning or sardonic; and it may

pale in comparison with the disincentives to academic achievement afforded by youth culture in the form of cars, clothing, dating, and athletics.

None of this is to say that encouragement, incentives, and good classroom morale should be abandoned; honey may indeed be better than vinegar. Yet, as cognitive psychologists point out, the main classroom value of reinforcement may lie in its capacity to inform the student about progress rather than in its power to reward.

PATTERNS OF TEACHING

As explained above, methods of teaching enact or combine more fundamental psychological elements. By further extension, *patterns* of teaching integrate elements and methods of teaching. The process of determining these more inclusive formulations was another step in the evolution of psychological research on education. Behavioral research evolved in the 1950s from psychological laboratories to short-term, controlled classroom experiments on one element at a time. In the 1970s, educational researchers tried to find patterns of effective practices from observations of ordinary teaching.

Thus behaviorists traded educational realism for theoretical parsimony and scientific rigor; later psychologists preferred realism until their insights could be experimentally confirmed. Fortunately, the results of both approaches appear to converge. Moreover, it seems possible to incorporate the work of cognitive psychologists of the 1980s into an enlarged understanding of teaching.

Explicit Teaching

Explicit teaching can be viewed as traditional or conventional whole-group teaching done well. Since most teaching has changed little in the last three-quarters of a century and may not change substantially in the near future,[7] it is worth knowing how to make the usual practice most productive. Since it has evolved from ordinary practice, explicit teaching seems natural to carry out and does not disrupt conventional institutions and expectations. Furthermore, it can incorporate many previously discussed elements and methods.

Systematic research was initiated in the early 1960s by N. L. Gage, Donald Medley, and others who employed "process–product" investigations of the association between what teachers do and how much their students learn. Jere Brophy, Carolyn Evertson, Thomas Good, and Jane Stallings later contributed substantially to this effort. Walter Doyle, Penelope Peterson, and Lee Shulman put the results into a psychological context. Barak Rosenshine has periodically reviewed the research, and Gage and Margaret Needels recently measured the results and pointed out their implications.

The various contributors to the knowledge base do not completely agree about the essential components of explicit teaching, and they refer to it by different names, such as process–product, direct, active, and effective teaching. The researchers weigh their own results heavily, but Rosenshine, a long-standing and comprehensive reviewer, has taken an eagle's-eye view of the results.[8]

In his early reviews of the correlational studies, Rosenshine discussed the traits of effective teachers, including clarity, task orientation, enthusiasm, and flexibility, as well as their tendency to structure their presentations and occasionally to use student ideas. From later observational and control-group research, Rosenshine identified six phased functions of explicit teaching: (1) daily review, checking of homework, and reteaching if necessary; (2) rapid presentation of new content and skills in small steps; (3) guided student practice with close monitoring by teachers; (4) corrective feedback and instructional reinforcement; (5) independent practice in seatwork and homework, with a success rate of more than 90 percent; and (6) weekly and monthly review.

Comprehension Teaching

The heirs of Aristotle and of the Anglo-American tradition of Bacon, Locke, Thorndike, and Skinner objected to philosophical "armchair" opinions; mid-century behaviorists, particularly John Watson, constructively insisted on hard empirical data about learning. But they also saw the child's mind as a blank tablet and seemed to encourage active teaching and passive acquisition of isolated facts.

Reacting to such atomism and to William James' "bucket" metaphor, cognitive psychologists in the early 1980s revived research on student-centered learning and "higher mental processes," in the tradition of Plato, Socrates, Kant, Rousseau, Dewey, Freud, and Piaget. In American hands, however, this European tradition has sometimes led to vacuity and permissiveness, as in the extremes of the "progressive education" movement of the 1930s.

Oddly, the Russian psychologist Lev Vygotsky hit on an influential compromise: emphasizing the two-way nature of teaching, he identified a "zone of proximal development," which extends from what learners can do independently to the maximum that they can do with the teacher's help.[9] Accordingly, teachers should set up "scaffolding" for building knowledge and then remove it when it becomes unnecessary. In mathematics, for example, the teacher can give prompts and examples, foster independent use, and then withdraw support. This approach is similar to the "prompting" and "fading" of the behavioral cues, and it seems commonsensical. It has revived interest in granting some autonomy to students.

During the 1980s, cognitive research on teaching sought ways to encourage self-monitoring, self-teaching, or "metacognition" to foster independence. Skills were seen as important, but the learner's monitoring and management of them had priority, as though the explicit teaching functions of planning, allocating time, and reviewing were partly transferred to the learner.

For example, David Pearson outlined three phases: (1) modeling, in which the teacher exhibits the desired behavior; (2) guided practice, in which students perform with help from the teacher; and (3) application, in which students perform independently of the teacher—steps that correspond to explicit teaching functions. Anne Marie Palincsar and Anne Brown described a program of "reciprocal teaching" that fosters comprehension by having students take turns in leading dialogues on pertinent features of a text. By assuming the kind of planning and executive control ordinarily exercised by teachers, students learn planning, structuring, and self-management. Perhaps that is why tutors learn from teaching and why we say that to learn something well, one should teach it.

Comprehension teaching encourages students to measure their progress toward explicit goals. If necessary, they can reallocate their time to different activities. In this way, self-awareness, personal control, and positive self-evaluation can be increased.[10]

LEARNER AUTONOMY IN SCIENCE

The National Science Foundation sponsored many studies of student inquiry and autonomy that showed that giving students opportunities to manipulate science materials, to contract with teachers about what to learn, to inquire on their own, and to engage in activity-based curricula all had substantial positive effects. Group- and self-direction, however, had smaller positive effects, and pass/fail and self-grading had small negative effects. Methods of providing greater learner autonomy may also work well in subjects other than science, as in the more radical approach that I discuss next.

OPEN EDUCATION

In the late 1960s, open educators expanded autonomy in the primary grades by enabling students to join teachers in planning educational purposes, means, and evaluation. In contrast to teacher- and textbook-centered education, open education gave students a voice in deciding what to learn—even to the point of writing their own texts to share with one another. Open educators tried to foster cooperation, critical thinking, constructive attitudes, and self-directed lifelong learning. They revived the spirit of the New England town meeting, Thoreau's self-reliance, Emerson's transcendentalism, and Dewey's progressivism. Their ideas also resonate with the "client-centered" psychotherapy of Carl Rogers, which emphasizes the "unconditional worth" of the person.

Rose Giaconia and Larry Hedges' synthesis of 153 studies showed that open education had worthwhile effects on creativity, independence, cooperation, attitudes toward teachers and schools, mental ability, psychological adjustment, and curiosity. Students in open programs had less motivation for grade grubbing, but they differed little from other students in actual achievement, self-concept, and anxiety.

However, Giaconia and Hedges also found that the open programs that were more effective in producing the positive outcomes with regard to attitudes, creativity, and self-concept sacrificed some academic achievement on standardized tests. These programs emphasized the role of the child in learning and the use of individualized instruction, manipulative materials, and diagnostic rather than norm-referenced evaluation. However, they did not include three other components thought by some to be essential to open programs: multi-age grouping, open space, and team teaching.

Giaconia and Hedges speculated that children in the most extreme open programs may do somewhat less well on conventional achievement tests because they have little experience with them. At any rate, it appears that open classrooms enhance several nonstandard outcomes without detracting from academic achievement unless they are radically extreme.[11]

INSTRUCTIONAL SYSTEMS

All the techniques discussed thus far can be planned and executed by a single teacher. They may entail some extra effort, encouragement, or training, but they do not call for unusual preparation or materials. In contrast, instructional systems require special arrangements and planning, and they often combine several components of instruction. Moreover, they tend to emphasize the adaptation of instruction to individual students rather than the adaptation of students to a fixed pattern of teaching. A little history will aid our understanding of current instructional systems.

Programmed Instruction

Developed in the 1950s, programmed instruction presents a series of "frames," each one of which conveys an item of information and requires a student response. *Linear programs* present a graduated series of frames that require such small increments in knowledge that learning steps may be nearly errorless and may be continuously reinforced by progression to the next frame. Able students proceed quickly under these conditions. *Branched programs* direct students back for re-teaching when necessary, to the side for correctives, and ahead when they already know parts of the material. The ideas of continuous progress and branching influenced later developers, who tried to optimize learning by individualization, mastery learning, and adaptive instruction.

Individualization adapts instruction to individual needs by applying variations in speed or branching and by using booklets, worksheets, coaching, and the like. Perhaps because they have been vaguely defined and poorly operationalized, individualized programs have had small effects. Other systems (discussed below) appear more effective for adapting instruction to the needs of individual learners.

Mastery Learning

Combining the psychological elements of instruction with suitable amounts of time, mastery learning employs formative tests to allocate time and to guide reinforcement and corrective feedback. In the most definitive synthesis of research on mastery learning, James Kulik and Chen-Lin Kulik reported substantial positive effects. Mastery programs that yielded larger effects established a criterion of 95 percent to 100 percent mastery and required repeated testing to mastery before allowing students to proceed to additional units (which yielded gigantic effects of one standard deviation). Mastery learning yielded larger effects with less-able students and reduced the difference between their performance and that of abler groups.

The success of mastery learning is attributable to several factors. The Kuliks, for example, found that when control groups were provided feedback from quizzes, the mastery groups' advantage was smaller. As Bloom pointed out, mastery learning takes additional time; the Kuliks found that mastery learning required a median of 16 percent (and up to 97 percent) more time than conventional instruction. The seven studies that provided equal time for mastery and control groups showed only a small advantage for mastery learning on standardized tests. However, the advantage was moderate on experimenter-made, criterion-referenced tests

for nine equal-time studies. These results illustrate the separate contributions to mastery learning of cuing, feedback, and time.

Mastery learning yielded larger effects in studies of less than a month's duration than in those lasting more than four months. Retention probably declines sharply no matter what the educational method, but the decline can be more confidently noted with regard to mastery learning since it has been more extensively studied than other methods.

Bloom and his students have reported larger effects than has Robert Slavin, who reviewed their work. Thomas Guskey and S. L. Gates, for example, reported an average effect size of .78 estimated from 38 studies of elementary and secondary students. In response to Slavin, Lorin Anderson and Robert Burns pointed out two reasons for larger effects in some studies, especially those under Bloom's supervision. Bloom has been more interested in what is possible than in what is likely; he has sought to find the limits of learning. His students, moreover, have conducted tightly controlled experiments over time periods of less than a semester or less than a year.[12]

Adaptive Instruction

Developed by Margaret Wang and others, adaptive instruction combines elements of mastery learning, cooperative learning, open education, tutoring, computer-assisted instruction, and comprehension teaching into a complex system whose aim is to tailor instruction to the needs of individuals and small groups. Managerial functions—including such activities as planning, allocating time, delegating tasks to aides and students, and quality control—are carried out by a master teacher. Adaptive instruction is a comprehensive program for the whole school day rather than a single method that requires simple integration into one subject or into a single teacher's repertoire. Its effects on achievement are substantial, but its broader effects are probably underestimated, since adaptive instruction aims at diverse ends—including student autonomy, intrinsic motivation, and teacher and student choice—which are poorly reflected by the usual outcome measures.

COMPUTER-ASSISTED INSTRUCTION

Ours is an electronic age, and computers have already had a substantial impact on learning. With the costs of hardware declining and with software becoming increasingly sophisticated, we may hope for still greater effects as computers are better integrated into school programs.

Computers show the greatest advantage for handicapped students—probably because they are more adaptive to their special needs than teachers might be. Computers may also be more patient, discreet, nonjudgmental, or even encouraging about progress. Perhaps for the same reasons, computers generally have bigger effects in elementary schools than in high schools or colleges.

Another explanation for the disparate results is also plausible. Elementary schools provide less tracking and fewer differentiated courses for homogeneous groups. Computers may be better adapted to larger within-class differences among elementary students because they allow them to proceed at their own pace without engaging in invidious comparisons.

Simulations and games, with or without computer implementation, require active, specific responses from learners and may strike a balance between vicarious book learning and the dynamic, complicated, and competitive "real world." The interactiveness, speed, intensity, movement, color, and sound of computers add interest and information to academic learning. Unless geared to educational purposes, however, computer games can also waste time.

STUDENT GROUPING

Teaching students what they already know and teaching them what they are yet incapable of learning are equally wasteful practices and may even be harmful to motivation. For this reason, traditional whole-class teaching of heterogeneous groups can present serious difficulties—a problem that is often unacknowledged in our egalitarian age. Outside of universities, however, most educators recognize that it is difficult to teach arithmetic and trigonometry at the same time. (Even some English professors might balk at teaching phonics and deconstructionism simultaneously.) If we want to teach students as much as possible rather than to make them all alike, we need to consider how they are grouped and try to help the full range of students.

Acceleration

Accelerated programs identify talented youth (often in mathematics and science) and group them together or with older students. Such programs provide counseling, encouragement, contact with accomplished adults, grade skipping, summer school, and the compression of the standard curriculum into fewer years. The effects are huge in elementary schools, substantial in junior high schools, and moderate in senior high schools. The smaller effects at more advanced levels may be attributable to the smaller advantage of acceleration over the tracking and differentiated course selection practiced in high schools.

The effects of acceleration on educational attitudes, vocational plans, participation in school activities, popularity, psychological adjustment, and character ratings have been mixed and often insignificant. These outcomes may not be systematically affected in either direction.

Ability Grouping

Students are placed in ability groups according to achievement, intelligence test scores, personal insights, and subjective opinions. In high school, ability grouping leaves deficient and average students unaffected, but it has beneficial effects on talented students and on attitudes toward the subject matter. In elementary school, the grouping of students with similar reading achievement but from different grades yields substantial effects. Within-class grouping in mathematics yields worthwhile effects, but generalized ability grouping does not.

Tutoring

Because it gears instruction to individual or small-group needs, tutoring is highly beneficial to both tutors and tutees. It yields particularly large effects in mathematics—perhaps because of the subject's well-defined scope and organization.

In whole-group instruction, teachers may ordinarily focus on average or deficient students to ensure that they master the lessons. When talented students are freed from repetition and slow progression, they can proceed quickly. Grouping may work best when students are accurately grouped according to their specific subject-matter needs rather than according to I. Q., demeanor, or other irrelevant characteristics.

Well-defined subject matter and student grouping may be among the chief reasons why Japanese students lead the world in academic achievement: the curriculum is explicit, rigorous, and nationally uniform. In primary schools, weaker students, with maternal help, study harder and longer to keep up with these explicit requirements. Subject-matter tests are administered to screen students for "lower" and "upper" secondary schools and for universities of various gradations of rigor and prestige. Each such screening determines occupational, marital, and other adult prospects; long-term adult rewards thus reinforce educational effort.[13]

SOCIAL ENVIRONMENT

Cooperative learning programs delegate some control of the pacing and methods of learning to groups of between two and six students, who work together and sometimes compete with other groups within classes. Such programs are successful for several reasons. They provide relief from the excessive teacher/student interaction of whole-group teaching, they free time for the interactive engagement of students, and they present opportunities for targeted cues, engagement, correctives, and reinforcement. As in comprehension teaching, the acts of tutoring and teaching may encourage students to think for themselves about the organization of subject matter and the productive allocation of time.

Many correlational studies suggest that *classroom morale* is associated with achievement gains, with greater interest in subject matter, and with the worthy outcome of voluntary participation in nonrequired subject-related activities. Morale is assessed by asking students to agree or disagree with such statements as "Most of the students know one another well" and "The class members know the purpose of the lessons."

Students who perceive the atmosphere as friendly, satisfying, focused on goals, and challenging and who feel that the classroom has the required materials tend to learn more. Those who perceive the atmosphere as fostering student cliques, disorganization, apathy, favoritism, and friction learn less. The research on morale, though plausible, lacks the specificity and causal confidence of the controlled experiments on directly alterable methods.

READING EFFECTS

Comprehension teaching, because it may extend to several subjects in elementary school, has already been discussed as a pattern of teaching. Several other methods have substantial effects on reading achievement.

Adaptive speed training involves principles that are similar to those of comprehension training. Students learn to vary their pace and the depth of their reflection according to the difficulty of the material and their reading purposes.

Reading methods vary widely, but their largest effects seem to occur when teachers are systematically trained, almost irrespective of particularities of method. Phonics or "word-attack" approaches, however, have a moderate advantage over guessing and "whole-word" approaches in the teaching of beginning reading—perhaps because early misconceptions are avoided. Phonics may also reduce the need for excessive reteaching and correctives.

Pictures in the text can be very helpful, although they add to the cost of a book and occupy space that could otherwise be used for prose. In order of their effectiveness, several types of pictures can be distinguished. Transformative pictures recode information into concrete and memorable form, relate information in a well-organized context, and provide links for systematic retrieval. Interpretive pictures, like advance organizers, make the text comprehensible by relating abstract terms to concrete ones and by connecting the unfamiliar and difficult to previously acquired knowledge. Organizational pictures, including maps and diagrams, show the coherence of objects or events in space and time. Representational pictures are photos or other concrete representations of what is discussed in the text. Decorative pictures present (possibly irrelevant or conflicting) information that is incidental to intended learning (although decoration may add interest if not information).

Pictures can provide vivid imagery and metaphors that facilitate memory, show what is important to learn, and intensify the effects of prose. Pictures may sometimes allow students to bypass the text, but memorable, well-written prose may obviate pictures.[14]

WRITING EFFECTS

Sixty well-designed studies of methods of teaching writing compared 72 experimental groups with control groups. The methods below are presented in the order of their effectiveness.

The *inquiry method* requires students to find and state specific details that convey personal experience vividly, to examine sets of data to develop and support explanatory generalizations, or to analyze situations that present ethical problems and arguments.

Scales are criteria or specific questions that students can apply to their own and others' writing to improve it.

Sentence combining shows students how to build complex sentences from simpler ones.

Models are presentations of good pieces of writing to serve as exemplars for students.

Free writing allows students to write about whatever occurs to them.

Grammar and mechanics include sentence parsing and the analysis of parts of speech.

SCIENCE EFFECTS

Introduced in response to the launch of *Sputnik I,* the "new" science curricula, sponsored by the National Science Foundation, yielded substantial effects on learning. They efficiently added value by producing superior learning on tests of their intended outcomes and on tests of general subject-matter goals. The new curricula also yielded effects ranging from small to substantial on such often-unmeasured outcomes as creativity, problem solving, scientific attitudes and skills, logical thinking, and achievement in nonscience subject matter.

Perhaps these advantages are attributable to the combined efforts of teachers, psychologists, and scientists, who collaborated to ensure that the curricula would be based on modern content and would foster effective teaching practices. The scientists may have been able to generate enthusiasm for teaching scientific methods, for laboratory work, and for other reforms.

The new science curricula worked well in improving achievement and other outcomes. Ironically, they are often forgotten today, despite the fact that, by international standards, U.S. students score poorly in mathematics and science.

Inquiry Teaching.   Often practiced in Japan, this method requires students to formulate hypotheses, reason about their credibility, and design experiments to test their validity. Inquiry teaching yields substantial effects, particularly on the understanding of scientific processes.

Audiotutorials.   These are tape-recorded instructions for using laboratory equipment, manipulatives, and readings for topical lessons or whole courses. This simple approach yields somewhat better results than conventional instruction, allows independent learning, and has the further advantage of individual pacing—allowing students to pursue special topics or to take courses on their own.

Original Source Papers.   This method derives from the Great Books approach of the late Robert Maynard Hutchins, former president of the University of Chicago, and his colleague Mortimer Adler. They saw more value in reading Plato or Newton than in resorting to predigested textbook accounts. The use of original sources in teaching trades breadth for depth in the belief that it is better to know a few ideas of transcending importance than to learn many unconnected bits of soon-forgotten information. Advocates of this approach have shown that such knowledge can be acquired by studying and discussing original scientific papers of historical or scientific significance.

Other methods of teaching science have effects that are near zero—that is, close to the effects of traditional methods of teaching. They include team teaching, departmentalized elementary programs, and media-based instruction. The equal results for media methods, however, suggest that choices can be based on cost and convenience. Since television programs and films can be broadcast, they can provide equally effective education in different and widespread locations (even in different parts of the world by satellite). Moreover, students today can interact online with teachers and fellow students who are far away.

There are some successful precedents for the use of media-based instruction. For a decade, the Chicago community colleges provided dozens of mainly one-way television courses to hundreds of thousands of students, who did most of their studying at home but participated in discussion and testing sessions at several sites in the metropolitan area. The best lecturers, media specialists, and test constructors could be employed, and tapes of the courses could be rebroadcast repeatedly.

In several Third World countries that are gaining in achievement and school enrollments, ministries of education make efficient and successful use of such low-cost, effective "distance education" for remote elementary and secondary schools.

The Oklahoma and Minnesota state departments of education apparently lead the nation in providing small high schools in rural areas with specialized television teachers and interactive courses in advanced science, mathematics, foreign language, and other subjects.

MATHEMATICS EFFECTS

In the heyday of its Education Directorate, the National Science Foundation sponsored considerable research not only on science but also on mathematics. Some worthwhile effects were found.

Manipulative Materials

The use of Cuisenaire rods, balance beams, counting sticks, and measuring scales allows students to engage directly in learning instead of passively following abstract presentations by the teacher.

Students can handle the materials, see the relation of abstract ideas and concrete embodiments, and check hypothesized answers by quick empirical testing without having to wait for quiz results or feedback from the teacher. This method apparently results in enormous effects.

Problem Solving

In mathematics teaching, a focus on problem solving yields worthwhile effects. Such an approach requires comprehension of terms and their application to varied examples. It may motivate students by showing them the application of mathematical ideas to "real-world" questions.

New Math

The so-called new math produced beneficial results, although it was not as successful as the new science curricula. Both reforms probably gained their learning advantages partly by testing what they taught.

SPECIAL POPULATIONS AND TECHNIQUES

We can also gain insights from programs that lie outside the usual scope of elementary and secondary classrooms.

Early Intervention

Programs of early intervention include educational, psychological, and therapeutic components for handicapped, at-risk, and disadvantaged children from the ages of one month to 5½ years. Studies of these programs found that the large, immediate effects of these programs declined rapidly and disappeared after three years.

Preschool Programs

Preschool programs also showed initial learning effects that were not sustained. It appears that young children can learn more than is normally assumed, but, like other learners, they can also forget. The key to sustained gains may be sustained programs and effective families—not one-shot approaches.

Programs for the Handicapped

Students classified as mentally retarded, emotionally disturbed, or learning disabled have been subjects in research that has several important implications. When they serve as tutors of one another and of younger students, handicapped students can learn well—a finding similar to those in comprehension-monitoring and tutoring studies of nonhandicapped children. Moreover, handicapped students are often spuriously classified, and we may underestimate their capacities.

Mainstreaming

Studies show that mildly to moderately handicapped students can prosper in regular classes and thereby avoid the invidious "labeling" that is often based on misclassification.

Psycholinguistic Training

Providing psycholinguistic training to special needs students yields positive effects. This approach consists of testing and remedying specific deficits in language skills.

Patient Education

Educating patients about diseases and treatments can affect mortality, morbidity, and lengths of illness and hospitalization. In studies of the acquisition of knowledge regarding drug usage for hypertension, diabetes, and other chronic conditions, one-to-one and group counseling (with or without instructional material) produced greater effects than providing instruction through labels on bottles or package inserts for patients.

Labels, special containers, memory aids, and behavior modification were successful in minimizing later errors in drug usage. The most efficacious educational principles were specification of intentions, relevance to the needs of the learner, provision of personal answers to questions, reinforcement and feedback on progress, facilitation of correct dosage (e.g., the use of unit-dose containers), and instructional and treatment regimens suited to personal convenience (e.g., prescribing drugs for administration at mealtimes).

In-Service Training of Physicians

Such training shows large effects on doctors' knowledge and on their classroom or laboratory performance but only moderate effects on the outcomes of treating actual patients. Knowledge and performance, even in practical training, may help, but they hardly guarantee successful application in practice. Can an accomplished mathematician handle the intricacies of federal income tax?

Panaceas and Shortcuts

At the request of the U.S. Army, the National Academy of Sciences evaluated exotic techniques for enhancing learning and performance that are described in popular psychology (and presumably are being exploited in California and Russia).[15] However, little or no evidence was found for the efficacy of learning during sleep; for mental practice of motor skills; for "integration" of left and right hemispheres of the brain; for parapsychological techniques; for biofeedback; for extrasensory perception, mental telepathy, and "mind over matter" exercises; or for "neurolinguistic programming," in which instructors identify the students' modes of learning and mimic the students' behaviors as they teach.

The Greeks found no royal road to geometry; even kings, if they desired mastery, had to sweat over Euclid's elements. Perhaps brain research will eventually yield a magic elixir or a panacea, but for proof of its existence educators should insist on hard data in refereed scientific journals.

EFFECTS ON TEACHERS

Programs to help teachers in their work have had substantial effects—notwithstanding complaints about typical in-service training sessions. Do physicians complain about the medical care they get?

Microteaching

Developed at Stanford University in the 1960s, microteaching is a behavioral approach for pre-service and in-service training that has substantial effects. It employs the explanation and modeling of selected teaching techniques; televised practice with small groups of students; discussion, correctives, and reinforcement while watching playback; and recycling through subsequent practice and playback sessions with new groups of students.

In-Service Education

In-service training for teachers also proves to have substantial effects. Somewhat like the case of in-service training of physicians, the biggest effects are on the teacher's knowledge, but effects on classroom behavior and student achievement are also notable.

For in-service training, authoritative planning and execution seem to work best; informal coaching by itself seems ineffective. Allowing the instructor to be responsible for the design and teaching of the sessions works better than relying on presentations by teachers and group discussions. The best techniques are observation and classroom practices, video/audio feedback, and practice. The most effective training combines lectures, modeling, practice, and coaching. The size of the training group, ranging from one to more than 60, makes no detectable difference.

Some apparent effects may be attributable to the selectivity of the program rather than to its superior efficacy. For example, federal-, state-, and university-sponsored programs appear more effective than locally initiated programs. Competitive selection of participants and the granting of college credit apparently work better as incentives than extra pay, renewal of certification, or no incentives. Independent study seems to have larger effects than workshops, courses, minicourses, and institutes.

CONCLUSION

Psychological research provides first-order estimates of the effects of instructional means on educational ends under various conditions. But some instructional practices may be costly—not in terms of dollars but in terms of new or complicated arrangements that may be difficult for some teachers and districts to adopt. Thus estimates of effects are only one basis for decision making. We need to consider the productivity or value of effects in relation to total costs, including the time and energies of educators and students.

Knowledge from the field of psychology alone is not sufficient to prescribe practices, since different means bring about different ends. Educators must decide whether the learning effort is to be directed by teachers, by students, or by the curriculum. They must choose among a range of facts and concepts, breadth and depth, short- and long-term ends, academic knowledge and knowledge that has direct application in the real world, equal opportunity and equal results. They must decide which aspect of Plato's triumvirate of thinking, feeling, and acting will take precedence. Once these choices are made, educators can turn to the researchers' estimates of effects as one basis for determining the most productive practices.

ENDNOTES

1. Herbert J. Walberg, Diane Schiller, and Geneva D. Haertel, "The Quiet Revolution in Educational Research," *Phi Delta Kappan,* November 1979, pp. 179–183; Herbert J. Walberg, "Improving the Productivity of America's Schools," *Educational Leadership,* vol. 41, 1984, pp. 19–27; and Barry J. Fraser, Herbert J. Walberg, Wayne W. Welch, and John A. Hattie, "Syntheses of Educational Productivity Research," *International Journal of Educational Research,* vol. 11, 1987, pp. 73–145.

2. Neal Miller and John Dollard, *Social Learning and Imitation* (New Haven, CT: Yale University Press, 1941); and John Dollard and Neal Miller, *Personality and Psychotherapy* (New York: McGraw-Hill, 1950).

3. Eric A. Hanushek, "Throwing Money at Schools," *Journal of Policy Analysis and Management,* vol. 1, 1981, pp. 19–41; and Herbert J. Walberg and William F. Fowler, "Expenditure and Size Efficiencies of Public School Districts," *Educational Researcher,* vol. 16, 1987, pp. 515–526.

4. Benjamin S. Bloom, *Human Characteristics and School Learning* (New York: McGraw-Hill, 1976); and John B. Carroll, "A Model of School Learning," *Teachers College Record,* vol. 64, 1963, pp. 723–733.

5. The effects are expressed as differences between experimental and control groups in units of standard deviations. For further details and references, see my chapter in Merlin C. Wittrock, ed., *Handbook of Research on Teaching* (New York: Macmillan, 1986).

6. Margo A. Mastropieri and Thomas E. Scruggs, *Effective Instruction for Special Education* (Boston: Little, Brown, 1987).

7. John Hoetker and William P. Ahlbrand, "The Persistence of the Recitation," *American Educational Research Journal,* vol. 6, 1969, pp. 145–167.

8. For a full account of most views, see Penelope L. Peterson and Herbert J. Walberg, eds., *Research on Teaching* (Berkeley, CA: McCutchan, 1979); and Wittrock, op. cit.

9. Lev Vygotsky, *Mind in Society* (Cambridge, MA: Harvard University Press, 1978).

10. Anne Marie Palincsar and Anne Brown, "Reciprocal Teaching of Comprehension-Fostering and Comprehension-Monitoring Activities," *Cognition and Instruction,* vol. 1, 1984, pp. 117–176; David Pearson, "Reading Comprehension Instruction: Six Necessary Steps," *Reading Teacher,* vol. 38, 1985, pp. 724–738; and Paul R. Pintrich et al., "Instructional Psychology," *Annual Review of Psychology,* vol. 37, 1986, pp. 611–651.

11. Rose M. Giaconia and Larry V. Hedges, "Identifying Features on Effective Open Education," *Review of Educational Research,* vol. 52, 1982, pp. 579–602.

12. James A. Kulik and Chen-Lin Kulik, "Mastery Testing and Student Learning," *Journal of Educational Technology Systems,* vol. 15, 1986, pp. 325–345; Lorin W. Anderson and Robert B. Burns, "Values, Evidence, and Mastery Learning," *Review of Educational Research,* vol. 57, 1988, pp. 215–223; Thomas R. Guskey and S. L. Gates, "Synthesis of Research on the Effects of Mastery Learning in Elementary and Secondary Classrooms," *Educational Leadership,* May 1986, pp. 73–80; and Robert E. Slavin, "Mastery Learning Reconsidered," *Review of Educational Research,* vol. 57, 1988, pp. 175–213.

13. Herbert J. Walberg, "What Can We Learn from Japanese Education?," *The World and I,* March 1988, pp. 661–665.

14. Joel R. Levin, Gary J. Anglin, and Russell N. Carney, "On Empirically Validating Functions of Pictures in Prose," in D. M. Willows and H. A. Houghton, eds., *The Psychology of Illustration* (New York: Springer-Verlag, 1987).

15. Daniel Druckman and John A. Swets, eds., *Enhancing Human Performance* (Washington, DC: National Academy Press, 1988).

DISCUSSION QUESTIONS

1. How can teachers use or improve cues, engagement, correctives, and reinforcement to facilitate student achievement?

2. How do explicit teaching and comprehension teaching differ in terms of methods and elements?

3. Consider the advantages and disadvantages of open education. Is open education appropriate for all educational settings and students? Why? Why not?

4. How can knowledge from the field of psychology be used to guide curriculum development?

5. In what ways have programs and techniques developed for special populations influenced elementary and secondary curriculum development?

11

Knowledge and Teaching:
Foundations of the New Reform

LEE S. SHULMAN

FOCUSING QUESTIONS

1. Why is a codified compendium of knowledge and skills insufficient for articulating a knowledge base of teaching?
2. What sources should comprise the knowledge base for teaching, according to the author?
3. What is pedagogical content knowledge?
4. Which role should the liberal arts college, school, and department of education assume in training teachers for the 21st century?
5. What is the purpose of transformation and reflection in the process of pedagogical reasoning and action?
6. What should be the goal of teacher education?

PROLOGUE: A PORTRAIT OF EXPERTISE

Richly developed portrayals of expertise in teaching are rare. While many characterizations of effective teachers exist, most of these dwell on the teacher's management of the classroom. We find few descriptions or analyses of teachers that give careful attention not only to the management of students in classrooms, but also to the management of *ideas* within classroom discourse. Both kinds of emphasis will be needed if our portrayals of good practice are to serve as sufficient guides to the design of better education. Let us examine one brief account.

> A twenty-five-year veteran English teacher, Nancy, was the subject of a continuing study of experienced teachers that we had been conducting. The class was nearing the end of the second week of a unit on *Moby Dick*. The observer had been well impressed with the depth of Nancy's understanding of that novel and her skill as a pedagogue, as she documented how Nancy helped a group

of California high school juniors grasp the many faces of that masterpiece. Nancy was a highly active teacher, whose classroom style employed substantial interaction with her students, through both recitations and more open-ended discussion. She was like a symphony conductor, posing questions, probing for alternative views, drawing out the shy while tempering the boisterous. Not much happened in the classroom that did not pass through Nancy, whose pacing and ordering, structuring and expanding, controlled the rhythm of classroom life.

Nancy characterized her treatment of literature in terms of a general theoretical model that she employed, breaking reading skills into four levels:

> *Level 1* is simply translation. . . . It is understanding the literal meaning, denotative, and frequently for students that means getting a dictionary.
>
> *Level 2* is connotative meaning and again you are still looking at the words. . . . What does that mean, what does that tell us about the character? . . . We looked at *The Scarlet*

Letter. Hawthorne described a rose bush in the first chapter. Literal level is: What is a rose bush? More important, what does a rose bush suggest, what is it that comes to mind, what did you picture?

Level 3 is the level of interpretation. . . . It is the implication of Levels 1 and 2. If the author is using a symbol, what does that say about his view of life? In *Moby Dick,* the example I used in class was the boots. The boots would be the literal level. What does it mean when he gets under the bed? And the students would say, he is trying to hide something. Level 3 would be what does Melville say about human nature? What is the implication of this? What does this tell us about this character?

Level 4 is what I call application and evaluation and I try, as I teach literature, to get the students to Level 4, and that is where they take the literature and see how it has meaning for their own lives. Where would we see that event occur in our own society? How would people that we know be behaving if they are doing what these characters are doing? How is this piece of literature similar to our common experiences as human beings? . . . So my view of reading is basically to take them from the literal on the page to making it mean something in their lives. In teaching literature I am always working in and out of those levels. (Gudmundsdottir, 1988)

Nancy employed this conceptual framework in her teaching, using it to guide her own sequencing of material and formulation of questions. She taught the framework explicitly to her students over the semester, helping them employ it like a scaffolding to organize their own study of the texts, to monitor their own thinking. Although as a teacher she maintained tight control of the classroom discourse, her teaching goals were to liberate her students' minds through literacy, eventually to use great works of literature to illuminate their own lives. Whichever work she was teaching, she understood how to organize it, frame it for teaching, divide it appropriately for assignments and activities. She seemed to possess a mental index for these books she had taught so often—*The Red Badge of Courage, Moby Dick, The Scarlet Letter, The Adventures of Huckleberry Finn*—with key episodes organized in her mind for different pedagogical purposes, different levels of difficulty, different kinds of pupils, different themes or emphases. Her combination of subject-matter understanding and pedagogical skill was quite dazzling.

When the observer arrived at the classroom one morning, she found Nancy sitting at her desk as usual. But her morning greeting elicited no response from Nancy other than a grimace and motion toward the pad of paper on her desktop. "I have laryngitis this morning and will not be able to speak aloud," said the note. What's more, she appeared to be fighting the flu, for she had little energy. For a teacher who managed her classroom through the power of her voice and her manner, this was certainly a disabling condition. Or was it?

Using a combination of handwritten notes and whispers, she divided the class into small groups by rows, a tactic she had used twice before during this unit. Each group was given a different character who had a prominent role in the first chapters of the novel, and each group was expected to answer a series of questions about that character. Ample time was used at the end of the period for representatives of each group to report to the whole class. Once again the class had run smoothly, and the subject matter had been treated with care. But the style had changed radically, an utterly different teaching technology was employed, and still the students were engaged, and learning appeared to occur.

Subsequently, we were to see many more examples of Nancy's flexible style, adapted to the characteristics of learners, the complexities of subject matter, and her own physical condition. When learners experienced serious problems with a particular text, she self-consciously stayed at the lower levels of the reading ladder, helping the students with denotative and connotative meanings, while emphasizing literary interpretations somewhat less. When teaching *Huck Finn,* a novel she saw as less difficult than *Moby Dick,* her style changed once again. She gave much more autonomy to the students and did not directly run the classroom as much.

For *Huck Finn,* she abandoned the stage early on and let the students teach each other. She had the students working independently in eight multi-ability groups, each group tracing one of eight themes: hypocrisy; luck and superstition; greed and materialism; romantic ideas and fantasy; religion and the Bible; social class and customs; family, racism, and prejudice; freedom and conscience. There were only two reading checks at the beginning and only two rounds of reporting. Once the groups were underway, Nancy took a seat at the back of the class and only interacted with students when she was called upon, and during group presentations. (Gudmundsdottir, 1988)

Thus Nancy's pattern of instruction, her style of teaching, is not uniform or predictable in some simple sense. She flexibly responds to the difficulty and character of the subject matter, the capacities of the students (which can change even over the span of a single course), and her educational purposes. She can not only conduct her orchestra from the podium; she can sit back and watch it play with virtuosity by itself.

What does Nancy believe, understand, and know how to do that permits her to teach as she does? Can other teachers be prepared to teach with such skill? The hope that teaching like Nancy's can become typical instead of unusual motivates much of the effort in the newly proposed reforms of teaching.

THE NEW REFORMS

The U.S. public and its professional educators have been presented with several reports on how to improve teaching as both an activity and a profession. One of the recurring themes of these reports has been the professionalization of teaching—the elevation of teaching to a more respected, more responsible, more rewarding, and better rewarded occupation. The claim that teaching deserves professional status, however, is based on a more fundamental premise: that the standards by which the education and performance of teachers must be judged can be raised and more clearly articulated. The advocates of professional reform base their arguments on the belief that there exists a "knowledge base for teaching"—a codified or codifiable aggregation of knowledge, skill, understanding, and technology, of ethics and disposition, of collective responsibility—as well as a means for representing and communicating it. The reports of the Holmes Group (1986) and the Carnegie Task Force (1986) rest on this belief and, furthermore, claim that the knowledge base is growing. They

argue that it should frame teacher education and directly inform teaching practice.

The rhetoric regarding the knowledge base, however, rarely specifies the character of such knowledge. It does not say what teachers should know, do, understand, or profess that will render teaching more than a form of individual labor, let alone be considered among the learned professions.

Here, I present an argument regarding the content, character, and sources for a knowledge base of teaching that suggests an answer to the question of the intellectual, practical, and normative basis for the professionalization of teaching. The questions that focus the argument are as follows: What are the sources of the knowledge base for teaching? In what terms can these sources be conceptualized? What are the implications for teaching policy and educational reform?[1]

In addressing these questions I am following in the footsteps of many eminent scholars, including Dewey (1904), Scheffler (1965), Green (1971), Fenstermacher (1978), Smith (1980), and Schwab (1983), among others. Their discussions of what qualities and understandings, skills and abilities, and traits and sensibilities render someone a competent teacher have continued to echo in the conference rooms of educators for generations. My approach has been conditioned, as well, by two current projects: a study of how new teachers learn to teach and an attempt to develop a national board for teaching.

First, my colleagues and I have been watching knowledge of pedagogy and content grow in the minds of young men and women. They have generously permitted us to observe and follow their eventful journeys from being teacher education students to becoming neophyte teachers. In this research, we are taking advantage of the kinds of insights Piaget provided from his investigations of knowledge growth. He discovered that he could learn a great deal about knowledge and its development from careful observation of the very young—those who were just beginning to develop and organize their intelligence. We are following this lead by studying those just learning to teach. Their development from students to teachers, from a state of expertise as learners through a novitiate

:achers, exposes and highlights the complex bodies of knowledge and skill needed to function effectively as a teacher. The result is that error, success, and refinement—in a word, teacher-knowledge growth—are seen in high profile and in slow motion. The neophyte's stumble becomes the scholar's window.

Concurrently, we have found and explored cases of veteran teachers such as Nancy (Baxter, 1988; Gudmundsdottir, 1988; Hashweh, 1985) to compare with those of the novices. What these studies show is that the knowledge, understanding, and skill we see displayed haltingly, and occasionally masterfully, among beginners are often demonstrated with ease by the expert. But, as we have wrestled with our cases, we have repeatedly asked what teachers knew (or failed to know) that permitted them to teach in a particular manner.

Second, I have engaged in quite a different project on the role of knowledge in teaching. In conjunction with the Carnegie initiative for the reform of the teaching profession, my colleagues and I have been studying ways to design a national board assessment for teaching, parallel in several ways to the National Board of Medical Examiners (Shulman & Sykes, 1986; Sykes, 1986). This challenge renders the questions about the definition and operationalization of knowledge in teaching as far more than academic exercises. If teachers are to be certified on the basis of well-grounded judgments and standards, then those standards on which a national board relies must be legitimized by three factors: they must be closely tied to the findings of scholarship in the academic disciplines that form the curriculum (such as English, physics, and history) as well as those that serve as foundations for the process of education (such as psychology, sociology, or philosophy); they must possess intuitive credibility (or "face validity") in the opinions of the professional community in whose interests they have been designed; and they must relate to the appropriate normative conceptions of teaching and teacher education.

The new reform proposals carry assumptions about the knowledge base for teaching: when advocates of reform suggest that requirements for the education of teachers should be augmented and periods of training lengthened, they assume there must be something substantial to be learned. When they recommend that standards be raised and a system of examinations introduced, they assume there must exist a body of knowledge and skill to examine. Our research and that of others (for example, Berliner, 1986; Leinhardt & Greeno, 1986) have identified the sources and suggested outlines of that knowledge base. Watching veterans such as Nancy teach the same material that poses difficulties for novice teachers helped focus our attention on what kinds of knowledge and skill were needed to teach demanding materials well. By focusing on the teaching of particular topics—*Huck Finn,* quadratic equations, the Indian subcontinent, photosynthesis—we learned how particular kinds of content knowledge and pedagogical strategies necessarily interacted in the minds of teachers.

What follows is a discussion of the sources and outlines of the required knowledge base for teaching. I divide this discussion into two distinct analyses. First, after providing an overview of one framework for a knowledge base for teaching, I examine the *sources* of that knowledge base—that is, the domains of scholarship and experience from which teachers may draw their understanding. Second, I explore the processes of pedagogical reasoning and action within which such teacher knowledge is used.

THE KNOWLEDGE BASE

Begin a discussion on the knowledge base of teaching, and several related questions immediately arise: What knowledge base? Is enough known about teaching to support a knowledge base? Isn't teaching little more than personal style, artful communication, knowing some subject matter, and applying the results of recent research on teaching effectiveness? Only the last of these, the findings of research on effective teaching, is typically deemed a legitimate part of a knowledge base.

The actions of both policy makers and teacher educators in the past have been consistent with the formulation that teaching requires basic skills, content knowledge, and general pedagogical skills. Assessments of teachers in most states consist of some combination of basic-skills tests, an examination of competence in subject matter, and observations in the classroom to ensure that certain kinds of general teaching behavior are present. In this manner, I would argue, teaching is trivialized, its complexities ignored, and its demands diminished. Teachers themselves have difficulty in articulating what they know and how they know it.

Nevertheless, the policy community at present continues to hold that the skills needed for teaching are those identified in the empirical research on teaching effectiveness. This research, summarized by Brophy and Good (1986), Gage (1986), and Rosenshine and Stevens (1986), was conducted within the psychological research tradition. It assumes that complex forms of situation-specific human performance can be understood in terms of the workings of underlying generic processes. In a study of teaching context, the research, therefore, seeks to identify those general forms of teaching behavior that correlate with student performance on standardized tests, whether in descriptive or experimental studies. The investigators who conduct the research realize that important simplifications must be made, but they believe that these are necessary steps for conducting scientific studies. Critical features of teaching, such as the subject matter being taught, the classroom context, the physical and psychological characteristics of the students, or the accomplishment of purposes not readily assessed on standardized tests, are typically ignored in the quest for general principles of effective teaching.

When policy makers have sought "research-based" definitions of good teaching to serve as the basis for teacher tests or systems of classroom observation, the lists of teacher behaviors that had been identified as effective in the empirical research were translated into the desirable competencies for classroom teachers. They became items on tests or on classroom-observation scales. They were accorded legitimacy because they had been "confirmed by research." While the researchers understood the findings to be simplified and incomplete, the policy community accepted them as sufficient for the definitions of standards.

For example, some research had indicated that students achieved more when teachers explicitly informed them of the lesson's objective. This seems like a perfectly reasonable finding. When translated into policy, however, classroom-observation competency-rating scales asked whether the teacher had written the objective on the blackboard and/or directly told the students the objectives at the beginning of class. If the teacher had not, he or she was marked off for failing to demonstrate a desired competency. No effort was made to discover whether the withholding of an objective might have been consistent with the form of the lesson being organized or delivered.

Moreover, those who hold with bifurcating content and teaching processes have once again introduced into policy what had been merely an act of scholarly convenience and simplification in the research. Teaching processes were observed and evaluated without reference to the adequacy or accuracy of the ideas transmitted. In many cases, observers were not expected to have content expertise in the areas being observed, because it did not matter for the rating of teacher performance. Thus, what may have been an acceptable strategy for research became an unacceptable policy for teacher evaluation.

Here, I argue that the results of research on effective teaching, while valuable, are not the sole source of evidence on which to base a definition of the knowledge base of teaching. Those sources should be understood to be far richer and more extensive. Indeed, properly understood, the actual and potential sources for a knowledge base are so plentiful that our question should not be, Is there really much one needs to know in order to teach? Rather, it should express our wonder at how the extensive knowledge of teaching can be learned at all during the brief period allotted to teacher preparation. Much of the rest of this chapter provides the details of the argument that there exists an elaborate knowledge base for teaching.

A View of Teaching

I begin with the formulation that the capacity to teach centers around the following commonplaces of teaching, paraphrased from Fenstermacher

6). A teacher knows something not understood by others, presumably the students. The teacher can transform understanding, performance skills, or desired attitudes or values into pedagogical representations and actions. These are ways of talking, showing, enacting, or otherwise representing ideas so that the unknowing can come to know, those without understanding can comprehend and discern, and the unskilled can become adept. Thus, teaching necessarily begins with a teacher's understanding of what is to be learned and how it is to be taught. It proceeds through a series of activities during which the students are provided specific instruction and opportunities for learning,[2] though the learning itself ultimately remains the responsibility of the students. Teaching ends with new comprehension by both the teacher and the student.[3] Although this is certainly a core conception of teaching, it is also an incomplete conception. Teaching must properly be understood to be more than the enhancement of understanding; but if it is not even that, then questions regarding performance of its other functions remain moot. The next step is to outline the categories of knowledge that underlie the teacher understanding needed to promote comprehension among students.

Categories of the Knowledge Base

If teacher knowledge were to be organized into a handbook, an encyclopedia, or some other format for arraying knowledge, what would the category headings look like?[4] At minimum, they would include

- content knowledge;
- general pedagogical knowledge, with special reference to those broad principles and strategies of classroom management and organization that appear to transcend subject matter;
- curriculum knowledge, with particular grasp of the materials and programs that serve as "tools of the trade" for teachers;
- pedagogical content knowledge, that special amalgam of content and pedagogy that is

uniquely the province of teachers, their own special form of professional understanding;
- knowledge of learners and their characteristics;
- knowledge of educational contexts, ranging from the workings of the group or classroom, the governance and financing of school districts, to the character of communities and cultures; and
- knowledge of educational ends, purposes, and values, and their philosophical and historical grounds.

Among those categories, pedagogical content knowledge is of special interest because it identifies the distinctive bodies of knowledge for teaching. It represents the blending of content and pedagogy into an understanding of how particular topics, problems, or issues are organized, represented, adapted to the diverse interests and abilities of learners, and presented for instruction. Pedagogical content knowledge is the category most likely to distinguish the understanding of the content specialist from that of the pedagogue. While far more can be said regarding the categories of a knowledge base for teaching, elucidation of them is not a central purpose of this chapter.

Enumerating the Sources

There are at least four major sources for the teaching knowledge base: (1) scholarship in content disciplines, (2) the materials and settings of the institutionalized educational process (for example, curricula, textbooks, school organizations and finance, and the structure of the teaching profession), (3) research on schooling, social organizations, human learning, teaching and development, and the other social and cultural phenomena that affect what teachers can do, and (4) the wisdom of practice itself. Let me elaborate on each of these.

Scholarship in Content Disciplines.   The first source of the knowledge base is content knowledge—the knowledge, understanding, skill, and disposition that are to be learned by school children. This knowledge rests on two foundations:

the accumulated literature and studies in the content areas, and the historical and philosophical scholarship on the nature of knowledge in those fields of study. For example, the teacher of English should know English and American prose and poetry, written and spoken language use and comprehension, and grammar. In addition, he or she should be familiar with the critical literature that applies to particular novels or epics that are under discussion in class. Moreover, the teacher should understand alternative theories of interpretation and criticism and how these might relate to issues of curriculum and of teaching.

Teaching is, essentially, a learned profession. A teacher is a member of a scholarly community. He or she must understand the structures of subject matter, the principles of conceptual organization, and the principles of inquiry that help answer two kinds of questions in each field: What are the important ideas and skills in this domain? and How are new ideas added and deficient ones dropped by those who produce knowledge in this area? That is, what are the rules and procedures of good scholarship or inquiry? These questions parallel what Schwab (1964) has characterized as knowledge of substantive and syntactic structures, respectively. This view of the sources of content knowledge necessarily implies that the teacher must have not only depth of understanding with respect to the particular subjects taught, but also a broad liberal education that serves as a framework for old learning and as a facilitator for new understanding. The teacher has special responsibilities in relation to content knowledge, serving as the primary source of student understanding of subject matter. The manner in which that understanding is communicated conveys to students what is essential about a subject and what is peripheral. In the face of student diversity, the teacher must have a flexible and multifaceted comprehension, adequate to impart alternative explanations of the same concepts or principles. The teacher also communicates, whether consciously or not, ideas about the ways in which "truth" is determined in a field and a set of attitudes and values that markedly influence student understanding. This responsibility places special demands on the teacher's own depth of understanding of the structures of the subject matter, as well as on the teacher's attitudes toward and enthusiasms for what is being taught and learned. These many aspects of content knowledge, therefore, are properly understood as a central feature of the knowledge base of teaching.

Educational Materials and Structures.   To advance the aims of organized schooling, materials and structures for teaching and learning are created. These include curricula with their scopes and sequences; tests and testing materials; institutions with their hierarchies, their explicit and implicit systems of rules and roles; professional teachers' organizations with their functions of negotiation, social change, and mutual protection; government agencies from the district through the state and federal levels; and general mechanisms of governance and finance. Because teachers necessarily function within a matrix created by these elements, using and being used by them, it stands to reason that the principles, policies, and facts of their functioning comprise a major source for the knowledge base. There is no need to claim that a specific literature undergirds this source, although there is certainly abundant research literature in most of these domains. But if a teacher has to "know the territory" of teaching, then it is the landscape of such materials, institutions, organizations, and mechanisms with which he or she must be familiar. These comprise both the tools of the trade and the contextual conditions that will either facilitate or inhibit teaching efforts.

Formal Educational Scholarship.   A third source is the important and growing body of scholarly literature devoted to understanding the processes of schooling, teaching, and learning. This literature includes the findings and methods of empirical research in the areas of teaching, learning, and human development, as well as the normative, philosophical, and ethical foundations of education.

The normative and theoretical aspects of teaching's scholarly knowledge are perhaps most important. Unfortunately, educational policy makers and staff developers tend to treat only the findings of empirical research on teaching and learning as relevant portions of the scholarly knowledge base. But these research findings, while important and worthy of careful study, represent only one facet of the contribution of scholarship. Perhaps the most enduring and powerful scholarly influences on teachers are those that enrich their images of the possible: their visions of what constitutes good education, or what a well-educated youngster might look like if provided with appropriate opportunities and stimulation.

The writings of Plato, Dewey, Neill, and Skinner all communicate their conceptions of what a good educational system should be. In addition, many works written primarily to disseminate empirical research findings also serve as important sources of these concepts. I count among these such works as Bloom's (1976) on mastery learning and Rosenthal and Jacobson's (1968) on teacher expectations. Quite independent of whether the empirical claims of those books can be supported, their impact on teachers' conceptions of the possible and desirable ends of education is undeniable. Thus, the philosophical, critical, and empirical literature which can inform the goals, visions, and dreams of teachers is a major portion of the scholarly knowledge base of teaching.

A more frequently cited kind of scholarly knowledge grows out of the empirical study of teaching effectiveness. This research has been summarized by Gage (1978, 1986), Shulman (1986a), Brophy and Good (1986), and Rosenshine and Stevens (1986). The essential goal of this program of research has been to identify those teacher behaviors and strategies most likely to lead to achievement gains among students. Because the search has focused on generic relationships—teacher behaviors associated with student academic gains irrespective of subject matter or grade level—the findings have been much more closely connected with the management of classrooms than with the subtleties of content pedagogy. That is, the effective-teaching principles deal with making classrooms places where pupils can attend to instructional tasks, orient themselves toward learning with a minimum of disruption and distraction, and receive a fair and adequate opportunity to learn. Moreover, the educational

purposes for which these research results are most relevant are the teaching of skills. Rosenshine (1986) has observed that effective teaching research has much less to offer to the teaching of understanding, especially of complex written material; thus, the research applies more to teaching a skill like multiplication than to teaching critical interpretations of, say, the *Federalist Papers.*

There are a growing number of such generic principles of effective teaching, and they have already found their way into examinations such as the National Teachers Examination and into state-level assessments of teaching performance during the first teaching year. Their weakness, that they essentially ignore the content-specific character of most teaching, is also their strength. Discovering, explicating, and codifying general teaching principles simplify the otherwise outrageously complex activity of teaching. The great danger occurs, however, when a general teaching principle is distorted into prescription, when maxim becomes mandate. Those states that have taken working principles of teaching, based solely on empirical studies of generic teaching effectiveness, and have rendered them as hard, independent criteria for judging a teacher's worth are engaged in a political process likely to injure the teaching profession rather than improve it.

The results of research on learning and development also fall within the area of empirical research findings. This research differs from research on teaching by the unit of investigation. Studies of teaching typically take place in conventional classrooms. Learning and development are ordinarily studied in individuals. Hence, teaching studies give accounts of how teachers cope with the inescapable character of schools as places where groups of students work and learn in concert. By comparison, learning and development studies produce principles of individual thought or behavior that must often be generalized to groups with caution if they are to be useful for schoolteaching.

The research in these domains can be both generic and content-specific. For example, cognitive psychological research contributes to the development of understanding of how the mind works to store, process, and retrieve information.

Such general understanding can certainly be a source of knowledge for teachers, just as the work of Piaget, Maslow, Erikson, or Bloom has been and continues to be. We also find work on specific subject matter and student developmental levels that is enormously useful; for example, we learn about student misconceptions in the learning of arithmetic by elementary school youngsters (Erlwanger, 1975) or difficulties in grasping principles of physics by university and secondary school students (for example, Clement, 1982). Both these sorts of research contribute to a knowledge base for teaching.

Wisdom of Practice.   The final source of the knowledge base is the least codified of all. It is the wisdom of practice itself, the maxims that guide (or provide reflective rationalization for) the practices of able teachers. One of the more important tasks for the research community is to work with practitioners to develop codified representations of the practical pedagogical wisdom of able teachers. As indicated above, much of the conception of teaching embodied in this chapter is derived from collecting, examining, and beginning to codify the emerging wisdom of practice among both inexperienced and experienced teachers.

The portrait of Nancy with which this chapter began is only one of the many descriptions and analyses of excellent teaching we have collected. As we organize and interpret such data, we attempt to infer principles of good practice that can serve as useful guidelines for efforts of educational reform. We attempt to keep the accounts highly contextualized, especially with respect to the content specificity of the pedagogical strategies employed. In this manner we contribute to the documentation of good practice as a significant source for teaching standards. We also attempt to lay a foundation for a scholarly literature that records the details and rationales for specific pedagogical practice.

One of the frustrations of teaching as an occupation and profession is its extensive individual and collective amnesia, the consistency with which the best creations of its practitioners are lost to both contemporary and future peers. Unlike fields such as architecture (which preserves its creations in both plans and edifices), law (which builds a case literature of opinions and interpretations), medicine (with its records and case studies), and even unlike chess, bridge, or ballet (with their traditions of preserving both memorable games and choreographed performances through inventive forms of notation and recording), teaching is conducted without an audience of peers. It is devoid of a history of practice.

Without such a system of notation and memory, the next steps of analysis, interpretation, and codification of principles of practice are hard to pursue. We have concluded from our research with teachers at all levels of experience that the potentially codifiable knowledge that can be gleaned from the wisdom of practice is extensive. Practitioners simply know a great deal that they have never even tried to articulate. A major portion of the research agenda for the next decade will be to collect, collate, and interpret the practical knowledge of teachers for the purpose of establishing a case literature and codifying its principles, precedents, and parables (Shulman, 1986b). A significant portion of the research agenda associated with the Carnegie program to develop new assessments for teachers involves the conducting of "wisdom-of-practice" studies. These studies record and organize the reasoning and actions of gifted teachers into cases to establish standards of practice for particular areas of teaching.[5]

A knowledge base for teaching is not fixed and final. Although teaching is among the world's oldest professions, educational research, especially the systematic study of teaching, is a relatively new enterprise. We may be able to offer a compelling argument for the broad outlines and categories of the knowledge base for teaching. It will, however, become abundantly clear that much, if not most, of the proposed knowledge base remains to be discovered, invented, and refined. As more is learned about teaching, we will come to recognize new categories of performance and understanding that are characteristic of good teachers, and will have to reconsider and redefine other domains. Our current "blueprint" for the knowledge base of teaching has many cells or categories with only the most rudimentary placeholders, much like the chemist's periodic table of a century ago. As we proceed, we will know that something can be known in principle about a particular aspect of teaching, but we will not yet know what that principle or practice entails. At base, however, we believe that scholars and expert teachers are able to define, describe, and reproduce good teaching.

THE PROCESSES OF PEDAGOGICAL REASONING AND ACTION

The conception of teaching I shall discuss has emerged from a number of sources, both philosophical and empirical. A key source has been the several dozen teachers whom we have been studying in our research. Through interviews, observations, structured tasks, and examination of materials, we have attempted to understand how they commute from the status of learner to that of teacher,[6] from being able to comprehend subject matter for themselves to becoming able to elucidate subject matter in new ways, reorganize and partition it, and clothe it in activities and emotions, in metaphors and exercises, and in examples and demonstrations, so that it can be grasped by students.

As we have come to view teaching, it begins with an act of reason, continues with a process of reasoning, culminates in performances of imparting, eliciting, involving, or enticing, and is then thought about some more until the process can begin again. In the discussion of teaching that follows, I will emphasize teaching as comprehension and reasoning, as transformation and reflection. This emphasis is justified by the resoluteness with which research and policy have so blatantly ignored those aspects of teaching in the past.

Fenstermacher (1978, 1986) provides a useful framework for analysis. The goal of teacher education, he argues, is not to indoctrinate or train teachers to behave in prescribed ways, but to educate teachers to reason soundly about their teaching as well as to perform skillfully. Sound reasoning requires both a process of thinking about what they are doing and an adequate base of facts, principles, and experiences from which to reason. Teachers must learn to use their knowledge base to provide the grounds for choices and

actions. Therefore, teacher education must work with the beliefs that guide teacher actions, with the principles and evidence that underlie the choices teachers make. Such reasons (called "premises of the practical argument" in the analysis of Green, 1971, on which Fenstermacher bases his argument) can be predominantly arbitrary or idiosyncratic ("It sure seemed like the right idea at the time!" "I don't know much about teaching, but I know what I like."), or they can rest on ethical, empirical, theoretical, or practical principles that have substantial support among members of the professional community of teachers. Fenstermacher argues that good teaching not only is effective behaviorally, but must rest on a foundation of adequately grounded premises.

When we examine the quality of teaching, the idea of influencing the grounds or reasons for teachers' decisions places the emphasis precisely where it belongs: on the features of pedagogical reasoning that lead to or can be invoked to explain pedagogical actions. We must be cautious, however, lest we place undue emphasis upon the ways teachers reason to achieve particular ends, at the expense of attention to the grounds they present for selecting the ends themselves. Teaching is both effective and normative; it is concerned with both means and ends. Processes of reasoning underlie both. The knowledge base must therefore deal with the purposes of education as well as the methods and strategies of educating.

This image of teaching involves the exchange of ideas. The idea is grasped, probed, and comprehended by a teacher, who then must turn it about in his or her mind, seeing many sides of it. Then the idea is shaped or tailored until it can in turn be grasped by students. This grasping, however, is not a passive act. Just as the teacher's comprehension requires a vigorous interaction with the ideas, so students will be expected to encounter ideas actively as well. Indeed, our exemplary teachers present ideas in order to provoke the constructive processes of their students and not to incur student dependence on teachers or to stimulate the flatteries of imitation.[7]

Comprehension alone is not sufficient. The usefulness of such knowledge lies in its value for judgment and action. Thus, in response to my aphorism "those who can, do; those who understand, teach" (Shulman, 1986b, p. 14), Petrie (1986) correctly observed that I had not gone far enough. Understanding, he argued, must be linked to judgment and action, to the proper uses of understanding in the forging of wise pedagogical decisions.

Aspects of Pedagogical Reasoning

I begin with the assumption that most teaching is initiated by some form of "text": a textbook, a syllabus, or an actual piece of material the teacher or student wishes to have understood. The text may be a vehicle for the accomplishment of other educational purposes, but some sort of teaching material is almost always involved. The following conception of pedagogical reasoning and action is taken from the point of view of the teacher, who is presented with the challenge of taking what he or she already understands and making it ready for effective instruction. The model of pedagogical reasoning and action is summarized in Table 11.1.

Given a text, educational purposes, and/or a set of ideas, pedagogical reasoning and action involve a cycle through the activities of

---

TABLE 11.1 A Model of Pedagogical Reasoning and Action

Comprehension
Of purposes, subject matter structures, and ideas within and outside the discipline

Transformation
Preparation: critical interpretation and analysis of texts, structuring and segmenting, development of a curricular repertoire, and clarification of purposes
Representation: use of a representational repertoire which includes analogies, metaphors, examples, demonstrations, explanations, and so forth
Selection: choice from among an instructional repertoire which includes modes of teaching, organizing, managing, and arranging
Adaptation and tailoring to student characteristics: consideration of conceptions, preconceptions, misconceptions, and difficulties; language, culture, and motivations; social class, gender, age, ability, aptitude, interests, self concepts, and attention

Instruction
Management, presentations, interactions, group work, discipline, humor, questioning, and other aspects of active teaching
Discovery or inquiry instruction
The observable forms of classroom teaching

Evaluation
Checking for student understanding during interactive teaching
Testing student understanding at the end of lessons or units
Evaluating one's own performance and adjusting for experiences

Reflection
Reviewing, reconstructing, reenacting, and critically analyzing one's own and the class's performance
Grounding explanations in evidence

New Comprehensions
Of purposes, subject matter, students, teaching, and self
Consolidation of new understandings and learnings from experience

comprehension, transformation, instruction, evaluation, and reflection.[8] The starting point and terminus for the process is an act of comprehension.

Comprehension.   To teach is first to understand. We ask that the teacher comprehend critically a set of ideas to be taught.[9] We expect teachers to understand what they teach and, when possible, to understand it in several ways. They should understand how a given idea relates to other ideas within the same subject area and to ideas in other subjects as well.

Comprehension of purposes is also central here. We engage in teaching to achieve educational purposes, to accomplish ends having to do with student literacy, student freedom to use and enjoy, and student responsibility to care and care for, to believe and respect, to inquire and discover, to develop understandings, skills, and values needed to function in a free and just society. As teachers, we also strive to balance our goals of fostering individual excellence with more general ends involving equality of opportunity and equity among students of different backgrounds and cultures. Although most teaching begins with some sort of text, and the learning of that text can be a worthy end in itself, we should not lose sight of the fact that the text is often a vehicle for achieving other educational purposes. The goals of education transcend the comprehension of particular texts, but may be unachievable without it.

Saying that a teacher must first comprehend both content and purposes, however, does not particularly distinguish a teacher from non-teaching peers. We expect a math major to understand mathematics or a history specialist to comprehend history. But the key to distinguishing the knowledge base of teaching lies at the intersection of content and pedagogy, in the capacity of a teacher to transform the content knowledge he or she possesses into forms that are pedagogically powerful and yet adaptive to the variations in ability and background presented by the students. We now turn to a discussion of transformation and its components.

Transformation.   Comprehended ideas must be transformed in some manner if they are to be taught. To reason one's way through an act of teaching is to think one's way from the subject matter as understood by the teacher into the minds and motivations of learners. Transformations, therefore, require some combination or ordering of the following processes, each of which employs a kind of repertoire: (1) preparation (of the given text materials) including the process of critical interpretation, (2) representation of the ideas in the form of new analogies, metaphors, and so forth, (3) instructional selections from among an array of teaching methods and models, and (4) adaptation of these representations to the general characteristics of the children to be taught, as well as (5) tailoring the adaptations to the specific youngsters in the classroom. These forms of transformation, these aspects of the process wherein one moves from personal comprehension to preparing for the comprehension of others, are the essence of the act of pedagogical reasoning, of teaching as thinking, and of planning—whether explicitly or implicitly—the performance of teaching.

Preparation involves examining and critically interpreting the materials of instruction in terms of the teacher's own understanding of the subject matter (Ben-Peretz, 1975). That is, one scrutinizes the teaching material in light of one's own comprehension and asks whether it is "fit to be taught." This process of preparation will usually include (1) detecting and correcting errors of omission and commission in the text and (2) the crucial processes of structuring and segmenting the material into forms better adapted to the teacher's understanding and, in prospect, more suitable for teaching. One also scrutinizes educational purposes or goals. We find examples of this preparation process in a number of our studies. Preparation certainly draws upon the availability of a curricular repertoire, a grasp of the full array of extant instructional materials, programs, and conceptions.

Representation involves thinking through the key ideas in the text or lesson and identifying the alternative ways of representing them to students. What analogies, metaphors, examples, demonstrations, simulations, and the like can help to build a bridge between the teacher's comprehension and that desired for the students? Multiple forms of representation are desirable. We speak of the importance of a representational repertoire in this activity.[10]

Instructional selections occur when the teacher must move from the reformulation of content through representations to the embodiment of representations in instructional forms or methods. Here the teacher draws upon an instructional repertoire of approaches or strategies of teaching. This repertoire can be quite rich, including not only the more conventional alternatives such as lecture, demonstration, recitation, or seatwork, but also a variety of forms of cooperative learning, reciprocal teaching, Socratic dialogue, discovery learning, project methods, and learning outside the classroom setting.

Adaptation is the process of fitting the represented material to the characteristics of the students. What are the relevant aspects of student ability, gender, language, culture, motivations, or prior knowledge and skills that will affect their responses to different forms of representation and presentation? What student conceptions, misconceptions, expectations, motives, difficulties, or strategies might influence the ways in which they approach, interpret, understand, or misunderstand the material? Related to adaptation is tailoring, which refers to the fitting of the material to the specific students in one's classrooms rather than to students in general. When a teacher thinks through the teaching of something, the activity is a bit like the manufacture of a suit of clothing. Adaptation is like preparing a suit of a particular style, color, and size that can be hung on a rack. Once it is prepared for purchase by a particular customer, however, it must be tailored to fit perfectly.

Moreover, the activity of teaching is rarely engaged with a single student at a time. This is a process for which the special term "tutoring" is needed. When we speak of teaching under typical school circumstances, we describe an activity which brings instruction to groups of at least fifteen—or more typically, twenty-five to thirty-five—students. Thus, the tailoring of instruction entails fitting representations not only to particular students, but also to a group of a particular size, disposition, receptivity, and interpersonal "chemistry."

All these processes of transformation result in a plan, or set of strategies, to present a lesson, unit, or course. Up to this point, of course, it is all a rehearsal for the performances of teaching which have not yet occurred. Pedagogical reasoning is as much a part of teaching as is the actual performance itself. Reasoning does not end when instruction begins. The activities of comprehension, transformation, evaluation, and reflection continue to occur during active teaching. Teaching itself becomes a stimulus for thoughtfulness as well as for action. We therefore turn next to the performance that consummates all this reasoning in the act of instruction.

Instruction. This activity involves the observable performance of the variety of teaching acts. It includes many of the most crucial aspects of pedagogy: organizing and managing the classroom; presenting clear explanations and vivid descriptions; assigning and checking work; and interacting effectively with students through questions and probes, answers and reactions, and praise and criticism. It thus includes management, explanation, discussion, and all the observable features of effective direct and heuristic instruction already well documented in the research literature on effective teaching.

We have compelling reasons to believe that there are powerful relationships between the comprehension of a new teacher and the styles of teaching employed. An example, based on the research of Grossman (1985), will illustrate this point.

> Colleen had completed a master's degree in English before entering a teacher education program. She expressed confidence in her command of the subject matter and began her internship with energy and enthusiasm. Her view of literature and its teaching was highly interpretive and interactive. She saw fine literature as layered communication, capable of many diverse readings and interpretations. Moreover, she felt that these various readings should be provided by her students through their own careful reading of the texts.
>
> Colleen was so committed to helping students learn to read texts carefully, a habit of mind not often found among the young or old, that she

constructed one assignment in which each student was asked to bring to school the lyrics of a favorite rock song. (She may have realized that some of these song lyrics were of questionable taste, but preferred to maximize motivation rather than discretion in this particular unit.) She then asked them to rewrite each line of the song, using synonyms or paraphrases to replace every original word. For many, it was the first time they had looked at any piece of text with such care.

When teaching a piece of literature, Colleen performed in a highly interactive manner, drawing out student ideas about a phrase or line, accepting multiple competing interpretations as long as the student could offer a defense of the construction by reference to the text itself. Student participation was active and hearty in these sessions. Based on these observations, one would have characterized Colleen's teaching style with descriptors such as student-centered, discussion-based, occasionally Socratic, or otherwise highly interactive.

Several weeks later, however, we observed Colleen teaching a unit on grammar. Although she had completed two university degrees in English, Colleen had received almost no preparation in prescriptive grammar. However, since a typical high school English class includes some grammar in addition to the literature and writing, it was impossible to avoid teaching the subject. She expressed some anxiety about it during a pre-observational interview.

Colleen looked like a different teacher during that lesson. Her interactive style evaporated. In its place was a highly didactic, teacher-directed, swiftly paced combination of lecture and tightly-controlled recitation: Socrates replaced by DISTAR. I sometimes refer to such teaching as the Admiral Farragut style, "Damn the questions, full speed ahead." Students were not given opportunities to raise questions or offer alternative views. After the session, she confessed to the observer that she had actively avoided making eye contact with one particular student in the front row because that youngster always had good questions or ideas and in this particular lesson Colleen really didn't want to encourage either, because she wasn't sure of the answers. She was uncertain about the content and adapted her instructional style to allay her anxiety.[11]

Colleen's case illustrates the ways in which teaching behavior is bound up with comprehension and transformation of understanding. The flexible and interactive teaching techniques that she uses are simply not available to her when she does not understand the topic to be taught. Having examined the processes of pedagogical reasoning and performance that are prospective and enactive in nature, we now move to those that are retrospective.

Evaluation.   This process includes the on-line checking for understanding and misunderstanding that a teacher must employ while teaching interactively, as well as the more formal testing and evaluation that teachers do to provide feedback and grades. Clearly, checking for such understanding requires all the forms of teacher comprehension and transformation described above. To understand what a pupil understands requires a deep grasp of both the material to be taught and the processes of learning. This understanding must be specific to particular school subjects and to individual topics within the subject. This represents another way in which what we call pedagogical content knowledge is used. Evaluation is also directed at one's own teaching and at the lessons and materials employed in those activities. In that sense it leads directly to reflection.

Reflection.   This is what a teacher does when he or she looks back at the teaching and learning that has occurred, and reconstructs, reenacts, and/or recaptures the events, the emotions, and the accomplishments. It is that set of processes through which a professional learns from experience. It can be done alone or in concert, with the help of recording devices or solely through memory. Here again, it is likely that reflection is not merely a disposition (as in "she's such a reflective person!") or a set of strategies, but also the use of particular kinds of analytic knowledge brought to bear on one's work (Richert, 1987). Central to this process is a review of the teaching in comparison to the ends that were sought.

New Comprehension.   Thus we arrive at the new beginning, the expectation that through acts of teaching that are "reasoned" and "reasonable" the teacher achieves new comprehension, both of the purposes and of the subjects to be taught, and also of the students and of the processes of pedagogy themselves. There is a good deal of transient experiential learning among teachers, characterized by the "aha" of a moment that is never consolidated and made part of a new understanding or a reconstituted repertoire (Brodkey, 1986). New comprehension does not automatically occur, even after evaluation and reflection. Specific strategies for documentation, analysis, and discussion are needed.

Although the processes in this model are presented in sequence, they are not meant to represent a set of fixed stages, phases, or steps. Many of the processes can occur in different order. Some may not occur at all during some acts of teaching. Some may be truncated, others elaborated. In elementary teaching, for example, some processes may occur that are ignored or given short shrift in this model. But a teacher should demonstrate the capacity to engage in these processes when called upon, and teacher education should provide students with the understandings and performance abilities they will need to reason their ways through and to enact a complete act of pedagogy, as represented here.

KNOWLEDGE, TEACHING POLICY, AND EDUCATIONAL REFORM

The investigations, deliberations, and debates regarding what teachers should know and know how to do have never been more active. Reform efforts are under way: they range from raising standards for admission into teacher education programs to establishing state and national examinations for teachers; from insisting that teacher preparation require at least five years of higher education (because there is so much to learn) to organizing elaborate programs of new-teacher induction and mentoring (because the most important learning and socialization can occur only in the workplace).

Most of the current reforms rest on the call for greater professionalization in teaching, with higher standards for entry, greater emphasis on the scholarly bases for practice, more rigorous

programs of theoretical and practical preparation, better strategies for certification and licensure, and changes in the workplace that permit greater autonomy and teacher leadership. In large measure, they call for teaching to follow the model of other professions that define their knowledge bases in systematic terms, require extended periods of preparation, socialize neophytes into practice with extended periods of internship or residency, and employ demanding national and state certification procedures.

Implicit in all these reforms are conceptions of teacher competence. Standards for teacher education and assessment are necessarily predicated on images of teaching and its demands. The conception of the knowledge base of teaching presented in this chapter differs in significant ways from many of those currently existing in the policy community. The emphasis on the integral relationships between teaching and the scholarly domains of the liberal arts makes clear that teacher education is the responsibility of the entire university, not the schools or departments of education alone. Moreover, teachers cannot be adequately assessed by observing their teaching performance without reference to the content being taught.

The conception of pedagogical reasoning places emphasis upon the intellectual basis for teaching performance rather than on behavior alone. If this conception is to be taken seriously, both the organization and content of teacher education programs and the definition of the scholarly foundations of education require revision. Teacher education programs would no longer be able to confine their activity to the content-free domains of pedagogy and supervision. An emphasis on pedagogical content knowledge would permeate the teacher preparation curriculum. A national board examination for teachers would focus upon the teacher's ability to reason about teaching and to teach specific topics, and to base his or her actions on premises that can bear the scrutiny of the professional community.

We have an obligation to raise standards in the interests of improvement and reform, but we must avoid the creation of rigid orthodoxies. We must achieve standards without standardization. We must be careful that the knowledge-base approach does not produce an overly technical image of teaching, a scientific enterprise that has lost its soul. The serious problems in medicine and other health professions arise when doctors treat the disease rather than the person, or when the professional or personal needs of the practitioner are permitted to take precedence over the responsibilities to those being served.

CONCLUSION

Needed change cannot occur without risk. The currently incomplete and trivial definitions of teaching held by the policy community comprise a far greater danger to good education than does a more serious attempt to formulate the knowledge base. Nancy represents a model of pedagogical excellence that should become the basis for the new reforms. A proper understanding of the knowledge base of teaching, the sources for that knowledge, and the complexities of the pedagogical process will make the emergence of such teachers more likely.

ENDNOTES

Preparation of this paper was made possible, in part, by grants to Stanford University from the Spencer Foundation for the project, Knowledge Growth in a Profession, and from the Carnegie Corporation of New York for research on the development of new modes of assessment for teachers, Lee S. Shulman, principal investigator. Suzanne Wilson, Pamela Grossman, and Judy Shulman provided criticism and counsel when it was most needed. The views expressed are the author's and are not necessarily shared by these organizations or individuals.

1. Most of the empirical work on which this essay rests has been conducted with secondary-school teachers, both new and experienced. While I firmly believe that much of the emphasis to be found here on the centrality of content knowledge in pedagogy holds reasonably well for the elementary level as well, I am reluctant to make that claim too boldly. Work at the elementary level, both by Leinhardt (1983) and her colleagues (for example, Leinhardt & Greeno, 1986; Leinhardt & Smith, 1985) and by our own research group, may help clarify this matter.

2. There are several aspects of this formulation that are unfortunate, if only for the impression they may leave. The rhetoric of the analysis, for example, is not meant to suggest that education is reduced to knowledge transmission, the conveying of information from an active teacher to a passive learner, and that this information is viewed as product rather than process. My conception of teaching is not limited to direct instruction. Indeed, my affinity for discovery learning and inquiry teaching is both enthusiastic and ancient (for example, Shulman & Keislar, 1966). Yet even in those most student-centered forms of education, where much of the initiative is in the hands of the students, there is little room for teacher ignorance. Indeed, we have reason to believe that teacher comprehension is even more critical for the inquiry-oriented classroom than for its more didactic alternative.

Central to my concept of teaching are the objectives of students learning how to understand and solve problems, learning to think critically and creatively as well as learning facts, principles, and rules of procedure. Finally, I understand that the learning of subject matter is often not an end in itself, but rather a vehicle employed in the service of other goals. Nevertheless, at least at the secondary level, subject matter is a nearly universal vehicle for instruction, whatever the ultimate goal.

3. This formulation is drawn from the teacher's perspective and, hence, may be viewed by some readers as overly teacher-centered. I do not mean to diminish the centrality of student learning for the process of education, nor the priority that must be given to student learning over teacher comprehension. But our analyses of effective teaching must recognize that outcomes *for teachers* as well as pupils must be considered in any adequate treatment of educational outcomes.

4. I have attempted this list in other publications, though, admittedly, not with great cross-article consistency (for example, Shulman, 1986b; Shulman & Sykes, 1986; Wilson, Shulman, & Richert, 1987).

5. It might be argued that the sources of skilled performances are typically tacit, and unavailable to the practitioner. But teaching requires a special kind of expertise or artistry, for which explaining and showing are the central features. Tacit knowledge among teachers is of limited value if the teachers are held responsible for explaining what they do and why they do it to their students, their communities, and their peers.

6. The metaphor of commuting is not used idly. The journey between learner and teacher is not one-way. In

the best teachers, as well as in the more marginal, new learning is constantly required for teaching.

7. The direction and sequence of instruction can be quite different as well. Students can literally initiate the process, proceeding by discovering, inventing, or inquiring to prepare their own representations and transformations. Then it is the role of the teacher to respond actively and creatively to those student initiatives. In each case the teacher needs to possess both the comprehension and the capacities for transformation. In the student-initiated case, the flexibility to respond, judge, nurture, and provoke student creativity will depend on the teacher's own capacities for sympathetic transformation and interpretation.

8. Under some conditions, teaching may begin with "given a group of students." It is likely that at the early elementary grades, or in special education classes or other settings where children have been brought together for particular reasons, the starting point for reasoning about instruction may well be at the characteristics of the group itself. There are probably some days when a teacher necessarily uses the youngsters as a starting point.

9. Other views of teaching will also begin with comprehension, but of something other than the ideas or text to be taught and learned. They may focus on comprehension of a particular set of values, of the characteristics, needs, interests, or propensities of a particular individual or group of learners. But some sort of comprehension (or self-conscious confusion, wonder, or ignorance) will always initiate teaching.

10. The centrality of representation to our conception of pedagogical reasoning is important for relating our model of teaching to more general approaches to the study of human thinking and problem solving. Cognitive psychologists (for example, Gardner, 1986; Marton, 1986; Norman, 1980) argue that processes of internal representation are key elements in any cognitive psychology. "To my mind, the major accomplishment of cognitive science has been the clear demonstration of the validity of positing a level of mental representation: a set of constructs that can be invoked for the explanation of cognitive phenomena, ranging from visual perception to story comprehension" (Gardner, 1986, p. 383). Such a linkage between models of pedagogy and models of more general cognitive functioning can serve as an important impetus for the needed study of teacher thinking.

11. In no way do I wish to imply that effective lectures are out of place in a high school classroom. On the contrary, good lecturing is an indispensable teaching technique. In this case I am more interested in the relationship between knowledge and teaching. It might be suggested that this teaching style is more suited to grammar than to literature because there is little to discuss or interpret in a grammar lesson. I do not agree, but will not pursue the matter here. In Colleen's case, the rationale for a linear lecture was not grounded in such an argument, but quite clearly in her concern for limiting the range of possible deviations from the path she had designed.

REFERENCES

Baxter, J. (1988). *Teacher Explanations in Computer Programming: A Study of Knowledge Transformation.* Unpublished doctoral dissertation, Stanford University.

Ben-Peretz, M. (1975). "The Concept of Curriculum Potential." *Curriculum Theory Network, 5:* 151–159.

Berliner, D. (1986). "In Pursuit of the Expert Pedagogue." *Educational Researcher, 15*(7): 5–13.

Bloom, B. S. (1976). *Human Characteristics and School Learning.* New York: McGraw-Hill.

Brodkey, J. J. (1986). *Learning While Teaching: Self-Assessment in the Classroom.* Unpublished doctoral dissertation, Stanford University.

Brophy, J. J., & Good, T. (1986). "Teacher Behavior and Student Achievement." In M. C. Wittrock (Ed.), *Handbook of Research on Teaching* (3rd ed., pp. 328–375). New York: Macmillan.

Carnegie Task Force on Teaching as a Profession. (1986). *A Nation Prepared: Teachers for the 21st Century.* Washington, DC: Carnegie Forum on Education and the Economy.

Clement, J. (1982). "Students' Preconceptions in Introductory Mechanics." *American Journal of Physics, 50:* 67–71.

Dewey, J. (1904). "The Relation of Theory to Practice in Education." In C. A. McMurry (Ed.), *The Relation of Theory to Practice in the Education of Teachers* (Third Yearbook of the National Society for the Scientific Study of Education, Part I). Bloomington, IL: Public School Publishing.

Erlwanger, S. H. (1975). "Case Studies of Children's Conceptions of Mathematics, Part I." *Journal of Children's Mathematical Behavior, 1:* 157–283.

Fenstermacher, G. (1978). "A Philosophical Consideration of Recent Research on Teacher Effectiveness." In L. S. Shulman (Ed.), *Review of Research in Education* (Vol. 6, pp. 157–185). Itasca, IL: Peacock.

Fenstermacher, G. (1986). "Philosophy of Research on Teaching: Three Aspects." In M. C. Wittrock (Ed.), *Handbook of Research on Teaching* (3rd ed., pp. 37– 49). New York: Macmillan.

Gage, N. L. (1978). *The Scientific Basis of the Art of Teaching*. New York: Teachers College Press.

Gage, N. L. (1986). *Hard Gains in the Soft Sciences: The Case of Pedagogy*. Bloomington, IN: Phi Delta Kappa.

Gardner, H. (1986). *The Mind's New Science: A History of Cognitive Revolution*. New York: Basic Books.

Green, T. F. (1971). *The Activities of Teaching*. New York: McGraw-Hill.

Grossman, P. (1985). *A Passion for Language: From Text to Teaching* (Knowledge Growth in Teaching Publications Series). Stanford: Stanford University, School of Education.

Gudmundsdottir, S. (1988). *Knowledge Use among Experienced Teachers: Four Case Studies of High School Teaching*. Unpublished doctoral dissertation, Stanford University.

Hashweh, M. Z. (1985). *An Exploratory Study of Teacher Knowledge and Teaching: The Effects of Science Teachers' Knowledge of Subject-Matter and Their Conceptions of Learning on Their Teaching*. Unpublished doctoral dissertation, Stanford University.

The Holmes Group. (1986). *Tomorrow's Teachers: A Report of the Holmes Group*. East Lansing, MI: Author.

Leinhardt, G. (1983). "Novice and Expert Knowledge of Individual Students' Achievement." *Educational Psychologist, 18:* 165–179.

Leinhardt, G., & Greeno, J. G. (1986). "The Cognitive Skill of Teaching." *Journal of Educational Psychology, 78:* 75–95.

Leinhardt, G., & Smith, D. A. (1985). "Expertise in Mathematics Instruction: Subject Matter Knowledge. *Journal of Educational Psychology, 77:* 247–271.

Marton, F. (1986). *Towards a Pedagogy of Content*. Unpublished manuscript, University of Gothenburg, Sweden.

Norman, D. A. (1980). "What Goes On in the Mind of the Learner?" In W. J. McKeachie (Ed.), *New Directions for Teaching and Learning: Learning,*

Cognition, and College Teaching (Vol. 2). San Francisco: Jossey-Bass.

Petrie, H. (1986, May). *The Liberal Arts and Sciences in the Teacher Education Curriculum*. Paper presented at the Conference on Excellence in Teacher Preparation through the Liberal Arts, Muhlenberg College, Allentown, PA.

Richert, A. (1987). *Reflex to Reflection: Facilitating Reflection in Novice Teachers*. Unpublished doctoral dissertation, Stanford University.

Rosenshine, B. (1986, April). *Unsolved Issues in Teaching Content: A Critique of a Lesson on Federalist Paper No. 10*. Paper presented at the meeting of the American Educational Research Association, San Francisco, CA.

Rosenshine, B., & Stevens, R. S. (1986). "Teaching Functions." In M. C. Wittrock (Ed.), *Handbook of Research on Teaching* (3rd ed., pp. 376–391). New York: Macmillan.

Rosenthal, R., & Jacobson, L. (1968). *Pygmalion in the Classroom*. New York: Holt, Rinehart & Winston.

Scheffler, I. (1965). *Conditions of Knowledge: An Introduction to Epistemology and Education*. Chicago: University of Chicago Press.

Schwab, J. J. (1964). "The Structure of the Disciplines: Meanings and Significances." In G. W. Ford & L. Pugno (Eds.), *The Structure of Knowledge and the Curriculum*. Chicago: Rand McNally.

Schwab, J. J. (1983). "The Practical Four: Something for Curriculum Professors to Do." *Curriculum Inquiry, 13:* 239–265.

Shulman, L. S. (1986a). "Paradigms and Research Programs for the Study of Teaching." In M. C. Wittrock (Ed.), *Handbook of Research on Teaching* (3rd ed., pp. 3–36). New York: Macmillan.

Shulman, L. S. (1986b). "Those Who Understand: Knowledge Growth in Teaching." *Educational Researcher, 15*(2): 4–14.

Shulman, L. S., & Keislar, E. R. (Eds.). (1966). *Learning by Discovery: A Critical Appraisal*. Chicago: Rand McNally.

Shulman, L. S., & Sykes, G. (1986, March). *A National Board for Teaching?: In Search of a Bold Standard*. Paper commissioned for the Task Force on Teaching as a Profession, Carnegie Forum on Education and the Economy.

Smith, B. O. (1980). *A Design for a School of Pedagogy*. Washington, DC: U.S. Department of Education.

Sykes, G. (1986). *The Social Consequences of Standard-Setting in the Professions.* Paper commissioned for the Task Force on Teaching as a Profession, Carnegie Forum on Education and the Economy.

Wilson, S. M., Shulman, L. S., & Richert, A. (1987). "150 Different Ways of Knowing: Representa-tions of Knowledge in Teaching." In J. Calderhead (Ed.), *Exploring Teacher Thinking.* Sussex, Eng.: Holt, Rinehart & Winston.

DISCUSSION QUESTIONS

1. Why is research on teacher effectiveness on its own an insufficient source for defining the knowledge base of teaching?
2. In what ways are (a) content area scholarship, (b) educational materials and struc-tures, (c) formal educational scholarship, and (d) wisdom of practice integral components of the teacher knowledge base?
3. Which domains should comprise the conception of teacher competence?
4. What do you think teachers should know and be able to do as a result of their training?
5. Should teacher education require national board examinations for certification? Why? Why not?

12

Honoring Diverse Styles
of Beginning Teachers

EDWARD F. PAJAK
ELAINE STOTKO
FRANK MASCI

FOCUSING QUESTIONS

1. How would you describe a teacher's style of teaching?
2. How does teacher style differ from teacher characteristics? Teacher behavior? Teacher effectiveness?
3. How is a teacher's style influenced by his or her educational philosophy?
4. How would you describe a teacher's cycle of learning?
5. How does a teacher's professional learning differ from problem solving? Critical thinking? Transfer of learning?
6. What kind of supervisor would you prefer to have observing and mentoring your teaching?

Schools today face the responsibility of guaranteeing high-quality instruction for every student, while simultaneously having to recruit and retain unprecedented numbers of new and second-career teachers. This dual challenge is achievable, we believe, only by supporting teachers in ways that are compatible with how they most naturally learn and teach. In other words, those educators who provide support to new teachers should strive to work with them in the same way that teachers are expected to work with students—by recognizing and celebrating a diversity of styles and responding to differences in ways that enhance learning for everyone.

The standards movement in education has set for itself the admirable goal of high expectations for all students. Because students differ in their styles of learning, experienced teachers recognize the importance of providing alternative paths for achieving these agreed-upon outcomes. Similarly, the time has come for us to realize that new teachers do not all learn or teach the same way. Talk to several new teachers about why they are teachers, what teaching means to them, how they know when they are successful, and what gives them the most satisfaction, and you'll discover that some teachers place great emphasis on imparting knowledge to students, while others stress the importance of helping students discover knowledge for themselves. Some teachers believe in getting actively involved in their students' lives, while others prefer to maintain a more distanced professional relationship. Some teachers dedicate themselves to social change and justice for all students, while others concentrate their efforts on individual students who show promise of becoming leaders of their generation.

These different perspectives of teaching reflect various experiences or styles of teaching— inventing, knowing, caring, and inspiring—that highlight differences in how individuals perceive and process information (Pajak, 2003). When *inventing* teachers talk about teaching, for example, they tend to emphasize the importance of "having students solve problems" and of "seeing students apply their learning to real situations." *Knowing* teachers are more likely to focus on "helping kids learn content" and to believe they are successful when they "see students mastering the subject matter." *Caring* teachers often say that "providing opportunities for student growth" is most important, and they define success in terms of "building a classroom community." Finally, *inspiring* teachers tend to view teaching as "an opportunity to shape the future" and derive satisfaction from "seeing students make independent decisions."

These four ways of experiencing teaching are clearly evident in the literature on education. The *inventing* perspective is expressed, for example, in the scholarship of Jean Piaget and Hilda Taba; advocacy for the *knowing* viewpoint may be found in the writings of Benjamin Bloom and Mortimer Adler; the importance of the *caring* attitude is explained to us by Nel Noddings and Parker Palmer; and the *inspiring* stance is articulated in the work of Paulo Freire and Maxine Greene. The four styles can also be seen in depictions of teachers in popular culture. Jaime Escalante, in the movie *Stand and Deliver,* is an example of an *inventing* teacher. Marva Collins in the made-for-TV movie *The Marva Collins Story,* represents a *knowing* teacher. Roberta Guaspari, in the film *Music of the Heart,* depicts a *caring* teacher, and LouAnne Johnson, in *Dangerous Minds,* an *inspiring* teacher.

A TEACHER-PROOF TEACHER?

Why do different teacher styles matter? Forty or more years ago, during the Cold War and post-Sputnik era, some experts in education tried to develop what has been termed the "teacher-proof curriculum," in the belief that if instruction and curriculum were controlled to a sufficient degree, teachers would be forced into teaching only what was prescribed by the experts. Today, we fear, the inflexible enforcement of standards for teaching is moving us toward a "teacher-proof teacher," one who is standardized to the point of being unable to think independently or to act on personal convictions. Yet, we know from the study of teaching styles that real teachers are more complex, as the following vignettes demonstrate.

Inventing

Students in Ken Garry's eleventh-grade world history class have come to expect the unexpected. Still, on one memorable day at the beginning of the Russian history unit, even they were surprised to see a somewhat disheveled, unshaven Mr. Garry enter the room. They were certainly not prepared for what happened next. He took out a razor and began to shave. Then he posed a series of questions, beginning with "What did my shaving have to do with an event in Russian history?" A very lively discussion ensued around the fact that Peter the Great, in one of his efforts to westernize the country, ordered his nobles, the Boyars, to shave off their flowing beards. The students were likely not only to remember this event but, as a result of the discussion, to place it within the larger context of the modernization of Russia.

Knowing

To an observer entering Pam Gilbert's twelfth-grade English classroom, it is immediately apparent that each student has a clear idea of her expectations. Daily objectives are posted; each student is given a detailed agenda of what is to be covered during the lesson; and posters that describe rules, submission requirements for papers, and assignment deadlines are prominent throughout the room. Ms. Gilbert's lesson plans reveal that instruction is largely teacher-directed and focused on the learning of factual information and key concepts. Group work is also part of her instructional strategy; she typically assigns students to groups, giving each student a specific responsibility within the group. The classroom climate is one of efficiency and purpose.

Caring

Gloria Silverman loves children, and her eighth-grade mathematics students, if pressed, would admit to affection for her as well. They would cite her keen interest in their lives, her close contact with their parents (they might even give grudging appreciation for this), and her willingness to "go the extra mile" to help them understand the sometimes bewildering intricacies of the rudiments of algebra. Surprisingly large numbers of students attend her daily lunchtime help sessions and are grateful for her tenacious insistence on learning the subject matter, always couched in an almost parental concern for their well-being.

Inspiring

Second graders, at the very beginning of their educational experience, certainly represent a wealth of untapped possibility. They are impressionable and usually very eager to please. No one realizes this more and capitalizes on it better than their teacher, Joanna Chakitis. To describe her classroom environment as a wonderland is an understatement. The walls are covered with colorful and stimulating instructional materials, stations for work on individualized assignments, and job charts for student helpers. Even the ceiling contains examples of student work. The students in Ms. Chakitis's class are the beneficiaries of exceptionally creative and innovative teaching practices that are carefully designed to promote their growth and development.

SUPPORTING NEW TEACHERS

Beginning teachers often find themselves facing expectations and advice from university supervisors, mentor teachers, peer coaches, principals, and district office supervisors. How should support systems for new teachers that are provided by universities and schools respond to these diverse teaching styles? Our fundamental principle

is simple, yet powerful. Those who provide support to new teachers—mentors, peer coaches, university supervisors, and principals—should make a deliberate effort to honor and legitimate perspectives and practices that differ from their own preferred styles of perceiving and judging reality. The starting point for helping new teachers succeed, in other words, should be the development of the teacher's preferred style. Once that style has been successfully developed, of course, the teacher should be encouraged to expand his or her repertoire of strategies and perspectives.

Teaching is much more than simply a job. For a great many people, teaching is a way of living their lives. Teaching is closely connected, in other words, to how teachers view themselves as people. Indeed, what teachers do in their classrooms is tightly wrapped up with, and difficult to separate from, their very identities. Support systems and mentoring practices that conflict with the teacher's identity and core values are, at the very least, useless and, at the worst, destructive.

Although any one of the experiences of teaching—*inventing, knowing, caring, inspiring*—can be a useful guide to practice, it is only a starting point. All of these paths must be traced if a teacher is to become truly effective. Supervisors (i.e., mentors, coaches, principals) are expected to ensure that new teachers know their subject matter and can teach, but in reality the support that new teachers need is much more complicated. An effective mentor is able to support the new teacher's personal and emotional needs and to help the teacher become an inquiring professional and reflective practitioner.

Each student that a teacher meets in the classroom requires different things at different times—explanations and reliable ways of thinking, high standards and understanding, nurturing care and emotional support, inspiration and values—and a teacher ought to be able to provide them all. Similarly, those who support beginning teachers should be able to offer differentiated support as well. Unfortunately, classroom observations and evaluations in most school systems rely on instruments or standards that favor only the organized and businesslike demeanor of the knowing teacher. The innovation, creativity, and democratic goals of caring, inventing, and inspiring teachers are usually de-emphasized or even implicitly discouraged.

Adult learning theorist David Kolb (1984) identified four types of learners that roughly correspond to the teaching styles described here. Most people develop preferences for a particular style of learning, he believes, as a result of events in their lives, personality differences, environmental circumstances, and education. No one style is necessarily better or worse than another, he insists. The important thing is to recognize that differences among learners do exist. His model portrays people as dynamic learners and problem solvers who constantly respond to their environments by engaging in new experiences, reflecting on these experiences from various perspectives, creating understandings and generalizations, and applying these understandings to their lives and to their work (Sims & Sims, 1995). Bernice McCarthy (1982, 1990) has long advocated linking Kolb's work to our understanding of teaching and learning.

Integrating the wisdom of three great educators—John Dewey, Jean Piaget, and Kurt Lewin—Kolb (1984) proposes a recurring cycle of learning that includes four phases. Teacher development can be understood as a recurring cycle of growth that begins with (a) concrete experience, followed by (b) empathic reflection, (c) construction of meaning, and (d) active experimentation. As teachers progress through the learning cycle, they complement their initial teaching style with functions that have lain dormant. Integrating the styles allows them to recognize and enact a wider range of choices and decisions when facing new situations. These phases of learning are best pursued with the support of a mentor, a clinical coach, or a team of colleagues. The descriptions of the four phases of learning, which appear below, are followed by an example of a clinical coach, Ms. Jeanette Greene, engaged in the process of observing and conferring with Gloria Silverman, the caring teacher described previously.

The Phases

1. The *concrete experience* phase of learning requires the clinical coach to actively engage the teacher in problem solving. Concrete data

concerning teacher and student behavior and their relationship to curriculum, standards, objectives, methods, materials, or classroom artifacts are considered. A key question for the teacher during this phase is "How well am I really doing?"

2. During the *empathic reflection* phase of learning, the coach displays and models empathy. Multiple perspectives are considered for the purpose of gaining insight into the subjective experience of students who inhabit the teacher's classroom. A question for the teacher to answer during this phase is "What is going on here for everyone involved, both for myself and for the students?"

3. In the *construction of meaning* phase of learning, the clinical coach encourages the teacher to raise theoretical and ethical issues, form generalizations, and propose hypotheses concerning cause and effect relationships. The central question for the teacher during this phase is "What does all this mean?"

4. Finally, during the *active experimentation* phase of learning, the coach steps back and empowers the teacher to take action. What has been learned is applied to practical problems in the classroom, accompanied by the collection of new data. The question for the teacher that guides this phase of the cycle is "How can I do things better?" (Pajak, 2003)

The key to applying these phases of learning is to help teachers enter the cycle at the phase that comes most naturally to them. When working with a caring teacher, for example, the mentor or coach should pay special attention to developing trust and a positive climate that will contribute to collaboration and mutual learning. Beginning a conversation that asks a caring teacher to empathically reflect on the experience of his or her students in the classroom will both be nonthreatening and serve to engage the teacher in the learning cycle.

The Example

Jeanette Greene, as clinical coach, has done her homework. The day prior to her observation of

Gloria Silverman, who exhibits a caring style of teaching, she scheduled a brief meeting for them to discuss the plan for the lesson. Having this conversation in advance demonstrates to Gloria that Jeanette respects her as a person and initiates the learning cycle by getting Gloria to focus on her teaching. The meeting also provides an opportunity for Jeanette to learn about the strategies that Gloria intends to use and how they relate to the purposes of the lesson.

The next day, Jeanette observes Gloria, recording a descriptive narrative of what is said and done by both the teacher and students, including some notes describing the feeling-tone within the classroom. Following the observation, Jeanette conducts an analysis of the data, looking for connections between observed events and student learning that will reinforce good practices, as well as patterns that relate to the interpersonal climate in the classroom. Later in the day, Jeanette meets with Gloria for the post-observation conference. For purposes of this example, we will assume that Gloria's lesson was generally positive, but there were several issues that Jeanette felt needed attention.

The first part of the conference, which corresponds to the *concrete experience* phase of learning, would be concerned chiefly with the data—in this case, a detailed discussion of the lesson that was observed. Jeanette would show Gloria the descriptive narrative she recorded along with specific events and patterns that relate to student learning and interpersonal behavior.

As Jeanette shifts to the *empathic reflection* phase, she needs to remember that caring teachers can be very sensitive and have their feelings easily hurt. While offering generous praise for positive aspects of the lesson, Jeanette should also tactfully introduce the areas of concern and even offer some concrete suggestions for Gloria to try. Since the major question of this phase is "What is going on here for everyone involved, both the teacher and the students?" Jeanette can tap into Gloria's intense concern for her students and ask how her actions directly affect them as she encourages Gloria to expand her teaching repertoire.

Jeanette can begin the *construction of meaning* phase of learning by restating the major issues

and by inviting Gloria to propose some strategies for modifying her instruction that are consistent with her personal values and beliefs about teaching and learning. Either Jeanette or Gloria might also propose concepts or theoretical perspectives that place their conversation within a broader framework. Again, by keeping the focus on the enhanced learning of Gloria's students, Jeanette honors Gloria's caring style, while facilitating her movement through the adult learning cycle.

The *active experimentation* phase of learning necessitates Gloria's implementing the recommendations collaboratively developed in the post-observation conference. Gloria's major motivation to carry out the recommendations should be in response to the questions "How can I do things better?" and "How can I become a better teacher?" Jeanette will work with Gloria to determine the focus of a subsequent observation to be conducted after Gloria has had time to try out some of the strategies identified. She will then establish with Gloria an appropriate time for the subsequent observation and follow-up conference to discuss Gloria's degree of success in implementing these innovations.

The intention is to gently nudge teachers out of their comfort zones and change their behavior by exposing them to alternative learning environments during each of the four phases (Rainey & Kolb, 1995). When Jeanette works with an inspiring teacher such as Joanna Chakitis, *construction of meaning* would be the starting point for discussion. In this case, Jeanette could begin with a conversation about personal values and beliefs about teaching and its purposes, and then encourage Joanna to move along to *active experimentation* by posing hypotheses about specific relationships between her behavior and student outcomes (How can I do things better?), with an eye toward the *concrete experience* phase (How well am I really doing?), which then would lead to *empathic* reflection.

When embedded in the reality of classroom experience, alternative learning environments structured around the four phases can allow teachers to take greater responsibility for their own professional growth and gradually develop a full range of teaching styles. Teams of teachers might be organized in a school according to their style preferences, perhaps by grade level or subject area, where they read and share instructional materials to more finely hone their natural abilities. Individual teachers could rotate through different teams as they gain fluency with different styles, or entire teams could explore different learning environments together over a period of time. The purpose of such teams is not to "track" teachers, but to create within a school "a cooperative human community that cherishes and utilizes individual uniqueness" (Kolb, 1984, p. 62). An awareness and appreciation of different styles can be helpful, for example, for improving communication, resolving conflicts amicably, selecting team members, and identifying mediators and as a framework for professional development.

MATCHING MENTORS AND TEACHERS

Honoring different teaching styles is not a technique to be used from time to time, but instead an entirely new way of thinking about support. At best, we typically offer teachers a "take it or leave it" form of support, because we have a natural tendency to want teachers to teach their classes the way we would if we were the teacher. But if a beginning teacher is forced to adopt a style of thinking and teaching by someone who is unsympathetic or inflexible, the beginning teacher is likely to become frustrated and discouraged and may never attain his or her full potential.

In an ideal world, every beginning teacher would be matched with a supervisor who shared his or her style, at least initially, to enhance communication and minimize frustration. Another workable strategy, however, may be to select clinical coaches who are knowledgeable about and sensitive to different teaching styles and who are comfortable allowing new teachers to teach to their strengths, while still understanding when and how to help the new teacher move out of his or her comfort zone and into an exploration of other styles.

Rather than advocating a particular way of behaving or thinking, this new form of support facilitates learning by modeling alternative behaviors and patterns of thinking. At each phase of the learning cycle, the supervisor or mentor becomes a clinical coach who is (a) a colleague who models and supports conscious awareness of the personal experience of teaching, (b) an empathic listener and sounding board who facilitates an understanding of the effect that teaching has on students, (c) a knowledgeable resource who helps interpret subjective and objective information to arrive at moral and conceptual meaning, and (d) a coach who empowers teachers toward action planning and hypothesis testing.

Attending to teacher differences requires flexibility and an environment that includes mutual respect, safety, shared responsibility for learning, and an emphasis on personal growth. Such change requires the clinical coach to meet teachers where they are and then build on their strengths, rather than relying on a remedial mentality. At a minimum, clinical coaches should

- Reflect on their own beliefs about learning, teaching, and support
- Assess and reflect on the needs of the new teacher as learner
- Be sensitive to preferences for perceiving and processing information, on the part of both the teacher and the coach
- Develop and use a variety of communication strategies
- Develop and use a range of supervisory approaches
- Clarify the roles of supervisor and teacher
- Begin building an inclusive community of learners that welcomes diverse learning styles and preferences

It is true that schools are not structured for individualized supervision, but then neither are classrooms designed for individualized instruction. Honoring diverse teaching styles is worth the extra effort, we believe, because it gives teachers greater choice and voice, which contributes to the coherence of their individual goals for professional development, is consistent with other reforms and classroom activities with which teachers are already involved, and can help build a schoolwide learning community that respects differences.

REFERENCES

Kolb, D. A. (1984). *Experiential Learning.* Englewood Cliffs, NJ: Prentice Hall.

McCarthy, B. (1982). "Improving Staff Development through CBAM and 4MAT." *Educational Leadership, 40*(1): 20–25.

McCarthy, B. (1990). "Using the 4MAT System to Bring Learning Styles to Schools." *Educational Leadership, 48*(2): 31–37.

Pajak, E. (2003). *Honoring Diverse Teaching Styles: A Guide for Supervisors.* Alexandria, VA: Association for Supervision and Curriculum Development.

Rainey, M. A., & Kolb, D. A. (1995). "Using Experiential Learning Theory and Learning Styles in Diversity Education." In, R. R. Sims & S. J. Sims (Eds.), *The Importance of Learning Styles.* Westport, CT: Greenwood Press.

Sims, R. R., & Sims, S. J. (1995). *The Importance of Learning Styles.* Westport, CT: Greenwood Press.

DISCUSSION QUESTIONS

1. Which best describes your own teaching style: knowing, caring, inventing, or inspiring? Why?
2. Do you agree with the authors' assessment that certain education policies are attempting to move us toward a "teacher-proof teacher"?
3. What advantages and drawbacks exist in having a variety of teaching styles represented in a school?
4. Which of the four styles of teaching identified in this chapter is most popular today? Which is most often disregarded or overlooked?
5. When you were a beginning teacher, would a system of support that honored your preferred teaching style have been helpful to you?

13

Keeping Good Teachers: Why It Matters, What Leaders Can Do

LINDA DARLING-HAMMOND

FOCUSING QUESTIONS

1. How can a comfortable learning/teaching environment be created?
2. Why is teacher attrition such a large problem?
3. How can qualified teachers be encouraged to continue teaching?
4. What types of programs may be instituted to help fight teacher attrition?
5. What are some of the reasons teachers leave the profession? Change schools?

How teachers are paid was a part of it, but overwhelmingly the things that would destroy the morale of teachers who wanted to leave were the working conditions . . . working in poor facilities, having to pay for supplies, and so on.

—A Los Angeles teacher talking
about a high-turnover school

The first-grade classroom in which I found myself five years ago had some two dozen ancient and tattered books, an incomplete curriculum, and a collection of outdated content standards. But I later came to thrive in my profession because of the preparation I received in my credential program: the practice I received developing appropriate curriculum; exposure to a wide range of learning theories; training in working with non-English-speaking students and children labeled "at risk."

It is the big things, though, that continue to sustain me as a professional and give me the courage to remain and grow: my understanding of the importance of asking questions about my own practice, the collegial relationships, and my belief in my responsibility to my students and to the institution of public education.

—A California teacher from a strong
urban teacher education program

What keeps some people in teaching while others give up? What can we do to increase the holding power of the teaching profession and to create a stable, expert teaching force in all kinds of districts? Some of the answers to these questions are predictable; others are surprising. The way schools hire and the way they use their resources can make a major difference.

Keeping good teachers should be one of the most important agenda items for any school leader. Substantial research evidence suggests that well-prepared, capable teachers have the largest impact on student learning (see Darling-Hammond, 2000b; Wilson, Floden, & Ferrini-Mundy, 2001). Effective teachers constitute a valuable human resource for schools—one that needs to be treasured and supported.

THE CHALLENGE OF TEACHER ATTRITION

The No Child Left Behind Act's requirement that schools staff all classrooms with "highly qualified teachers" creates a major challenge, especially for schools in inner-city and poor rural areas. The problem does not lie in the numbers of teachers available; we produce many more qualified

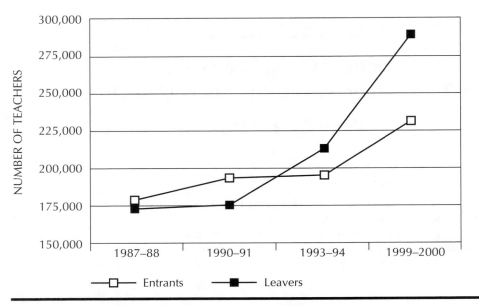

FIGURE 13.1 Trends in Teacher Entry and Attrition, 1987–2000
Source: Adapted from Ingersoll (2001).

teachers than we hire. The hard part is *keeping* the teachers we prepare.

The uphill climb to staff our schools with qualified teachers becomes steeper when teachers leave in large numbers. Since the early 1990s, the annual number of exits from teaching has surpassed the number of entrants by an increasing amount (Figure 13.1), putting pressure on the nation's hiring systems. Less than 20 percent of this attrition is due to retirement (Henke, Chen, & Geis, 2000; Ingersoll, 2001).

Steep attrition in the first few years of teaching is a longstanding problem. About one-third of new teachers leave the profession within five years. Rates of attrition from individual schools and districts include these leavers, plus movers who go from one school or district to another. Taken together, leavers and movers particularly affect schools that serve poor and minority students. Teacher turnover is 50 percent higher in high-poverty than in low-poverty schools (Ingersoll, 2001), and new teachers in urban districts exit or transfer at higher rates than their suburban counterparts do (Hanushek, Kain, & Rivkin, 1999).

High-poverty schools suffer higher rates of attrition for many reasons. Salary plays a part: Teachers in schools serving the largest concentrations of low-income students earn, at the top of the scale, one-third less than those in higher-income schools (National Center for Education Statistics [NCES], 1997). They also face fewer resources, poorer working conditions, and the stress of working with many students and families who have a wide range of needs. In addition, more teachers in these schools are underprepared and unsupported, factors that strongly influence attrition (Darling-Hammond, 2000a).

THE HEAVY COSTS OF ATTRITION

Early attrition from teaching bears enormous costs. A recent study in Texas, for example, estimated that the state's annual turnover rate of 15 percent, which includes a 40 percent turnover rate for public school teachers in their first three years, costs the state a "conservative" $329 million a year, or at least $8,000 per recruit who leaves in the first few years of teaching (Texas Center for

Educational Research, 2000). High attrition means that schools must take funds urgently needed for school improvements and spend them instead in a manner that produces little long-term payoff for student learning.

Given the strong evidence that teacher effectiveness increases sharply after the first few years of teaching (Kain & Singleton, 1996), this kind of churning in the beginning teaching force reduces productivity in education overall. The education system never gets a long-term payoff from its investment in novices who leave.

In addition, large concentrations of underprepared teachers create a drain on schools' financial and human resources. In a startling number of urban schools across the United States, a large share of teachers are inexperienced, underqualified, or both. One recent estimate indicates that more than 20 percent of schools in California have more than 20 percent of their staffs teaching without credentials. These inexperienced teachers are assigned almost exclusively to low-income schools serving students of color (Shields et al., 2001).

Such schools must continually pour money into recruitment efforts and professional support for these new teachers. Other teachers, including those who serve as mentors, are stretched thin and feel overburdened by the needs of their colleagues in addition to those of their students. Schools squander scarce resources trying to reteach the basics each year to teachers who come in with few tools and leave before they become skilled (Carroll, Reichardt, & Guarino, 2000). As a principal in one such school noted,

> Having that many new teachers on the staff at any given time meant that there was less of a knowledge base. . . . It meant there was less cohesion on the staff. It meant that every year, we had to recover ground in professional development that had already been covered and try to catch people up to where the school was heading. (cited in Darling-Hammond, 2002)

Most important, such attrition consigns a large share of students in high-turnover schools to a continual parade of ineffective teachers. Unless we develop policies to stem such attrition through better preparation, assignment, working conditions, and mentor support, we cannot meet the goal of ensuring that all students have qualified teachers.

FACTORS INFLUENCING TEACHER ATTRITION

In all schools, regardless of school wealth, student demographics, or staffing patterns, the most important resource for continuing improvement is the knowledge and skill of the school's best prepared and most committed teachers. Four major factors strongly influence whether and when teachers leave specific schools or the education profession entirely: salaries, working conditions, preparation, and mentoring support in the early years.

Salaries

Even though teachers are more altruistically motivated than are some other workers, teaching must compete with other occupations for talented college and university graduates each year. To attract its share of these graduates and to offer sufficient incentives for professional preparation, the teaching profession must be competitive in terms of wages and working conditions.

Unfortunately, teacher salaries are relatively low. Overall, teacher salaries are about 20 percent below the salaries of other professionals with comparable education and training. Data from the Bureau of Labor Statistics show that in 2001, the average teacher salary ($44,040) ranked below that of registered nurses ($48,240), accountants/auditors ($50,700), dental hygienists ($56,770), and computer programmers ($71,130) (National Commission on Teaching and America's Future [NCTAF], 2003).

Teachers are more likely to quit when they work in districts that offer lower wages and when their salaries are low relative to alternative wage opportunities, especially teachers in such high-demand fields as math and science (Brewer, 1996; Mont & Rees, 1996; Murnane & Olsen, 1990; Theobald & Gritz, 1996). Salary differences seem to matter more at the start of the teaching career

(Gritz & Theobald, 1996; Hanushek et al., 1999), whereas experienced teachers appear to place more importance on working conditions (Loeb & Page, 2000).

Working Conditions

Surveys of teachers have long shown that working conditions play a major role in teachers' decisions to switch schools or leave the profession. Teachers' feelings about administrative support, resources for teaching, and teacher input into decision making are strongly related to their plans to stay in teaching and to their reasons for leaving (Darling-Hammond, 2000a; Ingersoll, 2001, 2002). High- and low-wealth schools differ greatly, on average, in the support that they give teachers. Teachers in more advantaged communities experience easier working conditions, including smaller class sizes and pupil loads and greater influence over school decisions (NCES, 1997).

The high attrition of teachers from schools serving lower-income or lower-achieving students appears to be substantially influenced by the poorer working conditions typically found in those schools. For example, a survey of California teachers (Harris, 2002) found that teachers in high-minority, low-income schools report significantly worse working conditions, including poorer facilities, less access to textbooks and supplies, fewer administrative supports, and larger class sizes. Further, teachers surve yed were significantly more likely to say that they planned to leave the school soon if the working conditions were poor.

An analysis of these California data found that serious turnover problems at the school level were influenced most by working conditions, ranging from large class sizes and poor facilities to multitrack, year-round schedules and low administrative support (Loeb, Darling-Hammond, & Luczak, 2003). Together with salaries, these factors far outweighed the demographic characteristics of students in predicting turnover at the school level. This finding suggests that working conditions should be one target for policies aimed at retaining qualified teachers in high-need schools.

Teacher Preparation

A growing body of evidence indicates that teachers who lack adequate initial preparation are more likely to leave the profession. A recent National Center for Education Statistics report found that 29 percent of new teachers who had not had any student teaching experience left within five years, compared with only 15 percent of those who had done student teaching as part of a teacher education program (Henke et al., 2000). The same study found that 49 percent of uncertified entrants left within five years, compared with only 14 percent of certified entrants. In California, the state standards board found that 40 percent of emergency-permit teachers left the profession within a year, and two-thirds never received a credential (Darling-Hammond, 2002).

In Massachusetts, nearly half of all recruits from the Massachusetts Institute for New Teachers program had left within three years (Fowler, 2002), and in Houston, Texas, the attrition rate averaged 80 percent after two years for Teach for America recruits (Raymond, Fletcher, & Luque, 2001).

Other research evidence suggests that the more training prospective teachers receive, the more likely they are to stay. For example, a longitudinal study of 11 programs found that those who graduate from five-year teacher education programs enter and stay in teaching at much higher rates than do four-year teacher education graduates from the same institutions (Andrew & Schwab, 1995). These longer, redesigned programs provide a major in a disciplinary field, as well as intensive pedagogical training and long-term student teaching. As Figure 13.2 shows, both four-year and five-year teacher education graduates enter and stay in teaching positions at higher rates than do teachers hired through alternative programs that give them only a few weeks of training (Darling-Hammond, 2000a).

Taking into account the costs to states, universities, and school districts for preparation, recruitment, induction, and replacement due to attrition, the actual cost of preparing a career teacher in the more intensive five-year programs is actually less than the cost of preparing a greater number

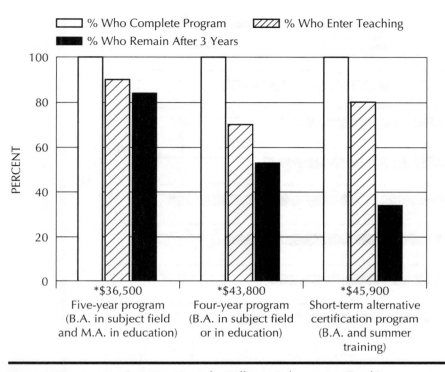

FIGURE 13.2   Average Retention Rates for Different Pathways into Teaching
*Estimated cost per third-year teacher.
Source: Darling-Hammond (2000a).

of teachers in short-term programs of only a few weeks' duration. Graduates of extended five-year programs also report higher levels of satisfaction with their preparation and receive higher ratings from principals and colleagues.

In 2000, new teachers who had received training in specific aspects of teaching (for example, selection and use of instructional materials, child psychology, and learning theory), who experienced practice teaching, and who received feedback on their teaching left the profession at rates one-half as great as those who had no training in these areas (NCTAF, 2003). Similarly, first-year teachers who felt that they were well prepared for teaching were much more likely to plan to stay in teaching than those who felt poorly prepared. On such items as preparation in planning lessons, using a range of instructional methods, and assessing students, two-thirds of those reporting strong

preparation intended to stay, compared with only one-third of those reporting weak preparation (see Figure 13.3). In these studies and others, graduates of teacher education programs felt significantly better prepared and more efficacious, and they planned to stay in teaching longer than did those entering through alternative routes or with no training (Darling-Hammond, Chung, & Frelow, 2002; NCTAF, 2003).

Mentoring Support

Schools can enhance the beneficial effects of strong initial preparation with strong induction and mentoring in the first years of teaching. A number of studies have found that well-designed mentoring programs raise retention rates for new teachers by improving their attitudes, feelings of efficacy, and instructional skills.

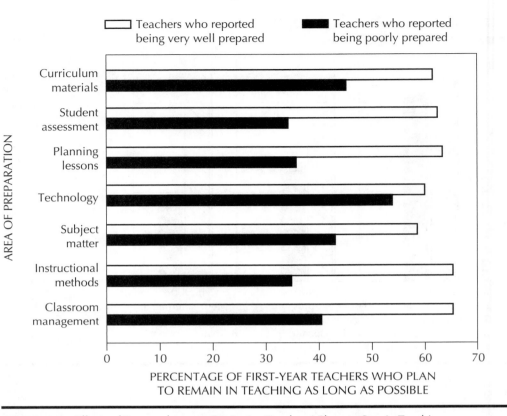

FIGURE 13.3 Effects of Preparedness on Beginning Teachers' Plans to Stay in Teaching
Source: Unpublished tabulations from Schools and Staffing Surveys, Teacher Questionnaire, 1999–2000.

Such districts as Rochester, New York, and Cincinnati, Columbus, and Toledo, Ohio, have reduced attrition rates of beginning teachers by more than two-thirds (often from levels exceeding 30 percent to rates of under 5 percent) by providing expert mentors with release time to coach beginners in their first year on the job (NCTAF, 1996). These young teachers not only stay in the profession at higher rates, but also become competent more quickly than those who must learn by trial and error.

Mentoring and induction programs produce these benefits only if they are well designed and well supported. Although the number of state induction programs has increased (from 7 states in 1996–1997 to 33 states in 2002), only 22 states provide funding for these programs, and not all of the programs provide on-site mentors (NCTAF, 2003). In an assessment of one of the oldest programs, California's Beginning Teacher Support and Assessment Program, early pilots featuring carefully designed mentoring systems found rates of beginning teacher retention exceeding 90 percent in the first several years of teaching. As the program has scaled up across the state, however, only half of the districts have provided mentors with time to coach novices in their classrooms (Shields et al., 2001).

Most effective are state induction programs that are tied to high-quality preparation. In Connecticut, for example, districts that hire beginning teachers must provide them with mentors who have received training in the state's teaching standards and its portfolio assessment system, which were introduced as part of reforms during the 1990s. These reforms also raised salaries and standards for teachers and created an assessment of teaching for professional licensure modeled after that of the National Board for Professional Teaching Standards. A beginning teacher noted of this connected system,

> One of the things that helped me a lot is that my cooperating teacher last year is a state assessor and she used to do live assessments. . . . She used to assess me using [state standards] for every lesson, every single day, which gave me a good idea of what is expected of me and how I will be assessed by the state. Also, I learned about the components that make good teaching. (Wilson, Darling-Hammond, & Berry, 2001)

As an additional benefit, these programs provide a new lease on life for many veteran teachers. Veterans need ongoing challenges to remain stimulated and excited about the profession. Many say that mentoring and coaching other teachers creates an incentive for them to remain in teaching as they learn from and share with their colleagues.

WHAT SCHOOL LEADERS CAN DO

The research reviewed here suggests several lessons for education policy and practice:

- Although investments in competitive salaries are important, keeping good teachers—both novices and veterans—also requires attention to the working conditions that matter to teachers. In addition to those often considered—class size, teaching load, and the availability of materials—key conditions include teacher participation in decision making, strong and supportive instructional leadership from principals, and collegial learning opportunities.
- Seeking out and hiring better-prepared teachers has many payoffs and savings in the long run in terms of both lower attrition and higher levels of competence.
- When the high costs of attrition are calculated, many of the strategic investments needed to keep good teachers—such as providing mentoring for beginners and creating ongoing learning and leadership challenges

for veterans—actually pay for themselves to a large degree.

School systems can create a magnetic effect when they make it clear that they are committed to finding, keeping, and supporting good teachers. In urban centers, just as in suburban and rural areas, good teachers gravitate to schools where they know they will be appreciated and supported in their work. These teachers become a magnet for others who seek environments in which they can learn from their colleagues and create success for their students. Great school leaders create nurturing school environments in which accomplished teaching can flourish and grow.

REFERENCES

Andrew, M., & Schwab, R. L. (1995). "Has Reform in Teacher Education Influenced Teacher Performance? An Outcome Assessment of Graduates of Eleven Teacher Education Programs." *Action in Teacher Education, 17:* 43–53.

Brewer, D. J. (1996). "Career Paths and Quit Decisions: Evidence from Teaching." *Journal of Labor Economics, 14(2):* 313–339.

Carroll, S., Reichardt, R., & Guarino, C. (2000). *The Distribution of Teachers among California's School Districts and Schools.* Santa Monica, CA: RAND.

Darling-Hammond, L. (2000a). *Solving the Dilemmas of Teacher Supply, Demand, and Quality.* New York: National Commission on Teaching and America's Future.

Darling-Hammond, L. (2000b). "Teacher Quality and Student Achievement: A Review of State Policy Evidence." *Educational Policy Analysis Archives, 8*(1) [Online journal]. Available: http://epaa.asu.edu/epaa/v8n1

Darling-Hammond, L. (2002). *Access to Quality Teaching: An Analysis of Inequality in California's Public Schools.* Stanford, CA: Stanford University.

Darling-Hammond, L., Chung, R., & Frelow, F. (2002). "Variation in Teacher Preparation: How Well Do Different Pathways Prepare Teachers to Teach?" *Journal of Teacher Education, 53*(4): 286–302.

Fowler, C. (2002). "Fast Track . . . Slow Going? Education Policy Clearinghouse Research Brief, Vol. 2, Issue 1 [Online]. Available: www.edpolicy.org/publications/documents/updatev2i1.pdf

Gritz, R. M., & Theobald, N. D. (1996). "The Effects of School District Spending Priorities on Length of Stay in Teaching." *Journal of Human Resources, 31*(3): 477–512.

Hanushek, E. A., Kain, J. F., & Rivkin, S. G. (1999). "Do Higher Salaries Buy Better Teachers? Working Paper No. 7082. Cambridge, MA: National Bureau of Economic Research.

Harris, P. (2002). *Survey of California Teachers.* Rochester, NY: Peter Harris Research Group.

Henke, R., Chen, X., & Geis, S. (2000). *Progress through the Teacher Pipeline: 1992–1993 College Graduates and Elementary/Secondary School Teaching as of 1997.* Washington, DC: National Center for Education Statistics, U.S. Department of Education.

Ingersoll, R. M. (2001). "Teacher Turnover and Teacher Shortages: An Organizational Analysis." *American Educational Research Journal, 38*(3): 499–534.

Ingersoll, R. M. (2002). *Out-of-Field Teaching, Educational Inequality, and the Organization of Schools: An Exploratory Analysis.* Seattle, WA: Center for the Study of Teaching and Policy, University of Washington.

Kain, J. F., & Singleton, K. (1996, May/June). "Equality of Educational Opportunity Revisited." *New England Economic Review,* 87–111.

Loeb, S., Darling-Hammond, L., & Luczak, J. (2003). *Teacher Turnover: The Role of Working Conditions and Salaries in Recruiting and Retaining Teachers.* Stanford, CA: Stanford University School of Education.

Loeb, S., & Page, M. (2000). "Examining the Link between Teacher Wages and Student Outcomes." *Review of Economics and Statistics, 82*(3): 393–408.

Mont, D., & Rees, D. I. (1996). "The Influence of Classroom Characteristics on High School Teacher Turnover." *Economic Inquiry, 34:* 152–167.

Murnane, R. J., & Olsen, R. J. (1990). "The Effects of Salaries and Opportunity Costs on Length of Stay in Teaching: Evidence from North Carolina." *The Journal of Human Resources, 25*(1): 106–124.

National Center for Education Statistics (NCES). (1997). *America's Teachers: Profile of a Profession, 1993–1994.* Washington, DC: U.S. Department of Education.

National Commission on Teaching and America's Future (NCTAF). (1996). *What Matters Most: Teaching for America's Future.* New York: Author.

National Commission on Teaching and America's Future (NCTAF). (2003). *No Dream Denied: A Pledge to America's Children.* New York: Author.

Raymond, M., Fletcher, S., & Luque, J. (2001). *Teach for America: An Evaluation of Teacher Differences and Student Outcomes in Houston, Texas.* Stanford, CA: Center for Research on Educational Outcomes, The Hoover Institution, Stanford University.

Shields, P. M., Humphrey, D. C., Wechsler, M. E., Riel, L. M., Tiffany-Morales, J., Woodworth, K., Youg, V. M., & Price, T. (2001). *The Status of the Teaching Profession, 2001.* Santa Cruz, CA: The Center for the Future of Teaching and Learning.

Texas Center for Educational Research. (2000). *The Cost of Teacher Turnover.* Austin, TX: Texas State Board for Teacher Certification.

Theobald, N. D., & Gritz, R. M. (1996). "The Effects of School District Spending Priorities on the Exit Paths of Beginning Teachers Leaving the District." *Economics of Education Review, 15*(1): 11–22.

Wilson, S., Darling-Hammond, L., & Berry, B. (2001). *A Case of Successful Teaching Policy: Connecticut's Long-Term Efforts to Improve Teaching and Learning.* Seattle, WA: Center for the Study of Teaching and Policy, University of Washington.

Wilson, S., Floden, R., & Ferrini-Mundy, J. (2001). *Teacher Preparation Research: Current Knowledge, Gaps, and Recommendations.* Seattle, WA: University of Washington, Center for the Study of Teaching and Policy.

DISCUSSION QUESTIONS

1. What were the reasons that you became a teacher?
2. What are the reasons that you remain in the profession?
3. Have you ever seriously thought about leaving the classroom? Why or why not?
4. Which do you think would do most to improve teachers' effectiveness: higher salaries, better working conditions, better preparation, or better mentoring?
5. Which do you think would make the least difference?

PRO-CON CHART 2

Should teachers be held accountable for their teaching?

PRO	CON
1. Teaching should be guided by clear objectives and outcomes.	1. Many factors influence teaching and learning that have little to do with measurable objectives and outcomes.
2. Students have a right to receive a quality education, whereby professionals are held accountable for their behavior.	2. Educational accountability is a cooperative responsibility of students, teachers, parents, and taxpayers.
3. Accountability will encourage teachers to uphold high standards for instruction.	3. Teachers can provide instruction but they cannot force students to learn.
4. Feedback from accountability evaluation measures will provide teachers with information about their instructional strengths and weaknesses.	4. Mandating accountability will demoralize teachers and reduce their professional status.
5. Accountability will provide standards that are derived through consensual agreement and will offer objective assessment.	5. There will always be disagreement on who is accountable, for what, and to whom.

CASE STUDY 2

School District Proposes Evaluations by Students

Kamhi County School District in West Suburb had proposed to vote on implementing a change to their current teacher evaluation procedures. The proposed change would permit junior high students to participate in the evaluation process of their teachers, beginning in the spring. As a way of gathering feedback, all thirty principals were asked to complete an anonymous three-part survey. In Parts One and Two, the principals were asked to cite the advantages and disadvantages of this proposed change. In Part Three, they were asked to provide a plan that outlined how they would implement this approach in their building site if it were enacted.

While reading the survey responses, Marilyn Lauter, assistant superintendent for instruction, noticed two items, unsigned letters from both a student and a teacher, that caught her attention. The student argued that because students are consumers of teachers' services, they should have a right to have their voices heard. The teacher's letter expressed complete opposition to the proposed change, citing that students lacked the maturity to provide feedback. The teacher's letter also stated that such a change would advocate the philosophy and teaching styles of certain administrators, thereby limiting the teacher's voice. Furthermore, the letter stated that if the district voted to enact this change as policy, the teachers would probably strike. Lauter was feeling very uncomfortable with both letters, but also knew that more discussion was needed before any policy change should be taken to a vote.

Discuss the issues raised by the student and the teacher and consider the following questions:

1. Should junior high students be involved in the evaluation of their teachers? Why? Why not?

2. If you were the assistant superintendent for instruction, how would you handle this situation?

3. What other approaches might have been used to elicit feedback from the teachers, parents, and students concerning the proposed policy change to the teacher evaluation process?

4. In what ways might students' evaluations of teachers affect their instruction or your own instruction?

5. What evidence does research provide about the ability of junior high students to evaluate teachers?

6. How might teachers and parents in your school district react to this proposed policy change in teacher evaluation procedures?

PART THREE

Curriculum and Learning

What is the relationship between learning and curriculum? What role does active participation play in student achievement? To what extent are higher-order thinking, creativity, and moral education emphasized in curriculum delivery? How has standardized testing influenced student confidence? What is the role of character education in students' learning experiences?

In Chapter 14, Theodore R. Sizer and Nancy Faust Sizer argue that moral or character education is an intellectual endeavor that must allow students opportunities to act and think. Students should be encouraged to deal with important and relevant ideas, even when the outcome of their grappling with difficult situations is uncertain. In Chapter 15, Matthew Lipman distinguishes between critical and ordinary thinking. He suggests that an emphasis on critical thinking will promote intellectual responsibility. He also describes the processes that encourage critical thinking.

Next, Robert Sternberg and Todd Lubart discuss the factors that characterize creative thinking. The authors describe the type of instruction that fosters creative thinking. They suggest that students should be given more responsibility for selecting the type of problems that they investigate, rather than relying on teacher-constructed problems. In Chapter 17, Lawrence Kohlberg describes how moral education promotes the aims of education. He compares the cognitive-developmental approach with other approaches to moral education. Alfie Kohn then presents a critical analysis of the limitations of current character education program strategies. He describes why divergent approaches would exemplify a program different from traditional approaches to moral development. The author suggests ways that reflection can be used to enhance students' moral growth.

In Chapter 19, Jeannie Oakes explains how the policy of tracking has affected student outcomes. She explores the reasons that the practice of tracking persists and explains how educators, despite evidence to the contrary, tend to justify the practice of tracking as being beneficial for students. Through actual case studies, Oakes examines the relationship among the practice of tracking, in-school segregation, and educational opportunity. In the final chapter in Part Three, Frederick Hess asks the question "What is public schooling?" The answer, he demonstrates, is more complicated than one might expect, and he argues that new realities require an expansion of our definition.

PROFESSIONAL PROFILE: LEARNING

Name:
Karen Bang-Jensen Kepler Zumwalt

Email:
kkz2@columbia.edu

Latest degree/university:
Ph.D., Education, The University of Chicago. My program was Curriculum and Philosophy in the Department of Education, Division of Social Sciences.

Position:
Edward Evenden Professor of Education, Department of Curriculum and Teaching, Teachers College, Columbia University

Previous positions:
I have been at Teachers College for 29 years, holding the titles of Instructor, Assistant Professor, Associate Professor, Professor, and Evenden Professor of Education. Major positions have included Director of the Elementary (N–9) Preservice Teacher Education Program; Department Chair, Department of Curriculum and Teaching; Director, Division of Institutions and Programs; and Dean of the College and Vice President for Academic Affairs.

Prior to coming to Teachers College, I was a Lecturer in the Department of Education and Child Study, Smith College, Northampton, Massachusetts after having taught middle school in Cleveland, Ohio, and Glencoe, Illinois, public schools.

Person most influential in your career:
I owe much to all the people who have supported, questioned, and stimulated me over the years. However, as I look back, perhaps the most defining influential person was a group of seventh-grade girls I worked with my first year of teaching in the largest junior high school in Ohio, the year after the riots in Cleveland. The students were mostly Black, as were the teachers. It was the year Martin Luther King was assassinated. This was a tough school—corporal punishment was still permitted and expected. But there was a lot of hope in the school, led by an inspiring Black principal who had instituted many experimental programs and had attracted some wonderful teachers.

To reach my girls, many of whom had been left back several times and none of whom was on grade level, I was constantly stretched as the curriculum unfolded with or without me. I did some things I never thought I would do, and there is much more I wish I had done. Thirty-six years later, I still reflect on the girls of 7-B. Not only did they teach me how to teach, but the issues I grappled with that year became the defining issues for my dissertation and later work in the field.

Number-one achievement:
All sorts of challenges face us in education today—continued racial and social class inequities, prescriptive mandated test-driven curriculum, professionally unsound teacher education programs, corporatization of academia—the list goes on. My biggest ac-

complishment is that I still remain positive, believing that groups of people working together—and, indeed, sometimes, one person—can make a meaningful difference.

Number-one regret:
Looking back on my career, I wish that I could have professionally afforded to return to the K–12 classroom as a classroom teacher. I believe that K–12 classroom teaching is an integral and valued part of being a professor of education, even at a research university.

Favorite educational journal:
Different kinds of journals serve different purposes, so a generic favorite is hard to choose. But forced to pick, I guess I would choose *Phi Delta Kappan.* Its articles and editorial material capture the intersection of current practice, policy, research, and theory in an intellectual but accessible style.

Favorite educational book:
Just as my first class of seventh graders was so influential in my career, the books I would choose as my favorites are those that grabbed my attention in graduate school, helping me understand the phenomena I had experienced and wanted to change. This cluster of books includes Dreeben's *On What Is Learned in School,* Jackson's *Life in Classrooms,* Rosenthal and Jacobson's *Pygmalion in the Classroom,* and Smith's *Complexity of an Urban Classroom.* Some of my students' favorites have become new favorites for me, but I realize that most of them are extensions of the ways of knowing I was introduced to in graduate school and the issues I grappled with in teaching seventh–ninth graders in economically diverse public schools.

Best book/chapter you wrote:
I would like to think that each piece of writing builds on past writing, so that each piece is better than the last. But choosing the "best" would mean that I would have to decide which *works* the "best" given the purpose of the piece and the intended audience. Since I have written with a variety of goals and audiences in mind, I can't name a "best" piece.

Of the works that articulate my point of view, perhaps the most memorable for me was the experience I had in writing a chapter in the *National Society for the Study of Education (NSSE) Yearbook,* for which I won AERA's first Interpretive Scholarship Award in 1983. The chapter, "Research on Teaching: Policy Implications for Teacher Education," was motivated by Teachers College President Larry Cremin telling me that I needed to articulate a Keplerian (my last name then) view of teacher education if I wanted tenure at Teachers College. When I look at the chapter, I realize that although I would have had the confidence today to write it without all the extensive quotations, it does articulate a point of view about a deliberative stance toward teaching and the interrelated relationship of curriculum and teaching that has defined, in today's parlance, my voice.

Additional interests:
Parenting has been my most absorbing interest over the last 25 years. It has challenged me and sustained me, an extraordinary experience that keeps unfolding. Seeing schools and teachers from a mother's perspective has also made me a better teacher.

Curriculum/learning relationship:
"What is curriculum?" was one of the central questions we pondered in our first years in the doctoral program at The University of Chicago, the home of so many greats in the curriculum field. Thinking of curriculum in the broadest sense gave the field intellectual depth and the analytic potential to capture the endemic questions in education. Since

then, curriculum to me encompasses the formal, intended, enacted, hidden, and experienced curriculum—it is everything that students learn in school.

Professional vision:

Over the past several years, teacher educators at Teachers College have been working on a conceptual framework for NCATE. We have adopted three stances—teaching as inquiring, teaching as curriculum making, and teaching for social justice—which capture the essence of my professional vision. These stances seem even more critical today if teachers are to be truly accountable.

Professional advice to teacher or curriculum specialist:

When I have asked teachers and administrators—even in the most test-conscious districts—to describe the best teachers they have known, they do not mention high test scores. Invariably, they describe teachers with high expectations for their students, teachers who engage their students in memorable curricular activities and who personally connect to individual students in meaningful ways. These are teachers who have made a difference in the lives of their students. As a teacher, curriculum specialist, or teacher educator, regardless of the circumstances we face, we all have the choice to be someone who makes a difference.

14

Grappling

THEODORE R. SIZER
NANCY FAUST SIZER

FOCUSING QUESTIONS

1. Why should teachers be concerned with moral or character education?
2. How can teachers involve students more actively in their learning?
3. Why is it important for students to think deeply about what they learn?
4. What are the characteristics of a demanding curriculum?
5. What role should values play in student learning?

School is a frustration for Carl. He just can't see the good it does him. Even more, he can't see the good he does it. In social studies, the teacher tells him which U.S. presidents were the greatest. At least she also tells him exactly why. His parents say he should be grateful for that; they only got to memorize the list, never to hear the explanations so it's more interesting to think about. Still, he'd like to have the chance to tell her why he thinks a president who manages to avoid a war is as good as one who leads a nation in a war.

In math, he's told that there is one right answer and one way to get to that right answer. In English, he's told that the music lyrics he dotes on are inferior poetry. Even when he is asked to write, he's told how many paragraphs he should use to get his ideas across to "the reader." Which reader? Wouldn't it matter who he or she was?

And when his teacher takes his class to the computer room only to find a substitute there who doesn't know how to run the new machines, Carl is not allowed to read the computer manual so that he can help to get the class started. He tries to argue that he's done this before at home and even at school and that he and his classmates need the time in the lab if they are to finish their projects.

But he gets a little too near to rudeness, and the teacher, visibly upset, cuts him off. "I don't know what's happened to kids these days," she says to us as she turns the class back toward her classroom to wait out the period. "They're so irresponsible."

In fact, this last situation requires some deeper consideration. There is, of course, no guarantee that Carl could have figured out how to run the new machines and thus saved the time for his classmates and his teacher. It's hard to predict how much time his grappling would have taken or what its outcome would have been. The problem could have been "solved" on a superficial level, or it might have needed a lot more work. Carl's energy might have given out; he might even have damaged the equipment. Nor is there any excuse for the rudeness that those who know more than others about technology or any other subjects often display.

Still, Carl had been treated as if he were an empty vessel, as if his skills and his opinions were of no value to those around him. In the computer room, he was told that there was nothing that he or anyone else could do. Instead, they were all to go back to their classroom and act as if nothing had happened. The result was an intellectual and a moral vacuum.

Why does an intellectual vacuum so often lead to a moral one as well? Schools exist for children, but children are often seen as the school's clients, as its powerless people. They are told that they are in school not because of what they know but because of what they don't know. All over the world, powerless people lose the instinct to help, because they are so often rebuffed. Yet, even if he had ultimately been unsuccessful, struggling with the computer manual would have been a good use of Carl's mind. He would have been fulfilling the real purpose of schooling: to equip himself to be of use both to himself and to others. He would have used what he already knew to reach out and learn more about how computers work. And he would have put himself on the line in a good cause.

Putting oneself on the line may be valuable, but it invites the kind of criticism that is rarely applied to the young. Raising the young is exquisitely tricky business. A fiftyish father grumped to us about his daughter who was just graduating from high school. The young woman had announced to her parents that she was determined to become a writer. "A writer?" her dad snorted to us. "What would she write about? She doesn't know anything."

The young woman was full of passion. She liked to string words out, playing with them. She wrote exclusively about her own world, casting it as a revelation. She labored hard in English courses and had had several intense pieces published in the school's literary magazine. She had skimmed over her other courses, doing only the minimum. Nonetheless, she was an honors student. She surely would get a book award at graduation and deservedly so.

And yet her dad had a telling point. Behind his daughter's enthusiasms was glibness. Her skill was admirable, and her joy in the application of that skill was palpable. Her ability to describe her own thoughts and feelings was unusual. But the young woman did not even know that she knew relatively little, that there was important knowledge that required a broader context than her own life.

The father, caught in the practical demands of earning a living and tired of years of teenage hubris, is understandably cautious. But if he is smart, he will keep his concerns to himself. The energy, even the presumption, of the young writer should not be reined in just because so much of it is based on self-absorption and naiveté. Instead, in taking herself seriously and wanting to write for an ever-widening audience, she will be motivated to take an increased interest in the ways of the world. Time will tell.

In case after case, this is how we have seen growing up work. A student's hope and sense of agency are often dependent on her belief that there is something she can do that is valued by others. Not just other kids, but adults as well. And not empty "self-esteem building activities," but the outcome of her best efforts, in which she has real confidence. From that point on, talent intertwines constantly with content, as the student challenges herself to perform at higher levels for a broader audience.

And so it is with learning the habits of civil behavior. The skills are important. Showing restraint. Being willing to listen. Having empathy. Feeling responsible for something and some people beyond oneself and one's personal coterie of friends. Being nice. Getting along in one's daily interactions.

But there must be more. Most interactions in life are complex; more than talent and good habits are needed to address them well. Few are mastered by merely applying a slogan such as "Just say no." Context is critical if not crucial. The thoughts and resultant actions of, say, a Polish-German day laborer working near Auschwitz in 1944, a person who sees the full trains come and the empty trains go, might be appreciably different from the conclusions about the Holocaust reached by an outraged American teenager sitting in an unthreatened high school classroom 50 years later. It will help the teenager to absorb the complexity of the situation if he can reflect as if from the shoes of the laborer, not necessarily to agree, but to empathize and to understand. In this Second World War moment there is powerful stuff: the particulars of a situation, in necessarily exquisite and painful detail. That stuff, if well and carefully considered, provides the perspective that is ultimately the heart of truly moral decisions. Educators call this content.

The habits of civil behavior can do much to bring safety to a school's halls. But the meanings of civil behavior are much tougher to present. They transcend one's immediate environment. When fully and painstakingly constructed, they provide a distant mirror, the meaning of one's immediate condition viewed against a sweep of human and environmental experience, past and present.

One has to grapple with those meanings. If not, "behavior" is reduced to glib catchwords that provoke little more than periodic puffs of self-righteousness. A curriculum rich in content will teach young people that important matters of sensitive living have everything to do with hard, substantive, and often agonizingly painful thought. The students will write plays or stories or imagined memoirs that will help them to get at the considerations inside that hypothetical day laborer's head.

Grappling is necessarily a balancing act. One tries to do what one has never done before and so learns more about what one wants to do. The reader's sense of his own power is built up by letting him try to understand the computer manual so the class can go forward. The writer's humility and appreciation of context are built up by asking her to take on another's complex identity before she tries to write about it. Each task is doable, but difficult; each requires that the student put him- or herself firmly on the line.

The first step in creating such a demanding curriculum is to believe that it can be done. Wise schoolpeople and parents should not underestimate the power that they can find in young minds, bodies, and hearts. Recently the newspapers reported that an 11-year-old took her younger cousin on a three-hour drive in the family car, crossing state lines, navigating effectively, looking for an uncle but settling for an aunt. Everyone who commented on the incident remarked on how naughty these children were, how neglectful was the mother who had left them and the keys in the car while she went to an exercise salon, how unobservant was the gas station attendant who sold them gas without noticing how young they were. No one wondered at the sheer competence lurking like a shadow underneath the youngsters' foolishness.

We're selling our children short when we believe that grappling is beyond them. In fact, most of them are engaging in dilemmas of intense seriousness while we're looking the other way. Most teenagers have watched one or another substance be abused, heard adults who are important to them treat each other harshly, and wondered why so many are poor in a rich country. Many have been mugged figuratively and some literally. The teenage mother or caregiver has been a fixture for centuries. Most modern wars have been fought (albeit neither started nor led) by teenage males. To treat adolescents as delicate flowers unable to act and think is a costly pretense, as patronizing as it is wasteful. Young people can do things, and they do do things now. Older folk should accept that fact and labor hard to provide the perspective that can affect, in a principled manner, the way that young people inform those actions that, willy-nilly, they will take.

Adolescents are no different from the rest of us. They resist mandates issued from on high, and most of them won't be forced into good habits. But they are willing to talk about moral choices, and they can decide that some courses of action are better than others. In fact, they are eager to formulate opinions on these matters, as long as they are trusted to take their time and examine their assumptions as carefully as they can. They can do this in school, by considering examples—some literary, some historical, some scientific—that are interesting and nuanced and in which a human must choose between possible actions. When they work it all through in a variety of assignments, they learn much about literature and history and about the human condition and the multiple ways in which it might develop. All of this considering is what helps the teenager to deepen his or her understanding of values and thus to construct a personal moral code. This last and most private step in the process is the most important one. Finally, the test of a good school is how its students behave when no one is looking, how they are in the mall as well as in the school's classrooms and corridors.

Most teachers are fond of the word "engagement," because it means that the students are really taking an interest in the work that the teacher has designed for them. Grappling, however, goes one step further. It presumes that the student has something to add to the story. Either hypothetically or actually, the student is asked to offer his or her input.

The input may be in the form of added information. High school students who are analyzing the racial and ethnic disagreements in their city may be asked to research immigration patterns, previous political relationships, or a number of other factors in order to get a clearer picture of what is in the minds of those who are involved in contemporary problems. The resultant information can be scrutinized carefully by their classmates, by their teacher, and by outside groups, both for the way it was gathered and for what it means. If it was gathered in the traditional ways of research, it can reinforce habits that are basically good ones: honesty, freedom from bias, the use of orderly procedures, and so forth. If it was gathered in unconventional ways, such as through chats with one's highly prejudiced uncle, those ways can be analyzed and even justified, at least on certain grounds. Once gathered, the research can be presented in graphs and photographs, essays and statistics, with much discussion of the way each format contributes to an overall understanding of the situation.

The students' input may also be in the form of opinion. Most high school students spend a lot of time considering such matters as pushing and shoving or even more violent activities and whether they are dangerous or are an inevitable part of life. They think about deterrence: when and how much a threatened punishment keeps them from doing something. They think about authority and about what its best and worst uses ought to be. They think about ethnicity and about how much it influences a person's overall approach to things. They question the religion that has been important to their family, the grandmother who believes that they ought to write thank-you notes, and the teacher who takes offense at sloppy work. They are at an unsettled time in their lives, while the many different thoughts they are having start to form themselves into opinions that they may keep all their lives.

We should be grateful for their confusion: it is part of life to think for oneself, and nature needs that little blip between generations. We can learn to live with and even harness (though that may be a "bad word" and suggest a "restrictive" concept) the energy of teenagers. The thoughts that are roiling around in the students' heads should be invited out and put to work. They should be applied to schoolwork, the better to develop and grow in the sunlight, the better to be made subject to others' questions.

Schoolwork is about violence and deterrence and authority and tradition and behavior. We should invite the students' input into the subject of whether the Civil War could have been avoided, of whether the southern states' desire to secede from the Union was legitimate self-determination or a dangerous threat to the very concept of democracy. School yard tensions and even family regroupings are not precisely analogous to the Civil War, of course. But the students' opinions will be refined and strengthened not by avoiding such analogies but by pressing to make them more accurate and appropriate. Insisting that the students tackle important and demonstrably relevant ideas, such as the meaning of justice, can be a tonic. It is one very important reason to be in school. And the students want more of it.

Text-based discussions are also amenable to grappling. For all sorts of reasons, many contemporary high school students read Harper Lee's *To Kill a Mockingbird,* a story of race, guilt, innocence, and courage set in the American South of the 1930s. The story shows the importance of evidence and argument. It portrays raw courage and the toughness of honesty. It is the sort of tale that usually provokes moral outrage and with that outrage the attention and engagement of high school students.

The litany of good questions that can arise is endless. To ponder them is to wrestle with specific and carefully described ideas that are freighted with values. Teachers can catch the heat that arises from the careful discussion of issues such as those raised by *To Kill a Mockingbird* and use it to deepen the talk, to broaden the questions, and to demand that the students use the text to support their arguments. Circling back over familiar ground, asking new sorts of questions about that ground, and looking for every scrap of data are necessary steps in building the habit of thoughtful grappling. A student who grapples is made aware of this complexity. And if there is an explicit assumption on the part of the school and its teachers that this sort of grappling is as worthy as it is complex, the student may get into the habit of the struggle.

When the students stick to a text such as *To Kill a Mockingbird* long enough to understand the abstractions in it, they are likely to apply that understanding to the next text they encounter. The exercise can thus lead a class into many places, with the depth of study growing as the interest deepens. Careful grappling is its own reward; it leads to further grappling.

Fiction is particularly useful in this kind of discussion because it gets the students outside of themselves. It provides a new and unfamiliar setting to play out enduring issues and thus avoids the pressures of the immediate. The sense of suspense in the narrative draws in even those students who do not feel comfortable in moral discussions. History itself is stories, and the line between fiction and fact is a necessarily fuzzy one when it comes to the consideration of moral dilemmas. Questions about who writes history and why, about the role of ideas and of personality in communities, and about the varied and changing nature of government are also subject to debate. In science, there are many prominent moral questions in need of discussion, both on the basis of scientific evidence and on the basis of belief. One of the most important technological questions in our time is clearly "Just because we can do something, should we?" This is a particularly pressing question for adolescents. John F. Kennedy thought the answer was yes when it came to exploring space. The issues of developing and testing nuclear weapons, cloning animals and humans, and reaching children through the Internet, however, may lead to different answers.

One difference between grappling and other forms of learning is that, when the questions become the student's own, so do the answers. When simple curiosity about the birds visiting a winter feeder leads to questions about territory, sharing, cruelty, and the relationship between animals and humans, the process becomes a reality check.

What is the evidence that some birds mate for life? That they return to the same feeder? How does this finding connect with other characteristics of birds? Is it real? Does it matter? If it matters, how am I affected? And finally and most important, How should I respond or behave? Should "last year's birds" have precedence over newcomers? Who am I to decide such things?

As adults, we must really be interested in what the students' "answers" are. If they are shallow, if they are biased, the teacher needs to help students develop them further but not necessarily replace them neatly with the teacher's own conclusions. The students may sense the teacher's personal views and be greatly influenced by them. However, they will also see that issues of weight are complex and that there are interpretations about which thoughtful, decent people can differ.

Few issues of value can be persuasively reduced to sharply painted absolutes. Even the dictum "Thou shalt not kill," for example, is a conflicted matter for those in the armed services or those in the part of the criminal justice system charged with carrying out legal executions. Depending on one's definition of when life begins, the issue of killing may arise in connection with abortion. There are few easy answers to central moral concerns. This is why young people must be given practice in grappling with them in as informed and principled a manner as possible.

In addition to providing additional information and offering informed opinion, a third kind of input that students can provide is their skills. Why should the local malls be the only agencies that know how to appreciate responsible teenagers? Besides the ability to do research, students have mathematical, artistic, writing, and speaking skills that can be valued in a complex world. Many high schools now have peer mediation programs, and students are learning much about identifying one another's needs and interests and finding common ground. These skills can be applied to a wider arena: at first in hypothetical role plays and under close supervision, but later with a somewhat more autonomous structure and in real situations, such as student-run businesses that raise money for the poor.

Unfortunately, the sort of grappling described here is all too rare in U.S. high schools. Few teachers have been offered the incentives or provided the support necessary to gain a deep grasp of their subjects. But a good deal of knowledge and authority on the teacher's part are usually required to teach in the interrogatory manner necessary to provoke the students to grapple. The larger the question, the more likely that the students will grow frustrated, at least at first. Only a confident coach can help his or her students move through that frustration to a greater clarity. It is much easier to give a lecture on the three causes of the French Revolution than to question the nature of revolution itself. The conventional metaphor for education is one of delivery, not of constructive, generative provocation. To teach grappling, teachers have to model it, which is difficult to do in a typical high school.

There are other factors as well. Given the sweeping nature of high school curricula—a bit of this and much of that, Cleopatra to Clinton, the history of China in two weeks, all branches of biology in a year—few schools are able to allow the time necessary for students to grapple. As long as the end result of high school is measured in "coverage" and as long as "coverage" is assessed by measuring the student's memory, there will be no time for students' own questions. Inquisitiveness, skepticism, and imagination are rarely priorities for state "curriculum frameworks" or, in all too many cases, for standardized tests. Indeed, the spiraling of ideas, the testing and retesting and testing again of hypotheses, the unpredictability of any one class, the messiness of this kind of inquiry will put the bravest and most effective teachers' students at a certain kind of short-term risk.

Another factor concerns deportment. High schools are such crowded places that certain norms seem only sensible. One is that people should listen to one another talk, which requires that only one person talk at a time. Most often, that person is the teacher, toward whom most students give the greatest respect. In many classrooms, the teacher has to shut a student up in order to open him up—that is, in order to give him the time to digest what is being said by the teacher or by other students.

In a classroom that puts a premium on developing ideas, everybody's hand would be up. No matter how pleased a teacher might be by this level of engagement, by the time it was any one student's turn to speak, any sense of coherence would be lost. Loosening up this structure by working in groups or by tolerating a certain amount of chaos would upset a lot of people. Some would be those students inside the classroom who need a degree of order and predictability to learn or who get intimidated by their classmates' ideas or even by their confidence. Other upset people might well be the folks who walk the school's halls. From such a distance, it is hard to tell the difference between excitement and cheekiness. Sometimes, it's the teacher whose initial convictions about the best kind of learning have been shaken or have put him on the line. He might be "grappling" with finding a new job by next spring.

And finally, many schools are afraid of the political ramifications of any sort of teaching that brings to the surface matters of value, matters that are often controversial and thus threatening. What if Susanna refuses to go to church on Sunday because she's offended by what she learned about abuses in the medieval church? What if Carlos can't sleep because he's upset about a predicted rise in the sun's temperature? What if Derek starts lecturing his parents about their smoking? If students take their education into their own hearts and begin to act according to their new discoveries, the dislocations in their own and their families' lives may well be difficult. The students will inevitably make some mistakes, and the school will be a convenient scapegoat.

Grappling with the tough issues is hard work. No matter how smart they sound, most students are new to the game of dealing with controversy. Recently, we observed a class that was learning about the Bill of Rights by discussing a case that involved downloading pornography, how much privacy a student should expect in school, who should decide what reasonable proof is, who has responsibility for the safety of students, and a host of other issues. One couldn't help but be struck not just by the students' commitment to the discussion but also by their skill at handling complex concepts, at looking at the background of the case, at imagining outcomes had the case been handled differently. One young man had an opinion on nearly every aspect; he was very well spoken and seemed confident and persuasive. Definitely a lawyer and a good one in the making, we thought. At the end of the class, though, he jumped up and, with a big smile, announced, "But what do we know? We're only children."

This young man wasn't undercutting the sophistication that he'd demonstrated so convincingly earlier. Indeed, he was adding to it by admitting that he had more that he needed to think about, more that he needed to learn. His perspective about his own place in life made it seem even more important to let him begin such discussions in school.

Few people in high schools believe that all young people are both capable of this level of work and ready to do it. Thus a self-fulfilling prophecy of lack of interest is at work. In matters such as the recent controversy over a national history curriculum, for example, adults with one perspective argued with adults with another perspective. The questions they argued over are important and enduring ones, such as how the experiences of Native Americans or African slaves or European immigrants should be presented. Much energy was being expended, and all these adults were honorable people trying to portray a complicated legacy in as fair and compelling a way as possible. They were mindful of the students they were teaching, in that they agreed that younger students should have a simpler and more complacent version of history than older ones. Teachers, too, try to design their lessons so carefully and to teach them so skillfully that there won't be any chance that they will misinform, or unnecessarily hurt, their students.

What these concerned adults leave out, however, is the dimension that each learner has to add to the material in order really to carry it in his or her head. There has to be a shred of interest present already on which the talented teacher can build. If the interest is based on a shared racial identity, a shared economic identity, or a shared psychological identity (such as seventh-graders often feel with the rebellious American colonists struggling to get out from under a "mother country"), so be it. Building on these existing interests seems more important than presenting each unit in the recommended number of days.

When the external tests are administered, however, the honest grappling that the teacher has encouraged may end up harming her students. Other teachers may have prepared their students better for the tests by sticking to the prescribed curriculum, which "covered" immigration and railroad regulation in the same number of days. However, by emphasizing accuracy, by which they mean the ability to sort through semi-right clues to get to the all-right answer on a machine-graded test to the exclusion of all other aspects of the material, those teachers (and the principals and parents who are flogging them to get the test scores up) are neglecting an important part of the process.

The material that stays in a student's head only until the test will never make it into his or her outlook. When it is in a student's outlook—when he thinks, for example, of the losses and gains that immigration brought to those who engaged in it, or when she compares the immigration experience with a recent move that her family made—it gains moral importance.

When a student has gotten his juices up in some way, he will think about such material outside of school, argue about it at the dinner table, take a book about it out of the library, choose the topic for his next paper. Accuracy will start to matter, but only if it follows engagement, only if the student has put himself on the line. Only then will he care if he gets his dates right or if he finds himself changing his interpretation of something. He has started to grapple with a question of importance to him, and it may well emerge into a lifelong interest and a lifelong habit.

Few schools place a high value on questioning, even though it is the habit that is most likely to lead to consequential scholarship and responsible adulthood. Schools are such crowded places: crowded not only with restless bodies but with parents' dreams for their children. No wonder so much emphasis is put on order. But order discourages questioning. Surrounded by the disorderliness of too many children, most teachers find themselves waiting for 3 p.m., waiting for Friday, and waiting for vacation all with a longing bordering on obsession, which makes them think in short-run rather than in long-run terms. In such a context, questions look messy and even rude. Besides, the students' own questions will take a lot more time to answer than the teachers' questions will, because the answers to most teachers' questions can be found on page 554 of the textbook. Better, most school systems seem to say, to present a watery diet of philosophical or psychological absolutes as a way to avoid conflict while appearing to attend to students' education in matters of value.

But more and more schoolpeople see things differently. They recognize that for humans the moral is embedded in the intellectual, that thinking hard by grappling in an informed and careful way is the most likely route to a principled and constructive life. The good person has both passion and restraint, respect for evidence and patience when evidence is not readily at hand.

These matters can be deeply embedded in the full academic curriculum. "Moral" or "character" education is neither a discrete curriculum added as an afterthought nor an unreflective activity, such as "community service," that has never been probed for its meaning. Truly moral education is an intellectual undertaking that must infuse the entire school. And it must be led by adults who know things, who themselves are regular grapplers with all the work and messiness and confusion that rich content entails.

DISCUSSION QUESTIONS

1. How does a teacher's concerns about moral or character education influence his or her instruction?
2. Why is grappling an important part of learning?
3. Is confusion a valuable or unavoidable step in the learning process?
4. What can adults do to provide a learning environment that challenges students to grapple?
5. Why is it important for moral education to infuse an entire school?

15

Critical Thinking—What Can It Be?

MATTHEW LIPMAN

FOCUSING QUESTIONS

1. What are the characteristics of critical thinking?
2. In what ways does critical thinking differ from ordinary thinking?
3. How does critical thinking assist students in becoming self-regulated learners?
4. What kind of curriculum needs to be implemented to encourage the development of critical thinking students?
5. How does the critical thinking model differ from (a) explicit instruction, (b) a generative model of teaching, (c) cooperative learning methods, and (d) a mastery model of learning?

If we are to foster and strengthen critical thinking in schools and colleges, we need a clear conception of what it is and what it can be. We need to know its defining features, its characteristic outcomes, and the underlying conditions that make it possible.

THE OUTCOMES OF CRITICAL THINKING ARE JUDGMENTS

Let's begin with outcomes. If we consult current definitions of critical thinking, we cannot help being struck by the fact that the authors stress the *outcomes* of such thinking but generally fail to note its essential characteristics. What is more, they specify outcomes that are limited to *solutions* and *decisions*. Thus, one writer defines critical thinking as "the mental processes, strategies, and representations people use to solve problems, make decisions, and learn new concepts."[1] Another conceives of critical thinking as "reasonable reflective thinking that is focused on deciding what to believe and do."[2]

These definitions provide insufficient enlightenment because the outcomes (solutions, deci-

sions, concept acquisition) are too narrow, and the defining characteristics (reasonable, reflective) are too vague. For example, if critical thinking is *thinking that results in decisions,* then selecting a doctor by picking a name at random out of a phone book would count as critical thinking. *We must broaden the outcomes, identify the defining characteristics, and then show the connection between them.*

Our contemporary conception of education as inquiry combines two aims—the transmission of knowledge and the cultivation of wisdom. But what is wisdom? Consulting a few dictionaries will yield such phrases as "intelligent judgment," "excellent judgment," or "judgment tempered by experience." But what is judgment?[3] Here again, recourse to dictionaries suggests that judgment is "the forming of opinions, estimates, or conclusions." It therefore includes such things as solving problems, making decisions, and learning new concepts; but it is more inclusive and more general.

The line of inquiry we are taking shows wisdom to be the characteristic outcome of good judgment and good judgment to be the characteristic of critical thinking. Perhaps the point where we are now, where we want to know how ordinary judgment and good judgment differ, is a good place to consider some illustrations.

Wherever knowledge and experience are not merely possessed but *applied to practice,* we see clear instances of judgment. Architects, lawyers, and doctors are professionals whose work constantly involves the making of judgments. It is true of any of us when we are in moral situations: we have to make moral judgments. It is true of teachers and farmers and theoretical physicists as well: all must make judgments in the practice of their occupations and in the conduct of their lives. There are practical, productive, and theoretical judgments, as Aristotle would have put it. Insofar as we make such judgments well, we can be said to behave wisely.

It should be kept in mind that good professionals make good judgments about their own practice as well as about the subject matter of their practice. A good doctor not only makes good diagnoses of patients and prescribes well for them, but also makes good judgments about the field of medicine and his or her ability to practice it. Good judgment takes everything into account, including itself.

A judgment, then, is a determination—of thinking, of speech, of action, or of creation. A gesture, such as the wave of a hand, can be a judgment; a metaphor, like "John is a worm," is a judgment; an equation, like $E = mc^2$, is a judgment. They are judgments because, in part, they have been reached in certain ways, relying on certain instruments or procedures in the process. They are likely to be *good* judgments if they are the products of *skillfully* performed acts guided by or facilitated by appropriate instruments and procedures. If we now look at the process of critical thinking and identify its essential characteristics, we can better understand its relationship to judgment. I will argue that critical thinking is *skillful, responsible thinking that facilitates good judgment because it (1) relies upon criteria,*[4] *(2) is self-correcting, and (3) is sensitive to context.*

CRITICAL THINKING RELIES ON CRITERIA

We suspect an association between the terms *critical* and *criteria* because they have a common ancestry. We are also aware of a relationship between criteria and judgments, for the very meaning of *criterion* is "a rule or principle utilized in the making of judgments." A criterion is an instrument for judging as an ax is an instrument for chopping. It seems reasonable to conclude, therefore, that there is some sort of logical connection between "critical thinking" and "criteria" and "judgment." The connection, of course, is to be found in the fact that judgment is a skill, critical thinking is skillful thinking, and skills cannot be defined without criteria by means of which allegedly skillful performances can be evaluated. So critical thinking is thinking that both employs criteria and can be assessed by appeal to criteria.

The fact that critical thinking relies upon criteria suggests that it is well-founded, structured, and reinforced thinking, as opposed to "uncritical" thinking, which is amorphous, haphazard, and unstructured. Critical thinking seems to be defensible and convincing. How does this happen?

Whenever we make a claim or utter an opinion, we are vulnerable unless we can back it up with *reasons.* What is the connection between reasons and criteria? Criteria *are* reasons: they are one kind of reason, but it is a particularly *reliable* kind. When we have to sort things out descriptively or evaluationally—and these are two very important tasks—we have to use the most reliable reasons we can find, and these are classificatory and evaluational criteria. Criteria may or may not have a high level of acceptance and respect in the community of inquiry. The competent use of such respected criteria is a way of establishing the objectivity of our prescriptive, descriptive, and evaluative judgments. Thus, architects will judge a building by employing such criteria as *utility, safety,* and *beauty;* and presumably, critical thinkers rely upon such time-tested criteria as *validity, evidential warrant,* and *consistency.* Any area of practice—architectural, cognitive, and the like—should be able to cite the criteria by which that practice is guided.

The intellectual domiciles we inhabit are often of flimsy construction; we can strengthen them by learning to reason more logically. But this will help little if their foundations are soft and spongy. We need to rest our claims and opinions—all of our thinking—upon footings as firm as bedrock. One way of putting our thinking upon a solid foundation is to rely upon sound criteria.

Here then is a brief list of the sorts of things we invoke or appeal to and that therefore represent specific kinds of criteria:

- standards;
- laws, by-laws, rules, regulations;
- precepts, requirements, specifications;
- conventions, norms, regularities;
- principles, assumptions, presuppositions, definitions;
- ideals, goals, objectives;
- tests, credentials, experimental findings;
- methods, procedures, policies.

All of these instruments are part of the apparatus of rationality. Isolated in categories in a taxonomy, as they are here, they appear inert and sterile. But when they are at work in the process of inquiry, they function dynamically—and critically.

As noted, by means of logic we can validly extend our thinking; by means of reasons such as criteria we can justify and defend it. The improvement of student thinking—from ordinary thinking to good thinking—depends heavily upon students' ability to identify and cite good reasons for their opinions (see Figure 15.1). Students can be brought to realize that, for a reason to be called good, it must be *relevant* to the opinion in question and *stronger* (in the sense of being more readily accepted, or assumed to be the case) than the opinion in question.

Critical thinking is a sort of *cognitive accountability.*[5] When we openly state the criteria we employ—for example, in assigning grades to students—we encourage students to do likewise. By demonstrating models of *intellectual responsibility,* we invite students to assume responsibility for their own thinking and, in a larger sense, for their own education.

When we have to select among criteria, we must of course rely on other criteria to do so. Some criteria serve this purpose better than others and can therefore be said to operate as *meta-criteria.* For example, when I pointed out earlier that criteria are especially reliable reasons and that good reasons are those that reveal strength and relevance, I was saying that *reliability, strength,* and *relevance* are important meta-criteria. *Coherence* and *consistency* are others.

Some criteria have a high level of generality and are often presupposed, explicitly or implicitly, whenever critical thinking takes place. Thus the notion of knowledge presupposes the criterion of *truth,* and so wherever scientific knowledge is claimed, the concomitant claim being made is that it is true. In this sense, philosophical domains such as epistemology, ethics, and aesthetics do not dictate the criteria relevant to them; rather, the criteria define the domains. Epistemology consists of judgments to which truth and falsity are the relevant criteria; ethics comprises judgments to which right and wrong are relevant; and aesthetics contains judgments to which beautiful and not-beautiful are relevant. *Truth, right, wrong, just, good, beautiful*—all of these are of such vast

Ordinary Thinking	Critical Thinking/Reasoning
Guessing	Estimating
Preferring	Evaluating
Grouping	Classifying
Believing	Assuming
Inferring	Inferring logically
Associating concepts	Grasping principles
Noting relationships	Noting relationships among other relationships
Supposing	Hypothesizing
Offering opinions without reasons	Offering opinions with reasons
Making judgments without criteria	Making judgments with criteria

FIGURE 15.1   Comparing Ordinary Thinking to Good Thinking

scope that we should probably consider them *mega-criteria*. And they in turn are instances of the great galactic criterion of *meaning*.

One of the primary functions of criteria is to provide a basis for comparisons. When a comparison is made and no basis or criterion is given (for example, "Tokyo is better than New York"), confusion results. On the other hand, if several competing criteria might be applicable (as when someone says "Tokyo is larger than New York" but does not specify whether in size or in population), the situation can be equally confusing. Just as opinions should generally be backed up with reasons, comparisons should generally be accompanied by criteria.

Sometimes criteria are introduced "informally" and extemporaneously, as when someone remarks that Tuesday's weather was good compared with Monday's, while Wednesday's weather was bad compared with Monday's. In this case, Monday's weather is being used as an informal criterion. Even figurative language can be understood as involving the use of informal criteria. Thus, an open simile such as "The school was like an army camp" suggests the regimentation of an army camp as an informal criterion against which to measure the orderliness of the school.

On the other hand, when criteria are considered by an authority or by general consent to be a basis of comparison, we might speak of them as "formal" criteria. When we compare the quantities of liquid in two tanks in terms of gallons, we are employing the unit of the gallon on the say-so of the Bureau of Weights and Measures. The gallon measure at the Bureau is the institutionalized paradigm case to which our gallon measure is comparable.

So things are compared by means of more or less formal criteria. But there is also the distinction between comparing things with one another and comparing them with an ideal standard, a distinction Plato addresses in *The Statesman*.[6] For example, in grading test papers, we may compare a student's performance with the performances of other students in the class (using "the curve" as a criterion); or we may compare it with the standard of an error-free performance.[7]

Standards and *criteria* are terms often used interchangeably in ordinary discourse. Standards, however, represent a vast subclass of criteria. It is vast because the concept of *standard* can be understood in many different ways. There is the interpretation cited in the preceding paragraph, where we are talking about a standard of perfection. There are, in contrast, standards as *minimal* levels of performance, as in the oft-heard cry "We must not lower our standards!" There is a sense in which standards are conventions of conduct: "When in Rome, do as the Romans do." There is also the sense in which standards are the units of measurement defined authoritatively by a bureau of standards.

There is, of course, a certain arbitrariness about even the most reliable standards, such as units of measurement, in that we are free to define them as we like. We could, if we liked, define a yard as containing fewer inches than it presently does. But the fact is that, once defined, we prefer such units to be unchanging: they are so much more reliable that way.

Perhaps we can sum up the relationship between criteria and standards by saying that criteria specify general requirements, while standards represent the degree to which these requirements need be satisfied in particular instances. Criteria—and particularly standards among them—are among the most valuable instruments of rational procedure. Teaching students to use them is essential to the teaching of critical thinking (see Figure 15.2).

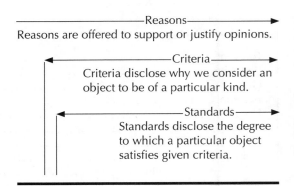

Reasons are offered to support or justify opinions.

Criteria disclose why we consider an object to be of a particular kind.

Standards disclose the degree to which a particular object satisfies given criteria.

FIGURE 15.2 Relationship of Standards to Criteria to Reasons

CRITICAL THINKING IS SELF-CORRECTING

The most characteristic feature of inquiry is that it aims to discover its own weaknesses and rectify what is at fault in its own procedures. Inquiry, then, is *self-correcting.*[8]

Much of our thinking unrolls impressionistically, from association to association, with little concern for either truth or validity, and with even less concern for the possibility that it might be erroneous. Among the many things we may reflect upon is our own thinking, yet we can do so in a way that is still quite uncritical. And so, "metacognition," or thinking about thinking, need not be equivalent to critical thinking.

One of the most important advantages of converting the classroom into a community of inquiry (in addition to the improvement of moral climate) is that the members of the community not only become conscious of their own thinking but begin looking for and correcting each other's methods and procedures. Consequently, insofar as each participant can internalize the methodology of the community as a whole, each participant is able to become self-correcting in his or her own thinking.

CRITICAL THINKING IS SENSITIVE TO CONTEXT

Just as critical thinking is sensitive to uniformities and regularities that are genetic and intercontextual, it is sensitive to situational characteristics that are holistic or context-specific. Thinking that is sensitive to context takes into account

(a) *exceptional or irregular circumstances and conditions*—for example, a line of investigation ordinarily considered *ad hominem* and therefore fallacious might be found permissible in a trial;

(b) *special limitations, contingencies, or constraints*—for example, the rejection of certain Euclidean theorems, such as that parallel lines never meet, in non-Euclidean geometries;

(c) *overall configurations*—for instance, a remark taken out of context may seem to be flagrantly in error but in the light of the discourse taken as a whole appears valid and proper, or vice versa;

(d) *the possibility that evidence is atypical*—for example, a case of overgeneralizing about national voter preferences based on a tiny regional sample of ethnically and occupationally homogeneous individuals;

(e) *the possibility that some meanings do not translate from one context or domain to another*—there are terms and expressions for which there are no precise equivalents in other languages and whose meanings are therefore wholly context-specific.

With regard to *thinking with criteria* and *sensitivity to context,* a suitable illustration might be an exercise involving the application of a particular criterion to a set of fictional situations. Suppose the criterion in question is *fairness* (which is itself a way of construing the still broader criterion of justice). One form that fairness assumes is *taking turns.* Figure 15.3 is an exercise taken from *Wondering at the World,*[9] the instructional manual accompanying *Kio and Gus,*[10] a Philosophy for Children program for children 9 to 10 years of age.

In performing this exercise, students apply the criterion of *turn-taking* (i.e., *fair play* or *justice*) to six situations requiring sensitivity to context. Classroom discussion should distinguish between those situations in which the procedure of turn-taking is appropriate and those in which it is dubious. Using exercises like these in a community of inquiry sets the stage for critical thinking in the classroom. It is not the only way to accomplish this, but it is one way.

THE PROMISE OF INTELLECTUAL EMPOWERMENT

What, then, is the relevance of critical thinking to the enhancement of elementary school, secondary school, and college education? Part of the answer lies in the gradual shift that is occurring in the focus of education—the shift from *learning* to *thinking.* We want students to think for themselves and not merely to learn what other people have thought.

But another part of the answer lies in the fact that we want students who can do more than merely think: it is equally important that they ex-

Taking Turns

To the teacher: There are times when people engage in sharing. For example, they go to a movie and share the pleasure of looking at the movie together. Or they can share a piece of cake by each taking half.

In other cases, however, simultaneous sharing is not so easily accomplished. If two people ride a horse, someone has to ride in front. They can take turns riding in front, but they can't both ride in front at the same time. Children understand this very well. They recognize that certain procedures must be followed in certain ways.

For example, ask your students to discuss the number of ways they "take turns" in the classroom during the ordinary day. They take turns washing the blackboard, going to the bathroom, going to the cloakroom, and passing out the papers. On the playground, they take turns at bat, they take turns lining up for basketball, and they take turns at the high bar.

Ask your students what they think the connection is between "taking turns" and "being fair." The resulting discussion should throw light on the fact that sometimes being fair involves the way children are to be treated simultaneously, while at other times it involves the way they are to be treated sequentially. For example, if it is one child's birthday and there is going to be a party with cupcakes, there should be at least one cupcake for every child. This is being fair simultaneously. Later, if you want to play "Pin the Tail on the Donkey," children should sequentially take turns in order to be fair. (The prospect of everyone *simultaneously* being blindfolded and searching about with a pin boggles the mind.)

Exercise: When is it appropriate to take turns?

	Appropriate	Not Appropriate	?
1. Pam: "Louise, let's take turns riding your bike. I'll ride it Mondays, Wednesdays, and Fridays, and you ride it Tuesdays, Thursdays, and Saturdays."	☐	☐	☐
2. Gary: "Burt, let's take turns taking Louise to the movies. I'll take her the first and third Saturday of every month, and you take her the second and fourth Saturday."	☐	☐	☐
3. Jack: "Louise, let's take turns doing the dishes. You wash and I'll dry."	☐	☐	☐
4. Chris: "Okay, Louise, let's take turns with the TV. You choose a half-hour program, then I'll choose one."	☐	☐	☐
5. Melissa: "Louise, what do you say we take turns doing our homework? Tonight I'll do yours and mine, and tomorrow you can do mine and yours."	☐	☐	☐
6. Hank: "Louise, I hate to see you struggle to school each day, carrying those heavy books! Let me carry yours and mine today, and you can carry yours and mine tomorrow."	☐	☐	☐

FIGURE 15.3 "Taking Turns" Exercise.

Reprinted from Matthew Lipman and Ann Margaret Sharp, *Wondering at the World* (Lanham, MD: University Press of America and IAPC, co-publishers, 1986).

ercise good judgment. It is good judgment that characterizes the sound interpretation of written text; the well-balanced, coherent composition; the lucid comprehension of what one hears; and the persuasive argument. It is good judgment that enables one to weigh and grasp what a statement or passage states, assumes, implies, or suggests. And this good judgment cannot be operative unless it rests upon proficient reasoning skills that can ensure competency in inference, as well as upon proficient inquiry, concept formation, and translation skills. Students who are *not* taught to use criteria in a way that is both sensitive to context and self-corrective are *not* being taught to think critically. If teaching critical thinking can improve education, it will be because it increases the quantity and quality of meaning that students derive from what they read and perceive and that they express in what they write and say.

CONCLUSION

Last, a word about the employment of criteria in critical thinking that facilitates good judgment. Critical thinking, as we know, is skillful thinking, and skills are proficient performances that satisfy relevant criteria. When we think critically, we are required to orchestrate a vast variety of cognitive skills, grouped in families such as reasoning skills, concept-formation skills, inquiry skills, and translation skills. Without these skills, we would be unable to draw meaning from written text or from conversation, nor could we impart meaning to a conversation or to what we write.

We all know that an otherwise splendid musical performance can be ruined if so much as a single instrumentalist performs below acceptable standards. Likewise, the mobilization and perfection of the cognitive skills that make up critical thinking cannot omit any of these skills without jeopardizing the process as a whole. We cannot be content, then, to give students practice in a handful of cognitive skills while neglecting all the others necessary for the competency in inquiry, in language, and in thought that is the hallmark of proficient critical thinkers. Instead of selecting and polishing a few skills that we think will do

the trick, we must begin with the raw subject matter of communication and inquiry—with reading, listening, speaking, writing, and reasoning—and we must cultivate all the skills that the mastery in such processes entails. It is only when we do this that we realize that the philosophical disciplines alone provide both the skills and the criteria that are presently lacking in the curriculum.

ENDNOTES

1. Robert Sternberg, "Critical Thinking: Its Nature, Measurement, and Improvement" in *Essays on the Intellect*, ed. Frances R. Link (Alexandria, VA: Association for Supervision and Curriculum Development, 1985), p. 46.
2. Robert H. Ennis, "A Taxonomy of Critical Thinking Dispositions and Abilities" in *Teaching Thinking Skills: Theory and Practice*, ed. Joan Boykoff Baron and Robert J. Sternberg (New York: W. H. Freeman and Co., 1987), p. 10.
3. For a penetrating discussion of judgment, see Justus Buchler, *Toward a General Theory of Human Judgment* (New York: Columbia University Press, 1951).
4. Useful discussions of the nature of criteria are to be found in Michael Anthony Slote, "The Theory of Important Criteria," *The Journal of Philosophy* LXIII, 8 (April 1966): 221–224; Michael Scriven, "The Logic of Criteria," *The Journal of Philosophy* 56 (October 1959): 857–868; and Stanley Cavell, *The Claim of Reason* (Oxford: Clarendon Press, 1979), pp. 3–36.
5. I see no inconsistency between urging "cognitive accountability" and urging the development of intellectual autonomy among students. There are times when we cannot let other people do our thinking for us; we must think for ourselves. And we must learn to think for ourselves by thinking for ourselves; no one can instruct us in how to do it, although a community of inquiry makes it relatively easy. The point is that students must be encouraged to become reasonable for their own good (i.e., as a step toward their own autonomy) and not just for our good (i.e., because the growing rationalization of the society requires it).
6. The Stranger remarks to young Socrates, "We must posit two types and two standards of greatness and smallness. . . . The standard of relative comparison will remain, but we must acknowledge a second standard, which is a standard of comparison with the due measure." *Statesman* (283e) in *Plato: The Collected Dialogues*, ed.

Edith Hamilton and Huntington Cairns (Princeton, NJ: Princeton University Press, 1969), p. 1051.

7. For a contemporary interchange regarding comparison of things with one another vs. comparison of things with an ideal, see Gilbert Ryle, "Perceiving" in *Dilemmas* (London: Cambridge University Press, 1966), pp. 93–102; and D. W. Hamlyn, *The Theory of Knowledge* (New York: Macmillan, 1970), pp. 16–21.

8. Charles Peirce, "Ideals of Conduct" in *Collected Papers of Charles Sanders Peirce,* ed. Charles Hartshorne and Paul Weiss (Cambridge, MA: Harvard University Press, 1931–35) discusses the connection between self-correcting inquiry, self-criticism, and self-control.

9. Matthew Lipman and Ann Margaret Sharp, *Wondering at the World* (Lanham, MD: University Press of America and IAPC, co-publishers, 1986), pp. 226–299.

10. Matthew Lipman, *Kio and Gus* (Upper Montclair, NJ: IAPC, 1982).

DISCUSSION QUESTIONS

1. How does critical thinking promote intellectual responsibility?
2. How do standards, criteria, and reasons differ?
3. How is good judgment related to critical thinking?
4. How can critical thinking be promoted in classroom instruction?
5. What modifications would you make to specific subject area content such as the art, science, reading, math, social studies, or science curriculum to help students become critical thinkers?

16

Creating Creative Minds

ROBERT J. STERNBERG
TODD I. LUBART

FOCUSING QUESTIONS

1. How are intelligence and creativity related?
2. What is the relationship between knowledge and creativity?
3. How are intellectual styles related to creativity?
4. What are the advantages and disadvantages of giving students the responsibility for selecting problems they would like to solve?
5. What distinguishes creative thinking and ordinary thinking?
6. How can the use of ill-structured problems help students to think insightfully?
7. How do the norms of a school's environment influence the development of creativity?

Creativity is not simply inborn. On the contrary, schooling can create creative minds—though it often doesn't. To create creativity, we need to understand the resources on which it draws and to determine how we can help children develop these resources. In particular, we need to know how we can invest in our children's futures by helping them invest in their own creative endeavors.

We propose an "investment theory of creativity."[1] The basic notion underlying our theory is that, when making any kind of investment, including creative investment, people should "buy low and sell high." In other words, the greatest creative contributions can generally be made in areas or with ideas that at a given time are undervalued. Perhaps people in general have not yet realized the importance of certain ideas, and hence there is a potential for making significant advances. The more in favor an idea is, the less potential there is for it to appreciate in value, because the idea is already valued.

A theory of creativity needs to account for how people can generate or recognize underval-

ued ideas. It also needs to specify who will actually pursue these undervalued ideas rather than join the crowd and make contributions that, while of some value, are unlikely to turn around our existing ways of thinking. Such a theory will enable us and our children to invest in a creative future.[2] As is sometimes said, nothing is as practical as a good theory.

We hold that developing creativity in children—and in adults—involves teaching them to use six resources: intelligence, knowledge, intellectual style, personality, motivation, and environmental context. Consider each of these resources in turn.

INTELLIGENCE

Two main aspects of intelligence are relevant to creativity. These aspects, based on the triarchic theory of human intelligence, are the ability to define and redefine problems and the ability to think insightfully.[3]

Problem Definition and Redefinition

Major creative innovations often involve seeing an old problem in a new way. For example, Albert Einstein redefined the field of physics by proposing the theory of relativity; Jean Piaget redefined the field of cognitive development by conceiving of the child as a scientist; Pablo Picasso redefined the field of art through his cubist perspective on the world.

In order to *re*define a problem, a student has to have the option of defining a problem in the first place. Only rarely do schools give students this luxury. Tests typically pose the problems that students are to solve. And if a student's way of seeing a problem is different from that of the test constructor, the student is simply marked wrong. Similarly, teachers typically structure their classes so that they, not the students, set the problems to be solved. Of course, textbooks work the same way. Even when papers or projects are assigned, teachers often specify the topics. Some teachers, who view themselves as more flexible, allow students to define problems for themselves. These same teachers may then proceed to mark students down when students' definitions of problems do not correspond to their own.

In the "thinking-skills movement," we frequently hear of the need for schools to emphasize more heavily the teaching of problem-solving skills. Educators are then pleased when students do not merely memorize facts but rather use the facts to solve problems. Certainly, there is much to be said for a problem-solving approach to education. But we need to recognize that creative individuals are often most renowned not for solving problems, but for posing them. It is not so much that they have found the "right" answers (often there are none); rather, they have asked the right questions—they recognized significant and substantial problems and chose to address them. One only has to open almost any professional journal to find articles that are the fruit of good problem solving on bad—or at least fairly inconsequential—problems.

If we are to turn schooling around and emphasize creative definition and redefinition of problems, we need to give our students some of the control we teachers typically maintain. Students need to take more responsibility for the problems they choose to solve, and we need to take less. The students will make mistakes and attempt to solve inconsequential or even wrongly posed problems. But they learn from their mistakes, and if we do not give them the opportunity to make mistakes, they will have no mistakes to learn from. Instead of almost always giving children the problems, we more often need to let them find the problems that they are to solve. We need to help them develop their skills in defining and redefining problems, not just in solving them.

Insight Skills

Insight skills are involved when people perceive a high-quality solution to an ill-structured problem to which the solution is not obvious. Being truly creative involves "buying low"—that is, picking up on an idea that is out of favor. But just picking up on any idea that is out of favor is not sufficient. Insight is involved in spotting the *good* ideas. We have proposed a theory of insight whereby insights are of three kinds.[4]

The first kind of insight involves seeing things in a stream of inputs that most people would not see. In other words, in the midst of a stream of mostly irrelevant information, an individual is able to zero in on particularly relevant information for his or her purposes. For example, the insightful reader observes clues to an author's meaning that others may miss. An insightful writer is often one whose observations about human behavior, as revealed through writing, go beyond those of the rest of us.

The second kind of insight involves seeing how to combine disparate pieces of information whose connection is nonobvious and usually elusive. For example, proving mathematical theorems requires seeing how to fit together various axioms and theorems into a coherent proof. Interpreting data from a scientific experiment often involves making sense of seemingly disparate pieces of information.

The third kind of insight involves seeing the nonobvious relevance of old information to a new problem. Creative analogies and metaphors are representative of this kind of insight. For example, the student of history comes to see how understanding events of long ago can help us understand certain events in the present. A scientist might recall a problem from the past that was solved by using a certain methodology and apply this methodology to a current scientific problem.

Problems requiring insightful solution are almost always ill-structured; that is, there are no readily available paths to solution. Rather, much of the difficulty in solving the problem is figuring out what the steps toward solution might be. For example, when James Watson and Francis Crick sought to find the structure of DNA, the nature of the problem was clear. The way in which to solve it was not clear at all.

Problems presented in schools, however, are usually well structured; that is, there is a clear path—or several paths—to a prompt and expedient solution. In standardized tests, for example, there is always a path that guarantees a "correct" solution. The examinee's problem is, in large part, to find that guaranteed path. Similarly, textbook problems are often posed so that there can be an answer key for the teacher that gives the "correct" answers. Problems such as these are unlikely to require insightful thinking. One ends up trying to "psych out" the thought processes of the person who formulated the problem, rather than to generate one's own insightful thought processes.

While not exclusively limited to ill-structured problems, creative innovations tend to address such problems—not the well-structured ones that we typically use in school settings. If we want students to think insightfully, we need to give them opportunities to do so by increasing our use of ill-structured problems that allow insightful thinking. Project work is excellent in this regard, for it requires students not only to solve problems but also to structure the problems for themselves.

KNOWLEDGE

In order to make a creative contribution to a field of knowledge, one must, of course, have knowledge of that field. Without such knowledge, one risks rediscovering what is already known. Without knowledge of the field, it is also difficult for an individual to assess the problems in the field and to judge which are important. Indeed, during the past decade or so, an important emphasis in psychology has been on the importance of knowledge of expertise.

Schools can scarcely be faulted for making insufficient efforts to impart knowledge. Indeed, that seems to be their main function. Yet we have two reservations about the extent to which the knowledge they impart is likely to lead to creativity.

First, there is a difference between knowledge and usable knowledge. Knowledge can be learned in a way that renders it inert. Knowledge may be stored in the brain, but an individual may nonetheless be unable to use it. For example, almost every college undergraduate who majors in psychology takes a course in statistics as a part of that major. Yet very few undergraduates who have taken statistics are able to use what they have learned in the design and analysis of scientific experiments. (At the secondary level, many physics and chemistry students are unable to use basic algebra when they need to apply it.) Undergraduates in psychology do fine as long as they are given highly structured problems in which it is obvious which statistical technique applies. But they have trouble when they have to figure out which technique to apply and when to apply it. The context in which they acquired their knowledge is so different from the context in which they must use it that their knowledge is simply unavailable.

Our experience with knowledge learned in statistics courses is, we believe, the rule rather than the exception. Students do not generally learn knowledge in a way that renders it useful to them. To the contrary, they are likely to forget much of what they learn soon after they are tested on it. We have all had the experience of studying for an exam and then quickly forgetting what we studied. The information was learned in such a way as to make it useful in the context of a structured exam; once the exam is finished, so is that use of the knowledge.

Our second reservation about the knowledge that schools typically impart is that students are not taught in a way that makes clear to them why the information they are learning is important.

Students do much better in learning if they believe that they can use what they learn. Foreign language provides a good example. People who need to use a foreign language learn it. Those who don't need it rarely retain much of it. Unless we show students why what they are learning should matter to them, we cannot expect them to retain what they are taught. Unfortunately, we often don't really know ourselves how students might use what we are teaching them. And if we don't know, how can we expect them to?

We also need to be concerned about the trade-off that can develop between knowledge and flexibility. We have suggested that increased expertise in terms of knowledge in a given domain often comes at the expense of flexibility in that domain.[5] We can become so automatic about the way we do certain things that we lose sight of the possibility of other ways. We can become entrenched and have trouble going beyond our very comfortable perspective on things. Because creativity requires one to view things flexibly, there is a danger that, with increasing knowledge, one will lose creativity by losing the ability to think flexibly about the domain in which one works. We need to recognize that sometimes students see things that we do not see—that they may have insights we have not had (and that initially we may not even recognize as insights). Teachers who have been doing the same thing year after year can become so self-satisfied and happy with the way they do things that they are closed to new ways of doing these things. They are unwilling to "buy low"—to try an idea that is different from those they have favored in the past.

On the one hand, we do not wish to underemphasize the importance of knowledge to creativity. On the other hand, we cannot overemphasize the importance of usable knowledge that does not undermine flexibility. Often we need to adopt the maintenance of flexibility as a goal to be achieved self-consciously. We might go to in-service training sessions, read new kinds of books, learn about a new domain of knowledge, seek to learn from our students, or whatever. If we want students to be creative, we have to model creativity for them, and we won't be able to do that if we seek to turn students' minds into safe-deposit boxes in which to store our assorted and often undigested bits of knowledge.

INTELLECTUAL STYLES

Intellectual styles are the ways in which people choose to use or exploit their intelligence as well as their knowledge. Thus intellectual styles concern not abilities, but how these abilities and the knowledge acquired through them are used in day-to-day interactions with the environment.

Elsewhere one of the authors has presented details of a theory of intellectual styles based on a notion of "mental self-government."[6] Hence we need not cover the theory in detail here. The basic idea is that people need to govern themselves mentally and that styles provide them with ways to do so. The ways in which people govern themselves are internal mirrors of the kinds of government we see in the external world.

Creative people are likely to be those with a legislative proclivity. A legislative individual is someone who enjoys formulating problems and creating new systems of rules and new ways of seeing things. Such a person is in contrast to an individual with an executive style: someone who likes implementing the systems, rules, and tasks of others. Both differ from an individual with a judicial style: someone who enjoys evaluating people, things, and rules. Thus the creative person not only has the ability to see things in new ways but likes to do so. The creative person is also likely to have a global—not just a local—perspective on problems. Seeing the forest despite all the trees is the mark of creative endeavor.

PERSONALITY

Creative people seem to share certain personality attributes. Although one can probably be creative in the short term without these attributes, long-term creativity requires most of them. The attributes are tolerance of ambiguity, willingness to surmount obstacles and persevere, willingness to grow, willingness to take risks, and courage of one's convictions.

Tolerance for Ambiguity

In most creative endeavors, there is a period of time during which an individual is groping—trying to figure out what the pieces of the puzzle are, how to put them together, how to relate them to what is already known. During this period, an individual is likely to feel some anxiety—possibly even alarm—because the pieces are not forming themselves into a creative solution to the problem being confronted. Creative individuals need to be able to tolerate such ambiguity and to wait for the pieces to fall into place.

In many schools, most of the assignments students are given are due the next day or within a very short period of time. In such circumstances students cannot develop a tolerance for ambiguity because they cannot spare the time to allow a situation to be ambiguous. If an assignment is due in a day or two, ambiguities need to be resolved quickly. A good way to help students develop a tolerance for ambiguity is to give them more long-term assignments and encourage them to start thinking about the assignments early on so that they can mull over whatever problems they face. Moreover, students need to realize that a period of ambiguity is the rule, not the exception, in creative work and that they should welcome this period as a chance to hatch their ideas, rather than dread it as a time when their ideas are not fully formed.

Willingness to Surmount Obstacles and Persevere

Almost every major creative thinker has surmounted obstacles at one time or another, and the willingness not to be derailed is a crucial element of success. Confronting obstacles is almost a certainty in creative endeavor because most such endeavors threaten some kind of established and entrenched interest. Unless one can learn to face adversity and conquer it, one is unlikely to make a creative contribution to one's field.

We need to learn to think of obstacles and the need to surmount them as part of the game, rather than as outside it. We should not think of obstacles as something only we have, but as something that everyone has. What makes creative people special is not that they have obstacles but how they face them.

Schools can be fairly good proving grounds for learning to surmount obstacles because we face so many of them while we are in school (whether as students or as teachers). But students sometimes leave school with the feeling that society is more likely to get in the way of creativity than to support it. Sometimes they are right, of course. And ultimately, they may have to fight for their ideas, as creative people have done before them. However, training to overcome resistance to new ideas shouldn't be the main contribution of the schools to students' creativity.

Willingness to Grow

When a person has a creative idea and is able to have others accept it, that person may be highly rewarded for the idea. It then becomes difficult to move on to still other ideas. The rewards for staying with the first idea are often great, and it feels comfortable to stick with that idea. At the same time, the person who has had a creative idea often acquires a deep-seated fear that his or her next idea won't be as good as the first one. Indeed, the phenomenon of "statistical" regression toward the mean would suggest that subsequent ideas actually will not be as good—that they will regress toward the mean. This is the same phenomenon that operates when the "rookie of the year" in baseball doesn't play as well in his second year as in his first or when a restaurant that seems outstanding when we first eat there isn't quite as good the second time. In short, there is a fair amount of pressure to stay with what one has and knows. But creativity exhibited over prolonged periods of time requires one to move beyond that first creative idea and even to see problems with what at one time may have seemed a superb idea. While schools often encourage the growth of a student's knowledge, such growth will by no means lead automatically to creativity, in part because schools do not encourage students to take risks with their newly acquired knowledge and abilities.

Willingness to Take Risks

A general principle of investment is that, on the average, greater return entails greater risk. For the most part, schools are environments that are not conducive to risk taking. On the contrary, students are as often as not punished for taking risks.

Taking a course in a new area or in an area of weakness is likely to lead to a low grade, which in turn may dim a student's future prospects. Risking an unusual response on an exam or an idiosyncratic approach in a paper is a step likely to be taken only with great trepidation because of the fear that a low or failing grade on a specific assignment may ruin one's chances for a good grade in the course. Moreover, there is usually some safe response that is at least good enough to earn the grade for which one is aiming.

In addition, many teachers are not themselves risk-takers. Teaching is not a profession that is likely to attract the biggest risk-takers, and hence many teachers may feel threatened by students who take large risks, especially if the teacher perceives those risks to be at his or her expense. Unfortunately, students' unwillingness to take risks derives from their socialization in the schools, which are environments that encourage conformity to societal norms. The result is often stereotyped thinking.

Courage of One's Convictions and Belief in Oneself

There are times in the lives of almost all creative people when they begin to doubt their ideas—and themselves. Their work may not be achieving the recognition it once achieved, or they may not have succeeded in getting recognition in the first place. At these times, it is difficult to maintain a belief in one's ideas or in oneself. It is natural for people to go through peaks and valleys in their creative output, and there are times when creative people worry that their most recent good idea will end up being their final good idea. At such times, one needs to draw upon deep-seated personal resources and to believe in oneself, even when others do not.

Schools do teach some students to believe in themselves: namely, those who consistently receive high grades. But the skills one needs to earn high grades are often quite different from those one needs to be creative. Thus those who go out and set their own course may receive little encouragement, whereas those who play the game and get good grades may develop a confidence in

themselves that, though justified, is not necessarily related to their past or potential creative contributions. Those who most need to believe in themselves may be given every reason not to.

MOTIVATION

There is now good evidence to suggest that motivation plays an important part in creative endeavors. Two kinds of motivation are particularly important: intrinsic motivation and the motivation to excel. Both kinds of motivation lead to a focus on tasks rather than on the external rewards that performance of these tasks might generate.

Intrinsic Motivation

Teresa Amabile has conducted and reviewed a number of studies suggesting the importance of intrinsic motivation to creativity.[7] People are much more likely to respond creatively to a task that they enjoy doing for its own sake, rather than a task that they carry out exclusively or even primarily for such extrinsic motivators as grades. Indeed, research suggests that extrinsic rewards undermine intrinsic motivation.[8]

There is little doubt as to the way in which most schools motivate students today: namely, through grades. Grades are the ultimate criterion of one's success in school, and if one's grades are not good, love of one's work is unlikely to be viewed as much compensation. Therefore, many students chart a path in school that is just sufficient to get them an A. (If they put too much effort into a single course, they risk jeopardizing their performance in the other courses they are taking.) Students who once may have performed well for love of an intellectual challenge may come to perform well only to get their next A. Whatever intrinsic motivation children may have had at the start is likely to be drummed out of them by a system that rewards extrinsically, not intrinsically.

Motivation to Excel

Robert White identified as an important source of motivation a desire to achieve competence in one or more of a person's endeavors.[9] In order to be creative in a field, one generally will need to be motivated not only to be competent, but also to excel. The best "investors" are almost always those who put in the work necessary to realize their goals. Success does not just come to them—they work for it.

Schools vary in the extent to which they encourage students to excel. Some schools seem to want nothing more than for all their students to be at some average or "golden mean." Many schools, however, encourage excellence. Unfortunately, it is rare in our experience for the kind of excellence that is encouraged to be *creative* excellence. It may be excellence in grades, which generally does not require great creativity to attain; it may be excellence in sports or in extracurricular activities. There is nothing wrong with excellence of these kinds. Indeed, they are undoubtedly important in today's world. But seeking such excellences does not foster creativity—and may even interfere with it. When a student is simultaneously taking five or six courses, there is not much opportunity to spend the time or to expend the effort needed to be creative in any of them.

ENVIRONMENTAL CONTEXT

Creativity cannot be viewed outside an environmental context. What would be viewed as creative in one context might be viewed as trivial in another. The role of context is relevant to the creative enterprise in at least three different ways: in sparking creative ideas, in encouraging follow-up of these ideas, and in rewarding the ideas and their fruits.

Sparking Creative Ideas

Some environments provide the bases for lots of creative sparks, whereas other environments may provide the basis for none at all. Do schools provide environments for sparking creative ideas? Obviously, the answer to this question is necessarily subjective. Given the discussion above, we would have difficulty saying that they do. Schools provide environments that encourage learning about and dealing with existing concepts rather than inventing new ones. There is a lot of em-

phasis on memorization and some emphasis on analysis, but there is little emphasis on creative synthesis. Indeed, it is difficult for us to remember more than a handful of tests we ever took in school that encouraged creative thinking. On the contrary, the tests students typically take reward them for spitting back what they have learned—or, at best, analyzing it in a fairly noncreative way.

Encouraging Follow-up of Creative Ideas

Suppose a student has a genuinely creative idea and would like to pursue it within the school setting. Is there any vehicle for such follow-up? Occasionally, students will be allowed to pursue projects that encourage them to develop their creative thinking. But again, spending a great deal of time on such projects puts them at risk in their other courses and in their academic work. It is quite rare that any allowance is made whereby students can be excused from normal requirements in order to pursue a special interest of their own.

Evaluating and Rewarding Creative Ideas

Most teachers would adamantly maintain that, when grading papers, they reward creativity. But, if the experience of other teachers is similar to that of the teachers with whom we have worked, they don't find a great deal of creativity to reward. And we sometimes worry whether they would recognize creativity in student work were they to meet it. Please note that we do not except ourselves from this charge. We have failed more than once to see the value of a student's idea when we first encountered it, only to see that value later on—after the student had decided to pursue some other idea, partly at our urging. Teachers genuinely believe that they reward creativity. But the rewards are few and far between.

Look at any school report card, and assess the skills that the report card values. You will probably not find creativity anywhere on the list. One of us actually analyzed the report cards given to children in several elementary schools. A number of skills were assessed. However, not a single one of the report cards assessed creativity in any field whatsoever. The creative child might indeed be valued by the teacher, but it would not show up in the pattern of check marks on the report card.

TEACHING FOR CREATIVITY

How can we help develop students' creativity in the classroom? Consider an example. One of us had the opportunity to teach a class of 9- and 10-year-olds in a New York City school. The children ranged fairly widely in abilities and came from various socioeconomic backgrounds. The guest teacher was asked to demonstrate how to "teach for thinking" and decided to do so in the context of teaching about psychology. However, he wanted to impart not merely a set of decontextualized "facts" about the field, but rather the way psychologists think when they develop ideas for creative scientific theory and research.

He didn't tell the students what problem they were going to solve or even offer them suggestions. Rather, he asked each of them to share with the class some aspect of human behavior—their own, their parents', their friends'—that intrigued them and that they would like to understand better. In other words, the students were asked to *define problems* rather than have the teacher do it for them. At first, no one said anything. The children may never have been asked to formulate problems for themselves. But the teacher waited. And then he waited some more (so as not to teach them that, if only they said nothing, he would panic and start to answer his own questions).

Eventually, one student spoke up, and then another, and then another. The ice broken, the children couldn't wait to contribute. Rather than adopting the executive and largely passive style to which they were accustomed, they were adopting a *legislative style* whereby they enjoyed and actively participated in the opportunity to create new ideas. And create ideas they did. Why do parents make children dress up on special occasions? Why do parents sometimes have unreasonable expectations for their children? Why do some siblings fight a lot while others don't? How do we choose our friends?

Because these problems were the children's own problems and not the teacher's, the children were *intrinsically motivated* to seek answers. And

they came up with some very perceptive answers indeed. We discussed their ideas and considered criteria for deciding which potential experiment to pursue as a group. The criteria, like the ideas, were the students' own, not the teacher's. And the students considered such factors as *taking risks* in doing experiments, *surmounting obstacles to doing an experiment,* and so on.

The children entered the class with almost no formal knowledge about psychology. But they left it with at least a rudimentary *procedural knowledge* of how psychologists formulate research. The teacher didn't give them the knowledge; they created it for themselves, in an environment that *sparked* and then *rewarded* creative ideas. To be sure, not all of the ideas were creative or even particularly good. But the students were encouraged to give it their best shot, and that's what they did.

The class didn't have time in one 75-minute period to complete the full design of an experiment. However, it did have time to demonstrate that even children can do the kind of creative work that we often reserve until graduate school. We can teach for creativity at any level, in any field. And if we want to improve our children and our nation, this is exactly what we need to do.

Does teaching for creativity actually work? We believe that it does. Moreover, the effectiveness of such teaching has been demonstrated.[10] After five weeks of insight training involving insight problems in language arts, mathematics, science, and social studies, students in grades 4 through 6 displayed significant and substantial improvements (from a pretest to a posttest) over an untrained control group on insight skills and general intelligence. In addition, the training transferred to insight problems of kinds not covered in the course, and a year later, the gains were maintained. These children had improved their creative skills with only a relatively small investment of instructional time.

Those who invest are taught that most obvious of strategies: buy low and sell high. Yet few people manage to do so. They don't know when a given security is really low or when it is really high. We believe that those who work in the schools do not have much better success in fostering creativity. We often don't recognize creativity when we see it. And although most of us believe that we encourage it, our analysis suggests that schools are probably as likely to work against the development of creativity as in its favor. The conventional wisdom is likely correct: schools probably do at least as much to undermine creativity as to support it.

It is important to realize that our theory of creativity is a "confluence" theory: the elements of creativity work together interactively, not alone. The implication for schooling is that addressing just one—or even a few—of the resources we have discussed is not sufficient to induce creative thinking. For example, a school might teach "divergent thinking," encouraging students to see multiple solutions to problems. But children will not suddenly become creative in the absence of an environment that tolerates ambiguity, encourages risk taking, fosters task-focused motivation, and supports the other aspects of creativity that we have discussed.

It is also important to realize that obtaining transfer of training from one domain to another is at least as hard with creative thinking as with critical thinking. If you use trivial problems in your classroom (e.g., "What are unusual uses of a paper clip?"), you are likely to get transfer only to trivial problems outside the classroom. We are not enthusiastic about many so-called tests of creativity, nor about many training programs, because the problems they use are trivial. We would encourage the use of serious problems in a variety of disciplines in order to maximize the transfer of training. Better to ask students to think of unusual ways to solve world problems—or school problems, for that matter—than to ask them to think of unusual ways to use a paper clip!

CONCLUSION

Perhaps the greatest block to the enhancement of creativity is a view of the "ideal student" that does not particularly feature creativity. Paul Torrance used an "Ideal Child Checklist," composed of characteristics that had been found empirically to differentiate highly creative people from less creative people.[11] A total of 264 teachers in the state of New York ranked the items in terms of

desirability. The teachers' rankings showed only a moderate relation with the rankings of ten experts on creativity. The teachers supported more strongly than the experts such attributes as popularity, social skills, and acceptance of authority. The teachers disapproved of asking questions, being a good guesser, thinking independently, and risk taking. A replication of this study in Tennessee showed only a weak relation between the views of teachers and those of experts on creativity.[12] Clearly, to engender creativity, first we must value it!

Schools could change. They could let students define problems, rather than almost always doing it for them. They could put more emphasis on ill-structured rather than well-structured problems. They could encourage a legislative rather than (or in addition to) an executive style, by providing assignments that encourage students to see things in new ways. They could teach knowledge for use, rather than for exams; they could emphasize flexibility in using knowledge, rather than mere recall. They could encourage risk taking and other personality attributes associated with creativity, and they could put more emphasis on motivating children intrinsically rather than through grades. Finally, they could reward creativity in all its forms, rather than ignore or even punish it.

But for schools to do these things, it would take a rather fundamental re*valuation* of what schooling is about. We, at least, would like to see that process start now. Rather than put obstacles in their paths, let's do all that we can to *value* and encourage the creativity of students in our schools.

ENDNOTES

1. Robert J. Sternberg, "A Three-Facet Model of Creativity," in R. J. Sternberg, ed., *The Nature of Creativity* (New York: Cambridge University Press, 1988), pp. 125–47; and Robert J. Sternberg and Todd I. Lubart, "An Investment Theory of Creativity and Its Development," *Human Development,* vol. 34, 1991, pp. 1–31.

2. Herbert J. Walberg, "Creativity and Talent as Learning," in Sternberg, *The Nature of Creativity,* pp. 340–61.

3. Robert J. Sternberg, *Beyond IQ: A Triarchic Theory of Human Intelligence* (New York: Cambridge University Press, 1985); and Sternberg, *The Triarchic Mind: A*

New Theory of Human Intelligence (New York: Viking, 1988).

4. Janet E. Davidson and Robert J. Sternberg, "The Role of Insight in Intellectual Giftedness," *Gifted Child Quarterly,* vol. 28, 1984, pp. 58–64; and Robert J. Sternberg and Janet E. Davidson, "The Mind of the Puzzler," *Psychology Today,* June 1982, pp. 37–44.

5. Robert J. Sternberg and Peter A. Frensch, "A Balance-Level Theory of Intelligent Thinking," *Zeitschrift für Pädagogische Psychologie,* vol. 3, 1989, pp. 79–96.

6. Robert J. Sternberg, "Mental Self-Government: A Theory of Intellectual Styles and Their Development," *Human Development,* vol. 31, 1988, pp. 197–224; and "Thinking Styles: Keys to Understanding Student Performance," *Phi Delta Kappan,* January 1990, pp. 366–71.

7. Teresa M. Amabile, *The Social Psychology of Creativity* (New York: Springer-Verlag, 1983).

8. Mark Lepper, David Greene, and Richard Nisbett, "Undermining Children's Intrinsic Interest with Extrinsic Rewards: A Test of the 'Overjustification' Hypothesis," *Journal of Personality and Social Psychology,* vol. 28, 1973, pp. 129–37.

9. Robert White, "Motivation Reconsidered: The Concept of Competence," *Psychological Review,* vol. 66, 1959, pp. 297–323.

10. Davidson and Sternberg, op. cit.

11. E. Paul Torrance, *Role of Evaluation in Creative Thinking* (Minneapolis: Bureau of Educational Research, University of Minnesota, 1964).

12. Bill Kaltsounis, "Middle Tennessee Teachers' Perceptions of Ideal Pupil," *Perceptual and Motor Skills,* vol. 44, 1977, pp. 803–806.

DISCUSSION QUESTIONS

1. How can curriculum workers plan instruction that encourages students to use legislative intellectual styles?
2. In what ways will the curriculum need to be structured to promote creative thinking?
3. What kinds of changes at the school level might be necessary to foster creative thinking?
4. What instructional approaches are most likely to promote creative thinking?
5. What personality attributes do creative people seem to share?

17

The Cognitive-Developmental Approach to Moral Education

LAWRENCE KOHLBERG

FOCUSING QUESTIONS

1. How does moral education promote the aims of education?
2. What are the levels of moral development?
3. How do moral judgment, content of moral judgment, and moral action differ?
4. How do conventional rules and principles influence moral choice?
5. How do indoctrination and values clarification differ as approaches to moral education?
6. What is the cognitive developmental approach to moral education?

In this chapter, I present an overview of the cognitive-developmental approach to moral education and its research foundations, compare it with other approaches, and report the experimental work my colleagues and I are doing to apply the approach.

MORAL STAGES

The cognitive-developmental approach was fully stated for the first time by John Dewey. The approach is called *cognitive* because it recognizes that moral education, like intellectual education, has its basis in stimulating the *active thinking* of the child about moral issues and decisions. It is called developmental because it sees the aims of moral education as movement through moral stages. According to Dewey:

> The aim of education is growth or *development,* both intellectual and moral. Ethical and psychological principles can aid the school in the *greatest of all the constructions—the building of a free and powerful character.* Only knowledge of the *order and connection of the stages in psychological de-*

> *velopment can insure this.* Education is the work of *supplying the conditions* which will enable the psychological functions to mature in the freest and fullest manner.[1]

Dewey postulated three levels of moral development: (1) the *pre-moral* or *preconventional* level "of behavior motivated by biological and social impulses with results for morals," (2) the *conventional* level of behavior "in which the individual accepts with little critical reflection the standards of his group," and (3) the *autonomous* level of behavior in which "conduct is guided by the individual thinking and judging for himself whether a purpose is good, and does not accept the standard of his group without reflection."[2]

Dewey's thinking about moral stages was theoretical. Building upon his prior studies of cognitive stages, Jean Piaget made the first effort to define stages of moral reasoning in children through actual interviews and through observations of children (in games with rules).[3] Using this interview material, Piaget defined the levels as follows: (1) the *premoral stage,* where there was no sense of obligation to rules; (2) the *heteronomous stage,* where the right was literal obedience to rules and an equation of obligation with submission to power and punishment (roughly ages four to eight); and (3) the *autonomous stage,* where the purpose and consequences of following rules are considered and obligation is based on reciprocity and exchange (roughly ages eight to twelve).[4]

In 1955, I started to redefine and validate (through longitudinal and cross-cultural study) the Dewey–Piaget levels and stages. The resulting stages are presented in Table 17.1.

We claim to have validated the stages defined in Table 17.1. The notion that stages can be *validated* by longitudinal study implies that stages have definite empirical characteristics.[5] The concept of stages (as used by Piaget and myself) implies the following characteristics:

1. Stages are "structured wholes," or organized systems of thought. Individuals are *consistent* in level of moral judgment.
2. Stages form an *invariant sequence.* Under all conditions except extreme trauma, movement is always forward, never backward. Individuals never skip stages; movement is always to the next stage up.
3. Stages are "hierarchical integrations." Thinking at a higher stage includes or comprehends within it lower-stage thinking. There is a tendency to function at or prefer the highest stage available.

Each of these characteristics has been demonstrated for moral stages. Stages are defined by responses to a set of verbal moral dilemmas classified according to an elaborate scoring scheme. Validating studies include

1. A twenty-year study of fifty Chicago-area boys, middle- and working-class. Initially interviewed at ages ten to sixteen, they have been reinterviewed at three-year intervals thereafter.
2. A small, six-year longitudinal study of Turkish village and city boys of the same age.
3. A variety of other cross-sectional studies in Canada, Britain, Israel, Taiwan, Yucatan, Honduras, and India.

With regard to the structured whole or consistency criterion, we have found that more than 50 percent of an individual's thinking is always at one stage, with the remainder at the next adjacent stage (which he is leaving or which he is moving into).

With regard to invariant sequence, our longitudinal results have been presented in the *American Journal of Orthopsychiatry* (see endnote 12), and indicate that on every retest individuals either were at the same stage as three years earlier or had moved up. This was true in Turkey as well as in the United States.

With regard to the hierarchical integration criterion, it has been demonstrated that adolescents exposed to written statements at each of the six stages comprehend or correctly put in their own words all statements at or below their own stage but fail to comprehend any statements more than one stage above their own.[6] Some individuals comprehend the next stage above their own; some do not. Adolescents prefer (or rank as best) the highest stage they can comprehend.

To understand moral stages it is important to clarify their relations to stages of logic or intelligence on the one hand and to moral behavior on the other. Maturity of moral judgment is not highly correlated with IQ or verbal intelligence (correlations are only in the 30s, accounting for 10 percent of the variance). Cognitive development, in the stage sense, however, is more important for moral development than such correlations suggest. Piaget has found that after the child learns to speak there are three major stages of reasoning: the intuitive, the concrete operational, and the formal operational. At around age seven, the child enters the stage of concrete logical thought: He can make logical inferences, classify, and handle quantitative relations about concrete things. In adolescence individuals usually enter the stage of formal operations. At this stage they can reason abstractly—i.e., consider all possibilities, form hypotheses, deduce implications from hypotheses, and test them against reality.[7]

Since moral reasoning clearly is reasoning, advanced moral reasoning depends upon advanced logical reasoning; a person's logical stage puts a certain ceiling on the moral stage he can

TABLE 17.1   Definition of Moral Stages

I. Preconventional level

At this level, the child is responsive to cultural rules and labels of good and bad, right or wrong, but interprets these labels either in terms of the physical or the hedonistic consequences of action (punishment, reward, exchange of favors) or in terms of the physical power of those who enunciate the rules and labels. The level is divided into the following two stages:

Stage 1: *The punishment-and-obedience orientation.* The physical consequences of action determine its goodness or badness, regardless of the human meaning or value of these consequences. Avoidance of punishment and unquestioning deference to power are valued in their own right, not in terms of respect for an underlying moral order supported by punishment and authority (the latter being Stage 4).

Stage 2: *The instrumental-relativist orientation.* Right action consists of that which instrumentally satisfies one's own needs and occasionally the needs of others. Human relations are viewed in terms like those of the marketplace. Elements of fairness, of reciprocity, and of equal sharing are present, but they are always interpreted in a physical, pragmatic way. Reciprocity is a matter of "You scratch my back and I'll scratch yours," not of loyalty, gratitude, or justice.

II. Conventional level

At this level, maintaining the expectations of the individual's family, group, or nation is perceived as valuable in its own right, regardless of immediate and obvious consequences. The attitude is not only one of *conformity* to personal expectations and social order, but of loyalty to it, of actively *maintaining,* supporting, and justifying the order, and of identifying with the persons or group involved in it. At this level, there are the following two stages:

Stage 3: *The interpersonal concordance or "good boy-nice girl" orientation.* Good behavior is that which pleases or helps others and is approved by them. There is much conformity to stereotypical images of what is majority or "natural" behavior. Behavior is frequently judged by intention—"he means well" becomes important for the first time. One earns approval by being "nice."

Stage 4: *The "law and order" orientation.* There is orientation toward authority, fixed rules, and the maintenance of the social order. Right behavior consists of doing one's duty, showing respect for authority, and maintaining the given social order for its own sake.

III. Postconventional level

At this level, there is a clear effort to define moral values and principles that have validity and application apart from the authority of the groups or persons holding these principles and apart from the individual's own identification with these groups. This level also has two stages:

Stage 5: *The social-contract, legalistic orientation,* generally with utilitarian overtones. Right action tends to be defined in terms of general individual rights and standards, which have been critically examined and agreed upon by the whole society. There is a clear awareness of the relativism of personal values and opinions and a corresponding emphasis upon procedural rules for reaching consensus. Aside from what is constitutionally and democratically agreed upon, the right is a matter of personal "values" and "opinion." The result is an emphasis upon the "legal point of view," but with an emphasis upon the possibility of changing law in terms of rational considerations of social utility (rather than freezing it in terms of Stage 4 "law and order"). Outside the legal realm, free agreement and contract is the binding element of obligation. This is the "official" morality of the American government and Constitution.

Stage 6: *The universal-ethical-principle orientation.* Right is defined by the decision of conscience in accord with self-chosen *ethical principles* appealing to logical comprehensiveness, universality, and consistency. These principles are abstract and ethical (the Golden Rule, the categorical imperative); they are not concrete moral rules like the Ten Commandments. At heart, these are universal principles of *justice,* of the *reciprocity* and *equality* of human *rights,* and of respect for the dignity of human beings as *individual persons.*

attain. A person whose logical stage is only concrete operational is limited to the preconventional moral stages (Stages 1 and 2). A person whose logical stage is only partially formal operational is limited to the conventional moral stages (Stages 3 and 4). While logical development is necessary for moral development and sets limits to it, most individuals are higher in logical stage than they are in moral stage. As an example, over 50 percent of late adolescents and adults are capable of full formal reasoning, but only 10 percent of these adults (all formal operational) display principled (Stages 5 and 6) moral reasoning.

The moral stages are *structures of moral judgment* or *moral reasoning. Structures* of moral judgment must be distinguished from the *content* of moral judgment. As an example, we cite responses to a dilemma used in our various studies to identify moral stage. The dilemma raises the issue of stealing a drug to save a dying woman. The inventor of the drug is selling it for ten times what it costs him to make it. The woman's husband cannot raise the money, and the seller refuses to lower the price or wait for payment. What should the husband do?

The choice endorsed by a subject (steal, don't steal) is called the *content* of his moral judgment in the situation. His reasoning about the choice defines the structure of his moral judgment. This reasoning centers on the following ten universal moral values or issues of concern to persons in these moral dilemmas:

1. Punishment
2. Property
3. Roles and concerns of affection
4. Roles and concerns of authority
5. Law
6. Life
7. Liberty
8. Distributive justice
9. Truth
10. Sex

A moral choice involves choosing between two (or more) of these values as they *conflict* in concrete situations of choice.

The stage or structure of a person's moral judgment defines (1) *what* he finds valuable in each of these moral issues (life, law), i.e., how he defines the value, and (2) *why* he finds it valuable, i.e., the reasons he gives for valuing it. As an example, at Stage 1 life is valued in terms of the power or possessions of the person involved; at Stage 2, for its usefulness in satisfying the needs of the individual in question or others; at Stage 3, in terms of the individual's relations with others and their valuation of him; at Stage 4, in terms of social or religious law. Only at Stages 5 and 6 is each life seen as inherently worthwhile, aside from other considerations.

MORAL JUDGMENT VS. MORAL ACTION

Having clarified the nature of stages of moral *judgment,* we must consider the relation of moral judgment to moral *action.* If logical reasoning is a necessary but not sufficient condition for mature moral judgment, mature moral judgment is a necessary but not sufficient condition for mature moral action. One cannot follow moral principles if one does not understand (or believe in) moral principles. However, one can reason in terms of principles and not live up to these principles. As an example, Richard Krebs and I found that only 15 percent of students showing some principled thinking cheated as compared to 55 percent of conventional subjects and 70 percent of preconventional subjects.[8] Nevertheless, 15 percent of the principled subjects did cheat, suggesting that factors additional to moral judgment are necessary for principled moral reasoning to be translated into "moral action." Partly, these factors include the situation and its pressures. Partly, what happens depends upon the individual's motives and emotions. Partly, what the individual does depends upon a general sense of will, purpose, or "ego strength." As an example of the role of will or ego strength in moral behavior, we may cite the study by Krebs: Slightly more than half of his conventional subjects cheated. These subjects were also divided by a measure of attention/will. Only 26 percent of the "strong-willed" conventional subjects cheated; however, 74 percent of the "weak-willed" subjects cheated.

If maturity of moral reasoning is only one factor in moral behavior, why does the cognitive-developmental approach to moral education focus so heavily upon moral reasoning? For the following reasons:

1. Moral judgment, while only one factor in moral behavior, is the single most important or influential factor yet discovered in moral behavior.
2. While other factors influence moral behavior, moral judgment is the only distinctively *moral* factor in moral behavior. To illustrate, we noted that the Krebs study indicated that "strong-willed" conventional stage subjects resisted cheating more than "weak-willed" subjects. For those at a preconventional level of moral reasoning, however, "will" had an opposite effect. "Strong-willed" Stages 1 and 2 subjects cheated more, not less, than "weak-willed" subjects; i.e., they had the "courage of their (amoral) convictions" that it was worthwhile to cheat. "Will," then, is an important factor in moral behavior, but it is not distinctively moral; it becomes moral only when informed by mature moral judgment.
3. Moral judgment change is long-range or irreversible; a higher stage is never lost. Moral behavior as such is largely situational and reversible or "losable" in new situations.

AIMS OF MORAL AND CIVIC EDUCATION

Moral psychology describes what moral development is, as studied empirically. Moral education must also consider moral philosophy, which strives to tell us what moral development ideally *ought to be*. Psychology finds an invariant sequence of moral stages; moral philosophy must be invoked to answer whether a later stage is a better stage. The "stage" of senescence and death follows the "stage" of adulthood, but that does not mean that senescence and death are better. Our claim that the latest or principled stages of moral reasoning are morally better stages, then, must rest on considerations of moral philosophy.

The tradition of moral philosophy to which we appeal is the liberal or rational tradition, in particular the "formalistic" or "deontological" tradition running from Immanuel Kant to John Rawls.[9] Central to this tradition is the claim that an adequate morality is *principled*—i.e., that it makes judgments in terms of *universal* principles applicable to all mankind. *Principles* are to be distinguished from *rules*. Conventional morality is grounded on rules, primarily "thou shalt nots" such as are represented by the Ten Commandments, prescriptions of kinds of actions. Principles are, rather, universal guides to making a moral decision. An example is Kant's "categorical imperative," formulated in two ways. The first is the maxim of respect for human personality, "Act always toward the other as an end, not as a means." The second is the maxim of universalization, "Choose only as you would be willing to have everyone choose in your situation." Principles like that of Kant state the formal conditions of a moral choice or action. In the dilemma in which a woman is dying because a druggist refuses to release his drug for less than the stated price, the druggist is not acting morally, though he is not violating the ordinary moral rules (he is not actually stealing or murdering). But he is violating principles: He is treating the woman simply as a means to his ends of profit, and he is not choosing as he would wish anyone to choose (if the druggist were in the dying woman's place, he would not want a druggist to choose as he is choosing). Under most circumstances, choice in terms of conventional moral rules and choice in terms of principles coincide. Ordinarily, principles dictate not stealing (avoiding stealing is implied by acting in terms of a regard for others as ends and in terms of what one would want everyone to do). In a situation where stealing is the only means to save a life, however, principles contradict the ordinary rules and would dictate stealing. Unlike rules which are supported by social authority, principles are freely chosen by the individual because of their intrinsic moral validity.[10]

The conception that a moral choice is a choice made in terms of moral principles is related to the claim of liberal moral philosophy that moral principles are ultimately principles of justice. In essence, moral conflicts are conflicts between the claims of persons, and principles for resolving these claims are principles of justice, "for giving each his due." Central to justice are the demands of *liberty, equality,* and *reciprocity.* At every moral stage, there is a concern for justice. The most damning statement a school child can make about a teacher is that "he's not fair." At each higher stage, however, the conception of justice is reorganized. At Stage 1, justice is punishing the bad in terms of "an eye for an eye and a tooth for a tooth." At Stage 2, it is exchanging favors and goods in an equal manner. At Stages 3 and 4, it is treating people as they desire in terms of the conventional rules. At Stage 5, it is recognized that all rules and laws flow from justice, from a social contract between the governors and the governed designed to protect the equal rights of all. At Stage 6, personally chosen moral principles are also principles of justice, the principles any member of a society would choose for that society if he did not know what his position was to be in the society and in which he might be the least advantaged.[11] Principles chosen from this point of view are, first, the maximum liberty compatible with the like liberty of others and, second, no inequalities of goods and respect which are not to the benefit of all, including the least advantaged.

As an example of stage progression in the orientation to justice, we may take judgments about capital punishment.[12] Capital punishment is only firmly rejected at the two principled stages, when the notion of justice as vengeance or retribution is abandoned. At the sixth stage, capital punishment is not condoned even if it may have some useful deterrent effect in promoting law and order. This is because it is not a punishment we would choose for a society if we assumed we had as much chance of being born into the position of a criminal or murderer as being born into the position of a law abider.

Why are decisions based on universal principles of justice better decisions? Because they are decisions on which all moral men could agree. When decisions are based on conventional moral rules, men will disagree, since they adhere to conflicting systems of rules dependent on culture and social position. Throughout history men have killed one another in the name of conflicting moral rules and values, most recently in Vietnam and the Middle East. Truly moral or just resolutions of conflicts require principles which are, or can be, universalizable.

Alternative Approaches

We have given a philosophic rationale for stage advance as the aim of moral education. Given this rationale, the developmental approach to moral education can avoid the problems inherent in the other two major approaches to moral education. The first alternative approach is that of indoctrinative moral education, the preaching and imposition of the rules and values of the teacher and his culture on the child. In America, when this indoctrinative approach has been developed in a systematic manner, it has usually been termed "character education."

Moral values, in the character education approach, are preached or taught in terms of what may be called the "bag of virtues." In the classic studies of character by Hugh Hartshorne and Mark May, the virtues chosen were honesty, service, and self-control.[13] It is easy to get superficial consensus on such a bag of virtues—until one examines in detail the list of virtues involved and the details of their definition. Is the Hartshorne and May bag more adequate than the Boy Scout bag (a Scout should be honest, loyal, reverent, clean, brave, etc.)? When one turns to the details of defining each virtue, one finds equal uncertainty or difficulty in reaching consensus. Does honesty mean one should not steal to save a life? Does it mean that a student should not help another student with his homework?

Character education and other forms of indoctrinative moral education have aimed at teaching universal values (it is assumed that honesty or service is a desirable trait for all men in all societies), but the detailed definitions used are relative; they are defined by the opinions of the teacher and the conventional culture and rest on the authority of the teacher for their justification. In this sense character education is close to the unreflective valuings by teachers which constitute the hidden curriculum of the school.[14] Because of the current unpopularity of indoctrinative approaches to moral education, a family of approaches called "values clarification" has become appealing to teachers. Values clarification takes the first step implied by a rational approach to moral education: the eliciting of the child's own judgment or opinion about issues or situations in which values conflict, rather than imposing the teacher's opinion on him. Values clarification, however, does not attempt to go further than eliciting awareness of values; it is assumed that becoming more self-aware about one's values is an end in itself. Fundamentally, the definition of the end of values education as self-awareness derives from a belief in ethical relativity held by many value-clarifiers. As stated by Peter Engel, "One must contrast value clarification and value inculcation. Value clarification implies the principle that in the consideration of values there is no single correct answer." Within these premises of "no correct answer," children are to discuss moral dilemmas in such a way as to reveal different values and discuss their value differences with each other. The teacher is to stress that "our values are different," not that one value is more adequate than others. If this program is systematically followed, students will themselves become relativists, believing there is no "right" moral answer. For instance, a student caught cheating might argue that he did nothing wrong, since his own hierarchy of values, which may be different from that of the teacher, made it right for him to cheat.

Like values clarification, the cognitive-developmental approach to moral education stresses open or Socratic peer discussion of value dilemmas. Such discussion, however, has an aim: stimulation of movement to the next stage of moral reasoning. Like values clarification, the developmental approach opposes indoctrination. Stimulation of movement to the next stage of reasoning is not indoctrinative, for the following reasons:

1. Change is in the way of reasoning rather than in the particular beliefs involved.
2. Students in a class are at different stages; the aim is to aid movement of each to the next stage, not convergence on a common pattern.
3. The teacher's own opinion is neither stressed nor invoked as authoritative. It enters in only as one of many opinions, hopefully one of those at a next higher stage.

4. The notion that some judgments are more adequate than others is communicated. Fundamentally, however, this means that the student is encouraged to articulate a position which seems most adequate to him and to judge the adequacy of the reasoning of others.

In addition to having more definite aims than values clarification, the moral development approach restricts value education to that which is moral or, more specifically, to justice. This is for two reasons. First, it is not clear that the whole realm of personal, political, and religious values is a realm which is nonrelative—i.e., in which there are universals and a direction of development. Second, it is not clear that the public school has a right or mandate to develop values in general. In our view, value education in the public schools should be restricted to that which the school has the right and mandate to develop: an awareness of justice, or of the rights of others in our Constitutional system.[15] While the Bill of Rights prohibits the teaching of religious beliefs, or of specific value systems, it does not prohibit the teaching of the awareness of rights and principles of justice fundamental to the Constitution itself.

When moral education is recognized as centered in justice and differentiated from value education or affective education, it becomes apparent that moral and civic education are much the same thing. This equation, taken for granted by the classic philosophers of education from Plato and Aristotle to Dewey, is basic to our claim that a concern for moral education is central to the educational objectives of social studies.

The term *civic education* is used to refer to social studies as more than the study of the facts and concepts of social science, history, and civics. It is education for the analytic understanding, value principles, and motivation necessary for a citizen in a democracy if democracy is to be an effective process. It is political education. Civic or political education means the stimulation of development of more advanced patterns of reasoning about political and social decisions and their implementation directly derivative of broader patterns of moral reasoning. Our studies show that reasoning and decision making about political decisions are directly derivative of broader patterns of moral reasoning and decision making. We have interviewed high school and college students about concrete political situations involving laws to govern open housing, civil disobedience for peace in Vietnam, free press rights to publish what might disturb national order, and distribution of income through taxation. We find that reasoning on these political decisions can be classified according to moral stage and that an individual's stage on political dilemmas is at the same level as on nonpolitical moral dilemmas (euthanasia, violating authority to maintain trust in a family, stealing a drug to save one's dying wife). Turning from reasoning to action, similar findings are obtained. In 1963 a study was made of those who sat in at the University of California, Berkeley, administration building and those who did not in the Free Speech Movement crisis. Of those at Stage 6, 80 percent sat in, believing that principles of free speech were being compromised, and that all efforts to compromise and negotiate with the administration had failed. In contrast, only 15 percent of the conventional (Stage 3 or Stage 4) subjects sat in. (Stage 5 subjects were in between.)[16]

From a psychological side, then, political development is part of moral development. The same is true from the philosophic side. In the *Republic,* Plato sees political education as part of a broader education for moral justice and finds a rationale for such education in terms of universal philosophic principles rather than the demands of a particular society. More recently, Dewey claims the same.

In historical perspective, the United States was the first nation whose government was publicly founded on postconventional principles of justice, rather than upon the authority central to conventional moral reasoning. At the time of our founding, postconventional or principled moral and political reasoning was the possession of the minority, as it still is. Today, as in the time of our founding, the majority of our adults are at the conventional level, particularly the "law and order" (fourth) moral stage. (Every few years the Gallup Poll circulates the Bill of Rights unidentified, and every year it is turned down.) The Founding Fathers intuitively understood this without benefit of our elaborate social science research; they constructed a document designing a government which would maintain principles of justice and the rights of man even though principled men were not the men in power. The machinery included checks and balances, the independent judiciary, and freedom of the press. Most recently, this machinery found its use at Watergate. The tragedy of Richard Nixon, as Harry Truman said long ago, was that he never understood the Constitution (a Stage 5 document), but the Constitution understood Richard Nixon.[17]

Watergate, then, is not some sign of moral decay of the nation, but rather of the fact that understanding and action in support of justice principles are still the possession of a minority of our society. Insofar as there is moral decay, it represents the weakening of conventional morality in the face of social and value conflict today. This can lead the less fortunate adolescent to fixation at the preconventional level, the more fortunate to movement to principles. We find a larger proportion of youths at the principled level today than was the case in their fathers' day, but also a larger proportion at the preconventional level.

Given this state, moral and civic education in the schools becomes a more urgent task. In the high school today, one often hears both preconventional adolescents and those beginning to move beyond convention sounding the same note of disaffection for the school. While our political institutions are in principle Stage 5 (i.e., vehicles for maintaining universal rights through the democratic process), our schools have traditionally been Stage 4 institutions of convention and authority. Today more than ever, democratic schools systematically engaged in civic education are required.

Our approach to moral and civic education relates the study of law and government to the actual creation of a democratic school in which moral dilemmas are discussed and resolved in a manner which will stimulate moral development.

Planned Moral Education

For many years, moral development was held by psychologists to be primarily a result of family upbringing and family conditions. In particular, conditions of affection and authority in the home were believed to be critical, some balance of warmth and firmness being optimal for moral development. This view arises if morality is conceived as an internalization of the arbitrary rules of parents and culture, since such acceptance must be based on affection and respect for parents as authorities rather than on the rational nature of the rules involved.

Studies of family correlates of moral stage development do not support this internalization view of the conditions for moral development. Instead, they suggest that the conditions for moral development in homes and schools are similar and that the conditions are consistent with cognitive-developmental theory. In the cognitive-developmental view, morality is a natural product of a universal human tendency toward empathy or role taking, toward putting oneself in the shoes of other conscious beings. It is also a product of a universal human concern for justice, for reciprocity or equality in the relation of one person to another. As an example, when my son was four, he became a morally principled vegetarian and refused to eat meat, resisting all parental persuasion to increase his protein intake. His reason was "It's bad to kill animals." His moral commitment to vegetarianism was not taught or acquired from parental authority; it was the result of the universal tendency of the young self to project its consciousness and values into other living things, other selves. My son's vegetarianism also involved a sense of justice, revealed when I read him a book about Eskimos in which a real hunting expedition was described. His response was to say, "Daddy, there is one kind of meat I would eat—Eskimo meat. It's all right to eat Eskimos because they eat animals." This natural sense of justice or reciprocity was Stage 1—an eye for an eye, a tooth for a tooth. My son's sense of the value of life was also Stage 1 and involved no differentiation between human personality and physical life. His morality, though Stage 1, was, however, natural and internal. Moral development past Stage 1, then, is not an internalization but the reconstruction of role taking and conceptions of justice toward greater adequacy. These reconstructions occur in order to

achieve a better match between the child's own moral structures and the structures of the social and moral situations he confronts. We divide these conditions of match into two kinds: those dealing with moral discussions and communication and those dealing with the total moral environment or atmosphere in which the child lives.

In terms of moral discussion, the important conditions appear to be

1. Exposure to the next higher stage of reasoning
2. Exposure to situations posing problems and contradictions for the child's current moral structure, leading to dissatisfaction with his current level
3. An atmosphere of interchange and dialogue combining the first two conditions, in which conflicting moral views are compared in an open manner

Studies of families in India and America suggest that morally advanced children have parents at higher stages. Parents expose children to the next higher stage, raising moral issues and engaging in open dialogue or interchange about such issues.[18]

Drawing on this notion of the discussion conditions stimulating advance, Moshe Blatt conducted classroom discussions of conflict-laden hypothetical moral dilemmas with four classes of junior high and high school students for a semester.[19] In each of these classes, students were to be found at three stages. Since the children were not all responding at the same stage, the arguments they used with each other were at different levels. In the course of these discussions among the students, the teacher first supported and clarified those arguments that were one stage above the lowest stage among the children; for example, the teacher supported Stage 3 rather than Stage 2. When it seemed that these arguments were understood by the students, the teacher then challenged that stage, using new situations, and clarified the arguments one stage above the previous one: Stage 4 rather than Stage 3. At the end of the semester, all the students were retested; they showed significant upward change when compared to the controls, and they maintained the change one year later. In the experimental classrooms, from one-fourth to one-half of the students moved up a stage, while there was essentially no change during the course of the experiment in the control group.

Given the Blatt studies showing that moral discussion could raise moral stage, we undertook the next step: to see if teachers could conduct moral discussions in the course of teaching high school social studies with the same results. This step we took in cooperation with Edwin Fenton, who introduced moral dilemmas in his ninth- and eleventh-grade social studies texts. Twenty-four teachers in the Boston and Pittsburgh areas were given some instruction in conducting moral discussions around the dilemmas in the text. About half of the teachers stimulated significant developmental change in their classrooms—upward stage movement of one-quarter to one-half a stage. In control classes using the text but no moral dilemma discussions, the same teachers failed to stimulate any moral change in the students. Moral discussion, then, can be a usable and effective part of the curriculum at any grade level. Working with filmstrip dilemmas produced in cooperation with Guidance Association, second-grade teachers conducted moral discussions yielding a similar amount of moral stage movement.

Moral discussion and curriculum, however, constitute only one portion of the conditions stimulating moral growth. When we turn to analyzing the broader life environment, we turn to a consideration of the *moral atmosphere* of the home, the school, and the broader society. The first basic dimension of social atmosphere is the role-taking opportunities it provides, the extent to which it encourages the child to take the point of view of others. Role taking is related to the amount of social interaction and social communication in which the child engages, as well as to his sense of efficacy in influencing attitudes of others. The second dimension of social atmosphere, more strictly moral, is the level of justice of the environment or institution. The justice structure of an institution refers to the perceived rules or principles for distributing rewards, punishments, responsibilities, and privileges among institutional members. This structure may exist or be perceived at any of our moral stages. As an example, a study of a traditional prison revealed that inmates perceived it as Stage 1, regardless of their own level.[20] Obedience to arbitrary command by power figures and punishment for disobedience were seen as the governing justice norms of the prison. A behavior-modification prison using point rewards for conformity was perceived as a Stage 2 system of instrumental exchange. Inmates at Stage 3 or 4 perceived this institution as more fair than the traditional prison, but not as fair in their own terms.

These and other studies suggest that a higher level of institutional justice is a condition for individual development of a higher sense of justice. Working on these premises, Joseph Hickey, Peter Scharf, and I worked with guards and inmates in a women's prison to create a more just community.[21] A social contract was set up in which guards and inmates each had a vote of one and in which rules were made and conflicts resolved through discussions of fairness and a democratic vote in a community meeting. The program has stimulated moral stage advance in inmates.

Fenton, Ralph Mosher, and I received a grant from the Danforth Foundation (with additional support from the Kennedy Foundation) to make moral education a living matter in two high schools in the Boston area (Cambridge and Brookline) and two in Pittsburgh. The plan had two components. The first was training counselors and social studies and English teachers in conducting moral discussions and making moral discussion an integral part of the curriculum. The second was establishing a just community school within a public high school.

We have stated the theory of the just community high school, postulating that discussing real-life moral situations and actions as issues of fairness and as matters for democratic decision would stimulate advance in both moral reasoning and moral action. A participatory democracy provides more extensive opportunities for role taking and a higher level of perceived institutional justice than does any other social arrangement. Most alternative schools strive to establish a democratic governance, but none we have observed has achieved a vital or viable participatory democracy. Our theory suggested reasons why we might succeed where others failed. First, we felt that democracy had to be a central commitment of a school, rather than a humanitarian frill. Democracy as moral education provides that commitment. Second, democracy in alternative schools often fails because it bores the students. Students prefer to let teachers make decisions about staff, courses, and schedules, rather than to attend lengthy, complicated meetings. Our theory said that the issues a democracy should focus on are issues of morality and fairness. Real issues concerning drugs, stealing, disruptions, and grading are never boring if handled as issues of fairness. Third, our theory told us that if large democratic community meetings were preceded by small-group moral discussion, higher-stage thinking by students would win out in later decisions, avoiding the disasters of mob rule.[22]

We can report that the school based on our theory makes democracy work or function where other schools have failed.

Our Cambridge just community school within the public high school was started after a small summer planning session of volunteer teachers, students, and parents. At the time the school opened in the fall, only a commitment to democracy and a skeleton program of English and social studies had been decided on. The school started with six teachers from the regular school and sixty students, twenty from academic professional homes and twenty from working-class homes. The other twenty were dropouts and troublemakers or petty delinquents in terms of previous record. The usual mistakes and usual chaos of a beginning alternative school ensued. Within a few weeks, however, a successful democratic community process had been established. Rules were made around pressing issues: disturbances, drugs, hooking. A student discipline committee or jury was formed. The resulting rules and enforcement have been relatively effective and reasonable. We do not see reasonable rules as ends in themselves, however, but as vehicles for moral discussion and an emerging sense of community. This sense of community and a resulting morale are perhaps the most immediate signs of success. This sense of community seems to lead to behavior change of a positive sort. An example is a fifteen-year-old student who started as one of the greatest combina-

tions of humor, aggression, light-fingeredness, and hyperactivity I have ever known. From being the principal disturber of all community meetings, he has become an excellent community meeting participant and occasional chairman. He is still more ready to enforce rules for others than to observe them himself, yet his commitment to the school has led to a steady decrease in exotic behavior. In addition, he has become more involved in classes and projects and has begun to listen and ask questions in order to pursue a line of interest.

CONCLUSION

We attribute such behavior change not only to peer pressure and moral discussion but to the sense of community which has emerged from the democratic process in which angry conflicts are resolved through fairness and community decision. This sense of community is reflected in statements of the students to us that there are no cliques—that the blacks and the whites, the professors' sons and the project students, are friends. These statements are supported by observation. Such a sense of community is needed where students in a given classroom range in reading level from fifth grade to college.

There is very little new in anything we are doing. Dewey wanted democratic experimental schools for moral and intellectual development seventy years ago. Perhaps Dewey's time has come.

ENDNOTES

1. John Dewey, "What Psychology Can Do for the Teacher," in Reginald Archambault, ed., *John Dewey on Education: Selected Writings* (New York: Random House, 1964).
2. These levels correspond roughly to our three major levels: the preconventional, the conventional, and the principled. Similar levels were propounded by William McDougall, Leonard Hobhouse, and James Mark Baldwin.
3. Jean Piaget, *The Moral Judgment of the Child,* 2nd ed. (Glencoe, IL: Free Press, 1948).
4. Piaget's stages correspond to our first three stages: Stage 0 (premoral), Stage 1 (heteronomous), and Stage 2 (instrumental reciprocity).

5. Lawrence Kohlberg, "Moral Stages and Moralization: The Cognitive-Developmental Approach," in Thomas Lickona, ed., *Moral Development and Behavior* (New York: Holt, Rinehart and Winston, 1976).

6. James Rest, Elliott Turiel, and Lawrence Kohlberg, "Relations Between Level of Moral Judgment and Preference and Comprehension of the Moral Judgment of Others," *Journal of Personality,* vol. 37, 1969, pp. 225–52; and James Rest, "Comprehension, Preference, and Spontaneous Usage in Moral Judgment," in Lawrence Kohlberg, ed., *Recent Research in Moral Development* (New York: Holt, Rinehart and Winston, 1986).

7. Many adolescents and adults only partially attain the stage of formal operations. They do consider all the actual relations of one thing to another at the same time, but they do not consider all possibilities and form abstract hypotheses. A few do not advance this far, remaining "concrete operational."

8. Richard Krebs and Lawrence Kohlberg, "Moral Judgment and Ego Controls as Determinants of Resistance to Cheating," in Lawrence Kohlberg, ed., *Recent Research.*

9. John Rawls, *A Theory of Justice* (Cambridge, MA: Harvard University Press, 1971).

10. Not all freely chosen values or rules are principles, however. Hitler chose the "rule" "exterminate the enemies of the Aryan race," but such a rule is not a universalizable principle.

11. Rawls, *A Theory of Justice.*

12. Lawrence Kohlberg and Donald Elfenbein, "Development of Moral Reasoning and Attitudes Toward Capital Punishment," *American Journal of Orthopsychiatry,* Summer, 1975.

13. Hugh Hartshorne and Mark May, *Studies in the Nature of Character: Studies in Deceit,* vol. 1; *Studies in Service and Self-Control,* vol. 2; *Studies in Organization of Character,* vol. 3 (New York: Macmillan, 1928–30).

14. As an example of the "hidden curriculum," we may cite a second-grade classroom. My son came home from this classroom one day saying he did not want to be "one of the bad boys." Asked "Who are the bad boys?" he replied, "The ones who don't put their books back and get yelled at."

15. Restriction of deliberate value education to the moral may be clarified by our example of the second-grade teacher who made tidying up of books a matter of moral indoctrination. Tidiness is a value, but it is not a moral value. Cheating is a moral issue, intrinsically one of fairness. It involves issues of violation of trust and taking advantage. Failing to tidy the room may under certain conditions be an issue of fairness, when it puts an undue burden on others. If it is handled by the teacher as a matter of cooperation among the group in this sense, it is a legitimate focus of deliberate moral education. If it is not, it simply represents the arbitrary imposition of the teacher's values on the child.

16. The differential action of the principled subjects was determined by two things. First, they were more likely to judge it right to violate authority by sitting in. But second, they were also in general more consistent in engaging in political action according to their judgment. Ninety percent of all Stage 6 subjects thought it right to sit in, and all 90 percent lived up to this belief. Among the Stage 4 subjects, 45 percent thought it right to sit in, but only 33 percent lived up to this belief by acting.

17. No public or private word or deed of Nixon ever rose above Stage 4, the "law and order" stage. His last comments in the White House were of wonderment that the Republican Congress could turn on him after so many Stage 2 exchanges of favors in getting them elected.

18. Bindu Parilch, "A Cross-Cultural Study of Parent-child Moral Judgment," unpublished doctoral dissertation, Harvard University, 1975.

19. Moshe Blatt and Lawrence Kohlberg, "Effects of Classroom Discussions upon Children's Level of Moral Judgment," in Lawrence Kohlberg, ed., *Recent Research.*

20. Lawrence Kohlberg, Peter Scharf, and Joseph Hickey, "The Justice Structure of the Prison: A Theory and an Intervention," *The Prison Journal,* Autumn-Winter, 1972.

21. Lawrence Kohlberg, Kelsey Kauffman, Peter Scharf, and Joseph Hickey, *The Just Community Approach to Corrections: A Manual, Part I* (Cambridge, MA: Education Research Foundation, 1973).

22. An example of the need for small-group discussion comes from an alternative school community meeting called because a pair of the students had stolen the school's video-recorder. The resulting majority decision was that the school should buy back the recorder from the culprits through a fence. The teachers could not accept this decision and returned to a more authoritative approach. I believe if the moral reasoning of students urging this solution had been confronted by students at a higher stage, a different decision would have emerged.

DISCUSSION QUESTIONS

1. Should moral and civic education be the responsibility of the schools? Why? Why not?
2. What type of curriculum design lends itself to promoting the aims of moral education?
3. How do the family and norms of school cultures influence children's moral development?
4. What is the role of the social atmosphere in moral education?
5. Should values be infused into the curriculum or explicitly taught? Why? Why not?

18

A Critical Examination of Character Education

ALFIE KOHN

FOCUSING QUESTIONS

1. What meanings are generally used to describe character education?
2. Why is understanding how individuals behave in context-specific situations relevant to analyzing the assumptions underlying character education programs?
3. In your opinion, is a negative view of human beings an appropriate orientation for creating character education programs? Why? Why not?
4. What essential components would traditional moralist and constructivists suggest for a character education program?
5. What should be the teachers' role in promoting students' moral development?

Were you to stand somewhere in the continental United States and announce, "I'm going to Hawaii," it would be understood that you were heading for those islands in the Pacific that collectively constitute the fiftieth state. Were you to stand in Honolulu and make the same statement, however, you would probably be talking about one specific island in the chain—the big one to your southeast. The word *Hawaii* would seem to have two meanings, a broad one and a narrow one; we depend on context to tell them apart.

The phrase *character education* also has two meanings. In the broad sense, it refers to almost anything that schools might try to provide outside of academics, especially when the purpose is to help children grow into good people. In the narrow sense, it denotes a particular style of moral training, one that reflects particular values as well as particular assumptions about the nature of children and how they learn.

Unfortunately, the two meanings of the term have become blurred, with the narrow version of character education dominating the field to the point that it is frequently mistaken for the broader concept. Thus educators who are keen to support

children's social and moral development may turn, by default, to a program with a certain set of methods and a specific agenda that, on reflection, they might very well find objectionable.

My purpose in this chapter is to subject these programs to careful scrutiny and, in so doing, to highlight the possibility that there are other ways to achieve our broader objectives. I address myself not so much to those readers who are avid proponents of character education (in the narrow sense), but to those who simply want to help children become decent human beings and may not have thought carefully about what they are being offered.

Let me get straight to the point. What goes by the name of character education nowadays is, for the most part, a collection of exhortations and extrinsic inducements designed to make children work harder and do what they're told. Even when other values are also promoted—caring or fairness, say—the preferred method of instruction is tantamount to indoctrination. The point is to drill students in specific behaviors, rather than to engage them in deep, critical reflection about certain ways of being. This is the impression one gets from reading articles and books by contemporary proponents of character education, as well as the curriculum materials sold by the leading national programs. The impression is only strengthened by visiting schools that have been singled out for their commitment to character education. To wit:

A huge, multiethnic elementary school in Southern California uses a framework created by the Jefferson Center for Character Education. Classes that the principal declares "well behaved" are awarded Bonus Bucks, which can eventually be redeemed for an ice cream party. On an enormous wall near the cafeteria, professionally painted Peanuts characters instruct children: "Never talk in line." A visitor is led to a fifth-grade classroom to observe an exemplary lesson on the current character education topic. The teacher is telling students to write down the name of the person they regard as the "toughest worker" in school. The teacher then asks them, "How many of you are going to be tough workers?" (Hands go up.) "Can you be a tough worker at home, too?" (Yes.)

A small, almost entirely African American school in Chicago uses a framework created by the Character Education Institute. Periodic motivational assemblies are used to "give children a good pep talk," as the principal puts it, and to reinforce the values that determine who will be picked as Student of the Month. Rule number one posted on the wall of a kindergarten room is "We will obey the teachers." Today students in this class are listening to the story of "Lazy Lion," who orders each of the other animals to build him a house, only to find each effort unacceptable. At the end, the teacher drives home the lesson: "Did you ever hear Lion say thank you?" (No.) "Did you ever hear Lion say please?" (No.) "It's good to always say . . . what?" (Please.) The reason for using these words, she points out, is that by doing so we are more likely to get what we want.

A charter school near Boston has been established specifically to offer an intensive, homegrown character education curriculum to its overwhelmingly white, middle-class student body. At weekly public ceremonies, certain children receive a leaf that will then be hung in the Forest of Virtue. The virtues themselves are "not open to debate," the headmaster insists, since moral precepts in his view enjoy the same status as mathematical truths. In a first-grade classroom, a teacher is observing

that "it's very hard to be obedient when you want something. I want you to ask yourself, 'Can I have it—and why not?'" She proceeds to ask the students, "What kinds of things show obedience?" and, after collecting a few suggestions, announces that she's "not going to call on anyone else now. We could go on forever, but we have to have a moment of silence and then a spelling test."

Some of the most popular schoolwide strategies for improving students' character seem dubious at face value. When President Clinton mentioned the importance of character education in his 1996 State of the Union address, the only specific practice he recommended was requiring students to wear uniforms. The premises here are, first, that children's character can be improved by forcing them to dress alike and, second, that if adults object to students' clothing the best solution is not to invite them to reflect together about how this problem might be solved, but instead to compel them all to wear the same thing.

A second strategy, also consistent with the dominant philosophy of character education, is an exercise that might be called "If It's Tuesday, This Must Be Honesty." Here, one value after another is targeted, with each assigned its own day, week, or month. This seriatim approach is unlikely to result in a lasting commitment to any of these values, much less a feeling for how they may be related. Nevertheless, such programs are taken very seriously by some of the same people who are quick to dismiss other educational programs, such as those intended to promote self-esteem, as silly and ineffective.

Then there is the strategy of offering students rewards when they are "caught" being good, an approach favored by right-wing religious groups[1] and orthodox behaviorists but also by leaders of—and curriculum suppliers for—the character education movement.[2] Because of its popularity and because a sizable body of psychological evidence germane to the topic is available, it is worth lingering on this particular practice for a moment.

In general terms, what the evidence suggests is this: the more we reward people for doing something, the more likely they are to lose interest in whatever they had to do to get the reward. Extrinsic motivation, in other words, not only is quite different from intrinsic motivation but actually tends to erode it.[3] This effect has been demonstrated under many different circumstances and with respect to many different attitudes and behaviors. Most relevant to character education is a series of studies showing that individuals who have been rewarded for doing something nice become less likely to think of themselves as caring or helpful people and more likely to attribute their behavior to the reward.

"Extrinsic incentives can, by undermining self-perceived altruism, decrease intrinsic motivation to help others," one group of researchers concluded on the basis of several studies. "A person's kindness, it seems, cannot be bought."[4] The same applies to a person's sense of responsibility, fairness, perseverance, and so on. The lesson a child learns from Skinnerian tactics is that the point of being good is to get rewards. No wonder researchers have found that children who are frequently rewarded—or, in another study, children who receive positive reinforcement for caring, sharing, and helping—are less likely than other children to keep doing those things.[5]

In short, it makes no sense to dangle goodies in front of children for being virtuous. But even worse than rewards are *a*wards—certificates, plaques, trophies, and other tokens of recognition whose numbers have been artificially limited so only a few can get them. When some children are singled out as "winners," the central message that every child learns is this: "Other people are potential obstacles to my success."[6] Thus the likely result of making students beat out their peers for the distinction of being the most virtuous is not only less intrinsic commitment to virtue but also a disruption of relationships and, ironically, of the experience of community that is so vital to the development of children's character.

Unhappily, the problems with character education (in the narrow sense, which is how I'll be using the term unless otherwise indicated) are not restricted to such strategies as enforcing sartorial uniformity, scheduling a value of the week, or offering students a "doggie biscuit" for being good. More deeply troubling are the fundamental assumptions, both explicit and implicit, that inform character education programs. Let us consider five

basic questions that might be asked of any such program: At what level are problems addressed? What is the view of human nature? What is the ultimate goal? Which values are promoted? And, finally, what is the theory of learning?

1. At what level are problems addressed?   One of the major purveyors of materials in this field, the Jefferson Center for Character Education in Pasadena, California, has produced a video that begins with some arresting images—quite literally. Young people are shown being led away in handcuffs, the point being that crime can be explained on the basis of an "erosion of American core values," as the narrator intones ominously. The idea that social problems can be explained by the fact that traditional virtues are no longer taken seriously is offered by many proponents of character education as though it were just plain common sense.

But if people steal or rape or kill solely because they possess bad values—that is, because of their personal characteristics—the implication is that political and economic realities are irrelevant and need not be addressed. Never mind staggering levels of unemployment in the inner cities or a system in which more and more of the nation's wealth is concentrated in fewer and fewer hands; just place the blame on individuals whose characters are deficient. A key tenet of the "Character Counts!" Coalition, which bills itself as a nonpartisan umbrella group devoid of any political agenda, is the highly debatable proposition that "negative social influences can [be] and usually are overcome by the exercise of free will and character."[7] What is presented as common sense is, in fact, conservative ideology.

Let's put politics aside, though. If a program proceeds by trying to "fix the kids"—as do almost all brands of character education—it ignores the accumulated evidence from the field of social psychology demonstrating that much of how we act and who we are reflects the situations in which we find ourselves. Virtually all the landmark studies in this discipline have been variations on this theme. Set up children in an extended team competition at summer camp, and you will elicit unprecedented levels of aggression. Assign adults to the roles of prisoners or guards in a mock jail, and they will start to become their roles. Move people to a small town, and they will be more likely to rescue a stranger in need. In fact, so common is the tendency to attribute to an individual's personality or character what is actually a function of the social environment that social psychologists have dubbed this the "fundamental attribution error."

A similar lesson comes to us from the movement concerned with Total Quality Management associated with the ideas of the late W. Edwards Deming. At the heart of Deming's teaching is the notion that the "system" of an organization largely determines the results. The problems experienced in a corporation, therefore, are almost always due to systemic flaws, rather than to a lack of effort or ability on the part of individuals in that organization. Thus, if we are troubled by the way students are acting, Deming, along with most social psychologists, would presumably have us transform the structure of the classroom, rather than try to remake the students themselves—precisely the opposite of the character education approach.

2. What is the view of human nature?   Character education's "fix the kids" orientation follows logically from the belief that kids need fixing. Indeed, the movement seems to be driven by a stunningly dark view of children—and, for that matter, of people in general. A "comprehensive approach [to character education] is based on a somewhat dim view of human nature," acknowledges William Kilpatrick, whose book *Why Johnny Can't Tell Right from Wrong* contains such assertions as "Most behavior problems are the result of sheer 'willfulness' on the part of children."[8]

Despite—or more likely because of—statements like that, Kilpatrick has frequently been invited to speak at character education conferences.[9] But that shouldn't be surprising in light of how many prominent proponents of character education share his views. Edward Wynne says his own work is grounded in a tradition of thought that takes a "somewhat pessimistic view of human nature."[10] The idea of character development "sees children as self-centered," in the opinion of Kevin Ryan, who directs the Center for the Advancement of Ethics and Character at Boston Univer-

sity, as well as heading up the character education network of the Association for Supervision and Curriculum Development.[11] Yet another writer approvingly traces the whole field back to the bleak world view of Thomas Hobbes: it is "an obvious assumption of character education," writes Louis Goldman, that people lack the instinct to work together. Without laws to compel us to get along, "our natural egoism would lead us into 'a condition of warfare one against another.'"[12] This sentiment is echoed by F. Washington Jarvis, headmaster of the Roxbury Latin School in Boston, one of Ryan's favorite examples of what character education should look like in practice. Jarvis sees human nature as "mean, nasty, brutish, selfish, and capable of great cruelty and meanness. We have to hold a mirror up to the students and say, 'This is who you are. Stop it.'"[13]

Even when proponents of character education don't express such sentiments explicitly, they give themselves away by framing their mission as a campaign for self-control. Amitai Etzioni, for example, does not merely include this attribute on a list of good character traits; he *defines* character principally in terms of the capacity "to control impulses and defer gratification."[14] This is noteworthy because the virtue of self-restraint—or at least the decision to give special emphasis to it—has historically been preached by those, from St. Augustine to the present, who see people as basically sinful.

In fact, at least three assumptions seem to be at work when the need for self-control is stressed: (1) we are all at war not only with others but with ourselves, torn between our desires and our reason (or social norms); (2) these desires are fundamentally selfish, aggressive, or otherwise unpleasant; and (3) these desires are very strong, constantly threatening to overpower us if we don't rein them in. Collectively, these statements describe religious dogma, not scientific fact. Indeed, the evidence from several disciplines converges to cast doubt on this sour view of human beings and, instead, supports the idea that it is as "natural" for children to help as to hurt. I will not rehearse that evidence here, partly because I have done so elsewhere at some length.[15] Suffice it to say that even the most hard-headed empiricist might well conclude that the promotion of prosocial values consists to some extent of supporting (rather than restraining or controlling) many facets of the self. Any educator who adopts this more balanced position might think twice before joining an educational movement that is finally inseparable from the doctrine of original sin.

3. What is the ultimate goal? It may seem odd even to inquire about someone's reasons for trying to improve children's character. But it is worth mentioning that the whole enterprise—not merely the particular values that are favored—is often animated by a profoundly conservative, if not reactionary, agenda. Character education based on "acculturating students to conventional norms of 'good' behavior . . . resonates with neoconservative concerns for social stability," observed David Purpel.[16] The movement has been described by another critic as a "yearning for some halcyon days of moral niceties and social tranquillity."[17] But it is not merely a *social* order that some are anxious to preserve (or recover): character education is vital, according to one vocal proponent, because "the development of character is the backbone of the economic system" now in place.[18]

Character education, or any kind of education, would look very different if we began with other objectives—if, for example, we were principally concerned with helping children to become active participants in a democratic society (or agents for transforming a society *into* one that is authentically democratic). It would look different if our top priority were to help students to develop into principled and caring members of a community or advocates for social justice. To be sure, these objectives are not inconsistent with the desire to preserve certain traditions, but the point would then be to help children to decide which traditions are worth preserving and why, based on these other considerations. That is not at all the same as endorsing anything that is traditional or making the preservation of tradition our primary concern. In short, we want to ask character education proponents what goals they emphasize—and ponder whether their broad vision is compatible with our own.

4. Which values? Should we allow values to be taught in school? The question is about as sensible as asking whether our bodies should be allowed to contain bacteria. Just as humans are teeming with microorganisms, so schools are teeming with values. We can't see the former because they're too small; we don't notice the latter because they're too similar to the values of the culture at large. Whether or not we deliberately adopt a character or moral education program, we are always teaching values. Even people who insist that they are opposed to values in school usually mean that they are opposed to values other than their own.[19]

And that raises the inevitable question: Which values, or whose, should we teach? It has already become a cliché to reply that this question should not trouble us because, while there may be disagreement on certain issues, such as abortion, all of us can agree on a list of basic values that children ought to have. Therefore, schools can vigorously and unapologetically set about teaching all those values.

But not so fast. Look at the way character education programs have been designed and you will discover, alongside such unobjectionable items as "fairness" or "honesty," an emphasis on values that are, again, distinctly conservative—and, to that extent, potentially controversial. To begin with, the famous Protestant work ethic is prominent: children should learn to "work hard and complete their tasks well and promptly, even when they do not want to," says Ryan.[20] Here the Latin question *cui bono?* comes to mind. Who benefits when people are trained not to question the value of what they have been told to do but simply to toil away at it—and to regard this as virtuous?[21] Similarly, when Wynne defines the moral individual as someone who is not only honest but also "diligent, obedient, and patriotic,"[22] readers may find themselves wondering whether these traits really qualify as *moral*—as well as reflecting on the virtues that are missing from this list.

Character education curricula also stress the importance of things like "respect," "responsibility," and "citizenship." But these are slippery terms, frequently used as euphemisms for uncritical deference to authority. Under the headline "The Return of the 'Fourth R'"—referring to "respect, responsibility, or rules"—a news magazine recently described the growing popularity of such practices as requiring uniforms, paddling disobedient students, rewarding those who are compliant, and "throwing disruptive kids out of the classroom."[23] Indeed, William Glasser observed some time ago that many educators "teach thoughtless conformity to school rules and call the conforming child 'responsible.'"[24] I once taught at a high school where the principal frequently exhorted students to "take responsibility." By this he meant specifically that they should turn in their friends who used drugs.

Exhorting students to be "respectful" or rewarding them if they are caught being "good" may likewise mean nothing more than getting them to do whatever the adults demand. Following a lengthy article about character education in the *New York Times Magazine,* a reader mused, "Do you suppose that if Germany had had character education at the time, it would have encouraged children to fight Nazism or to support it?"[25] The more time I spend in schools that are enthusiastically implementing character education programs, the more I am haunted by that question.

In place of the traditional attributes associated with character education, Deborah Meier and Paul Schwarz of the Central Park East Secondary School in New York nominated two core values that a school might try to promote: "empathy and skepticism: the ability to see a situation from the eyes of another and the tendency to wonder about the validity of what we encountered."[26] Anyone who brushes away the question "Which values should be taught?" might speculate on the concrete differences between a school dedicated to turning out students who are empathic and skeptical and a school dedicated to turning out students who are loyal, patriotic, obedient, and so on.

Meanwhile, in place of such personal qualities as punctuality or perseverance, we might emphasize the cultivation of autonomy so that children come to experience themselves as "origins" rather than "pawns," as one researcher put it.[27] We might, in other words, stress self-determination at least as much as self-control. With such an agenda, it would be crucial to give students the chance to participate in making decisions about their learning and about how they want their classroom to be.[28] This stands in sharp contrast to a philosophy of character education like Wynne's, which decrees that "it is specious to talk about

student choices" and offers students no real power except for when we give "some students authority over other students (for example, hall guard, class monitor)."[29]

Even with values that are widely shared, a superficial consensus may dissolve when we take a closer look. Educators across the spectrum are concerned about excessive attention to self-interest and are committed to helping students to transcend a preoccupation with their own needs. But how does this concern play out in practice? For some of us, it takes the form of an emphasis on *compassion;* for the dominant character education approach, the alternative value to be stressed is *loyalty,* which is, of course, altogether different.[30] Moreover, as John Dewey remarked at the turn of the century, anyone seriously troubled about rampant individualism among children would promptly target for extinction the "drill and skill" approach to instruction: "The mere absorbing of facts and truths is so exclusively individual an affair that it tends very naturally to pass into selfishness."[31] Yet conservative champions of character education are often among the most outspoken supporters of a model of teaching that emphasizes rote memorization and the sequential acquisition of decontextualized skills.

Or take another example: all of us may say we endorse the idea of "cooperation," but what do we make of the practice of setting groups against one another in a quest for triumph, such that cooperation becomes the means and victory is the end? On the one hand, we might find this even more objectionable than individual competition. (Indeed, we might regard a "We're Number One!" ethic as a reason for schools to undertake something like character education in the first place.) On the other hand, "school-to-school, class-to-class, or row-to-row academic competitions" actually have been endorsed as part of a character education program,[32] along with contests that lead to awards for things like good citizenship.

The point, once again, is that it is entirely appropriate to ask which values a character education program is attempting to foster, notwithstanding the ostensible lack of controversy about a list of core values. It is equally appropriate to put such a discussion in context—specifically, in the context of which values are *currently* promoted in schools. The fact is that schools are already powerful socializers of traditional values—although, as noted above, we may fail to appreciate the extent to which this is true because we have come to take these values for granted. In most schools, for example, students are taught—indeed, compelled—to follow the rules regardless of whether the rules are reasonable and to respect authority regardless of whether that respect has been earned. (This process isn't always successful, of course, but that is a different matter.) Students are led to accept competition as natural and desirable and to see themselves more as discrete individuals than as members of a community. Children in U.S. schools are even expected to begin each day by reciting a loyalty oath to the Fatherland, although we call it by a different name. In short, the question is not whether to adopt the conservative values offered by most character education programs, but whether we want to consolidate the conservative values that are already in place.

5. What is the theory of learning?
We come now to what may be the most significant, and yet the least remarked on, feature of character education: the way values are taught and the way learning is thought to take place.

> The character education coordinator for the small Chicago elementary school also teaches second grade. In her classroom, where one boy has been forced to sit by himself for the last two weeks ("He's kind of pesty"), she is asking the children to define tolerance. When the teacher gets the specific answers she is fishing for, she exclaims, "Say that again," and writes down only those responses. Later comes the moral: "If somebody doesn't think the way you think, should you turn them off?" (No.)
> Down the hall, the first-grade teacher is fishing for answers on a different subject. "When we play games, we try to understand the—what?" (Rules.) A moment later, the children scramble to get into place so she will pick them to tell a visitor their carefully rehearsed stories about conflict resolution. Almost every child's account, narrated with considerable prompting by the teacher, concerns name-calling or some other unpleasant incident that was "correctly" resolved by finding an adult. The teacher never asks the children how they felt

about what happened or invites them to reflect on what else might have been done. She wraps up the activity by telling the children, "What we need to do all the time is clarify—make it clear—to the adult what you did."

The schools with character education programs that I have visited are engaged largely in exhortation and directed recitation. At first one might assume that this is due to poor implementation of the programs on the part of individual educators. But the programs themselves—and the theorists who promote them—really do seem to regard teaching as a matter of telling and compelling. For example, the broad-based "Character Counts!" Coalition offers a framework of six core character traits and then asserts that "young people should be specifically and repeatedly told what is expected of them." The leading providers of curriculum materials walk teachers through highly structured lessons in which character-related concepts are described and then students are drilled until they can produce the right answers.

Teachers are encouraged to praise children who respond correctly, and some programs actually include multiple-choice tests to ensure that students have learned their values. For example, here are two sample test questions prepared for teachers by the Character Education Institute, based in San Antonio, Texas: "Having to obey rules and regulations (a) gives everyone the same right to be an individual, (b) forces everyone to do the same thing at all times, (c) prevents persons from expressing their individually [sic]"; and "One reason why parents might not allow their children freedom of choice is (a) children are always happier when they are told what to do and when to do it, (b) parents aren't given a freedom of choice; therefore, children should not be given a choice either, (c) children do not always demonstrate that they are responsible enough to be given a choice." The correct answers, according to the answer key, are (a) and (c), respectively.

The Character Education Institute recommends "engaging the students in discussions," but only discussions of a particular sort: "Since the lessons have been designed to logically guide the students to the right answers, the teacher should allow the students to draw their own conclusions.

However, if the students draw the wrong conclusion, the teacher is instructed to tell them why their conclusion is *wrong.*"[33]

Students are told what to think and do, not only by their teachers but by highly didactic stories, such as those in the Character Education Institute's "Happy Life" series, which end with characters saying things like "I am glad that I did not cheat," or "Next time I will be helpful," or "I will never be selfish again." Most character education programs also deliver homilies by way of posters and banners and murals displayed throughout the school. Children who do as they are told are presented with all manner of rewards, typically in front of their peers.

Does all of this amount to indoctrination? Absolutely, says Wynne, who declares that "school is and should and must be inherently indoctrinative."[34] Even when character education proponents tiptoe around that word, their model of instruction is clear: good character and values are *instilled in* or *transmitted to* students. We are "planting the ideas of virtue, of good traits in the young," says William Bennett.[35] The virtues or values in question are fully formed and, in the minds of many character education proponents, divinely ordained. The children are—pick your favorite metaphor—so many passive receptacles to be filled, lumps of clay to be molded, pets to be trained, or computers to be programmed.

Thus, when we see Citizen-of-the-Month certificates and "Be a good sport!" posters, when we find teachers assigning preachy stories and principals telling students what to wear, it is important that we understand what is going on. These techniques may appear merely innocuous or gimmicky; they may strike us as evidence of a scattershot, let's-try-anything approach. But the truth is that these are elements of a systematic pedagogical philosophy. They are manifestations of a model that sees children as objects to be manipulated, rather than as learners to be engaged.

Ironically, some people who accept character education without a second thought are quite articulate about the bankruptcy of this model when it comes to teaching academic subjects. Plenty of teachers have abandoned the use of worksheets, textbooks, and lectures that fill children full of disconnected facts and skills. Plenty of administrators are working to create schools where students can actively construct meaning around scientific and historical and literary concepts. Plenty of educators, in short, realize that memorizing right answers and algorithms doesn't help anyone to arrive at a deep understanding of ideas.

And so we are left scratching our heads. Why would all these people, who know that the "transmission" model fails to facilitate intellectual development, uncritically accept the very same model to promote ethical development? How could they understand that mathematical truths cannot be shoved down students' throats, but then participate in a program that essentially tries to shove moral truths down the same throats? In the case of individual educators, the simple answer may be that they missed the connection. Perhaps they just failed to recognize that "a classroom cannot foster the development of autonomy in the intellectual realm while suppressing it in the social and moral realms," as Constance Kamii and her colleagues put it.[36]

In the case of the proponents of character education, I believe the answer to this riddle is quite different. The reason they are promoting techniques that seem strikingly ineffective at fostering autonomy or ethical development is that, as a rule, they are not *trying* to foster autonomy or ethical development. The goal is not to support or facilitate children's social and moral growth, but simply to "demand good behavior from students," in Ryan's words.[37] The idea is to get compliance, to *make* children act the way we want them to.

Indeed, if these are the goals, then the methods make perfect sense—the lectures and pseudodiscussions, the slogans and the stories that conk students on the head with their morals. David Brooks, who heads the Jefferson Center for Character Education, frankly states, "We're in the advertising business." The way you get people to do something, whether it's buying Rice Krispies or becoming trustworthy, is to "encourage conformity through repeated messages"[38] The idea of selling virtues like cereal nearly reaches the point of self-parody in the Jefferson Center's curriculum, which includes the following activity: "There's a new product on the market! It's Considerate Cereal. Eating it can make a person more considerate. Design a label for the box. Tell why someone should buy and eat this cereal. Then list the ingredients."[39]

If "repeated messages" don't work, then you simply force students to conform: "Sometimes compulsion is what is needed to get a habit started," says William Kilpatrick.[40] We may recoil from the word "compulsion," but it is the premise of that sentence that really ought to give us pause. When education is construed as the process of inculcating *habits*—which is to say, unreflective actions—then it scarcely deserves to be called education at all. It is really, as Alan Lockwood saw, an attempt to get "mindless conformity to externally imposed standards of conduct."[41]

Notice how naturally this goal follows from a dark view of human nature. If you begin with the premise that "good conduct is not our natural first choice," then the best you can hope for is "the development of good habits"[42]—that is, a system that gets people to act unthinkingly in the manner that someone else has deemed appropriate. This connection recently became clear to Ann Medlock, whose Giraffe Project was designed to evoke "students' own courage and compassion" in thinking about altruism, but which, in some schools, was being turned into a traditional, authoritarian program in which students were simply told how to act and what to believe. Medlock recalls suddenly realizing what was going on with these educators: "Oh, *I* see where you're coming from. You believe kids are no damn good!"[43]

The character education movement's emphasis on habit, then, is consistent with its view of children. Likewise, its process matches its product. The transmission model, along with the use of rewards and punishments to secure compliance, seems entirely appropriate if the values you are trying to transmit are things like obedience and loyalty and respect for authority. But this approach overlooks an important distinction between product and process. When we argue about which traits to emphasize—compassion or loyalty, cooperation or competition, skepticism or obedience—we are trafficking in value judgments. When we talk about how best to teach these things, however, we are being descriptive rather than just prescriptive.

Even if you like the sort of virtues that appear in character education programs, and even if you regard the need to implement those virtues as urgent, the attempt to transmit or instill them dooms the project because that is just not consistent with the best theory and research on how people learn. (Of course, if you have reservations about many of the values that the character educators wish to instill, you may be *relieved* that their favored method is unlikely to be successful.)

I don't wish to be misunderstood. The techniques of character education may succeed in temporarily buying a particular behavior. But they are unlikely to leave children with a *commitment* to that behavior, a reason to continue acting that way in the future. You can turn out automatons who utter the desired words or maybe even "emit" (to use the curious verb favored by behaviorists) the desired actions. But the words and actions are unlikely to continue—much less transfer to new situations—because the child has not been invited to integrate them into his or her value structure. As Dewey observed, "The required beliefs cannot be hammered in; the needed attitudes cannot be plastered on."[44] Yet watch a character education lesson in any part of the country and you will almost surely be observing a strenuous exercise in hammering and plastering.

For traditional moralists, the constructivist approach is a waste of time. If values and traditions and the stories that embody them already exist, then surely "we don't have to reinvent the wheel," remarks Bennett.[45] Likewise an exasperated Wynne: "Must each generation try to completely reinvent society?"[46] The answer is no—and yes. It is not as though everything that now exists must be discarded and entirely new values fashioned from scratch. But the process of learning does indeed require that meaning, ethical or otherwise, be actively invented and reinvented, from the inside out. It requires that children be given the opportunity to make sense of such concepts as fairness or courage, regardless of how long the concepts themselves have been around. Children must be invited to reflect on complex issues, to recast them in light of their own experiences and questions, to figure out for themselves—and with one another—what kind of person one ought to be, which traditions are worth keeping, and how to proceed when two basic values seem to be in conflict.[47]

In this sense, reinvention is necessary if we want to help children to become moral people, as opposed to people who merely do what they are told—or reflexively rebel against what they are told. In fact, as DeVries and Zan add (in a book that offers a useful antidote to traditional character education), "If we want children to resist [peer pressure] and not be victims of others' ideas, we have to educate children to think for themselves about all ideas, including those of adults."[48]

Traditionalists are even more likely to offer another objection to the constructivist approach, one that boils down to a single epithet: *relativism!* If we do anything other than insert moral absolutes in students, if we let them construct their own meanings, then we are saying that anything goes, that morality collapses into personal preferences. Without character education, our schools will just offer programs such as Values Clarification, in which adults are allegedly prohibited from taking a stand.

In response, I would offer several observations. First, the Values Clarification model of moral education, popular in some circles a generation ago, survives today mostly in the polemics of conservatives anxious to justify an indoctrinative approach. Naturally, no statistics are ever cited as to the number of school districts still telling students that any value is as good as any other—assuming the program actually said that in the first place.[49] Second, conservative critics tendentiously try to connect constructivism to relativism, lumping together the work of the late Lawrence Kohlberg with programs like Values Clarification.[50] The truth is that Kohlberg, while opposed to what he called the "bag of virtues" approach to moral education, was not much enamored of Values Clarification either, and he spent a fair amount of time arguing against relativism in general.[51]

If Kohlberg can fairly be criticized, it is for emphasizing moral reasoning, a cognitive process, to the extent that he may have slighted the affective components of morality, such as caring. But the traditionalists are not much for the latter either: caring is seen as an easy or soft virtue (Ryan) that

isn't sufficiently "binding or absolute" (Kilpatrick). The objection to constructivism is not that empathy is eclipsed by justice, but that children—or even adults—should not have an active role to play in making decisions and reflecting on how to live. They should be led instead to an uncritical acceptance of ready-made truths. The character educator's job, remember, is to elicit the right answer from students and tell those who see things differently "why their conclusion is *wrong*." Any deviation from this approach is regarded as indistinguishable from full-blown relativism; we must "plant" traditional values in each child or else morality is nothing more than a matter of individual taste. Such either/or thinking, long since discarded by serious moral philosophers,[52] continues to fuel character education and to perpetuate the confusion of education with indoctrination.

To say that students must construct meaning around moral concepts is not to deny that adults have a crucial role to play. The romantic view that children can basically educate themselves so long as grown-ups don't interfere is not taken seriously by any constructivists I know of—certainly not by Dewey, Piaget, Kohlberg, or their followers. Rather, like Values Clarification, this view seems to exist principally as a straw man in the arguments of conservatives. Let there be no question, then: educators, parents, and other adults are desperately needed to offer guidance, to act as models (we hope), to pose challenges that promote moral growth, and to help children to understand the effects of their actions on other people, thereby tapping and nurturing a concern for others that is present in children from a very young age.[53]

Character education rests on three ideological legs: behaviorism, conservatism, and religion. Of these, the third raises the most delicate issues for a critic; it is here that the charge of *ad hominem* argument is most likely to be raised. So let us be clear: it is of no relevance that almost all the leading proponents of character education are devout Catholics. But it is entirely relevant that, in the shadows of their writings, there lurks the assumption that only religion can serve as the foundation for good character. (William Bennett, for example, has flatly asserted that the difference between right and wrong cannot be taught "without reference to religion."[54]) It is appropriate to consider the personal beliefs of these individuals if those beliefs are ensconced in the movement they have defined and directed. What they do on Sundays is their own business, but if they are trying to turn our public schools into Sunday schools, that becomes everybody's business.

Even putting aside the theological underpinnings of the character education movement, the five questions presented in this chapter can help us to describe the natural constituency of that movement. Logically, its supporters should be those who firmly believe that we should focus our efforts on repairing the characters of children, rather than on transforming the environments in which they learn, those who assume the worst about human nature, those who are more committed to preserving than to changing our society, those who favor such values as obedience to authority, and those who define learning as the process of swallowing whole a set of preexisting truths. It stands to reason that readers who recognize themselves in this description would enthusiastically endorse character education in its present form.

The rest of us have a decision to make. Either we define our efforts to promote children's social and moral development as an *alternative* to "character education," thereby ceding that label to the people who have already appropriated it, or we try to *reclaim* the wider meaning of the term by billing what we are doing as a different kind of character education.

The first choice—opting out—seems logical: it strains the language to use a single phrase to describe practices as different as engaging students in reflecting about fairness, on the one hand, and making students dress alike, on the other. It seems foolish to pretend that these are just different versions of the same thing, and thus it may be unreasonable to expect someone with a constructivist or progressive vision to endorse what is now called character education. The problem with abandoning this label, however, is that it holds considerable appeal for politicians and members of the public at large. It will be challenging to explain that "character education" is not synonymous with helping children to grow into good people and, indeed, that the movement associated with the term is a good deal more controversial than it first appears.

The second choice, meanwhile, presents its own set of practical difficulties. Given that the individuals and organizations mentioned in this chapter have succeeded in putting their own stamp on character education, it will not be easy to redefine the phrase so that it can also signify a very different approach. It will not be easy, that is, to organize conferences, publish books and articles, and develop curricular materials that rescue the broad meaning of "character education."

Whether we relinquish or retain the nomenclature, though, it is vital that we work to decouple most of what takes place under the banner of "character education" from the enterprise of helping students become ethically sophisticated decision makers and caring human beings. Wanting young people to turn out that way doesn't require us to adopt traditional character education programs, any more than wanting them to be physically fit requires us to turn schools into Marine boot camps.

What does the alternative look like? Return once more to those five questions: in each case, an answer different from that given by traditional character education will help us to sketch the broad contours of a divergent approach. More specifically, we should probably target certain practices for elimination, add some new ones, and reconfigure still others that already exist. I have already offered a catalogue of examples of what to eliminate, from Skinnerian reinforcers to lesson plans that resemble sermons. As examples of what to add, we might suggest holding regular class meetings in which students can share, plan, decide, and reflect together.[55] We might also provide children with explicit opportunities to practice "perspective taking"—that is, imagining how the world looks from someone else's point of view. Activities that promote an understanding of how others think and feel, that support the impulse to imaginatively reach beyond the self, can provide the same benefits realized by holding democratic class meetings—that is, helping students become more ethical and compassionate while simultaneously fostering intellectual growth.[56]

A good example of an existing practice that might be reconfigured is the use of literature to teach values. In principle, the idea is splendid: it makes perfect sense to select stories that not only help students develop reading skills (and an appreciation for good writing) but also raise moral issues. The trouble is that many programs use simplistic little morality tales in place of rich, complex literature. Naturally, the texts should be developmentally appropriate, but some character educators fail to give children credit for being able to grapple with ambiguity. (Imagine the sort of stories likely to be assigned by someone who maintains that "it is ridiculous to believe children are capable of objectively assessing most of the beliefs and values they must absorb to be effective adults."[57])

Perhaps the concern is not that students will be unable to make sense of challenging literature, but that they will not derive the "correct" moral. This would account for the fact that, even when character education curricula include impressive pieces of writing, the works tend to be used for the purpose of drumming in simple lessons. As Kilpatrick sees it, a story "points to these [characters] and says in effect, 'Act like this; don't act like that.'"[58] This kind of lesson often takes the form of hero worship, with larger-than-life characters—or real historical figures presented with their foibles airbrushed away—held up to students to encourage imitation of their actions.

Rather than employ literature to indoctrinate or induce mere conformity, we can use it to spur reflection. Whether the students are 6-year-olds or 16-year-olds, the discussion of stories should be open ended rather than relentlessly didactic. Teachers who refrain from tightly controlling such conversations are impressed again and again by the levels of meaning students prove capable of exploring and the moral growth that they exhibit in such an environment. Instead of announcing "This man is a hero; do what he did," such teachers may involve the students in *deciding* who (if anyone) is heroic in a given story—or in contemporary culture[59]—and why. They may even invite students to reflect on the larger issue of whether it is desirable to have heroes. (Consider the quality of discussion that might be generated by ask-

ing older students to respond to the declaration of playwright Bertolt Brecht: "Unhappy is the land that needs a hero.")

More than specific practices that might be added, subtracted, or changed, a program to help children grow into good people begins with a commitment to change the way classrooms and schools are structured—and this brings us back to the idea of transcending a fix-the-kid approach. Consider the format of classroom discussions. A proponent of character education, invoking such traditional virtues as patience or self-control, might remind students that they must wait to be recognized by the teacher. But what if we invited students to think about the best way to conduct a discussion? Must we raise our hands? Is there another way to avoid having everyone talk at once? How can we be fair to those who aren't as assertive or as fast on their feet? Should the power to decide who can speak always rest with the teacher? Perhaps the problem is not with students who need to be more self-disciplined, but with the whole instructional design that has students waiting to be recognized to answer someone else's questions. And perhaps the real learning comes only when students have the chance to grapple with such issues.

One more example. A proponent of character education says we must make students understand that it is wrong to lie; we need to teach them about the importance of being honest. But why do people lie? Usually because they don't feel safe enough to tell the truth. The real challenge for us as educators is to examine that precept in terms of what is going on in our classrooms, to ask how we and the students together can make sure that even unpleasant truths can be told and heard. Does pursuing this line of inquiry mean that it's acceptable to fib? No. It means that the problem has to be dissected and solved from the inside out. It means behaviors occur in a context that teachers have helped to establish; therefore, teachers have to examine (and consider modifying) that context even at the risk of some discomfort to themselves. In short, if we want to help children grow into compassionate and responsible people, we have to change the way the classroom works and feels, not just the way each separate member of that class acts. Our emphasis should not be on forming individual characters so much as on transforming educational structures.

Happily, programs do exist whose promotion of children's social and moral development is grounded in a commitment to change the culture of schools. The best example of which I am aware is the Child Development Project, an elementary school program designed, implemented, and researched by the Developmental Studies Center in Oakland, California. The CDP's premise is that, by meeting children's needs, we increase the likelihood that they will care about others. Meeting their needs entails, among other things, turning schools into caring communities. The CDP offers the additional advantages of a constructivist vision of learning, a positive view of human nature, a balance of cognitive and affective concerns, and a program that is integrated into all aspects of school life (including the curriculum).[60]

Is the CDP an example of what character education ought to be—or of what ought to replace character education? The answer to that question will depend on tactical, and even semantic, considerations. Far more compelling is the need to reevaluate the practices and premises of contemporary character education. To realize a humane and progressive vision for children's development, we may need to look elsewhere.

ENDNOTES

1. See, for example, Linda Page, "A Conservative Christian View on Values," *School Administrator,* September 1995, p. 22.

2. See, for example, Kevin Ryan, "The Ten Commandments of Character Education," *School Administrator,* September 1995, p. 19; and program materials from the Character Education Institute and the Jefferson Center for Character Education.

3. See Alfie Kohn, *Punished by Rewards: The Trouble with Gold Stars, Incentive Plans, A's, Praise, and Other Bribes* (Boston: Houghton Mifflin, 1993); and Edward L. Deci and Richard M. Ryan, *Intrinsic Motivation and Self-Determination in Human Behavior* (New York: Plenum, 1985).

4. See C. Daniel Batson et al., "Buying Kindness: Effect of an Extrinsic Incentive for Helping on Perceived Altruism," *Personality and Social Psychology Bulletin,*

vol. 4, 1978, p. 90; Cathleen L. Smith et al., "Children's Causal Attributions Regarding Help Giving," *Child Development,* vol. 50, 1979, pp. 203–10; and William Edward Upton III, "Altruism, Attribution, and Intrinsic Motivation in the Recruitment of Blood Donors," *Dissertation Abstracts International* 34B, vol. 12, 1974, p. 6260.

5. Richard A. Fabes et al., "Effects of Rewards on Children's Prosocial Motivation: A Socialization Study," *Developmental Psychology,* vol. 25, 1989, pp. 509–15; and Joan Grusec, "Socializing Concern for Others in the Home," *Developmental Psychology,* vol. 27, 1991, pp. 338–42.

6. See Alfie Kohn, *No Contest: The Case Against Competition,* rev. ed. (Boston: Houghton Mifflin, 1992).

7. This statement is taken from an eight-page brochure produced by the "Character Counts!" Coalition, a project of the Josephson Institute of Ethics. Members of the coalition include the American Federation of Teachers, the National Association of Secondary School Principals, the American Red Cross, the YMCA, and many other organizations.

8. William Kilpatrick, *Why Johnny Can't Tell Right from Wrong* (New York: Simon & Schuster, 1992), pp. 96, 249.

9. For example, Kilpatrick was selected in 1995 to keynote the first in a series of summer institutes on character education sponsored by Thomas Lickona.

10. Edward Wynne, "Transmitting Traditional Values in Contemporary Schools," in Larry P. Nucci, ed., *Moral Development and Character Education: A Dialogue* (Berkeley, CA: McCutchan, 1989), p. 25.

11. Kevin Ryan, "In Defense of Character Education," in Nucci, p. 16.

12. Louis Goldman, "Mind, Character, and the Deferral of Gratification," *Educational Forum,* vol. 60, 1996, p. 136. As part of "educational reconstruction," he goes on to say, we must "connect the lower social classes to the middle classes who may provide role models for self-discipline" (p. 139).

13. Jarvis is quoted in Wray Herbert, "The Moral Child," *U.S. News & World Report,* June 3, 1996, p. 58.

14. Amitai Etzioni, *The Spirit of Community: The Reinvention of American Society* (New York: Simon & Schuster, 1993), p. 91.

15. See Alfie Kohn, *The Brighter Side of Human Nature: Altruism and Empathy in Everyday Life* (New York: Basic Books, 1990); and "Caring Kids: The

Role of the Schools," *Phi Delta Kappan,* March 1991, pp. 496–506.

16. David E. Purpel, "Moral Education: An Idea Whose Time Has Gone," *The Clearing House,* vol. 64, 1991, p. 311.

17. This description of the character education movement is offered by Alan L. Lockwood in "Character Education: The Ten Percent Solution," *Social Education,* April/May 1991, p. 246. It is a particularly apt characterization of a book like *Why Johnny Can't Tell Right from Wrong,* which invokes an age of "chivalry" and sexual abstinence, a time when moral truths were uncomplicated and unchallenged. The author's tone, however, is not so much wistful about the past as angry about the present: he denounces everything from rock music (which occupies an entire chapter in a book about morality) and feminism to the "multiculturalists" who dare to remove "homosexuality from the universe of moral judgment" (p. 126).

18. Kevin Walsh of the University of Alabama is quoted in Eric N. Berg, "Argument Grows That Teaching of Values Should Rank with Lessons," *New York Times,* January 1, 1992, p. 32.

19. I am reminded of a woman in a Houston audience who heatedly informed me that she doesn't send her child to school "to learn to be nice." That, she declared, would be "social engineering." But a moment later this woman added that her child ought to be "taught to respect authority." Since this would seem to be at least as apposite an example of social engineering, one is led to conclude that the woman's real objection was to the teaching of *particular* topics or values.

20. Kevin Ryan, "Mining the Values in the Curriculum," *Educational Leadership,* November 1993, p. 16.

21. Telling students to "try hard" and "do their best" begs the important questions. *How,* exactly, do they do their best? Surely it is not just a matter of blind effort. And *why* should they do so, particularly if the task is not engaging or meaningful to them, or if it has simply been imposed on them? Research has found that the attitudes students take toward learning are heavily influenced by whether they have been led to attribute their success (or failure) to innate ability, to effort, or to other factors—and that traditional classroom practices such as grading and competition lead them to explain the results in terms of ability (or its absence) and to minimize effort whenever possible. What looks like "laziness" or insufficient perseverance, in other words, often turns out to be a rational decision to avoid challenge; it is rational because this route proves most expedient for performing well or maintaining an image of oneself as smart. These systemic factors, of course, are complex and often threatening for educators to address; it is much easier just to impress on children the importance of doing their best and then blame them for lacking perseverance if they seem not to do so.

22. Edward A. Wynne, "The Great Tradition in Education: Transmitting Moral Values," *Educational Leadership,* December 1985/January 1986, p. 6.

23. Mary Lord, "The Return of the 'Fourth R,'" *U.S. News & World Report,* September 11, 1995, p. 58.

24. William Glasser, *Schools Without Failure* (New York: Harper & Row, 1969), p. 22.

25. Marc Desmond's letter appeared in the *New York Times Magazine,* May 21, 1995, p. 14. The same point was made by Robert Primack, "No Substitute for Critical Thinking: A Response to Wynne," *Educational Leadership,* December 1985/January 1986, p. 12.

26. Deborah Meier and Paul Schwarz, "Central Park East Secondary School," in Michael W. Apple and James A. Beane, eds., *Democratic Schools* (Alexandria, VA: Association for Supervision and Curriculum Development, 1995), pp. 29–30.

27. See Richard de Charms, *Personal Causation: The Internal Affective Determinants of Behavior* (Hillsdale, NJ: Erlbaum, 1983). See also the many publications of Edward Deci and Richard Ryan.

28. See, for example, Alfie Kohn, "Choices for Children: Why and How to Let Students Decide," *Phi Delta Kappan,* September 1993, pp. 8–20; and Child Development Project, *Ways We Want Our Class to Be: Class Meetings That Build Commitment to Kindness and Learning* (Oakland, CA: Developmental Studies Center, 1996).

29. The quotations are from Wynne, "The Great Tradition," p. 9; and Edward A. Wynne and Herbert J. Walberg, "The Complementary Goals of Character Development and Academic Excellence," *Educational Leadership,* December 1985/January 1986, p. 17. William Kilpatrick is equally averse to including students in decision making; he speaks longingly of the days when "schools were unapologetically authoritarian," declaring that "schools can learn a lot from the Army," which is a "hierarchial [sic], authoritarian, and undemocratic institution" (see *Why Johnny Can't,* p. 228).

30. The sort of compassion I have in mind is akin to what the psychologist Ervin Staub described as a "prosocial orientation" (see his *Positive Social Behavior and Morality,* vols. 1 and 2 [New York: Academic Press, 1978 and 1979])—a generalized inclination to

care, share, and help across different situations and with different people, including those we don't know, don't like, and don't look like. Loyally lending a hand to a close friend is one thing; going out of one's way for a stranger is something else.

31. John Dewey, *The School and Society* (Chicago: University of Chicago Press, 1900; reprint, 1990), p. 15.

32. Wynne and Walberg, p. 17. For another endorsement of competition among students, see Kevin Ryan, "In Defense," p. 15.

33. This passage is taken from page 21 of an undated 28-page "Character Education Curriculum" produced by the Character Education Institute. Emphasis in original.

34. Wynne, "Great Tradition," p. 9. Wynne and other figures in the character education movement acknowledge their debt to the French social scientist Emile Durkheim, who believed that "all education is a continuous effort to impose on the child ways of seeing, feeling, and acting which he could not have arrived at spontaneously. . . . We exert pressure upon him in order that he may learn proper consideration for others, respect for customs and conventions, the need for work, etc." (See Durkheim, *The Rules of Sociological Method* [New York: Free Press, 1938], p. 6.)

35. This is from Bennett's introduction to *The Book of Virtues* (New York: Simon & Schuster, 1993), pp. 12–13.

36. Constance Kamii, Faye B. Clark, and Ann Dominick, "The Six National Goals: A Road to Disappointment," *Phi Delta Kappan,* May 1994, p. 677.

37. Kevin Ryan, "Character and Coffee Mugs," *Education Week,* May 17, 1995, p. 48.

38. The second quotation is a reporter's paraphrase of Brooks. Both it and the direct quotation preceding it appear in Philip Cohen, "The Content of Their Character: Educators Find New Ways to Tackle Values and Morality," *ASCD Curriculum Update,* Spring 1995, p. 4.

39. See B. David Brooks, *Young People's Lessons in Character: Student Activity Workbook* (San Diego, CA: Young People's Press, 1996), p. 12.

40. Kilpatrick, p. 231.

41. To advocate this sort of enterprise, he adds, is to "caricature the moral life." See Alan L. Lockwood, "Keeping Them in the Courtyard: A Response to Wynne," *Educational Leadership,* December 1985/January 1986, p. 10.

42. Kilpatrick, p. 97.

43. Personal communication with Ann Medlock, May 1996.

44. John Dewey, *Democracy and Education* (New York: Free Press, 1916; reprint, 1966), p. 11.

45. Bennett, p. 11.

46. Wynne, "Character and Academics," p. 142.

47. For a discussion of how traditional character education fails to offer guidance when values come into conflict, see Lockwood, "Character Education."

48. Rheta DeVries and Betty Zan, *Moral Classrooms, Moral Children: Creating a Constructivist Atmosphere in Early Education* (New York: Teachers College Press, 1994), p. 253.

49. For an argument that critics tend to misrepresent what Values Clarification was about, see James A. Beane, *Affect in the Curriculum* (New York: Teachers College Press, 1990), pp. 104–106.

50. Wynne, for example, refers to the developers of Values Clarification as "popularizers" of Kohlberg's research (see "Character and Academics," p. 141), while Amitai Etzioni, in the course of criticizing Piaget's and Kohlberg's work, asserts that "a typical course on moral reasoning starts with something called 'values clarification'" (see *The Spirit of Community,* p. 98).

51. Kohlberg's model, which holds that people across cultures progress predictably through six stages of successively more sophisticated styles of moral reasoning, is based on the decidedly nonrelativistic premise that the last stages are superior to the first ones. See his *Essays on Moral Development, Vol. 1: The Philosophy of Moral Development* (San Francisco: Harper & Row, 1981), especially the essays titled "Indoctrination versus Relativity in Value Education" and "From *Is* to *Ought.*"

52. See, for example, James S. Fishkin, *Beyond Subjective Morality* (New Haven, CT: Yale University Press, 1984); and David B. Wong, *Moral Relativity* (Berkeley: University of California Press, 1984).

53. Researchers at the National Institute of Mental Health have summarized the available research as follows: "Even children as young as 2 years old have (a) the cognitive capacity to interpret the physical and psychological states of others, (b) the emotional capacity to effectively experience the other's state, and (c) the behavioral repertoire that permits the possibility of trying to alleviate discomfort in others. These are the capabilities that, we believe, underlie children's caring behavior in the presence of another person's distress. . . . Young children seem to show patterns of moral internalization that are not simply fear based or solely responsive to parental commands. Rather, there are signs that children feel responsible for (as well as

connected to and dependent on) others at a very young age." (See Carolyn Zahn-Waxler et al., "Development of Concern for Others," *Developmental Psychology,* vol. 28, 1992, pp. 127, 135. For more on the adult's role in light of these facts, see Kohn, *The Brighter Side.*)

54. "Education Secretary Backs Teaching of Religious Values," *New York Times,* November 12, 1985, p. B-4.

55. For more on class meetings, see Glasser, chaps. 10–12; Thomas Gordon, *T. E.T: Teacher Effectiveness Training* (New York: David McKay Co., 1974), chaps. 8–9; Jane Nelsen, Lynn Lott, and H. Stephen Glenn, *Positive Discipline in the Classroom* (Rocklin, CA: Prima, 1993); and Child Development Project.

56. For more on the theory and research of perspective taking, see Kohn, *The Brighter Side,* chaps. 4–5; for practical classroom activities for promoting perspective-taking skills, see Norma Deitch Feshbach et al., *Learning to Care: Classroom Activities for Social and Affective Development* (Glenview, IL: Scott, Foresman, 1983). While specialists in the field distinguish between perspective taking (imagining what others see, think, or feel) and empathy (*feeling* what others feel), most educators who talk about the importance of helping children to become empathic really seem to be talking about perspective taking.

57. Wynne, "Great Tradition," p. 9.

58. Kilpatrick, p. 141.

59. It is informative to discover whom the proponents of a hero-based approach to character education themselves regard as heroic. For example, William Bennett's nominee for "possibly our greatest living American" is Rush Limbaugh. (See Terry Eastland, "Rush Limbaugh: Talking Back," *American Spectator,* September 1992, p. 23.)

60. See Victor Battistich et al., "The Child Development Project: A Comprehensive Program for the Development of Prosocial Character," in William M. Kurtines and Jacob L. Gewirtz, eds., *Moral Behavior and Development: Advances in Theory, Research, and Applications* (Hillsdale, NJ: Erlbaum, 1989); and Daniel Solomon et al., "Creating a Caring Community: Educational Practices That Promote Children's Prosocial Development," in Fritz K. Oser, Andreas Dick, and Jean-Luc Patry, eds., *Effective and Responsible Teaching* (San Francisco: Jossey-Bass, 1992). For more information about the CDP program or about the research substantiating its effects, write the Developmental Studies Center at 2000 Embarcadero, Suite 305, Oakland, CA 94606.

DISCUSSION QUESTIONS

1. According to the author, how is character education most accurately described?
2. What are the fundamental limitations of current character education program strategies?
3. Why do many educators contest the goals and values that typify character education programs?
4. What divergent approaches would exemplify a program that is different from traditional approaches to moral development?
5. How can reflection be used to enhance students' moral growth?
6. How can classroom norms thwart or facilitate students' moral development?

19

Limiting Students' School Success and Life Chances: The Impact of Tracking

JEANNIE S. OAKES

FOCUSING QUESTIONS

1. Why has tracking been considered to be a fair educational practice by educators and psychologists?
2. How has tracking affected student outcomes?
3. How do educators tend to justify the practice of tracking?
4. In what ways were criteria used to assign students to tracks?
5. What procedures were used to ensure that parents were informed about tracking and their rights to influence placements?
6. What role did teacher assessment and perception play in assigning students to tracks?

Evidence from two school systems whose ability-grouping and tracking systems were subject to scrutiny in 1993 in conjunction with school desegregation cases demonstrates how grouping practices can create within-school segregation and discrimination against African American and Latino students. In both school systems, tracking created racially unbalanced classes at all three levels—elementary, middle, and senior high, with African American or Latino students consistently overrepresented and white and Asian students consistently underrepresented in low-ability tracks in all subjects. Neither district's placement practices created classrooms with a range of measured student ability and achievement in classrooms sufficiently narrow to be considered homogeneous "ability groups," and African American and Latino students were much less likely than whites or Asians with comparable scores to be placed in high-track courses. These disproportionate lower-track placements worked to disadvantage minority students' achievement outcomes. Whether students began with relatively high or relatively

low achievement, those who were placed in lower-level courses showed lesser gains over time than similarly situated students placed in higher-level courses. In both systems, grouping practices created a cycle of restricted opportunities and diminished outcomes and exacerbated differences between African American and Latino and white students.

Since the 1920s, most elementary and secondary schools have tracked their students into separate "ability" groups designed for bright, average, and slow learners and into separate programs for students who are expected to follow different career routes after high school graduation. Tracking has seemed appropriate and fair, given the way psychologists have defined differences in students' intellectual abilities, motivation, and aspirations. Tracking has seemed logical because it supports a nearly century old belief that a crucial job of schools is to ready students for an economy that requires workers with quite different knowledge and skills. According to this logic, demanding academic classes would prepare bright, motivated students heading for jobs that require college degrees, while more rudimentary academic classes and vocational programs would ready less able and less motivated students for less-skilled jobs or for post–high school technical training. With the development early in the 20th century of standardized tests for placement, most people viewed a tracked curriculum with its ability-grouped academic classes as functional, scientific, and democratic—an educationally sound way to accomplish two important tasks: (1) providing students with the education that best suits their abilities and (2) providing the nation with the array of workers it needs.

Despite its widespread legitimacy, there is no question that tracking, the assessment practices that support it, and the differences in educational opportunity that result from it limit many students' schooling opportunities and life chances. These limits affect schoolchildren from all racial, ethnic, and socioeconomic groups. However, schools far more often judge African American and Latino students to have learning deficits and limited potential. Not surprisingly, then, schools place these students disproportionately in low-track, remedial programs.

Educators justify these placements by pointing out that African American and Latino children typically perform less well on commonly accepted assessments of ability and achievement. Moreover, conventional school wisdom holds that low-track, remedial, and special education classes help these students, since they permit teachers to target instruction to the particular learning deficiencies of low-ability students. However, considerable research demonstrates that students do not profit from enrollment in low-track classes; they do not learn as much as comparably skilled students in heterogeneous classes; they have less access than other students to knowledge, engaging learning experiences, and resources.[1] Thus school tracking practices create racially separate programs that provide minority children with restricted educational opportunities and outcomes.

In what follows, I will illustrate these points with evidence from two school systems whose ability grouping and tracking systems have been subject to scrutiny in conjunction with school desegregation cases. The first system, Rockford Public Schools, in Rockford, Illinois (previously under an interim court order), was the target of a liability suit brought by a community group, The People Who Care. Among other complaints, the group charged the school system with within-school segregation through ability grouping and discrimination against the district's nearly 30 percent African American and Latino students. The second system, San Jose Unified School District, in San Jose, California, approached the court hoping to be released from its desegregation order of 1985. The plaintiffs in the San Jose case argued, among other things, that the district had used its ability-grouping system to create within-school segregation and, thereby, circumvented the intent of the court order with regard to its approximately 30 percent Latino student population. I analyzed data about the grouping practices in both these cities, prepared reports for the court, and testified. The San Jose system reached a settlement prior to the formal hearing date. The Rockford system was found liable by the court.

To shed light on the grouping practices in these two systems, I conducted analyses and reported my conclusions about tracking and ability-grouping practices around several questions:

1. Does the school system employ tracking and/or ability grouping? If so, what is the specific nature of these practices?
2. Does the system's use of tracking and/or ability grouping create racially imbalanced classrooms?
3. Does the system's use of these grouping practices reflect sound, consistent, and educationally valid considerations?
4. Are the racial disproportionalities created by the system's ability-grouping practices explained by valid educational considerations?
5. What are the consequences of the system's grouping and tracking practices for the classroom instructional opportunities of Latino children?
6. What are the consequences of the system's grouping and tracking practices for the educational outcomes of Latino children?
7. Does the system have the necessary support and capacity to dismantle racially identifiable tracking and create heterogeneously grouped classrooms?

I addressed these questions with analyses using data specific to the two school systems. These data were gathered from a variety of sources: district and individual school curriculum documents (e.g., curriculum guides, course catalogs, course descriptions, etc.); school plans; computerized student enrollment and achievement data; prior reports prepared by court monitors; and depositions taken from school district employees in the course of the discovery process.[2]

Several analytic methods were applied to these data, all of which had been used in prior published research on tracking and ability grouping. In both systems, I used statistical methods to calculate the achievement range within each track, the distribution of students from various ethnic groups into various tracks, and the probability of placement of students from each ethnic group whose prior achievement "qualified" them for various tracks. In San Jose, but not in Rockford, I was also able to calculate rather precisely the impact of track placement on achievement gains of students with comparable prior achievement. I applied content analysis techniques to district and school curriculum documents in order to classify courses into various track levels, determine placement criteria and processes, and identify curricular goals, course content, and learning opportunities. These documents constitute official district policy statements about the levels and content of the districts' programs and courses, as well as the criteria and procedures by which students enroll in various programs and courses.

The scope of possible analyses was limited, more in Rockford than in San Jose, by a lack of some essential data. Even so, the available data permitted comprehensive analyses of many aspects of the district's grouping practices. They provided a clear picture of tracking and ability grouping in the two systems and enabled me to place the district's practices in light of national research.

PROLIFERATION OF TRACKING

Grouping practices and their effects on minority children were remarkably similar in both systems. Both systems used tracking extensively. At most grade levels and in most academic subject areas at nearly all schools, educators assigned students to classes based on judgments about students' academic abilities. The schools then tailored the curriculum and instruction within classes to the students' perceived ability levels. The districts' tracking systems were not only very comprehensive (in terms of the subject areas and grade levels that are tracked), but also very rigid and stable. That is, the districts tended to place students at the same ability level for classes in a variety of subject areas and to lock students into the same or a lower ability-level placement from year to year.

RACIALLY DISPROPORTIONATE TRACK ENROLLMENTS

In both school systems, tracking had created racially imbalanced classes at all three levels—elementary, middle, and senior high. This imbalance took two forms: (1) white (and Asian, in San Jose) students were consistently overrepresented and African American and Latino students were consistently underrepresented in high-ability classes in all subjects; (2) in contrast, African American or Latino students were consistently overrepresented while white and Asian students were consistently underrepresented in low-ability tracks in all subjects.

INCONSISTENT APPLICATION OF PLACEMENT CRITERIA

The criteria used to assign students to particular tracks were neither clearly specified nor consistently applied. Accordingly, neither district's tracking policies and practices could be construed as the enactment of valid educational purposes; neither did either district present an educational justification for the racial imbalance that results from tracking. Moreover, my analyses demonstrate clearly that neither district's placement practices—practices that result in racially imbalanced tracked classrooms—could be justified by a racially neutral policy of creating classrooms that are distinctly different from one another in terms of students' academic ability or achievement. To the contrary, neither district had enacted ability grouping and tracking in ways that narrow the range of measured student ability and achievement in classrooms sufficiently so that these classrooms can be considered bona fide ability groups.

Both school systems honored parent requests for students' initial track placements and for subsequent changes. This policy undermined the basis of student assignments in either objective measures of students' abilities or more subjective professional judgments. Making matters worse, not all parents were informed about tracking practices or about parents' right to influence their children's placements. Specifically, African American and Latino parents had less access than others to this knowledge.

Additionally, teacher and counselor recommendations at the critical transitions between elementary and middle school and between middle and high school included a formal mechanism to take into account highly subjective judgments about students' personalities, behavior, and motivation. For example, the screening process for gifted programs usually began with a subjective teacher identification of potentially gifted children, who were then referred for formal testing. Such referrals were often based on subjective judgments about behavior, personality, and attitudes.

TRACKS ACTUALLY HETEROGENEOUS GROUPS

The theory of tracking argues that, to facilitate learning, children should be separated into groups so that they may be taught together with peers of similar ability and apart from those with higher or lower abilities. But in both school systems, classes that were supposed to be designated for students at a *particular* ability level actually enrolled students who spanned *a very wide range* of measured ability. These ranges demonstrate dramatically that in both Rockford and San Jose racially imbalanced tracked classes have borne little resemblance to homogeneous ability groups—even though they have been labeled and treated as such by schools. While the mean scores in each of the tracks followed expected patterns—with average achievement score for students in the low track less than average score for students in the standard or accelerated tracks—the extraordinarily broad range of achievement in each of the three tracks makes clear how far these classes are from being ho-

mogeneous ability groups. In sum, the district's practices do not represent what tracking advocates would claim is a trustworthy enactment of a "theory" of tracking and ability grouping.

For example, at one Rockford middle school, the range of eighth-grade reading scores in Honors English (31–99 National Percentile [NP]) overlapped considerably with the range in Regular English (1–95 NP), which overlapped considerably with the range in Basic English (1–50 NP). At one of the senior highs, the math scores of tenth graders in the normal progress college prep math track (26–99 NP) overlapped considerably with those in the slow progress college prep courses (1–99), and both overlapped considerably with the scores of those in non–college preparatory classes (1–99). I found similar patterns of large, overlapping ranges of qualifying scores throughout the system.

The same was true in San Jose. For example, sixth graders placed in a low-track mathematics course demonstrated abilities that ranged all the way from rock-bottom Normal Curve Equivalent (NCE) achievement scores of 1 to extraordinarily high scores of 86. Even more striking, sixth graders in standard-track math classes had achievement scores that spanned the entire range, from NCE scores of 1 to 99. And, while sixth graders in accelerated courses had a somewhat more restricted ability range, they too scored all the way from 52 to 99 NCEs. I found similar patterns in a number of other subjects in most middle and senior high school grades.

PLACEMENTS RACIALLY SKEWED BEYOND THE EFFECTS OF ACHIEVEMENT

As a group, African American and Latino students scored lower on achievement tests than whites and Asians in Rockford and San Jose. However, African American and Latino students were much less likely than white or Asian students *with the same test scores* to be placed in accelerated courses. For example, in San Jose, Latino eighth graders with average scores in mathematics were three times less likely than whites with the same scores to be placed in an accelerated math course. Among ninth graders, the results were similar. Latinos scoring between 40 and 49, 50 and 59, and 60 and 69

NCEs were less than half as likely as their white and Asian counterparts to be placed in accelerated tracks. The discrimination is even more striking among the highest scoring students. While only 56 percent of Latinos scoring between 90 and 99 NCEs were placed in accelerated classes, 93 percent of whites and 97 percent of Asians gained admission to these classes.

In Rockford's tracks and class ability levels, the groups of *higher*-track students whose scores fell within a range that would qualify them for participation in either a higher or a lower track (i.e., their scores were the same as students in the lower track) were consistently "whiter" than groups of students whose scores fell within that same range but were placed in the *lower* track. In a number of cases, Rockford's high-track classes included students with exceptionally low scores, but rarely were these students African Americans. Conversely, high-scoring African Americans were enrolled in low-track classes; again, this was seldom the case for high-scoring whites. For example, in 1987, none of the African American students who scored in the top quartile (75–99 NP) on the California Assessment Program (CAP) reading comprehension test at two of Rockford's large high schools were placed in high-track English, compared with about 40 percent of top-quartile whites who were enrolled in the high track at those schools. In contrast, at three of the system's senior high schools, a small fraction of white students who scored in the bottom quartile (1–25 NP) were in high-track classes, while no similarly low-scoring African Americans were so placed. At two other senior highs, while some top-quartile African Americans were placed in Honors English, many more top-scoring African Americans were in the basic classes. No low-scoring whites were so placed. I found similar patterns in other subjects at the district's high schools.

I found other striking examples of racially skewed placements in Rockford's junior highs. For example, at one, the range of reading comprehension scores among eighth graders enrolled in Basic English classes was from the first to the seventy-second national percentile. Of these, ten students scored above the national average of 50 NP. Six of the highest scoring, above-average students were African American, including the highest achieving student in the class. One other of the above-average students was Latino.

In both San Jose and Rockford, placement practices skewed enrollments in favor of whites over and above that which can be explained by measured achievement.

LOW TRACKS PROVIDING LESS OPPORTUNITY

In both school systems, African American and Latino students in lower-track classes had fewer learning opportunities. Teachers expected less of them and gave them less exposure to curriculum and instruction in essential knowledge and skills. Lower-track classes also provided African American and Latino students with less access to a whole range of resources and opportunities: to highly qualified teachers, to classroom environments conducive to learning, to opportunities to earn extra grade points that could bolster their grade-point averages, and to courses that would qualify them for college entrance and a wide variety of careers as adults.

LOW TRACKS AND LOWER ACHIEVEMENT

Not only did African American and Latino students receive a lower-quality education as a result of tracking in San Jose and Rockford; their academic achievement suffered as well. In Rockford, the initial average achievement gap (i.e., the difference in group mean achievement scores between white and African American and/or white and Latino students on district-administered achievement tests in first grade) did not diminish in higher grades. To the contrary, eleventh graders exhibited gaps somewhat larger than those of first graders. For example, on the 1992 Stanford Achievement Test in reading comprehension, the gap between African American and white first graders was 25 percent; that between African American and white eleventh graders was 30 percent. Undoubtedly more telling, at the time of the seventh-grade test—probably the last point before considerable numbers of lower-achieving minority students drop out of school—the achievement gap between African Americans and whites had grown considerably wider, to 36 percent. A similar pattern was found in students' raw scores in reading comprehension and mathematics for grades 1–6 on the 1992 Stanford Achievement Test. Here, the reading achievement gap between African American and white students was .88 of a standard deviation at first grade and grew to .99 by grade 6. The Latino–white gap grew from .67 to .70 over the same grades. In math, the African American–white gap grew from .87 to 1.01; in contrast, the Latino–white gap dropped from .98 to .79. Clearly, the district's tracked programs failed to close the minority–white gap between average group scores. Neither did these practices correct the overrepresentation of black and Latino students in the group of lowest-scoring students in the district. For example, in 1992, 37 percent of the first-grade children scoring between the first and the twenty-fifth national percentiles in reading comprehension on the Stanford Achievement Test were African American; at seventh grade, the percentage of African Americans in this low-scoring group had risen to 46 percent, and by grade 11 (following a disproportionately high incidence of dropping out by low-achieving African American students), African American students still made up 35 percent of this group. Neither did student placements in various instructional programs enable minority students to rise into the group of the district's highest achievers. In fact, *the proportion of minority students in the highest-achieving group of students dropped precipitously.* For example, in 1992, 10 percent of the first-grade children scoring between the seventy-fifth and the ninety-ninth national percentiles in reading comprehension on the Stanford Achievement Test were African American; at seventh grade, the percentage of African Americans in this high-scoring group had dropped by half, to only 5 percent (28 in number); this low proportion was also found at grade 11 (even though the actual number of students, 20, was smaller).

Rockford's grouping practices that created racially identifiable classrooms and provided unequal opportunities to learn (with fewer such opportunities provided to minority students) *did not serve a remedial function for minority students.* To the contrary, these practices did not even enable minority students to sustain their position, relative to white students, in the district's achievement hierarchy.

In San Jose, better data permitted me to analyze the impact of track placement on individual students over time. Students who were placed in lower-level courses—disproportionately Latino students—consistently demonstrate lesser gains in achievement over time than their peers placed in high-level courses. For example, among the students with preplacement math achievement between 50 and 59 NCEs, those who were placed in a low-track course began with a mean of 54.4 NCEs, but lost an average of 2.2 NCEs after one year and had lost a total of 1.9 NCEs after three years. Students who scored between 50 and 59 NCEs and were placed in a standard-track course, by contrast, began with a mean of 54.6 NCEs, gained 0.1 NCE after one year, and had gained 3.5 NCEs after three years. The largest gains were experienced by students who were placed in an accelerated course, who began with a mean of 55.4 NCEs, gained 6.5 NCEs after one year, and had gained a total of 9.6 NCEs after three years.

These results are consistent across achievement levels: Whether students began with relatively high or relatively low achievement, those who were placed in lower-level courses showed lesser gains over time than similarly situated students who were placed in higher-level courses.

IN SUM, CONSIDERABLE HARM

The findings from my analyses of San Jose and Rockford support disturbing conclusions about tracking and within-school segregation and discrimination. The districts' tracking systems pervade their schools. The harm that accrues to African Americans and Latinos takes at least three demonstrable forms: (1) unjustifiable, disproportionate, and segregative assignment to low-track classes and exclusion from accelerated classes; (2) inferior opportunities to learn; and (3) lower achievement. In both systems, grouping practices have created a cycle of restricted opportunities and diminished outcomes and have exacerbated differences between African American and Latino and white students. That these districts have not chosen to eliminate grouping practices that so clearly discriminate against their African American and Latino children warrants serious concern and strong remedial action.

IMPLICATIONS FOR REMEDIAL ACTIVITIES AND SCHOOL REFORM

Is it technically possible or politically feasible to abandon these discriminatory practices in San Jose, Rockford, or other school systems that are like them? The two systems are currently charged with making significant progress toward that end.

Both Rockford and San Jose school systems have considerable technical capacity to reform their placement practices so that they teach all children in heterogeneous settings, including the gifted, for part or all of the school day in most or all core academic courses. Conspicuous examples of successful heterogeneous grouping exist currently in San Jose schools. Much of the professional expertise and some of the support structures needed to implement such practices districtwide are already in place. Moreover, in both systems, administrative and teaching staff demonstrate considerable knowledge of the harms of tracking and ample ability to implement educationally sound alternatives.

Furthermore, both districts are situated in a national and state policy environment that encourages the development and use of such alternatives. For example, such national policy groups as the National Governors' Association and federally supported efforts to create national standards in each of the curriculum areas all recommend against tracking. In California, the State Department of Education's major policy documents on the reform of K–12 schooling (*It's Elementary, Caught in the Middle,* and *Second to None*) and the state's subject matter frameworks caution schools about problems with tracking and strongly recommend that they not use it.[3] Similar state-led initiatives promote heterogeneity in Illinois—for example, the state's involvement in middle-school reform and its adoption of the Accelerated Schools model.

However, racially mixed school systems that have tackled this issue around the country have experienced considerable difficulty creating alternatives. Amy Stuart Wells and I are currently studying ten such schools.[4] While each has made considerable progress toward integrated classrooms and a more even distribution of educational opportunities, most have been the target of considerable fear and anger. As with the nation's experiences with between-school segregation, the pursuit of court sanctions against tracking and ability grouping may be critical to ensuring educational equality. However, like that earlier effort, remedies are neither easily specified nor readily accepted.

ENDNOTES

1. For a comprehensive review of the literature, see Jeannie Oakes, Adam Gamoran, and Reba Page, "Curriculum Differentiation: Opportunities, Outcomes, and Meanings," in *Handbook of Research on Education,* ed. Philip Jackson (New York: Macmillan, 1992).
2. These previously unpublished analyses are available in the form of a 1993 report to the court in *The People Who Care* v. *Rockford Board of Education School District no. 205* and in my July 1993 deposition in conjunction with *Jose B. Vasquez* v. *San Jose Unified School District et al.*
3. California State Department of Education, *It's Elementary* (Sacramento: Author, 1993); *Caught in the Middle* (Sacramento: Author, 1988); and *Second to None* (Sacramento: Author, 1991).
4. The study "Beyond Sorting and Stratification: Creating Alternatives to Tracking in Racially Mixed Schools" is sponsored by the Lilly Endowment.

DISCUSSION QUESTIONS

1. What important purposes was tracking designed to fulfill?
2. In your opinion, is tracking (a) a fair practice, (b) a beneficial practice, or (c) a disadvantageous practice? Why?
3. Does research support the practice of tracking? Why? Why not?
4. What educational opportunities are typically provided to students in lower-class tracks?
5. How did lower-track placement affect students' quality of education and student outcomes?
6. What is the relationship among the practice of tracking, in-school segregation, and educational equality?

20

What Is a "Public School"?
Principles for a New Century

FREDERICK M. HESS

FOCUSING QUESTIONS

1. How is "public education" defined?
2. What are "public schools"? What are not?
3. What are the components of an "ideal school"?
4. How much governmental input should be provided to public schools?
5. What kind of education is appropriate for a student in public education? Is a basic reading/writing/arithmetic curriculum enough? Is developing critical thought part of public education?
6. Is education for the nation or for the individual?
7. Is neutral schooling possible? Is it desired?

The phrase "public schooling" has become more a rhetorical device than a useful guide to policy. As our world evolves, so too must our conception of what "public" means. James Coleman eloquently made this point more than two decades ago, implying a responsibility to periodically reappraise our assumptions as to what constitutes public schooling.[1] In a world where charter schooling, distance education, tuition tax credits, and other recent developments no longer fit neatly into our conventional mental boxes, it is clearly time for such an effort. Nonetheless, rather than receiving the requisite consideration, public schooling has served as a flag around which critics of these various reforms can rally. It is because the phrase resonates so powerfully that critics of proposals like charter schooling, voucher programs, and rethinking teacher licensure have at times abandoned substantive debate in order to attack such measures as anti–public schooling.[2]

Those of us committed to the promise of public education are obliged to see that the ideal does not become a tool of vested interests. The perception that public schooling has strayed from its purpose and been captured by self-interested parties has fueled lacerating critiques in recent years. Such critics as Andrew Coulson and Douglas Dewey find a growing audience when they suggest that the ideal of public schooling itself is nothing more than a call to publicly subsidize the private agendas of bureaucrats, education school professors, union officials, and leftist activists.[3] Although I believe such attacks are misguided, answering them effectively demands that we discern what it is that makes schooling public and accept diverse arrangements that are consistent with those tenets. Otherwise, growing numbers of reformers may come to regard public schooling as a politicized obstacle rather than a shared ideal.

While I do not aim to provide a precise answer as to what public schooling should mean in the early 21st century, I will argue that public schools are broadly defined by their commitment to preparing students to be productive members of a social order, aware of their societal responsibilities, and respectful of constitutional strictures;

that such schools cannot deny access to students for reasons unrelated to their educational focus; and that the system of public schools available in any community must provide an appropriate placement for each student. In short, I suggest that it is appropriate to adopt a much more expansive notion of public schooling than the one the education community holds today.

WHAT ISN'T PUBLIC?

Traditionally, public schools are deemed to be those directly accountable to elected officials or funded by tax dollars.[4] As a practical matter, such definitions are not very useful, largely because there are conventional public schools that do not fit within these definitions, while there are private providers that do.

We generally regard as public schools those in which policy making and oversight are the responsibility of governmental bodies, such as a local school board. Nongovernmental providers of educational services, such as independent schools or educational management organizations (EMOs), are labeled "nonpublic." The distinction is whether a formal political body is in charge, since these officials are accountable by election or appointment to the larger voting public.

There are two particular problems here. First, how hands on must the government be for us to regard a service as publicly provided? The National Aeronautics and Space Administration, the Environmental Protection Agency, the U.S. Department of Education, and most other state, federal, and local government agencies contract with for-profit firms for support, services, and evaluation of service delivery. Yet we tend to regard the services as public because they were initiated in response to a public directive and are monitored by public officials. It is not clear when government-directed activity ceases to be public. For instance, if a for-profit company manages a district school, is the school less public than it was when it purchased its texts from a for-profit textbook publisher and its professional development from a private consultant?

A second approach to defining "public" focuses on inputs. By this metric, any activity that involves government funds is public because it involves the expenditure of tax dollars. However, this distinction is more nebulous than we sometimes suppose. For instance, schools in the Milwaukee voucher program receive Wisconsin tax dollars. Does this mean that voucher schools ought to be regarded as de facto public schools? Similarly, Wisconsin dairy farmers receive federal subsidies. Does this make their farms public enterprises?

A particular complication is that many traditional public schools charge families money. For instance, during 2002–2003, the families of more than 2,300 Indiana students were paying tuition of as much as $6,000 to enroll their children in a public school in another district. Public schools routinely charge fees to families that participate in interdistrict public choice plans, and they frequently charge families fees if a child participates in extracurricular activities. Would proponents of a revenue-based definition suggest that such practices mean that these schools are no longer public?

A third approach, famously advanced by John Dewey, the esteemed champion of public education, recognizes that private institutions may serve public ends and that public institutions may fail to do so.[5] Such a recognition suggests that public schools are those that serve public ends, regardless of the monitoring arrangements or revenue sources. This approach is ultimately problematic, however, because we do not have clear agreement on appropriate public purposes. I'll have more to say on this point shortly.

WHAT IS PUBLIC SCHOOLING?

Previously, I have posed five questions to guide our efforts to bring more precision to our understanding of public schooling.[6] Here, I offer these questions as a way to sketch principles that may help shape a contemporary conception of public schooling.

What are the purposes of public schooling? Schooling entails both public and private purposes, though we often fail to note the degree to which the private benefits may serve the public interest. In particular, academic learning serves the individual and also the needs of the state. Successful democratic communities require a high level of literacy and numeracy and are anchored by the knowledge and the good sense of the population. Citizens who lack these skills are less likely to contribute effectively to the well-being of their communities and more likely to be a drain on public resources. Therefore, in a real sense, any school that helps children master reading, writing, mathematics, and other essential content is already advancing some significant public purposes.[7] It is troubling that prominent educational thinkers, including Frank Smith, Susan Ohanian, Deborah Meier, and Alfie Kohn, have rejected this fundamental premise and encouraged public schools to promote preferred social values even at the expense of basic academic mastery.[8]

More fundamentally, there are two distinct ways to comprehend the larger public purposes of education. One suggests that schools serve a public interest that transcends the needs of individuals. This line of thought, understood by Rousseau as the "general will," can be traced to Plato's conviction that nations need a farsighted leader to determine their true interests, despite the shortsighted preferences of the mob. A second way of thinking about the public purposes of education accepts the classically "liberal" understanding of the public interest as the sum of the interests of individual citizens and rejects the idea of a transcendent general will. This pragmatic stance helped shape U.S. public institutions that protect citizens from tyrannical majorities and overreaching public officials.

While neither perspective is necessarily "correct," our government of limited powers and separate branches leans heavily toward the more modest dictates of liberalism. Despite our tendency to suffuse education with the sweeping rhetoric of a disembodied national interest, our freedoms are secured by a system designed to resist such imperial visions.

The public components of schooling include the responsibility for teaching the principles, habits, and obligations of citizenship. While schools of education typically interpret this to mean that educators should preach tolerance or affirm diversity, a firmer foundation for citizenship education would focus on respect for law, process, and individual rights. The problem with phrases like "tolerance" and "diversity" is that they are umbrella terms with multiple interpretations. When we try to define them more precisely—in policy or practice—it becomes clear that we must privilege some values at the expense of others. For instance, one can plausibly argue that tolerant citizens should respectfully hear out a radical Muslim calling for jihad against the United States or that tolerance extends only to legalistic protection and leaves one free to express social opprobrium. If educators promote the former, as their professional community generally advises, they have adopted a particular normative view that is at odds with that held by a large segment of the public.

Promoting any one particular conception of tolerance does not make schools more public. In a liberal society, uniformly teaching students to accept teen pregnancy or homosexuality as normal and morally unobjectionable represents a jarring absolutism amidst profound moral disagreement.

Nonetheless, many traditional public schools (such as members of the Coalition of Essential Schools) today explicitly promote a particular world view and endorse a particular social ethos. In advancing "meaningful questions," for instance, faculty members at these schools often promote partisan attitudes toward U.S. foreign policy, the propriety of affirmative action, or the morality of redistributive social policies. Faculty members in these schools can protest that they have no agenda other than cultivating critical inquiry, but observation of classrooms or perusal of curricular materials makes clear that most of these schools are not neutral on the larger substantive questions. This poses an ethical problem in a pluralist society where the parents of many students may reject the public educators' beliefs and where the educators have never been clearly empowered to stamp out "improper" thoughts.

Public schools should teach children the essential skills and knowledge that make for productive citizens, teach them to respect our constitutional order, and instruct them in the framework of rights and obligations that secure our democracy and protect our liberty. Any school that does so should be regarded as serving public purposes.

How should we apportion responsibility between families and public schools? The notion that schools can or should serve as a "corrective" against the family was first promulgated in the early 19th century by reformers who viewed the influx of immigrants as a threat to democratic processes and American norms. In the years since, encouraged by such thinkers as George Counts, Paulo Freire, Michael Apple, Peter McLaren, and Amy Gutmann, educational thinkers have unapologetically called for schooling to free students from the yoke of their family's provincial understandings.

The problem is that this conception of the public interest rests uneasily alongside America's pluralist traditions. American political thought, dating back to Madison's pragmatic embrace of "faction," has presumed that our various prejudices and biases can constructively counter one another, as long as the larger constitutional order and its attendant protections check our worst impulses.

The notion that schools are more public when they work harder to stamp out familial views and impress children with socially approved beliefs is one that ought to give pause to any civil libertarian or pluralist. Such schools are more attuned to the public purposes of a totalitarian regime than those of a democratic one. While a democratic nation can reasonably settle on a range of state/family relationships, there is no reason to imagine that a regime that more heavily privileges the state is more public. The relative "publicness" of education is not enhanced by having schools intrude more forcefully into the familial sphere.

Who should be permitted to provide public schooling? Given publicly determined purposes, it is not clear that public schooling needs to impose restrictions on who may provide services. There is no reason why for-profit or religious providers, in particular, ought to be regarded as suspect.

While traditional public schools have always dealt with for-profit providers of textbooks, teaching supplies, professional development, and so on, profit-seeking ventures have recently emerged as increasingly significant players in reform efforts. For instance, the for-profit, publicly held company Edison Schools is today managing scores of traditional district schools across the nation. Yet these are still regarded as public schools. In fact, Edison is managing the summer school programs, including curricula and personnel, for more than 70 public school districts. Yet those communities continue to regard summer school as public schooling.

Such arrangements seem to run afoul of our conventional use of the term "public," but the conflict is readily resolved when we recognize that all public agencies, including public hospitals and public transit systems, routinely harness the services of for-profit firms. Just as a public university is not thought to lose its public status merely because portions of it enter into for-profit ventures with regard to patents or athletics, so the entry of for-profit providers into a K–12 public school does not necessarily change the institution's fundamental nature. What matters in public higher education is whether the for-profit unit is controlled and overseen by those entrusted with the university's larger public mission. What matters in public schooling is whether profit seekers are hired to serve public ends and are monitored by public officials.

The status of religious providers has raised great concern among such groups as People for the American Way and the Center on Education Policy. However, the nation's early efforts to provide public education relied heavily on local church officials to manage public funds, to provide school facilities, and to arrange the logistics of local schooling. It was not until the anti-Catholic fervor of the mid- and late-19th century that states distanced themselves from religious schooling. It was not until the mid-20th century that advocacy groups such as the American Civil Liberties Union pushed the remnants of religion out of state-run schools.

In recent decades, the U.S. Supreme Court has made clear that the push for a "wall of separation" has overreached and run afoul of First Amendment language protecting the "free exercise" of religion. Moreover, contemporary America has continued to evolve since the anti-Catholic zeal of the 19th century and the anti-religious intellectualism of the mid-20th century. Those conflicts were of a particular time and place. Today, church officials have less local sway and lack the unquestioned authority they once held, while they are more integrated into secular society. Just as some onetime opponents of single-sex schools can now, because of changes in the larger social order, imagine such schools serving the public interest, so too we should not reflexively shrink from viewing religious schools in a similar light. In most industrial democracies, including such nations as Canada, France, and the Netherlands, religious schools operate as part of the public system and are funded and regulated accordingly.

What obligations should public schools have to ensure opportunity for all students? We have never imagined that providing opportunity to all students means treating all students identically. The existence of magnet schools, special education, gifted classes, and exam schools makes it clear that we deem it appropriate for schools to select some children and exclude others in order to provide desirable academic environments. Our traditional school districts have never sought to ensure that every school or classroom should serve a random cross-section of children, only that systems as a whole should appropriately serve all children.

Given the tension between families who want their child schooled in an optimal environment and public officials who must construct systems that address competing needs, the principle that individual schools can exclude children but that systems cannot is both sensible and morally sound. That said, this principle does mean that some children will not attend school with the peers their parents might prefer.

The dilemma this presents is that no solitary good school can serve all the children who might wish to attend and that randomly admitting students may impede a school's effectiveness. Demanding that a science magnet school accept students with minimal science accomplishments or that any traditional school accept a habitually violent student threatens the ability of each school to accomplish its basic purposes. This is clearly not in the public interest. The same is true when a constructivist school is required to admit students from families who staunchly prefer back-to-basics instruction and will agitate for the curricula

and pedagogy they prefer. In such cases, allowing schools to selectively admit students is consistent with the public interest—so long as the process furthers a legitimate educational purpose and the student has access to an appropriate alternative setting. Such publicly acceptable exclusion must be pursued for some reasonable educational purpose, and this creates a gray area that must be monitored. However, the need to patrol this area does not require that the practice be preemptively prohibited.

Moreover, self-selected or homogeneous communities are not necessarily less public than others. For instance, no one suggests that the University of Wyoming is less public than the University of Texas, though it is less geographically and ethnically representative of the nation. It has never been suggested that elections in San Francisco or Gopher Springs, West Virginia, would be more public if the communities included more residents who had not chosen to live there or whose views better reflected national norms. Nor has it been suggested that selective public institutions, such as the University of Michigan, are less public than are community colleges, even though they are selective about whom they admit. Moreover, there is always greater homogeneity in self-selected communities, such as magnet schools, as they attract educators and families who share certain views. None of this has been thought to undermine their essential publicness.

Even champions of public education, such as Deborah Meier and Ted Sizer, argue that this shared sense of commitment helps cultivate a participatory and democratic ethos in self-selected schools. In other words, heightened familial involvement tends to make self-selected schools more participatory and democratic. Kneeling before the false gods of heterogeneity or nonselectivity undermines our ability to forge participatory or effective schools without making schools commensurately more public.

Nowhere, after all, does the availability of a public service imply that we get to choose our fellow users. In every field—whether public medicine, public transportation, or public higher education—the term "public" implies our right to a service, not our right to have buses serve a particular route or to have a university cohort configured to our preferences. Even though such considerations influence the quality of the service, the need for public providers to juggle the requirements of all the individuals they must serve necessarily means that each member of the public cannot necessarily receive the service in the manner he or she would ultimately prefer. Public schooling implies an obligation to ensure that all students are appropriately served, not that every school is open to all comers.

What parts of public schooling are public? Debates about publicness focus on the classroom teaching and learning that is central to all schools. Maintenance, accounting, payroll, and food services are quite removed from the public purposes of education discussed above. Even though these peripheral services may take place in the same facility as teaching and learning, their execution does not meaningfully affect the publicness of schooling. Rather, we understand that it is sufficient to have ancillary services provided in a manner that is consistent with the wishes of a public education provider. For example, federal courts and state legislatures are indisputably public institutions, yet they frequently procure supplies, services, and personnel from privately run, for-profit enterprises. We properly regard these institutions as public because of their core purposes, not because of the manner in which they arrange their logistics.

TODAY'S PUBLIC SCHOOLS OFTEN AREN'T

Given the haphazard notion of public schooling that predominates today, it comes as little surprise that we offer contemporary educators little guidance in serving the public interest. This poses obvious problems, given that employment as an educator doesn't necessarily grant enhanced moral wisdom or personal virtue. If schools are to serve as places where educators advance purposes and cultivate virtues that they happen to prefer, it is not clear in what sense schools are serving "public purposes."

Blindly hoping that educators have internalized shared public purposes, we empower individuals to proselytize under the banner of public schooling. This state of affairs has long been endorsed by influential educational theorists like George Counts, Paulo Freire, Henry Giroux, and Nel Noddings, who argue that teachers have a charge to use their classrooms to promote personal visions of social change, regardless of the broader public's beliefs. For these thinkers, public schooling ironically implies a community obligation to support schools for the private purposes of educators. The problem is that public institutions are not personal playthings. Just as it is unethical for a judge to disregard the law and instead rule on the basis of personal whimsy, so it is inappropriate for public school teachers to use their office to impose personal views on a captive audience.

One appropriate public response is to specify public purposes and to demand that teachers reflect them, though we are reasonably cautious about adopting such an intrusive course. To the extent that explicit direction is absent, however, educators are left to their own devices. In such a case, our liberal tradition would recommend that we not subject children to the views of educators at an assigned school but allow families to avail themselves of a range of schools with diverse perspectives, so long as each teaches respect for our democratic and liberal tradition.

CONCLUSION

Today, our system of public schooling does little to ensure that our schools serve public purposes, while permitting some educators to use a publicly provided forum to promote their personal beliefs. Meanwhile, hiding behind the phrase's hallowed skirts are partisans who furiously attack any innovation that threatens their interests or beliefs.

There are many ways to provide legitimate public education. A restrictive state might tightly regulate school assignment, operations, and content, while another state might impose little regulation. However, there is no reason to regard the schools in the one state as more public than those in the other. The publicness of a school does not depend on class size, the use of certified teachers, rules governing employee termination, or the rest of the procedural apparatus that ensnares traditional district schools. The fact that public officials have the right to require public schools to comply with certain standards does not mean that schools subjected to more intrusive standards are somehow more public. The inclusion of religious schools in European systems, for instance, has been accompanied by intensive regulation of curricula and policy. Regulation on that order is not desirable, nor is it necessary for schools to operate as part of a public system; it is merely an operational choice made by officials in these relatively bureaucratic nations.

As opportunities to deliver, structure, and practice education evolve, it is periodically necessary to revisit assumptions about what constitutes public schooling. The ideology and institutional self-interest that infuse the dominant current conception have fueled withering attacks on the very legitimacy of public schooling itself. Failure to address this impoverished status quo will increasingly offer critics cause to challenge the purpose and justification of public education. Maintaining and strengthening our commitment to public schooling requires that we rededicate ourselves to essential principles of opportunity, liberal democracy, and public benefit, while freeing ourselves from political demands and historic happenstance.

In an age when social and technological change have made possible new approaches to teaching and learning, pinched renderings of public schooling have grown untenable and counterproductive. They stifle creative efforts, confuse debates, and divert attention from more useful questions. A more expansive conception is truer to our traditions, more likely to foster shared values, and better suited to the challenges of the new century.

ENDNOTES

1. James Coleman, "Public Schools, Private Schools, and the Public Interest," *Public Interest,* Summer 1981, pp. 19–30. See also "Quality and Equality in American Education," *Phi Delta Kappan,* November 1981, pp. 159–64.

2. For the best empirical examination of the scope and nature of the public school ideology, see Terry Moe, *Schools, Vouchers, and the American Public* (Washington, D.C.: Brookings, 2001).

3. See Andrew Coulson, *Market Education: The Unknown History* (New Brunswick, N. J.: Transaction Publishers, 1999); and Douglas Dewey, "An Echo, Not a Choice: School Vouchers Repeat the Error of Public Education," *Policy Review,* November/December 1996, www.policyreview.org/nov96/backup/dewey/html.

4. See Frederick M. Hess, "Making Sense of the 'Public' in Public Education," unpublished paper, Progressive Policy Institute, Washington, D.C., 2002.

5. John Dewey, *The Public and Its Problems* (1927; reprint, Athens, Ohio University Press, 1954).

6. See Frederick M. Hess, "What Is 'Public' About Public Education?," *Education Week,* January 8, 2003, p. 56.

7. An extended discussion of this point can be found in Paul T. Hill, "What Is Public About Public Education?," in Terry Moe, ed., *A Primer on America's Schools* (Stanford, CA: Hoover Institution, 2001), pp. 285–316.

8. Frank Smith, "Overselling Literacy," *Phi Delta Kappan,* January 1989, pp. 353–59; Alfie Kohn, *No Contest: The Case Against Competition* (Boston: Houghton Mifflin, 1986); Susan Ohanian, "Capitalism, Calculus, and Conscience," *Phi Delta Kappan,* June 2003, pp. 736–47; and Deborah Meier, "Educating a Democracy," in *Will Standards Save Public Education?* (Boston: Beacon Press, 2000).

DISCUSSION QUESTIONS

1. What does "public schooling" mean to you?
2. What are the purposes of public schooling?
3. Should schools try to "correct" the thinking that students learn from their families?
4. Should public schools be obligated to ensure opportunity for all students?
5. Should teachers use their classrooms to promote their personal visions of social change, regardless of the broader public's belief?

PRO-CON CHART 3

Should special education students be grouped (mainstreamed) into regular education classes?

PRO

1. Schools should be organized so that all students achieve their maximum potential.

2. Schools should implement a curriculum that is student-centered and responsive to the students' learning needs.

3. Students need to work side by side with peers who have different learning needs.

4. Teachers must develop a broad-based repertoire of instructional strategies so that they can teach students with different needs and abilities in the same classroom.

5. Mainstreaming can improve the social acceptance of special education students.

CON

1. Serving the special education population diminishes resources for students who are most likely to benefit from public schooling.

2. Schools should not have to provide an alternative curriculum designed for a small group of special needs students within a regular classroom setting.

3. Legislating to require teachers to fulfill the role of parent, home, and counselor for special education students is unrealistic and unproductive.

4. Students who cannot conform to classroom structure and attend to learning tasks will not benefit from regular education instruction.

5. Most educators have not been adequately prepared to work with special education students.

CASE STUDY 3

Language and Standardized Testing

East High School in the big city has a large ethnic minority/immigrant population. Most of the immigrant students are placed in English as a Second Language (ESL) classes because of their initial English skill level. At East High School, ESL classes move at a slower pace than mainstream classes and reading selections are often remedial to give students ample time to adapt to their new surroundings.

The ESL language teacher, Fred Davis, drills the students hard, and many become miraculously fluent in a short period of time. To pass out of the ESL classes into the mainstream classes, students must receive 85 percent or higher on the administered English test for ESL students. Many students in ESL find this practice unfair. They claim that their English skill levels surpass those of many of the mainstream students and that they are being unfairly held back in all of their schoolwork because of unfair scoring expectations on one English test. Only students in the mainstream classes are able to take advanced coursework, and ESL students believe that East High is hurting their ultimate potential.

Further, ESL students wishing to continue on to colleges and universities are afraid that they will not be prepared for future tests; that their scores will be adversely affected by their remedial coursework in high school. They also fear that the institutions of higher education will penalize them during the admission process because they were unable to advance into "normal" classes.

1. Is it fair for schools to use standardized testing as the sole measure of ability for determining advancement? Why? Why not? What are other methods that can be used?

2. Should subject tests be administered in a language of the student's choosing?

3. Is it good practice to separate non-English or limited-English immigrant students in all areas of coursework? Should they be integrated into mainstream courses even if their English language ability is limited?

4. How might a teacher handle a class differently if it were integrated with students of different cultural backgrounds? Different academic abilities? Is this beneficial? Why? Why not?

5. How does a cultural knowledge background affect a student's understanding?

PART FOUR
Curriculum and Instruction

How do curriculum and instruction influence each other? Which instructional strategies are most effective for learners? Why are students' learning experiences still based on highly structured curricula? How can we really know if a school is doing well? What role should standards play in education? In what ways are electronic and information technologies affecting instruction?

In Chapter 21, Benjamin Bloom describes the advantages and disadvantages of conventional instruction, mastery learning, and tutoring. He explains how context variables, including home environment, school learning, and teachers' differential interaction with students, are related to outcomes. In the next chapter, William Glasser outlines choice theory, a way to nurture warm human relationships to support student success in school. The application of choice theory by faculty and administrators in an elementary school and an urban middle school is described.

In Chapter 23, Evans Clinchy focuses on the elusive goal of ensuring equity for all students. Noting that the Civil Rights movement of the 20th century was not wholly successful, he calls for a "new education civil rights movement" based on principles adopted by the United Nations. In the next chapter, Andrew Gitlin and Stacey Ornstein challenge the factual orientation to curriculum and the alienation from work that they believe many teachers experience. Questioning assumptions that arise from commonsense thinking, they propose political humanism as an alternative. In Chapter 25, Geneva Gay highlights a variety of multicultural issues that increasingly influence schools today. She offers a number of ideas that demonstrate the relevance of multiculturalism for professional practice, curriculum development, and closing the achievement gap.

In Chapter 26, David Perkins argues for inclusion of what he calls "knowledge arts" in the curriculum. The ability to communicate strategically and effectively, to think critically and creatively, and to apply knowledge to real-world problems can help to enliven teaching and learning. In the last chapter in Part Four, Don Tapscott discusses trends in electronic interactive learning. New technologies require teachers to think differently about what they do and to learn new strategies, tools, and skills. He suggests that teachers can best adjust to this transition by turning the tools of learning over to students and allowing them to guide the development of schools into places where learning is both relevant and effective.

PROFESSIONAL PROFILE: INSTRUCTION

Name:
Herbert J. Walberg

Email:
hwalberg@yahoo.com

Latest degree/university:
Ph.D., University of Chicago

Position:
University Scholar, University of Illinois at Chicago; Distinguished Visiting Scholar, Stanford University

Previous positions:
Assistant Professor, Harvard University; Research Psychologist, Educational Testing Service

Person most influential in your career:
Benjamin S. Bloom inspired me because of his work on the taxonomies of educational objectives, his synthesis of research on the causes of learning, his studies of highly accomplished learners, and his clear writing style.

Number-one achievement:
My theory of education productivity specifies the complete set of factors proved to affect student learning, serves as a framework for planning research projects, organizing the results systematically, and planning effective and efficient education.

Number-one regret:
Only one life to lead.

Favorite educational journal:
I most like *Education Next* because it criticizes the status quo, offers constructive alternatives, publishes the work of distinguished scholars, and is exceedingly well written.

Favorite educational book:
My favorite book is *Cultural Literacy* (Houghton Mifflin) by E. Donald Hirsch, although I admire his *The Schools We Need and Why We Don't Have Them* as well as his series starting with *What Your Kindergartner Needs to Know*. Although controversial in traditional curriculum circles, Hirsch is the single most influential, living curriculum expert. In his *Core Knowledge* curriculum, he specifies in detail what students should learn at each grade level.

Best book/chapter you wrote:
Edited with Geneva Haertel, *Psychology and Educational Practice* contains chapters by 27 leading authorities on what psychology has to say about intelligence, teaching, educational technologies, moral and social understandings, assessment, home, classroom and school environments, and related topics.

Additional interests:
I have enjoyed collaborating with colleagues in Europe and Asia and sharing research findings with educators and policy makers.

Curriculum/instruction relationship:
Instruction should provide the best opportunities for learners to achieve intended outcomes most efficiently. Explicit, evidence-based instructional principles should guide curriculum content delivery.

Professional vision:
For a quarter of a century, I concentrated on original research on instruction and other factors that affect learning. For the next decade, I synthesized my own and others' research on teaching for other scholars and educators. During that period and particularly since I retired from my professorship in 2000 and accepted a new appointment at the Hoover Institution at Stanford University, I have testified before Congress and federal and state courts, served on and chaired foundation and education boards, and written editorials and books aimed at the general public and at policy makers.

Professional advice to teacher or curriculum specialist:
As a presidentially nominated and Senate-approved founding member of the National Board for Educational Sciences, I think that curriculum workers should base their work in part on scientific evidence about teaching and learning.

21

The Search for Methods of Instruction

BENJAMIN S. BLOOM

FOCUSING QUESTIONS

1. What is the difference between conventional instruction, mastery learning, and tutoring?
2. How does mastery learning influence student achievement?
3. What are the advantages and disadvantages of the mastery learning model and tutoring?
4. In what ways are home environment processes and a student's school learning related?
5. How does tutoring influence student achievement?

Two University of Chicago doctoral students in education, Anania (1982, 1983) and Burke (1984), completed dissertations in which they compared student learning under the following three conditions of instruction:

1. *Conventional.* Students learn the subject matter in a class with about 30 students per teacher. Tests are given periodically for marking the students.
2. *Mastery learning.* Students learn the subject matter in a class with about 30 students per teacher. The instruction is the same as in the conventional class (usually with the same teacher). Formative tests (the same tests used with the conventional group) are given for feedback, followed by corrective procedures and parallel formative tests to determine the extent to which the students have mastered the subject matter.
3. *Tutoring.* Students learn the subject matter with a good tutor for each student (or for two or three students simultaneously). This tutoring instruction is followed periodically by formative tests, feedback-corrective procedures, and parallel formative tests as in the

mastery learning classes. It should be pointed out that the need for corrective work under tutoring is very small.

The students were randomly assigned to the three learning conditions, and their initial aptitude test scores, previous achievement in the subject, and initial attitudes and interests in the subject were similar. The amount of time for instruction was the same in all three groups except for the corrective work in the mastery learning and tutoring groups. Burke (1984) and Anania (1982, 1983) replicated the study with four different samples of students at grades 4, 5, and 8 and with two different subject matters, probability and cartography. In each substudy, the instructional treatment was limited to 11 periods of instruction over a three-week block of time.

Most striking were the differences in final achievement measures under the three conditions. Using the standard deviation (sigma) of the control (conventional) class, it was typically found that the average student under tutoring was about two standard deviations above the average of the control class (the average tutored student was above 98 percent of the students in the control class).[1] The average student under mastery learning was about one standard deviation above the average of the control class (the average mastery learning student was above 84 percent of the students in the control class).

The variation of the students' achievement also changed under these learning conditions such that about 90 percent of the tutored students and 70 percent of the mastery learning students attained the level of summative achievement reached by only the highest 20 percent of the students under conventional instructional conditions (see Figure 21.1).

There were corresponding changes in students' time on task in the classroom (65 percent under conventional instruction, 75 percent under Mastery Learning, and 90+ percent under tutoring) and students' attitudes and interests (least positive under conventional instruction and most positive under tutoring). There were great reductions in the relations between prior measures (aptitude or achievement) and the summative achievement measures. Typically, the aptitude-achievement correlations changed from +.60 under conventional to +.35 under mastery learning and +.25 under tutoring. It is recognized that the correlations for the mastery learning and tutoring groups were so low because of the restricted range of scores under these learning conditions. However,

the most striking of the findings is that under the best learning conditions we can devise (tutoring), the average student is 2 sigma above the average control student taught under conventional group methods of instruction.

The tutoring process demonstrates that *most* of the students do have the potential to reach this high level of learning. I believe an important task of research and instruction is to seek ways of accomplishing this under more practical and realistic conditions than one-to-one tutoring, which is too costly for most societies to bear on a large scale. This is the *2 sigma* problem. Can researchers and teachers devise teaching-learning conditions that will enable the majority of students under *group instruction* to attain levels of achievement that can at present be reached only under good tutoring conditions?

It has taken almost a decade and a half to develop the Mastery Learning (ML) strategy to a point where large numbers of teachers at every level of instruction and in many countries can use the feedback-corrective procedures to get the 1 sigma effect (the average ML student is above 84 percent of the students under conventional instruction—even with the same teacher teaching both the ML and the conventional classes). If the research on the 2 sigma problem yields *practical methods* (methods that the average teacher or school faculty can learn in a brief period of time and use with little more cost or time than conventional instruction), that would be an educational contribution of the greatest magnitude. It would change popular notions about human potential and would have significant effects on what the schools can and should do with the educational years each society requires of its young people.

This chapter is a brief presentation of the work on solutions to the 2 sigma problem. It is hoped that it will interest both educational researchers and teachers in further research and application of these ideas.

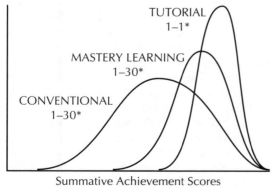

TUTORIAL
1–1*

MASTERY LEARNING
1–30*

CONVENTIONAL
1–30*

Summative Achievement Scores

*Teacher–student ratio

FIGURE 21.1   Achievement Distribution for Students under Conventional, Master Learning, and Tutorial Instruction

THE SEARCH

In a number of articles, my graduate students and I have attempted to contrast alterable educational variables with more stable or static variables

(Bloom, 1980). In our treatment of this topic, we summarized the literature on such alterable variables as the *quality of teaching,* the *use of time* by teachers and students, *cognitive* and *affective* entry characteristics of students, *formative testing, rate of learning,* and the *home environment.* In each case, we contrasted these alterable variables with the more *stable* variables (e.g., personal characteristics of teachers, intelligence measures, achievement tests for grading purposes, socioeconomic status of the family, etc.) and indicated some of the ways in which the alterable variables influence learning and the processes by which these variables have been altered.

But not all alterable variables are likely to have equal effects on learning. Our research summaries were intended to emphasize the alterable variables that have had the strongest effects on school learning. This search has been aided by the rapid growth of the meta-analysis literature. In this literature, writers have summarized the research literature on a particular set of alterable variables to indicate the effect size between control and experimental groups of students. They have standardized the results in terms of the *difference* between the experimental and control groups divided by the standard deviation of the control group.[2]

In each study, the reviewer also analyzed the effect size under different conditions—level of school, sex of student, school subject, size of sample, and so on. Such reviews are very useful in selecting alterable variables that are most likely to contribute significantly to the 2 sigma solution.

Table 21.1 is adapted from a summary of effect sizes of key variables by Walberg (1984) who, with other co-authors, has contributed greatly to this literature. In Table 21.1 he has listed the selected variables in order of magnitude of effect size. (We have added other variables and indicated the equivalent percentile for each effect size.) Thus, in the first entry, *tutorial instruction,* we have indicated the effect size (2 sigma) and indicated that under tutorial instruction, the average student is above 98 percent of the students under the control teaching conditions. A list of effect size studies appears in the Appendix at the end of this chapter.

In our own attempts to solve the 2 sigma problem we assume that two or three alterable variables must be used that *together* contribute

more to the learning than any one of them alone. Because of more than 15 years of experience with ML at different levels of education and in different countries, we have come to rely on ML as one of the possible variables to be combined with selected other variables. ML (the feedback corrective process) under good conditions yields approximately a 1 sigma effect size. We have systematically tried other variables which, in combination with ML, might approach the 2 sigma effect size. So far, we have *not* found any two-variable combination that has exceeded the 2 sigma effect. Thus some of our present research reaches the 2 sigma effect but does not go beyond it.

We have classified the variables in Table 21.1 in terms of the direct object of the change process: (a) the learner; (b) the instructional material; (c) the home environment or peer group; and (d) the teacher and the teaching process.

We have speculated that two variables involving different objects of the change process may, in some instances, be additive, whereas two variables involving the same object of the change process are less likely to be additive (unless they occur at different times in the teaching–learning process). Our research is intended to determine when these rules are true and when they are not. Several of the studies done so far suggest that they may be true. Thus the ML process (which affects the learner most directly), when combined with changes in the teaching process (which affects the teacher most directly), yields additive results. (See Tenenbaum, 1982, and Mevarech, 1980.) Although we do not believe these two rules are more than *suggestive* at present, future research on this problem will undoubtedly yield a stronger set of generalizations about how the effects of separable variables may be best combined.

In our work so far, we have restricted the search to two or three variables, each of which is likely to have a .5 or greater sigma effect. We suspect that the research, as well as the applications to school situations, would get too complex if more than three alterable variables were used.

In our research with two variables, we have made use of a 2 × 2 randomized design with ML and one other variable. So far we have not done research with three variables. Where possible, we try to replicate the study with at least two subject

TABLE 21.1   Effect of Selected Alterable Variables on Student Achievement

OBJECT OF CHANGE PROCESS[a]	ALTERABLE VARIABLE	EFFECT SIZE	PERCENTILE EQUIVALENT
D	Tutorial instruction	2.00	98
D	Reinforcement	1.20	
A	Feedback-corrective (ML)	1.00	84
D	Cues and explanations	1.00	
(A)D	Student classroom participation	1.00	
A	Student time on task	1.00[b]	
A	Improved reading/study skills	1.00	
C	Cooperative learning	.80	79
D	Homework (graded)	.80	
D	Classroom morale	.60	73
A	Initial cognitive prerequisites	.60	
C	Home environment intervention	.50[b]	69
D	Peer and cross-age remedial tutoring	.40	66
D	Homework (assigned)	.30	62
D	Higher order questions	.30	
(D)B	New science & math curricula	.30[b]	
D	Teacher expectancy	.30	
C	Peer group influence	.20	58
B	Advance organizers	.20	
	Socioeconomic status (for contrast)	.25	60

Source: This table was adapted from Walberg (1984) by Bloom. See the Appendix for effect size references.

[a]A—Learner; B—Instructional Material; C—Home environment or peer group; D—Teacher.

[b]Averaged or estimated from correlational data or from several effect sizes.

fields, two levels of schooling, or some combination of subject fields and levels of schooling. We hope that others will take up this 2 sigma search and that some guidelines for the research can be set up to make the combined results more useful and to reduce the time and costs for experimental and demonstration studies.

IMPROVING STUDENT PROCESSING OF CONVENTIONAL INSTRUCTION

In this section, we are concerned with ways in which schools can help students learn more effectively without basically changing the teaching. If students develop good study habits, devote more time to the learning, improve their reading skills, and so on, they will be better able to

learn from a particular teacher and course—even though neither the course nor the teacher has undergone a change process.

For example, the ML feedback-corrective approach is addressed primarily to providing students with the cognitive and affective prerequisites for each new learning task. As we have noted before, when the ML procedures are done systematically and well, the school achievement of the average student under ML is approximately 1 sigma (84th percentile) above the average student in the control class, even when both classes are taught by the *same teacher* with much the same instruction and instructional material. We view the ML process as a method of improving the students' learning from the same teaching over a series of learning tasks.

The major changes under the ML process are that more of the students have the cognitive prerequisites for each new learning task, they become more positive about their ability to learn the subject, and they put in more active learning time than do the control students. As we observe the students' learning and the test results in the ML and the conventional class, we note the improvements in the student learning under ML and the lack of such improvement in conventional classes.

One of our University of Chicago doctoral students, Leyton (1983), suggested that one approach to the 2 sigma problem would be to use ML during the advanced course in a sequence, but in addition attempt to *enhance the students' initial cognitive entry prerequisites* at the beginning of the course. Working with high school teachers in Algebra 2 and French 2, Leyton and others developed an initial test of the prerequisites for each of these courses. The procedure in developing the initial test was to take the final examination in the prior course (Algebra 1 or French 1) and have a committee of four to six teachers in the subject independently check each test item that they believed measured an idea or skill that was a necessary prerequisite for the next course in the subject. There was very high agreement on most of the selected items, and discussion among the teachers led to consensus about some of the remaining items.

Two of the classes were helped to review and relearn the specific prerequisites they lacked. This was not done for the students in the other two classes—they spent the time on a more general and informal review of the content taught in the previous course (Algebra 1 or French 1). The method of enhancing the prerequisites was much like the ML feedback-corrective process: the teacher retaught the items that the majority of students had missed, small groups of students helped each other over items that had been missed, and the students reviewed items they were not sure about by referring to the designated pages in the instructional material. The corrective process took about 3 to 4 hours during the first week of the course. After the students completed the corrective process, they were given a parallel test. As a result of the corrective process, most of the students reached the mastery standard (80 percent) on the parallel test given at the end of the first week of the course. In a few cases, students who didn't reach this standard were given further help.

More important was the improved performance of the enhanced classes over the other two classes on the first *formative* test in the advanced course (French 2 or Algebra 2). The two enhanced classes, which had been helped on the initial prerequisites, were approximately .7 sigma higher than the other two classes on the first formative test given at the end of a 2-week period of learning in the advanced course.

When one of the enhanced classes was also provided with ML feedback-corrective procedures over a series of learning tasks, the final result after a 10- to 12-week period of instruction was that this experimental group was approximately 1.6 sigma above the control group on the summative examination. (The average student in the ML plus enhanced initial prerequisites was above 95 percent of the control students on this examination.) There were also attitudinal and other affective differences in students related to these achievement differences. These included positive academic self-concept, greater interest in the subject, and greater desire to learn more in the subject field.

In Leyton's (1983) study, he found that the average effect of initial enhancement of prerequisites alone is about .6 sigma (see differences between conventional and conventional plus enhanced prerequisites and between ML and ML plus enhanced prerequisites in Figure 21.2). That is, we have two processes—*ML* and *initial enhancement of cognitive prerequisites*—that have sizable but separate effects. When they are combined, their separate effects tend to be additive. We believe these two variables are additive because they occur at different times. The enhancement of the initial prerequisites is completed during the first week of the new course, while the ML feedback-corrective process takes place every 2 or 3 weeks during the course, after the initial enhancement.

This solution to the 2 sigma problem is likely to be applicable to sequential courses in most school subjects. (In the United States, over two-thirds of the academic courses in elementary-secondary schools are sequential courses.) This solution, of course, applies most clearly to the second courses in a sequence. It probably will

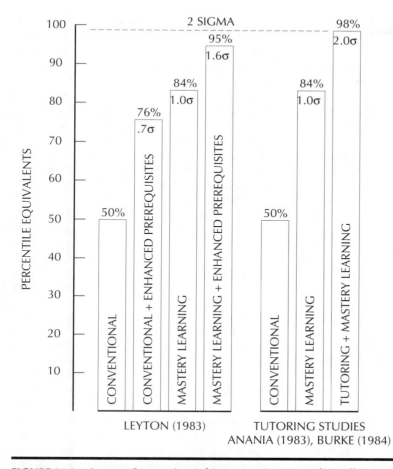

FIGURE 21.2   Average Summative Achievement Scores Under Different Learning Conditions. Comparison of Tutoring Studies, Mastery Learning, and Enhanced Prerequisites

not work as well with the third, fourth, or later courses in a sequence if there has been no earlier use of initial enhancement of prerequisites or ML procedures. We hope these ideas will be further explored in the United States as well as in other countries. We believe this solution is relevant at all levels of education, including elementary-secondary, college, and even the graduate and professional school level.

We also regard this approach as widely applicable within a country because the prerequisites for a particular sequential subject or course are likely to be very similar even though different textbooks and teachers may be involved. Thus, a well-made test of the initial prerequisites for a particular sequential course—Arithmetic 2, French 2, Reading 2, and so on—may with only minor changes apply to other versions of the same course within a particular country. Also, the procedures that work well in enhancing these prerequisites in one school should work equally well in other schools. Further research is needed to establish the sequential courses in which this approach is most effective.

Finally, the time cost of the initial enhancement procedures is limited to the class hours of the course during the first week of the sequential course, while the time or other costs of the ML procedures have usually been very small. We hope that this approach to the 2 sigma problem will be found to be a widely applicable as well as economical solution available to most teachers who wish to improve student learning, student academic self-concept, and student attitudes and interest in the learning.

Our graduate students have written papers on several other approaches for improving student processing of conventional instruction:

1. Help students develop a student support system in which groups of two or three students study together, help each other when they encounter difficulties in the course, help each other review in advance of taking tests, and review their learning periodically. A student support system that provides support, encouragement and even help when needed can do much to raise the level of learning of the participants. There is evidence that these and other cooperative learning efforts are almost as effective as ML procedures. [Cooperative learning—effect size .80 (79th percentile); Slavin, 1980.]
2. There is evidence that students who take special programs to improve their reading and/or their study and learning methods tend to learn more effectively. Ideally, such special programs should be available at the beginning of each new school level—that is, junior high school, high school, and so on. One would hope that the special programs would be closely related to the academic courses the student is currently taking. [Improved reading/study skills—effect size 1.00 (84th percentile); Pflaum, Walberg, Karegianes, & Rasher, 1980.]

IMPROVE INSTRUCTIONAL MATERIALS AND EDUCATIONAL TECHNOLOGY

In the United States, as well as in most advanced countries in the world, the textbook is an almost universal part of school instruction. There has been much work on the improvement of the textbooks

for reading and, to some extent, arithmetic, mathematics, and science subjects. Most of these are in relation to special curricular improvements, which include improvements in the sequential nature of the topics, the attempt to find important ideas or schema that help to interrelate the different parts of the subject, and improvements in the illustrations and exercises in the books. However, as far as we can find, these improvements have not had very significant effects on student achievement unless the teachers were provided with much inservice education for the new curriculum or the new textbook.

My graduate students and I have been intrigued by the possibility that a particular section (or chapter) of the textbook might be better integrated or the parts of the section more closely related to each other. Preorganizers or advance organizers (Ausubel, 1960) have been moderately effective when provided in the textbook or provided by the teacher at the beginning of the new unit of the course. These may be provided in the form of objectives, some ideas about what will be learned in the unit, or a brief discussion of the relation between what has already been learned and what will be learned in the unit. Such advanced organizers (Luiten, Ames, & Ackerson, 1980) appear to have an average effect size on achievement of about .2 sigma. (Incidentally, such advance organizers have about a .4 sigma effect on retention of the learning.) Although this effect is rather consistent, by itself it is not enough to contribute significantly to the 2 sigma effect. It is likely that a *combination* of advance organizers at the beginning of a new topic, further organizational aids during the chapter or unit, and appropriate questions, summaries, or other organizational aids at the end of the unit, may have a substantial effect on the student's learning of that chapter.

Other suggestions for the improvement of instructional materials and educational technology include the following:

1. Some of our students have used computer learning courses, such as the Plato system, which appear to work very well for highly motivated students. We believe that it should be possible to determine whether particular

computer courses enable sizable proportions of students to attain the 2 sigma achievement effect. The effectiveness of the computer courses can be determined in terms of the time required, completion rates, student performance on achievement tests, and student retention of the learned material. It is hoped that the more effective computer courses will also have positive effects on such affective characteristics as academic self-concept, interest in the subject, and desire to learn further with computer learning methods.

2. Although the average effect size for new science and math curricula in the United States is only .3 sigma, some of the new curricula (or textbooks) in these and other subjects may be much more effective than others. We propose a careful search of the new curricula and textbooks to determine which ones are more effective and to determine what characteristics make them more effective than the others.

HOME ENVIRONMENT AND THE PEER GROUP

In this section, we are primarily concerned with the out-of-school support that the student receives from the home or the peer group. We are interested in the ways in which the student's achievement, academic aspirations and goals, and progress in learning are influenced by these types of support. We know that the home environment does have great influence on the pupil's school learning and that this influence is especially effective at the elementary school level or earlier. The peer group's influence is likely to be strongest (both positively or negatively) at the secondary school level.

Home Environment Processes

There have been a large number of studies of the home environment processes that affect the students' school learning. These studies involve interviews and observations directed at determining the relevant interactions between parents and their children. The studies find correlations of +.70 to +.80 between an index of the home environment

processes and the children's school achievement.[3] Some of the home environment processes that appear to have high relationships with school achievement include the following:

1. Work habits of the family—the degree of routine in the home management, the emphasis on regularity in the use of space and time, and the priority given to schoolwork over other more pleasurable activities.
2. Academic guidance and support—the availability and quality of the help and encouragement parents give the child for his or her schoolwork and the conditions they provide to support the child's schoolwork.
3. Stimulation in the home—the opportunity provided by the home to explore ideas, events, and the larger environment.
4. Language development—opportunities in the home for the development of correct and effective language usage.
5. Academic aspirations and expectations—the parents' aspirations for the child, the standards they set for the child's school achievement, and their interest in and knowledge of the child's school experiences.

These studies of the home environment processes began with the work of Dave (1963) and Wolf (1964, 1966), and since then have been replicated in other studies done in the United States and other countries (Marjoribanks, 1974; Kalinowski & Sloane, 1981).

These previous studies of the relationship between the home and the children's school achievement suggest a strong effect of the home environment on the school learning of the children, but they do not provide evidence on the extent to which the home environment can be *altered* and the effect of such alteration on changes in the children's school achievement.

A study done in Thailand by Janhom (1983) involved a control group and three experimental groups of parents (and their children). In this study, the most effective treatment of the parents was for the group of parents to meet with a parent educator for about 2 hours twice a month for 6 months. In these meetings, the parents discussed ways in which they could support their children's learning in the school. There was usually an initial presentation made by the parent educator on one of the home environment processes, and then the parents discussed what they did as well as what they hoped to do to support their children's school learning.

Another experimental approach included visits to each home separately by a parent educator twice a month for 6 months. A third experimental approach was that newsletters about the same topics were sent to the home twice a month for 6 months.

The parents of all four groups were observed and interviewed at the beginning and end of the 6-month period using the Dave (1963) interview and observational methods. Although the three experimental approaches show significantly greater changes in the parents' home environment index than the control group, the most effective method was the series of meetings between groups of parents and the parent educator. The changes in the home environment of this group were highly significant when compared with the changes in the other three groups of parents.

The fourth-grade children of all these parents were given a national standardized test on reading and mother tongue as well as arithmetic at the beginning and end of the 6-month period. It was found that the achievement of the children of the meeting group of parents at the end was 1 sigma above that of the control group of children. In comparison, the parent educators' visit to each of the homes every other week had only a .5 sigma effect on the children's school achievement.

Other methods of changing the home environment have been reported by Dolan (1980), Bronfenbrenner (1974), and Kalinowski and Sloane (1981). Again, the most effective approaches to changing the home environment processes result in changes in the children's school achievement. [Home environment—effect size .50 (69th percentile), Iverson & Walberg, 1982.]

The methods of changing the home environments are relatively costly in terms of parent educators meeting with groups of parents over a series of semi-monthly meetings, but the payoff of this approach is likely to be very great. If parents continue to encourage and support each of

their children to learn well in school throughout the elementary school years, this should greatly help the children during the years they will attend schools and colleges.

Although such research has not been done as yet, we hope that others will explore an approach to the 2 sigma problem of providing effective parent education combined with the mastery learning method. Because parent support takes place in the home and ML takes place in the school, we expect that these two effects will be additive. The result should be close to a 2 sigma improvement in student learning.

Ideally, if both methods began with first- or second-grade children, one might hope that the combination would result in consistently good learning, at least through the elementary school years, with less and less need for effort expended by the parents or the use of ML procedures in the school.

Peer Group

During the adolescent years, it is likely that the peer group will have considerable influence on the student's activities, behavior, attitudes, and academic expectations. The peer group(s) to which the individual "belongs" also has some effect on the student's high school achievement level as well as further academic aspirations. These effects appear to be greatest in urban settings. Although it is difficult to influence the student's choice of friends and peer groups, the availability in the school of a variety of extracurricular activities and clubs (e.g., athletics, music, science, mathematics, social, etc.) should enable students to be more selective in their peer choices within the school setting. [Peer group influence—effect size .20 (58th percentile); Ide, Haertel, Parkerson, & Walberg, 1981.]

IMPROVEMENT OF TEACHING

When we compare student learning under conventional instruction and tutoring, we note that approximately 20 percent of the students under conventional instruction do about as well as the tutored students (see Figure 21.1). That is, tutoring probably would not enable these top students to do any better than they already do under conventional instruction. In contrast, about 80 percent of the students do poorly under conventional instruction relative to what they might do under tutoring. We have pondered these facts and believe that this in part results from the unequal treatment of students within most classrooms.

Observations of teacher interaction with students in the classroom reveal that teachers frequently direct their teaching and explanations to some students and ignore others. They give much positive reinforcement and encouragement to some students but not to others, and they encourage active participation in the classroom from some students and discourage it from others. The studies find that typically teachers give students in the top third of the class the greatest attention, and students in the bottom third of the class receive the least attention and support. These differences in the interaction between teachers and students provide some students with much greater opportunity and encouragement for learning than is provided for other students in the same classroom (Brophy & Good, 1970).

It is very different in a one-to-one tutoring situation where there is a constant feedback and corrective process between the tutor and the tutee. If the explanation is not understood by the tutee, the tutor soon becomes aware of it and explains it further. There is much reinforcement and encouragement in the tutoring situation, and the tutee must be actively participating in the learning if the tutoring process is to continue. In contrast, there is less feedback from each student in the group situation to the teacher—and frequently the teacher gets most of the feedback on the clarity of his or her explanations, the effect of the reinforcements, and the degree of active involvement in the learning from a *small* number of high-achieving students in the typical class of 30 students.

Teachers are frequently unaware of the fact that they are providing more favorable conditions of learning for some students than they are for other students. Generally, they are under the impression that all students in their classes are given equality of opportunity for learning. One basic assumption of our work on teaching is the belief that when teachers are helped to secure a more accurate picture of their own teaching methods and styles of interaction with their students, they will increasingly be able to provide more favorable learning conditions for more of their students, rather than just for the top fraction of the class.

In some of our research on the 2 sigma problem, we have viewed the task of teaching as providing for more equal treatment of students. We have been trying to give teachers feedback on their differential treatment of students. We attempt to provide teachers with a mirror of what they are now doing and have them develop techniques for equalizing their interactions with the students. These include such techniques as (a) attempting to find something positive and encouraging in each student's response, (b) finding ways of involving more of the students in active engagement in the learning process, (c) securing feedback from a small random sample of students to determine when they comprehend the explanations and illustrations, and (d) finding ways of supplying additional clarification and illustrations as needed. The major emphasis in this work was *not* to change the teachers' *methods* of instruction, but to have the teacher become more aware of the ways in which he or she could more directly teach to a cross section of the students at each class section.

The first of our studies on improving instruction was done by Nordin (1979, 1980), who found ways of improving the cues and explanations for students as well as increasing the active participation of students.

He found it helpful to meet frequently with the teachers to explain these ideas as well as to observe the teachers and help them determine when they still needed to improve these qualities of the instruction. He also had independent observers noting the frequency with which the experimental teachers were using these ideas well or poorly. Similarly, he had students note the frequency with which they were actively participating in the learning and any problems they had with understanding the ideas or explanations.

In this research he compared student learning under conventional instruction and under enhanced cues (explanations) and participation conditions. During the experiment, observers noted that the student participation and the explanations and directions were positive in about 57 percent of the observations in the control class as compared with about 67 percent in the enhanced cue + participation classes. Students in the control classes noted that the cues and participation were positive for them about 50 percent of the time as compared with about 80 percent of the time for the students in the enhanced cue + participation classes.

In terms of final achievement, the average student in the enhanced cue and participation group was 1.5 sigma higher than the average student in the control classes. (The average student in the enhanced group was above 93 percent of the students in the control classes.) (See Figure 21.3.) Nordin (1979, 1980) also made use of the ML procedures in other classes and found that they worked even better than the enhanced cue + participation procedures. Unfortunately, he did not use the ML in combination with the enhanced cue + participation methods.

In any case, Nordin (1979, 1980) did demonstrate that teachers could be taught ways to be more responsive to most of the students in the class, secure increased participation of the students, and ensure that most of the students understood the explanations and illustrations that the teacher provided. The observers noted that the students in the enhanced participation and cue classes were actively engaged in learning (time on task) about 75 percent of the classroom time, whereas the control students were actively learning only about 57 percent of the time.

In a later study, Tenenbaum (1982) compared control groups, ML groups, and enhanced cues, participation, and reinforcement in combination with ML (CPR + ML). Tenenbaum studied these three methods of teaching with randomly assigned students in two different courses—sixth-grade science and ninth-grade algebra.

Tenenbaum also used student observation of their own classroom processes on cues, participation, and reinforcement. He found that under the CPR + ML, students responded positively about their own participation about 87 percent of the time as contrasted with 68 percent in the control classes.

The results of this study demonstrated large differences between the three methods of instruction, with the final achievement scores of the CPR + ML group about 1.7 sigma above those of the control students (the average student in this group was above 96 percent of the students in the control group). The average student in the ML groups was the usual 1 sigma above the control students (see Figure 21.3).

We believe that this research makes it clear that teachers in both the Nordin and Tenenbaum studies could (at least temporarily) change their teaching methods to provide more equal treatment of the students in their classes. When this more equal treatment is provided and supplemented with the ML feedback and corrective procedures, the average student approaches the level of learning found under tutoring methods of instruction.

We believe there are a variety of methods of giving feedback to teachers on the extent to which they are providing equality of interaction with their students. The tactic of providing a "mirror" to the teacher of the ways in which he or she is providing cues and explanations and appropriate reinforcement and securing overt as well as covert participation of the students in the learning seems to us to be an excellent approach. This may be in the form of an observer's notes on what the teacher and students did or student observations of their own interactions with the teaching (preferably anonymous, but coded as to whether the students are in the top third, middle third, or bottom third of the class in achievement), such as their understanding of the cues and explanations, the extent of their overt and covert participation, and the amount of reinforcement they are getting. Perhaps a videotape or audiotape recording of the class could serve the same purpose if the teacher were given brief training on ways of summarizing the classroom interaction between the teacher and the students in the class.

It is our hope that when teachers are helped to secure a more accurate picture of their own teaching methods and styles of interaction with their students, they will be better able to provide favorable learning conditions for most of their students.

IMPROVEMENT OF TEACHING OF THE HIGHER MENTAL PROCESSES

Although there is much rote learning in schools through the world, in some of the national cur-

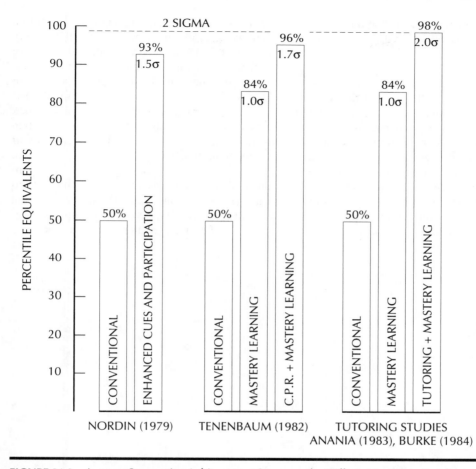

FIGURE 21.3 Average Summative Achievement Scores under Different Learning Conditions: Comparison of Tutoring Studies, Mastery Learning, and Enhanced Instructional Methods

riculum centers in different countries (e.g., Israel, Malaysia, South Korea) I find great emphasis on problem solving, application of principles, analytical skills, and creativity. Such higher mental processes are emphasized because these centers believe that they enable the student to relate his or her learning to the many problems he or she encounters in day-to-day living. These abilities are also stressed because they are retained and used long after the individual has forgotten the detailed specifics of the subject matter taught in the schools. These abilities are regarded as one set of essential characteristics needed to continue learning and to cope with a rapidly changing world.

Some curriculum centers believe that these higher mental processes are important because they make learning exciting and constantly new and playful. In these countries, subjects are taught as methods of inquiry into the nature of science, mathematics, the arts, and the social studies. The subjects are taught as much for the ways of thinking they represent as for their traditional content. Much of this learning makes use of observations, reflections on these observations, experimentation with phenomena, and first-hand data and daily experiences, as well as primary printed sources. All of this is reflected in the materials of instruction, the learning and teaching processes used, and the questions and problems used in the quizzes and formative testing, as well as on the final summative examinations.

In sharp contrast with teachers in some of these other countries, teachers in the United States typically make use of textbooks that rarely pose real problems. These textbooks emphasize specific content to be remembered and give students little opportunity to discover underlying concepts and principles and even less opportunity to attack real problems in the environments in which they live. The teacher-made tests (and standardized tests) are largely tests of remembered information. After the sale of over one million copies of the *Taxonomy of Educational Objectives—Cog-*

nitive Domain (Bloom, Engelhart, Furst, Hill, & Krathwohl, 1956) and over a quarter of a century of use of this domain in preservice and in-service teacher training, it is estimated that over 90 percent of test questions that U.S. public school students are *now* expected to answer deal with little more than information. Our instructional material, our classroom teaching methods, and our testing methods rarely rise above the lowest category of the taxonomy-knowledge.

In the tutoring studies reported at the beginning of this paper, it was found that the tutored students' Higher Mental Process (HMP) achievement was 2.0 sigma above the control students' (see Figure 21.4). (The average tutored student was above

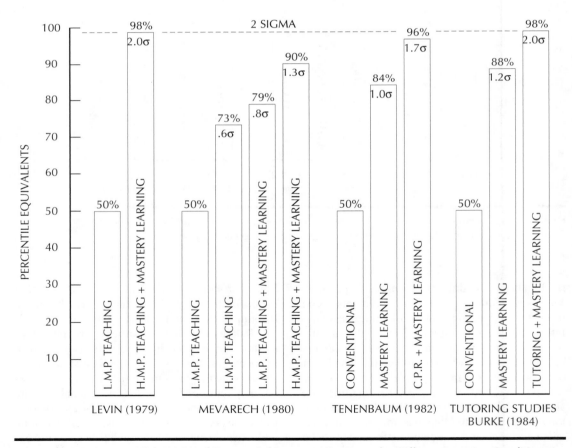

FIGURE 21.4   Average Higher Mental Process Achievement Scores under Different Learning Conditions: Comparison of Tutoring Studies, Mastery Learning, and Higher Mental Process Instructional Methods

98 percent of the control students on the HMP part of the summative examination.) It should be noted that in these studies higher mental process as well as lower mental process questions were included in the formative tests used in the feedback-corrective processes for both the ML and tutored groups. Again, the point is that students can learn the higher mental processes if they become more central in the teaching-learning process.

Several studies have been made in which the researcher was seeking to improve the higher mental processes.

We have already referred to the Tenenbaum (1982) study, which emphasized changing teacher-student interaction. In this study, the cue-participation-reinforcement + mastery learning student group was 1.7 sigma higher than the control students on the higher mental process part of the summative examination. (The average CPR + ML student was above 96 percent of the control students on the higher mental processes.) (See Figure 21.4.)

Another study done by Levin (1979) was directed to improving the higher mental processes by emphasizing the mastery of the lower mental processes and providing learning experiences in which the students applied principles in a variety of different problem situations. On the summative examinations, the students were very high on the knowledge of principles and facts and in their ability to apply the principles in new problem situations. These experimental students were compared with a control group that was taught only the principles (but not their application). On the higher mental processes, the experimental group was 2 sigma above the control students (the average experimental student was above 98 percent of the control students) in the ability to apply the principles to new problem situations.

A third study by Mevarech (1980) was directed at improving the higher mental processes by emphasizing heuristic problem solving and including higher and lower mental process questions in the formative testing and in the feedback-corrective processes. On the higher mental process part of the summative tests, the group using the heuristic methods + ML (HMP Teaching + ML) was 1.3 sigma above the control group

(LMP Teaching) taught primarily by learning algorithms—a set of rules and procedures for solving particular math problems (the average student in this experimental group was above 90 percent of the control students).

In all of these studies, attempts to improve higher mental processes included group instruction emphasizing higher mental processes and feedback-corrective processes, which also emphasized higher mental processes. In addition, the tutoring studies included an instructional emphasis on both higher and lower mental processes, as well as the feedback-corrective processes, which included both higher and lower mental processes. It was evident in all of these studies that in the formative feedback and corrective processes the students needed and received more corrective help on the higher mental processes questions and problems than they did on the lower mental process questions.

CONCLUSION

The Anania (1982, 1983) and Burke (1984) studies comparing student learning under one-to-one tutoring, ML, and conventional group instruction began in 1980. As the results of these separate studies at different grade levels and in different school subjects began to emerge, we were astonished at the consistency of the findings as well as the great differences in student cognitive achievement, attitudes, and academic self-concept under tutoring as compared with the group methods of instruction.

For 4 years, the graduate students in my seminars at the University of Chicago and Northwestern University considered various approaches to the search for group methods of instruction that might be as effective as one-to-one tutoring. This chapter reports on the research studies these students completed and some of the other ideas we explored in these seminars.

Although all of us at first thought it was an impossible task, we did agree that if we succeeded in finding *one* solution, there would soon be a great many solutions. In this chapter, I report on six solutions to the 2 sigma problem. In spite of the difficulties, our graduate students found the problem to be very intriguing because the goal was so clear and specific—*find methods of group instruction as effective as one-to-one tutoring.*

Early in the work, it became evident that more than group instruction in the school had to be considered. We also needed to find ways of improving the students' learning processes, the curriculum and instructional materials, as well as the home environmental support of the students' school learning. This chapter is only a preliminary report on what has been accomplished to date, but it should be evident that much can now be done to improve student learning in the schools. However, the search is far from complete. We look for additional solutions to the 2 sigma problem to be reported in the next few years. I hope some of the readers of this chapter will also find this problem challenging.

APPENDIX: EFFECT SIZE REFERENCES

Tutorial Instruction*

Anania, J. (1982). "The Effects of Quality of Instruction on the Cognitive and Affective Learning of Students (doctoral dissertation, University of Chicago, 1981). *Dissertation Abstracts International, 42,* 4269A.

Burke, A. J. (1984). "Students' Potential for Learning Contrasted under Tutorial and Group Approaches to Instruction (doctoral dissertation, University of Chicago, 1983). *Dissertation Abstracts International, 44,* 2025A.

Reinforcement

Lysakowski, R. S., & Walberg, H. J. (1981). "Classroom Reinforcement: A Quantitative Synthesis." *Journal of Educational Research, 75:* 69–77.

Feedback-Corrective, Cues & Explanations, and Student Classroom Participation

Lysakowski, R. S., & Walberg, H. J. (1982). "Instructional Effects of Cues, Participation, and Corrective Feedback: A Quantitative Synthesis." *American Educational Research Journal, 19:* 559–578.

Student Time on Task (in the classroom)

Frederick, W. C., & Walberg, H. J. (1980). "Learning as a Function of Time." *Journal of Educational Research, 73:* 183–194.

Improved Reading/Study Skills

Pflaum, S. W., Walberg, H. J., Karegianes, M. L., & Rasher, S. (1980). "Reading Instruction: A Quantitative Synthesis." *Educational Researcher, 9:* 12–18.

Cooperative Learning

Slavin, R. E. (1980). "Cooperative Learning." *Review of Educational Research, 50:* 315–342.

Home Work (graded) and Home Work (assigned)

Paschal, R., Weinstein, T., & Walberg, H. J. (1984). "Effects of Homework: A Quantitative Synthesis." *Journal of Educational Research, 78:* 97–104.

Classroom Morale

Haertel, G. D., Walberg, H. J., & Haertel, E. H. (1981). "Social-Psychological Environments and Learning: A Quantitative Synthesis." *British Educational Research Journal, 7:* 27–36.

Initial Cognitive Prerequisites*

Leyton, F. S. (1983). "The Extent to Which Group Instruction Supplemented by Mastery of the Initial Cognitive Prerequisites Approximates the Learning Effectiveness of One-to-One Tutorial Instruction (doctoral dissertation, University of Chicago, 1983). *Dissertation Abstracts International, 44,* 974A.

Home Environment Intervention (parental educational program)

Iverson, B. K., & Walberg, H. J. (1982). Home environment and learning: A quantitative synthesis. *Journal of Experimental Education, 50:* 144–151.

Peer & Cross-Age Remedial Tutoring

Cohen, P. A., Kulik, J. A., & Kulik, C. C. (1982). "Educational Outcomes of Tutoring: A Meta-Analysis of Findings." *American Educational Research Journal 19:* 237–248.

Higher Order Questions

Redfield, D. L., & Rousseau, E. W. (1981). "Meta-Analysis of Experimental Research on Teacher Questioning Behavior." *Review of Educational Research, 51:* 235–245.

New Science & Math Curricula and Teacher Expectancy

Walberg, H. J. (1984). "Improving the Productivity of America's Schools." *Educational Leadership, 41:* 8, 19–27.

* Not effect size studies

Peer Group Influence

Ide, J., Haertel, G. D., Parkerson, J. A., & Walberg, H. J. (1981). "Peer-Group Influences on Learning: A Quantitative Synthesis." *Journal of Educational Psychology, 73,* 472–484.

Advance Organizers

Luiten, J., Ames, W., & Ackerson, G. (1980). "A Meta-Analysis of the Effects of Advance Organizers on Learning and Retention." *American Educational Research Journal, 17:* 211–218.

ENDNOTES

1. In giving the percentile equivalent we make use of the normal curve distribution. The control class distributions were approximately normal, although the mastery learning and tutoring groups were highly skewed.

2. $\dfrac{\text{Mean experimental} - \text{Mean control}}{\text{Standard deviation of the control}}$

$$= \frac{\text{Mex} - \text{Mc}}{\text{Sigma of control}} = \textit{effect size}$$

3. When questionnaires rather than interviews and observations have been used, the correlations are somewhat lower, with the average being between +.45 and +.55.

REFERENCES

Anania, J. (1982). "The Effects of Quality of Instruction on the Cognitive and Affective Learning of Students." Doctoral dissertation, University of Chicago, 1981. *Dissertation Abstracts International, 42,* 4269A.

Anania, J. (1983). "The Influence of Instructional Conditions on Student Learning and Achievement." *Evaluation in Education: An International Review Series, 7*(1): 1–92.

Ausubel, D. (1960). "The Use of Advanced Organizers in the Learning and Retention of Meaningful Verbal Material." *Journal of Educational Psychology, 51:* 267–272.

Bloom, B. S. (1980). "The New Direction in Educational Research: Alterable Variables." *Phi Delta Kappan, 61*(6): 382–385.

Bloom, B. S., Engelhart, M. D., Furst, E. J., Hill, W. H., & Krathwohl, D. R. (1956). *Taxonomy of Educational Objectives: Handbook I, Cognitive Domain.* New York: Longman.

Bronfenbrenner, U. (1974). "Is Early Intervention Effective?" In H. J. Leichter, (Ed.), *The Family as Educator.* New York: Teachers College Press.

Brophy, J. E., & Good, T. L. (1970). "Teachers' Communication of Differential Expectations for Children's Classroom Performance: Some Behavioral Data." *Journal of Educational Psychology, 61:* 365–374.

Burke, A. J. (1984). "Students' Potential for Learning Contrasted under Tutorial and Group Approaches to Instruction." Doctoral dissertation, University of Chicago, 1983. *Dissertation Abstracts International, 44,* 2025A.

Dave, R. H. (1963). "The Identification and Measurement of Environment Process Variables that are Related to Educational Achievement." Unpublished doctoral dissertation, University of Chicago.

Dolan, L. J. (1980). "The Affective Correlates of Home Concern and Support, Instructional Quality, and Achievement." Unpublished doctoral dissertation, University of Chicago.

Ide, J., Haertel, G. D., Parkerson, J. A., & Walberg, H. J. (1981). "Peer Group Influences on Learning: A Quantitive Synthesis." *Journal of Educational Psychology, 73:* 472–484.

Iverson, B. K., & Walberg, H. J. (1982). "Home Environment and Learning: A Quantitative Synthesis." *Journal of Experimental Education, 50:* 144–151.

Janhom, S. (1983). "Educating Parents to Educate Their Children." Unpublished doctoral dissertation, University of Chicago.

Kalinowski, A., & Sloane, K. (1981). "The Home Environment and School Achievement." *Studies in Educational Evaluation, 7:* 85–96.

Levin, T. (1979). "Instruction Which Enables Students to Develop Higher Mental Processes." *Evaluation in Education: An International Review Series, 3*(3): 173–220.

Leyton, F. S. (1983). "The Extent to Which Group Instruction Supplemented by Mastery of the Initial Cognitive Prerequisites Approximates the Learning Effectiveness of One-to-One Tutorial Methods." Doctoral dissertation, University of Chicago, 1983. *Dissertation Abstracts International, 44,* 974A.

Luiten, J., Ames, W., & Ackerson, G. (1980). "A Meta-Analysis of the Effects of Advance Organizers on Learning and Retention." *American Educational Research Journal, 17:* 211–218.

Marjoribanks, K. (1974). *Environments for Learning.* London: National Foundation for Educational Research.

Mevarech, Z. R. (1980). "The Role of Teaching-Learning Strategies and Feedback-Corrective Procedures in Developing Higher Cognitive Achievement." Unpublished doctoral dissertation, University of Chicago.

Nordin, A. B. (1979). "The Effects of Different Qualities of Instruction on Selected Cognitive, Affective, and Time Variables." Unpublished doctoral dissertation, University of Chicago.

Nordin, A. B. (1980). "Improving Learning: An Experiment in Rural Primary Schools in Malaysia." *Evaluation in Education: An International Review Series, 4*(2): 143–263.

Pflaum, S. W., Walberg, H. J., Karegianes, M. L., & Rasher, S. (1980). "Reading Instruction: A Quantitative Synthesis." *Educational Researcher, 9:* 12–18.

Slavin, R. E. (1980). "Cooperative Learning." *Review of Educational Research, 50:* 315–342.

Tenenbaum, G. (1982). "A Method of Group Instruction Which Is as Effective as One-to-One Tutorial Instruction." Doctoral dissertation, University of Chicago, 1982. *Dissertation Abstracts International, 43,* 1822A.

Walberg, H. J. (1984). "Improving the Productivity of America's Schools." *Educational Leadership, 41,* 8, 19–27.

Wolf, R. M. (1964). "The Identification and Measurement of Home Environmental Process Variables That Are Related to Intelligence." Unpublished doctoral dissertation, University of Chicago.

Wolf, R. M. (1966). "The Measurement of Environments." In A. Anastasi (Ed.), *Testing Problems in Perspective.* Washington, DC: American Council on Education.

DISCUSSION QUESTIONS

1. Is the mastery learning approach appropriate for all students?
2. How does a teacher's differential interaction with students influence student achievement?
3. How are conditions of learning integrally related to student outcomes?
4. What type of staff development initiatives might be undertaken to provide teachers with an accurate perception of the quality of learning conditions that they provide for their students?
5. How effective are conventional instruction, mastery learning, and tutoring?

22

A New Look at School Failure and School Success

WILLIAM GLASSER

FOCUSING QUESTIONS

1. Why do some students do poorly in school?
2. How can teachers provide warm, supportive relationships?
3. What psychological needs motivate students in the classroom?
4. Can teachers be trained to respond to student needs?
5. What is choice theory and how does it work?

John is 14 years old. He is capable of doing good work in school. Yet he reads and writes poorly, has not learned to do more than simple calculations, hates any work having to do with school, and shows up more to be with his friends than anything else. He failed the seventh grade last year and is well on his way to failing it again. Essentially, John chooses to do nothing in school that anyone would call educational. If any standards must be met, his chances of graduation are nonexistent.

We know from our experience at the Schwab Middle School, which I will describe shortly, that John also knows that giving up on school is a serious mistake. The problem is he doesn't believe that the school he attends will give him a chance to correct this mistake. And he is far from alone. There may be five million students between the ages of 6 and 16 who come regularly to school but are much the same as John. If they won't make the effort to become competent readers, writers, and problem solvers, their chances of leading even minimally satisfying lives are over before they reach age 17.

Janet is 43 years old. She has been teaching math for 20 years and is one of the teachers who is struggling unsuccessfully with John. She considers herself a good teacher but admits that she does not know how to reach John. She blames him, his home, his past teachers, and herself for this failure. All who know her consider her a warm, competent person. But for all her warmth, five years ago, after 15 years of marriage, Janet divorced. She is doing an excellent job of caring for her three children, but, with only sporadic help from their father, her life is no picnic. If she and her husband had been able to stay together happily, it is almost certain that they and their children would be much better off than they are now.

Like many who divorce, Janet was aware that the marriage was in trouble long before the separation. But in the context of marriage as she knew it, she didn't know what to do. "I tried, but nothing I did seemed to help," she says. She is lonely and would like another marriage but, so far, hasn't been able to find anyone she would consider marrying. There may be more than a million men and women teaching school who, like Janet, seem capable of relationships but are either divorced or unhappily married. No one doubts that marriage failure is a huge problem. It leads to even more human misery than school failure.

I bring up divorce in reducing school failure because there is a much closer connection between these two problems than almost anyone realizes. So close, in fact, that I believe the cause of both these problems may be the same. As soon as I wrote those words, I began to fear that my readers would jump to the conclusion that I am blaming Janet for the failure of her marriage or for her inability to reach John. Nothing could be further from the truth. The fact that she doesn't know something that is almost universally unknown cannot be her fault.

If you doubt that the problems of John and Janet are similar, listen to what each of them has to say. John says, "I do so little in school because no one cares for me, no one listens to me, it's no fun, they try to make me do things I don't want to do, and they never try to find out what I want to do." Janet says, "My marriage failed because he didn't care enough for me, he never listened to me, each year it was less fun, he never wanted to do what I wanted, and he was always trying to make me do what he wanted." These almost identical complaints have led John to "divorce" school, and Janet, her husband.

Are these Greek tragedies? Are all these students and all these marriages doomed to failure no matter what we do? I contend they are not. The cause of both school failure and marriage failure is that almost no one, including Janet, knows how he or she functions psychologically. Almost all people believe in and practice an ancient, commonsense psychology called stimulus/response (SR) psychology. I am one of the leaders of a small group of people who believe that SR is completely wrongheaded and, when put into practice, is totally destructive to the warm, supportive human relationships that students need to succeed in school and that couples need to succeed in marriage. The solution is to give up SR theory and replace it with a new psychology: choice theory.

To persuade a teacher like Janet to give up what she implicitly believes to be correct is a monumental task. For this reason I have hit upon the idea of approaching her through her marriage failure as much as through her failure to reach students like John. I think she will be more open to learning something that is so difficult to learn if she can use it in both her personal and her professional lives. From 20 years of experience teaching choice theory, I can also assure her that learning this theory can do absolutely no harm.

If John could go to a school where choice theory was practiced, he would start to work. That was conclusively proved at the Schwab Middle School. To explain such a change in behavior, John would say, "The teachers care about me, listen to what I have to say, don't try to make me do things I don't want to do, and ask me what I'd like to do once in a while. Besides, they make learning fun." If Janet and her husband had practiced choice theory while they still cared for each other, it is likely that they would still be married. They would have said, "We get along well because every day we make it a point to show each other we care. We listen to each other, and when we have differences we talk them out without blaming the other. We never let a week go by without having fun together, and we never try to make the other do what he or she doesn't want to do."

Where school improvement is concerned, I can cite hard data to back up this contention. I also have written two books that explain in detail all that my staff and I try to do to implement choice theory in schools. The books are *The Quality School* and *The Quality School Teacher.*[1] Where marriage failure is concerned, I have no hard data yet. But I have many positive responses from readers of my most recent book, *Staying Together,*[2] in which I apply choice theory to marriage.

The most difficult problems are human relationship problems. Technical problems, such as landing a man on the moon, are child's play compared to persuading all students like John to start working hard in school or helping all unhappily married couples to improve their marriages. Difficult as they may be to solve, however, relationship problems are surprisingly easy to understand. They are all some variation of "I don't like the way you treat me, and, even though it may destroy my life, your life, or both our lives, this is what I am going to do about it."

Readers familiar with my work will have figured out by now that choice theory used to be called control theory because it teaches that the only person whose behavior we can control is our own. I find choice theory to be a better and more positive-sounding name. Accepting that you can control only your own behavior is the most difficult lesson that choice theory has to teach. It is so difficult that almost all people, even when they are given the opportunity, refuse to learn it. This is because the whole thrust of SR theory is that we do not control our own behavior; rather, our behavior is a response to a stimulus from outside ourselves. Thus we answer a phone in response to a ring.

Choice theory states that we never answer a phone because it rings, and we never will. We answer a phone—and do anything else—because it is the most satisfying choice for us at the time. If we have something better to do, we let it ring. Choice theory states that the ring of the phone is not a stimulus to do anything; it is merely information. In fact, all we can ever get from the outside world, which means all we can give one another, is information. But information, by itself, does not make us do anything. Janet can't make her husband do anything. Nor can she make John do anything. All she can give them is information, but she, like all SR believers, doesn't know this.

What she "knows" is that, if she is dissatisfied with someone, she should try to "stimulate" that person to change. And she wastes a great deal of time and energy trying to do this. When she discovers, as she almost always does, how hard it is to change another person, she begins to blame the person, herself, or someone else for the failure. And from blaming, it is a very short step to punishing. No one takes this short step more frequently and more thoroughly than husbands, wives, and teachers. As they attempt to change their mates, couples develop a whole repertoire of coercive behaviors aimed at punishing the other for being so obstinate. When teachers attempt to deal with students such as John, punishment—masquerading as "logical consequences"—rules the day in school.

Coercion in either of its two forms, reward or punishment, is the core of SR theory. Punishments are by far the more common, but both are destructive to relationships. The difference is that rewards are more subtly destructive and generally less offensive. Coercion ranges from the passive behaviors of sulking and withdrawing to the active behaviors of abuse and violence. The most common and, because it is so common, the most destructive of coercive behaviors is criticizing—and nagging and complaining are not far behind.

Choice theory teaches that we are all driven by four psychological needs that are embedded in our genes: the need to belong, the need for power, the need for freedom, and the need for fun. We can no more ignore these psychological needs than we can ignore the food and shelter we must have if we are to satisfy the most obvious genetic need, the need for survival.

Whenever we are able to satisfy one or more of these needs, it feels very good. In fact, the biological purpose of pleasure is to tell us that a need is being satisfied. Pain, on the other hand, tells us that what we are doing is not satisfying a need that we very much want to satisfy. John suffers in school, and Janet suffers in marriage because neither is able to figure out how to satisfy these needs. If the pain of this failure continues, it is almost certain that in two years John will leave school, and of course Janet has already left her marriage.

If we are to help Janet help John, she needs to learn and to use the most important of all the concepts from choice theory, the idea of the quality world. This small, very specific, personal world is the core of our lives because in it are the people, things, and beliefs that we have discovered are most satisfying to our needs. Beginning at birth, as we find out what best satisfies our needs, we build this knowledge into the part of our memory that is our quality world and continue to build and adjust it throughout our lives. This world is best thought of as a group of pictures, stored in our brain, depicting with extreme precision the way we would like things to be—especially the way we want to be treated. The most important pictures are of people, including ourselves, because it is almost impossible to satisfy our needs without getting involved with other people.

Good examples of people who are almost always in our quality worlds are our parents and our children—and, if our marriages are happy, our husbands or wives. These pictures are very specific. Wives and husbands want to hear certain words, to be touched in certain ways, to go to certain places, and to do specific activities together. We also have special things in our quality world. For example, the new computer I am typing this article on is very much the computer I wanted. I also have a strong picture of myself teaching choice theory, something I believe in so strongly that I spend most of my life doing it.

When we put people into our quality worlds, it is because we care for them, and they care for us. We see them as people with whom we can satisfy our needs. John has long since taken pictures of Janet and of most other teachers—as well as a picture of himself doing competent schoolwork—out of his quality world. As soon as he did this, neither Janet nor any other SR teacher could reach him. As much as they coerce, they cannot make him learn. This way of teaching is called "bossing." Bosses use coercion freely to try to make the people they boss do what they want.

To be effective with John, Janet must give up bossing and turn to "leading." Leaders never coerce. We follow them because we believe that they have our best interests at heart. In school, if he senses that Janet is now caring, listening, encouraging, and laughing, John will begin to consider putting her into his quality world. Of course, John knows nothing about choice theory or about the notion of a quality world. But he can be taught and, in a Quality School, this is what we do. We have evidence to show that the more students know about why they are behaving as they do, the more effectively they will behave.

Sometime before her divorce, Janet, her ex, or both of them took the other out of their quality worlds. When this happened, the marriage was over. If they had known choice theory and known how important it is to try to preserve the picture of a spouse in one's quality world, they could have made a greater effort than they did to care, listen, encourage, and laugh with each other. They certainly would have been aware of how destructive bossing is and would have tried their best to avoid this destructive behavior.

As I stated at the outset, I am not assigning blame for the failure of Janet's marriage. I am saying that, as soon as one or the other or both partners became dissatisfied, the only hope was to care, listen, encourage, and laugh and to completely stop criticizing, nagging, and complaining. Obviously, Janet and her ex-husband would have been much more likely to have done this if they had known that the only behavior you can control is your own.

When Janet, as an SR teacher, teaches successfully, she succeeds with students because her students have put her or the math she teaches (or both) into their quality worlds. If both she and the math are in their quality worlds, the students will be a joy to teach. She may also succeed with a student who does not particularly want to learn math, but who, like many students, is open to learning math if she gives him a little attention.

John, however, is hard core. He is more than uninterested; he is disdainful, even disruptive at times. To get him interested will require a real show of interest on her part. But Janet resents any suggestion that she should give John what he needs. Why should she? He's 14 years old. It's his job to show interest. She has a whole classroom full of students, and she hasn't got the time to give him special attention. Because of this resentment, all she can think of is punishment.

When Janet punishes John, she gives him more reasons to keep her and math out of his quality world. Now he can blame her; from his standpoint, his failure is no longer his fault. Thus the low grades and threats of failure have exactly the opposite effect from the one she intends. That is why she has been so puzzled by students like John for so many years. She did the "right thing," and, even though she can see John getting more and more turned off, she doesn't know what else to do. She no more knows why she can't reach John than she knows why she and her husband found it harder and harder to reach each other when their marriage started to fail.

From the beginning to the end of the 1994–1995 school year, my wife Carleen and I worked to introduce Quality School concepts into the Schwab Middle School, a seventh- and eighth-grade school that is part of the Cincinnati Public School System. (Carleen actually began training many staff members in choice theory during the second semester of the 1993–1994 school year.) This school of 600 regularly attending students (750 enrolled) has at least 300 students like John, who come to school almost every day. With the help of the principal, who was named best principal in Ohio in 1996, and a very good staff, we turned this school around.

By the end of the year, most of the regularly attending students who were capable of doing passable schoolwork were doing it.[3] Indeed, some of the work was much better than passable. None of the students like John were doing it when we arrived. Discipline problems that had led to 1,500 suspensions in the previous year slowly came under control and ceased to be a significant concern by the end of the school year.

By mid-February, after four months of preparation, we were able to start a special program in which we enrolled all the students (170) who had failed at least one grade and who also regularly attended school. Most had failed more than one grade, and some, now close to 17 years of age, had failed four times. Teachers from the regular school staff volunteered for this program. Our special program continued through summer school, by the end of which 147 of these 170 students were promoted to high school. The predicted number of students who would go to high school from this group had been near zero. Getting these students out of the "on-age" classes where they had been disruptive freed the regular teachers to teach more effectively, and almost all the "on-age" students began to learn. The "on-age" seventh-graders at Schwab had a 20 percent increase in their math test scores, another positive outcome of the program.

We were able to achieve these results because we taught almost all the teachers in the school enough choice theory to understand how students need to be treated if they are to put us into their quality worlds. Using these concepts, the teachers stopped almost all coercion—an approach that was radically different from the way most of these students had been treated since kindergarten. When we asked the students why they were no longer disruptive and why they were beginning to work in school, over and over they said, "You care about us." And sometimes they added, "And now you give us choices and work that we like to do."

What did we do that they liked so much? With the district's permission, we threw out the regular curriculum and allowed the students to work at their own pace. We assigned lessons that, when successfully completed, proved that the students were ready for high school. The seven teachers in the special program (called the Cambridge Program)—spurred on by the challenge that this was their school and that they could do anything they believed necessary—worked day and night for almost two months to devise these lessons, in which the students had to demonstrate that they could read, write, solve problems, and learn the basics of social studies and science.

We told the students that they could not fail but that it was up to them to do the work. We said that we would help them learn as much as we could, and teachers from the "on-age" classes volunteered their free periods to help. Some of the students began to help one another. The fear began to dissipate as the staff saw the students begin to work. What we did was not so difficult that any school staff, with the leadership of its principal, could not do it as well. Because we had so little time, Carleen and I were co-leaders with the principal. A little extra money (about $20,000) from a state grant was also spent to equip the room for the Cambridge Program with furniture, carpeting, and computers, but it was not more than any school could raise if it could promise the results we achieved.

These Quality School ideas have also been put to work for several years in Huntington Woods Elementary School in Wyoming, Michigan. This nearly 300-student K–5 school is located in a small middle-class town and is the first school to be designated a Quality School. There were very few Johns in this school to begin with, so the task was much easier than at Schwab. Nonetheless, the outcomes at Huntington Woods have been impressive.

- All students are doing competent schoolwork, as measured by the Michigan Education Assessment Program (MEAP). The percentages of Huntington Woods students who score satisfactorily as measured against a state standard are 88 percent in reading and 85 percent in math (compared to state averages of 49 percent in reading and 60 percent in math).

- As measured by both themselves and their teachers, all students are doing some quality work, and many are doing a great deal of quality work.
- While there are occasional discipline incidents, there are no longer any discipline problems.
- The regular staff works very successfully with all students without labeling them learning disabled or emotionally impaired.
- Even more important than these measurable outcomes, the school is a source of joy for students, teachers, and parents.

I emphasize that no extra money was spent by the district to achieve these results. The school, however, did some fund raising to pay for staff training.

I cite Schwab and Huntington Woods because I have worked in one of these schools myself and have had a great deal of contact with the other. They are both using the ideas in my books. Huntington Woods has changed from an SR-driven system, and Schwab has made a strong start toward doing so. Moreover, Schwab's start has produced the results described above. And more than 200 other schools are now working with me in an effort to become Quality Schools.

So far only Huntington Woods has evaluated itself and declared itself a Quality School. Even Schwab, as improved as it is, is far from being a Quality School. But, in terms of actual progress made from where we found it, what Schwab has achieved is proportionally greater than what Huntington Woods has achieved.

While many schools have shown interest in what has been achieved at Huntington Woods and at Schwab, very few of them have accepted the core idea: change the system from SR theory to choice theory. Indeed, there are many successful SR schools around the country that are not trying to change the fundamental system in which they operate, and I believe their success is based on two things.

First, for a school to be successful, the principal is the key. When an SR school succeeds, as many do, it is led by a principal whose charisma has inspired the staff and students to work harder than they would ordinarily work. This kind of success will last only as long as the principal remains. I am not saying that some charismatic principals do not embrace many of the ideas of the Quality School, or that the principal doesn't have to lead the systemic change that choice theory makes possible. However, once the system has been changed, it can sustain itself (with the principal's support, of course, but without a charismatic leader).

Second, the SR schools that are working well have strong parental support for good education and few Johns among their students. Where such support is already present or can be created by hard-working teachers and principals, schools have a very good chance of being successful without changing their core system. After all, it is these schools that have traditionally made the SR system seem to work. In such schools, Janet would be a very successful teacher.

While Huntington Woods had the kind of support that would have made it a good school without changing the system, the staff wanted it to become a Quality School and set about changing the system from the outset. With the backing of the superintendent, the staff members were given an empty building and the opportunity to recruit new staff members, all of whom were anxious to learn the choice theory needed to change the system. The fact that Huntington Woods has a charismatic leader is certainly a plus, but it is her dedication to the ideas of choice theory that has led to the school's great success. With very high test scores, no discipline problems, and no need for special programs, Huntington Woods has gone far beyond what I believe the typical SR school could achieve. Many educators who have visited the school have said that it is "a very different kind of school."[4]

Schwab today is also very different from the school it was. And what has been accomplished at Schwab has been done with almost no active parental support. The largest number of parents we could get to attend any meeting—even when we served food and told them to bring the whole family—was 20, and some of them were parents of the few students who live in the middle-class neighborhood where the school is located. Almost all the Schwab students who are like John are bused in from low-income communities far from the school, a fact that makes parents' participation more difficult.

At Schwab an effort was made to teach all the teachers choice theory. Then Carleen and I reminded them continually to use the theory as they worked to improve the school. At Huntington Woods, not only were the teachers and principal taught choice theory in much more depth than at Schwab and over much more time than we had at Schwab, but all the students and many parents were also involved in learning this theory and beginning to use it in their lives.

Unfortunately, Janet has never taught in a school that uses choice theory. When she brings up her problems with John in the teachers' lounge, she is the beneficiary of a lot of SR advice: "Get tough!" "Show him right away who's boss." "Don't let him get away with anything." "Call his mother, and demand she do something about his behavior." "Send him to the principal." Similarly, like almost everyone whose marriage is in trouble, Janet has been the beneficiary of a lot of well-intended SR advice from family and friends—some of which, unfortunately, she took.

Her other serious problem is that she works in an SR system that is perfectly willing to settle for educating only those students who want to learn. The system's credo says, "It's a tough world out there. If they don't make an effort, they have to suffer the consequences." Since Janet is herself a successful product of such a system, she supports it. In doing so, she believes it is right to give students low grades for failing to do what she asks them to do. She further believes it is right to refuse to let them make up a low grade if they don't have a very good attitude—and sometimes even if they do.

In her personal life, she and her husband had seen so much marriage failure that, when they started to have trouble, it was easy for them to think of divorce as almost inevitable. This is bad information. It discourages both partners from doing the hard work necessary to learn what is needed to put their marriage back together. Life is hard enough without the continuing harangues of the doomsayers. In a world that uses choice theory, people would be more optimistic.

There has been no punishment in the Huntington Woods School for years. There is no such thing as a low grade that cannot be improved. Every student has access to a teacher or another student if he or she needs personal attention. Some students will always do better than others, but, as the MEAP scores show, all can do well. This is a Quality system, with an emphasis on continual improvement, and there is no settling for good enough.

Unfortunately for them, many Schwab students who experience success in school for the first time will fail in high school. The SR system in use there will kill them off educationally, just as certainly as if we shot them with a gun. They didn't have enough time with us and were too fragile when we sent them on. However, if by some miracle the high school pays attention to what we did at Schwab, many will succeed. There was some central office support for our efforts, and there is some indication that this support will continue.

The Huntington Woods students are less fragile. They will have had a good enough start with choice theory so that, given the much stronger psychological and financial support of their parents, they will probably do well in middle school. Indeed, data from the first semester of 1995–1996 confirm that they are doing very well.

It is my hope that educators, none of whom are immune to marriage failure, will see the value of choice theory in their personal lives. If this happens, there is no doubt in my mind that they will begin to use it with their students.

ENDNOTES

1. William Glasser, *The Quality School* (New York: HarperCollins, 1990); and *The Quality School Teacher* (New York: HarperCollins, 1994).
2. William Glasser, *Staying Together* (New York: HarperCollins, 1995).
3. The school also had about four classes of special education students who were in a special program led by capable teachers and were learning as much as they were capable of learning.
4. Dave Winans, "This School Has Everything," *NEA Today,* December 1995, pp. 4–5.

DISCUSSION QUESTIONS

1. Does Glasser's model explain human relationships as you have experienced them?
2. Can you identify other psychological needs that must be met for human relationships to continue?
3. Can coercion ever be beneficial in a student's education?
4. Do you think Glasser's model would work in your school? Why or why not?
5. What are the implications of Glasser's thinking for curriculum?

23

Needed: A New Educational
Civil Rights Movement

EVANS CLINCHY

FOCUSING QUESTIONS

1. Why was true desegregation never realized?
2. What are steps that can be taken to reduce the segregation problem (especially for inner-city schools)?
3. What are solutions to overcome the inequalities?
4. How is a student harmed by being held back? How is she or he benefited?
5. What are the benefits of "tracking" programs? The pitfalls?
6. What steps can be taken to "level the playing field" of education?
7. What aspects of an education make up a "proper" public education?

Now that the great U.S. post–World War II civil rights movement in education has apparently run its course and appears to be moving backwards, it is time to launch a new educational civil rights movement. Or at least it's time to take the old one in a new and more comprehensive direction for the 21st century.

I think we might all agree that the Supreme Court's 1954 decision in *Brown v. Board of Education* was the single greatest recognition in the 20th century that the parents and children of this country really do have educational rights. In that sense, it was the high-water mark of that century's educational civil rights movement.

The Brown decision made two vitally important points. The first was that the "segregation of children in public schools solely on the basis of race deprives children of the minority group of equal educational opportunities, even though the physical facilities and other 'tangible' factors may be equal." The second and equally important finding was that "where a state has undertaken to provide an opportunity for an education in its public schools, such opportunity is a right which must be made available to all on equal terms."[1]

NOT WHOLLY A SUCCESS

Following the Brown decision and subsequent court decisions, this country embarked on the long effort to desegregate all our public schools and provide all U.S. children of every racial and ethnic group with those "equal educational opportunities." But if we look at what has happened since 1954, we can see all too clearly that that movement has turned out to be only a qualified success. While legal segregation has ended in this country and Southern school districts can no longer run officially segregated schools, many school districts—especially inner-city districts in both the North and the South—are at least as segregated as they were in 1954. Indeed, many districts, such as those in Boston, Chicago, New York, and other major cities, are *more* segregated.[2]

What's more, both federal and state courts are now moving toward declaring that many of our formerly segregated districts have made "good faith"—if unsuccessful—efforts to desegregate and are therefore legally "unified" and relieved of any further duty to integrate their schools. These same courts are also declaring that "race-based admissions policies" are unconstitutional and that districts may now return to the policy of racially identifiable neighborhood schools, the very policy that originally caused the de facto segregation of schools in the North.

In addition, we are experiencing an increase in economic segregation throughout our system of public education. Those inner-city schools that house most of our minority children also house large concentrations of our poor children. What's more, the nation's rural schools serve disproportionately large numbers of just plain poor (though mainly nonminority) children.

And all of these schools are still very clearly victims of Jonathan Kozol's "savage inequalities." While suburban school districts may spend $12,000 to $15,000 on every student, city and rural school districts are fortunate if they can raise $7,000 per student, a situation that puts every state in the union except Hawaii in violation of the Brown ruling that requires states to provide public education on equal terms to all children and young people. Urban students and their teachers are all too often housed in ancient, crumbling buildings. Their schools are all too often staffed by poorly trained and underpaid teachers. Classes can be as large as 40 to 45 students and are often supplied with ancient materials and little or no modern electronic equipment. At the same time, there is an inadequate array of community support services to assist the many children and young people and their families who live lives of extreme poverty.

All of this is happening at a time when the United States is not only the richest nation the world has ever seen but also a nation in which the already rich are garnering an ever increasing share of the national wealth while 20 million children still live in poverty. Neither those children nor their parents have adequate health insurance, adequate schools, adequate social services, or adequate jobs. In short, despite the Brown decision, the nation has signally failed to provide anything close to equal educational opportunity to all our children and young people.

MAKING THINGS WORSE

As if all these inequities were not bad enough, we have now embarked on a new national agenda in education that, if it is perhaps not as overtly immoral as segregation, is surely as inhumane, undemocratic, and (many of us devoutly hope and believe) unconstitutional. This is the Goals 2000 federal agenda that is causing every state except Iowa to impose on all students and all schools a single standardized curriculum that embodies new, "higher," "tougher," "world-class" academic standards.[3]

Many of these new academic standards, according to many of the teachers, principals, and school administrators who must impose them, are hopelessly abstruse, excessively demanding, and quite inappropriate for the age and intellectual development of the children and young people who are forced to attempt to meet them. Indeed, a study conducted by staff members of Midcontinent Research for Education and Learning has estimated that it would take as much as 22 years of schooling for a student to meet all the standards in all the core subject areas that are being mandated by most states.[4]

This attempt to impose on all students a narrow, authoritarian, uniform definition of what it is to be an educated person is being cemented in place in nearly every state by the imposition of new, "tougher," "high-stakes," standardized, pencil-and-paper, most often multiple-choice tests that all students must pass before they can be promoted to the next grade or permitted to graduate from high school. All public schools are now being forced to "align" their curricula with these tests—that is, to teach to and only to the academic orthodoxy that is contained in and thus authorized by the tests.[5]

The National Center for Fair and Open Testing (FairTest) and many testing experts believe that the single, high-stakes tests currently in use are too long, too complicated, and both academically unfair and inaccurate because they often test what has not been studied and pose questions that are well above any student's level of cognitive development. They are also often badly administered and in thousands of cases incorrectly scored. All of these testing malfeasances are causing unjustified anguish for children and parents across the land.[6]

One fact that renders invalid the practice of using any single high-stakes test to determine whether students can be promoted from grade to grade or allowed to graduate from high school is that none of the high-prestige colleges and universities would ever dream of using any single measure to determine whether to admit students. Even though the SAT is used by these institutions, the *New York Times* has pointed out that an institution such as Wesleyan University will "weigh a student's race, ethnicity, home town as well as course selection, athletic prowess, alumni connections, artistic skill, musical talent, writing ability, community service and the quality of the school" from which the student comes. High-prestige colleges and universities want to make sure that their entering classes are "not only academically sound and ethnically and racially diverse but also well-stocked with poets, running backs, activists, politicians, painters, journalists and cellists." And they will often use a variety of criteria in choosing to admit students who have lower test scores than other applicants.[7] The practices of these highly selective institutions clearly spell out the kind of broad, inclusive, and all-encompassing criteria we should be using in assessing the progress of all students as they move from kindergarten through high school.

But to this range of sterling and necessary human endeavors we need to add the full range of technical and mechanical skills, few of which are going to be acquired by going to college. Just as we need poets, running backs, and cellists, we need skilled (and equally well-paid) farmers, carpenters, electricians, plumbers, sheet metal workers, auto mechanics, construction workers, chefs, and so on, and the full range of skilled and even unskilled service industry people. After all, it is these skilled and unskilled workers, many with

only a high school education or less, who actually keep the social and economic worlds working.

PUNISHING STUDENTS
FOR THE FAILURE OF SCHOOLS

But there is more to this sad story. In an effort to end what the school authorities call "social promotion," policies are being adopted that force students who do not pass the tests to go to summer school and to be "retained" in grade if they still fail to pass the tests. Or take the case of Boston, where students who don't pass the eighth-grade state test are not held back but are instead forced to go to summer school and, if they still fail the test, are then placed in "transition" classes in the ninth grade. This, according to Judith Baker, a veteran Boston high school teacher,

> is the same exact thing as tracking used to be. [The students] are denied electives or creative programs, they take double English and math, and if they fail these, they will probably go into transition 10th-grade and 11th-grade classes. . . . Although there is an attempt to bolster these courses, they are essentially remedial. They create "higher" and "lower" tracks, just by taking the majority of entering ninth-graders into what automatically becomes the school's "lower" track. These "transition" classes throw the entire curriculum sequence off, because they delay until later grades many required courses, and by the time students fulfill their requirements, they will never have had a chance to take an elective, an honors or AP course, anything remotely interesting.
>
> Students are responding by being sullen and bored, by failing (the guidance counselor for grade 9 went home with a stuffed shopping bag full of warning notices), and by other negative behavior. I have heard of no positive behavior, academic or other, associated with the "transition" course.[8]

So what are the utterly expectable results of this wave of so-called school reform? The reformers say that "all children can and now will learn"—if only they and their teachers settle down, work hard, and concentrate on those lessons that will help them raise their test scores. Forget about those "savage inequalities." Success can be achieved solely by hard work and teaching to the standards and the tests.

But there is no secret about who the children and young people are who are going to fail those tests and, indeed, are already failing them all over the country. They are precisely the poor and minority children and young people—especially those with limited proficiency in English—who inhabit those savagely unequal schools. (Madison Park High School, where Judith Baker teaches, has a student body that is made up almost entirely of minority students and students who qualify for federally subsidized lunches.)

Indeed, the latest figures on dropouts in Boston, according to the Massachusetts Advocacy Center, are that over the period 1995–1999, during which the state and local high-stakes testing program was instituted, the annual dropout rate for all students increased by 34 percent. For African Americans, the rate of increase has been 28 percent; for Hispanics, 40 percent; for Asians, 43 percent; and for whites, 37 percent.

NOT GOOD FOR ANYBODY

Now I hasten to add that I am not suggesting that the largely majority and most often suburban students who pass the tests are thereby being supplied with a good and proper education. I steadfastly maintain that the narrow, authoritarian, uniform, "high-standards," academically and politically orthodox definition of what it means to be an educated person is no better for well-to-do, white suburbanites than it is for low-income, inner-city minorities. Indeed, the kind of education that everyone should be getting is precisely the kind of schooling that will produce those poets, running backs, activists, politicians, painters, journalists, and cellists that the elite colleges want and need, as well as the farmers, carpenters, electricians, auto mechanics, and service providers that American society as a whole wants and needs.

So the expected is happening. The poor and minority children and young people who do not pass the tests are being humiliated and labeled as failures. It is interesting to note here that most states, including Massachusetts, are not imposing such tests on students in private schools, thus en-abling rich parents to buy their children's way out of any such humiliation. The always unlevel playing field is growing even steeper for the poor and for minorities as each day passes.

And it is not just the students who are being punished. If those poor and minority children in public schools don't pass the tests, their teachers and principals will also be labeled failures and threatened with the loss of their jobs or the takeover of their schools by the state.

As these thousands of poor and minority children and young people continue to fail the tests and to be publicly excoriated as failures, what is going to be their inevitable reaction? As at Madison Park, they will believe the labels certifying them as failures, they will realize what that failure means in terms of their chances in life, and large numbers of them will drop out of school as quickly as they legally—or illegally—can. And if you, as a school administrator, can rid your school of its low-scoring failures, you have hit upon a surefire way to guarantee that the test scores of your school and school district will go up and that your school and district will be considered successes.

A SUSPICIOUS AGENDA

This scenario leads to the dark suspicion that this is precisely what some of the reformers—not all of them, of course—may have had in mind all along. They certainly seem to be seeking to build an increasingly two-tiered system of American society: one tier for the small number of successfully "educated," largely nonminority winners who have succeeded in school and a second tier for the many failures who will be left to serve the needs of the increasingly wealthy successes.

Many of these reformers, having given up on the possibility of building a truly democratic system of public education that can provide a high-quality education for all children, now advocate that we abandon any such attempt and move instead toward a completely privatized system by providing all children with vouchers that can be used to pay at least part of the tuition at private schools. There is also a burgeoning movement to create publicly supported charter schools that parents can choose, schools that are for the most part independent of local school districts and are usually directly responsible to state governments.

Insofar as these charters are and remain genuinely public schools with guaranteed access for all poor and minority students and are not exempted from the standards and tests required of other public schools, they constitute a legitimate choice for both parents and teachers. Unfortunately, many of these charters are being run by profit-making corporations, and in many instances they are not being adequately supervised by the states. Thus charter schools appear to be increasingly serving the nonminority, middle-class portion of the population, including many students whose parents either have been paying or at least could pay for tuition at private schools. (Recall that charter schools tend to be located in urban centers where large numbers of minorities reside; thus statewide figures for charter school attendance can be skewed to make minority enrollments appear proportionally larger than they are.)

WHO IS DOING ALL OF THIS?

This authoritarian, antidemocratic national educational regime of high standards and high-stakes testing is being imposed almost entirely by self-appointed experts with, at best, weak credentials in education—primarily state and local politicians, including governors and state legislators, and state department of education bureaucrats. These are the folks who have attended three national education "summits" called by the National Governors' Association, by foundation officials, and by the CEOs of such leading corporations as IBM. The rallying cry at these gatherings is that the new, viciously competitive, capitalistic world economy requires that any nation that hopes to survive must produce large numbers of technologically adept, well-behaved, mentally skillful workers to staff those multinational corporations and the vast service industries that support not only the corporations but society as a whole.

Over the past several years, this strictly economic argument has been revealed as a deceptive myth, for despite our purported educational woes, the U.S. economy has somehow managed to be-

come the most powerful economic engine in the history of the world. As the eminent social and educational thinker Richard Rothstein has pointed out, when *A Nation at Risk* was published in 1983 the economy appeared to be in big trouble. It was then widely believed that this poor economic performance was the result of the shoddy quality of the nation's public schools. In those days, the unemployment rate (and in many minds the unemployability rate) was over 6 percent, and the school dropout rate was twice that.

Now, in these early years of the new millennium, the unemployment rate is 3.9 percent, and even high school dropouts are finding jobs. The U.S. system of public education, however, is not being credited as one of the chief causes of this economic miracle. Nor have those governors and state legislators, those state department of education bureaucrats, those foundation officials, and those corporate CEOs held another national education summit to announce that their highly touted reform agenda of high standards and high-stakes testing may be totally wrongheaded, educationally damaging, and even economically counterproductive.[9]

BUT NO DEVILS HERE

Now, before I attempt any further exploration of what is going on here, let me be very clear on one point. Despite any and all suspicions to the contrary, I refuse to believe that those governors and legislators, those corporate leaders and foundation executives, the many state bureaucrats, and even those leaders of teacher unions and learned professors in our colleges and universities who support and help implement this arrogant, inhumane agenda are evil people. Nor are they uniformly ultraconservative "right wingers" or "leftist revolutionaries." Indeed, they inhabit every niche of the political spectrum, sharing only the undemocratic, authoritarian belief that they have the right and, indeed, the moral duty to impose their limited and limiting version of educational truth on all children, all young people, all parents, all teachers and other educators, and thus on all public schools throughout the land. I do not doubt that they genuinely believe that what they are advocating is in the best interests of the nation and even in the best interests of the schoolchildren—and especially the poor and minority children—of this country and their parents.

A NEW CIVIL RIGHTS MOVEMENT

But a growing number of parents, older students, teachers, frontline school administrators, school board members, and leading educational thinkers have come to believe that these self-appointed experts could not be more misguided in their efforts to impose what they call school reform on all of our public schools. Indeed, we see this movement as a flagrant and open violation of the basic human educational rights of the citizens of this nation.

By "basic human educational rights," I mean not only the two set forth in the Brown decision but also those contained in the United Nations' Universal Declaration of Human Rights. Article 26 of that Declaration says first that "everyone has a right to education. Education shall be free [i.e., publicly supported] at least at the elementary and fundamental stages. Technical and professional education shall be made generally available, and higher education shall be equally accessible to all on the basis of merit."

The Declaration then goes on to state the two fundamental rights that have the most relevance to the argument here: "Education shall be directed to the full development of the human personality and to the strengthening of respect for human rights and fundamental freedoms," and "Parents have a prior right to choose the kind of education that shall be given to their children."[10]

Article 26 clearly states that all children have a right to an education that is aimed at the "full development" of the individual human personalities of all children—not just their academic capacities but all their social, political, and artistic capacities as well. The full range of these capacities is what the developmental psychologist Howard Gardner believes are the "multiple intelligences" that all children have: not only the verbal and logico/mathematical intelligences (the only ones usually dealt with in school and tested on the tests), but also the visual, kinetic, musical, naturalistic, social, and personal intelligences—in short, the

range of capacities that will produce those poets, running backs, activists, politicians, painters, journalists, and cellists.

BOTH DIVERSITY AND CHOICE

The part of Article 26 that guarantees parental choice recognizes two of the most stubborn and important facts about any truly democratic system of education. The first is that children and young people do not come in any single size, shape, or collection of attributes, capacities, talents, or intelligences. The second fact is a corollary truism: there cannot be any single educational environment that is going to be suitable and appropriate for all children. As Susan Ohanian has put it, "One size fits few."[11]

It is in part because of the broad diversity among children and young people that there is an equivalent diversity of educational philosophies, curricula, and methodologies. At one end of that diverse spectrum are the very conservative, traditional, rigorously academic, "back-to-basics" approaches, such as the Paideia Schools of Mortimer Adler and the Core Knowledge Schools of E. D. Hirsch, Jr. Somewhere in the middle of the spectrum are schools such as those advocating the "continuous progress" of students and those that specialize in particular areas of the conventional curriculum, such as the arts or science and technology. At the other end of the spectrum are the schools that would most likely call themselves progressive—such as Montessori and Waldorf schools, "open" schools, integrated day schools, or microsociety schools. It is from this broad array of educational possibilities that parents have a right to choose the kind of public schooling they believe best fits the individual educational needs of each of their children.

Those of us who reject the new totalitarian educational agenda believe that this right of choice is guaranteed not only by the United Nations Universal Declaration but by the U.S. Constitution through its guarantees of free speech and free assembly. Surely, under those guarantees and under the basic democratic principle that governments may act only with the consent of the governed, parents have the right to specify the kind of public schooling they want their children to have and thus what they wish to have taught to their children in a publicly supported institution called a school. This right of choice is limited only by the First Amendment separation of church and state and by the now watered-down Fourteenth Amendment civil rights decisions that still say that all public schools should be at least as integrated as the school district in which they exist.

BUT NOT JUST PARENTAL CHOICE

It is those two unbending facts—the diversity among our students and the diversity of educational belief and practice—that make educational diversity and choice absolute requirements of any reasonably fair, just, and democratic U.S. education system. And I don't mean just parental choice of the schools their children will go to. Teachers and other professional educators also have the right—called "academic freedom" by college and university professors and guaranteed by the First Amendment—to choose the kind of schooling they wish to practice, since they share with parents that diversity of educational belief. It is this dual right of choice for both parent and professional— along with the right to the full development of each child's personality—that must overrule any state's power to impose a single standardized curriculum and a single high-stakes testing system on all children, all parents, and all professionals.

A DIVERSITY OF STANDARDS
AND ASSESSMENTS

Let me also be clear about one more thing. To say that one is against the imposition of a single set of solely academic standards and a single high-stakes, solely academic test—which together add up to the establishment of a single, solely academic intellectual orthodoxy—is not to say that there should be no high educational expectations and no system of public accountability in U.S. public education. Has anyone ever heard of a school that does not propose that its students read and write well and do all appropriate forms of basic arithmetic?

But above and beyond providing these valuable "basics" and quite possibly a commitment

to help students develop their capacity for high-level reasoning, it is the task of the parents and the professional staff of each freely chosen public school to decide and spell out in detail what that school conceives its educational mission to be. This would include what its intellectual (rather than academic) standards are, what and how it proposes that teachers should teach and students should learn, and how it proposes to measure its progress toward achieving those desired ends. And if a school decides that a standardized test would be useful, it is, of course, free to use one.

What's more, there is also the basic right of parents operating within such a system of strictly public school choice to opt out of manifestly failing schools and to choose other public schools that they believe will provide the better quality of education they are seeking. This same principle of "free market" public school choice allows teachers to leave failing schools and choose "better" ones. As both parents and teachers abandon failing schools and opt for schools they see as "better," the overall quality of the system is not only likely—but perhaps bound—to improve. At the very least, this is an organizational theory that many people would like to see put to the test.

How then might this new system of U.S. education be organized and operated? After each school selected by both parents and professional staff members has spelled out its educational mission, it is the task and responsibility of the locally elected school board, acting as the agent of state government, to review each school's stated mission and goals to make sure that what the school plans to do falls within the broad limits of democratic belief and practice and the U.S. Constitution. The board would then monitor each school's yearly performance as measured against its stated goals.

It is then the task of the state to monitor the civil rights performance of local school districts and to make sure that every school in every district is equally and adequately funded. And it is the task of the federal government to monitor the civil rights performance of the states and to make sure that the schools of every state are equally and adequately funded. No savage inequalities are permitted anywhere.

NOT A NEW IDEA

It is interesting—but not at all surprising—that what I am proposing here is hardly a new idea. Indeed, back in the latter part of the 19th century, Alfred Russel Wallace, the co-constructor with Charles Darwin of the theory of evolution by natural selection, set forth these ideas in the following fashion:

> In our present society the bulk of the people have no opportunity for the full development of all their powers and capacities. . . . The accumulation of wealth is now mainly effected by the misdirected energy of competing individuals; and the power that wealth so obtained gives them is often used for purposes which are hurtful to the nation. There can be no true individualism, no fair competition, without equality of opportunity for all. This alone is social justice, and by this alone can the best that is in each nation be developed and utilised for the benefit of all its citizens.

"Equality of opportunity," Wallace went on to say,

> is absolute fair play as between man and man in the struggle for existence. It means that all shall have the best education they are capable of receiving; that their faculties shall all be well trained, and their whole nature obtain the fullest moral, intellectual, and physical development. This does not mean that we shall all have the same education, that all shall be made to learn the same things and go through the same training, but that all shall be so trained as to develop fully all that is best in them. It must be an adaptive education, modified in accordance with the peculiar mental and physical nature of the pupils, not a rigid routine applied to all alike, as is too often the case now.[12]

THE PATH TO A NEW MOVEMENT

Now it is unfortunately true that recent federal court decisions, one in Florida and one in Texas, have ruled that those two states have the right to set academic standards and to administer a single high-stakes test to all students in order to determine whether those standards are being met, even though poor and minority students in those states are failing the tests at an alarming rate. This, of course, suggests that, until there is an eventual rul-

ing by the U.S. Supreme Court, all states are free to pursue their present autocratic course.[13]

Concerned parents, teachers, school administrators, and test experts in all the states, refusing to accept these decisions as final, are preparing further challenges to the authoritarian agenda of standards and testing in state legislatures and in state and federal courts all across the land. No court decision is unalterable. After all, it was the Supreme Court's 1896 decision in *Plessy v. Ferguson* that established the doctrine of "separate but equal," which was eventually overturned by the 1954 Brown decision.

It will almost certainly take a new educational civil rights movement, such as the one proposed here, to bring about the kind of just, fair, equal, and truly democratic system of U.S. public education we want and deserve. Let us hope as well that we are not in for another century of continued educational injustice before we set the record straight and achieve that just, fair, and equitable system.

ENDNOTES

1. *Brown v. Board of Education,* 347 U.S. 483 (1954), p. 1.
2. See Gary Orfield and John T. Yun, *Resegregation in American Schools* (Cambridge, MA: Harvard Civil Rights Project, June 1999), for data on increased racial, ethnic, and economic segregation.
3. For more on this movement, see Marion Brady, "The Standards Juggernaut," *Phi Delta Kappan,* May 2000, pp. 649–51; and Susan Ohanian, *One Size Fits Few: The Folly of Educational Standards* (Portsmouth, NH: Heinemann, 1999).
4. Robert J. Marzano and John S. Kendall, *Awash in a Sea of Standards* (Aurora, CO: Midcontinent Research for Education and Learning, 1998).
5. See Gary Natriello and Aaron M. Pallas, *The Development and Impact of High-Stakes Testing* (Cambridge, MA: Harvard Civil Rights Project, November 1999); and Linda McNeil and Angela Valenzuela, "Harmful Effects of the TAAS System of Testing in Texas: Beneath the Accountability Rhetoric," in Mindy Kornhaber, Gary Orfield, and Michal Kurlaendar (Eds.), *Raising Barriers? Inequality and High-Stakes Testing in Public Education* (New York: Century Foundation, 2000).
6. For details, see the newsletters and publications of the National Center for Fair and Open Testing, 342

Broadway, Cambridge, MA 02139; or send e-mail to info@fairtest.org.

7. Jacques Sternberg, "For Gatekeepers at Colleges, a Daunting Task of Sorting," *New York Times,* February 27, 2000, pp. A–1, A–24.

8. Judith Baker, personal e-mail communication, June 12, 1999.

9. Richard Rothstein, "Education and Job Growth," *New York Times,* May 10, 2000, p. A–23.

10. Universal Declaration of Human Rights (Geneva: Office of the United Nations High Commissioner for Human Rights, United Nations Department of Public Information, 1998).

11. Ohanian, *One Size Fits Few.*

12. Harry Clements, *Alfred Russel Wallace: Biologist and Social Reformer* (London: Hutchinson, 1983), pp. 96–98.

13. For the Texas decision, see *G. I. Forum et al. v. Texas Education Agency et al.,* Civil Action No. SA-97-CA-1278EP (www.txwd.uscourts.gov).

DISCUSSION QUESTIONS

1. Do you agree that the civil rights movement in the United States during the last half of the 20th century was not wholly successful? What evidence do you see?
2. Do you agree that the federal government's current policies are making our society less equitable?
3. Can high-stakes testing serve the purpose of ensuring equity in public schooling or is it an obstacle to that end?
4. Should the United Nations Universal Declaration of Human Rights be used to guide education policy in the United States?
5. What kind of "new educational civil rights movement" does the author propose? Do you think it would be successful?

24

A Political Humanist Curriculum
for the 21st Century

ANDREW GITLIN
STACEY ORNSTEIN

FOCUSING QUESTIONS

1. What is a curriculum embodied in politics?
2. How are teachers alienated? What are the downfalls of this alienation?
3. What is common sense? How is it enlisted in schools? Why is it harmful? How might it help?
4. How do the humanities follow a political curriculum?
5. How does cross-referencing subjects aid learning?
6. What is the core of a curriculum based in political humanism? How does it work?

Curriculum, as a specialized educational orientation, combines teaching with an understanding of human relationships (e.g., student/teacher, community/school, cultural group/school/classroom, societal hierarchies/school/classroom, etc.) that is textured by institutional structures and widely held beliefs and ideologies. The forces that shape curriculum, however, are not unidirectional. For the most part, the emphasis on testing, standards, and teacher accountability (see, for example, Eitle, 2003 and Florida Commission on Educational Reform and Accountability, 1994) has discouraged classroom teachers from investigating some of the more political aspects of the curriculum. Practitioners, today, are encouraged by these reforms, and the institutions and ideologies that support them, to operate in a survival mode, where not only are they teaching to the test but also attempting to deflect the strong criticisms directly and indirectly pointed toward them by pejorative accountability schemes. Conversely, there has been a vocal segment of curriculum workers in the academy that has encouraged teachers to take a more political stance as they investigate and put into practice multicultural, bilingual programs, and dual language, democratic, peace, and tolerance curricula (Gandara, 1995; Hernandez, 1997; Rosenblum & Travis, 1996).

Given the dominance of the more rote, factual orientation to curriculum during the last century, it is important for those who see a political orientation to curriculum as an essential and embodied aspect of teaching to understand why a political orientation to curriculum is not a dominant aspect of the policy and practice of teaching. With this understanding in mind, we can then consider how forces that currently constrain a more political orientation to curriculum might be altered. We begin this investigation by considering the issue of politics itself, asking the question "How can the concept of politics be reconfigured to occupy a more prominent place within the educational landscape?" To address this query, we begin by considering how politics can be connected to a form of humanism, a humanism that stands in contrast to the alienated self that is and has been so much a part of capitalist life.

THE ROOTS OF POLITICAL HUMANISM

Alienation

To understand humanism, it is important, if not essential, to consider what is holding us back from our human potential. For Marx and other sociologists (Fromm, 1961), the signature of this constraint is alienation. Alienation, in its most facile characterization, occurs when work has lost its purposefulness. Yes, work brings money, but the work itself does not connect directly to human needs and human potential. Instead, for the vast majority of workers, work or labor is experienced as establishing authority/novice relationships that focus workers' attention on finding leisure time. When this is the case, the character of the labor process is determined by superiors. At best, the work is only a means to an end. This alienation applies not only to production workers, but also to teachers (Gitlin, 1983). If teachers are alienated, as we believe many are, then in fact any reform or change proposal that leaves their "alienated state" intact will be mediated in the direction of the status quo. Put differently, teachers will attempt to minimize their workload, and this limiting effect often keeps things the same if for no other reason than that reform or change, in general, creates additional work (Apple, 1983; Gitlin, 2001). So, to challenge this alienation, where it exists among teachers, is to alter not only their work but, more importantly, their alienation and, ultimately, the possible ways they interact and connect with students. A brief example might clarify this point.

An English teacher has a choice to assign an essay or a multiple-choice test. Educationally, the teacher feels the essay would be best. However, this particular secondary teacher sees 175 students a day, and unless she gives an objective assessment she is likely to be confronted by any number of students (and parents) who think the grade given is unfair or unjust. Now, if the structures of schooling did not require a teacher to see so many students or have as a priority the sorting of students—if the teacher operated in a non-alienating or less alienating environment—the choice would be open and the essay test might reasonably be selected if it would make the educational process more meaningful for the teacher and students. Yet many teachers, when faced with this choice, would choose the multiple-choice test. Why? Because, in part, the context of work has limited or taken away their control and forced them to treat students as sorted commodities, not engaged learners. Teachers are alienated, and that alienation influences (not determines) the nature of their work and relations with students.

So what is to be done to foster a more humanistic view of politics? Teachers should engage in a form of inquiry that allows them to see and then rethink the forces that shape their alienation. If they do so in a way that confronts or challenges alienation, teachers will be engaging in relations of freedom. In this sense, politics of a humanistic kind makes a double move to challenge alienation and engage in a freedom quest. Part of this freedom quest is to focus knowledge production, and therefore a humanistic politics, on common sense as an object of inquiry.

Common Sense as an Object of Inquiry

In her 1899 novel *The Awakening,* Kate Chopin chronicles the journey of the protagonist, Edna, from her early life as a wealthy lady of privilege, schooled in the traditions of her society, to her arrival at a place of creative self-awareness. Here, she is able and willing to interrogate the societal structures that she feels circumscribe her life to a small, suffocating existence. At one point in the novel, the author talks about Edna's husband and his unease with the changes he finds in his wife: "He could see plainly that she was not herself. That is, he could not see that she was becoming herself and daily casting aside that fictitious self which we assume like a garment with which to appear before the world" (p. 96). And what is this fictitious self? It is the alienated self that has its roots in common sense.

Because the meaning we attach to common sense is somewhat unique, it might be helpful to say a few words about how this term speaks to us.

Common sense, in our view, is a catchall phrase that refers to normative discourses, the broad-based circulating value systems that often move across multiple contexts, and local discourses, the specific normative systems found in a particular locale. Common sense, however, is not a free-floating "sense," but a sense or normative account that is tied to context or contexts. When we use the word *context,* we are referring to architectures such as political and economic systems, the influence of the state, institutional rules and organizations, and even the layout of a particular space, among a variety of contextual structures. As such, common sense opens a window into our alienated state. Marcuse (1964) speaks to the influence of context on common sense when he notes that even social and economic systems as different as those in the United States and the Soviet Union (in the 1950s) have common institutional structures that coordinate particular alienated perspectives and orientations (p. 66). This coordinating function has the effect of helping to produce a common sense; in this case, an unnamed conformism to the structural priorities becomes the watchword of a secular faith—a faith that suffocates the exploration of cultural needs and interests—and relations that are defined by economics, bureaucracies, and mass media (Reitz, 2003, p. 162). Now, this unnamed conformism is not guaranteed; rather, it is a contextual priority that requires cultural participation. In this way, common sense emerges from the interaction of contextual priorities and cultural participation.

Common sense, however, does not operate simply on the wide planes of governmental and institutional systems and structures; it is also in our homes and communities and moves back and forth between these broad boundaries and local contexts. An example closer to our educational homes might clarify this point. If a teacher is going to produce knowledge (i.e., reflect on her experience) as part of her attempt to develop a sixth-grade social studies curriculum, the knowledge she produces is likely to be influenced by a dominant discourse found in many, if not most, schools—that education functions to sort students from best to worst. This assumption or commonsense position about sorting may also operate in conjunction with a local discourse found at a particular school or community—that U.S. history should focus on the accomplishments of government throughout time, not on its controversies or conflicts. The normative nature of these discourses may give teachers and others the impression that they are being neutral as they sort students based on their understanding of the accomplishments of government. However, it is also possible that this impression of neutrality may hide the way in which sorting serves a legitimating function in supporting differential social and cultural group opportunities, while focusing on accomplishments may further political quiescence and the maintenance of existing distributions of power and rationality in society (Apple, 1983, p. 84).

The problem with these commonsense discourses is not that they are always to be avoided, but rather that they act behind the backs of actors such as teachers and therefore discourage them from challenging or even further supporting their content and form. It is not as if each teacher necessarily thought about the decision to sort students or avoid controversies; rather, it is often the case that this is just "the way we do things here [in schools]." And even if they did carefully investigate these issues, some teachers simply wouldn't have the authority to significantly challenge many of these commonsense discourses because the textbooks and the grading systems are mandated (Gitlin, 2001). Nevertheless, even in these constrained situations, teachers almost always have the ability to find small places in which to make alterations in, for example, the way sorting takes place in their classrooms and the use of controversies—they can teach against the grain (Cochran-Smith, 1991). Teachers who see common sense can point to the connections between context and alienation and can exploit our human potential to be free—to free ourselves from alienation and common sense in general. By doing so, teachers who engage in knowledge production of the kind we discuss here are simultaneously engaging in a form of humanistic politics.

The common sense of schooling that we refer to in the above example moves back and forth between the classroom and the school district and, of course, wider forms of common sense found at the governmental and institutional level, to focus attention on competition, producing hierarchies (this is the sorting function) and minimizing controversies and protest-oriented histories—which have been documented in various art and aesthetic forms. You might be asking yourself, "What is the problem?" The problem, from our point of view, is not that competition and sorting are inherently evil, or that history should focus solely on controversies or protests, or that the teacher role is fundamentally flawed. Instead, our problem is that all these aspects of common sense direct our attention to the *is,* the way things *are,* and encourage conformism to political and social reality. As such, the educational common sense we mention stands in opposition to freedom, the "unquestioned ethical and political value to social nonconformism" (Marcuse, 1978, pp. 55–56). To build on Marcuse's (1964) language, cultural common sense has made us one-dimensional, and part of becoming multi-dimensional is to emerge from the saturating aspects of common sense that deny us the ability to perceive and act beyond the known of everyday life and normative considerations. By doing so, we hope to create a knowledge/politics that will enable educators and others to see their world through relations of freedom—a freedom that is centered in protest.

Relations of Freedom

What is being protested against? We are protesting the affirming, commonsense aspects of culture that limit human freedom. We are protesting static forms of knowledge that simply become new and improved forms of common sense that obstruct the free unfolding of life (Reitz, 2003, pp. 185–186). In the form of knowledge we desire, "[t]he object of knowledge, of the knower, does not in this case stand 'over against' him as a different entity 'foreign' to him . . . but 'lives with him. . . .'" (Marcuse, 1968, p. 4). The object of inquiry in this sense is life itself; there is a living unity between the inquirer and the themes of inquiry, or, more specifically, the commonsense aspects of life become the thematic emphasis of scholarly inquiry. But the focus on life itself concerns not only the "is," the current realities, but also the relation of

those current realities with the possibilities for a better social order that acknowledges the importance of taboos and illusory insights (Marcuse, 1968, p. 1). When this is the case, knowledge/politics has the potential to free civilization from its own brutality, its own insufficiency, and its own blindness and lead to the rehumanization of history, in which man inquires about his essence in order to see anew in ways less saturated with aspects of affirming culture, or cultural common sense.

However, moving toward relations of freedom should do more than engage actors with common sense; it should promote freedom by enlarging our horizons, increasing our autonomy, and making more complex our visions and our imagination. Vision and imagination are particularly critical for freedom, for they speak to what is unique about our humanness—our ability to begin somewhat anew and to find something previously unseen (Arendt, 1968). To do so, knowledge/politics needs to address the specific relation between mind/body/soul (self) and the articulation of commonsensical *texts*. What we see as possible, our horizon, should be enlarged if knowledge/politics moves in the direction of relations of freedom (Gadamer, 1988). Further, the relation between texts and teachers should also be enhanced, such that new meaning flows into these texts and into our own values and prejudices.

One such space is what we call the borderland between differences. This is a space in the knowledge-production/political process that is neither that of the text nor that of the teacher. Instead, it is a space that emerges out of the differences in perspectives between text and teacher. As such, borderland spaces, spaces of freedom in our view, are one terrain on which new possibilities can develop when the influences of common sense do not totally saturate teachers' perspectives. Relations of freedom, therefore, include not only knowledge/political production of a certain type, but also the intimate connection between producing a certain type of knowledge/politics and expanding possibilities to act on the social world (Giroux, 1988).

What we mean by the ideal or purpose of relations of freedom and its link to knowledge/political production may become clearer if we use an example from our context as educators. If a teacher sees being in control as a primary prerequisite for student learning, knowledge/politics attempting to move toward relations of freedom might push the teacher to consider whether there are other ways to enhance learning and, if so, what values (e.g., cultural relevance) these new orientations might hold, as well as what advantages or disadvantages they might have in relation to viewing learning as emerging from a controlled situation. If this process is successful, and the knowledge/politics produced points to other possibilities such as cultural relevance, the question of how to create spaces in which to put this new learning foundation into practice might come to the fore. When the teacher's horizons have been broadened, and when she has acted in ways that experiment with new points of view, the knowledge-production/political process will certainly move toward enhancing relations of freedom. Freedom, in this view, is, in part, a movement away from forms of common sense that reinforce what is typically understood to be the case—for example, the need in schools for educational sorting and competition (Spring, 1976).

To move toward relations of freedom is not only a movement away; it is also a movement toward. Put more simply, movement toward relations of freedom requires a double move—a movement away from common sense and a movement toward a knowledge-production/political process and a form of inquiry that allows new horizons, as well as spaces of freedom, to emerge. It is this double move, in our view, that fuels the importance of relations of freedom as a purpose for knowledge/political production. However, an important caveat is in order. We use the phrase "moving toward relations of freedom" quite intentionally. The importance of the phrase "moving toward" is that it connotes that relations of freedom are an ideal—the long-term, lifelong process is never complete. Therefore, a movement away from common sense is not something that is accomplished in any absolute way. Instead, it is something that must be struggled with on a constant basis, even though in most instances knowledge production will fall short of achieving this ideal.

In sum, we think about politics in humanistic terms, as an orientation that begins with a chal-

lenge to alienation. With this challenge setting the stage, a politics of curriculum proceeds with common sense as an object of inquiry and sets teachers and other curriculum workers on an exploration of freedom to exploit our human potential to see anew, without that vision being totally saturated with the past traditions, categories, and ways of seeing the world.

Curriculum Influences

With this orientation to politics in mind, we can now move closer to our curriculum homes by looking at the forces that have pushed and pulled on curriculum workers. One of the most important sets of forces in this regard is the push toward facts and the pull toward educating the "whole child" to become a problem solver.

Rousseau (1762) suggested that education springs forth from a child's natural inclinations and argued that educating the full child (body, brain, and soul) would foster a free-thinking *person* and a more humane society. In reality, the curriculum emphasis in both the United States and Europe in the 19th century was on facts and memorization. This was best expressed by Charles Dickens in his novel *Hard Times* (1854) when Mr. Gradgrind, the school patron, demonstrated his teaching prowess for the school teacher by saying, "Now what I want is facts. Teach these boys and girls nothing but the Facts. Facts alone are wanted in life. Plant nothing else, and root out everything else. You can only form the minds of reasoning animals upon Facts: nothing else will ever be of service to them . . . Stick to the facts, Sir!" (p. 1).

While a factual orientation dominated the curriculum landscape of this time, other forces were at play, not the least of which was the progressive movement of the 20th century, with its emphasis on problem solving and reasoning. Dewey's (1910, 1916) notion of *reflective thinking* and Bruner's (1959) idea of *subject [matter] structure* seemed to embody this movement. These ideals were conceived as the be-all-and-end-all concepts for teaching, learning, and developing curriculum: "The sole direct path to enduring improvement in the methods of instruction and learning consists in centering upon conditions which exact, promote and test thinking"—that is, fostering and challenging natural interests to encourage life learners (Dewey, 1916, p. 153). It is therefore essential that we foster a child's natural interests and creative mind, as well as desires for a true education—one that society and the student will see as useful, enjoyable, and generative.

Bruner (1959) also tried to differentiate himself from the domination of facts within the curriculum by arguing that learning bits of information is limited; only by understanding relationships is the learner able to continually and independently relate additional information to a field study or across subjects (Suarez-Orozco and Qin-Hilliard, 2004). From Bruner's point of view (1959), only by understanding relationships is the learner able to continually and independently relate additional information to a field of study or subject (and ultimately cross-reference and inter-relate), based on Piaget's ideas of *assimilation* (whereby the child incorporates new experiences into existing experiences) and *accommodation* (whereby the child's experiences are modified and adapted in response to his or her environment). Learning the same things or facts should not be an end of learning but, as Dewey (1910) and later Piaget (1932) and Bruner (1959) suggest, should be related to other aspects of subject matter and should be general enough to apply in other problems, situations, and contexts.

It is important to note that Rousseau, Dewey, and Bruner were not political humanists per se. They did, however, pave the way for thinking about curriculum in much more humane ways than would have been possible with an emphasis on facts. In particular, Rousseau's focus on allowing the child to blossom links with the optimism that most humanists have concerning human potential. Dewey adds to a humanist perspective by suggesting that not only can and should we encourage problem solving and reasoning abilities, but these abilities allow us to escape some of the commonsense assumptions that can seductively infiltrate our lives. And Bruner's focus on relationships goes hand in hand with confronting relationships that may be alienating in one sense or another and furthering relations of freedom that exploit our human potential to move beyond the taken-for-granted, the

commonsense dictates that limit our creativity and human potential to see anew.

Nevertheless, it is still the case that while these great academics laid the foundation for a political humanist curriculum, they were overshadowed by the realities of schooling during the last century. Many teachers are still being asked to stick to a script and teach to the facts so that students can pass a knowledge-based test. This mandate leaves almost no time for any other classroom instruction in which students might have a chance to use problem-solving skills or teachers might focus on the whole child by structuring subject matter around relationships. One reason why the forces of fact have dominated over the more political humanist orientation to curriculum is that parents want to know how their child's education fares in comparison with that of others and thus believe that standards in education should not be eliminated. We become increasingly dependent on facts and numbers to prove an education—the *product* rather than the *process* is paramount. The areas of education that are difficult (or time consuming) to objectify, test, and quantify are often eliminated. The arts and humanities—an aesthetic curriculum, which allows the mind to traverse into the unknown, to ask "Why are we here?"—often fall to the wayside.

And yet it is naïve to provide a child with an education of yesterday when it is increasingly obvious that this knowledge base is obsolete from the start. Sadker and Zittleman (2004) post a challenge to readers to answer questions from an 1895 eighth-grade exam, questions such as "Define the following terms and give examples of each: Trigraph, subvocals, diphthong, cognate letter, linguals" and "Name all the republics of Europe and give the capital of each." The test contains questions that would be difficult for today's college student to answer and only proves that "what is essential knowledge at one time may eventually be irrelevant or erroneous" (p. 741). Hot topics, fads, and fashions become outdated in the twelve to eighteen years it takes for a child to reach the workforce.

Increasingly, the corporate sector complains that those entering the workforce must endure costly training sessions because the knowledge base is not up to working world standards (Winter, 2005; Jennings, 1996). Big business informs us that we are failing to educate our children, and news magazines such as *Newsweek* (Carmichael, 2004) and *Time* (Winters, 2002; Morse, 2002) report that U.S. students score an F on international tests. Students today need to understand how to redevelop and re-evaluate current techniques and procedures in order to survive competitively in a political future (Suarez-Orozco and Qin-Hilliard, 2004). The assembly-line education that exists today for test-regurgitation throughout school does not support this free-thought process; rather, it blocks it from developing, causing students to be dependent on rote learning that rules their whole life. Low-level, quick, question-response standardized tests develop only the quick-thinking intellect required for limited multiple-choice answers. The thought processes needed to solve larger problems with greater social and political consequences are not encouraged in a classroom driven by right answers. (What is the capital of Brazil? What is the sine of an angle?) The "whys" and "what ifs" in society have enormously diverse answers that need classroom time and consideration. The problem is, according to David Posner (2004), that "individuals equipped only with the ability to solve routine problems would be those most vulnerable to displacement by automation" (p. 750). Sadly, the majority of our children and teachers are concerned only with the right answer in class and the right answer on the test.

Why Move toward Political Humanism?

The humanities celebrate individual critical thinking. A humanities orientation focuses on morals, ethics, and the politics needed in a heterogeneous, global society. A political orientation to curriculum, as we are using the term, "emerges when men are confronted with situations in which different desires promise opposed goods and in which incompatible courses of action seem to be morally justified. Only such a conflict of good ends and of standards and rules of right and wrong calls for the personal inquiry into the bases of morals" (Dewey, 1932, p. 5).

A political humanist curriculum cannot be taught through standardized tests. These concepts cannot be made into objects or objectives to be taught as tiny pieces of information. Tolerance and democracy, two concepts that inundate our media constantly today, cannot be taught in terms of right answers or by memorizing lists of information. Rather, these media should allow us to question and theorize, expand and develop our own thoughts and feelings. It is because these concepts are not tangible subjects, but rather virtues that need discussion, contemplation, and thought into why a person believes or acts the way she does, that they need attention (Barzun, 1944/1972). "Thinking means shuffling, relating, selecting the contents of one's mind so as to assimilate novelty, digest it, and create order" (p. 34). It takes imagination and integration across subjects to fully comprehend, connect, and create meaning of ideas.

This expanded curriculum offers *divergent* rather than *convergent* thought processes and ultimately directs the mind to broader ways of thinking and problem-solving skills. In this light, the arts complement a "standard" curriculum because they provide different modes of thought (Fowler, 1996). Humanities and the arts do not allow for one correct answer. They "require students to apply standards to their own work, to be self-critical, and to be able to self-correct. Through the arts, students learn self-discipline and how to handle frustration and failure in pursuit of their goals" (p. 49). These skills are important to competently survive in the world as a functional, compassionate, global citizen. In an era of nationalistic struggle, ethnic cleansing, and religious zealousness, the humanities provide a forum and consciousness to transcend demeaning national, racial, ethnic, and religious struggles, cultural assumptions, and the political trauma and upheaval shaping many parts of the globe.

Political Humanism and the Arts

With the discussion of the forces of curriculum and an argument for a political humanist curriculum in mind, it is now time to turn to the foundation for such a curriculum. In our view, such a foundation is found in the arts.

Deeper questions of humanity are often ignored in a curriculum of alienation. It is the testing industry that reinforces competition and glorifies test outcomes in an already highly competitive and materialistic world. It is not competition that the world needs. Competition ultimately breeds jealousy, hatred, misunderstanding, and war. Compassion, amity, and understanding (especially on a global basis) are needed today to propel the world into the future and to help people to work cooperatively.

Literature, poetry, music, art, and drama cannot supply absolute answers or furnish water-tight explanations. What they can do is raise political humanist questions and encourage people to think about their cultural life, experiences, personal possibilities, and responsibilities in the context of history, present society, and the future. These questions make us think and feel about life and the world around us and clarify our own human relations. They help us analyze the shadows of society—persistent poverty, malnutrition, exploitation, injustice, class, caste and gender issues, child labor practices, immigration and refugee problems, and the horrors of war. They also provide hope and renewal, a new way of thinking, and a better way of creating a new person and new society. They help define who we are and serve as benchmarks for our political consciousness.

The current system of testing reinforces and reminds us of achievement gaps by race and class that make the divide between the "haves" and the "have-nots" stronger. We perpetuate the "culture of poverty" by this system of testing, in which immediate outcomes reflect the results of economic and social deprivation. Animosity between those who figure out the system early and those who fall along the wayside grows more powerful. As we encourage standards and testing, verbal and mathematical achievement, now the ultimate test for academic acceptance, become increasingly more important. Budget cuts are imposed, and importance is taken away from the arts and humanities, which emancipate the soul into deeper notions of feeling and understanding.

In a world that increasingly celebrates sex and violence (just turn on a television), it grows ever more important to find a freedom that challenges this commonsense way of being in the world. The arts and humanities are a tool of expression and communication in that they cast and capture our own and others' perceptions. "To become an expressive, communicative being is the essence of our personal human spirit. When that possibility is denied to young people, they acquire little pride and less enthusiasm" (Fowler, 1996, p. 61). When arts and humanities are cut from school programs, the responsibility for discussing values and virtues is left to already busy parents. The more this important aspect of education is neglected, "the more schooling tends to legitimate existing inequalities, since its effectiveness is a function of the existing (and unevenly distributed) competence of the individuals being schooled" (Bourdieu and Darbel, 1990, p. 66). Some may say it is the parents' responsibility to pass on to their children the difficult morals, values, and virtues of society. But we believe it is better to discuss the larger concepts of life in the comfortable platform of the school, where multiple ideas can be bounced off each other and the student has the opportunity to come to a conclusion on his or her own, a conclusion that he or she genuinely believes. To implement such an ideal requires a curriculum based on grappling with ideas, not focusing on facts in order to pass a standardized test.

Education must reveal itself as a necessity of life to a child because ultimately it emancipates humans. Education is shown as a tool to pull societies out of poverty, inform leadership, and promote health and social (especially for women) growth (Bloom, 2004; Suarez-Orozco, 2004). John Dewey (1915) was a supporter of encouraging lifelong learning (in whatever form), not because it is dull and time consuming, but because it liberates humans to find freedom and their calling in life. The 19th century American author Edgar Allan Poe (1850/2004) once said, "Beauty, of whatever kind, invariably excites the human soul to tears." This beauty is found in the curriculum we too often neglect and set aside as frivolous. The arts, whatever their form, connect the human spirit on a globally understood, deeply emotional, *human* level. Arts and humanities encourage respect because they share the universal values and emotions—love, dignity, compassion, caring and also hate, suffering, jealousy, pain—the good and the bad. These feelings help educators and students to escape the common sense that limits human potential to see anew and aid them in moving forward without that movement being totally dependent on what has been. In this respect, the humanities, and the arts in particular, provide a path to political humanism that offers an understanding of what all cultures and people are—human. One aspect of this humanness is our ability to imagine.

IMAGINATION AND A POLITICAL HUMANIST CURRICULUM

Without an active imagination that was allowed to wander beyond the planned curriculum and standard way of thinking, would Albert Einstein have developed such groundbreaking theories? Would Maya Angelou have so much compassion in her writing? Would Susan B. Anthony have had the audacity to stand up for what she saw as a natural right? Would Martin Luther King Jr. have been an eloquent speaker of his beliefs? The list goes on: Freud, Gandhi, Picasso, Bocelli, Geronimo, Mother Teresa. Without the development of natural human tendencies to inquire into the way things are and how they *could* be (not just what they *are*), these great individuals would not have accomplished what they did. The active and imaginative parts of our mind must be encouraged to develop if out-of-the-box thinking is expected.

Standardized tests, knowledge-based curriculum, and right-answer teaching and learning have overtaken school policies and programs. The student is confined to a box with no innovation allowed—no time to reflect, to question, to imagine, to ask "why?" or "what if?" The idea too often is to conform and to spit out the right answer—that is, the answer the teacher expects.

The understandings that are enlisted in viewing a play, listening to or performing music, or appreciating paintings, sculptures, and films express deep thoughts that connect the human spirit. It is these understandings that allow people to un-

derstand cultures other than their own. The arts and humanities express community and ethnicity, allowing us to define who and what we are. They "can help young people acquire inter- and intra-cultural understanding. The arts are not just multicultural, they are trans-cultural, inviting cross-cultural communication and understanding and teaching openness toward those who are different from us" (Fowler, 1996, p. 52).

The world is always at our door, hammering to be let in. We can try to ignore or forget about it by overlooking the voices of more than 6 billion people, each trying to be heard in his or her own way, each one's thoughts striving for equal importance, and each one claiming a right to live life with dignity. We can continue to teach the facts, nothing but the facts, and try to raise test scores, thus ignoring the demands of what lies outside the classroom, or we can let in some of the uncomfortable surroundings that may or may not shatter our optimistic illusions and visions of the world. This involves addressing the questions about the purpose and value of life that we find by reading and discussing literature, poetry, art, music, film, and drama. It involves revealing the everyday inequalities, injustices, and violence around the globe. In practical terms, it means that a critical mass of educators in a school or school district stand up and say, "Fewer facts, more ideas! Less rote knowledge, more values, and a curriculum based on imagination!" The arts can then be part of a freedom quest to exploit our human potential to see beyond the common sense that drives us toward the status quo.

REFERENCES

Apple, M. (1983). *Education and Power.* Boston: Routledge and Kegan Paul.

Apple, M. (1986). *Teachers and Texts: A Political Economy of Class and Gender Relations in Education.* New York: Routledge.

Apple, M. (1990). *Ideology and Curriculum* (2nd ed.). New York: Routledge.

Arendt, H. (1968). *Between Past and Future: Eight Exercises in Political Thought.* New York: Penguin Books.

Barzun, J. (1972). *Teacher in America.* New York: University Press of America. (Originally published 1944.)

Bloom, D. E. (2004). "Globalization and Education: An Economic Perspective." In M. Suarez-Orozco, and D. B. Qin-Hilliard, *Globalization and Education*. Berkeley: University of California Press.

Bourdieu, P., & Darbel, A. (1990). "Cultural Works and Cultivated Disposition." in P. Bourdieu and A. Darbel, eds., *The Love of Art: European Art Museums and Their Public*. Trans. by C. Beattie and N. Merriman. Stanford: Stanford University Press.

Bruner, J. S. (1959). *The Process of Education*. Cambridge, MA: Harvard University Press.

Carmichael, M. (2204, Dec. 12). "Stirring Up Science." *Newsweek,* pp. 54–55.

Chopin, K. (1899/1972). *The Awakening*. New York: Avon Books.

Cochran-Smith, M. (1991). "Learning to Teach Against the Grain." *Harvard Educational Review, 61,* 279–310.

Dewey, J. (1932). *Theory of the Moral Life*. New York: Irvington Publishers.

Dewey, J. (1916). *Democracy and Education*. New York: Macmillan Company.

Dewey, J. (1915). *Schools of Tomorrow*. New York: Dutton.

Dewey, J. (1910). *How We Think*. Boston: D.C. Heath.

Dickens, C. (1989). *Hard Times*. New York: Oxford University Press. (Originally published 1854.)

Eitle, T. M. (2003). "Diversity, Segregation and Accountability in Florida Schools." Paper presented at the meeting of the American Sociological Association, Atlanta, Georgia.

Florida Commission on Education Reform and Accountability. (1994). Blueprint 2000. Tallahassee, FL: Author.

Fowler, C. (1996). *Strong Arts, Strong Schools*. New York: Oxford University Press.

Fromm, E. (1961). *Marx's Concept of Man*. New York: Frederick Ungar Publishing.

Gadamer, H. G. (1988). *Truth and Method* (J. Weinsheimer & D. G. Marshall, trans.). New York: Continuum.

Gandara, P. (1995). *Over the Ivy Walls: The Educational Mobility of Low-Income Chicanos*. New York: SUNY Press.

Giroux, H. (1988). *Teachers as Intellectuals: Toward a Critical Pedagogy of Learning*. South Hadley, MA: Bergin and Harvey.

Giroux, H., & Simon, R. (1989). "Popular Culture and Critical Pedagogy: Everyday Life as a Basis for Curriculum Knowledge." In H. Giroux and P. McLaren, eds., *Critical Pedagogy, the State and Cultural Struggle.* (pp. 237–252) New York: SUNY Press. .

Gitlin, A. (1983). "School Structure, Teachers Work and Reproduction." In M. Apple and L. Weiss, eds., *Ideology and Practice in Education* (pp. 193–212). Philadelphia: Temple University Press.

Gitlin, A. (2001). "Bounding Teacher Decision Making: The Threat of Intensification." *Educational Policy, 15*(2): 227–258.

Hernandez, H. (1997). *Teaching in Multicultural Classrooms: A Teacher's Guide to Context, Process and Content*. Upper Saddle River, NJ: Merrill.

Jennings, J. F. (1996). "Using Standards to Improve Education." In R. Lafayette and J. Draper, eds., *National Standards*. Chicago: National Textbook Company.

Marcuse, H. (1964). *One Dimensional Man: Studies into Ideology in Advanced Industrial Society*. Boston: Beacon Press.

Marcuse, H. (1968). "Philosophy and Critical Theory." In *Negations: Essays in Critical Theory*. Trans. J. Shapiro. Boston: Beacon Press.

Marcuse, H. (1978). "Theory and Politics: A Discussion with Herbert Marcuse, Jurgen Habermas, Heinz Lubasz, and Tilman Spengler." *Telos, 38:* 24–153.

Morse, J. (2002, Sept. 23). "Anything to Avoid an F." *Time,* p. 22.

Piaget, J. (1932). *The Child's Conception of Physical Causality*. New York: Harcourt.

Poe, Edgar Allan. (1850/2004). *Criticism*. Whitefish, MT: Kessinger Publishing.

Posner, D. (2004, June). "What's Wrong with Teaching to the Test?" *Phi Delta Kappan, 85*(10): 749–751.

Reitz, C. (2003). *Art, Alienation and the Humanities: A Critical Engagement with Herbert Marcuse*. New York: SUNY Press.

Rosenblum, K., & Travis, T. (1996). *The Meaning of Difference: American Constructions of Race, Sex and Gender, Social Class and Sexual Orientation*. New York: McGraw Hill.

Rousseau, J. (1979). *Emile*. New York: Basic Books. (Originally published 1762.)

Sadker, D. & Zittleman, K. (2004, June). "Test Anxiety: Are Students Failing Tests—or Are Tests Failing Students?" *Phi Delta Kappan,* 740–744, 751.

Spring, J. (1976). *The Sorting Machine: National Educational Policy Since 1945*. New York: Longman.

Suarez-Orozco, C. (2004). "Formulating Identity in a Globalized World." In M. Suarez-Orozco and

D. B. Qin-Hilliard, eds., *Globalization and Education.* Berkeley: University of California Press.

Suarez-Orozco, M., & Qin-Hilliard, D. B. (2004). "Globalization: Culture and Education in the New Millennium." In M. Suarez-Orozco and D. B. Qin-Hilliard, eds., *Globalization and Education.* Berkeley: University of California Press.

Winter, Greg. (2005, February 23). "Governors Seek Rise in High School Standards." *New York Times.*

Winters, Rebecca. (2002, May 27). "Trouble for School Inc." *Time,* pp. 53–55.

DISCUSSION QUESTIONS

1. Does the definition of "curriculum" proposed at the beginning of this chapter conform to your experience with the term?
2. What role should politics have in determining what students should learn? Who should make those decisions?
3. Do you agree that most teachers feel alienated from their work? If so, what would make teaching more engaging?
4. Why do the authors find fault with reliance on common sense when it comes to schooling? How do they propose we move beyond it?
5. What do the authors mean by the term "political humanism"? Do you agree that the changes proposed would improve schooling for both teachers and students?

25

The Importance of Multicultural Education

GENEVA GAY

FOCUSING QUESTIONS

1. How has multiculturalism changed in the United States?

2. How does lack of ethnic, racial, and cultural community harm schools? How does this extend into society?

3. How can multicultural education extend beyond the arts/humanities? Why is this important?

4. What are some steps to incorporating multicultural content into a curriculum?

5. How does cross-referencing subjects aid multicultural learning?

6. How do reality/representation and relevance shape a multicultural curriculum? How do they shape student learning?

Multiculturalism in U.S. schools and society is taking on new dimensions of complexity and practicality as demographics, social conditions, and political circumstances change. Domestic diversity and unprecedented immigration have created a vibrant mixture of cultural, ethnic, linguistic, and experiential plurality.

Effectively managing such diversity in U.S. society and schools is at once a very old and a very new challenge. Benjamin Barber (1992) eloquently makes the point that

> America has always been a tale of peoples trying to be a People, a tale of diversity and plurality in search of unity. Cleavages among [diverse groups] . . . have irked and divided Americans from the start, making unity a civic imperative as well as an elusive challenge. (p. 41)

Accomplishing this end is becoming increasingly important as the 21st century unfolds. People coming from Asia, the Middle East, Latin America, Eastern Europe, and Africa differ greatly from earlier generations of immigrants who came primarily from western and northern Europe.

These unfamiliar groups, cultures, traditions, and languages can produce anxieties, hostilities, prejudices, and racist behaviors among those who do not understand the newcomers or who perceive them as threats to their safety and security. These issues have profound implications for developing, at all levels of education, instructional programs and practices that respond positively and constructively to diversity.

A hundred years ago, W. E. B. Du Bois (1994) proposed that the problem of the 20th century was conflict and controversy among racial groups, particularly between African and European Americans. He concluded,

> Between these two worlds [black and white], despite much physical contact and daily intermingling, there is almost no community of intellectual life or point of transference where the thoughts and feelings of one race can come into direct contact and sympathy with the thoughts and feelings of the other. (p. 110)

Although much has changed since Du Bois's declarations, too much has not changed nearly enough. Of course, the color line has become more complex and diverse, and legal barriers against racial intermingling have been dismantled. People from different ethnic, racial, and cultural groups live in close physical proximity. But coexistence does not mean that people create genuine communities in which they know, relate to, and care deeply about one another. The lack of a genuine community of diversity is particularly evident in school curriculums that still do not regularly and systematically include important information and deep study about a wide range of diverse ethnic groups. As disparities in educational opportunities and outcomes among ethnic groups have continued to grow, the resulting achievement gap has reached crisis proportions.

Multicultural education is integral to improving the academic success of students of color and preparing all youths for democratic citizenship in a pluralistic society. Students need to understand how multicultural issues shape the social, political, economic, and cultural fabric of the United States as well as how such issues fundamentally influence their personal lives.

CONCEPTIONS OF MULTICULTURAL EDUCATION

Even though some theorists (Banks & Banks, 2002) have argued that multicultural education is a necessary ingredient of quality education, in actual practice educators most often perceive it either as an addendum prompted by some crisis or as a luxury. Multicultural education has not yet become a central part of the curriculum regularly offered to all students; instead, educators have relegated it primarily to social studies, language arts, and the fine arts and have generally targeted instruction for students of color.

These attitudes distort multicultural education and make it susceptible to sporadic and superficial implementation, if any. Textbooks provide a compelling illustration of such an attitude: The little multicultural content that they offer is often presented in sidebars and special-events sections (Loewen, 1995).

Another obstacle to implementing multicultural education lies with teachers themselves. Many are unconvinced of its worth or its value

in developing academic skills and building a unified national community. Even those teachers who are more accepting of multicultural education are nevertheless skeptical about the feasibility of its implementation. "I would do it if I could," they say, "but I don't know how." "Preparing students to meet standards takes up all my time," others point out. "School curriculums are already overburdened. What do I take out to make room for multicultural education?"

A fallacy underlies these conceptions and the instructional behaviors that they generate: the perception of multicultural education as separate content that educators must append to existing curriculums as separate lessons, units, or courses. Quite the contrary is true. Multicultural education is more than content; it includes policy, learning climate, instructional delivery, leadership, and evaluation (see Banks, 1994; Bennett, 2003; Grant & Gomez, 2000). In its comprehensive form, it must be an integral part of everything that happens in the education enterprise, whether it is assessing the academic competencies of students or teaching math, reading, writing, science, social studies, or computer science. Making explicit connections between multicultural education and subject- and skill-based curriculum and instruction is imperative.

It is not pragmatic for K–12 educators to think of multicultural education as a discrete entity, separated from the commonly accepted components of teaching and learning. These conceptions may be fine for higher education, where specialization is the rule. But in K–12 schools, where the education process focuses on teaching eclectic bodies of knowledge and skills, teachers need to use multicultural education to promote such highly valued outcomes as human development, education equality, academic excellence, and democratic citizenship (see Banks & Banks, 2001; Nieto, 2000).

To translate these theoretical conceptions into practice, educators must systematically weave multicultural education into the central core of curriculum, instruction, school leadership, policy making, counseling, classroom climate, and performance assessment. Teachers should use multicultural content, perspectives, and experiences to teach reading, math, science, and social studies.

For example, teachers could demonstrate mathematical concepts, such as less than/greater than, percentages, ratios, and probabilities, using ethnic demographics. Younger children could consider the ethnic and racial distributions in their own classrooms, discussing which group's representation is greater than, less than, or equal to another's. Older students could collect statistics about ethnic distributions on a larger scale and use them to make more sophisticated calculations, such as converting numbers to percentages and displaying ethnic demographics on graphs.

Students need to apply such major academic skills as data analysis, problem solving, comprehension, inquiry, and effective communication as they study multicultural issues and events. For instance, students should not simply memorize facts about major events involving ethnic groups, such as civil rights movements, social justice efforts, and cultural accomplishments. Instead, educators should teach students how to think critically and analytically about these events, propose alternative solutions to social problems, and demonstrate understanding through such forms of communication as poetry, personal correspondence, debate, editorials, and photo essays.

Irvine and Armento (2001) provide specific examples for incorporating multicultural education into planning language arts, math, science, and social studies lessons for elementary and middle school students and connecting these lessons to general curriculum standards. One set of lessons demonstrates how to use Navajo rugs to explain the geometric concepts of perimeter and area and to teach students how to calculate the areas of squares, rectangles, triangles, and parallelograms.

These suggestions indicate that teachers need to use systematic decision-making approaches to accomplish multicultural curriculum integration. In practice, this means developing intentional and orderly processes for including multicultural content. The decision-making process might involve the following steps:

- Creating learning goals and objectives that incorporate multicultural aspects, such as "Developing students' ability to write persuasively about social justice concerns."

- Using a frequency matrix to ensure that the teacher includes a wide variety of ethnic groups in a wide variety of ways in curriculum materials and instructional activities.
- Introducing different ethnic groups and their contributions on a rotating basis.
- Including several examples from different ethnic experiences to explain subject matter concepts, facts, and skills.
- Showing how multicultural content, goals, and activities intersect with subject-specific curricular standards.

Virtually all aspects of multicultural education are interdisciplinary. As such, they cannot be adequately understood through a single discipline. For example, teaching students about the causes, expressions, and consequences of racism and how to combat racism requires the application of information and techniques from such disciplines as history, economics, sociology, psychology, mathematics, literature, science, art, politics, music, and health care. Theoretical scholarship already affirms this interdisciplinary need; now, teachers need to model good curricular and instructional practice in elementary and secondary classrooms. Putting this principle into practice will elevate multicultural education from impulse, disciplinary isolation, and simplistic and haphazard guesswork to a level of significance, complexity, and connectedness across disciplines.

MULTICULTURALISM AND CURRICULUM DEVELOPMENT

How can teachers establish linkages between multicultural education and the disciplines and subject matter content taught in schools? One approach is to filter multicultural education through two categories of curriculum development: reality/representation and relevance.

Reality/Representation

A persistent concern of curriculum development in all subjects is helping students understand the realities of the social condition and how they came to be, as well as adequately representing those realities. Historically, curriculum designers have been more exclusive than inclusive of the wide range of ethnic and cultural diversity that exists within society. In their haste to promote harmony and avoid controversy and conflict, they gloss over social problems and the realities of ethnic and racial identities, romanticize racial relations, and ignore the challenges of poverty and urban living in favor of middle-class and suburban experiences. The reality is distorted and the representations incomplete (Loewen, 1995).

An inescapable reality is that diverse ethnic, racial, and cultural groups and individuals have made contributions to every area of human endeavor and to all aspects of U.S. history, life, and culture. When students study food resources in the United States, for example, they often learn about production and distribution by large-scale agribusiness and processing corporations. The curriculum virtually ignores the contributions of the many ethnically diverse people involved in planting and harvesting vegetables and fruits (with the Mexican and Mexican American farm labor unionization movement a possible exception). School curriculums that incorporate comprehensive multicultural education do not perpetuate these exclusions. Instead, they teach students the reality—how large corporations and the food industry are directly connected to the migrant workers who harvest vegetables and pick fruits. If we are going to tell the true story of the United States, multicultural education must be a central feature in its telling.

School curriculums need to reverse these trends by also including equitable representations of diversity. For example, the study of American literature, art, and music should include the contributions of males and females from different ethnic groups in all genres and in different expressive styles. Thus, the study of jazz would examine various forms and techniques produced not just by African Americans but also by Asian, European, and Latino Americans.

Moreover, educators should represent ethnically diverse individuals and groups in all strata of human accomplishment instead of typecasting particular groups as dependent and helpless victims who make limited contributions of significance. Even under the most oppressive conditions, diverse groups in the United States have been creative, activist, and productive on broad scales. The way in which Japanese Americans handled their internment during World War II provides an excellent example. Although schools must not overlook or minimize the atrocities this group endured, students should also learn how interned Japanese Americans led dignified lives under the most undignified circumstances, elevating their humanity above their circumstances. The curriculum should include both issues.

Relevance

Many ethnically diverse students do not find schooling exciting or inviting; they often feel unwelcome, insignificant, and alienated. Too much of what is taught has no immediate value to these students. It does not reflect who they are. Yet most educators will agree that learning is more interesting and easier to accomplish when it has personal meaning for students.

Students from different ethnic groups are more likely to be interested and engaged in learning situations that occur in familiar and friendly frameworks than in those occurring in strange and hostile ones. A key factor in establishing educational relevance for these students is cultural similarity and responsiveness (see Bruner, 1996; Hollins, 1996; Wlodkowski & Ginsberg, 1995). For example, immigrant Vietnamese, Jamaican, and Mexican students who were members of majority populations in their home countries initially may have difficulty understanding what it means to be members of minority groups in the United States. Students who come from education environments that encourage active participatory learning will not be intellectually stimulated by passive instruction that involves lecturing and completing worksheets. Many students of color are bombarded with irrelevant learning experiences, which dampen their academic interest, engagement, and achievement. Multicultural education mediates these situations by teaching content about the cultures and contributions of many ethnic groups and by using a variety of teaching techniques that are culturally responsive to different ethnic learning styles.

Using a variety of strategies may seem a tall order in a classroom that includes students from many different ethnic groups. Research indicates, however, that several ethnic groups share some learning style attributes (Shade, 1989). Teachers need to understand the distinguishing characteristics of different learning styles and use the instructional techniques best suited to each style. In this scenario, teachers would provide alternative teaching techniques for clusters of students instead of for individual students. In any given lesson, the teacher might offer three or four ways for students to learn, helping to equalize learning advantages and disadvantages among the different ethnic groups in the classroom.

Scholars are producing powerful descriptions of culturally relevant teaching for multiethnic students and its effects on achievement. Lipka and Mohatt (1998) describe how a group of teachers, working closely with Native Alaskan (Yup'ik) elders, made school structure, climate, curriculum, and instruction more reflective of and meaningful to students from the community. For ten years, the teachers translated, adapted, and embedded Yup'ik cultural knowledge in math, literacy, and science curriculums. The elders served as resources and quality-control monitors of traditional knowledge, and they provided the inspiration and moral strength for the teachers to persist in their efforts to center the schooling of Yup'ik students around the students' own cultural orientations. In math, for instance, the teachers now habitually make connections among the Yup'ik numeration system, body measurements, simple and complex computations, geometry, pattern designs, and tessellations.

Similar attributes apply to the work of such scholars as Moses and Cobb (2001), Lee (1993), and Boykin and Bailey (2000), who are studying the effects of culturally relevant curriculum and instruction on the school performance of African American students. Moses and his colleagues are making higher-order math knowledge accessible to African American middle school students by teaching this material through the students' own cultural orientations and experiences. To teach algebra, they emphasize the experiences and familiar environments of urban and rural low-income students, many of whom are at high risk for academic failure. A key feature of their approach is making students conscious of how algebraic principles and formulas operate in their daily lives and getting students to understand how to explain these connections in nonalgebraic language before converting this knowledge into the technical notations and calculations of algebra. Students previously considered by some teachers as incapable of learning algebra are performing at high levels—better, in fact, than many of their advantaged peers.

Evidence increasingly indicates that multicultural education makes schooling more relevant and effective for Latino American, Native American, Asian American, and Native Hawaiian students as well (see McCarty, 2002; Moll, Amanti, Neff, & Gonzalez, 1992; Park, Goodwin, & Lee, 2001; Tharp & Gallimore, 1988). Students perform more successfully at all levels when there is greater congruence between their cultural backgrounds and such school experiences as task interest, effort, academic achievement, and feelings of personal efficacy or social accountability.

As the challenge to better educate underachieving students intensifies and diversity among student populations expands, the need for multicultural education grows exponentially. Multicultural education may be the solution to problems that currently appear insolvable: closing the achievement gap; genuinely not leaving any children behind academically; revitalizing faith and trust in the promises of democracy, equality, and justice; building education systems that reflect the diverse cultural, ethnic, racial, and social contributions that forge society; and providing better opportunities for all students.

Multicultural education is crucial. Classroom teachers and educators must answer its clarion call to provide students from all ethnic groups with the education they deserve.

REFERENCES

Banks, J. A. (1994). *Multiethnic Education: Theory and Practice* (3rd ed.). Boston: Allyn and Bacon.

Banks, J. A., & Banks, C. A. M. (Eds.). (2001). *Multicultural Education: Issues and Perspectives* (4th ed.). Boston: Allyn and Bacon.

Banks, J. A., & Banks, C. A. M. (Eds.). (2002). *Handbook of Research on Multicultural Education* (2nd ed.). San Francisco: Jossey-Bass.

Barber, B. R. (1992). *An Aristocracy of Everyone: The Politics of Education and the Future of America.* New York: Oxford University Press.

Bennett, C. I. (2003). *Comprehensive Multicultural Education: Theory and Practice.* Boston: Allyn and Bacon.

Boykin, A. W., & Bailey, C. T. (2000). "The Role of Cultural Factors in School Relevant Cognitive Functioning: Synthesis of Findings on Cultural Context, Cultural Orientations, and Individual Differences." (ERIC Document Reproduction Service No. ED 441 880).

Bruner, J. (1996). *The Culture of Education.* Cambridge, MA: Harvard University Press.

Du Bois, W. E. B. (1994). *The Souls of Black Folk.* New York: Gramercy Books.

Grant, C. A., & Gomez, M. L. (Eds.). (2000). *Making School Multicultural: Campus and Classroom* (2nd ed.). Upper Saddle River, NJ: Merrill/Prentice-Hall.

Hollins, E. R. (1996). *Culture in School Learning: Revealing the Deep Meaning.* Mahwah, NJ: Erlbaum.

Irvine, J. J., & Armento, B. J. (Eds.). (2001). *Culturally Responsive Teaching: Lesson Planning for Elementary and Middle Grades.* New York: McGraw-Hill.

Lee, C. (1993). "Signifying as a Scaffold to Literary Interpretation: The Pedagogical Implications of a Form of African American Discourse" (NCTE Research Report No. 26). Urbana, IL: National Council of Teachers of English.

Lipka, J., & Mohatt, G. V. (1998). *Transforming the Culture of Schools: Yup'ik Eskimo Examples.* Mahwah, NJ: Erlbaum.

Loewen, J. W. (1995). *Lies My Teacher Told Me: Everything Your American History Textbook Got Wrong.* New York: New Press.

McCarty, T. L. (2002). *A Place to Be Navajo: Rough Rock and the Struggle for Self-Determination in Indigenous Schooling.* Mahwah, NJ: Erlbaum.

Moll, L. C., Amanti, C., Neff, D., & Gonzalez, N. (1992). "Funds of Knowledge for Teaching: Using a Qualitative Approach to Connect Homes and Classrooms." *Theory into Practice, 31*(1): 132–141.

Moses, R. P., & Cobb, C. E., Jr. (2001). *Radical Equations: Math Literacy and Civil Rights.* Boston: Beacon Press.

Nieto, S. (2000). *Affirming Diversity: The Sociopolitical Context of Multicultural Education* (3rd ed.). New York: Longman.

Park, C. C., Goodwin, A. L., & Lee, S. J. (Eds.). (2001). *Research on the Education of Asian and Pacific Americans.* Greenwich, CT: Information Age Publishers.

Shade, B. J. (Ed.). (1989). *Culture, Style, and the Educative Process.* Springfield, IL: Charles C Thomas.

Tharp, R. G., & Gallimore, R. (1988). *Rousing Minds to Life: Teaching, Learning, and Schooling in Social Context.* Cambridge, UK: Cambridge University Press.

Wlodkowski, R. J., & Ginsberg, M. B. (1995). *Diversity and Motivation: Culturally Responsive Teaching.* San Francisco: Jossey-Bass.

DISCUSSION QUESTIONS

1. What issues related to multiculturalism have emerged in your school in recent years?

2. Do you agree with the author's claim that many teachers remain unconvinced that multicultural education has value?

3. What would be needed to bring theoretical concepts of multiculturalism into practice? Would this be of benefit to students? How?

4. How should considerations of multiculturalism influence the process of curriculum development?

5. Would a greater emphasis on multiculturalism help close the achievement gap? Why or why not?

26

Knowledge Alive

DAVID PERKINS

FOCUSING QUESTIONS

1. How are knowledge arts used in society? How does this translate to schools?
2. How do schools fail to transmit the knowledge arts between subjects?
3. What are the ways listed by which a teacher can make knowledge visible? How does this relate to student understanding?
4. How can a teacher provide a culture of learning?

Perhaps the broadest and most basic question for educators—before matters of method, testing, or grading—is "What should we teach?" And perhaps the most basic answer is "knowledge." Knowledge in the broad sense—facts, ideas, and skills—provides the mainstay of the school curriculum from kindergarten through college.

But then there's the question of what you do with knowledge. Education has always been more generous about exposing learners to large volumes of knowledge than about teaching them the diverse skills involved in handling knowledge well—the knowledge arts.

The knowledge arts include communicating strategically, insightfully, and effectively; thinking critically and creatively; and putting school knowledge to work in what educators sometimes humbly call the "real world." The knowledge arts bundle together deep reading, compelling writing, strong problem solving and decision making, and the strategic and spirited self-management of learning itself, within and across the disciplines.

We need to put the knowledge arts on the table—to celebrate them for the depth and power they provide and for the ways they make knowl-edge meaningful. And we need to worry about their neglect.

THE KNOWLEDGE ARTS IN SOCIETY

To get a picture of how the knowledge arts work in schools, let's start with the bigger picture of how they work in society. We can tell the broad story of knowledge in four chapters, starting with creating it and moving on to communicating it, organizing it, and acting on it.

People create knowledge in various ways. Scientists examine the sky or the sea or quarks or viruses; historians puzzle over ancient documents and artifacts; pollsters survey public opinion; engineers design and test prototypes; newspaper reporters investigate political dogfights; police officers comb for evidence about crimes. Then we communicate that knowledge in various ways: through writing and reading; mathematical equations, maps, and diagrams; news broadcasts; electronic mailing lists; and works of art. We organize knowledge in various ways for ready access (notes, concept maps, Web sites) or for particular purposes, judgments, plans, and decisions (the court's verdict, the advertising campaign, the blueprints for a new building). And eventually, we act on all this knowledge: We carry out the judgment, erect the building, or launch the mission.

Of course, the story of knowledge in the form of these four chapters is far too linear. Creating, communicating, organizing, and acting on knowledge mix with one another in complex and generative ways. However, the four chapters provide a rough and ready overview.

THE KNOWLEDGE ARTS IN SCHOOL: A REPORT CARD

Keeping the four chapters in mind, how well does schooling develop the knowledge arts of learners? The report card for business-as-usual schooling would look like this:

> Creating knowledge: D
> Communicating knowledge: B
> Organizing knowledge: C
> Acting on knowledge: D

The first D reflects the fact that in typical schools, investigative, inquiry-oriented activities in which learners create knowledge are sparse. Of course, such activities occur here and there—for instance, in some kinds of science learning—but even then they often entail simply going through the motions of a laboratory experiment rather than genuinely wrestling with ideas.

Acting on knowledge also earns a D. We rarely ask students to do much with their learning outside school—except homework, of course. As a result, knowledge tends to become passive or inert. In both academic and practical contexts, learners fail to connect what they have learned to new situations or to act effectively on that knowledge (Bransford, Franks, Vye, & Sherwood, 1989). Students may memorize key information about biology for the science test but never ponder what that knowledge says about personal health care or public health issues.

Problems of transfer of learning have long plagued education (Bransford & Schwartz, 1999; Detterman & Sternberg, 1992; Perkins & Salomon, 1988). Typical schooling does not even encourage students to carry their knowledge from one classroom to another. Science instructors

often complain that the math from math class somehow evaporates in the science room. History instructors grumble that some cognitive Bermuda Triangle in the corridor between the English and history classrooms has sucked away students' knowledge of writing.

Conventional education probably does best at communicating knowledge, so why does it rate only a B in this area? On the receptive side of communication, although learners spend a great deal of time loading up on knowledge, schools do not typically teach them to do so strategically. Many young readers can decode competently but have never learned to ask themselves what they are reading for, to monitor their reading as they go, to assess themselves afterward, and to fill in what they missed. The productive side of communication includes not only writing but also artistic expression, presentations, multimedia work, and so on. These areas, except for the mechanics of writing, typically receive little time or guidance.

Further, some schools direct dogged attention to skill and content learning in a narrow sense, with the unsettling consequence that skills become ritualized into mere recipes to follow (Perkins, 1992). For instance, students who know how to add, subtract, multiply, and divide can become quite confused about how to apply these operations to story problems, and they often fall back on limited keyword strategies, such as "all together means add." Students learn what they are supposed to say in class without really understanding it. Science educator Marcia Linn amusingly noted what one student made of a Newtonian principle of motion: "Objects in motion remain in motion in the classroom, but come to rest on the playground" (2002).

Organizing knowledge also receives little attention in typical schools—thus, the grade of C. In most school settings, strategic guidance in this skill appears only during review sessions or around such products as essays. Yet learning logs, concept mapping, debates, group presentations, and many other activities can dramatically expand students' skills in organizing knowledge.

At this point, dedicated educators will object: "My kids are deeply engaged in inquiry-oriented science learning!" "My students keep learning journals and review their learning every week!" "We stage a debate after every unit!" "Teams of youngsters are out there in the community investigating local history!" Good. These undertakings certainly cultivate the knowledge arts and deserve kudos when and where they occur. But we need to ask, How often is this kind of teaching and learning happening, and how well? Between the oases of glory stretch deserts of neglect.

BRINGING KNOWLEDGE TO LIFE

What does it look like to enliven teaching and learning through the knowledge arts? The following examples come from the work of my colleagues at Project Zero of the Harvard Graduate School of Education (www.pz.harvard.edu).

Making Thinking Visible

One way to advance the knowledge arts is to use thinking routines (Ritchhart, 2002) to make students' thinking visible, thus increasing their awareness of what goes into creating, communicating, organizing, and acting on knowledge.

For instance, Shari Tishman (2002) explored a simple way to make certain kinds of thinking visible by asking two key questions: "What's going on here?" and "What do you see that makes you say so?" She adapted this approach from a procedure for thoughtfully examining works of visual art (Housen, Yenawine, & Arenas, 1991), but learners can apply these questions to many different objects—for example, a short poem or a satellite photograph of a hurricane. Or a history instructor might show a historical artifact, like a crossbow, accompanied by the slightly tweaked questions "How does this work?" and "What do you see that makes you think so?"

Tina Grotzer and I have developed inquiry-oriented activities that engage students in communicating about the complex causal models that can often make science concepts difficult to understand—models that involve such invisible features as electrons, causal loops, and simultaneous cause and effect (Grotzer, 2003; Perkins & Grotzer, 2000). For instance, fourth graders studying electrical circuits compare different ideas about what

the current does. Does it start at the battery and fill the circuit, as when a hot-water radiator system is turned on for the first time, and then continue to cycle? Or does the current of electrons move all at once, like a bicycle chain? Young learners lean toward the first idea, but the second is more scientifically accurate. The following discussion shows how the teacher can help students make visible their thinking about the scientific explanation of electrical flow (Grotzer, 2000):

TEACHER: Let's compare how cause and effect works in these two different kinds of cyclic models. In the cyclic sequential model [as in the radiator system analogy], what makes the electrons move?

STUDENT 1: They want to get out of the battery because of all the electrons so they go onto the wire.

TEACHER: And then what happens?

STUDENT 2: They go along the wire till they get to the bulb and that makes the bulb light up.

TEACHER: Why do the electrons move in the cyclic simultaneous model [as in the bicycle chain analogy]?

STUDENT 1: The electrons push the one in front but at the same time they are pushed by the one behind them. So everything moves at the same time.

TEACHER: Yes, each electron repels the next one but is repelled by the one behind it. It's both a cause and an effect at the same time. The whole thing turns like the chain on a bicycle. What causes the bulb to light?

STUDENT 3: When the electrons start to flow.

Grotzer's research shows that conversations like this one, along with simple experiments and activities, can make causal thinking visible and lead to higher levels of understanding.

Teaching for Understanding

Understanding is one of the most cherished goals of education. Teaching for understanding can bring knowledge to life by requiring students to manipulate knowledge in various ways. For instance, understanding a historical event means going beyond the facts to explain it, explore the remote causes, discuss the incident as different people might see it from their own perspectives, and skeptically critique what various sources say.

A number of years ago, several colleagues and I developed the Teaching for Understanding framework, which centers on the idea of performances of understanding (Blythe & Associates, 1998; Gardner, 1999; Perkins & Blythe, 1994). Here are two examples of classrooms using this framework, drawn from Wiske (1998).

Joan Soble employed the Teaching for Understanding framework to organize and deliver an introductory writing course for at-risk ninth graders—students whom she described as "perpetually overwhelmed." The students engaged in a wide range of understanding performances, including work with collages as preparation for writing; keeping and critically reviewing portfolios; and setting and pursuing goals individually, using a form that listed writing skills they wanted to improve, from sentence structure to revision practices to aspects of self-management. Thus, these students worked directly on the knowledge art of writing, learning how to practice it with more skill, confidence, and flair. Soble's approach also helped students with another knowledge art: the thoughtful management of their own learning.

Lois Hetland's seventh-grade class examined fundamental questions about Colonial America throughout the year. Some questions concerned the land: How does land shape human culture? How do people think about the land? How do people change the land? Another line of questioning concerned historical truth: How do we find out the truth about things that happened long ago or far away? How do we see through bias in sources? There throughlines, as Hetland called them, provided abiding points of reference for the learners. Discussing the same throughlines in connection with topic after topic helped students to develop not only a deeper understanding of Colonial America but also important knowledge arts: the ins and outs of historical inquiry and the management of their own learning through sustained questioning.

Such practices engage students in various mixes of the four broad activities identified earlier—creating, communicating, organizing, and acting on knowledge—in ways linked to the disciplines. Moreover, research has revealed something quite striking: Students who participate in Teaching for Understanding classrooms display shifts in their attitudes toward understanding. Compared with other students, they think of understanding in a more dynamic and exploratory way, rather than as a collection of facts and skills (Wiske, 1998). This stance toward understanding amounts to a knowledge art that equips students for deeper learning.

Creating a Culture of Learning

The knowledge arts—like any art—are more than skills: They involve passion, energy, and commitment (Tishman, Perkins, & Jay, 1995). Teachers promote the knowledge arts when they strive to establish a classroom culture of inquiry and excitement.

Ritchhart (2002) describes an algebra teacher who began the first day of school by displaying a mathematical puzzle problem from the newspaper, noting that a student had brought it in, saying that he loved little problems, and encouraging students to provide other puzzle problems throughout the year. Then he wrote on the chalkboard an elaborate arithmetic computation drawn from an episode in *The Phantom Tollbooth,* asking students to work out the answer and commenting that he had better figure it out himself. Inevitably, students came up with a variety of answers. The teacher gave his own answer but warned that he didn't think it was correct. He challenged students to find the right answer.

Through these actions and others like them—informal, welcoming, and inquiring—this teacher signaled that the coming school year would bring knowledge alive.

THE SECOND CURRICULUM

One natural reaction to these examples—and others from ingenious teachers across the world—is that they simply illustrate good teaching methods. They show ways of teaching content that enhance student engagement and make knowledge more meaningful.

True enough, but the knowledge arts are more than just tools for teachers to teach with; they encompass ideas, skills, and attitudes for learners to learn—a second curriculum. Thinking of the knowledge arts in this way creates new responsibilities for educators. As teachers teach science, history, or literature, they should be able to specify what skills of inquiry, strategies of communication, methods of organization, and ranges of application they are striving to develop in students; how they are spending time doing so; and how they are exciting students' interest and providing serious guidance. Without such an account, the second curriculum does not exist in any substantive sense.

The bad news: All this amounts to one more agenda in an era in which educators must prepare students for high-stakes tests that often emphasize *having* knowledge far more than *doing* something with it. The good news: The second curriculum is not just an add-on to the first. Instead, it's a meld, a fusion, an infiltration designed to bring knowledge to life and keep it alive. Taking the second curriculum seriously will not only equip students with knowledge-handling skills they need but also deepen and broaden their mastery of the first curriculum.

Behind the second curriculum is a simple idea: Education is not just about acquiring knowledge, but also about learning how to do significant things with what you know. It's not about dead knowledge, but about bringing knowledge to life. To educate for today and tomorrow, every school and every classroom should teach the knowledge arts seriously and well.

REFERENCES

Blythe, T., & Associates. (1998). *The Teaching for Understanding Guide.* San Francisco: Jossey-Bass.

Bransford, J. D., Franks, J. J., Vye, N. J., & Sherwood, R. D. (1989). "New Approaches to Instruction: Because Wisdom Can't Be Told." In S. Vosniadou & A. Ortony (Eds.), *Similarity and Analogical Reasoning* (pp. 470–497). New York: Cambridge University Press.

Bransford, J. D., & Schwartz, D. L. (1999). "Rethinking Transfer: A Simple Proposal with Interesting Implications." In A. Iran-Nejad & P. D. Pearson (Eds.), *Review of Research in Education* (Vol. 24, pp. 61–101). Washington, DC: American Educational Research Association.

Detterman, D., & Sternberg, R. (Eds.). (1992). *Transfer on Trial.* Norwood, NJ: Ablex.

Gardner, H. (1999). *The Disciplined Mind.* New York: Simon and Schuster.

Grotzer, T. A. (2000, April). *How Conceptual Leaps in Understanding the Nature of Causality Can Limit Learning: An Example from Electrical Circuits.* Paper presented at the annual conference of the American Educational Research Association, New Orleans, LA.

Grotzer, T. A. (2003). "Learning to Understand the Forms of Causality Implicit in Scientific Explanations." *Studies in Science Education, 39:* 1–74.

Housen, A., Yenawine, P., & Arenas, A. (1991). *Visual Thinking Curriculum.* (Unpublished but used for research purposes). New York: Museum of Modern Art.

Linn, M. (2002, May). *The Role of Customization of Innovative Science Curricula: Implications for Design, Practice, and Professional Development.* Symposium at the annual meeting of the National Association for Research in Science Teaching, New Orleans, LA.

Perkins, D. N. (1992). *Smart Schools: From Training Memories to Educating Minds.* New York: Free Press.

Perkins, D. N., & Blythe, T. (1994). "Putting Understanding Up Front." *Educational Leadership, 51*(5): 4–7.

Perkins, D. N., & Grotzer, T. A. (2000, April). *Models and Moves: Focusing on Dimensions of Causal Complexity to Achieve Deeper Scientific Understanding.* Paper presented at the annual conference of the American Educational Research Association, New Orleans, LA.

Perkins, D. N., & Salomon, G. (1988). "Teaching for Transfer." *Educational Leadership, 46*(1), 22–32.

Ritchhart, R. (2002). *Intellectual Character: What It Is, Why It Matters, and How to Get It.* San Francisco: Jossey-Bass.

Tishman, S. (2002). "Artful Reasoning." In T. Grotzer, L. Howick, S. Tishman, & D. Wise, (Eds.), *Art Works for Schools.* Lincoln, MA: DeCordova Museum and Sculpture Park.

Tishman, S., Perkins, D. N., & Jay, E. (1995). *The Thinking Classroom.* Boston: Allyn and Bacon.

Wiske, M. S. (Ed.). (1998). *Teaching for Understanding: Linking Research with Practice.* San Francisco: Jossey-Bass.

DISCUSSION QUESTIONS

1. What types of learning does the author include in the category "knowledge arts"?
2. Why does the author give schools low grades in the teaching of knowledge arts?
3. What suggestions are offered for enlivening teaching and learning?
4. Do the suggestions offered make you think differently about what goes on in your own classroom or school?
5. Which of the suggested changes would be easiest to make and which would be most difficult?

27

Educating the Net Generation

DON TAPSCOTT

FOCUSING QUESTIONS

1. What effect is interactive technology having on teaching?
2. What effect is interactive technology having on student learning?
3. What are the implications of interactive technology for teachers' professional development?
4. What are the implications of interactive technology for society?
5. What part can students play in making schools relevant and effective?

Every time I enter a discussion about efforts to get computers into schools, someone insists that computers aren't the answer. "It won't help to just throw computers at the wall, hoping something will stick. I've seen lots of computers sitting unused in classrooms."

Agreed. Computers alone won't do the trick. They are a necessary but insufficient condition for moving our schools to new heights of effectiveness. We've still got to learn how best to use this technology. And I have become convinced that the most potent force for change is the students themselves.

Why look to the kids? Because they are different from any generation before them. They are the first to grow up surrounded by digital media. Computers are everywhere—in the home, school, factory, and office—as are digital technologies—cameras, video games, and CD-ROMs. Today's kids are so bathed in bits that they think technology is part of the natural landscape. To them, digital technology is no more intimidating than a VCR or a toaster. And these new media are increasingly connected by the Internet, that expanding web of networks that is attracting one million new users a month.

THE NET GENERATION

The Net affects us all—the way we create wealth, the nature of commerce and marketing, the deliv-

ery system for entertainment, the role and dynamics of learning, and the nature of government. It should not surprise us that those first to grow up with this new medium are defined by their relationship to it. I call them the Net Generation—the N-Geners.

According to Teenage Research Unlimited (1997), teens feel that being online is as "in" as dating and partying! And this exploding popularity is occurring while the Net is still in its infancy and, as such, is painfully slow; primitive; limited in capabilities; lacking complete security, reliability, and ubiquity; and subject to both hyperbole and ridicule. Nevertheless, children love it and keep coming back after each frustrating experience. They know its potential.

What do students do on the Net? They manage their personal finances; organize protest movements; check facts; discuss zits; check the scores of their favorite team and chat online with its superstars; organize groups to save the rain forest; cast votes; learn more about the illness of their little sister; go to a virtual birthday party; or get video clips from a soon-to-be-released movie.

Chat groups and computer conferences are populated by young people hungry for expression and self-discovery. Younger kids love to meet people and talk about anything. As they mature, their communications center on topics and themes. For all ages, "E-mail me" has become the parting expression of a generation.

DIGITAL ANXIETY

For many adults, all this digital activity is a source of high anxiety. Are kids really benefiting from the digital media? Can technology truly improve the process of learning, or is it dumbing down and misguiding educational efforts? What about Net addiction? Is it useful for children to spend time in online chat rooms, and what are they doing there? Are some becoming glued to the screen? What about cyberdating and cybersex? Aren't video games leading to a violent generation? Is technology stressing kids out—as it seems to be doing to adults? Has the Net become a virtual world—drawing children away from parental authority and responsible adult influence—where untold new problems and dangers lie? What is the real risk of online predators, and can children be effectively protected? How can we shield kids from sleaze and porn? As these children come of age, will they lack the social skills for effective participation in the work force?

These questions are just a sampling of the widespread concern raised not just by cynics, moralists, and technophobes, but also by reasonable and well-meaning educators, parents, and members of the community.

Everybody, relax. The kids are all right. They are learning, developing, and thriving in the digital world. They need better tools, better access, better services—more freedom to explore, not less. Rather than convey hostility and mistrust, we need to change our way of thinking and behaving. This means all of us—parents, educators, lawmakers, and business leaders alike.

Digital kids are learning precisely the social skills required for effective interaction in the digital economy. They are learning about peer relationships, teamwork, critical thinking, fun, friendships across geographies, self-expression, and self-confidence.

Conventional wisdom says that because children are multitasking—jumping from one computer-based activity to another—their attention span is reduced. Research does not support this

view. Ironically, the same people who charge that today's kids are becoming "glued to the screen" also say that kids' attention spans are declining.

At root is the fear that children will not be able to focus and therefore will not learn. This concern is consistent with the view that the primary challenge of learning is to absorb specific information. However, many argue—and I agree—that the content of a particular lesson is less important than learning how to learn. As John Dewey wrote, "Perhaps the greatest of all pedagogical fallacies is the notion that a person learns only the particular thing he is studying at the time. Collateral learning . . . may be and often is more important than the spelling lesson or lesson in geography or history that is learned" (1963, p. 48).

THE CHALLENGE OF SCHOOLING

The new technologies have helped create a culture for learning (Papert, 1996) in which the learner enjoys enhanced interactivity and connections with others. Rather than listen to a professor regurgitate facts and theories, students discuss ideas and learn from one another, with the teacher acting as a participant in the learning. Students construct narratives that make sense out of their own experiences.

Initial research strongly supports the benefits of this kind of learning. For example, in 1996, 33 students in a social studies course at California State University in Northridge were randomly divided into two groups, one taught in a traditional classroom and the other taught virtually on the Web. The teaching model wasn't fundamentally changed—both groups received the same texts, lectures, and exams. Despite this, the Web-based class scored, on average, 20 percent higher than the traditional class. The Web class had more contact with one another and were more interested in the class work. The students also felt that they understood the material better and had greater flexibility to determine how they learned (Schutte, n.d.).

The ultimate interactive learning environment is the Internet itself. Increasingly, this technology includes the vast repository of human knowledge, the tools to manage this knowledge, access to people, and a growing galaxy of services ranging from sandbox environments for preschoolers to virtual laboratories for medical students studying neural psychiatry. Today's baby will tomorrow learn about Michelangelo by walking through the Sistine Chapel, watching Michelangelo paint, and perhaps stopping for a conversation. Students will stroll on the moon. Petroleum engineers will penetrate the earth with the drill bit. Doctors will navigate the cardiovascular system. Researchers will browse through a library. Auto designers will sit in the back seat of the car they are designing to see how it feels and to examine the external view.

EIGHT SHIFTS OF INTERACTIVE LEARNING

The digital media are causing educators and students alike to shift to new ways of thinking about teaching and learning.

1. From linear to hypermedia learning.
Traditional approaches to learning are linear and date back to using books as a learning tool. Stories, novels, and other narratives are generally linear. Most textbooks are written to be tackled from the beginning to the end. TV shows and instructional videos are also designed to be watched from beginning to end.

But N-Geners' access to information is more interactive and nonsequential. Notice how a child channel surfs when watching television. I've found that my kids go back and forth among various TV shows and video games when they're in the family room. No doubt that as TV becomes a Net appliance, children will increasingly depend on this nonlinear way of processing information.

2. From instruction to construction and discovery.
Seymour Papert says, "The scandal of education is that every time you teach something, you deprive a child of the pleasure and benefit of discovery" (de Pommereau, 1997, p. 68).

With new technologies, we will experience a shift away from traditional types of pedagogy to the creation of learning partnerships and learning cultures. This is not to say that teachers should not plan activities or design curriculums. They might, however, design the curriculum in partnership with learners or even help learners design the curriculum themselves.

This constructivist approach to teaching and learning means that rather than assimilate knowledge that is broadcast by an instructor, the learner constructs knowledge anew. Constructivists argue that people learn best by doing rather than simply by listening. The evidence supporting constructivism is persuasive, but that shouldn't be too surprising. When youngsters are enthusiastic about a fact or a concept that they themselves discovered, they will better retain the information and use it in creative, meaningful ways.

3. From teacher-centered to learner-centered education.
The new media focus the learning experience on the individual rather than on the transmitter. Clearly, learner-centered education improves the child's motivation to learn.

The shift from teacher-centered to learner-centered education does not suggest that the teacher is suddenly playing a less important role. A teacher is equally crucial and valuable in the learner-centered context, for he or she creates and structures what happens in the classroom.

Learner-centered education begins with an evaluation of abilities, learning styles, social contexts, and other important factors that affect the student. Evaluation software programs can tailor the learning experience for each individual child. Learner-centered education is also more active, with students discussing, debating, researching, and collaborating on projects with one another and with the teacher.

4. From absorbing material to learning how to navigate and how to learn.
This means learning how to synthesize, not just analyze. N-Geners can assess and analyze facts—a formidable challenge in a data galaxy of easily accessible information sources. But more important, they can synthesize. They are engaged in information sources and people on the Net, and then they construct higher-level structures and mental images.

5. From school to lifelong learning.
For young baby boomers looking forward to the world of work, life often felt divided—between the

period when you learned and the period when you did. You went to school and maybe to university and learned a trade or profession. For the rest of your life, your challenge was simply to keep up with developments in your field. But things have changed. Today, many boomers reinvent their knowledge base constantly. Learning has become a continuous, lifelong process. The N-Gen is entering a world of lifelong learning from day one, and unlike the schools of the boomers, today's educational system can anticipate how to prepare students for lifelong learning.

6. From one-size-fits-all to customized learning.

The digital media enable students to be treated as individuals—to have highly customized learning experiences based on their backgrounds, individual talents, age levels, cognitive styles, and interpersonal preferences.

As Papert puts it,

> What I see as the real contribution of digital media to education is a flexibility that could allow every individual to find personal paths to learning. This will make it possible for the dream of every progressive educator to come true: In the learning environment of the future, every learner will be "special." (1996, p. 16)

In fact, Papert believes in a "community of learning" shared by students and teachers:

> Socialization is not best done by segregating children into classrooms with kids of the same age. The computer is a medium in which what you make lends itself to be modified and shared. When kids get together on a project, there is abundant discussion; they show it to other kids, other kids want to see it, kids learn to share knowledge with other people—much more than in the classroom. (1996, p. 11)

7. From learning as torture to learning as fun.

Maybe torture is an exaggeration, but for many kids, class is not exactly the highlight of their day. Some educators have decried the fact that a generation schooled on *Sesame Street* expects to be entertained at school—and to enjoy the learning experience. They argue that learning and entertainment should be clearly separated.

Why shouldn't learning be entertaining? In *Merriam-Webster's Collegiate Dictionary,* the third definition of the verb *to entertain* is "to keep, hold, or maintain in the mind" and "to receive and take into consideration." In other words, entertainment has always been a profound part of the learning process, and teachers throughout history have been asked to convince their students to entertain ideas. From this perspective, the best teachers were the entertainers. Using the new media, the learner also becomes the entertainer and, in doing so, enjoys, is motivated toward, and feels responsible for learning.

8. From the teacher as transmitter to the teacher as facilitator.

Learning is becoming a social activity, facilitated by a new generation of educators.

The topic is saltwater fish. The sixth-grade teacher divides the class into teams, asking each team to prepare a presentation on a fish of its choice. Students have access to the Web and are allowed to use any resources. They must cover the topics of history, breathing, propulsion, reproduction, diet, predators, and "cool facts." They must also address questions to others in their team or to others in the class, not to the teacher.

Two weeks later, Melissa's group is first. The students have created a shark project home page with hot links for each topic. As the students talk, they project their presentation onto a screen at the front of the class. They have video clips of different types of sharks and also a clip from Jacques Cousteau discussing the shark as an endangered species. They then use the Web to go live to Aquarius, an underwater site located off the Florida Keys. The class can ask questions of the Aquarius staff, although most inquiries are directed to the project team. One such discussion focuses on which is greater: the dangers posed by sharks to humans or the dangers posed by humans to sharks.

The class decides to hold an online forum on this topic and invites kids from classes in other countries to participate. The team asks students to browse through its project at any time, from any location, because the forum will be up for the rest of the school year. In fact, the team decides to maintain the site by adding new links and fresh information throughout the year. The assignment becomes a living project. Learners from around the world find the shark home page helpful and build links to it.

In this example, the teacher acts as consultant to the teams, facilitates the learning process, and participates as a technical consultant on the new media. The teacher doesn't have to compete with Jacques Cousteau's expertise on underwater life; her teaching is supported by his expertise.

TURNING TO THE NET GENERATION

A whole generation of teachers needs to learn new tools, new approaches, and new skills. This will be a challenge, not just because of resistance to change by some teachers, but also because of the current atmosphere of financial cutbacks, low teacher morale, increased workloads, and reduced retraining budgets.

But as we make this inevitable transition, we may best turn to the generation raised on and im-

mersed in new technologies. Give students the tools, and they will be the single most important source of guidance on how to make their schools relevant and effective places to learn.

REFERENCES

de Pommereau, I. (1997, April 21). "Computers Give Children the Key to Learning." *Christian Science Monitor,* p. 68.

Dewey, J. (1963). *Experience and Education.* London: Collier Books.

Papert, S. (1996). *The Connected Family: Bridging the Digital Generation Gap.* Marietta, GA: Longstreet Press.

Schutte, J. G. (n.d.). Virtual teaching in higher education [On-line]. Available: http://www.csun.edu/sociology/virtexp.htm

Teenage Research Unlimited, Inc. (1997, Spring). *Teenage Marketing and Lifestyle Update.* Northbrook, IL: Author.

DISCUSSION QUESTIONS

1. Is the Net Generation different from the generations of students preceding it in really important ways? What does it have in common with earlier generations?
2. At what age should students be introduced to interactive technology in classrooms?
3. Is interactive technology the best way to teach all students or only those who have a strong interest in computers?
4. Can substantive learning be made entertaining, or are hard work and persistence necessary to achieve true excellence?
5. Does learning in groups undermine or reinforce individual effort?

PRO-CON CHART 4

Should academic content standards be used in place of curriculum guides?

PRO	CON

PRO

1. Content standards ensure high expectations for every student in every classroom.

2. Standards make public what all students should know and be able to do.

3. Standards ensure that important content is not overlooked and that students are exposed to new content at each grade.

4. Standards focus teaching, student work, and assessment on the knowledge and skills that are most important for success in life.

5. Standards can reduce the wide variability in the quality of curriculum, instruction, and assessment that exists from one classroom to another.

6. Rubrics and scoring guides that describe the specific criteria that must be met at each level of achievement help to communicate what students should know to both students and parents.

CON

1. Raising expectations will hurt students who are already not achieving by making a difficult challenge impossible.

2. Curriculum guides and textbooks are public documents that already exist and serve the same purpose.

3. Teachers need flexibility when covering content to meet the needs of diverse groups of students who may be at different stages in their development.

4. Students need to learn how to be responsible for their own learning, because no one really knows what knowledge and skills will be most important in the future.

5. Teachers deserve to be treated as professionals who employ academic freedom to help students to construct knowledge that is personally meaningful.

6. Standards are really nothing but a smokescreen for one-shot, high-stakes tests.

CASE STUDY 4

An Advocate for Longer School Days

Jack Pierce, curriculum coordinator of Ipsid Elementary District, handed a written proposal to the superintendent, Dick Bosio, which suggested that the district lengthen the school day by forty minutes beginning in the fall. Pierce cited research to support his claim that academic learning time is the most important variable associated with student learning for most types of learners. He also reported research that showed significant relationships between increased academic time and gains in student achievement. While explaining his rationale for increasing the length of the school day, Pierce said he felt confident that overall the district would demonstrate an increase in students' Iowa Test of Basic Skills scores. He suggested that this change would probably satisfy the public that Ipsid was promoting excellence in education.

Pierce emphasized that since time spent on relevant academic tasks is measurable, the district would be able to show that better test scores were the result of the increased academic instruction. Furthermore, he said that increased instructional time was advisable according to the research on teaching that emphasized student outcomes.

The Ipsid superintendent listened closely to Pierce's proposal. He had some concerns, but decided that Pierce had analyzed almost all the critical factors. Noting some of the considerations that might need to be addressed, Bosio thought to himself that because engaged time was equivalent to time devoted to actual work, asking teachers to stay a little longer each day would not be an issue. Bosio turned to Pierce and said, "I think this is a good idea. Go ahead and implement this change."

1. Assume you are Bosio and discuss how you would implement an extension of your school's instructional day by forty minutes.

2. Do you think that student achievement is directly correlated with academic engaged time? Why? Why not?

3. Based on your experience, what factors other than time on task influence student outcomes?

4. In what ways does the use of different instructional models influence student outcomes?

5. What alternatives might be considered to promote student outcomes, instead of lengthening the school day?

6. What is the relationship among content, quality of teaching, academic engaged time, and student outcomes?

7. How do subject matter content and social atmosphere of the classroom affect academic engaged time?

PART FIVE
Curriculum and Supervision

How do developments in supervision and curriculum influence each other? What are the issues changing our views of supervision and leadership? How would new conceptions of supervision influence practice and professional programs of preparation?

In Chapter 28, Thomas Sergiovanni describes how conceptions of school leadership practice would be reconceived if the politics of division were replaced with the politics of virtue. He explores how the role of the principal as steward differs from perceptions of transformational leadership. He also claims that students as well as teachers will be able to embrace the concept of civic virtue. In the next chapter, Dennis Sparks and Susan Loucks-Horsley provide an overview of the models that characterize effective staff development. They discuss the theory and research that support each model. The authors also consider how organizational climate, administrative structures, policy, and participant involvement support or impede the implementation of each approach.

In Chapter 30, Harry Wong, Ted Britton, and Tom Ganser point out that induction of new teachers in the United States is either entirely lacking or not well structured, typically involving support from a single mentor. The authors describe more systematic approaches to induction that other countries have adopted. In Chapter 31, Thomas Guskey discusses why professional development is essential to educational reform. He identifies components that are characteristic of successful professional development programs. He offers suggestions for how successful development programs should be designed.

Edward Pajak next describes how various models of clinical supervision are linked to the concept of psychological style. He explains why and how clinical supervisors can better communicate by applying approaches that coincide with teachers' psychological types. Pajak also suggests that supervisors should strive to work with teachers in ways that are consistent with how teachers are expected to work with students—by celebrating diversity and responding to that diversity in ways that enhance learning for all. In the final chapter in Part Five, Frank Levy and Richard Murnane suggest that teachers can be thought of as managers of students and classrooms who can benefit from four lessons learned at IBM, where technology has been used successfully to improve the quality of professional development.

PROFESSIONAL PROFILE: SUPERVISION

Name:
Larry Cuban

Email:
cuban@stanford.edu

Latest degree/university:
Ph.D., History of Education, Stanford
University

Position:
Professor Emeritus of Education, Stanford
University

Previous positions:
Professor of Education, Stanford University;
Superintendent, Arlington (VA) public schools;
high school history teacher, Washington, D.C.;
high school history teacher, Cleveland (OH)

Person most influential in your career:
Oliver Deex, principal of Glenville High School in the 1950s. He introduced me—a
young, raw, and ambitious social studies teacher—to the intellectual play of ideas through
the books and magazines he gave me and, for the first time in my life, engaged me in intense reflective conversations about what I had read. I acknowledged my debt to him in
the first book I wrote, *To Make a Difference: Teaching in the Inner City* (Free Press, 1970).

Number-one achievement:
Moving from being a high school teacher for 13 years to being a school superintendent
in a district undergoing major demographic changes, serving 7 years in that post, and
then becoming a professor for 20 years and being able to research and publish on the
history of reform, teaching, technology, and administration

Number-one regret:
Not being bilingual

Favorite educational journal:
Education Week because it has become very valuable to me as the paper of record in
K–12 public education

Favorite educational book:
Philip Jackson's *Life in Classrooms* (1968) because its content reconceptualized my experiences and thoughts as a teacher and served as a classic model of clear, insightful prose

Best book/chapter you wrote:
The book *How Teachers Taught*. The question that led to this book first arose when I
was a superintendent, visiting hundreds of classrooms in Arlington, Virginia. I noticed
so many echoes of teaching from my student days that I wanted to find out how much
change and constancy had marked teaching over the past century. My historical research
in cities and rural schools took me across the country and had a profound impact on my
thinking about the limitations of so many school reforms that try to alter routine teaching practices.

Additional interests:

Being with family and close friends, biking, reading, and gardening

Curriculum/supervision relationship:

As superintendent, I supervised administrators and curriculum specialists and engaged in many conversations about academic content and supervision of teachers. I taught late-afternoon courses at the Administration Building to interested teachers, administrators, and curriculum specialists on subjects such as critical thinking skills, framing and solving problems, and using different perspectives to understand events.

Professional vision:

There is no one right way to teach, to learn, to know, or to supervise.

Professional advice to teacher or curriculum specialist:

Be able to distinguish between problems and dilemmas and be especially skilled in framing and reframing problems. The essence of leadership is to help people see issues from different perspectives and engage in alternative thinking. That is what administrators and curriculum specialists need to do.

28

The Politics of Virtue: A New Framework for School Leadership

THOMAS J. SERGIOVANNI

FOCUSING QUESTIONS

1. What is the politics of virtue?
2. In what ways are the politics of virtue and the democratic legacy related?
3. How would practice emanating from a pluralistic conception of politics influence school leadership?
4. What are the basic principles of formal organization theories?
5. If the politics of division were replaced with the politics of virtue, how would conceptions of leadership need to be redefined?
6. In what ways does the role of the principal as steward differ from current conceptions of school leadership?
7. What are the similarities and differences between conceptions of stewardship and transformational leadership?

Margaret Mead once remarked, "Never doubt that a small group of thoughtful, committed citizens can change the world; indeed, it's the only thing that ever has." Her thought suggests that perhaps there is something to the 1,000 points of light theory of change. Is it possible to rally enough small groups of thoughtful and committed citizens to create the kind of schools we want? I think so, if we are willing to change the way politics is thought about in schools.

Rarely does a day go by without the media telling us still another story about divisions, hostilities, factions, and other symptoms of disconnectedness in schools. Teachers disagreeing over methods; parents bickering with teachers over discipline problems; board members squabbling over curriculum issues; administrators complaining about encroachments on their prerogatives; everyone disagreeing on sex education; and students, feeling pretty much left out of it all, making it difficult for everyone in the school by tediously trad-

ing their compliance and goodwill for things that they want. This mixture of issues and this mixture of stakeholders, all competing for advantage, resembles a game of bartering where self-interest is the motivator and individual actors engage in the hard play of the politics of division. The purpose of this game is to win more for yourself than you have to give back in return. Allison (1969) summarizes the game of *politics of division* as follows:

> Actions emerge neither as the calculated choice of a unified group nor as a formal summary of a leader's preferences. Rather the context of shared power but separate judgment concerning important choices determines that politics is the mechanism of choice. Note the environment in which the game is played: inordinate uncertainty about what must be done, the necessity that something be done and crucial consequences of whatever is done. These features force responsible men to become active players. The *pace of the game*—hundreds of is-

sues, numerous games, and multiple channels—compels players to fight to "get others' attention," to make them "see the facts," to assure that they "take the time to think seriously about the broader issue." The *structure of the game*—power shared by individuals with separate responsibilities—validates each player's feeling that "others don't see my problem," and "others must be persuaded to look at the issue from a less parochial perspective." The *rules of the game*—he who hesitates loses his chance to play at that point, and he who is uncertain about his recommendation is overpowered by others who are sure—pressures players to come down on the side of a 51–49 issue and play. The *rewards of the game*—effectiveness, i.e., impact on outcomes, as the immediate measure of performance—encourage hard play. (p. 710)

The politics of division is a consequence of applying formal organization theories of governance, management, and leadership to schools. At root, these theories assume that human nature is motivated by self-interest and that leadership requires the bartering of need fulfillment for compliance. Would things be different if we applied community theories instead? Communities, too, "play the game" of politics. But it is a different game. It is a game of politics more like that envisioned by James Madison, Alexander Hamilton, John Jay, Thomas Jefferson, and other American Founders and enshrined in such sacred documents as the Declaration of Independence, the Constitution of the United States, and the amendments to that Constitution that represent a bill of rights and a bill of responsibilities for all Americans. It is a game called the *politics of virtue*—a politics motivated by shared commitment to the common good and guided by protections that ensure the rights and responsibilities of individuals.

CIVIC VIRTUE

Is it possible to replace the politics of division with a politics of virtue? I think so, if we are willing to replace the values that have been borrowed from the world of formal organizations with traditional democratic values that encourage a commitment to civic virtue. This would entail development and use of different theories of human nature and leadership. For example, the rational

choice theories of human nature we now use will need to be replaced with a normative and moral theory of human nature. And the executive images of leadership that we now rely on will need to be replaced with collegial images aimed at problem solving and ministering.

Creating a politics of virtue requires that we renew commitments to the democratic legacy that gave birth to our country. This is the legacy that can provide the foundation for leadership in schools. The American Founders had in mind the creation of a covenantal polity within which "The body is one but has many members. There can be unity with diversity. . . . The great challenge was to create a political body that brought people together and created a 'we' but still enabled people to separate themselves and recognize and respect one another's individualities. This remains the great challenge for all modern democracies" (Elshtain, 1994, p. 9). The cultivation of commitment to civic virtue is a key part of this challenge.

During the debate over passing the Constitution of 1787, America was faced with a choice between two conceptions of politics: *republican* and *pluralist*. In republican politics, civic virtue was considered to be the cornerstone principle—the prerequisite for the newly proposed government to work. Civic virtue was embodied in the willingness of citizens to subordinate their own private interests to the general good (e.g., see Sunstein, 1993) and was therefore the basis for creating a politics of virtue. This politics of virtue emphasized self-rule by the people, but not the imposition of their private preferences on the new government. Instead, preferences were to be developed and shaped by the people themselves for the benefit of the common good.

Haefele (1993) believes that it is easier to provide examples of how civic virtue is expressed than to try to define it with precision. In his words:

It is fashionable nowadays for both the left and the right to decry the loss of civic virtue; the left on such issues as industry rape of the environment and the right because of the loss of patriotism. Both sides are undoubtedly right, as civic virtue belongs to no single party or creed. It is simply a quality of caring about public purposes and public destinations. Sometimes the public purpose is chosen over private purposes. A young Israeli economist investigating a Kibbutz came across the following case. The Kibbutz had money to spend. The alternatives were a TV antenna and TV sets for everyone or a community meeting hall. The economist found that everyone preferred the TV option but that, when they voted, they unanimously chose the meeting hall. Call it enlightened self-interest, a community preference or something else, it is civic virtue in action. (p. 211)

When the republican conception of politics is applied to schools, both the unique shared values that define individual schools as communities and our common democratic principles and conceptions of goodness that provide the basis for defining civic virtue are important.

The pluralist conception of politics differs from the republican. Without the unifying power of civic virtue, factions are strengthened and the politics of division reigns. In the ideal, the challenge of this politics is to play people and events in a way that the self-interests of individuals and factions are mediated in some orderly manner. "Under the pluralist conception, people come to the political process with pre-selected interests that they seek to promote through political conflict and compromise" (Sunstein, 1993, p. 176). Deliberate governmental processes of conflict resolution and compromise, of checks and balances, are needed in the pluralist view because preferences are not shaped by the people themselves as they strive to control self-interests that happen to dominate at the time.

Civic virtue was important to both Federalists, who supported the proposed Constitution, and Anti-Federalists, who opposed the Constitution, though it was the centerpiece of Anti-Federalist thinking. The Anti-Federalists favored decentralization in the form of democracy tempered by a commitment to the common good. The Federalists, by contrast, acknowledged the importance of civic virtue, but felt the pull of pluralistic politics was too strong for the embodiment of virtue to be left to chance. They proposed a representative rather than a direct form of government that would be guided by the principles of a formal constitution that specified a series of governmental checks and balances to control factionalism and self-interest.

Both the positions of the Federalists and the Anti-Federalists have roles to play in the governance of schools. In small communities, for example, the politics of virtue expressed within a direct democracy that is guided by *citizen* devotion to the public good seems to make the most sense. Small schools and small schools within schools would be examples of such communities. They would be governed by autonomous school councils that are responsible for both educational policy and site-based management—both ends and means. This approach to governance represents a significant departure from present policies that allow principals, parents, and teachers in local schools to decide how they will do things, but not what they will do. The decisions that local school councils make would be guided by shared values and beliefs that parents, teachers, and students develop together. Schools, in this image, would not function as markets where self-interests reign or bureaucracies where entrenched rule systems reign, but as morally based direct democracies within which parents, teachers, and students, guided by civic virtue, make the best decisions possible for learning.

At the school district level, by contrast, the position of the Federalists might make the most sense. A representative form of government spearheaded by elected school boards, guided by an explicit constitution that contains the protections and freedoms needed to enable individual school communities to function both responsibly and autonomously, would be the model. School communities would have to abide by certain school district regulations regarding safety, due process, equity, fiscal procedures, and a few basic academic standards. But, beyond these, schools would be free to decide for themselves not only their management processes, but their policy structures as well. They would be responsible for deciding their own educational purposes, educational programs, scheduling and ways of operating, and means to demonstrate to the school district and to the public that they are functioning responsibly. Accountability in such a system would be both responsive to each school's purposes and, in light of those purposes, to tough standards of proof.

How can schools be held accountable for different standards? First, we will need to create standards for standards. Then we will be able to assess whether the standards that individual schools set for themselves are good ones. Once standards are accepted, each school is then assessed on its own terms. Here is how such a strategy would work: Schools make promises to the people; the promises must be good ones; school boards and states hold schools accountable for keeping their promises.

THE RATIONAL CHOICE QUESTION

Formal organization theories of human nature can be traced back to a few principles that are at the center of classical economic theory. Prime among them is the *utility function,* which is believed to explain all consumer behavior. The reasoning behind this belief is as follows. Humans are by their nature selfish. They are driven by a desire to maximize their self-interests and thus continually calculate the costs and benefits of their actions. They choose courses of action that either make them winners (they get a desired payoff) or keep them from losing (they avoid penalties). So dominant is this view and so pervasive is the concept of utility function that emotions such as love, loyalty, obligation, sense of duty, belief in goodness, commitment to a cause, and a desire to help make things better are thought to count very little in determining the courses of actions that humans choose. This view of human nature comprises a model of economics called *rational choice theory.*

Rational choice theory, expressed simply as "What gets rewarded gets done," undergirds much of the thinking in schools about how to motivate teachers to perform, how to introduce school improvement initiatives in schools, how to motivate people to accept change, and how to motivate students to learn and to behave. By emphasizing self-interest, rational choice theory discourages the development of civic virtue.

Two additional motivational rules need to be recognized if we are to have a more complete picture of human nature: "What is *rewarding* gets done," and "What people value and believe in gets done." Both rules compel people to perform, improve, change, and meet their commitments from within, even if doing so requires that self-interest be sacrificed. Both rules address the intrinsic and moral nature of human nature. Both rules are essential to the cultivation of civic virtue.

IS CIVIC VIRTUE FOR STUDENTS, TOO?

Some readers might concede that perhaps we should move away from a rational choice view of motivation. Perhaps we should acknowledge the capacity of parents and teachers to respond less in terms of their self-interest and more in terms of what they believe is right and good. But what about students? Can they too respond to the call of virtue?

Children and young adults in schools have different needs and different dispositions. They function developmentally at different levels of moral reasoning than do adults. But the evidence is clear that students from kindergarten to grade 12 have the capacity to understand what civic virtue is and to respond to it in ways that are consistent with their own levels of maturation.

Reissman (1993) and several other teachers in New York City's District 25, for example, have been working with elementary school children (even first and second graders) on developing "bills of responsibilities." The bills are designed to teach the meaning of civic virtue and to introduce students to sources of authority that are more morally based than the usual behavioristic ways to get students to do things. Key is the emphasis on reciprocal responsibilities—a critical ingredient in community building. Communities of mind, for example, evolve from commitments to standards that apply to everyone in the school, not just to students. Thus, if students must be respectful, so must parents, teachers, principals, and everyone else who is a member of the school community or who visits the school.

Events at the Harmony School in Bloomington, Indiana, illustrate civic virtue in action (Panasonic Foundation, Inc., 1994). A well-known sculptor had removed his limestone rhinoceros from its place in front of an art gallery in Bloomington to keep it from being vandalized. The kindergarten through twelfth grade students at the Harmony School launched a campaign to return the rhino to Bloomington. They raised $6,000 and purchased the rhino, which now stands in front of the school for the entire community to enjoy.

One year Harmony High School students decided that, instead of the traditional field trip to Chicago, they would go to Quincy, Illinois, where the Mississippi floods had devastated the city. One of the students explained, "They have plenty of food, and plenty of relief supplies, but they don't have anybody to help get life in order." Harmony students helped by clearing mud, garbage, and debris from the streets and by planting flowers and shrubs. Many similar stories, I know, are coming to your mind as you read about and think about the events at Harmony.

Harmony School is private, and Bloomington, Indiana, is hardly downtown Kansas City, Miami, or San Antonio. But students everywhere are pretty much the same. They have the capacity to care. They want to be called to be good, and they know the difference between right and wrong. The fact is that students, too, under the right conditions, not only will be responsive to the calls of civic virtue, but they need to be responsive if they are to develop into the kinds of adults that we want them to be.

NEW LEADERSHIP IMAGES

Replacing the politics of division with a politics of virtue requires a redefined leadership. Civic virtue is encouraged when leadership aims to develop a web of moral obligations that administrators, teachers, parents, and even students must accept. One part of this obligation is to share in the responsibility for exercising leadership. Another part of this obligation is to share in the responsibility for ensuring that leadership, whatever its source, is successful. In this redefinition, teachers continue to be responsible for providing leadership in classrooms. But students, too, have a moral obligation to help make things work. They, too, provide leadership where they can and try as best they can to make the teacher's leadership

effective. Similarly, administrators, parents, and teachers would accept responsibility together for the provision and the success of leadership.

Key to leadership in a democracy is the concept of social contract. Heifetz (1994) notes, "In part, democracy requires that average citizens become aware that they are indeed the principals, and that those upon whom they confer power are the agents. They have also to bear the risks, the costs, and the fruits of shared responsibility and civic participation" (p. 61).

It is through morally held role responsibilities that we can understand school administration as a profession in its more traditional sense. School administration is bound not just to standards of technical competence, but to standards of public obligation as well (Bellah et al., 1985, p. 290). The primacy of public obligation leads us to the roots of school leadership—stewardship defined as a commitment to administer to the needs of the school by serving its purposes, by serving those who struggle to embody these purposes, and by acting as a guardian to protect the institutional integrity of the school.

Principals function as stewards by providing for the overseeing and caring of their schools. As stewards, they are not so much managers or executives but administrators. According to Webster, to "manage" means to handle, to control, to make submissive, to direct an organization. "Superintend," in turn, means attending to, giving attention to, having oversight over what is intended. It means, in other words, supervision. As supervisor, the principal acts in loco parentis in relationship to students, ensuring that all is well for them. And as supervisor the principal acts as steward, guarding and protecting the school's purposes and structures.

Supervision in communities implies accountability, but not in the tough, inspectoral sense suggested by factory images of inspection and control. Instead, it implies an accountability embedded in tough and tender caring. Principals care enough about the school, the values and purposes that undergird it, the students who are being served, the parents whom they represent, and the teachers upon whom they depend that they will do whatever they can to protect school values and purposes, on the one hand, and to enable their accomplishment on the other.

In a recent interview, Deborah Meier, then co-director of the celebrated Central Park East Secondary School in New York City, was asked, "What is the role of the principal in an effective school?" (Scherer, 1995). Her response shows how the various ministerial roles of the principal are brought together by supervision understood as an expression of stewardship:

> Someone has to keep an eye on the whole and alert everyone when parts need close- or long-range attention. A principal's job is to put forth to the staff an agenda. The staff may or may not agree, but they have an opportunity to discuss it. I'll say, "Listen, I've been around class after class, and I notice this, don't notice this, we made a commitment to be accountable for one another, but I didn't see anybody visiting anybody else's class. . . ." Paul [Schwartz, Meier's co-director] and I also read all the teachers' assessments of students. Once we noticed that the 9th and the 10th grade math teachers often said the kids didn't seem to have an aptitude for math. We asked the math staff, "How can these kids do nicely in 7th and 8th grade, and then seem inept in 9th and 10th? Are we fooling ourselves in 7th and 8th, or are we fooling ourselves in 9th and 10th? Because they are the same kids." (p. 7)

Meier and Schwartz both practiced leadership that is idea based. The source of authority that they appealed to are the values that are central to the school and the commitments that everyone has made to them. And because of this, their supervisory responsibilities do not compromise democratic principles, dampen teacher empowerment, or get in the way of community building. Both directors were committed to creating a staff-run school with high standards—one where staff must know each other, be familiar with each other's work, and know how the school operates. As Meier (1992) explained,

> Decisions are made as close to each teacher's own classroom setting as possible, although all decisions are ultimately the responsibility of the whole staff. The decisions are not merely on minor matters—length of classes or the number of field trips. The teachers collectively decide on content, pedagogy, and assessment as well. They teach what

they think matters . . . governance is simple. There are virtually no permanent standing committees. Finally, we work together to develop assessment systems for our students, their families, ourselves, and the broader public. Systems that represent our values and beliefs in as direct a manner as possible. (p. 607)

This process of shared decision making is not institutionalized into a formal system, but is embedded in the daily interactions of everyone working together.

In stewardship the legitimacy of leadership comes in part from the virtuous responsibilities associated with the principal's role and in part from the principal's obligation to function as the head follower of the school's moral compact. In exercising these responsibilities and obligations, it is not enough to make the right moves for just any purpose or just any vision. The noted historian and leadership theorist James MacGregor Burns (1978) pointed out that purposes and visions should be socially useful, should serve the common good, should meet the needs of followers, and should elevate followers to a higher moral level. He calls this kind of leadership *transformational.*

Many business writers and their imitators in educational administration have secularized this original definition of transformational leadership to make it more suitable to the values of formal organizations. They "conceive of transformation, not in Burns's sense of elevating the moral functioning of a polity, but in the sense of inspiration, intellectual stimulation, and personal considerations . . . , or altering the basic normative principles that guide an institution . . ." (Heifetz, 1994, pp. 228–289; see also Bass, 1985, and Hargrove, 1989). This revisionist concept of transformational leadership might be alright for managers and CEOs in business organizations. But when it comes to the kind of leadership that they want for their children's schools, few businesspersons are likely to prefer the corporate definition over Burns's original definition.

When principals practice leadership as stewardship, they commit themselves to building, serving, caring for, and protecting the school and its purposes. They commit themselves to helping others to face problems and to make progress in getting problems solved. Leadership as steward-ship asks a great deal of leaders and followers alike. It calls both to higher levels of commit-ment. It calls both to higher levels of goodness. It calls both to higher levels of effort. And it calls both to higher levels of accountability. Leadership as stewardship is the *sine qua non* for cultivating civic virtue. Civic virtue can help to transform in-dividual stakeholders into members of a commu-nity who share common commitments and who feel a moral obligation to help each other to em-body those commitments.

ENDNOTE

This chapter is drawn from *Leadership for the School-house: How Is It Different? Why Is It Important?* San Francisco: Jossey-Bass, 1996.

REFERENCES

Allison, G. T. (1969). "Conceptual Models and the Cuban Missile Crisis." *American Political Science Review, 63* (3): 689–718.

Bass, B. M. (1985). *Leadership and Performance be-yond Expectations.* New York: Free Press.

Bellah, R. N., and others. (1985). *Habits of the Heart: Individualism and Commitment in American Life.* New York: HarperCollins.

Burns, J. M. (1978). *Leadership.* New York: Harper-Collins.

Elshtain, J. B. (1994). "Democracy and the Politics of Difference." *Responsive Community, 4* (2): 9–20.

Haefele, E. T. (1993). "What Constitutes the American Republic?" In S. L. Elkin and K. E. Soltan (eds.), *A New Constitutionalism.* Chicago: University of Chicago Press: 207–233.

Hargrove, E. C. (1989). "Two Conceptions of Institu-tional Leadership. In B. D. Jones (ed.), *Leadership and Politics: New Perspectives in Political Science.* Lawrence: University of Kansas Press.

Heifetz, R. (1994). *Leadership without Easy Answers.* Cambridge, MA: Harvard University Press.

Meier, D. (1992). "Reinventing Teaching." *Teacher's College Record, 93* (4): 594–609.

Panasonic Foundation. (1994). *Panasonic Partnership Program.* A newsletter of the Panasonic Founda-tion, *4* (1).

Reissman, R. (1993). "A Bill of Responsibilities." *Edu-cational Leadership, 51* (4): 86–87.

Samuelson, P. (1947). *Foundations of Economic Analy-sis.* Cambridge, MA: Harvard University Press.

Scherer, M. (1995). "On Schools Where Students Want to Be: A Conversation with Deborah Meier." *Edu-cational Leadership, 52* (1): 4–8.

Sunstein, C. R. (1993). "The Enduring Legacy of Re-publicanism." In S. L. Elkin and K. E. Soltan (eds.), *A New Constitutionalism.* Chicago: Univer-sity of Chicago Press: 174–207.

van Mannen, M. (1991). *The Tact of Teaching: The Meaning of Pedagogical Thoughtfulness.* Albany: State University of New York Press.

DISCUSSION QUESTIONS

1. What is the relationship between the politics of division and the application of for-mal organization theories of governance, management, and leadership in schools?
2. What are the implications of applying the politics of virtue to the practice of school leadership?
3. What are the disadvantages of applying rational choice theory to change initia-tives and student motivation?
4. What evidence is there to support the belief that students of all ages have the ca-pacity to understand and support civic virtue?
5. Why are the concepts of social contract and obligation key to the practice of lead-ership in a democracy?
6. In your opinion, is the notion of school leadership based on the politics of virtue a (a) practical, (b) feasible, or (c) desirable idea? Why? Why not?

29

Five Models of Staff Development
for Teachers

DENNIS SPARKS
SUSAN LOUCKS-HORSLEY

FOCUSING QUESTIONS

1. How are staff development and school restructuring initiatives related?
2. For what kind of person is the individually guided model of staff development most suitable?
3. How are cognitive levels and types of feedback related?
4. What activities are characteristic of the peer-coaching, clinical supervision, and evaluation supervisory approaches?
5. How can training facilitate school improvement efforts?
6. What are the common elements within organizations that have successful staff development programs?
7. How can staff development contribute to the professionalization of teaching?

In the early 1970s, a growing concern about the effectiveness of inservice education resulted in a spate of studies to determine the attitudes of educators about these programs (Ainsworth, 1976; Brim & Tollett, 1974; Joyce & Peck, 1977; Zigarmi, Betz, & Jensen, 1977). The findings indicated nearly unanimous dissatisfaction with current efforts, but a strong consensus that inservice was critical if school programs and practices were to be improved (Wood & Kleine, 1987).

During the late 1970s and early 1980s, several major studies and reviews contributed to our understanding of the characteristics of effective staff development, focusing not on attitudes, but on actual practices (Berman & McLaughlin, 1978; Kells, 1981; Lawrence, 1974; Yarger, Howey, & Joyce, 1980). The resulting list of effective practices, well known by now, included:

- Programs conducted in school settings and linked to school-wide efforts

- Teachers participating as helpers to each other and as planners, with administrators, of inservice activities
- Emphasis on self-instruction, with differentiated training opportunities
- Teachers in active roles, choosing goals and activities for themselves
- Emphasis on demonstration, supervised trials, and feedback; training that is concrete and ongoing over time
- Ongoing assistance and support available on request

Staff development came of age in the 1980s. It was the focus of countless conferences, workshops, articles, books, and research reports. State legislators and administrators of local school districts saw staff development as a key aspect of school improvement efforts. Many school districts initiated extensive staff development projects to improve student learning.

Research on these projects and craft knowledge generated by staff developers have substantially advanced our understanding of effective staff development practices beyond the overview studies of the early 1980s referred to above.

INTRODUCTION

In spite of this intense, widespread interest in staff development, much remains to be learned about the process. This chapter organizes what is known about effective staff development into five models that are espoused and used by staff developers. A review of the supporting theory and research on these models is followed by a description of what is known about the organizational context that is required to support successful staff development efforts. The conclusion discusses what can be said with confidence about effective staff development practice and what remains to be learned. First, however, are definitions of the key terms and a description of the literature that is used throughout the article.

Definitions

Staff development is defined as those processes that improve the job-related knowledge, skills, or attitudes of school employees. While participants in staff development activities may include school board members, central office administrators, principals, and non-certified staff, this article focuses on staff development for teachers. In particular, it examines what is known about staff development that is intended to improve student learning through enhanced teacher performance.

Two uses of the word "model" have been combined in an effort to both conceptualize staff development and make this conceptualization useful to staff developers. First, borrowing from Ingvarson's (1987) use of the term, a model can be seen as a design for learning which embodies a set of assumptions about (a) where knowledge about teaching practice comes from, and (b) how teachers acquire or extend their knowledge. Models chosen for discussion differ in their assumptions. Second, adapting Joyce and Weil's (1972) definition of a model of teaching, a staff development model is a pattern or plan which can be used to guide the design of a staff development program.

Each staff development model presented below is discussed in terms of its theoretical and research underpinnings, its critical attributes (including its underlying assumptions and phases of activities), and illustrations of its impact on teacher growth and development. The literature supporting these models is of several types. First, for each model, the theoretical and research bases that support its use in improving teachers' knowledge, skills, or attitudes are considered. The question asked was: Why should one believe that this model *should* affect teachers' classroom behavior? Second, program descriptions were reviewed in which these models were applied. The question asked was: What evidence exists that demonstrates that this model can be implemented by staff developers in schools and school districts? Third, data about outcomes were sought. The question asked was: What evidence indicates that this model actually makes a difference in teacher performance?

An Overview

This chapter presents five models of staff development: (a) individually guided staff development, (b) observation/assessment, (c) involvement in a development/improvement process, (d) training, and (e) inquiry.

Individually guided staff development refers to a process through which teachers plan for and pursue activities they believe will promote their own learning. The observation/assessment model provides teachers with objective data and feedback regarding their classroom performance. This process may in itself produce growth or it can provide information that may be used to select areas for growth.

Involvement in a development/improvement process engages teachers in developing curriculum, designing programs, or engaging in a school improvement process to solve general or particular problems. The training model (which may be synonymous with staff development in the minds of many educators) involves teachers in acquiring knowledge or skills through appropriate individual or group instruction. The inquiry model requires that teachers identify an area of instructional interest, collect data, and make changes in their instruction based on an interpretation of those data.

Next, this chapter examines the organizational context that is required to support these models. Our discussion includes organizational climate, leadership and support, district policies and systems, and participant involvement.

The final section looks for gaps in the knowledge base of staff development, identifying areas about which there is still more to learn and areas that as yet remain unexplored by researchers. The hope is that this chapter will serve as both a signpost for how far we have come in our understanding of effective staff development practices and a spring-board for future research in this vital area.

Five Models of Staff Development

1. Individually Guided Staff Development.
Teachers learn many things on their own. They read professional publications, have discussions with colleagues, and experiment with new instructional strategies, among other activities. All of these may occur with or without the existence of a formal staff development program.

It is possible, however, for staff development programs to actively promote individually guided activities. While the actual activities may vary widely, the key characteristic of the individually guided staff development model is that the learning is designed by the teacher. The teacher determines his or her own goals and selects the activities that will result in the achievement of those goals. Perhaps a sense of this model is best represented in an advertisement for the Great Books Foundation, which reads: "At 30, 50, or 70, you are more self-educable than you were at 20. It's time to join a Great Books reading and discussion group."

Underlying Assumptions.   This model assumes that individuals can best judge their own learning needs and that they are capable of self-direction and self-initiated learning. It also assumes that adults learn most efficiently when they initiate and plan their learning activities rather than spending their time in activities that are less relevant than those they would design. (It is, however, true that when individual teachers design their own learning there is much "reinventing of the wheel," which may seem inefficient to some observers.) The model also holds that individuals will be most motivated when they select their own learning goals based on their personal assessment of their needs.

Theoretical and Research Underpinnings.   According to Lawrence's (1974) review of 97 studies of inservice programs, programs with individualized activities were more likely to achieve their objectives than were those that provided identical experiences for all participants. Theory supporting the individually guided model can be found in the work of a number of individuals. Rogers's (1969) client-centered therapy and views on education are based on the premise that human beings will seek growth given the appropriate conditions. "I have come to feel," Rogers wrote, "that the only learning which significantly influences behavior is self-discovered, self-appropriated learning" (p. 153).

The differences in people and their needs are well represented in the literature on adult learning theory, adult development, learning styles, and the change process. Adult learning theorists (Kidd, 1973; Knowles, 1980) believe that adults become increasingly self-directed and that their readiness to learn is stimulated by real-life tasks and problems. Stage theorists (Levine, 1989) hold that individuals in different stages of development have different personal and professional needs. Consequently, staff development that provides practical classroom management assistance to a 22-year-old beginning teacher may be inappropriate for a teaching veteran who is approaching retirement.

Learning styles researchers (Dunn & Dunn, 1978; Gregorc, 1979) argue that individuals are different in the ways they perceive and process information and in the manner in which they most effectively learn (e.g., alone or with others, by doing as opposed to hearing about). Research on the Concerns-Based Adoption Model (CBAM) (Hall & Loucks, 1978) indicates that as individuals learn new behaviors and change their practice, they experience different types of concerns that require different types of responses from staff developers. For instance, when first learning about a new instructional technique, some teachers with personal concerns require reassurance that they will not be immediately evaluated on the use of the strategy, while a teacher with management concerns wants to know how this technique can be used in the classroom.

Taken together, these theorists and researchers recognize that the circumstances most suitable for one person's professional development may be quite different from those that promote another individual's growth. Consequently, individually guided staff development allows teachers to find answers to self-selected professional problems using their preferred modes of learning.

Phases of Activity.   Individually guided staff development consists of several phases: (a) the identification of a need or interest, (b) the development of a plan to meet the need or interest, (c) the learning activity(ies), and (d) assessment of whether the learning meets the identified need or interest. These phases might be undertaken informally and almost unconsciously, or they may be part of a formal, structured process. Each phase is explained in greater detail below.

With the identification of a need or interest, the teacher considers what he or she needs to learn. This assessment may be done formally (e.g., the completion of a needs assessment process or as a result of evaluation by a supervisor) or occur more spontaneously (e.g., a conversation with a colleague or reflection upon an instructional problem). The need or interest may be remedial (e.g., "I've really come to dislike my work because of the classroom management problems I'm having") or growth-oriented (e.g., "I'm intrigued by recent research on the brain and want to better understand its implications for student learning").

Having identified the need or interest, the teacher selects a learning objective and chooses activities that will lead to accomplishing this objective. Activities may include workshop attendance, reading, visits to another classroom or school, or initiation of a seminar or similar learning program.

The learning activity may be single session (e.g., attendance at a workshop on new approaches to reading in the content areas) or occur over time (e.g., examination of the research on retaining students in grade). Based on the individual's preferred mode of learning, it may be done alone (e.g., reading or writing), with others (e.g., a seminar that considers ways of boosting the self-esteem of high school students), or as a combination of these activities.

When assessing formal individually guided processes, the teacher may be asked to make a brief written report to the funding source or an oral report to colleagues. In other instances the teacher may simply be aware that he or she now better understands something. It is not uncommon that as a result of this assessment phase the teacher may realize how much more there is to be learned on the topic or be led to a newly emerging need or interest.

Illustrations and Outcomes.   Individually guided staff development may take many forms. It may be as simple as a teacher reading a journal article on a topic of interest. Other forms of individually guided staff development are more complex. For instance, teachers may design and carry out special professional projects supported by incentive grants such as a competitive "teacher excellence fund" promoted by Boyer (1983) or "mini-grants" described by Mosher (1981). Their projects may involve research, curriculum development, or other learning activities. While evidence of outcomes for such programs is not substantial, there are indications that they can empower teachers to address their own problems, create a sense of professionalism, and provide intellectual stimulation (Loucks-Horsley, Harding, Arbuckle, Murray, Dubea, & Williams, 1987). This strategy proved effective in New York City and Houston, where teachers were supported to develop and disseminate their own exemplary programs through Impact II grants. They reported changes in their classroom practices, as well as increases in student attendance, discipline, and motivation (Mann, 1984–85).

Teacher evaluation and supervision can be a source of data for individually guided staff development. McGreal (1983) advocates that goal setting be the principal activity of teacher evaluation.

Supervisors would assist in the establishment of those goals based on the motivation and ability of the teacher. The type of goals, the activities teachers engage in to meet the goals, and the amount of assistance provided by supervisors would differ from teacher to teacher based upon developmental level, interests, concerns, and instructional problems.

Similarly, Glatthorn's (1984) "differentiated supervision" calls for "self-directed development" as one form of assistance to teachers. Self-directed development is a goal-based approach to professional improvement in which teachers have access to a variety of resources for meeting their collaboratively identified needs.

Research on teacher centers also demonstrates the value of individually guided staff development. Hering and Howey (1982) summarized research conducted on 15 teacher centers sponsored by the Far West Laboratory for Educational Research and Development from 1978 to 1982. They concluded that, "the most important contribution of teachers' centers is their emphasis on working with individual teachers over time" (p. 2). Such a focus on individual teachers is absent from many traditional staff development programs, which teacher centers appear to complement quite effectively.

Hering and Howey (1982) reported that minigrants of up to $750 provided by the St. Louis Metropolitan Teacher Center were used to fund a variety of classroom-oriented projects. Interviews with participants found that teachers made extensive use of the ideas and products they developed. Some of these projects eventually affected not only an individual classroom, but a school or the entire district. Regarding this project, Hering and Howey concluded:

> As would be expected, teachers who were given money and support reported high levels of satisfaction and a sense of accomplishment. Also not surprisingly, they developed projects anchored in the realities of the classroom and responsive to the needs and interests of their students. Perhaps most important, however, is the strong suggestion that they can, indeed, influence change and innovation in other classrooms, as well as their own, through projects they design at minimal costs. (p. 6)

Hering and Howey (1982) also report the findings for a study done on individualized services provided at the Northwest Staff Development Center in Livonia, Michigan. Even though these awards rarely exceeded $50, 78 percent of the recipients reported that they had considerable control over their own learning and professional development. Almost 85 percent of the recipients thought that these services made a substantive difference in their classrooms. In summarizing the value of individualized services, the researchers wrote, "Individual teacher needs and concerns have to be attended to, as well as school-wide collective ones, or enthusiasm for the collective approach will quickly wane" (p. 6).

While there are many illustrations of an individualized approach to staff development in the literature and many more in practice, research on its impact on teaching is largely perceptual and self-reported. Perhaps as more resources are directed to supporting this strategy—particularly in the form of incentive grants to teachers—more will be learned about its contribution to teacher, as well as student, growth.

2. Observation/Assessment.   "Feedback is the breakfast of champions" is the theme of Blanchard and Johnson's (1982) popular management book, *The One Minute Manager.* Yet many teachers receive little or no feedback on their classroom performance. In fact, in some school districts teachers may be observed by a supervisor as little as once every 3 years, and that observation/feedback cycle may be perfunctory in nature.

While observation/assessment can be a powerful staff development model, in the minds of many teachers it is associated with evaluation. Because this process often has not been perceived as helpful (Wise & Darling-Hammond, 1985), teachers frequently have difficulty understanding the value of this staff development model. However, once they have had an opportunity to learn about the many forms this model can take (for instance, peer coaching and clinical supervision, as well as teacher evaluation), it may become more widely practiced.

Underlying Assumptions.   One assumption underlying this model, according to Loucks-Horsley and her associates (1987), is that "Reflection and analysis are central means of professional growth" (p. 61). Observation and assessment of instruction provide the teacher with data that can be reflected upon and analyzed for the purpose of improving student learning.

A second assumption is that reflection by an individual on his or her own practice can be enhanced by another's observations. Since teaching is an isolated profession, typically taking place in the presence of no other adults, teachers are not able to benefit from the observations of others. Having "another set of eyes" gives a teacher a different view of how he or she is performing with students.

Another assumption is that observation and assessment of classroom teaching can benefit both involved parties—the teacher being observed and the observer. The teacher benefits by another's view of his or her behavior and by receiving helpful feedback from a colleague. The observer benefits by watching a colleague, preparing the feedback, and discussing the common experience.

A final assumption is that when teachers see positive results from their efforts to change, they are more apt to continue to engage in improvement. Because this model may involve multiple observations and conferences spread over time, it can help teachers see that change is possible. As they apply new strategies, they can see changes in both their own and their students' behavior. In some instances, measurable improvements in student learning will also be observed.

Theoretical and Research Underpinnings. Theoretical and research support for the observation/assessment model can be found in the literature on teacher evaluation, clinical supervision, and peer coaching. Each of these approaches is based on the premise that teaching can be objectively observed and analyzed and that improvement can result from feedback on that performance.

McGreal's (1982) work on teacher evaluation suggests a key role for classroom observation, but expresses a major concern about reliability of observations. The author points to two primary ways to increase the reliability of classroom observations. The first is to narrow the range of what is

looked for by having a system that takes a narrowed focus on teaching (for instance, an observation system based on the Madeline Hunter approach to instruction) or by using an observation guide or focusing instrument. The second way is to use a pre-conference to increase the kind and amount of information the observer has prior to the observation. Glatthorn (1984) recommends that clinical supervisors (or coaches) alternate unfocused observations with focused observations. In unfocused observation the observer usually takes verbatim notes on all significant behavior. These data are used to identify some strengths and potential problems that are discussed in a problem-solving feedback conference. A focus is then determined for the next observation, during which the observer gathers data related to the identified problem.

Glickman (1986) suggests that the type of feedback provided teachers should be based on their cognitive levels. Teachers with a "low-abstract" cognitive style should receive directive conferences (problem identification and solution come primarily from the coach or supervisor); "moderate-abstract" teachers should receive collaborative conferences (an exchange of perceptions about problems and a negotiated solution); and "high-abstract" teachers should receive a nondirective approach (the coach or supervisor helps the teacher clarify problems and choose a course of action).

Peer coaching is a form of the observation/assessment model that promotes transfer of learning to the classroom (Joyce & Showers, 1982). In peer observation, teachers visit one another's classrooms, gather objective data about student performance or teacher behavior, and give feedback in a follow-up conference. According to Joyce and Showers (1983):

> Relatively few persons, having mastered a new teaching skill, will then transfer that skill into their active repertoire. In fact, few will use it at all. Continuous practice, feedback, and the companionship of coaches are essential to enable even highly motivated persons to bring additions to their repertoire under effective control. (p. 4)

Joyce (Brandt, 1987) says that up to 30 trials may be required to bring a new teaching strategy under "executive control." Similarly, Shalaway (1985) found that 10 to 15 coaching sessions may be necessary for teachers to use what they have learned in their classrooms.

Phases of Activity. The observation/assessment model—whether implemented through evaluation, clinical supervision, or peer coaching—usually includes a pre-observation conference, observation, analysis of data, post-observation conference, and (in some instances) an analysis of the observation/ assessment process (Loucks-Horsley et al., 1987). In the pre-observation conference, a focus for the observation is determined, observation methods selected, and any special problems noted.

During the observation, data are collected using the processes agreed upon in the pre-observation conference. The observation may be focused on the students or on the teacher, and can be global in nature or narrowly focused. Patterns found during instruction may become evident. Hunter (1982) recommends three points of analysis: (a) behaviors that contribute to learning, (b) behaviors that interfere with learning, and (c) behaviors that neither contribute nor interfere, but use time and energy that could be better spent.

In the post-observation conference both the teacher and observer reflect on the lesson and the observer shares the data collected. Strengths are typically acknowledged and areas for improvement suggested (by either the teacher or observer, depending upon the goals established in the pre-observation conference). An analysis of the supervisory (or coaching) process itself, while not necessarily a part of all forms of this model, provides participants with an opportunity to reflect on the value of the observation/assessment process and to discuss modifications that might be made in future cycles.

Illustrations and Outcomes. Acheson and Gall (1980) report a number of studies in which the clinical supervision model has been accepted by teachers when they and their supervisors are taught systematic observation techniques. They further note that this process is viewed as productive by teachers when the supervisor uses "indirect" behaviors (e.g., accepting feelings and ideas, giving praise and encouragement, asking questions). While the authors report that trained supervisors helped teachers make improvements in a number of instructional behaviors, they were unable to find any studies that demonstrated student effects.

The most intensive and extensive studies of the impact of observation/assessment on learning come from the work of Showers and Joyce. Discussed in more detail in the training section, these authors and their associates have found that powerful improvements have been made to student learning when the training of teachers in effective instructional practices is followed by observations and coaching in their classrooms (Joyce & Showers, 1988). In a study that contrasted different sources of coaching, Sparks (1986) contrasted a workshop-only approach with peer coaching and with consultant coaching. Her findings indicated that peer coaching was most powerful in improving classroom performance.

The research, then, provides reason to believe that teacher behaviors can be positively influenced by the use of an observation/assessment model of staff development. It still remains to be learned, however, whether this model must be combined with particular kinds of training if student learning is to be enhanced.

3. Involvement in a Development/Improvement Process.

Teachers are sometimes asked to develop or adapt curriculum, design programs, or engage in systematic school improvement processes that have as their goal the improvement of classroom instruction and/or curriculum. Typically these projects are initiated to solve a problem. Their successful completion may require that teachers acquire specific knowledge or skills (e.g., curriculum planning, research on effective teaching, group problem-solving strategies). This learning could be acquired through reading, discussion, observation, training, and/or trial and error. In other instances, the process of developing a product itself may cause significant learnings (e.g., through experiential learning), some of which may have been difficult or impossible to predict in advance. This model focuses on the combination of learnings that result from the involvement of teachers in such development/improvement processes.

Underlying Assumptions.   One assumption on which this model is based is that adults learn most effectively when they have a need to know or a problem to solve (Knowles, 1980). Serving on a school improvement committee may require that teachers read the research on effective teaching and that they learn new group and interpersonal skills. Curriculum development may demand new content knowledge of teachers. In each instance, teachers' learning is driven by the demands of problem solving.

Another assumption of this model is that people working closest to the job best understand what is required to improve their performance. Their teaching experiences guide teachers as they frame problems and develop solutions. Given appropriate opportunities, teachers can effectively bring their unique perspectives to the tasks of improving teaching and their schools.

A final assumption is that teachers acquire important knowledge or skills through their involvement in school improvement or curriculum development processes. Such involvement may cause alterations in attitudes or the acquisition of skills as individuals or groups work toward the solution of a common problem. For instance, teachers may become more aware of the perspectives of others, more appreciative of individual differences, more skilled in group leadership, and better able to solve problems. While the learnings may be unpredictable in advance, they are often regarded as important by teachers.

Theoretical and Research Underpinnings.   We have chosen to represent curriculum development and school improvement as types of staff development; involvement in these processes nurtures teachers' growth. Others see staff development (perhaps viewed more narrowly as training) as a key component of effective curriculum development and implementation. As Joyce and Showers (1988) write, "It has been well established that curriculum implementation is demanding of staff development—essentially, without strong staff development programs that are appropriately designed a very low level of implementation occurs" (p. 44).

Whichever perspective one has, staff development and the improvement of schools and cur-

riculum go hand in hand. Glickman (1986), who argues that the aim of staff development should be to improve teachers' ability to think, views curriculum development as a key aspect of this process. He believes that the intellectual engagement required in curriculum development demands that teachers not only know their content, but that they also acquire curriculum planning skills. He recommends that curriculum development be conducted in heterogeneous groups composed of teachers of low, medium, and high abstract reasoning abilities. According to Glickman, the complexity of the curriculum development task should be matched to the abstract reasoning ability of the majority of teachers in the group.

Glatthorn (1987) describes three ways in which teachers can modify a district's curriculum guide. They may operationalize the district's curriculum guide by taking its lists of objectives and recommended teaching methods and turning them into a set of usable instructional guides. Or they may adapt the guide to students' special needs (e.g., remediation, learning style differences). Finally, teachers may enhance the guide by developing optional enrichment units. Glatthorn recommends that these activities be done in groups, believing that, in doing so, teachers will become more cohesive and will share ideas about teaching and learning in general, as well as on the development task at hand.

The involvement of teachers in school improvement processes, while similar in its assumptions and process to curriculum development, finds its research and theory base in other sources. General approaches to school improvement come from the literature on change and innovation. For example, Loucks-Horsley and Hergert (1985) describe seven action steps in a school improvement process that are based in research on implementation of new practices in schools (Crandall & Loucks, 1983; Hall & Loucks, 1978; Louis & Rosenblum, 1981). The research on effective schools underpins other approaches to school improvement (Cohen, 1981). Finally, an approach to school improvement through staff development developed by Wood and his associates was derived from an analysis of effective staff development practices as represented in the research and in reports from educational practitioners (Thompson, 1982; Wood, 1989). The result is a five-stage RPTIM model (Readiness, Planning, Training, Implementation, and Maintenance) used widely in designing and implementing staff development efforts (Wood, Thompson, & Russell, 1981). As a result of involvement in such improvement efforts, schools (and the teachers within them) may develop new curriculum, change reporting procedures to parents, enhance communication within the faculty, and improve instruction, among many other possibilities.

Phases of Activity. This model begins with the identification of a problem or need by an individual, a group of teachers (e.g., a grade-level team or a secondary department), a school faculty, or a district administrator. The need may be identified informally through discussion or a growing sense of dissatisfaction, through a more formal process such as brainstorming or the use of a standardized instrument (such as a school improvement survey or needs assessment), or through examination of student achievement or program evaluation data.

After a need has been identified, a response is formulated. This response may be determined informally or formally. In some cases, the necessary action may become immediately evident (e.g., the need for new lunchroom rules). At other times, teachers may need to brainstorm or search out alternatives, weigh them against a set of predetermined criteria, develop an action plan, and determine evaluation procedures. This process may take several sessions to complete and require consultation with a larger group (e.g., the school-wide staff development committee may receive feedback on the tentative plan from the entire faculty).

Typically it becomes evident during this phase that specific knowledge or skills may be required to implement the plan. For instance, the faculty may decide that it wants to study several discipline systems before implementing the new lunchroom management system. The improvement of students' higher-order thinking may involve the selection of new textbooks, requiring that committee members better understand which features to look for in a textbook to support this goal. The development or selection of a new elementary science curriculum may require study of the latest research on science teaching and the examination of other curricula.

At this point the plan is implemented or the product developed. This process may take several days, several months, or several years. As a final step, the success of the program is assessed. If teachers are not satisfied with the results, they may return to an earlier phase (e.g., acquisition of knowledge or skills) and repeat the process.

Illustrations and Outcomes. While teachers have long been involved in curriculum development, little research on the impact of these experiences on their professional development has been conducted. The research that has been done has assessed the impact of such involvement on areas other than professional development (for example, job satisfaction, costs, and commitment to the organization) (Kimpston & Rogers, 1987). Similarly, although the engagement of teachers in school improvement processes has increased in the last few years, little research has been conducted on the effects of that involvement on their professional development. There are, however, numerous examples that illustrate the various ways schools and districts have enhanced teacher growth by engaging them in the development/improvement process.

In the past few years, many state education agencies have supported implementation of state-initiated reforms through the encouragement (and sometimes mandating) of school improvement processes. For example, the Franklin County (Ohio) Department of Education used a staff development process to assist five school districts to meet mandated state goals (Scholl & McQueen, 1985). Teachers and administrators from the districts learned about the state requirements and developed goals and planning strategies for their districts. A major product of the program was a manual that included a synthesis of information and worksheets that could be used to guide small group activities in the five districts.

School districts have also initiated programs which involve teachers in improvement planning. In the Hammond (Indiana) Public Schools, decision making is school based (Casner-Lotto, 1988). School improvement committees (each composed of 15–20 members, including teachers, administrators, parents, students, and community members) receive training in consensus building, brainstorming, creative problem solving, and group dynamics. After this training, each committee develops a "vision of excellence" for its school. As a result, schools have initiated projects in individualized learning, peer evaluation, cross-grade-level reading, and teacher coaching/mentoring.

Sparks, Nowakowski, Hall, Alec, and Imrick (1985) reported on two elementary school improvement projects that led to large gains on state reading tests. The first school's staff decided to review the reading curriculum and to investigate alternative instructional approaches. Teachers task-analyzed the six lowest-scoring objectives on the state test, studied effective instructional techniques, and participated in self-selected professional growth activities. In 2 years the number of students who scored above the average rose from 72 percent to 100 percent. In the second school, teachers adopted a new reading series, revised the kindergarten program, and created a booklet that included practice test items and effective instructional practices for improving student achievement. The percentage of students achieving the reading objectives increased almost 20 percent in 3 years.

The Jefferson County (Colorado) School District has long involved teachers in curriculum development and adaptation (Jefferson County Public Schools, 1974). A cyclical process of needs assessment, curriculum objective statements, curriculum writing, pilot testing and evaluation, and district-wide implementation has been used on a regular basis in the major content areas. Teachers involved in writing and pilot test teams hone their skills as curriculum planners and developers and as masters of the new techniques that are incorporated into the curriculum (these have included such strategies as cooperative learning and individualized instruction). They also often take on the role of teacher trainers for the district-wide implementation that follows pilot and field tests (Loucks & Pratt, 1979).

E. J. Wilson High School in Spencerport (New York) is one of many across the country that has implemented elements of effective schools through a systematic school improvement process.

Teachers in the school participate with building administrators on a Building Planning Committee which spearheads the achievement of "ideal practices" within the school through a seven-step process that engages the entire faculty in assessment, planning, implementation, and evaluation. As a result, the school climate and student achievement have improved, as have the knowledge, skills, and attitudes of the teachers involved. This school's outcome is representative of other schools that have implemented similar improvement processes (Kyle, 1985).

These state, school, and district-level efforts illustrate the wide variety of ways in which this model of staff development is being used. While the research and evaluation evidence regarding the impact of these processes on teacher knowledge and skills is not substantial, research does support many of the ingredients contained within these processes. These include commitment to the process by school and building administrators, which includes giving authority and resources to the team to pursue and then implement its agenda; development of knowledge and skills on the part of the teacher participants; adequate, quality time to meet, reflect, and develop; adequate resources to purchase materials, visit other sites, and hire consultants to contribute to informed decision making; leadership that provides a vision, direction and guidance, but allows for significant decision making on the part of the teacher participants; and integration of the effort into other improvement efforts and into other structures that influence teaching and learning in the school (Loucks-Horsley et al., 1987). When these factors are present, a limited amount of research data and a great deal of self-report data indicate clearly that the desired outcomes of staff development are achieved.

4. Training.   In the minds of many educators, training is synonymous with staff development. Most teachers are accustomed to attending workshop-type sessions in which the presenter is the expert who establishes the content and flow of activities. Typically the training session is conducted with a clear set of objectives or learner outcomes. These outcomes frequently include awareness or knowledge (e.g., participants will be able to explain the five principles of cooperative learning) and skill development (e.g., participants will demonstrate the appropriate use of open-ended questions in a class discussion). Joyce and Showers (1988) cite changes in attitudes, transfer of training, and "executive control" (the appropriate and consistent use of new strategies in the classroom) as additional outcomes. It is the trainer's role to select activities (e.g., lecture, demonstration, role-playing, simulation, micro-teaching) that will aid teachers in achieving the desired outcomes.

Whatever the anticipated outcomes, the improvement of teachers' thinking is an important goal. According to Showers, Joyce, and Bennett (1987):

> . . . the purpose of providing training in any practice is not simply to generate the external visible teaching "moves" that bring that practice to bear in the instructional setting but to generate the conditions that enable the practice to be selected and used appropriately and integratively. . . . a major, perhaps the major, dimension of teaching skill is cognitive in nature. (pp. 85–86)

Underlying Assumptions. An assumption that undergirds the training model of staff development is that there are behaviors and techniques that are worthy of replication by teachers in the classroom. This assumption can certainly be supported by the large number of research-based effective teaching practices that have been identified and verified in past years (Sparks, 1983).

Another assumption underlying this model is that teachers can change their behaviors and learn to replicate behaviors in their classroom that were not previously in their repertoire. As Joyce and Showers (1983) point out, training is a powerful process for enhancing knowledge and skills. "It is plain from the research on training," they say, "that teachers can be wonderful learners. They can master just about any kind of teaching strategy or implement almost any technique as long as adequate training is provided" (p. 2).

Because of a high participant-to-trainer ratio, training is usually a cost-efficient means for teachers to acquire knowledge or skills. Many instructional skills require that teachers view a demonstration of their use to fully understand their

implementation. Likewise, certain instructional techniques require for their classroom implementation that teachers have an opportunity to practice them with feedback from a skilled observer. Training may be the most efficient means for large numbers of teachers to view these demonstrations and to receive feedback as they practice.

Theoretical and Research Underpinnings. The theoretical and research underpinnings for the training model come from several sources, but the most intensive research has been conducted by Joyce and Showers (1988). They have determined that, depending upon the desired outcomes, training might include exploration of theory, demonstration or modeling of a skill, practice of the skill under simulated conditions, feedback about performance, and coaching in the workplace. Their research indicates that this combination of components is necessary if the outcome is skill development.

In addition to those components identified by Joyce and Showers, Sparks (1983) cites the importance of discussion and peer observation as training activities. She notes that discussion is useful both when new concepts or techniques are presented and as a problem-solving tool after teachers have had an opportunity to try out new strategies in their classrooms. Training sessions that are spaced 1 or more weeks apart so that content can be "chunked" for improved comprehension and so that teachers have opportunities for classroom practice and peer coaching are shown to be more effective than "one-shot" training (Loucks-Horsley et al., 1987; Sparks, 1983).

Sparks (1983), Wu (1987), and Wood and Kleine (1987) point out the value of teachers as trainers of their peers. Sparks indicates that teachers may learn as much from their peers as from "expert" trainers. She also argues that school districts can afford the type of small-group training that she recommends when peers are used rather than more expensive external consultants. In reviewing the research, Wood and Kleine found that teachers preferred their peers as trainers. Wu's review of the research also confirmed this, finding that when their peers are trainers, teachers feel more comfortable exchanging ideas, play a more active role in workshops, and report that they receive more practical suggestions. There is, however, evidence that indicates that expert trainers who have the critical qualities teachers value in their peers (e.g., a clear understanding of how a new practice works with real students in real classroom settings) can also be highly effective (Crandall, 1983).

Phases of Activities.   According to Joyce and Showers (1988), "Someone has to decide what will be the substance of the training, who will provide training, when and where the training will be held and for what duration" (p. 69). While training content, objectives, and schedules are often determined by administrators or by the trainer, Wood, McQuarrie, and Thompson's (1982) research-based model advocates involving participants in planning training programs. Participants serve on planning teams which assess needs (using appropriate sources of data), explore various research-based approaches, select content, determine goals and objectives, schedule training sessions, and monitor implementation of the program.

Joyce and Showers (1988) point out that there are specific "learning-to-learn" attitudes and skills that teachers possess or can develop that aid the training process. They cite persistence, acknowledgment of the transfer problem (the need for considerable practice of new skills in the classroom), teaching new behaviors to students, meeting the cognitive demands of innovations (developing a "deep understanding" of new practices), the productive use of peers, and flexibility. The authors list several conditions of training sessions that foster these aptitudes and behaviors: adequate training, opportunities for collegial problem solving, norms that encourage experimentation, and organizational structures that support learning. Sparks' (1983) review of staff development research suggests that a diagnostic process (such as detailed profiles of teaching behaviors based upon classroom observations) may be an important first step in the training process.

After training, in-classroom assistance in the form of peer observation and coaching is critical to the transfer of more complex teaching skills (Joyce & Showers, 1988). The process of data gathering and analysis that accompanies most forms of peer observation is valuable to the observer as well as the observed teacher (Brandt, 1987; Sparks, 1986). A more thorough discussion of this topic can be found in the observation/assessment model described earlier in this article.

Illustrations and Outcomes.   The power of training to alter teachers' knowledge, attitudes, and instructional skills is well established. Its impact on teachers, however, depends upon its objectives and the quality of the training program. Joyce and Showers (1988) have determined that when all training components are present (theory, demonstration, practice, feedback, and coaching), an effect size of 2.71 exists for knowledge-level objectives, 1.25 for skill-level objectives, and 1.68 for transfer of training to the classroom. (The effect size describes the magnitude of gains from any given change in educational practice; the higher the effect size, the greater the magnitude of gain. For instance, an effect size of 1.0 indicates that the average teacher in the experimental group outperformed 84% of the teachers in the control group.) "We have concluded from these data," Joyce and Showers (1988) report, "that teachers can acquire new knowledge and skill and use it in their instructional practice when provided with adequate opportunities to learn" (p. 72). Coaching and peer observation research cited earlier in the observation/assessment model also supports the efficacy of training.

Wade (1985) found in her meta-analysis of inservice teacher education research that training affected participants' learning by an effect size of .90 and their behavior by .60. An effect size of .37 was found for the impact of teacher training on student behavior. Wade also concluded that training groups composed of both elementary and secondary teachers achieved higher effect sizes than did those enrolling only elementary or only secondary teachers.

Gage (1984) traces the evolution of research on teaching from observational and descriptive studies to correlational studies to nine experiments that were designed to alter instructional practices. "The main conclusion of this body of research," Gage wrote, "is that, in eight out of the nine cases, inservice education was fairly effective—not with all teachers and not with all teaching practices but effective enough to change teachers and improve student achievement, or attitudes, or behavior" (p. 92).

Numerous specific illustrations of training programs are available that have demonstrated impact on teacher behavior and/or student learning. For instance, studies indicate that teachers who have been taught cooperative learning strategies for their classrooms have students who have higher achievement, display higher reasoning and greater critical thinking, have more positive attitudes toward the subject area, and like their fellow students better (Johnson, Johnson, Holubec, & Roy, 1984).

Good and Grouws (1987) describe a mathematics staff development program for elementary teachers. In this 10-session program teachers learned more about mathematics content and about instructional and management issues. As a result of the training, the researchers found changes in teachers' classroom practice and improved mathematics presentations. Student mathematics performance was also improved.

Kerman (1979) reports a 3-year study in which several hundred K–12 teachers were trained to improve their interactions with low-achieving students. The five-session training program included peer observation in the month interval between each session. The researchers found that low-achieving students in experimental classes made significant academic gains over their counterparts in control groups.

Rauth (1986) describes an American Federation of Teachers training program that brought research on teaching to its members. Teacher Research Linkers (TRLs) first determine which aspects of the research will be most valuable in their teaching. Between sessions they carry out implementation plans in their own classrooms. TRLs are then taught how to effectively share this research with their colleagues. A study of this program indicated that teachers made significant changes in their practice and that, in addition, their morale and collegiality increased dramatically.

Robbins and Wolfe (1987) discuss a 4-year staff development project designed to increase elementary students' engaged time and achievement. Evaluation of the training program documented steady improvement for 3 years in teachers' instructional skills, student engaged time, and student achievement in reading and math. While scores in all these areas dropped in the project's fourth and final year, Robbins and Wolfe argue that this decline was due to insufficient coaching and peer observation during that year.

As the preceding discussion indicates, there is a much more substantial research literature on training than on the models presented earlier. Under the appropriate conditions, training has the potential for significantly changing teachers' beliefs, knowledge, and behavior and the performance of their students.

5. Inquiry.   Teacher inquiry can take different forms. A high school teacher wonders if an alteration in her lesson plan from her first period class will produce improved student understanding in second period. A brief written quiz given at the end of the class indicates that it did. A group of teachers gathers weekly after school for an hour or two at the teacher center to examine the research on ability grouping. Their findings will be shared with the district's curriculum council. Several elementary teachers study basic classroom research techniques, formulate research questions, gather and analyze data, and use their findings to improve instruction in their classrooms.

Teacher inquiry may be a solitary activity, be done in small groups, or be conducted by a school faculty. Its process may be formal or informal. It may occur in a classroom or at a teacher center or result from a university class. In this section teacher inquiry is explored as a staff development model.

Underlying Assumptions.   Inquiry reflects a basic belief in teachers' ability to formulate valid questions about their own practice and to pursue objective answers to those questions. Loucks-Horsley and her associates (1987) list three assumptions about a teacher inquiry approach to staff development:

- Teachers are intelligent, inquiring individuals with legitimate expertise and important experience.
- Teachers are inclined to search for data to answer pressing questions and to reflect on the data to formulate solutions.

- Teachers will develop new understandings as they formulate their own questions and collect their own data to answer them.

The overarching assumption of the model is that

> the most effective avenue for professional development is cooperative study by teachers themselves into problems and issues arising from their attempts to make their practice consistent with their educational values. . . . [The approach] aims to give greater control over what is to count as valid educational knowledge to teachers. (Ingvarson, 1987, pp. 15, 17)

Theoretical and Research Underpinnings. The call for inquiry-oriented teachers is not new. Dewey (1933) wrote of the need for teachers to take "reflective action." Zeichner (1983) cites more than 30 years of advocacy for "teachers as action researchers," "teacher scholars," "teacher innovators," "self-monitoring teachers," and "teachers as participant observers."

More recently, various forms of inquiry have been advocated by a number of theorists and researchers. Tikunoff and Ward's (1983) model of interactive research and development promotes teacher inquiry into the questions they are asking through close work with researchers (who help with methodology) and staff developers (who help them create ways of sharing their results with others). Lieberman (1986) reports on a similar process in which teachers serving on collaborative teams pursued answers to school-wide rather than classroom problems. Watts (1985) discusses the role of collaborative research, classroom action research, and teacher support groups in encouraging teacher inquiry. Simmons and Sparks (1985) describe the use of action research to help teachers better relate research on teaching to their unique classrooms.

Glickman (1986) advocates action research in the form of quality circles, problem-solving groups, and school improvement projects as means to develop teacher thought. Cross (1987) proposes classroom research to help teachers evaluate the effectiveness of their own teaching. Glatthorn (1987) discusses action research by teams of teachers as a peer-centered option for promoting professional growth. Loucks-Horsley and her colleagues (1987) discuss teachers-as-researchers as a form of teacher development that helps narrow the gap between research and practice. Sparks and Simmons (1989) propose inquiry-oriented staff development as a means to enhance teachers' decision-making abilities.

One of the important tenets of the inquiry approach is that research is an important activity in which teachers should be engaged, although they rarely participate in it other than as "subjects." Gable and Rogers (1987) "take the terror out of research" by describing ways in which it can be used as a staff development tool. They discuss both qualitative and quantitative methodology, providing specific strategies that teachers can use in their classrooms. They conclude by saying ". . . the desire and ability to do research is an essential attribute of the professional teacher" (p. 695).

Phases of Activity. While the inquiry model of staff development can take many forms, these forms have a number of elements in common. First, individuals or a group of teachers identify a problem of interest. Next, they explore ways of collecting data that may range from examining existing theoretical and research literature to gathering original classroom or school data. These data are then analyzed and interpreted by an individual or the group. Finally, changes are made, and new data are gathered and analyzed to determine the effects of the intervention.

This process can be adapted to the unique needs of a particular approach to inquiry. For instance, Hovda and Kyle (1984) provide a 10-step process for action research that progresses from identifying interested participants, through sharing several study ideas, to discussing findings, to considering having the study published or presented. Glatthorn (1987) describes a four-step process for action research. Collaborative research teams (a) identify a problem, (b) decide upon specific research questions to be investigated and methodology to be used, (c) carry out the research design, and (d) use the research to design an intervention to be implemented in the school.

Watts (1985) describes "reflective conversations" in which teachers carefully observe and thoughtfully consider a particular child or practice. Using a standard procedure, the group shares observations, reviews previous records and information, summarizes the findings, and makes recommendations. As a final step, the group reviews the process to assess how well it went, looks for gaps, and identifies ideas to repeat in future conversations.

Organizational support and/or technical assistance may be required throughout the phases of an inquiry activity. Organizational support may take the form of structures such as teacher centers or study groups or of resources such as released time or materials. Technical assistance may involve training in research methodologies, data-gathering techniques, and other processes that aid teachers in making sense of their experiences.

Illustrations and Outcomes. The forms inquiry as a staff development model may take are limited only by the imagination. Simmons and Sparks (1985) describe a "Master of Arts in Classroom Teaching" degree designed to help teachers meet their individually identified improvement goals. Teachers in this program learn about educational research, identify and analyze classroom problems, pursue topics of professional interest, and improve their overall teaching ability. The authors report evidence of change in participant knowledge (e.g., concerning effective teaching-learning), thinking (e.g., enhanced problem-solving skills, increased cognitive complexity), and patterns of communication and collegiality.

Watts (1985) presents a number of ways in which teachers act as researchers. She discussed collaborative research in teacher centers funded by the Teachers' Center Exchange (then located at the Far West Laboratory for Educational Research and Development) that was conducted in the late 1970s and early 1980s. Fourteen projects were funded in which teachers collaborated with researchers on topics of interest to the individual teachers' center. Watts also described ethnographic studies of classrooms conducted collaboratively by teachers and researchers. In addition, she provided examples of classroom action research and teachers' study groups as forms of inquiry. Watts concluded that these three approaches share several outcomes. First, as a result of learning more about research, teachers make more informed decisions about when and how to apply the research findings of others. Second, teachers experience more supportive and collegial relationships. And third, teaching improves as teachers learn more about it by becoming better able to look beyond the immediate, the individual, and the concrete.

The effects of the teacher inquiry model of staff development may reach beyond the classroom to the school. An example of school-wide impact comes from the report of a high school team convened to reflect on a lack of communication and support between teachers and administrators (Lieberman & Miller, 1984). As a result of working together to define the problem, learn each other's perspectives, gather evidence, and formulate solutions, teachers and administrators address important school problems collaboratively. Note that there is a substantial overlap between this kind of "school-based" inquiry and some of the school improvement processes discussed earlier in the model described as involvement in a development/improvement process.

ORGANIZATIONAL CONTEXT

Teacher development in school districts does not take place in a vacuum. Its success is influenced in many ways by the district's organizational context (McLaughlin & Marsh, 1978; Sparks, 1983). Key organizational factors include school and district climate, leadership attitudes and behaviors, district policies and systems, and the involvement of participants.

While staff development fosters the professional growth of individuals, organizational development addresses the organization's responsibility to define and meet changing self-improvement goals (Dillon-Peterson, 1981). Consequently, effective organizations have the capacity to continually renew themselves and solve problems. Within this context, individuals can grow.

In earlier sections of this chapter, five models of staff development were discussed that have solid foundations in research and/or practice and are being used in increasingly robust forms throughout the country. While each model requires somewhat different organizational supports to make it successful, it is also true that research points to a common set of attributes of the organizational context without which staff development can have only limited success (Loucks-Horsley et al., 1987). In organizations where staff development is most successful:

- Staff members have a common, coherent set of goals and objectives that they have helped formulate, reflecting high expectations of themselves and their students.
- Administrators exercise strong leadership by promoting a "norm of collegiality," minimizing status differences between themselves and their staff members, promoting informal communication, and reducing their own need to use formal controls to achieve coordination.
- Administrators and teachers place a high priority on staff development and continuous improvement.
- Administrators and teachers make use of a variety of formal and informal processes for monitoring progress toward goals, using them to identify obstacles to such progress and ways of overcoming these obstacles, rather than using them to make summary judgments regarding the "competence" of particular staff members (Conley & Bacharach, 1987).
- Knowledge, expertise, and resources, including time, are drawn on appropriately, yet liberally, to initiate and support the pursuit of staff development goals.

This section briefly highlights the research that supports these organizational attributes.

Organizational Climate

Little (1982) found that effective schools are characterized by norms of collegiality and experimentation. Simply put, teachers are more likely to persist in using new behaviors when they feel the support of colleagues and when they believe that professional risk taking (and its occasional failures) are encouraged. Fullan (1982) reports that the degree of change is strongly related to the extent to which teachers interact with each other and provide technical help to one another. "Teachers need to participate in skill-training workshops," Fullan writes, "but they also need to have one-to-one and group opportunities to receive and give help, and more simply to converse about the meaning of change" (p. 121).

Joyce and Showers (1983) point out that "in a loose and disorganized social climate without clear goals, reticent teachers may actually subvert elements of the training process not only for themselves but also for others" (p. 31). While teacher commitment is desirable, it need not necessarily be present initially for the program to be successful. Miles (1983) found that teacher/administrator harmony was critical to the success of improvement efforts, but that it could develop over the course of an improvement effort. Initially, working relationships between teachers and administrators had to be clear and supportive enough so that most participants could "suspend disbelief," believing that the demands of change would be dealt with together (Crandall, 1983). In their study of school improvement efforts that relied heavily on staff development for their success, both Miles and Crandall found that in projects where a mandated strategy caused some initial disharmony between teachers and administrators, the climate changed as the new program's positive impact on students became clear. When a new program was selected carefully and teachers received good training and support, most who were initially skeptical soon agreed with and were committed to the effort. Showers, Joyce, and Bennett (1987) support the position that, at least initially, teachers' ability to use a new practice in a competent way may be more important than commitment.

Few would disagree with the importance of a school and district climate that encourages experimentation and supports teachers to take risks, i.e., establishes readiness for change (Wood, Thompson, & Russell, 1981). Yet a supportive context consists of more than "good feelings." The quality of the recommended practices is also critical. Research conducted by Guskey (1986) and Loucks and Zacchei (1983) indicates that the new practices developed or chosen by or for teachers need to be effective ones—effective by virtue of evaluation results offered by the developer or by careful testing by the teachers who have developed them. These researchers found that only when teachers see that a new program or practice enhances the learning of their students will their beliefs and attitudes change in a significant way.

Leadership and Support

According to the Rand Change Agent Study (McLaughlin & Marsh, 1978), active support by principals and district administrators is critical to the success of any change effort. According to McLaughlin and Marsh (1978):

> The Rand research sets the role of the principal as instructional leader in the context of strengthening the school improvement process through team building and problem solving in a "project-like" context. It suggests that principals need to give clear messages that teachers may take responsibility for their own professional growth. (p. 92)

Stallings and Mohlman (1981) determined that teachers improved most in staff development programs where the principal supported them and was clear and consistent in communicating school policies. Likewise, Fielding and Schalock (1985) report a study in which principals' involvement in teachers' staff development produced longer-term changes than when principals were not involved.

In their discussion of factors that affect the application of innovations, Loucks and Zacchei (1983) wrote ". . . administrators in successful improvement sites take their leadership roles seriously and provide the direction needed to engage teachers in the new practices" (p. 30).

According to Huberman (1983), teachers' successful use of new skills often occurs when administrators exert strong and continuous pressure for implementation. He argues that ". . . administrators, both at the central office and building levels, have to go to center stage and stay there if school improvement efforts are to succeed" (p. 27). While administrator presence is important, administrators must also act as gate-keepers of change so that "innovation overload" can be avoided (Anderson & Odden, 1986).

While much research points to administrators as being key leaders in staff development and change, it is also true that others can take on leadership and support roles—and may in fact be better placed to do so. Research on school improvement indicates that a team approach can help orchestrate leadership and support "functions" which can be shared by administrators (building and district level), district coordinators or staff developers, teachers, and external trainers and consultants (Loucks-Horsley & Hergert, 1985). For example, Cox (1983) reports that while principals seem to play an important role in clarifying expectations and goals and stabilizing the school organization, central office coordinators, who often know more about a specific practice, can effectively coach teachers in their attempts to change their classroom behavior. Coordinated leadership can also help avoid situations such as a school's textbooks and curriculum not matching the instructional models teachers are being taught to use (Fielding & Schalock, 1985).

District Policies and Systems

Staff development activities occur within the context of a school district's staff development program. According to Ellis (1989), a comprehensive staff development program includes a philosophy, goals, allocation of resources, and coordination. The philosophy spells out beliefs that guide the program. District, school, and individual goals (and their accompanying action plans) provide direction to staff development efforts. Resources need to be allocated at the district, school, and individual levels so that these goals have a reasonable chance of being achieved. Staff development programs need to be coordinated by individuals who have an assigned responsibility for this area. Ellis also supports the use of a district-level staff development committee to aid in coordination of programs.

The selection, incorporation, or combination of the models of staff development described in this chapter are the responsibility of the district's staff development structure. Decisions about their use need to match the intended outcomes if they are to be effective (Levine & Broude, 1989), but these decisions are also influenced by state and/or community initiatives aimed at the improvement of schools and/or teaching (Anderson & Odden, 1986).

Participant Involvement

Research clearly indicates that involving participants in key decisions about staff development is necessary for a program to have its greatest impact. According to Lieberman and Miller (1986), a supportive context for staff development requires both a "top-down" and a "bottom-up" approach. The top-down component sets a general direction for the district or school and communicates expectations regarding performance. The bottom-up processes involve teachers in establishing goals and designing appropriate staff development activities.

The establishment of common goals is important to the success of staff development efforts (Ward & Tikunoff, 1981). Odden and Anderson's (1986) research indicates that a clearly defined process of data collection, shared diagnosis, and identification of solutions to problems must be employed during the planning phase. Collaboration, from initial planning through implementation and institutionalization, is a key process in determining these goals and in influencing lasting change (Lambert, 1984; McLaughlin & Marsh, 1978; Wood, Thompson, & Russell, 1981).

Lortie (1986) argues that when teachers perceive that they can participate in important school-level decisions, the relationship between the extra efforts required by school improvement and the benefits of these efforts becomes clearer. Following this argument, he recommends that schools be given relatively little detailed supervision, but be monitored instead for results based on explicit criteria.

Others report that, when teachers cannot be involved in initial decisions regarding staff development (e.g., when it is mandated by state legislation or when it supports the use of district-wide curriculum), their involvement in decisions about the "hows" and "whens" of implementation can be important to success. Furthermore, teachers' involvement in developing curriculum and as trainers for staff development programs can contribute in important ways to the success of an effort (Loucks & Pratt, 1979).

Odden and Anderson (1986) capture the reciprocal relationship between organization and individual development in this discussion of their research:

> When instructional strategies, which aim to improve the skills of individuals, were successful, they had significant effects on schools as orga-

nizations. When school strategies, which aim to improve schools as organizations, were successful, they had significant impacts on individuals. (p. 585)

The importance of paying attention to the context of staff development is underscored by Fullan (1982). He responds to educators who say that they cannot provide the elements required to support change (e.g., supportive principals, a 2- or 3-year time period for implementation):

> Well don't expect much implementation to occur . . . I say this not because I am a cynic but because it is wrong to let hopes blind us to the actual obstacles to change. If these obstacles are ignored, the experience with implementation can be harmful to the adults and children directly involved—more harmful than if nothing had been done. (p. 103)

CONCLUSION

Staff development is a relatively young "science" within education. In many ways the current knowledge base in staff development is similar to what was known about teaching in the early 1970s. During the 1970s and early 1980s research on teaching advanced from descriptive to correlational to experimental (Gage, 1984). With the exception of research on training, much of the staff development literature is theoretical and descriptive rather than experimental. The remaining two sections describe what can be said with some confidence about the research base for the staff development models and what remains to be learned.

What Can Be Said with Confidence

Staff development possesses a useful "craft knowledge" that guides the field. This craft knowledge includes ways to organize, structure, and deliver staff development programs (Caldwell, 1989). It was disseminated in the 1980s through publications such as *The Journal of Staff Development, Educational Leadership,* and *Phi Delta Kappan,* and through thousands of presentations at workshops and conventions. As a result, hundreds of staff development programs were established in urban, suburban, and rural school districts throughout the United States and Canada. This craft knowledge serves another useful purpose: It can guide researchers in asking far better questions than they could have asked previously.

Of the five models discussed in this chapter, the research on training is the most robust. It is the most widely used form of staff development and the most thoroughly investigated. As a result, it is possible to say with some confidence which training elements are required to promote the attainment of specific outcomes. Likewise, research on coaching has demonstrated the importance of in-classroom assistance to teachers (by an "expert" or by a peer) for the transfer of training to the classroom.

The consensus of "expert opinion" is that school improvement is a systemic process (Fullan, 1982). This ecological approach recognizes that changes in one part of a system influence the other parts. Consequently, staff development both influences and is influenced by the organizational context in which it takes place. The impact of the staff development models that have been discussed depends not only upon their individual or blended use, but upon the features of the organization in which they are used.

While this appears to relate to the "art" of making staff development work (i.e., the judgment with which one combines and juggles the various organizational interactions), there is also much "science" that can be drawn from when it comes to the organizational supports necessary for effective staff development. Study after study confirms the necessity of:

- Schools possessing norms that support collegiality and experimentation
- District and building administrators who work with staff to clarify goals and expectations and who actively commit to and support teachers' efforts to change their practice
- Efforts that are strongly focused on changes in curricular, instructional, and classroom management practices with improved student learning as the goal
- Adequate, appropriate staff development experiences with follow-up assistance that continues long enough for new behaviors to be incorporated into ongoing practice

Interestingly enough, it appears that these factors apply to a wide variety of school improvement and staff development efforts. While there are little hard research data on some of the models discussed above (see next section), most if not all of these factors will certainly persist as being important, regardless of what is learned about other models.

What We Need to Learn More About

While the work of staff developers during the 1980s was grounded in theory and research from various disciplines (e.g., adult learning, organization development, training), the scientific base of their own practice (with the exception of training and coaching) was quite thin. Unfortunately, the systematic study of some of the models discussed earlier is difficult because their use is not widespread. Listed below are areas for further study.

1. We need research to determine the potency of the models described above (with the exception of training).   We need to learn which models are most effective for which outcomes with which teachers. For instance, we might ask: How effective is individually guided staff development for knowledge level outcomes for self-directed experienced teachers? Or: How effective is an inquiry approach in helping beginning teachers learn their craft?

2. We need a better understanding of the impact on student learning of the four non-training staff development models.   Do non-training models alter teacher knowledge or skills in a way that improves student learning?

3. We need to know more about the impact on teachers of blending the models described above in a comprehensive staff development program.   How are teachers' attitudes, knowledge, and skills altered when they choose among and blend various models as the means of reaching one or more "growth" goals? For instance, what would be the result if a teacher blended individually guided staff development (e.g., reading research on tracking), observation/assessment (e.g., peer observation), and training (e.g., in co-operative learning) as means to alter classroom practices that are viewed as disadvantageous to a subgroup of students?

4. We need a systemic view of comprehensive staff development at the district level. Most districts provide a variety of staff development opportunities to teachers. Some purposely support individual, school-based, and district-based activities. We need descriptive studies of what these programs look like, both from the overall, coordination point of view and from the individual teacher point of view. We need to know: How are goals set and coordinated? How are resources allocated? How equitable are opportunities for individual teachers? How do different contextual factors (e.g., resources, state mandates) influence success?

5. We need to understand more about the relative costs of different staff development models and combinations of the models. Moore and Hyde (1978, 1981) have conducted some useful analyses of how many school district resources actually go for staff development purposes. But more micro-analyses would be useful to understand the cost-effectiveness of relatively labor-intensive models (e.g., coaching) versus those that rely only on the activity of a single teacher (e.g., individually guided staff development).

6. Finally, we need to look at staff development as it contributes to teacher professionalism and teacher leadership. Many believe that teacher professionalism and leadership must characterize our education system in the future if that system is to survive. Yet there are as many different definitions of the terms as there are ideas of how to implement them. One role of staff development research is to help identify and clarify the various meanings given to these concepts. We then need descriptive studies of staff development's contributions to these efforts, with special attention to how these efforts influence the conduct of staff development.

It is possible that future research may contradict current craft knowledge (this, for example, has occurred with the learning that attitude change

does not always have to precede behavior change), or, as is likely, future research will support current practice. Many questions about effective staff development remain unanswered. The need is great for well-designed, long-term studies of school improvement efforts that are based on staff development. The field of staff development seeks a solid base that moves beyond description and advocacy to a better understanding of those factors that support and improve classroom practice.

ENDNOTE

This chapter was adapted from "Models of Staff Development," in W. Robert Houston (Ed.), *Handbook of Research on Teacher Education.* New York: Macmillan, 1990.

REFERENCES

Acheson, K. A., & Gall, M. D. (1980). *Techniques in the Clinical Supervision of Teachers.* White Plains, NY: Longman.

Ainsworth, A. (1976). "Teachers Talk about In-service Education." *Journal of Teacher Education, 27:* 107–109.

Anderson, B., & Odden, A. (1986). "State Initiatives Can Foster School Improvement." *Phi Delta Kappan, 67*(8): 578–581.

Berman, P., & McLaughlin, M. (1978). *Federal Programs Supporting Educational Change: Vol. 8. Implementing and Sustaining Innovation.* Santa Monica, CA: Rand Corporation.

Blanchard, K., & Johnson, S. (1982). *The One Minute Manager.* New York: William Morrow.

Boyer, E. (1983). *High School: A Report on Secondary Education in America.* New York: Harper & Row.

Brandt, R. (1987). "On Teachers Coaching Teachers: A Conversation with Bruce Joyce." *Educational Leadership, 44*(5): 12–17.

Brim, J., & Tollett, D. (1974). "How Do Teachers Feel about Inservice Education?" *Educational Leadership, 31:* 21–25.

Caldwell, S. (Ed.). (1989). *Staff Development: A Handbook of Effective Practices.* Oxford, OH: National Staff Development Council.

Casner-Lotto, J. (1988). "Expanding the Teacher's Role: Hammond's School Improvement Process." *Phi Delta Kappan, 69*(5): 349–353.

Cohen, M. (1981). "Effective Schools: What the Research Says." *Today's Education, 70*: 466–469.

Conley, S., & Bacharach, S. (1987). "The Holmes Group Report: Standards, Hierarchies, and Management." *Teachers College Record, 88*(3): 340–347.

Cox, P. L. (1983). "Complementary Roles in Successful Change." *Educational Leadership, 41*(3): 10–13.

Crandall, D. (1983). "The Teacher's Role in School Improvement." *Educational Leadership, 41*(3): 6–9.

Crandall, D., & Loucks. S. (1983). *A Roadmap for School Improvement.* Executive Summary of *People, Policies, and Practices: Examining the Chain of School Improvement.* Andover, MA: The NETWORK, Inc.

Cross, P. (1987). "The Adventures of Education in Wonderland: Implementing Education Reform." *Phi Delta Kappan, 68*(7): 496–502.

Dewey, J. (1933). *How We Think.* Chicago: Henry Regnery Co.

Dillon-Peterson, B. (1981). "Staff Development/Organizational Development—Perspective 1981." In B. Dillon-Peterson (Ed.), *Staff Development/Organization Development* (pp. 1–10). Alexandria, VA: Association for Supervision and Curriculum Development.

Dunn, R., & Dunn, K. (1978). *Teaching Students through Their Individual Learning Styles: A Practical Approach.* Reston, VA: Reston Publishing Co.

Ellis, S. (1989). "Putting It All Together: An Integrated Staff Development Program." In S. Caldwell (Ed.), *Staff Development: A Handbook of Effective Practices* (pp. 58–69). Oxford, OH: National Staff Development Council.

Fielding, G., & Schalock, H. (1985). *Promoting the Professional Development of Teachers and Administrators.* Eugene, OR: ERIC Clearinghouse on Educational Management. (ERIC Document Reproduction Service No. EA 017 747).

Fullan, M. (1982). *The Meaning of Educational Change.* Toronto: OISE Press.

Gable, R., & Rogers, V. (1987). "Taking the Terror out of Research." *Phi Delta Kappan, 68*(9): 690–695.

Gage, N. (1984). "What Do We Know about Teaching Effectiveness?" *Phi Delta Kappan, 66*(2): 87–93.

Glatthorn, A. (1984). *Differentiated Supervision.* Alexandria, VA: Association for Supervision and Curriculum Development.

Glatthorn, A. (1987). "Cooperative Professional Development: Peer-centered Options for Teacher Growth." *Educational Leadership, 45*(3): 31–35.

Glickman, E. (1986). "Developing Teacher Thought." *Journal of Staff Development, 7*(1): 6–21.

Good, T., & Grouws, D. (1987). "Increasing Teachers' Understanding of Mathematical Ideas through Inservice Training." *Phi Delta Kappan, 68*(10): 778–783.

Gregorc, A. (1979). "Learning/Teaching Styles: Their Nature and Effects." In *Student Learning Styles: Diagnosing and Prescribing Programs.* Reston, VA: National Association of Secondary School Principals.

Guskey, T. (1986). "Staff Development and the Process of Teacher Change." *Educational Researcher, 15*(5): 5–12.

Hall, G., & Loucks, S. (1978). "Teacher Concerns as a Basis for Facilitating and Personalizing Staff Development." *Teachers College Record, 80*(1): 36–53.

Hering, W., & Howey, K. (1982). *Research in, on, and by Teachers' Centers.* Occasional Paper No. 10. San Francisco: Teachers' Center Exchange, Far West Laboratory for Educational Research and Development.

Hovda, R., & Kyle, D. (1984). "A Strategy for Helping Teachers Integrate Research into Teaching." *Middle School Journal, 15*(3): 21–23.

Huberman, A. (1983). "School Improvement Strategies That Work: Some Scenarios." *Educational Leadership, 41*(3): 23–27.

Hunter, M. (1982). *Mastery Teaching.* El Segundo, CA: TIP Publications.

Ingvarson, L. (1987). *Models of Inservice Education and Their Implications for Professional Development Policy.* Paper presented at a conference on "Inservice Education: Trends of the Past, Themes for the Future," Melbourne, Australia.

Jefferson County Public Schools (1974). *Report of the Task Force to Define the Process of Developing Curriculum.* Lakewood, CO: Author.

Johnson, D., Johnson, R., Holubec, E., & Roy, P. (1984). *Circles of Learning.* Alexandria, VA: Association for Supervision and Curriculum Development.

Joyce, B., & Peck, L. (1977). *Inservice Teacher Education Project Report II: Interviews.* Syracuse, NY: Syracuse University.

Joyce, B., & Showers, B. (1982). "The Coaching of Teaching." *Educational Leadership, 40*(1): 4–10.

Joyce, B., & Showers, B. (1983). *Power in Staff Development through Research in Training.* Alexandria, VA: Association for Supervision and Curriculum Development.

Joyce, B., & Showers, B. (1988). *Student Achievement through Staff Development.* New York: Longman.

Joyce, B., & Weil, M. (1972). *Models of Teaching.* Englewood Cliffs, NJ: Prentice-Hall.

Kells, P. (1981, January). "Quality Practices in Inservice Education." *The Developer.* Oxford, OH: National Staff Development Council.

Kerman, S. (1979). "Teacher Expectations and Student Achievement." *Phi Delta Kappan, 60*(10): 716–718.

Kidd, J. (1973). *How Adults Learn.* Chicago: Follett Publishing Co.

Kimpston, R., & Rogers, K. (1987). "The Influence of Prior Perspectives, Differences in Participatory Roles, and Degree of Participation on Views about Curriculum Development: A Case Study." *Journal of Curriculum and Supervision, 2*(3): 203–220.

Knowles, M. (1980). *The Modern Practice of Adult Education.* Chicago: Association/Follett Press.

Kyle, R. (Ed.) (1985). *Reaching for Excellence: An Effective School Sourcebook.* Washington, DC: U.S. Government Printing Office.

Lambert, L. (1984). *How Adults Learn: An Interview Study of Leading Researchers, Policy Makers, and Staff Developers.* Paper presented at the annual meeting of the American Educational Research Association, New Orleans, LA.

Lawrence, G. (1974). *Patterns of Effective Inservice Education: A State of the Art Summary of Research on Materials and Procedures for Changing Teacher Behaviors in Inservice Education.* Gainesville: University of Florida College of Education. (ERIC Document Reproduction Service No. ED 176 424)

Levine, S. (1989). *Promoting Adult Growth in Schools: The Promise of Professional Development.* Boston: Allyn and Bacon.

Levine, S., & Broude, N. (1989). "Designs for Learning." In S. Caldwell (Ed.), *Staff Development: A Handbook of Effective Practices.* Oxford, OH: National Staff Development Council.

Lieberman, A. (1986). "Collaborative Research: Working With, Not Working On." *Educational Leadership, 43*(5): 28–32.

Lieberman, A., & Miller, L. (1984). *Teachers, Their World and Their Work: Implications for School Improvement.* Alexandria, VA: Association for Supervision and Curriculum Development.

Lieberman, A., & Miller, L. (1986). "School Improvement: Themes and Variations." In A. Lieberman (Ed.), *Rethinking School Improvement: Research,*

Craft, and Concept. New York: Teachers College Press.

Little, J. (1982). "Norms of Collegiality and Experimentation: Work-Place Conditions of School Success." *American Educational Research Journal, 19*(3): 325–340.

Lortie, D. (1986). "Teacher Status in Dade County: A Case of Structural Strain?" *Phi Delta Kappan, 67*(8): 568–575.

Loucks, S., & Pratt, H. (1979). "A Concerns-Based Approach to Curriculum Change." *Educational Leadership, 37*(3): 212–215.

Loucks, S., & Zacchei, D. (1983). "Applying Our Findings to Today's Innovations." *Educational Leadership, 41*(3): 28–31.

Loucks-Horsley, S., & Hergert, L. (1985). *An Action Guide to School Improvement.* Alexandria, VA: Association for Supervision and Curriculum Development. Andover, MA: The NETWORK, Inc.

Loucks-Horsley, S., Harding, C., Arbuckle, M., Murray, L., Dubea, C., & Williams, M. (1987). *Continuing to Learn: A Guidebook for Teacher Development.* Andover, MA: Regional Laboratory for Educational Improvement of the Northeast and Islands, and the National Staff Development Council.

Louis, K., & Rosenblum, S. (1981). *Linking R & D with Schools: A Program and Its Implications for Dissemination and School Improvement Policy.* Washington, DC: National Institute of Education.

Mann, D. (1984–85). "Impact II and the Problem of Staff Development." *Educational Leadership, 42*(4): 44–47.

McGreal, T. (1982). "Effective Teacher Evaluation Systems." *Educational Leadership, 39*(4): 303–305.

McGreal, T. (1983). *Successful Teacher Evaluation.* Alexandria, VA: Association for Supervision and Curriculum Development.

McLaughlin, M., & Marsh, D. (1978). "Staff Development and School Change." *Teachers College Record, 80*(1): 69–94.

Miles, M. (1983). "Unraveling the Mystery of Institutionalization." *Educational Leadership, 41*(3): 14–19.

Moore, D., & Hyde, A. (1978). *Rethinking Staff Development: A Handbook for Analyzing Your Program and Its Costs.* New York: Ford Foundation.

Moore, D., & Hyde, A. (1981). *Making Sense of Staff Development Programs and Their Costs in Three Urban Districts.* Chicago: Designs for Change.

Mosher, W. (1981). *Individual and Systemic Change Mediated by a Small Educational Grant Program.*

San Francisco: Far West Laboratory for Educational Research and Development.

Odden, A., & Anderson, B. (1986). "How Successful State Education Improvement Programs Work." *Phi Delta Kappan, 67*(8): 582–585.

Rauth, M. (1986). "Putting Research to Work." *American Educator, 10*(4): 26–31.

Robbins, P., & Wolfe, P. (1987). "Reflections on a Hunter-Based Staff Development Project." *Educational Leadership, 44*(5): 56–61.

Rogers, C. (1969). *Freedom to Learn.* Columbus, OH: Charles E. Merrill.

Scholl, S., & McQueen, P. (1985). "The Basic Skills Articulation Plan: Curriculum Development through Staff Development." *Journal of Staff Development, 6*(2): 138–142.

Shalaway, T. S. (1985). "Peer Coaching . . . Does It Work?" *R & D Notes.* Washington, DC: National Institute of Education.

Showers, B., Joyce, B., & Bennett, B. (1987). "Synthesis of Research on Staff Development: A Framework for Future Study and a State-of-art Analysis." *Educational Leadership, 45*(3): 77–87.

Simmons, J., & Sparks, G. (1985). "Using Research to Develop Professional Thinking about Teaching." *Journal of Staff Development, 6*(1): 106–116.

Sparks, G. (1983). "Synthesis of Research on Staff Development for Effective Teaching." *Educational Leadership, 41*(3): 65–72.

Sparks, G. (1986). "The Effectiveness of Alternative Training Activities in Changing Teaching Practices." *American Educational Research Journal, 23*(2): 217–225.

Sparks, G., & Simmons, J. (1989). "Inquiry-Oriented Staff Development: Using Research as a Source of Tools, Not Rules." In S. Caldwell (Ed.), *Staff Development: A Handbook of Effective Practices* (pp. 126–139). Oxford, OH: National Staff Development Council.

Sparks, G., Nowakowski, M., Hall, B., Alec, R., & Imrick, J. (1985). "School Improvement through Staff Development." *Educational Leadership, 42*(6): 59–61.

Stallings, J., & Mohlman, G. (1981). *School Policy, Leadership Style, Teacher Change, and Student Behavior in Eight Schools, Final Report.* Washington, DC: National Institute of Education.

Thompson, S. (1982). *A Survey and Analysis of Pennsylvania Public School Personnel Perceptions of Staff Development Practices and Beliefs with a View to Identifying Some Critical Problems or Needs.* Unpublished Dissertation, The Pennsylvania State University, University Park, PA.

Tikunoff, W., & Ward, B. (1983). "Collaborative Research on Teaching." *The Elementary School Journal, 83*(4): 453–468.

Wade, R. (1985). "What Makes a Difference in Inservice Teacher Education? A Meta-analysis of Research." *Educational Leadership, 42*(4): 48–54.

Ward, B., & Tikunoff, W. (1981, September). "The Relationship between Inservice Training, Organizational Structure and School Climate." *Inservice,* 7–8.

Watts, H. (1985). "When Teachers Are Researchers, Teaching Improves." *Journal of Staff Development, 6*(2): 118–127.

Wise, A., & Darling-Hammond, L. (1985). "Teacher Evaluation and Teacher Professionalism." *Educational Leadership, 42*(4): 28–33.

Wood, F. (1989). "Organizing and Managing School-based Staff Development." In S. Caldwell (Ed.), *Staff Development: A Handbook of Effective Practices* (pp. 26–43). Oxford, OH: National Staff Development Council.

Wood, F., & Kleine, P. (1987). *Staff Development Research and Rural Schools: A Critical Appraisal.* Unpublished paper, University of Oklahoma, Norman.

Wood, F., McQuarrie, F., & Thompson, S. (1982). "Practitioners and Professors Agree on Effective Staff Development Practices." *Educational Leadership, 43*: 63–66.

Wood, F., Thompson, S., & Russell, F. (1981). "Designing Effective Staff Development Programs." In B. Dillon-Peterson (Ed.), *Staff Development/Organization Development* (pp. 59–91). Alexandria, VA: Association for Supervision and Curriculum Development.

Wu, P. (1987). "Teachers as Staff Developers: Research, Opinions, and Cautions." *Journal of Staff Development, 8*(1): 4–6.

Yarger, S., Howey, K., & Joyce, B. (1980). *Inservice Teacher Education.* Palo Alto, CA: Booksend Laboratory.

Zeichner, K. (1983). "Alternative Paradigms of Teacher Education." *Journal of Teacher Education, 34*(3): 3–9.

Zigarmi, P., Betz, L., & Jensen, D. (1977). "Teacher Preference in and Perceptions of Inservice." *Educational Leadership, 34*: 545–551.

DISCUSSION QUESTIONS

1. How is knowledge of adult learning theory integrated into the underlying assumptions of the five staff development models described?
2. In what ways can staff development programs aid teachers in school improvement or curriculum development?
3. What kind of staff development program would you design to assist your colleagues in mainstreaming students?
4. Discuss the similarities and differences between the inquiry model of staff development, reflective action, and an independent research initiative.
5. How do school district attitudes and climate variables influence staff development program efforts?

30

What the World Can Teach Us about New Teacher Induction

HARRY K. WONG
TED BRITTON
TOM GANSER

FOCUSING QUESTIONS

1. What are some new teacher induction techniques?
2. How does extended teacher assistance training shape a new teacher's experience? What are the benefits?
3. How does teacher induction aid in teacher retention?
4. How can teacher induction aid seasoned teachers (those that have been teaching over 5 years)? The administration? The community?
5. What are some ways to combat isolation/alienation in U.S. schools? What are ways that teachers, administration, and community can do this?

An effective teacher is perhaps the most important factor in producing consistently high levels of student achievement.[1] Thus the profession must see to it that teachers are continually learning throughout their careers, and that process begins with those newest to the profession. A new teacher induction program can acculturate newcomers to the idea that professional learning must be a lifelong pursuit.

A book edited by Ted Britton, Lynn Paine, David Pimm, and Senta Raizen provides a more detailed look at how five countries—Switzerland, Japan, France, New Zealand, and China (Shanghai)—acculturate their new teachers, specifically their science and mathematics teachers, and shape their entry into the profession.[2] In this chapter, we share a brief summary of the findings reported in that volume.

The five countries studied provide well-funded support that reaches all beginning teachers, incorporates multiple sources of assistance, typically lasts at least two years, and goes beyond the imparting of mere survival skills. For example, in Switzerland, new teachers are involved in practice groups, in which they network to learn effective problem solving. In Shanghai, new teachers join lesson-preparation and teaching-research groups. New teachers in New Zealand take part in a 25-year-old Advice and Guidance program that extends for 2 years. Lesson study groups are the mode in Japan, while in France, new teachers work for an extended time with groups of peers who share experiences, practices, tools, and professional language.

Before we go into more detail about these programs, a basic definition of induction is in order. *Induction* is a highly organized and comprehensive form of staff development, involving many people and components, that typically continues as a sustained process for the first 2 to 5 years of a teacher's career. Mentoring is often a component of the induction process.

The exponential growth in the number of induction programs in the United States attests to the value that staff developers and other school leaders ascribe to them. Educational leaders have eagerly adapted their approaches to induction to reflect the many changes in the teaching profession.[3] But induction programs are a global phenomenon, and here we offer to U.S. leaders a summary of the best practices of the international programs reported by Britton and his colleagues.

SWITZERLAND

In the Swiss system, teachers are assumed to be lifelong learners. From the start, beginning teachers are viewed as professionals, and induction focuses on the development of the person as well as on the development of the professional.

Induction begins during student teaching as teams of three students network with one another. It continues for beginning teachers in practice groups of about half a dozen teachers and is carried forward in mutual classroom observations between beginning teachers and experienced teachers. Thus induction moves seamlessly from a teacher's preservice days to novice teaching to continuing professional learning.

The Swiss philosophy explicitly rejects a deficit model of induction, which assumes that new teachers lack training and competence and thus need mentors. Instead, several cantons provide a carefully crafted array of induction experiences for new teachers, including

- *Practice groups.* These are a form of structured, facilitated networking that supports beginning teachers from different schools as they learn to be effective solvers of practical problems.
- *Standortbestimmung.* Practice groups generally conclude with a group Standortbestimmung—a form of self-evaluation of the first year of teaching that reflects the Swiss concern with developing the whole person as well as the teacher.
- *Counseling.* Counseling is generally available for all teachers, but a greater number of

beginning teachers take part. It can grow out of the practice groups and can involve one-on-one mentoring of classroom practice. In some cantons, counseling is mandatory for beginning teachers.
- *Courses.* Course offerings range from obligatory courses to voluntary courses available on a regular basis to impulse courses, which are put together on short notice to meet a short-term need.

These practices are supported with training for practice-group leaders, counselors, and mentors.

A professional team heads the whole set of induction activities and is in charge of the practice-group leaders. These leaders, all active teachers themselves, are the key to the quality of the practice groups and other components of induction, such as classroom visits and individual counseling. These individuals are relieved of some of their teaching duties to make time for their responsibilities as practice-group leaders. They also receive additional pay and are themselves supported by the central team. The group leaders are trained to carry out their responsibilities and take part in a wide range of professional development offerings to increase their competence as leaders.

CHINA (SHANGHAI)

The teaching culture in Shanghai features research groups and collective lesson planning. It is a culture in which all teachers learn to engage in joint work to support their teaching and their personal learning, as well as the learning of their pupils. The induction process is designed to help bring new teachers into this culture.

There is an impressive array of learning opportunities at both the school and the district level, among them

- Welcoming ceremonies at the school
- District-level workshops and courses
- District-organized teaching competitions
- District-provided mentoring
- A district hot line for new teachers that connects them with subject specialists
- District awards for outstanding novice/mentor work

- Half-day training sessions at colleges of education and in schools for most weeks for the first year of teaching
- Peer observation, both in and outside of school
- Public, or open, lessons, with debriefing and discussion of the lesson afterwards
- Report lessons, in which a new teacher is observed and given comments, criticisms, and suggestions
- Talk lessons, in which a teacher (new or experienced) talks through a lesson and provides justification for its design, but does not actually teach it
- Inquiry projects and action research carried out by new teachers, with support from those on the school or district teaching research section or induction staff
- District- or school-developed handbooks for new teachers and mentors
- End-of-year celebrations of teachers' work and collaboration

In keeping with the collective and collaborative focus of the teaching culture in Shanghai, a number of other critical components play a role in the induction process for new teachers.

Lesson-Preparation Groups

The heart of the professional learning culture is the lesson-preparation group. These groups engage new and veteran teachers in discussing and analyzing the lessons they are teaching.

Teaching-Research Groups

A beginning teacher is also a member of a teaching-research group, which provides a forum for the discussion of teaching techniques. Each teacher, new or experienced, must observe at least eight lessons a semester, and most teachers observe more. It is very common for teachers to enter others' classrooms and to engage in discussion about mutually observed teaching. These conversations help new teachers acquire the language and adopt the norms of public conversation about teaching, and that conversation becomes a natural part of the fabric of any teacher's professional life.

Teaching Competitions

Districts organize teaching competitions with the goal of motivating new teachers and encouraging the serious study of and preparation for teaching. The competitions also identify and honor outstanding accomplishment. Lessons are videotaped so that the district can compile an archive for future use. Teaching thus becomes community property, not owned privately by one teacher, but shared by all.

NEW ZEALAND

In New Zealand, the induction phase is called the Advice and Guidance (AG) program. The AG program is seen as the initial phase of the life-long professional development of teachers. Every beginning teacher is released from 20 percent of work time to participate in the program.

Teachers and school-level administrators are willing to invest in the effort to support beginning teachers partly because schools are required to provide an AG program. Provisionally registered teachers must document the AG support they received during their first 2 years when they apply for a permanent certificate. But many of those who provide support for new teachers view their assistance as a commitment to the teaching profession.

The National Ministry of Education also provides limited regional resources for professional development services to beginning teachers. Regional meetings, which attract teachers from different schools, provide for the free exchange of induction experiences among a wide variety of participants. Although there is a national handbook outlining the goals of the AG program, the extent, nature, and quality of the local programs vary widely.

At the local school, an administrator or a staff member is typically the coordinator of the AG program. The people involved most directly in supporting beginning teachers are typically the AG coordinator, department heads, "buddy teachers," and, to a lesser extent, all other school staff members. In schools that have more than one beginning teacher, the AG coordinator convenes all the beginning teachers every 2 weeks throughout most of the year. Observation of teaching is a key activity in school-level induction programs and comes in several varieties. As in Switzerland, facilitated peer support is an important induction strategy.

Ted Britton explains that one reason New Zealand was chosen as a subject for study was the contrast it offered to countries that place a great deal of the responsibility for assisting beginning teachers on a single mentor or on just a couple of people. (He was alluding to the United States.) Indeed, we were struck by the variety of the sources of support in New Zealand and by how the schools make use of a range of induction activities. Throughout the education system in New Zealand, there is a universal commitment to supporting beginning teachers.

JAPAN

Teaching in Japan is regarded as a high-status occupation, a dignified profession. New teachers have a reduced teaching load and are assigned guiding teachers. The guiding teacher is the key to success in the Japanese system.

In-School Teacher Education

In their first year, all new teachers typically teach two or more demonstration lessons, which are viewed by prefectural administrators, the guiding teacher, the school principal or assistant principal, and other teachers in the school. The demonstration, or "study teaching," lesson, a traditional Japanese method for improving teaching, is a formal public lesson, which is observed and then subjected to critique by colleagues.

James Stigler and James Hiebert view these lessons and their subsequent public analysis as the core activity of in-school teacher education.[4] To prepare for their public lessons, the new teachers write and rewrite their lesson plans, practice teaching the lesson with one of their classes, and modify the lesson with the help of a guiding teacher. They might even call teachers from neighboring schools, whom they know from their university or prefectural classes, and seek their help and advice.

In Japan, as in Shanghai, teaching is viewed as a public activity, open to scrutiny by many. The induction process welcomes beginners into that open practice and provides beginning teachers with many regular opportunities to observe their peers, their guiding teachers, and other teachers in their school, as well as those in other schools. No special arrangements need to be made, for schools and teaching are organized to allow for such open observations. Indeed, the method is so universal that all teachers have experienced it, and all seem to see its wisdom and believe in its efficacy. The most critical factor is that it is the lesson that is criticized, not the teacher.

New teachers are also required to submit a culminating "action research" project based on a classroom lesson they would like to investigate. This project is usually about 30–40 pages in length and is handed in to the prefectural education office (though no formal feedback on it is provided). These projects are accumulated in the prefectural inservice offices and are available for other teachers to use.

Japanese teachers do not have their own, isolated offices. Rather, teams or even an entire staff occupy one large room with individual desks and the accompanying equipment and supplies. Thus a new teacher receives help from many teachers, since most veteran teachers believe it is their responsibility to help new teachers become successful.

Out-of-School Teacher Education

Most out-of-school activity occurs under the guidance of a city or prefectural inservice center. Such a center is usually housed in a rather large building, is well staffed with specialists in most disciplines, and is dedicated to the inservice development of local teachers

Induction is only the first phase of a teacher's professional learning. All Japanese teachers must participate in sponsored inservice programs 5, 10, and 20 years after their induction program has been completed.

FRANCE

To become a certified secondary teacher in France, one must successfully pass a highly competitive national recruitment examination, both oral and written. A new teacher is referred to as a *stagiaire*, which translates roughly as someone who is undertaking a stage of development or formation.

A pedagogical advisor, appointed by a regional pedagogical inspector, is provided for all secondary school stagiaires. When new teachers need advice, the advisors give it, but the teachers are encouraged to proceed on their own. Stagiaires observe one another's classes on numerous occasions.

All new teachers are required to attend off-campus sessions several days per week at the nearest Institut Universitaire de Formation des Mâitres (IUFM), an institution created in 1991 specifically to handle teacher education and development. The main goal of the IUFM is to increase both the intellectual status of teacher education and the professionalism of teachers.

At the IUFM, groups of stagiaires meet, and their work is directed by their *formateur*, an experienced teacher educator who teaches in the classroom part time and is employed part time by the IUFM. *Formation,* which translates roughly as development or shaping, is the process a new teacher undergoes to become a member of the teaching profession, and the formateur is the person who provides formative experiences. A typical day for a new teacher might include

- Preparing several lessons, teaching the lessons, and marking the pupils' homework
- Tutoring a smaller group of pupils
- Observing the pedagogical advisor teach and discussing features of the lesson
- Observing, participating in, and discussing lessons taught by a teacher in a different school in the same town
- Working on aspects of teaching for a day and a half at the IUFM

A professional *memoir*, written under the guidance of a memoir tutor, is required of every new teacher. The memoir is a report on some detailed exploratory work relating to some aspect of teaching practice or to an academic issue. It can be done either individually or by a pair of stagiaires.

The compulsory learning opportunities for stagiaires are varied. In France, first-year teaching and learning about teaching take place in a number of settings, and a certain amount of flexibility is required, as stagiaires move between institutional settings. The French view working with different teachers as ideal for formation, because these experiences bring the stagiaires into contact with a considerable number of different people in varied roles: the formateurs, the pedagogical advisors; the school staff in different schools, including administrators and teachers of various subjects; the memoir tutor; different groups of pupils; parents; and possibly the regional pedagogical inspectors.

Stagiaires can come to think of the group with which they work at the IUFM as a "tribe," a group of same-subject teachers working together in their joint area of specialization. And the notion of tribe is an important one. Various things support the integrity of a tribe: shared experience, shared practices, shared tools, and shared language.

To an outsider, this process might look like induction that ends after the first year of teaching. But the French view it as simply part of teacher formation; it is the method by which the system takes in new members.

APPLICATION TO U.S. SCHOOLS

Although the approaches to the induction of new teachers in these five countries differ from one another, they do have three major similarities that can provide useful ideas for staff developers responsible for induction programs in the United States First, the induction approaches are highly structured, comprehensive, rigorous, and seriously monitored. There are well-defined roles for staff developers, administrators, and instructors, mentors, or formateurs.

In contrast, the professional development programs in the United States are often sporadic, incoherent, and poorly aligned, and they lack adequate follow-up.[5] The amount of time devoted to professional development in a given area is most commonly about 1 day during the year for any given teacher.[6]

Second, the induction programs of the five countries focus on professional learning and on the growth and professionalism of teachers. They achieve these ends through an organized, sustained professional development system that employs a variety of methods. These countries all consider their induction programs to be one phase or a single part of a total lifelong professional learning process.

In contrast, in more than 30 states, the nearly universal U.S. practice seems remarkably narrow: mentoring predominates, and often there is little more.[7] In many schools, one-on-one mentoring is the dominant or even the sole strategy for supporting new teachers, and it often lacks real structure and relies on the willingness of the veteran teacher and the new teacher to seek each other out. Many mentors are assigned to respond to new teachers' need for day-to-day survival tips, and so they function primarily as a safety net for the new teachers.

Third, collaboration is a strength of each of these five induction programs. Collaborative group work is understood, fostered, and accepted as a part of the teaching culture in all five countries surveyed. Experiences, practices, tools, and language are shared among teachers. And it is the function of the induction phase to engender this sense of group identity in new teachers and to help experienced teachers begin treating them as colleagues.

In contrast, isolation is the common thread and complaint among new teachers in U.S. schools. New teachers want more than a job. They want to experience success. They want to contribute to a group. They want to make a difference. Thus collegial interchange, not isolation, must become the norm for U.S. teachers.[8]

Indeed, the most successful U.S. induction programs go beyond mentoring.[9] They are structured, sustained, intensive professional development programs that allow new teachers to observe others, to be observed by others, and to be part of networks or study groups, in which all teachers share with one another and learn to respect one another's work. Michael Garet and his colleagues confirmed this finding when they showed that teachers learn more in teacher networks and study groups than with mentoring.[10]

In their examination of over 30 new teacher induction programs in the United States, Annette Breaux and Harry Wong also found the inevitable presence of a leader.[11] These leaders have created organized and comprehensive induction programs that stress collaboration and professional growth. Teacher induction programs that rely on networking and collaboration can be found in such places as the Flowing Wells Schools in Tucson, Arizona (the Institute for Teacher Renewal and Growth); the Lafourche Parish Schools in Lafourche, Louisiana (the Framework for Inducting, Retaining, and Supporting Teachers program); and the Dallas Public Schools in Dallas, Texas (New Teacher Initiatives: New Teacher Support and Development Programs and Services).

The district staff developer and the building principal are the keys to establishing the commitment to teacher improvement and student achievement. But the bottom line remains: Good teachers make the difference. Districts that provide structured, sustained induction, training, and support for their teachers achieve what every school district seeks to achieve—improved student learning through improved professional learning.

ENDNOTES

1. Eric A. Hanushek, John F. Kain, and Steven G. Rivkin, "Why Public Schools Lose Teachers," Working Paper 8599, National Bureau of Economic Research (Cambridge, Mass., 2001); and Aubrey Wang et al., *Preparing Teachers around the World* (Princeton, N. J.: Educational Testing Service, 2003), available at *www. ets.org/research/pic.*

2. Edward Britton et al., eds., *Comprehensive Teacher Induction: Systems for Early Career Learning* (Dordrecht, Netherlands: Kluwer Academic Publishers and WestEd, 2003), available at *www.WestEd.org.*

3. Tom Ganser, "The New Teacher Mentors: Four Trends That Are Changing the Look of Mentoring Programs for New Teachers," *American School Board Journal*, December 2002, pp. 25–27; and Tom Ganser, "Sharing a Cup of Coffee Is Only a Beginning," *Journal of Staff Development*, Fall 2002, pp. 28–32.

4. James Stigler and James Hiebert, *The Teaching Gap* (New York: Free Press, 1999).

5. Wang et al., *Preparing Teachers.*

6. Basmat Parsad, Laurie Lewis, and Elizabeth Farris, *Teacher Preparation and Professional Development, 2000* (Washington, D.C.: National Center for Education Statistics, 2001).

7. Edward Britton et al., "More Swimming, Less Sinking. Perspectives from Abroad on U.S. Teacher Induc-

tion," paper prepared for the National Commission on Mathematics and Science Teaching in the 21st Century, San Francisco, 2000.

8. Harry K. Wong, "Collaborating with Colleagues to Improve Student Learning," Eisenhower National Clearinghouse, ENC Focus, vol. 11, no. 6, 2003, available at *www.enc.org/features/focus;* and "Induction Programs That Keep Working," in Marge Scherer, ed., *Keeping Good Teachers* (Alexandria, Va.: Association for Supervision and Curriculum Development, 2003),

chap. 5, available at *www.newteacher.com*—click on "Published Papers."

9. Annette L. Breaux and Harry K. Wong, *New Teacher Induction: How To Train, Support, and Retain New Teachers* (Mountain View, Calif.: Harry K. Wong Publications, 2003).

10. Michael Garet, "What Makes Professional Development Effective?" *American Educational Research*, Winter 2001, pp. 915–946.

11. Breaux and Wong, *New Teacher Induction*.

DISCUSSION QUESTIONS

1. What kind of professional support did you receive when you first became a teacher? Was this support adequate?
2. Is the support that beginning teachers receive today any better than the support that you received?
3. Which country's induction program described in this chapter sounds most appealing to you?
4. Which induction practices do you think are least likely to be adopted in the United States? Why?
5. What changes in induction practices would be of most benefit to teachers in the United States?

31

Results-Oriented Professional Development

THOMAS R. GUSKEY

FOCUSING QUESTIONS

1. What is professional development?
2. What evidence is there to confirm that professional development programs are effective?
3. How can meta-analysis help to identify the elements of a successful professional development program?
4. In what ways does consideration of context influence the design of a professional development program?
5. Why should change efforts be introduced in a gradual and incremental fashion?
6. How are teamwork and collaboration related to successful professional development programs?
7. In what ways are support and pressure integral to successful professional development programs?

Never before in the history of education has there been greater recognition of the importance of professional development. Every proposal to reform, restructure, or transform schools emphasizes professional development as a primary vehicle in efforts to bring about needed change. With this increased recognition, however, has come increased scrutiny.

Questions are being raised about the effectiveness of all forms of professional development. And with these questions have come increased demands for demonstrable results. Legislators, policy makers, funding agencies, and the general public all want to know if professional development programs really make a difference. If they do, what evidence is there to show that they are effective?

To address these questions, professional developers are considering more seriously the issues of program evaluation. They are beginning to gather information more regularly on the outcomes of professional development activities. And this information is no longer limited to surveys of teachers' attitudes and practices. Increasingly, information on crucial measures of student learning is also being considered (Guskey & Sparks, 1991).

But perhaps more importantly, professional developers are looking more seriously at the research on professional development in education. They are examining what is known about the various forms of professional development, not only for teachers but for all those involved in the educational process. They also are considering what is known about various organizational characteristics and structures, especially those that facilitate ongoing professional growth.

This chapter will examine what that research says about the effectiveness of professional development. In particular, I will consider the mixed messages reformers are getting from this research and how we might make sense of those messages. I will then turn to a series of guidelines for professional development, drawn principally from the research on individual and organizational change. Finally, I will consider the potential impact of implementing these guidelines.

RESEARCH ON PROFESSIONAL DEVELOPMENT

The research base on professional development in education is extensive. For the most part, however, this research has documented the inadequacies of professional development and, occasionally, proposed solutions (Epstein, Lockard, & Dauber, 1988; Griffin, 1983; Guskey, 1986; Joyce & Showers, 1988; Lieberman & Miller, 1979; Orlich, 1989; Wood & Thompson, 1980, 1993).

Still, reformers attempting to make sense of these various solutions quickly find themselves faced with seemingly incompatible dichotomies. For instance:

- Some researchers suggest that professional development efforts designed to facilitate change must be teacher specific and focus on the day-to-day activities at the classroom level (McLaughlin, 1990; Weatherley & Lipsky, 1977; Wise, 1991). Others indicate that an emphasis on individuals is fundamental to progress, and more systemic or organizational approaches are necessary (Tye & Tye, 1984; Waugh & Punch, 1987).
- Some experts stress that reforms in professional development must be initiated and carried out by individual teachers and school-based personnel (Joyce, McNair, Diaz, & McKibbin, 1976; Lambert, 1988; Lawrence, 1974; Massarella, 1980). Others emphasize that the most successful programs are guided by a clear vision that transcends the walls of individual classrooms and schools, since individual teachers and school-based individuals generally lack the opportunity to conceive and implement worthwhile improvements (Barth, 1991; Clune, 1991; Mann, 1986; Wade, 1984).
- Some reviewers argue that the most effective professional development programs are those that approach change in a gradual and incremental fashion, not expecting too much at one

time (Doyle & Ponder, 1977; Fullan, 1985; Mann, 1978; Sparks, 1983). Others insist that the broader the scope of a professional development program is, the more effort required of teachers, and the greater the overall change in teaching style attempted, the more likely the program is to elicit the enthusiasm of teachers and to be implemented well (Berman, 1978; McLaughlin & Marsh, 1978).

These and other similar dichotomies in the professional development literature leave reformers feeling confused. Many question how they can be expected to design and implement successful professional development programs when even researchers and experts in the field cannot agree on what should be done. While the critical issues seem clear, solutions remain elusive. As a result, reformers struggle desperately in their attempts to address educators' many and highly diverse professional development needs.

THE SEARCH FOR AN OPTIMAL MIX

A major problem in these efforts to identify elements of successful professional development programs is that they are generally looking for "one right answer." Most begin by gathering evidence from a variety of studies, investigations, and program evaluations. This evidence is then combined and synthesized to identify those characteristics that are consistently associated with some measure of effectiveness. The modern technique many researchers use to conduct such a synthesis is called *meta-analysis* (Hedges & Olkin, 1985).

In most cases, program effectiveness is judged by an index of participants' satisfaction with the program or some indication of change in participants' professional knowledge. Only rarely is change in professional practice considered, and rarer still is the assessment of any impact on student learning (Guskey & Sparks, 1991). The result of such an effort is usually a prescription composed of general practices described in broad and nebulous terms. Unfortunately, such prescriptions offer little guidance to practically minded reformers who want to know precisely what to do and how to do it.

What is neglected in nearly all of these efforts is the powerful impact of *context*. In fact, synthesizing the evidence across studies is done specifically to eliminate the effects of context, or to decontextualize the data. Yet, as Clark, Lotto, and Astuto (1984), Firestone and Corbett (1987), Fullan (1985), Huberman and Miles (1984), and others suggest, the uniqueness of the individual setting will always be a critical factor in education. While there may be some general principles that apply throughout, most will need to be adapted, at least in part, to the unique characteristics of that setting.

Businesses and industries operating in different parts of the country or in different regions around the world may successfully utilize identical processes to produce the same quality product. But reforms based on assumptions of uniformity in the educational system repeatedly fail (Elmore & McLaughlin, 1988). The teaching and learning process is a complex endeavor that is embedded in contexts that are highly diverse. This combination of complexity and diversity makes it difficult, if not impossible, for researchers to come up with universal truths (Guskey, 1993; Huberman, 1983, 1985).

We know with certainty that reforms in education today succeed to the degree that they adapt to and capitalize on this variability. In other words, they must be shaped and integrated in ways that best suit local values, norms, policies, structures, resources, and processes (Griffin & Barnes, 1984; McLaughlin, 1990; Talbert, McLaughlin, & Rowan, 1993).

Recognizing the importance of contextual differences brings clarity to the dichotomies described earlier. That is, successful change efforts in some contexts require professional development that focuses on teacher-specific activities (Porter, 1986; Wise, 1991), while other contexts demand a more systemic or organizational approach (Sarason, 1990).

In some contexts, teacher-initiated efforts work best (Weatherley & Lipsky, 1977), while in others a more administratively directed approach may be needed (Mann, 1986). And while some contexts demand that professional development take a gradual approach to change (Sparks, 1983), others require immediate and drastic alterations at all levels of the organization (McLaughlin, 1990).

Acknowledging the powerful influence of context also shows the futility of any search for "one right answer." Rather than one right answer, there will be a collection of answers, each specific to a context. Our search must focus, therefore, on finding the *optimal mix*—that assortment of professional development processes and technologies that will work best in a particular setting.

We also must recognize, however, that the optimal mix in a particular setting changes over time. Contexts, like the people who shape them, are dynamic. They change and adapt in response to a variety of influences. Some of these influences may be self-initiated, while others are environmentally imposed. Because of this dynamic nature, the optimal mix for a particular context evolves over time, changing as various aspects of the context change. What works today may be quite different from what worked five years ago, but also is likely to be different from what will work five years hence.

GUIDELINES FOR SUCCESS

Because of the powerful and dynamic influence of context, it is impossible to make precise statements about the elements of an effective professional development program. Even programs that share a common vision and seek to attain comparable goals may need to follow very different pathways to succeed. The best that can be offered, therefore, are *procedural guidelines* that appear to be critical to the professional development process.

These guidelines are derived from research on professional development specifically and on the change process generally (Crandall et al., 1982; Fullan, 1991; Guskey, 1986; Huberman & Miles, 1984; Prochaska, DiClemente, & Norcross, 1992; McLaughlin, 1990). Rather than representing strict requirements, these guidelines reflect a framework for developing that optimal mix of professional development processes and technologies that will work best in a specific context at a particular time.

In reviewing these guidelines, it is important to keep in mind that at present we know far more about professional development processes that fail than we do about those that succeed (Gall

& Renchler, 1985; Showers, Joyce, & Bennett, 1987). There is no guarantee, therefore, that following these guidelines will result in successful professional development programs. Nevertheless, substantial evidence indicates that neglecting the issues described in these guidelines at best will limit success and, at worst, will result in programs that fail to bring about significant or enduring change.

1. Recognize that change is both an individual and an organizational process.

An important lesson learned from the past is that we cannot improve schools without improving the skills and abilities of the teachers and principals within them. In other words, we must see change as an *individual process* and be willing to invest in the intellectual capital of those individuals who staff our schools (Wise, 1991).

Success in any improvement effort always hinges on the smallest unit of the organization and, in education, that is the classroom (McLaughlin, 1991). Teachers are the ones chiefly responsible for implementing change. Therefore, professional development processes, regardless of their form (Sparks & Loucks-Horsley, 1989), must not only be relevant to teachers, but must directly address their needs and concerns (Hall & Loucks, 1978; Weatherley & Lipsky, 1977).

Yet to see change as *only* an individual process can limit the effectiveness of professional development. Even changes that are empowering bring a certain amount of anxiety. And teachers, like professionals in many fields, are reluctant to adopt new practices or procedures unless they feel sure that they can make them work (Lortie, 1975). To change or to try something new means to risk failure, and that is both highly embarrassing and threatening to one's sense of professional pride (Pejouhy, 1990).

Furthermore, it is important to keep in mind that organizations, like individuals, must change (Sarason, 1982; Shroyer, 1990; Waugh & Punch, 1987). To focus exclusively on individuals in professional development efforts and to neglect factors such as organizational features and system politics severely limit the likelihood of success (Berman, 1978; Clift, Holland, & Veal, 1990; Deal, 1987; Fullan & Pomfret, 1977; Parker,

1980). A debilitating environment can quash any change effort, no matter how much we exhort individuals to persist (Beane, 1991).

To focus on change as *only* an organizational matter, however, is equally ineffective. Fiddling with the organizational structure is a favorite device of educational policy makers and administrators, because it communicates to the public symbolically that they are concerned with the performance of the system. But, as Elmore (1992) argues, evidence is scant that such structural change leads in any reliable way to changes in how teachers teach, what they teach, or how students learn. McLaughlin (1990) describes this as the difference between macro-level concerns and micro-level realities. To facilitate change, we must look beyond policy and consider the embedded structure that most directly affects the actions and choices of the individuals involved.

The key is to find the optimal mix of individual *and* organizational processes that will contribute to success in a particular context. In some situations, individual initiative and motivation might be high, but organizational structures stand in the way of significant improvement. In others, progressive and supportive organizational structures may be in place, but the lack of personal incentives for collaboration and experimentation inhibit any meaningful change in classroom practice. Viewing change as both an individual *and* an organizational process that must be adapted to contextual characteristics will help to clarify the steps necessary for success in professional development.

2. Think big but start small.

There is no easier way to sabotage change efforts than to take on too much at one time. In fact, if there is one truism in the vast research literature on change, it is that the magnitude of change that people are asked to make is inversely related to their likelihood of making it (Guskey, 1991). Professionals at all levels generally oppose radical alterations to their present procedures. Hence, the probability of their implementing a new program or innovation depends largely on their judgment of the magnitude of change required for implementation (Doyle & Ponder, 1977; Fullan, 1982; Mann, 1978).

Successful professional development programs are those that approach change in a gradual and incremental fashion. Efforts are made to illustrate how the new practices can be implemented in ways that are not too disruptive and do not require a great deal of extra work (Sparks, 1983). If a new program does require major changes, it is best to ease into its use rather than expect comprehensive implementation at once (Fullan, 1985).

But while the changes advocated in a professional development program must not be so ambitious that they require too much too soon, they need to be sufficient in scope to challenge professionals and kindle interest (McLaughlin, 1990). Crandall, Eisemann, and Louis (1986) argue that the greatest success is likely when the size of the change is not so massive that typical users find it necessary to adopt a coping strategy that seriously distorts the change, but large enough to require noticeable, sustained effort. Modest, narrowly conceived projects seldom bring about significant improvement. This is what is meant by "think big."

The key again is to find the optimal mix. Professional development efforts should be designed with long-term goals based on a grand vision of what is possible. A program might seek to have *all* students become successful learners, for example. At the same time, that vision should be accompanied by a strategic plan that includes specific incremental goals for three to five years into the future, gradually expanding on what is successful in that context and offering support to those engaged in the change (Fullan, 1992; Louis & Miles, 1990).

3. Work in teams to maintain support.   The discomfort that accompanies change is greatly compounded if the individuals involved perceive that they have no say in the process or if they feel isolated and detached in their implementation efforts. For this reason it is imperative that all aspects of a professional development program be fashioned to involve teams of individuals working together. This means that planning, implementation, and follow-up activities should be seen as joint efforts, providing opportunities for those with diverse interests and responsibilities to offer their input and advice (Massarella, 1980).

To ensure that the teams function well and garner broad-based support for professional development efforts, it is important that they involve individuals from all levels of the organization. In school improvement programs, for example, the best professional development teams include teachers, noninstructional staff members, and building and central office administrators (Caldwell & Wood, 1988).

In some contexts the involvement of parents and community members also can be helpful (Lezotte, 1989). Although the roles and responsibilities of these individuals in the professional development process will be different, all have valuable insights and expertise to offer.

Still, the notion of teamwork must be balanced. There is evidence to show, for instance, that large-scale participation during the early stages of a change effort is sometimes counterproductive (Huberman & Miles, 1984). Elaborate needs assessments, endless committee and task force meetings, and long and tedious planning sessions often create confusion and alienation in the absence of any action. Extensive planning can also exhaust the energy needed for implementation so that, by the time change is to be enacted, people are burned out (Fullan, 1991).

Furthermore, broad-based participation in many decisions is not always essential or possible on a large scale (Dawson, 1981; Hood & Blackwell, 1980). As Little (1989) argues, there is nothing particularly virtuous about teamwork or collaboration *per se.* It can serve to block change or inhibit progress just as easily as it can serve to enhance the process.

To facilitate change, teamwork must be linked to established norms of continuous improvement and experimentation. In other words, teamwork and collaboration must be balanced with the expectation that all involved in the process—teachers, administrators, and noninstructional staff members—are constantly seeking and assessing potentially better practices (Little, 1989). Such a balance promotes collegial interaction and acknowledges the naturally occurring relationships among professionals.

The most successful professional development programs, for example, are those that provide regular opportunities for participants to share perspectives and seek solutions to common problems in an atmosphere of collegiality and professional respect (Fullan, Bennett, & Rolheiser-Bennett, 1989; Little, 1982). Working in teams also allows tasks and responsibilities to be shared. This not only reduces the workload of individual team members, but it also enhances the quality of the work produced. Additionally, working in teams helps to focus attention on the shared purposes and improvement goals that are the basis of the professional development process in that context (Leithwood & Montgomery, 1982; Rosenholtz, 1987; Stevenson, 1987).

4. Include procedures for feedback on results. If the use of new practices is to be sustained and changes are to endure, the individuals involved need to receive regular feedback on the effects of their efforts. It is well known that successful actions are reinforcing and likely to be repeated, while those that are unsuccessful tend to be diminished.

Similarly, practices that are new and unfamiliar will be accepted and retained when they are perceived as increasing one's competence and effectiveness. This is especially true of teachers, whose primary psychic rewards come from feeling certain about their capacity to affect student growth and development (Bredeson, Fruth, & Kasten, 1983; Guskey, 1989; Huberman, 1992).

New practices are likely to be abandoned, however, in the absence of any evidence of their positive effects. Hence, specific procedures to provide feedback on results are essential to the success of any professional development effort.

Personal feedback on results can be provided in a variety of ways, depending on the context. In professional development programs involving the implementation of mastery learning (Bloom, 1968, 1971), for example, teachers receive this feedback from their students through regular formative assessments (Bloom, Madaus, & Hastings, 1981).

In mastery learning classrooms, formative assessments are used to provide students with detailed feedback on their learning progress and to diagnose learning problems. As such, they can take many forms, including writing samples, skill demonstrations, projects, reports, performance tasks, or other, more objective assessment devices such as quizzes or tests. These assessments are then paired with corrective activities designed to help students to remedy any learning errors identified through the assessment.

But, in addition to the feedback that they offer students, formative assessments also offer teachers specific feedback on the effectiveness of their application of mastery learning. These regular checks on student learning provide teachers with direct evidence of the results of their teaching efforts. They illustrate what improvements have been made and where problems still exist. This information then can be used to guide revisions in the instructional process so that even greater gains are achieved (Guskey, 1985).

Of course, results from assessments of student learning are not the only type of personal feedback that teachers find meaningful. Brophy and Good (1974) discovered that providing feedback to teachers about their differential treatment of students resulted in significant change in their interactions with students.

Information on increased rates of student engagement during class sessions and evidence of improvements in students' sense of confidence or self-worth also have been shown to be powerful in reinforcing the use of new instructional practices (Dolan, 1980; Stallings, 1980). Information from informal assessments of student learning and moment-to-moment responses during instruction can also provide a basis for teachers to judge the effectiveness of alternative techniques (Fiedler, 1975; Green, 1983; Smylie, 1988).

Yet, despite its importance, the procedure for gathering feedback on results must be balanced with other concerns. The methods used to obtain feedback, for example, must not be disruptive to instructional procedures. Furthermore, they should not require inordinate amounts of time or extra work from those engaged in the difficult process of implementation.

Timing issues are also critical, for it is unfair to expect too much too soon from those involved in implementation. As Loucks-Horsley et al. (1987) point out, this is analogous to pulling a plant out of the ground each day to check its roots for growth. In other words, the need for feedback must be adapted to the characteristics of the program and the setting. Feedback procedures must focus on outcomes that are meaningful to the professionals involved, but also timed to best suit program needs and the constraints of the context.

5. *Provide continued follow-up, support, and pressure.* Few persons can move from a professional development experience directly into successful implementation. In fact, few will even venture into the uncertainty of implementation unless there is an appreciation of the difficulties and potential problems involved (Fullan & Miles, 1992).

Fitting new practices and techniques to unique on-the-job conditions is an uneven process that requires time and extra effort, especially when beginning (Berman, 1978; Joyce and Showers, 1980). Guidance, direction, and support with pressure are crucial when these adaptations are being made (Baldridge & Deal, 1975; Fullan, 1991; Parker, 1980; Waugh & Punch, 1987).

What makes the early stages of implementation so complicated is that the problems encountered at this time are often multiple, pervasive, and unanticipated. Miles and Louis (1990) point out that developing the capacity to deal with these problems promptly, actively, and in some depth may be "the single biggest determinant of program success" (p. 60). And, regardless of how much advanced planning or preparation takes place, it is when professionals actually implement the new ideas or practices that they have the most specific problems and doubts (Berman, 1978; Fullan & Pomfret, 1977).

Support coupled with pressure at this time is vital for continuation. Support allows those engaged in the difficult process of implementation to tolerate the anxiety of occasional failures. Pressure is often necessary to initiate change among those with little self-impetus for change (Airasian, 1987; Huberman & Crandall, 1983). In addition, it provides the encouragement, motivation, and occasional nudging that many practitioners require to persist in the challenging tasks that are intrinsic to all change efforts.

Of all aspects of professional development, this aspect of support with pressure is perhaps the most neglected. It makes clear that, to be successful, professional development must be seen as a *process,* not an event (Loucks-Horsley et al., 1987). Learning to be proficient at something new or finding meaning in a new way of doing things is difficult and sometimes painful. Furthermore, any change that holds great promise for increasing individuals' competence or enhancing an organization's effectiveness is likely to be slow and require extra work (Huberman & Miles, 1984). It is imperative, therefore, that improvement be seen as a continuous and ongoing endeavor (McLaughlin & Marsh, 1978).

If a new program or innovation is to be implemented well, it must become a natural part of practitioners' repertoire of professional skills and built into the normal structures and practices of the organization (Fullan & Miles, 1992; Miles & Louis, 1987). For advances to be made and professional improvements to continue, the new practices and techniques that were the focus of the professional development effort must be used automatically. And, for this to occur, continued support and encouragement, paired with subtle pressure to persist, are essential.

This crucial support with pressure can be offered in a variety of ways. McLaughlin and Marsh (1978) recommend that local resource personnel or consultants be available to provide on-line assistance when difficulties arise. They emphasize, however, that the quality of the assistance is critical and that it is better to offer no assistance than poor or inappropriate assistance.

Joyce and Showers (1988) suggest that support for change take the form of coaching—providing practitioners with technical feedback, guiding them in adapting the new practices to their unique contextual conditions, helping them to analyze the effects of their efforts, and urging them to continue despite minor setbacks. In other words, coaching is personal, practical, on-the-job assistance that can be provided by consultants, administrators, directors, or professional colleagues. Simply offering opportunities for practitioners to interact and share ideas with each other also can be valuable (Massarella, 1980; McLaughlin & Marsh, 1978).

Here, again, the notion of balance is critical. In some contexts a substantial amount of pressure from leaders may be necessary to overcome inertia, recalcitrance, or outright resistance (Mann, 1986). It is possible, for example, when making decisions about instructional practices to overemphasize teachers' personal preferences and underemphasize concern about student learning (Buchmann, 1986). Yet, in contexts where there is considerable individual initiative, such pressure may be seen as a strong-armed tactic and unprofessional (Leiter & Cooper, 1978). The key is to find the optimal mix for that context, understanding well the interpersonal dynamics of the individuals involved and the culture of the organization in which they work.

6. Integrate programs.

More so than any other profession, education seems fraught with innovation. In fact, innovations seem to come and go in education about as regularly as the seasons change. Each year new programs are introduced in schools without any effort to show how they relate to the ones that came before or those that may come afterward. Furthermore, there is seldom any mention of how these various innovations contribute to a growing professional knowledge base. The result is an enormous overload of fragmented, uncoordinated, and ephemeral attempts at change (Fullan & Miles, 1992).

The steady stream of innovations in education causes many practitioners to view all new programs as isolated fads that will soon be gone, only to be replaced by yet another bandwagon (Latham, 1988). This pattern of constant, yet unrelated, short-term innovations not only obscures improvement and provokes cynicism, but it also imposes a sense of affliction. Having seen a multitude of innovations come into and go out of fashion, veteran teachers frequently calm the fears of their less experienced colleagues who express concern about implementing a new program with the advice, "Don't worry; this too shall pass."

If professional development efforts that focus on the implementation of innovations are to succeed, they must include precise descriptions of how these innovations can be integrated. That is, each new innovation must be presented as part of a coherent framework for improvement. It is difficult enough for practitioners to learn the particular features of one innovation, let alone to figure out how it can be combined with others. And, because no single innovation is totally comprehensive, implementing only one will leave many problems unresolved. It is only when several strategies are carefully and systematically integrated that substantial improvements become possible. Doyle (1992), Sarason (1990), and others also emphasize that coordinating programs and combining ideas release great energy in the improvement process.

In recent years, insightful researchers have described how different combinations of innovations can yield impressive results (e.g., Arredondo & Block, 1990; Davidson & O'Leary, 1990; Guskey, 1988, 1990a; Mevarech, 1985; Weber, 1990). In addition, several frameworks for integrating a collection of programs or innovations have been developed that practitioners are finding especially useful.

One example is a framework developed by Marzano, Pickering, and Brandt (1990) based on various dimensions of learning. Another developed by Guskey (1990b) is built around five major components in the teaching and learning process. These frameworks allow skilled practitioners to see more clearly the linkages between various innovations. They also offer guidance to the efforts of seriously minded reformers seeking to pull together programs that collectively address the problems that are most pressing in a particular context.

A crucial point here is that the particular collection of programs or innovations that is best undoubtedly will vary from setting to setting. As a result, the way linkages are established and applications integrated will need to vary as well.

Fullan (1992) stresses that "schools are not in the business of managing single innovations; they are in the business of contending with multiple innovations simultaneously" (p. 19). By recognizing the dimensions of learning that a particular innovation stresses or the components of the teaching and learning process that it emphasizes, savvy educators can pull together innovations that collectively address what is most needed in that context at a particular time.

CONCLUSION

The ideas presented in these procedural guidelines are not really new and certainly cannot be considered revolutionary. They may, in fact, appear obvious to those with extensive experience in the professional development process. Yet, as self-evident as they may seem, it is rare to find a professional development program today that is designed and implemented with thorough attention to these guidelines or the factors that underlie them. It is rarer still to find professional development programs that evaluate the implementation of these guidelines in terms of their effects on student learning.

What is evident from these guidelines is that the key to greater success in professional development, which translates to improvements in student learning, rests not so much in the discovery of new knowledge, but in our capacity to deliberately and wisely use the knowledge that we have. This is true regardless of whether professional development is viewed as an integral part of one's career cycle, as a self-directed journey to find meaning and appreciation in one's work, or as a structured effort to keep professionals abreast of advances in their field. To develop this capacity requires a clear vision of the process by which those goals can be attained.

In the minds of many today, there is a clear vision of what would be ideal in professional development. That ideal sees educators at all levels constantly in search of new and better ways to address the diverse learning needs of their students. It sees schools as learning communities in which teachers and students are continually engaged in inquiry and stimulating discourse. It sees practitioners in education respected for their professional knowledge and pedagogic skill.

The exact process by which that vision can be accomplished, however, is blurred and confused. The reason, as we have argued here, is that the process is so highly contextualized. There is no "one right answer" or "one best way." Rather,

there are a multitude of ways, all adapted to the complex and dynamic characteristics of specific contexts. Success, therefore, rests in finding the optimal mix of process elements and technologies that can then be carefully, sensibly, and thoughtfully applied in a particular setting.

While it is true that the ideas presented here offer an optimistic perspective on the potential of professional development in education, these ideas are not far-fetched. They illustrate that, although the process of change is difficult and complex, we are beginning to understand how to facilitate that process through pragmatic adaptations to specific contexts so that ongoing professional growth and improved professional practice are ensured. Doing so is essential to the improved learning of all students.

ENDNOTE

This chapter is adapted from a chapter in T. R. Guskey and M. Huberman (Eds.), *Professional Development in Education: New Paradigms and Practices,* Teachers College Press. Copyright T. Guskey, 1995.

REFERENCES

Airasian, P. W. (1987). "State Mandated Testing and Educational Reform: Context and Consequences." *American Journal of Education, 95*: 393–412.

Arredondo, D. E., & Block, J. H. (1990). "Recognizing the Connections Between Thinking Skills and Mastery Learning." *Educational Leadership, 47*(5): 4–10.

Baldridge, J. V., & Deal, T. (1975). *Managing Change in Educational Organizations.* Berkeley, CA: McCutchan.

Barth, R. S. (1991). "Restructuring Schools: Some Questions for Teachers and Principals." *Phi Delta Kappan, 73*(2): 123–128.

Beane, J. A. (1991). "Sorting Out the Self-Esteem Controversy." *Educational Leadership, 49*(1): 25–30.

Berman, P. (1978). "The Study of Macro- and Micro-implementation." *Public Policy, 26*(2): 157–184. In P. Berman & M. W. McLaughlin (Eds.), *Federal Programs Supporting Educational Change. Vol. VIII: Implementing and Sustaining Innovations.* Santa Monica, CA: Rand Corporation.

Bloom, B. S. (1968). "Learning for Mastery." *Evaluation Comment, 1*(2): 1–12.

Bloom, B. S. (1971). "Mastery Learning." In J. H. Block (Ed.), *Mastery Learning: Theory and Practice.* New York: Holt, Rinehart & Winston.

Bloom, B. S., Madaus, G. F., & Hastings, J. T. (1981). *Evaluation to Improve Learning.* New York: McGraw-Hill.

Bredeson, P. V., Fruth, M. J., & Kasten, K. L. (1983). "Organizational Incentives and Secondary School Teaching." *Journal of Research and Development in Education, 16*: 24–42.

Brophy, J. E., & Good, T. L. (1974). *Teacher—Student Relationships: Causes and Consequences.* New York: Holt, Rinehart & Winston.

Buchmann, M. (1986). "Role over Person: Morality and Authenticity in Teaching." *Teachers College Record, 87*: 529–543.

Caldwell, S., & Wood, F. (1988). "School-based Improvement—Are We Ready?" *Educational Leadership, 46*(2): 50–53.

Clark, D., Lotto, S., & Astuto, T. (1984). "Effective Schools and School Improvement: A Comparative Analysis of Two Lines of Inquiry." *Educational Administration Quarterly, 20*(3): 41–68.

Clift, R. T., Holland, P. E., & Veal, M. L. (1990). "School Context Dimensions That Affect Staff Development." *Journal of Staff Development, 11*(1): 34–38.

Clune, W. H. (1991). *Systemic Educational Policy.* Madison, WI: Wisconsin Center for Educational Policy, University of Wisconsin-Madison.

Crandall, D., Eisemann, J., & Louis, K. (1986). "Strategic Planning Issues That Bear on the Success of School Improvement Efforts." *Educational Administration Quarterly, 22*(3): 21–53.

Crandall, D. P., Loucks-Horsley, S., Bauchner, J. E., Schmidt, W. B., Eiseman, J. W., Cox, P. L., Miles, M. B., Huberman, A. M., Taylor, B. L., Goldberg, J. A., Shive, G., Thompson, C. L., & Taylor, J. A. (1982). *People, Policies, and Practices: Examining the Chain of School Improvement.* Andover, MA: The Network.

Davidson, N., & O'Leary, P. W. (1990). "How Cooperative Learning Can Enhance Mastery Teaching." *Educational Leadership, 47*(5): 30–34.

Dawson, J. (1981). *Teacher Participation in Educational Innovation: Some Insights into Its Nature.* Philadelphia: Research for Better Schools.

Deal, T. (1987). "The Culture of Schools." In L. Sheive & M. Schoeheit (Eds.), *Leadership: Examining the Elusive* (pp. 3–15). Alexandria, VA: Association for Supervision and Curriculum Development.

Dolan, L. J. (1980). *The Affective Correlates of Home Support, Instructional Quality, and Achievement.* Unpublished doctoral dissertation, University of Chicago.

Doyle, D. P. (1992). "The Challenge, the Opportunity." *Phi Delta Kappan, 73*(7): 512–520.

Doyle, W., & Ponder, G. (1977). "The Practical Ethic and Teacher Decision-making." *Interchange, 8*(3): 1–12.

Elmore, R. F. (1992). "Why Restructuring Alone Won't Improve Teaching." *Educational Leadership, 49*(7): 44–48.

Elmore, R. F., & McLaughlin, M. W. (1988). *Steady Work: Policy, Practice, and Reform in American Education* (R-3574-NIE/RC). Santa Monica, CA: Rand Corporation.

Epstein, J. L., Lockard, B. L., & Dauber, S. L. (1988). *Staff Development Policies Needed in the Middle Grades.* Paper presented at the annual meeting of the American Educational Research Association, New Orleans, LA.

Fiedler, M. (1975). "Bidirectionality of Influence in Classroom Interaction." *Journal of Educational Psychology, 67*: 735–744.

Firestone, W., & Corbett, H. D. (1987). "Planned Organizational Change." In N. Boyand (Ed.), *Handbook of Research on Educational Administration* (pp. 321–340). New York: Longman.

Fullan, M. G. (1982). *The Meaning of Educational Change.* New York: Teachers College Press.

Fullan, M. G. (1985). "Change Processes and Strategies at the Local Level." *Elementary School Journal, 85*: 391–421.

Fullan, M. G. (1991). *The New Meaning of Educational Change.* New York: Teachers College Press.

Fullan, M. G. (1992). "Visions That Blind." *Educational Leadership, 49*(5): 19–20.

Fullan, M. G., & Miles, M. B. (1992). "Getting Reform Right: What Works and What Doesn't." *Phi Delta Kappan, 73*(10): 745–752.

Fullan, M., & Pomfret, A. (1977). "Research on Curriculum and Instruction Implementation." *Review of Educational Research, 27*(2): 355–397.

Fullan, M. G., Bennett, B., & Rolheiser-Bennett, C. (1989). *Linking Classroom and School*

Improvement. Paper presented at the annual meeting of the American Educational Research Association, San Francisco, CA.

Gall, M. D., & Renchler, R. S. (1985). *Effective Staff Development for Teachers: A Research-based Model.* Eugene, OR: ERIC Clearinghouse on Educational Management, University of Oregon.

Green, J. (1983). "Research on Teaching as a Linguistic Process: A State of the Art." In E. Gordon (Ed.), *Review of Research in Education* (Vol. 10, pp. 151–252). Washington, DC: American Educational Research Association.

Griffin, G. A. (Ed.) (1983). *Staff Development. Eighty-second Yearbook of the National Society for the Study of Education.* Chicago: University of Chicago Press.

Griffin, G. A., & Barnes, S. (1984). "School Change: A Craft-derived and Research-based Strategy." *Teachers College Record, 86*: 103–123.

Guskey, T. R. (1985). *Implementing Mastery Learning.* Belmont, CA: Wadsworth.

Guskey, T. R. (1986). "Staff Development and the Process of Teacher Change." *Educational Researcher, 15*(5): 5–12.

Guskey, T. R. (1988). "Mastery Learning and Mastery Teaching: How They Complement Each Other." *Principal, 68*(1): 6–8.

Guskey, T. R. (1989). "Attitude and Perceptual Change in Teachers." *International Journal of Educational Research, 13*(4): 439–453.

Guskey, T. R. (1990a). "Cooperative Mastery Learning Strategies." *Elementary School Journal, 91*(1): 33–42.

Guskey, T. R. (1990b). "Integrating Innovations." *Educational Leadership, 47*(5): 11–15.

Guskey, T. R. (1991). "Enhancing the Effectiveness of Professional Development Programs." *Journal of Educational and Psychological Consultation, 2*(3): 239–247.

Guskey, T. R. (1993, February). "Why Pay Attention to Research If Researchers Can't Agree?" *The Developer,* pp. 3–4.

Guskey, T. R., & Sparks, D. (1991). "What to Consider When Evaluating Staff Development." *Educational Leadership, 49*(3): 73–76.

Hall, G. E., & Loucks, S. (1978). "Teachers' Concerns as a Basis for Facilitating and Personalizing Staff Development." *Teachers College Record, 80*: 36–53.

Hedges, L. V., & Olkin, I. (1985). *Statistical Methods for Meta-analysis.* Orlando, FL: Academic Press.

Hood, P., & Blackwell, L. (1980). *The Role of Teachers and Other School Practitioners in Decision-making and Innovations.* San Francisco: Far West Laboratory.

Huberman, M. (1983). "Recipes for Busy Teachers." *Knowledge: Creation, Diffusion, Utilization, 4*: 478–510.

Huberman, M. (1985). "What Knowledge Is of Most Worth to Teachers? A Knowledge-use Perspective." *Teaching and Teacher Education, 1*: 251–262.

Huberman, M. (1992). "Teacher Development and Instructional Mastery." In A. Hargreaves & M. G. Fullan (Eds.), *Understand Teacher Development* (pp. 122–142). New York: Teachers College Press.

Huberman, M., & Crandall, D. (1983). *People, Policies and Practice: Examining the Chain of School Improvement, Vol. 9. Implications for Action: A Study of Dissemination Efforts Supporting School Improvement.* Andover, MA: The Network.

Huberman, M., & Miles, M. B. (1984). *Innovation Up Close: How School Improvement Works.* New York: Plenum.

Joyce, B., & Showers, B. (1980). "Improving Inservice Training: The Messages of Research." *Educational Leadership, 37*(5): 379–385.

Joyce, B., & Showers, B. (1988). *Student Achievement through Staff Development.* New York: Longman.

Joyce, B., McNair, K. M., Diaz, R., & McKibbin, M. D. (1976). *Interviews: Perceptions of Professionals and Policy Makers.* Stanford, CA: Stanford Center for Research and Development in Teaching, Stanford University.

Lambert, L. (1988). "Staff Development Redesigned." *Educational Leadership, 45*(8): 665–668.

Latham, G. (1988). "The Birth and Death Cycles of Educational Innovations." *Principal, 68*(1): 41–43.

Lawrence, G. (1974). *Patterns of Effective Inservice Education: A State of the Art Summary of Research on Materials and Procedures for Changing Teacher Behavior in Inservice Education.* Tallahassee, FL: Florida State Department of Education.

Leiter, M., & Cooper, M. (1978). "How Teacher Unionists View Inservice Education." *Teachers College Record, 80*: 107–125.

Leithwood, K., & Montgomery, D. (1982). "The Role of the Elementary School Principal in Program Improvement." *Review of Educational Research, 52*: 309–339.

Lezotte, L. W. (1989). "The Open Book." *Focus in Change, 1*(2): 3.

Lieberman, A., & Miller, L. (1979). *Staff Development: New Demands, New Realities, New Perspectives.* New York: Teachers College Press.

Little, J. W. (1982). "Norms of Collegiality and Experimentation: Workplace Conditions of School Success." *American Educational Research Journal, 19*: 325–340.

Little, J. W. (1989). *The Persistence of Privacy: Autonomy and Initiative in Teachers' Professional Relations.* Paper presented at the annual meeting of the American Educational Research Association, San Francisco.

Lortie, D. C. (1975). *Schoolteacher: A Sociological Study.* Chicago: University of Chicago Press.

Loucks-Horsley, S., Harding, C. K., Arbuckle, M. A., Murray, L. B., Dubea, C., & Williams, M. K. (1987). *Continuing to Learn: A Guidebook for Teacher Development.* Andover, MA: Regional Laboratory for Educational Improvement of the Northeast & Islands.

Louis, K. S., & Miles, M. B. (1990). *Improving the Urban High School: What Works and Why.* New York: Teachers College Press.

Mann, D. (1978). "The Politics of Training Teachers in Schools." In D. Mann (Ed.), *Making Change Happen* (pp. 3–18). New York: Teachers College Press.

Mann, D. (1986). "Authority and School Improvement: An Essay on "Little King" Leadership." *Teachers College Record, 88*(1): 41–52.

Marzano, R. J., Pickering, D. J., & Brandt, R. S. (1990). "Integrating Instructional Programs through Dimensions of Learning." *Educational Leadership, 47*(5): 17–24.

Massarella, J. A. (1980). "Synthesis of Research on Staff Development." *Educational Leadership, 38*(2): 182–185.

McLaughlin, M. W. (1990). "The Rand Change Agent Study Revisited: Macro Perspectives and Micro Realities." *Educational Researcher, 19*(9): 11–16.

McLaughlin, M. W. (1991). "Test-based Accountability as a Reform Strategy." *Phi Delta Kappan, 73*(3): 248–251.

McLaughlin, M. W., & Marsh, D. D. (1978). "Staff Development and School Change." *Teachers College Record, 80*(1): 70–94.

Mevarech, Z. R. (1985). "The Effects of Cooperative Mastery Learning Strategies on Mathematics Achievement." *Journal of Educational Research, 78*: 372–377.

Miles, M. B., & Louis, K. S. (1987). "Research on Institutionalization: A Reflective Review" (pp. 24–44). In M. B. Miles, M. Ekholm, & R. Vandenberghe (Eds.), *Lasting School Improvement: Exploring the Process of Institutionalization.* Leuven, Belgium: Acco.

Miles, M. B., & Louis, K. S. (1990). "Mustering the Will and Skill for Change." *Educational Leadership, 47*(8): 57–61.

Orlich, D. C. (1989). *Staff Development: Enhancing Human Potential.* Boston: Allyn and Bacon.

Parker, C. A. (1980). "The Literature on Planned Organizational Change: A Review and Analysis." *Higher Education, 9*: 429–442.

Pejouhy, N. H. (1990). "Teaching Math for the 21st Century." *Phi Delta Kappan, 72*(1): 76–78.

Porter, A. C. (1986). "From Research on Teaching to Staff Development: A Difficult Step." *Elementary School Journal, 87*: 159–164.

Prochaska, J. O., DiClemente, C. C., & Norcross, J. C. (1992). "In Search of How People Change." *American Psychologist, 47*: 1102–1114.

Rosenholtz, S. (1987). "Education Reform Strategies: Will They Increase Teacher Commitment?" *American Journal of Education, 95*: 534–562.

Sarason, S. (1982). *The Culture of School and the Problem of Change.* Boston: Allyn and Bacon.

Sarason, S. (1990). *The Predictable Failure of Educational Reform.* San Francisco: Jossey-Bass.

Showers, B., Joyce, B., & Bennett, B. (1987). "Synthesis of Research on Staff Development: A Framework for Future Study and a State-of-the-art Analysis." *Education Leadership, 45*(3): 77–87.

Shroyer, M. G. (1990). "Effective Staff Development for Effective Organizational Development." *Journal of Staff Development, 11*(1): 2–6.

Smylie, M. A. (1988). "The Enhancement Function of Staff Development: Organizational and Psychological Antecedents to Individual Teacher Change." *American Educational Research Journal, 25*(1): 1–30.

Sparks, D., & Loucks-Horsley, S. (1989). "Five Models of Staff Development for Teachers." *Journal of Staff Development, 10*(4): 40–57.

Sparks, G. M. (1983). "Synthesis of Research on Staff Development for Effective Teaching." *Educational Leadership, 41*(3): 65–72.

Stallings, J. (1980). "Allocated Academic Learning Time Revisited, or Beyond Time on Task." *Educational Researcher, 9*(11): 11–16.

Stevenson, R. B. (1987). "Staff Development for Effective Secondary Schools: A Synthesis of Research." *Teaching and Teacher Education, 3*(2): 233–248.

Talbert, J. E., McLaughlin, M. W., & Rowan, B. (1993). "Understanding Context Effects on Secondary School Teaching." *Teachers College Record, 95*(1): 45–68.

Tye, K. A., & Tye, B. B. (1984). "Teacher Isolation and School Reform." *Phi Delta Kappan, 65*(5): 319–322.

Wade, R. K. (1984). "What Makes a Difference in In-service Teacher Education? A Meta-analysis of Research." *Educational Leadership, 42*(4): 48–54.

Waugh, R. F., & Punch, K. F. (1987). "Teacher Receptivity to Systemwide Change in the Implementation Stage." *Review of Educational Research, 57*(3): 237–254.

Weatherley, R., & Lipsky, M. (1977). "Street-level Bureaucrats and Institutional Innovation: Implementing Special Education Reform." *Harvard Educational Review, 47*(2): 171–197.

Weber, A. (1990). "Linking ITIP and the Writing Process." *Educational Leadership, 47*(5): 35–39.

Wise, A. E. (1991). "On Teacher Accountability." In *Voices from the Field* (pp. 23–24). Washington, DC: William T. Grant Foundation. Commission on Work, Family and Citizenship *and* Institute for Educational Leadership.

Wood, F. H., & Thompson, S. R. (1980). "Guidelines for Better Staff Development." *Educational Leadership, 37*: 374–378.

Wood, F. H., & Thompson, S. R. (1993). "Assumptions about Staff Development Based on Research and Best Practice." *Journal of Staff Development, 14*(4): 52–57.

DISCUSSION QUESTIONS

1. Why is successful professional program development essential to educational reform?
2. What is the relationship between professional development and student outcomes?
3. Based on the research on professional development, how should such programs be redesigned?
4. In what ways is context critical to the impact of a professional development program?
5. Why is change considered both an individual and an organizational process?
6. Why is feedback essential to professional development?
7. What can be done to ensure that the implementation of an innovation is successful?

32

Clinical Supervision and Psychological Functions

EDWARD F. PAJAK

FOCUSING QUESTIONS

1. What is clinical supervision, and how has it evolved over time?
2. What are psychological functions?
3. How do psychological functions influence communication styles?
4. What are the implications of psychological functions for the practice of clinical supervision?
5. How can supervisor–teacher relationships be improved?

Clinical supervision of instruction has a fairly long history in the United States, stretching back more than three decades. The seminal work began with Morris Cogan (1973) and Robert Goldhammer (1969) at Harvard University in the 1960s and continued later at the University of Pittsburgh. Since its inception, scholars have commented and elaborated on the fundamental clinical cycle at great length and from a wide variety of perspectives. So many volumes and articles have been published about clinical supervision over the years, in fact, that fresh insights and refinements may seem improbable at this point. This article asserts, on the contrary, that the theory of psychological functions introduced by Carl Jung (1971) and popularized by others (Briggs & Myers, 1977; Keirsey, 1998) can bring some conceptual clarity to the field of clinical supervision and also serve as a guide to practitioners when communicating with teachers.

Because the number of authors who have written about clinical supervision during recent decades is so very large, a complete account of every perspective is well beyond the scope of this article. The most prominent approaches, how-ever, have been classified according to certain shared qualities into four families (see Figure 32.1). These four families of clinical supervision emerged chronologically in approximately the order in which they are listed (Pajak, 2000). The *original clinical* models of Goldhammer (1969) and Cogan (1973), which appeared in the late 1960s and early 1970s, for example, were followed during the mid- to late 1970s by what may be described as the *humanistic–artistic* models of Blumberg (1974) and Eisner (1979). In turn, the *technical–didactic* models advocated by Acheson and Gall (1980) and Hunter (1984) gained ascendancy in the early to mid-1980s and were followed by the *developmental–reflective* models. The latter category arose during the mid-1980s and continued proliferating through the 1990s; it includes models proposed by Glickman (1985), Costa and Garmston (1994), and Zeichner and Liston (1996), among others (Garman, 1986; Waite, 1995). These four families of clinical supervision and the models comprising them differ greatly in the purposes toward which they strive, their relative emphasis on objectivity versus subjectivity, the type of data collected and the procedures for

Original clinical models	The models proposed by Goldhammer, Mosher and Purpel, and Cogan offer an eclectic blending of empirical, phenomenological, behavioral, and developmental perspectives. These models emphasize the importance of collegial relations between supervisors and teachers, cooperative discovery of meaning, and development of individually unique teaching styles.
Humanistic–artistic models	The perspectives of Blumberg and Eisner are based on existential and aesthetic principles. These models forsake step-by-step procedures and emphasize open interpersonal relations and personal intuition, artistry, and idiosyncrasy. Supervisors are encouraged to help teachers to understand the expressive and artistic richness of teaching.
Technical–didactic models	The work of Acheson and Gall, Hunter, and Joyce and Showers draws on process–product and effective teaching research. These models emphasize techniques of observation and feedback that reinforce certain effective behaviors or predetermined models of teaching to which teachers attempt to conform.
Developmental–reflective models	The models of Glickman; Costa and Garmston; Schon; Zeichner and Liston; Garman; Smyth and Retallick; Bowers and Flinders; and Waite are sensitive to individual differences and the organizational, social, political, and cultural contexts of teaching. These models call for supervisors to encourage reflection among teachers, foster professional growth, discover context-specific principles of practice, and promote justice and equity.

FIGURE 32.1   Four Families of Clinical Supervision

Source: Pajak (2000).

recording it, the number and series of steps or stages involved, the degree of control exercised by the supervisor versus the teacher, and the nature and structure of pre- and postobservation conferences (Pajak, 2000).

What could possibly be the source of so many divergent perspectives on what is essentially a straightforward process involving a pre-observation conference, a classroom observation, and a postobservation conference? How can such a multiplicity of models that differ among themselves in fundamental ways conceivably coexist and retain adherents among theorists and school practitioners? More practically, how can anyone sort through this profusion of advice and reasonably decide which version of clinical supervision may actually be appropriate for oneself or for any given situation? A number of supervision scholars have recently suggested that concepts derived from the psychology of Carl Jung may offer a promising perspective for answering these and other questions related to the supervision of instruction (Champagne & Hogan, 1995; Garmston, Lipton, & Kaiser, 1998; Hawthorne & Hoffman, 1998; Norris, 1991; Oja & Reiman, 1998; Shapiro & Blumberg, 1998).

JUNG'S PSYCHOLOGICAL FUNCTIONS

Among many other important discoveries related to conscious and unconscious mental processes, Jung (1971) proposed that people exhibit four psychological functions with respect to their perceptions. Two of these functions, intuition (N) and sensing (S), characterize the way that we gather data about and perceive reality, while another two functions, thinking (T) and feeling (F), refer to the ways that we appraise or judge the reality that is perceived. Although gathering data and making judgments about perceptions are obviously central issues for clinical supervision, Champagne and Hogan (1995) appear to be alone in having applied Jung's formulations to the field in a thorough and systematic way. (Their book includes a useful assessment instrument for determining psychological type and function and speculates about the effect that these mental processes have on both teaching and supervision.) The concept of psychological functions already productively informs other areas of study, including learning styles (Silver, Strong, & Perini, 1997), leadership (Fitzgerald & Kirby, 1997), and organizational dynamics (Hirsch & Kummerow, 1998), all of which have clear relevance for understanding classrooms and schools. It seems worthwhile, therefore, to further explore the implications of Jung's formulations for clinical supervision.

According to Jung (1971), people who draw primarily on *intuition* to collect data and perceive reality prefer exploring and discussing ideas and theories, untried possibilities, and what is new. They easily become bored with specifics, details, data, and facts that are unrelated to concepts. Intuitive people tend to think and communicate with spontaneous leaps of intuition and may omit or neglect details. In contrast, those who draw on the *sensing* function to gather data and perceive reality prefer focusing on what is real, concrete, and tangible in the here and now. They tend to be more concerned with facts and data than with theory and abstractions. Sensing people think and communicate carefully and accurately, referring to and emphasizing facts and details, but may miss seeing the *gestalt,* or big picture.

People who favor *thinking* over feeling when making judgments about the reality that they perceive prefer using evidence, analysis, and logic. They are more concerned with being rational than with empathy, emotions, and values. Thinking types communicate in an orderly and linear manner, emphasizing if–then and cause–effect linkages. On the other hand, those who prefer using *feeling* to guide their judgments do so on the basis of empathy, warmth, personal convictions, and a consistent value system that underlies all their decision processes. They are more interested in

people, emotions, and harmony than in logic, analysis, or attaining impersonal goals. Feeling people communicate by expressing personal likes and dislikes, as well as feelings about what is good versus bad and right versus wrong.

Jung (1971) compared the four functions to the points on a compass and suggested that their interplay was just as indispensable as this navigational device for psychological orientation and discovery. Displaying the functions in a compass-like configuration (see Figure 32.2) highlights the manner in which the two psychological processes of getting information and making decisions interact, resulting in four possible function pairs: sensory–thinking (S–T), sensory–feeling (S–F), intuitive–thinking (N–T), and intuitive–feeling (N–F). These four combinations (bracketed by parentheses in the quadrants illustrated in Figure 32.2) have distinctive effects on how individuals relate to the world. They also appear to correspond well with the four families of clinical supervision described earlier.

People characterized by an intuitive–thinking (N–T) function pair, for example, are concerned with competence and tend to concentrate on the future, ideas, and possibilities. They are guided by theoretical concepts and work by testing hypotheses. N–Ts are likely to consider the big picture and are distressed by what they view as incorrect or faulty principles. This worldview most closely parallels the original clinical models, particularly those of Goldhammer (1969) and Cogan (1973).

In comparison, those individuals who display a sensory–feeling (S–F) combination primarily want to be helpful to others. They focus attention on the present and facts, but are most concerned with people. S–Fs want to provide support and are guided by a sense of service. They work by meeting people's needs and are troubled by conflict and disagreements. An S–F orientation, in turn, would seem to most closely resemble the humanistic–artistic family of models represented by Blumberg (1974) and Eisner (1979).

People possessing a sensory–thinking (S–T) orientation mainly strive to be efficient. They focus on the present and facts and attend closely to current reality. They prefer to follow established policies and procedures and believe that

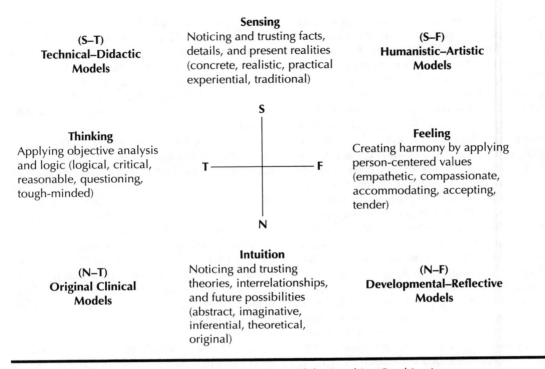

Sensing
Noticing and trusting facts, details, and present realities (concrete, realistic, practical experiential, traditional)

**(S–T)
Technical–Didactic
Models**

**(S–F)
Humanistic–Artistic
Models**

S

Thinking
Applying objective analysis and logic (logical, critical, reasonable, questioning, tough-minded)

T ——————— F

Feeling
Creating harmony by applying person-centered values (empathetic, compassionate, accommodating, accepting, tender)

N

**(N–T)
Original Clinical
Models**

Intuition
Noticing and trusting theories, interrelationships, and future possibilities (abstract, imaginative, inferential, theoretical, original)

**(N–F)
Developmental–Reflective
Models**

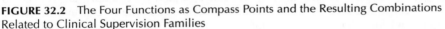

FIGURE 32.2   The Four Functions as Compass Points and the Resulting Combinations Related to Clinical Supervision Families

their work and the work of others is facilitated by having such processes and structures in place. S–Ts want to see results produced and are annoyed when work is done incorrectly. The technical–didactic models of Acheson and Gall (1980) and Hunter (1984) appear to match up well with this perspective.

Finally, people who possess an intuitive–feeling (N–F) combination seek to empower others and are strongly concerned with the future, people, and possibilities. Guided by ideals that they believe are worthy, N–Fs work by expressing and acting on their values. These individuals seek to promote growth and are troubled when values are absent or are viewed as incorrect. The developmental–reflective models, represented by a range of contemporary authors, would seem to be associated with the N–F viewpoint.

Applying the concept of psychological functions in this way illustrates how the four clinical

supervision families are related and complement one another despite their obvious differences. Rather than solely expressing the *Zeitgeist* of the decade when it emerged or the worldview of particular authors, each family of models may be viewed as expressing a logic that is complete only in relation to the other three families. Chronologically, the intuitive–thinking qualities of the original clinical supervision models that emerged in the 1960s were mirrored by their psychological opposite, the sensory–feeling orientation of the humanistic–artistic models in the 1970s, following what could be conceived as a sort of Hegelian thesis–antithesis dialectic (Friedrich, 1954). The tension between them was then resolved by a synthesis of the two, which incorporated the sensing and thinking functions of each and resulted in the technical–didactic models that were prominent in the 1980s. This synthesis became a new thesis, in turn, giving rise to its own antithesis, the N–F-oriented developmental–reflective models of the 1990s. This final grouping, thus, rounded out the range of psychological possibilities.

Does this mean that the potential for developing entirely new approaches to clinical supervision has been exhausted? Probably. Could this *fin de siecle* explain the dearth of new clinical supervision models during the last five years or so? Perhaps. Should it be a cause of concern for theorists and practitioners? Probably not. Rather, this completion of the pattern may provide an unprecedented foundation for further theory building and research, as well as a basis for more precise and successful practice.

THE COMMUNICATION WHEEL

Thompson (2000) has recently adapted and applied Jung's concept of psychological functions to the purpose of better understanding and improving communication within organizations. He notes that communication is effective only when information and understanding are passed along accurately from a sender to a receiver. Problems are likely to arise when individuals or groups encode or decode messages differently while trying to communicate with one another. Not all communication problems can be traced to differences in psychological type, he cautions, but communication preferences do serve as filters that influence our perceptions. These perceptions ultimately become the realities to which we all respond.

Of particular relevance and interest to theorists and practitioners of clinical supervision is Thompson's (2000) assertion that attending to psychological functions can enhance the quality of interaction between coaches (i.e., supervisors) and their clients within all types of organizations. He proposes that the functions (S, N, T, and F) can be thought of as four languages that people use when communicating. Thompson further hypothesizes the existence of eight communication dialects (T–N, N–T, S–T, T–S, S–F, F–S, N–F, and F–N), which are determined by whether an individual usually relies more heavily on his or her dominant or auxiliary function. Everyone can use both, but people tend to rely more heavily on their dominant function during times of stress. Draw-

ing on this finer differentiation, the relationship among the various models of clinical supervision can be depicted in terms of these eight communication dialects, as in Figure 32.3.

Communication works best, Thompson (2000) suggests, when both parties speak the same primary language. If they differ, one or the other must adjust or else communication will break down. On the other hand, the better an individual can approximate the language and dialect of others, the more communication should improve. Understanding how psychological type affects communication can be useful for diagnosing causes of communication problems, both interpersonally and in groups. Possible solutions to existing problems can be identified and potential problems in supervisory situations may be avoided entirely by anticipating communication difficulties in advance. In any case, listening for cues about the communication preferences of other people is obviously the key.

By aligning the models of clinical supervision with the function-based communication dialects, fine conceptual distinctions among the models that fall within the various families can be explained (see Figure 32.3). Despite many similarities between the perspectives of Goldhammer (1969) and Cogan (1973), for example, these models of clinical supervision differ substantially in their respective justifications for clinical supervision. Goldhammer (1969) begins his book by "generating images of what school can be like, particularly in the children's experience" (p. 1). He offers a scathing indictment of the meaninglessness of much that occurs in classrooms and recommends clinical supervision as a way of making instruction more consciously purposeful and responsive to students' needs. Cogan (1973) grounds his argument for clinical supervision, in contrast, along organizational and professional development lines. He advocates clinical supervision as a practical means for "disseminating and implementing new practices" more effectively and for professionalizing the teaching corps (p. 3). Cogan and Goldhammer also differ in the relative importance that each places on objective versus subjective issues. Both authors are concerned with observable behaviors and meanings and the relationship between them as expressed in the teacher's unique teaching style. Cogan (1973) urges supervisors to focus attention primarily on teacher behaviors, however, arguing that a change in style will naturally follow if behavior changes: "The proper domain of the clinical supervisor is the classroom behavior of the teacher. That is, the proper subject of supervision is the teacher's classroom behavior, not the teacher as a person" (p. 58). Goldhammer (1969), on the other hand, advocates consideration of how supervisory processes affect the teacher's "ideas and feelings about himself," beyond "substantive technical learning" (p. 133). Supervisors themselves are advised by Goldhammer (1969) to submit their own behavior to "reflexive examination" during the postconference analysis stage (p. 337), intriguingly anticipating the reflective practice associated with the adjacent N–F perspective (see Figure 32.3).

Such differences between the two seminal theorists may be due to the communication dialect that each expresses in his writings. Although both original models of clinical supervision are highly consistent with an intuitive–thinking function pair, Goldhammer's views lean closer to conceptual abstraction, while Cogan clearly places greater emphasis on issues of practical application. Goldhammer's model appears to reflect a communication preference for intuition over thinking (N–T), in other words, while Cogan's model demonstrates a stronger preference for thinking over intuition (T–N). Although we will never know if such preferences were rooted in the personalities of these men, it is interesting to note that Goldhammer, who was Cogan's student, published his book on clinical supervision in 1969. Cogan had spoken and written articles about clinical supervision many years before, however, and he is said

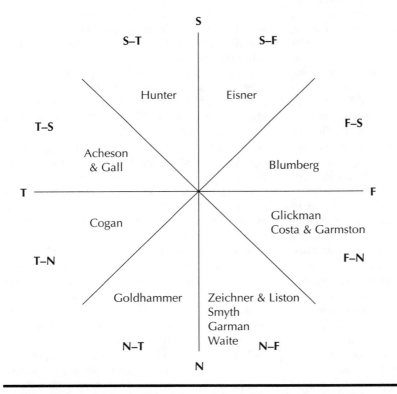

FIGURE 32.3   Models of Clinical Supervision as Communication Dialects

to have finished three or four drafts of his own book before deciding in 1973 that his ideas were finally ready for public scrutiny (personal communications with Robert H. Anderson and David W. Champagne). Even then, he referred to his work rather tentatively as a "rationale," apparently anticipating further refinement.

Moving to the technical–didactic family, the approaches to clinical supervision advocated both by Acheson and Gall and by Hunter plainly give voice to a sensory–thinking (S–T) combination (see Figure 32.3). Yet the former carry objective analysis to an extreme. Where Goldhammer had five stages and Cogan had eight phases, Acheson and Gall (1980) propose no less than *thirty-two* discrete behavioral techniques for classroom observation and conferencing, indicating an exceptionally heavy reliance on the thinking function. They contrast their *techniques* with competing texts, noting that other authors "have emphasized theory and research on clinical supervision. Our book is practical in intent. We emphasize the techniques of clinical supervision, the 'nuts and bolts' of how to work with teachers to help them improve their classroom teaching" (p. xiii).

In comparison, Hunter (1984) draws heavily on her personal experience to inform practice and is concerned with obtaining a complete and accurate record, through "script-taping" of everything that is said and done in the classroom by teachers and students. While every bit as linear and rational as Acheson and Gall's approach, Hunter's version requires the clinical supervisor to directly experience and record sensory input, unmediated and unimpeded by observation instruments or mechanical devices. A major advantage of script-taping, she notes, is that "the observer can quickly 'swing' focus from one part of the group to another (something not possible for a camera). This enables an observer to scan and record many parts of the room almost simultaneously" (pp. 185–186). Thus, although both models express an S–T preference, Acheson and Gall place greater emphasis on the thinking function (T–S), whereas Hunter emphasizes sensing (S–T) more heavily.

Blumberg's (1974) model of clinical supervision is highly sensing as well, but, coupled with a dominant feeling function, the primary focus is on people and the quality of their interpersonal relations. As typifies an F–S function pair, Blumberg's model of clinical supervision is built on the assumption that much of the difficulty that teachers and supervisors face in working together stems from behavioral conflicts that originate in the organizational context of schools. Blumberg (1974) advises supervisors to concentrate on issues of trust, affection, and influence that he believes create psychological barriers between teachers and supervisors. He suggests that three conditions must be in place for instructional supervision to be successful: "the teacher must want help, the supervisor must have the resources to provide the kind of help required or know where the resources may be found, and the interpersonal relationships between a teacher and supervisor must enable the two to give and receive in a mutually satisfactory way" (p. 18).

Along with Blumberg, Eisner (1979) eschews following a step-by-step formula, as would be expected of any S–F combination. But Eisner is considerably less concerned with improving interpersonal relations. By relying on personal sensitivities and experiences, Eisner proposes that an instructional supervisor can become the major instrument through which the classroom and its context are perceived and understood. He views clinical supervisors ideally as "connoisseurs" who perceive what is important yet subtle in classroom behavior and who can eloquently describe its essential expressive value. This esthetic aspect of Eisner's (1979) model suggests an affinity with the N–F function pairing, but a closer reading of the process that he outlines indicates a very strong emphasis on visual, auditory, and kinaesthetic sensing accompanied by the subjective feeling function, (S–F dialect). That is, a combination of heightened sensing and feeling are critical for informing an artistic appreciation of the teaching act:

> By artistic I mean using an approach to supervision that relies on the sensitivity, perceptivity, and knowledge of the supervisor as a way of appreciating the significant subtleties occurring in the classroom, and that exploits the expressive, poetic, and often metaphorical potential of language to convey to teachers or to others whose decisions

affect what goes on in schools, what has been observed. (p. 59)

Finally, the developmental and reflective models, respectively, appear to represent the F–N and N–F communication dialects, as depicted in Figure 32.3. Costa and Garmston's (1994) and Glickman's (1985) versions of clinical supervision place a high premium on both feeling and intuition (F–N), with a focus on facilitating the cognitive growth and decision-making ability of teachers through empathetic understanding and flexible response to teachers' current levels of functioning. Both aim to influence the way that teachers mentally process information and strongly favor abstract over concrete thinking as a goal to pursue. They concentrate primarily on the matter of how supervisors can guide teachers toward conscious understanding and control of their actions in the individual classroom, as well as when working collectively, to attain desirable learning outcomes for students. For example, Glickman (1985) defines "the key to successful schools as instructional supervision that fosters teacher development by promoting greater abstraction, commitment and collective action" (p. 381). Similarly, Costa and Garmston (1994) explain that "cognitive coaching enhances the intellectual capacities of teachers, which in turn produces greater intellectual achievement in students" (p. 6). A major goal of cognitive coaching is "enhancing growth toward *holonomy*," which they define as "individuals acting *autonomously* while simultaneously acting *interdependently* with the group" (p. 3).

Advocates of reflective practice, such as Zeichner and Liston (1987), Garman (1986), Waite (1995), and Smyth (1985), also seek to influence cognitive processes, but their position more closely approximates the value-driven N–F orientation. Accordingly, these authors urge supervisors and teachers to question the hierarchical nature of interpersonal relationships in schools, to raise issues of gender, race, and culture to conscious levels, and to challenge the knowledge embodied in the books, curriculum, lessons, and examinations that are part of schooling. Teachers and supervisors are encouraged to consider those aspects of classrooms and schools (including their own professional identities) that disempower other educators and debilitate students. This potential transformation of schooling is to be fueled by collaborative inquiry and guided by the moral principles of justice and equity.

DISCUSSION AND IMPLICATIONS

Choosing the proper communication style when working with teachers has been a perennial concern in the clinical supervision literature. Although general consensus exists that the process of selecting a communication style should include consideration of the needs of teachers, experts conflict substantively in the specific advice that they offer on this point. Goldhammer (1969), writing from an intuitive–thinking point of view, for example, cautions supervisors to refrain from being overly direct when working with inexperienced teachers lest these teachers become dependent on the supervisor and fail to develop a personal teaching identity. He advises that experienced veterans can more easily tolerate a supervisor's forthrightness and assimilate into their teaching repertoire what seems appropriate to them, without feeling unduly pressured or intimidated. In contrast, Hunter (1984), writing from a sensing–thinking perspective, asserts that a direct communication style is exactly the tonic for inducting newcomers into the teaching profession, because novices are inexperienced and sorely need the expert advice that a supervisor can readily provide. Collaborative communication, she believes, should be reserved for teachers who possess the experience and expertise to engage in dialogue with the supervisor on a more equal footing.

Which of these rationales is correct? Each view seems sound and plausible until the other is considered, because both positions are consistent within their own internal logic. Yet each remains diametrically opposed to the other. Rather than quibble about the *right* way and the *wrong* way to treat teachers with varying levels of experience and expertise on the basis of general principles, an understanding of psychological functions and communication dialects allows us to accept *both—and* a range of other alternatives that may be appropriate under different sets of circumstances. Instead of stereotyping beginning teachers and experienced teachers as being all alike, a *functional* perspective on clinical supervision enables us to see that each situation is defined by the psychological processes of the individuals who happen to be involved in the teacher–supervisor relationship. While this insight greatly complicates things for both supervision theorists and practitioners, it also promises a refinement of our understanding and an improvement of our chances for success by moving us beyond the *direct* versus *indirect* communication controversy.

The application of psychological functions to clinical supervision sheds light on another contemporary issue, as well: shaping the content of communication with teachers on the basis of the hierarchical goals that a supervisor hopes to accomplish. Several authors, all writing from a developmental–reflective perspective, have independently recommended that a supervisor's practice should be guided by whether the object is to improve a teacher's technical competence, conceptual understanding, or sensitivity to issues of an ethical nature (e.g., Grimmett, 1989; Zeichner & Liston, 1996). In each instance, a preference for goals favoring moral sensitivity over technical competence is explicitly stated. A view of clinical supervision that considers psychological functions suggests that this hierarchical device is essentially arbitrary, except from the perspective of those who favor intuition and feeling as ways of perceiving and evaluating reality. A supervisor with a sensing–thinking preference, in contrast, is likely to consider an idealistic and well-intentioned teacher who lacks the skills needed to help students to learn as more problematic than a motivated and technically proficient teacher who expresses little concern for principles of social justice. A view informed by psychological functions suggests, as well, that in addition to technical (S–T), conceptual (N–T), and moral (N–F) considerations, a relational (S–F) dimension of growth is also possible, desirable, and seriously worth considering as an outcome of instruction and supervision. Without questioning the value of moral commitment or more abstract thinking, in other words, the legitimacy and importance of development along other lines for students, teachers, and supervisors become evident.

The major implication of psychological functions for practice, however, is that clinical supervisors ought to interact with teachers in the manner through which the teachers, themselves, learn best. Wiles (2001) reported preliminary findings that Florida teachers who were nominated by their superintendents as "the best" differ from other teachers on a learning styles inventory based on Jung's psychological functions and other measures. The teachers who were nominated as exemplary "tend to be more flexible, more experimental, and more student-centered than the regular population of teachers in Florida" (p. 7). Yet much of what supervisors do, say, and think when they interact with teachers, consciously or unconsciously, is typically determined by their own psychological preferences for perceiving and judging. Indeed, Goldhammer (1969) very clearly anticipated this very point. Until supervisors become conscious of their own preferences and more sensitive to those of teachers, they will inadvertently tend to favor, reward, and reinforce teachers who behave, speak, and think as they do, while misunderstanding and failing to communicate with teachers who differ from themselves.

The bases of a true collegial relationship include trust and a willingness to share and understand personal meanings, understandings, and frames of reference. Clinical supervision should provide support for teachers with an aim toward increasing professional responsibility and openness and the capacity for self-analysis and self-direction. By attending carefully to psychological functions, clinical supervisors can recognize and build on existing strengths. Instead of calling attention to deficits and shortcomings, supervisors can open alternative paths for teachers to reach their professional goals. Teachers can be helped to perfect their uniquely personal teaching styles and also round out their repertoires by developing styles that reflect other modes of thinking. Clinical supervisors should initially be willing to accept each teacher's unique style and enter into dialogue with the assumption that the teacher is professionally competent, even though the two of them may experience and respond to the world very differently. Indeed, tracking teachers according to the supervisor's subjective judgments of their ability is as indefensible as the placing of students into different curriculum tracks according to the teacher's perceptions of their academic aptitude.

Clinical supervisors, no less than teachers, should make a deliberate effort to honor and legitimate perspectives and strategies that are not harmonious with their own preferred tendencies for perceiving and judging reality. That is to say, clinical supervisors should strive to work with teachers in ways that are consistent with how teachers are expected to work with students—by celebrating diversity and responding to that diversity in ways that enhance learning for all.

REFERENCES

Acheson, K. A., & Gall, M. D. (1980). *Techniques in the Clinical Supervision of Teachers* (White Plains, NY: Longman).

Blumberg, A. (1974). *Supervisors and Teachers: A Private Cold War* (Berkeley, CA: McCutchan).

Briggs, K. A., & Myers, I. B. (1977). *Myers–Briggs Type Indicator* (Palo Alto, CA: Consulting Psychologists Press).

Champagne, D. W., & Hogan, R. C. (1995). *Consultant Supervision: Theory and Skill Development,* 3rd Ed. (Wheaton, IL: CH Publications).

Cogan, M. L. (1973). *Clinical Supervision* (Boston: Houghton Mifflin).

Costa, A. L., & Garmston, R. J. (1994). *Cognitive Coaching: A Foundation for Renaissance Schools* (Norwood, MA: Christopher–Gordon).

Eisner, E. W. (1979). *The Educational Imagination: On the Design and Evaluation of Educational Programs* (New York: Macmillan).

Fitzgerald, C., & Kirby, L. (Eds.) (1997). *Developing Leaders: Research and Applications in Psychological Type and Leadership Development* (Palo Alto, CA: Davies–Black).

Friedrich, C. J. (1954). *The Philosophy of Hegel* (New York: Random House).

Garman, N. B. (1986). Reflection, the Heart of Clinical Supervision: A Modern Rationale for Practice. *Journal of Curriculum and Supervision, 2*(1), 1–24.

Garmston, R. J., Lipton, L. E., & Kaiser, K. (1998). The Psychology of Supervision. In Gerald R. Firth and Edward F. Pajak (Eds.), *Handbook of Research on School Supervision,* pp. 242–286. (New York: Simon & Schuster Macmillan).

Glickman, C. D. (1985). *Supervision of Instruction: A Developmental Approach* (Boston: Allyn and Bacon).

Goldhammer, R. (1969). *Clinical Supervision: Special Methods for the Supervision of Teachers* (New York: Holt, Rinehart & Winston).

Hawthorne, R. D., & Hoffman, N. E. (1998). Supervision in Non-Teaching Professions. In Gerald R. Firth and Edward F. Pajak (Eds.), *Handbook of Research on School Supervision,* pp. 555–580 (New York: Simon & Schuster Macmillan).

Hirsch, S. K., & Kummerow, J. M. (1998). *Introduction to Type in Organizations* (Palo Alto, CA: Consulting Psychologists Press).

Hunter, M. (1984). Knowing, Teaching, and Supervising. In P. L. Holford (Ed.), *Using What We Know about Teaching* (Alexandria, VA: Association for Supervision and Curriculum Development).

Jung, C. G. (1971). *Psychological Types.* A revision by R. F. C. Hull of the translation by H. G. Baynes. (Princeton, NJ: Princeton University Press).

Keirsey, D. (1998). *Please Understand Me II: Temperament, Character, Intelligence* (Del Mar, CA: Prometheus Nemesis).

Norris, C. J. (1991). Supervising with Style. *Theory Into Practice, 30* (Spring 1991), 129–133.

Oja, S. N., & Reiman, A. J. (1998). Supervision for Teacher Development across the Career Span. In Gerald R. Firth and Edward F. Pajak (Eds.), *Handbook of Research on School Supervision,* pp. 463–487 (New York: Simon & Schuster Macmillan).

Pajak, E. F. (2000). *Approaches to Clinical Supervision: Alternatives for Improving Instruction,* 2nd Ed. (Norwood, MA: Christopher–Gordon).

Shapiro, A. S., & Blumberg, A. (1998). Social Dimensions of Supervision. In Gerald R. Firth and Edward F. Pajak (Eds.), *Handbook of Research on School Supervision,* pp. 1055–1084 (New York: Simon & Schuster Macmillan).

Silver, H., Strong, R., & Perini, M. (1997). Integrating Learning Styles and Multiple Intelligences, *Educational Leadership, 55* (September), 22–27.

Smyth, J. W. (1985). Developing a Critical Practice of Clinical Supervision. *Journal of Curriculum Studies, 17* (January–March), 1–15.

Thompson, H. L. (2000). *Introduction to the Communication Wheel* (Watkinsville, GA: Wormhole Publishing).

Waite, D. (1995). *Rethinking Instructional Supervision: Notes on Its Language and Culture* (Washington, DC: Falmer Press).

Wiles, J. (2001). Some of Our Best Teachers. *Wingspan, 13* (March), 4–9.

Zeichner, K. M., & Liston, D. P. (1987). Teaching Student Teachers to Reflect. *Harvard Educational Review, 57* (February), 23–48.

Zeichner, K. M., & Liston, D. P. (1996). *Reflective Teaching: An Introduction* (Mahwah, NJ: Erlbaum).

DISCUSSION QUESTIONS

1. How effective and how collegial have your experiences been with clinical supervision?

2. In your experience, do teachers tend to exhibit the various psychological types described?

3. How could a principal or peer coach apply the concept of psychological functions when working with a teacher?

4. Would understanding and use of psychological types make clinical supervision more collegial? Why or why not?

5. Would understanding and use of psychological types make clinical supervision more effective? Why or why not?

33

A Role for Technology in Professional Development? Lessons from IBM

FRANK LEVY
RICHARD J. MURNANE

FOCUSING QUESTIONS

1. In what ways can professional development be altered to become more useful? What challenges are faced in making such changes?
2. What is an educator?
3. How can technology aid in training educators?
4. How can corporate training techniques translate to educator training in schools?
5. How does follow-up enhance the training process?
6. In what way can technology be implemented to enhance training programs?

Standards-based accountability systems challenge American educators to accomplish something that has never been done in the nation's history: teaching all children to master a demanding set of skills. The challenge makes sense today because technological changes and outsourcing have left American workers who lack strong skills unable to earn a decent living wage. However, the magnitude of the challenge is frequently underestimated. Working harder will not by itself allow American educators to meet this challenge. Indeed, most already work so hard that burnout is a continual danger. Instead, educators need to learn how to work together more effectively.

Professional development, the primary strategy for improving the effectiveness of educators, has not worked well. As Mike Schmoker has pointed out, too often professional development consists of workshops led by an outside speaker, with little or no follow-up.[1] These efforts do not change how well teachers teach or how effectively

children learn. Nor do they improve the quality of administrators' leadership.

One response to the professional development challenge has been to make greater use of technology. Initiatives that use the Internet in professional development include TeachScape, LessonLab, and the Center for Online Professional Education. What role should technology play in professional development? Can it substitute for face-to-face meetings that are expensive and hard to schedule? Can it make face-to-face meetings more valuable? Does it change how meeting time should be spent and require new skills of those who facilitate these meetings?

In this chapter, we describe how IBM answered these questions in the process of revamping its training program for new managers. We then consider how the IBM experience can inform efforts to improve professional development for educators. At this point, readers may well ask, What can educators learn from a profit-making company engaged in a business so different from teaching children? Our answer has three parts.

First, for reasons we explain below, the challenges IBM managers face have much in common with those educators face. We want to be clear that we are using the term *educators* to include teachers as well as school administrators. We see teachers as "managers" in that they are responsible for the well-being and development of a large number of children. In the differentiated staffing models that many school reformers advocate, experienced teachers also serve as mentors and supervisors for beginning teachers.[2] Second, as a technology-based company, IBM has significant expertise in developing and implementing new ways to use computer networks in its training programs. Third, because IBM operates in an extremely competitive industry, it has both a great incentive to design efficient training programs and the freedom to do so.

WHAT INFORMATION TECHNOLOGY CAN AND CANNOT DO

Computers excel at conveying information. Because using information lies at the center of teachers' and administrators' jobs, it makes intuitive sense that networked computers could be valuable in improving the effectiveness of teachers and administrators. Indeed, we believe this is true. Networked computers can improve teachers' and administrators' access to a wide range of potentially useful information, including patterns in student test scores, ideas for lesson plans, and school district rules and strategies for dealing with disruptive students.

Yet, for information to be useful, it needs to be interpreted in context. Suppose in the course of conversation, a friend speaks the word *bill*. How do we interpret it? As a person's first name? As the front end of a duck? As a piece of legislation? As a request for payment? As a piece of currency? The answer depends on the context of the conversation. The same is true for much of the information teachers and administrators receive. Seeing an Internet video of a teacher explaining to third-graders how to write topic sentences may spark useful ideas. However, only by talking with

fellow teachers about the strengths and limitations of the lesson and about what happened when each teacher tried it in her or his own classroom will the information result in constructive changes in instruction.

Similarly, accessing the district's network to read the policy for dealing with disruptive students may provide some guidance in dealing with a particular student. However, the rules alone will not be sufficient to tell a teacher or administrator what to do. She will need to learn how to find out why the student misbehaved and the consequences of that misbehavior for the rest of the class. She will have to deal with her own emotions in this situation. Educators learn to do this by practicing and receiving constructive feedback. Computer simulations can be useful in creating opportunities for practice, but they cannot provide the intense learning experiences that discussions of specific cases, role-playing, and other face-to-face activities can.

It follows that designing professional development efforts to improve the skills of educators requires an understanding of what ideas can be conveyed adequately by text and video—and consequently can be transmitted electronically—and what ideas and skills need to be learned through face-to-face interactions. This is the question IBM faced.

THE GENESIS OF BASIC BLUE

Strong management training is part of the IBM tradition. Formerly, novice managers went to the company headquarters in Armonk, New York, for New Managers School, a week of polished lectures on IBM policies and practices. Participants found the week stimulating and worthwhile. Their positive responses reflected the week's content— but also its timing. Managers arrived 4–6 months after their appointment. Their initial experiences had made them well aware of what they did not know. Unfortunately, the timing also meant that they faced their first months of managing with relatively few resources.

During the 1990s, changes at IBM put the New Managers School under pressure not unlike that now placed on U.S. schools. Lou Gerstner, the new chairman hired to turn the company around, soon developed an ambitious training agenda. He wanted IBM managers to learn how to manage in a different way, to become more active in coaching—developing and supporting the skills of the people who reported to them. He knew that managing by following rules would not work in a rapidly changing business environment.

As IBM's management development team faced its new challenge, its options were bounded by two extremes. It could have expanded the face-to-face professional development time in Armonk from one week to, say, three weeks. But tight training budgets ruled out this option immediately.

Alternatively, the team could have put all the relevant material into text, stored it on CDs or on Web pages, and instructed new managers to read it (videos were ruled out because new managers in many locations lacked high-speed connections). We have already seen one objection to this option: The team knew that the skills needed to manage effectively could not be learned by reading text alone. A second objection would have been a lack of accountability. Like teachers, new managers face a stream of daily problems that require immediate attention. Simply giving these managers access to written information was no guarantee they would read the material, much less understand it.

The new training program steered between these extremes. The team responsible for revamping new manager training recognized that much of the material presented in New Managers School was essential rules: IBM's policies governing promotions, leaves, and other aspects of employment. While rules are open to interpretation, their basic substance could be conveyed in text, provided the text was easily accessible and a new manager was given incentives to read it. At the same time, many of the skills needed to manage effectively were too complex to be conveyed in text. They would have to be learned through direct interactions, but even here the proper text could complement face-to-face interactions by defining coaching and similar concepts.

The resulting program, dubbed Basic Blue, was introduced in 1999. It extends through three phases over a full year and covers several times as much material as the earlier New Managers School. The first phase takes about two hours a week over a period of 6 months to complete. All the Phase 1 work is done with text-based training materials downloaded from IBM's intranet site.

Each new manager is placed in a training cohort of 75 individuals who are collectively assigned a Lotus Learning Space, a Web-based collaborative learning tool that allows cohort members to correspond as they tackle the online material. To get new managers' attention, the first two program modules, to be completed in 30 days, cover "keep out of jail" topics, including business conduct and sexual harassment. Each module contains one or more Management Quick Views, short summaries of best-practice strategies for such commonly occurring tasks as running a meeting, conducting an employee evaluation, and coaching an employee. Management Quick Views also contain links to more detailed information. Each module ends with a brief multiple-choice test of mastery to be completed online and sent electronically to an IBM site for scoring. The test is "open book," and a new manager may take it as often as necessary to achieve a passing score. Scores are returned electronically in a few hours.

Several of the modules contain text-based simulations, short cases in which the new manager chooses among alternative responses at several steps of a personal interaction. One simulation explores strategies for coaching a team member who is not performing well in a new position. The simulations contain links to relevant online material and provide instant reactions to the selected responses. In terms of learning by doing, the simulations fall well short of group role-playing and discussion, but they do stimulate thinking about applying IBM policies to situations managers face frequently.

To ensure that managers actually read these modules, the Basic Blue team designed two-way information flows. The same software that scores new managers' tests keeps the management development team informed of the managers' progress. This tracking is crucial. Often, the time new managers budget for online work is taken up dealing with clients' questions instead. Managers who don't keep up receive e-mails and sometimes follow-up phone calls urging them to get back on schedule.

The reward for completing Phase 1 is admission to Phase 2, the week spent at the IBM Learning Center in Armonk. For that week, each cohort is divided into three groups of 25 new managers. Throughout the week, the work of each group is facilitated by an experienced IBM manager who knows the pressures IBM managers face and has learned how to facilitate intense discussions. The facilitator leads the group through a variety of interactive tasks to help them become more aware of their strengths and limitations as managers and to experiment with strategies for improvement. He assures the participants that their performances during the week will not be graded and that reports will not be sent to their managers. In the words of one facilitator, this is a week to "discuss the undiscussable."

REALLOCATING HUMAN EFFORT

There is more to describe about Basic Blue, but it is useful to take a step back to see how computers complement the face-to-face interactions. In designing Basic Blue, IBM's management development team used Web-based technology in five ways:

1. To convey text-based training materials, including company policies and tips on managing the IBM way
2. To keep track of new managers' progress in studying these materials
3. To create virtual collaboration forums in which new managers in the same training cohort could discuss training materials and tests
4. To provide hypertext links to fully documented company policies, providing greater detail than the training course materials
5. To provide interactive text-based simulations that offer new managers opportunities to apply IBM policies to specific management challenges, such as evaluating and coaching staff members who report directly to them

TEACHING COMPLEX COMMUNICATION SKILLS

The week at Armonk begins with an exploration of different managerial styles—a topic as complex as, say, teaching strategies, for which text descriptions only scratch the surface. For this reason, much of the teaching and learning comes through role-playing followed by discussion. In one role-playing exercise, Carol Dorsey, a new IBM manager from Atlanta, demonstrated coercion by demanding that an angry employee who might have brought a gun to work (played by another new manager) give her his security badge and leave the building. Carol's performance was compelling, in part because she had faced a similar situation as a new manager for another company. The other class members watched in rapt silence as the skit unfolded. Their expressions made it clear that they were watching a dress rehearsal of something they could actually face. As the first day at Armonk progresses, the group uses role-playing and discussion to explore other management styles in the context of completing various tasks, such as setting a pace or democratically eliciting team members' views.

The group returns to the subject of management styles later in the week when discussing detailed cases in which it is not clear which management styles are appropriate. The managers identify with the problems—among them a rancorous interaction between an IBM project manager and a client and an employee who might have an alcohol problem. Increasingly, the managers begin to explore how they can elicit information—verbal and nonverbal—that might reveal early signs of trouble. The managers also begin to mention policies they studied in Phase 1. The discussions are sometimes heated, in part because the managers are revisiting decisions they made on their own jobs.

In the middle of the week, the facilitator leads the new managers through assessments of their own management styles, using information that they, their managers, their colleagues, and the people they supervise provided during Phase 1. Because the group has now spent several days examining management styles, understanding one's own tendencies takes on greater importance. Equally important is understanding how others see you and translating this knowledge into ideas for managing more effectively.

FROM KNOWLEDGE TO ACTION

In management as in teaching, behavior change rarely occurs without follow-up. For this reason, one of the final activities in the week requires the new managers to construct "individual development plans" and "organizational action plans." These are detailed descriptions of concrete steps they will take to translate the week's lessons into improvements in their own managing and into enhancements in their team's skills. The new managers share their plans with one another, swapping ideas for improving them.

The individual and organizational plans are a natural transition into Phase 3 of Basic Blue. One part of Phase 3 is another round of online learning, similar to Phase 1. New managers work to develop their skills in such areas as creating strong teams, networking, and making mobile management work. While some of these topics are mandatory, others reflect learning commitments managers made in their individual development plans.

In addition, as part of Phase 3, each new manager is required to schedule meetings with both his or her supervisor and the members of the team he or she leads. In the meeting with team members, the new manager explains the goals for the group and his or her plans to realize these goals. The meeting between the new manager and his or her boss, which takes place 90 days after completion of Phase 2, serves to review progress toward the individual and organizational goals. Completion of this work starts the clock counting down to the next round of professional development, a process of ongoing structured learning that continues as long as the manager is with IBM.

MAKING BASIC BLUE WORK

Face-to-face debate, discussion, and role-playing are central to Basic Blue. However, computers complement these expensive activities by helping participants to learn text-based information outside of class. In the process of making this hybrid model work, the IBM design team learned four lessons.

1. *Know the audience and the curriculum.* To design training that would help new managers to pursue IBM's goals effectively, the team responsible for creating Basic Blue had to understand the problems new managers encountered in trying to manage the "IBM way" as Lou Gerstner had defined it, the skills and knowledge the managers needed to solve these problems, and what aspects of the appropriate curriculum new managers could learn by reading Web-based text and which parts required face-to-face interactions.

2. *Get the right mix of teaching skills.* The content of the curriculum dictated the requirements for instructors. The team had first thought that Basic Blue could use the instructors who had lectured in the New Managers School. It soon learned otherwise: Facilitating rich discussions of management issues required different skills from those needed to lecture about company policies. In Basic Blue, the facilitator needed to know how to guide intense discussions among very different people who worked in a variety of settings. Instead of searching for experts on particular company policies, the management development team recruited individuals who had IBM management experience and were interested in spending two years working with new managers. It then helped the interested managers to strengthen their facilitation skills.

3. *Get the technology right.* Basic Blue was designed for new IBM managers all over the world, many of whom access the Web via telephone modems rather than high-speed fiber-optic cables. Faced with this problem, the management development team could have placed the curriculum on CDs, but it rejected this approach because frequent curriculum revisions would be required in response to both weaknesses identified by program participants and changes in company policies—the subject of much of the online curriculum. The Web-based approach made it possible to give all users immediate access to curriculum revisions. The team also learned that the technology had to include the ability to track student progress.

4. *Create the right incentives.* When the management development team launched Basic Blue, it assumed a good curriculum and the chance to come to Armonk would be incentive enough for new managers to devote two

hours each week to completing the learning tasks. It soon learned that job pressures caused many new managers to fall behind. The team adopted a variety of tactics to keep the new managers working at the Phase 1 tasks, including using the tracking system to trigger e-mails and telephone calls to spur on lagging managers.

Incentives are also required in Phase 3, when knowledge is turned into performance. The Basic Blue curriculum focuses directly on the skills managers need to manage effectively. But even the best training can be ineffective as people, confronted with the stress of their jobs, fall back into familiar habits. The requirement to design an individual development plan and an organizational action plan is intended to focus the new manager's attention on concrete goals and the steps needed to reach them. The required Phase 3 meetings with supervisors and team members make visible the commitments of Basic Blue participants to translate new learning into new behavior.

FROM IBM TO THE CLASSROOM

In many respects, the work of teachers and administrators is very different from that of IBM managers. For example, K–12 educators are responsible for helping all clients (children) succeed, not just those who can pay the bill. However, despite many differences between the work educators and IBM managers do, the lessons from IBM shed light on opportunities for improving professional development for educators.

Before turning to the applicability of these lessons, let's consider some of the factors that hinder the creation of effective professional development for teachers and administrators. One is a lack of time. For most teachers and administrators, the school day is filled with pressing responsibilities to children. It is difficult in most schools to find opportunities for teachers to watch one another work with children and then to work collaboratively to improve instruction.

A second problem is a lack of capacity. Under the pressure of standards-based education reforms,

schools are introducing new curricula, especially in mathematics, that require instructional methods quite different from the ones teachers are familiar with. Many schools lack resource people who know a new curriculum well and can demonstrate how to teach it effectively.

A third problem is the information deluge. Educators do their work in highly regulated environments. They need to follow a variety of policies and rules—for example, how to place and teach English-language learners, how to create Individualized Education Programs for learning-disabled students, and what disciplinary steps they may take with a misbehaving student. The policies and rules that govern educators' work often change. As a result, considerable time that could be devoted to improving instruction is spent listening to descriptions of new rules and policies. With this context in mind, we turn to the lessons from IBM.

1. *Know the audience and the curriculum.* In many school districts, teachers and administrators spend much of the first days back at school after the summer vacation listening to descriptions of new policies. This is typically not an effective use of time, both because educators don't remember what they hear and because the limited time together has more valuable uses. Posting the new information on a Web site and asking educators to answer questions online about the new policies would free up professional development time. The obligation to respond to the online questionnaire would also help educators to learn where to look for the information when they need it.

    Just as IBM used collaborative learning tools to help busy new managers communicate with their peers, these same tools can enable educators to share ideas and information about curriculum and teaching strategies. Technology can also allow teachers to view from home demonstrations of the teaching of new curricula or videos of a colleague teaching a particular topic. By themselves, these activities will not result in improved instruction. However, they can provide busy educators with ideas and bring up questions that will catalyze focused conversations about how to improve instruction. In other words, technology can increase the effectiveness of the time educators spend in face-to-face interactions. However, technology cannot substitute for the development of face-to-face learning communities.

2. *Get the right mix of teaching skills.* Just as IBM learned that the lecturers in its New Managers School could not function effectively as facilitators of intense conversations among new managers in Basic Blue, schools that change the format of professional development are likely to confront the same problem. Consider the consequences of changing the format of beginning-of-the-year professional development.

In preparation for the first day back to work, school principals are asked to read online the district's new policy for evaluating teachers' instructional strengths and weaknesses, watch a 30-minute video of a teacher providing mathematics instruction, write an evaluation of the instruction following the new guidelines, and submit this evaluation electronically. Then on the first morning back to work, principals meet in small groups, read one another's evaluations, watch segments of the video, and then discuss the evaluations that they wrote. The goal of the session is to use the advice of their colleagues to revise their evaluations. After lunch, the principals role-play the meeting they would have with the teacher in the video, explaining the points in the evaluation and helping the teacher develop a plan to improve the weak aspects of his or her instruction. It seems unlikely that many central office officials accustomed to explaining the district's teacher evaluation policies each August would know how to effectively facilitate the intense face-to-face interactions that the new format would produce.

3. *Get the technology right.* Whether it is software to provide school-based educators with information on student test results, videos of classroom instruction, or descriptions of state learning standards, most busy K–12 educators will use the electronic tools only if the technology works reliably on the computer they typically use, most often their home computer. Many efforts to use technology for training fall by the wayside because insufficient attention is paid to ensuring that members of the learning community using computers of different vintages and running different operating systems can access the relevant information reliably.

4. *Create the right incentives.* Most K–12 educators want to improve their skills, just as new managers at IBM do. However, like the new IBM managers, teachers are often sidetracked by unexpected demands of jobs and families. As a result, investments in professional development will result in improved teaching and learning only if time is set aside in the school schedule for the face-to-face interactions necessary for improving instruction. Just as critical are incentives for educators to prepare for the face-to-face sessions and to translate the professional development initiatives into instructional change. Getting the incentives right is not easy. However, facing the incentive problem is just as important when working with educators as it is when working with IBM managers.

SUMMING UP

The four lessons that the developers of Basic Blue learned are not new to K–12 educators or to groups developing online professional development tools for an audience of educators. However, they are easy to forget, especially given the pressures to improve instruction rapidly and the difficulty of creating time in the school schedule for educators to work together on improving instruction.

The lure of substituting technology for face-to-face interactions can be great. Realizing that these same lessons held for IBM, a company with enormous technical expertise and with the resources to apply technology intensively to solve its training problems, may help K–12 educators to remember their importance. Keeping in mind what computers are good at and what they are not good at will be critical to using technology in ways that will help K–12 educators meet the unprecedented challenge of preparing all students to meet high learning standards.

ENDNOTES

1. Michael Schmoker, *Phi Beta Kappan*, February 2004, pp. 424–432.

2. See, for example, Vivian Troen and Katherine C. Boles, *Who's Teaching Your Children?* (New Haven, CT: Yale University Press, 2003).

DISCUSSION QUESTIONS

1. Are you convinced that technology can be a useful tool for improving professional development opportunities for teachers?
2. What advantages or disadvantages arise from thinking of teachers as "managers"?
3. What are the author's specific recommendations for improving professional development in schools?
4. Can models developed in the business world translate successfully to the world of education?
5. What would have to change in your school to make the approach to professional development described in this chapter work successfully?

PRO-CON CHART 5

Should the person who helps teachers to improve instruction also evaluate their performance?

PRO

1. The threat of evaluation can stimulate reluctant teachers to improve.

2. Evaluation is simply the final step in an extended period of formative supervisory feedback.

3. Trust and honesty are built by people working closely together over a long period of time.

4. The relationship between supervisor and teacher is very similar to the relationship between teacher and student.

5. The person who has been working with a teacher all year long is best qualified to make a judgment about whether the teacher's employment should continue.

CON

1. Supervision requires an environment where new skills can be safely practiced without threat.

2. Supervision and evaluation, like formative and summative assessment, are entirely separate categories of thought and practice.

3. The threat of evaluation irrevocably eliminates trust and makes open communication impossible.

4. Supervisors should always treat teachers as professional colleagues, not as subordinates who know less than they do.

5. The person who has been working with a teacher all year long in a helping relationship cannot be relied on to provide an objective judgment of performance.

CASE STUDY 5

A Principal Works for Inclusion

Imagine you are the principal at Northmore High School, in a small, rural town. Northmore's surrounding population is fairly homogenous, as is the student body. The school counselor has approached you concerning a number of students who are mildly handicapped or have special needs and who have recently become targets of unwelcoming comments in the hallways and schoolyard. The comments come from a specific group of students who participate on various athletic teams.

It is a basic concern of yours that all students feel welcomed at the school and do not have to be subjected to behavior or remarks that make them uncomfortable.

1. Do you approach the teachers first and discuss how to deal with the issue in the classroom?

2. How should the teachers approach the subject in the classroom to establish a healthy relationship among all students?

3. What programs can you present in the school to make the environment more accepting: clubs, peer and outside discussion groups, films, classroom discussions, parent-teacher conferences, guest speakers, etc.?

4. Is it better to work with outside groups to provide a forum for discussion that puts the issue in a larger community or national context? To what extent should the issue be put in a larger sociological perspective, and to what extent should it be dealt with locally?

5. Should the coaches of the respective athletic teams be notified so that they can announce that they will suspend the athletes or limit playing time if there is another occurrence?

6. Is it better to inform parents in writing about their children's misbehavior and warn them that another incident could lead to suspension or worse?

7. To what extent, if at all, should the school district's attorney be consulted? Are the incidents a legal matter?

PART SIX
Curriculum and Policy

In Part Six, the relationship between policy and curriculum is considered. What are the implications of current demographic trends for curriculum? How are issues of diversity, homosexuality, educational equity, and practice-based assessment influencing the curriculum? Does academic tracking help or hinder the pursuit of equitable student learning outcomes? How are school reform and restructuring efforts affecting the curriculum, and what policy alternatives are available?

In Chapter 34, Harold Hodgkinson identifies key demographic changes that are influencing educational policy and offers recommendations for teachers who work with diverse students in their classrooms. His ideas include practices such as valuing all students, understanding student backgrounds, helping new students to get settled, paying close attention to students who are eligible for free or reduced-price lunches, and emphasizing that students are all Americans, regardless of their differences. Next, Robert Slavin argues that the use of randomized experiments, now beginning to affect education policy, has the potential to revolutionize education. With their greater use, confidence in educational research will grow among policymakers and educators, and better educational programs for children will result.

In Chapter 36, James Sears calls attention to the growing number of school-aged children who come from nontraditional families. He suggests that educators need to be responsive to the issues that children with gay or lesbian parents might encounter in gender and social development, as well as in the classroom. He advocates integrating issues about homosexuality into the school curriculum. He also describes some ways that educators can assume proactive roles on behalf of lesbian, gay, or bisexual students and families. Next, Allan Odden describes how standards-based reform necessitates a change of focus in educational funding. Attempting to ensure equity of resources must give way to providing for an adequate level of resources if we seriously hope to close the achievement gap between low-income and minority students and all other students.

In Chapter 38, Carl Glickman argues that single models, structures, methods, and systems of education should be avoided. A diversity of approaches is preferable, he contends, as long as every school and district is held responsible for providing an education for all students that increases their choices for exercising their rights to life, liberty, and the pursuit of happiness. Next, Richard Rothstein offers evidence that the cumulative effects of social class more strongly influence student achievement than does schooling. He recommends a comprehensive strategy that includes greater access to learning opportunities, improved health and social services, and other policies for reducing inequality. In the concluding chapter in Part Six, Allan Ornstein examines how his thinking on education, equality, and equity has changed over the span of his career, especially in light of current events, policies, and societal trends that seem to signal growing inequality in American society. He challenges educators to ask whether and how schools can serve as equalizers of differences.

PROFESSIONAL PROFILE: POLICY

Name:
Gerald W. Bracey

Email:
gbracey1@verizon.net

Latest degree/university:
Ph.D., Psychology, Stanford University

Position:
Associate Professor, George Mason University; Associate, High Scope Educational Research Foundation, Ypsilanti, Michigan; Fellow, Educational Policy Studies Laboratory, Arizona State University

Previous positions:
Director of Research and Evaluation, Cherry Creek (CO) Schools; Director of Research, Evaluation and Testing, Virginia Department of Education; Associate Director, Institute for Child Study, Indiana University; Associate Research Psychologist, Educational Testing Service

Person most influential in your career:
Stanley Williams. Stan was a friend before becoming a mentor. He chaired the psychology department at the College of William and Mary and, after my freshman year there, was my next-door neighbor. Stan and his wife, Betty, were night owls. I worked every other night from four to midnight as a police dispatcher and would often drop in on them when I got off work. We sometimes watched Jack Paar, sometimes gossiped about various college characters, and sometimes talked about psychology. It was in these conversations that I learned a great deal of psychology that could not be found in a textbook.

Number-one achievement:
Waking at least some people up to the real performances of American schools and to the true purposes of No Child Left Behind

Number-one regret:
I really don't have any "number one." It's not a functional game. As a freshman in college, my literature professor pulled me aside one day and said that I seemed to be able to turn a phrase and that if I took the time to write extra material, he'd read it and advise me on it. I had a full course load, a girlfriend, and a job and never got around to it. It could have changed things.

Favorite educational journal:
Phi Delta Kappan. Not because I've written a column for it since 1984, but because since that time and before, it has been the place to find the most lucid essays on education policy issues.

Favorite educational book:
James Herndon's *How To Survive in Your Native Land.* The nation missed a great opportunity in 1971 when this book appeared. It should have declared a moratorium on

writing about schools until everyone had a chance to digest this small volume. Funny, biting, angry, profane, and wise, it describes, in no particular order, Jim's at the time 10-year-long career as a teacher in South San Francisco (after he had been fired after 1 year from a school in Oakland as "unfit to teach").

Best book/chapter you wrote:
Setting the Record Straight: Responses to Misconceptions about Education in the United States, Revised Edition (2004). In truth, I like to give the same answer I've heard composers and movie directors give: the last one. I think, hope, that I see progress in the craft of writing with each new volume.

Additional interests:
Travel. In 1965–1966 I spent a year in Hong Kong and traveled extensively through Southeast Asia, the Middle East, and Europe on the way home. That whetted my appetite to take off and go until the money ran out. I did that in 1973, returning home in late-1976 with net assets of $300, two Canon F-1 bodies, and four lenses.

Food. An earlier trip to Paris (1964) had led me to conclude that heaven would be working for *Guide Michelin*. I got a chance to do newspaper restaurant reviews in Richmond, Virginia, in the early 1980s and then for the rest of the decade in Denver.

Also music, opera, and film.

Curriculum/school policy relationship:
Policy should flow from the curriculum, which in turn should relate to someone's vision. For instance, the vision at the Key School, a public magnet school in Indianapolis, was that Howard Gardner's theories of multiple intelligences offered an excellent approach to developing a curriculum and that the school should be integrated into the community. One of the initial policy decisions was about whether to develop all intelligences or to diagnose kids' intelligences and play to their strengths. They decided to develop all intelligences, which led to everyone learning to play an instrument and everyone learning a foreign language, as well as to a number of original activities to develop interpersonal and intrapersonal intelligences, and so forth.

Professional vision:
To develop an education system in which people once again realize that the root of educate, *educare,* means "to lead out." The system now insists on externally imposing instruction and "standards" through programs like No Child Left Behind and the National Governors Association initiative on high schools. That will never work. I'd also like to use the example of Finland to show that you don't have to use tests. The Finns don't use tests to evaluate students, teachers, or schools. Yet when Finland takes part in international test programs, it outscores all Western nations and often some of the Asian countries as well. The Finns trust teachers to know what they're doing.

Professional advice to teacher or curriculum specialist:
Know your field. Know pedagogy. Understand that nothing works for everyone. Alan Roses, vice president of GlaxoSmithKline, observed that 90 percent of FDA-approved drugs work for only 30–50 percent of the people who take them. The same is true of curricula and instructional methods. The randomized field trials so touted by some educational researchers don't advance the needed knowledge at all.

34

Educational Demographics:
What Teachers Should Know

HAROLD HODGKINSON

FOCUSING QUESTIONS

1. What key demographic trends are affecting educational policy today?
2. How can teachers use demographics in their daily practice?
3. How will changes in the racial and age composition of the U.S. population influence education in coming years?
4. What different worldviews will students be bringing to classrooms?
5. What are some things teachers can do to help students to adjust to school?

Teachers are, unfortunately, rarely invited to participate in policy discussions affecting their schools—either by local or state boards of education or by various legislative bodies, from state legislatures to the United States Congress. Over the last two decades, the field of demographics has become vitally important to education policymakers at all levels. What are the key demographics affecting educational policy? How can teachers make good use of demographics in their daily practice?

KEY DEMOGRAPHICS

Nothing is distributed evenly across the United States. Not race, not religion, not age, not fertility, not wealth, and certainly not access to higher education. For example, only five states will have a 20 percent (or more) increase in school enrollments; most states will have smaller increases and about nine states will have declines. "Tidal Wave II," as former U.S. Secretary of Education Richard Riley likes to call the new increases in enrollments, is a statistical fiction for the vast majority of states.

But what will happen where you work? That depends on your state and your location. About one-quarter of Americans live in big cities, half live in suburbs, and a quarter live in small towns or rural areas. If you live in a central city in the eastern half of the country, you can expect almost no enrollment increases and some decreases. Those who can flee to the suburbs.

The inner suburban ring (where there is nothing between you and the city limits) will see a major increase in student diversity—more minorities, more immigrants, more students learning English as a second language (ESL), and more students from poverty. Teaching in an inner suburb will increasingly resemble teaching in an inner city. The second suburban ring (with one suburb between you and the city) will see some expansion in student enrollments, especially as you reach the beltway, which used to contain growth—like a belt—but is now the jumping-off place for growth. In these areas, parents do not commute to the central city; they live in one suburb and work in another.

Finally, enrollments in small towns or rural areas will be flat. But these places will have increasingly large percentages of elderly people. Older residents tend to "age in place," and whereas the young move away, some elderly do seek out small-town life.

Inner cities in the West tend to be economically flexible and porous, whereas those in the East and Midwest rigidly segregate low-income people in the cities. Racial and economic segregation are almost the same thing in the East and Midwest, which have the 10 most racially segregated cities in the nation; none of the 10 most racially segregated cities is in the South.

Consider another kind of diversity: the percentage of youth who by age 19 have graduated from high school and have been admitted to a college. Attaining this status is, of course, the American Dream. Some states have 65 percent of their 19-year-olds in this category, whereas others have 25 to 30 percent—a range that is far greater than any differences in scores between the United States and other nations.

One form of diversity that affects every teacher is transiency. Although about 3 million children are born each year, up to 40 million Americans move in that same time period, making mobility far more important than births in explaining population changes. Many teachers have 22 students in the fall and 22 in the following spring, but 20 out of the 22 are different students. Hospitals in these regions spend most of their time taking case histories from strangers. Each Sunday, ministers preach to congregations, a third of whose members are new. Transiency also relates to crime—knowing your neighbor will prevent you from stealing his lawnmower.

In addition, the states with the lowest rates of high school graduation and college admissions are the five most transient states in the United States. Most migration occurs within the same state, but about 6 to 8 million people move to another state each year. People in the New England, Middle Atlantic, and Midwestern states are moving to the Southeast and Southwest. In addition, a million immigrants each year are settling mainly in California, Texas, and Florida.

RACE FACTS

The nature of race is changing. Fact one: About 65 percent of America's population growth in the next two decades will be "minority," particularly from Hispanic and Asian immigrants. These groups have higher fertility rates than Caucasians, whose fertility level is too low to even replace the current population.

Fact two: The 2000 Census allows you to check as many race boxes as you wish. As a result, Tiger Woods, who is a "Cablinasian," will be able to check Caucasian, Black, Indian, and Asian. But how do we score his four checks? Does he count as four people? Is each check mark exactly one-quarter of Tiger? Can he be counted as white for housing surveys and black for civil rights actions?

Fact three: Three million black Hispanics in the United States, mostly dark-skinned Spanish speakers from the Caribbean, have checked black on the census form because Hispanic is not a race. Although race is vitally important politically, economically, and historically, it remains scientific nonsense—Office of Management and Budget Directive 15, the guide for the census for more than 20 years, states that the racial categories in the census have no scientific validity.

Fact four: At least 40 percent of all Americans have had some racial mixing in the last three generations—including President Bill Clinton and Martin Luther King, Jr.—but only 2 to 4 percent will admit it on Census 2000. The blurring of racial identity will grow rapidly, however; children of Asian and Hispanic immigrants are marrying out of their parents' heritage at rates between 30 to 60 percent. In the 1900 immigration wave, an Italian's marriage to a German was called miscegenation, and the families would not speak to each other. Today, only 15 percent of European Americans are married to a spouse from the same country of origin, and we laugh about this outdated notion. Soon, Asians and Hispanics may do the same.

Diversity is increasingly unevenly distributed. In fact, the 65 percent increase in diverse populations will be absorbed by only about 230 of our 3,068 counties; California, Texas, and Florida will get about three-fifths of the increase. Remember that more than half of our entire population lives in only nine states—those three, plus New York, Pennsylvania, Ohio, Illinois, Michigan, and New

Jersey—yet only California, Texas, and Florida are growing so quickly; the other six seem to be "wealthy but tired." Forty-one states compete for the other half of the population. Although we talk of "minority majorities," this phenomenon is only possible in a handful of counties. Whites will become a minority of the U.S. population around 2050, and you will have retired before then.

But the blurring of racial lines suggests the declining importance of race, and many people are lobbying for race data to be excluded from the next census because it tells many things that are not accurate. Most poor children in the United States are white, but a higher percentage of black and Hispanic kids are poor. Being black is no longer a universal handicap; over one-quarter of black households have a higher income than the white average, and rates of blacks who go to college and own homes continue to grow. But poverty is a universal handicap. If you have poor kids of diverse ethnicities as well as middle-class minorities in your classes, you know exactly what I mean.

Racial desegregation has not led to economic equality. Twenty percent of U.S. kids are below the poverty line today—exactly the same percentage as 15 years ago—even though most of the nation is less segregated and wealthier. This poverty rate is inexcusable in the wealthiest nation on earth. It is time to do what Kentucky has done—build an economic "floor" under every child in the state to equalize the investment in each child's education. That is economic desegregation, and many states are doing it. Our new understanding of the importance of children's preschool years has led many states to mandate a preschool program for all poverty-level children in the state, another attempt to equalize investment in every child and economically desegregate.

AN AGING POPULATION

We grow old. Although immigration and high minority fertility stall the trend, the U.S. population is steadily getting older, as are populations in other developed or industrialized nations. Census 2000 added an extra box for the state-your-age question because 57,000 Americans are now over 100 years of age, and 1.4 million are in their 90s. President Clinton, born in 1946 (a leading-edge baby boomer), will be 65 in 2011. By then, 65 will not be considered old—today, geriatrics defines middle age as 50 through 75 and old age as 75 and older. Of the baby boomers, born between 1946 and 1964, one in four will live past 85. Today, only one household in four has a child in the public schools.

President and Mrs. Clinton now have an empty nest, since their daughter graduated from college and moved out. The question for schools: Will baby boomers (70 million of them) maintain their interest in public schools after their kids have left the educational system? Will they vote for bond issues for someone else's children? Or for raises for teachers to benefit someone else's children? The answer is key to the future of public school finance. Already, many school board meetings are dominated by today's much smaller group of citizens ages 65 and older who wish to be removed from the public school tax rolls. And remember the mantra from demographics to politics: As you get older, you vote more often. How will we convince seniors that their Social Security and Medicare trust funds will be replenished by today's high school students when they join the work force?

DIFFERENCES IN WORLDVIEWS

A final issue for teachers concerns the switch from race to national origin. This new category will tell much more about students and their parents. Knowing that students and parents are Hispanic tells very little—15 percent of California's Hispanics do not even speak Spanish. Knowing that they are Cuban or Panamanian tells lots more. The following is a collection of important differences in how people see the world.

- *The sense of time.* Americans believe in the future as if it were a religion (except Californians, who seem to live in the eternal now). Many immigrants have a sophisticated sense of the past that puts us all to shame. Yet teachers usually motivate students on the grounds of a brighter future—when consistency with the past might be a better motivator for some students.
- *The sense of family.* Whereas most Americans are only aware of their nuclear family

(parents plus their children), some Americans are from extended families—for them, a loan to buy a house might come from an uncle; a medical problem might be solved by an aunt. The extended family provides comfort, stability, and many services that the U.S. government typically provides.

- *The sense of hierarchy.* America is as "flat" as you can get on this score, but many newcomers are from rigidly structured societies in which children (and women) are considered inferior beings. Thus, the child enters school having been told by parents that teachers are authority figures. To show respect, they look at the floor when the teacher addresses them. Most teachers see this behavior as evasive and prefer students to look them straight in the eye, indicating honesty, trust, and interest in the class.

In many seminars, students are encouraged to disagree with their teachers to show their individuality. But in many nations and cultures, such behavior is called "putting yourself forward," often a major sin. Asian, Hispanic, and Native American kids seldom leap into the air, fists extended, saying "Yes! I'm wonderful!" Indeed, at one high school graduation I attended, the valedictorian downplayed her own talent and hard work, declaring that the award belonged to her entire family and that her family should be on the stage with her (they later joined her there). This behavior was not excessive modesty: The young lady truly believed that the honor was her family's achievement, not just her own.

DEMOGRAPHIC TIPS FOR TEACHERS

Some simple actions can help teachers work with the diverse students in their classrooms.

- If a student is presented in records as "Hispanic," make sure you know what country that student's family is from, what language the family uses at home, and whether the parents also speak English and how well. If parents speak only Spanish and you speak none, try to get a colleague who is bilingual to be on the line during your first phone call home.

- If a student won't look you in the eye during the first week of school, don't make a big deal of it in front of the class. Take a minute to ask the student about it privately.

- Find out as soon as possible which of your students is new to the area and may need some help in getting settled. If half your students (or fellow teachers) are new in town, be prepared for some problems. Transiency often brings out the worst in people at any age.

- Even though students may choose to sit with their racial or ethnic groups in the cafeteria or in other informal settings, your classroom must value all students. Rather than "color blind," your goal should be "culture fair."

- Pay particular attention to your students who are eligible for free or reduced-price lunches—they may need extra help and may not get enough to eat on weekends. (There should be no "Title I pullout program" that identifies low-income students in your classroom.)

- If you have lots of diversity in your classroom, try to use as many different visual presentations as possible. Pictures can often convey meaning when words do not.

- Some students may be genuinely confused about their ethnic ancestry. Several state courts have indicated that it is illegal to force a child to choose between the mother's and father's backgrounds. Although it's a sensitive issue, you can communicate clearly to your class that you value all children and that you expect them to do their best. The important thing is the understanding that we are all Americans, regardless of our backgrounds.

- Make a list of student successes for any ethnic group in your school, whether in your class or not. It's the perfect defense against the student who says, "You just don't understand! No one from [country x] can do [math/ English/science]."

- Some students may be the responsibility of grandparents—more than 1 million public school students are. If so, make sure that the grandparents get the same level of attention that you give to biological parents—they may need even more help.

THE IMPORTANCE OF DEMOGRAPHICS

We have only scratched the surface regarding the impact of demographics on education and on the president of the classroom—the teacher. All of these demographic changes are coming soon to a classroom near you.

DISCUSSION QUESTIONS

1. Which demographic changes are likely to have the greatest impact on your classroom or school?
2. Which demographic changes are likely to have the greatest impact on the United States as a whole?
3. Should newcomers to the United States be expected to adjust quickly to American culture?
4. Why is it important for teachers to be sensitive to student differences?
5. What implications do changes in demographics have for curriculum and instruction?

35

Evidence-Based Education Policies:
Transforming Educational Practice
and Research

ROBERT E. SLAVIN

FOCUSING QUESTIONS

1. What is scientific-based research? What promises does it hold for education?
2. How does scientific-based research aid noneducational fields? What is the potential it can translate to education? What are the difficulties that the field of education must overcome in adapting some of these practices?
3. List some of the reasons why educational development lags behind other advanced fields.
4. What are some of the vital considerations when doing educational research?
5. What are some of the differences in results obtained from nonexperimental versus experimental research? What can be learned from each?

Education is on the brink of a scientific revolution that has the potential to profoundly transform policy, practice, and research. Consider the following:

- In 1998, Congress appropriated $150 million per year to provide schools funds to adopt "proven, comprehensive reform models" (U.S. Department of Education, 1999). This unprecedented legislation, introduced by Congressmen David Obey and John Porter, defined "proven" in terms of experimental-control comparisons on standards-based measures. To my knowledge, this was the first time in history that federal education funding had been linked directly to evidence of effectiveness (see Slavin, 1997). In 2001, Comprehensive School Reform (CSR) funding was progressively increased to $310 million annually and provided funding to more than 2,600 mostly high-poverty schools (Southwest Educational Research Laboratory, 2002).

- Kent McGuire, Director of the Office of Educational Research and Improvement (OERI) in the Clinton administration, convinced Congress that the CSR funding program warranted a substantial increase in education research and development. Under his leadership, an array of capacity building, program development, and evaluation efforts were launched. All of these were intended to put programs with rigorous evidence of effectiveness into thousands more schools, particularly those serving many at-risk children.

- The Bush administration's first domestic initiative, the reauthorization of the Elementary and Secondary Education Act (ESEA), called No Child Left Behind, took the idea of scientifically based practice to an even higher level. No Child Left Behind (U.S. Congress, 2001) mentions "scientifically based research" 110 times. It defines "scientifically based research" as "rigorous, systematic and objective procedures to obtain valid knowledge," which includes research that "is evaluated using experimental or quasi-experimental designs," preferably with random assignment. Scientifically based research is intended to serve as the basis for Title I programs, Reading First programs for reading in grades K–3, Early Reading First programs for pre-kindergarten, CSR, and many other components. Funding for ESEA overall was increased by 18 percent, the largest increase ever.

- Grover Whitehurst, the Bush Administration's OERI director, took a strong line in support of randomized experiments (Whitehurst, 2002). In a request for proposals that is a revolutionary document in its own right, OERI invited early childhood programs to subject themselves to randomized evaluations in which data would be collected by third-party evaluators (U.S. Department of Education, 2002a). Requests for proposals of this kind in other areas are in the pipeline. Not since the Follow Through Planned Variation studies of the 1970s (Rhine, 1981) have rigorous, experimental designs with common measures been applied to programs capable of broad scale replication.

- OERI has been reorganized to consider randomized and rigorous matched experimental research on programs and policies that are central to the education of large numbers of children. The U.S. Department of Education's (2002b) strategic plan for 2002–2007 anticipated having 75 percent of all OERI-funded research that addresses causal questions use random assignment designs by 2004. (Previously, such research probably represented less than 5 percent of causal research funded by OERI.) As a direct result, Congress is likely to substantially increase funding for educational research.

It is important to note that none of these policy developments have yet produced the revolution I am anticipating. The CSR funding program, despite a clear focus on proven programs, has so far provided most of its funds to programs with little or no rigorous evidence of effectiveness, including many "programs" slapped together for the purpose of obtaining funding. A 1999 review of the research on 24 comprehensive reform models by the American Institutes of Research (AIR) (Herman, 1999) categorized them as having strong evidence of effectiveness; promising, marginal, mixed, weak, or no effects; or no research. Among 2,665 CSR grants made from 1998 to 2002 (Southwest Educational Research Laboratory, 2002), only 20.8 percent of grants went to programs rated by AIR as having strong evidence and 16.0 percent to programs rated as promising or marginal. Most of the grants (63.2%) went either to programs rated as mixed or unresearched or to national or homegrown models not even considered by AIR. The ESEA reauthorization tightened up the definition of proven and comprehensive and placed more emphasis on programs with scientifically based evidence of effectiveness (U.S. Department of Education, 2002c), but state officials who review CSR proposals still have broad discretion and could continue to minimize or ignore the research base behind the programs they fund. No Child Left Behind and other initiatives emphasizing rigorous research are too new to have had any impact on practice or funding. Yet these and other developments, if not yet proven, still create the potential for changes with far-reaching consequences. It is possible that these policy reforms could set in motion a process of research and development on programs and practices affecting children everywhere. This process could create the kind of progressive, systematic improvement over time that has characterized successful parts of our economy and society throughout the 20th century, in fields such as medicine, agriculture, transportation, and technology. In each of these fields, processes of development, rigorous evaluation, and dissemination have produced a pace of innovation and improvement that is unprecedented in history (see Shavelson & Towne, 2002). These innovations have transformed the world. Yet education has failed to embrace this dynamic, and as a result, education moves from fad to fad. Educational practice does change over time, but the change process more resembles the pendulum swings characteristic of tastes in art or fashion (think hemlines) than the progressive improvements characteristic of science and technology (see Slavin, 1989).

WELCOME TO THE 20TH CENTURY

At the dawn of the 21st century, education is finally being dragged, kicking and screaming, into the 20th century. The scientific revolution that utterly transformed medicine, agriculture, transportation, technology, and other fields early in the 20th century almost completely bypassed the field of education. If Rip Van Winkle had been a physician, a farmer, or an engineer, he would be unemployable if he awoke today. If he had been a good elementary school teacher in the 19th century, he would probably be a good elementary school teacher today. It is not that we have not learned anything since Rip Van Winkle's time. It is that applications of the findings of educational research remain haphazard; furthermore, evidence is respected only occasionally, and only if it happens to correspond to current educational or political fashions.

Early in the 20th century, the practice of medicine was at a similar point. For example, research had long since identified the importance of bacteria in disease, and by 1865 Joseph Lister had demonstrated the effectiveness of antiseptic procedures in surgery. In the 1890s, William Halsted at Johns Hopkins University introduced rubber gloves, gauze masks, and steam sterilization of surgical instruments and demonstrated the effectiveness of these procedures. Yet it took 30 years to convince tradition-bound physicians to use sterile procedures. If he dropped his scalpel, a physician in 1910 was as likely as not to give it a quick wipe and carry on.

Today, of course, the linkage between research and practice in medicine is so tight that no physician would dream of ignoring the findings of rigorous research. Because medical practice is so closely based on medical research, funding for medical research is vast, and advances in medicine take place at breathtaking speed. My father's cardiologist recommended that he wait a few years to

have a necessary heart valve operation because the doctor was sure that within that short span of time research would advance far enough to make the wait worthwhile. As it turned out, he was right.

The most important reason for the extraordinary advances in medicine, agriculture, and other fields is the acceptance by practitioners of evidence as the basis for practice. In particular, it is the randomized clinical trial—more than any single medical breakthrough—that has transformed medicine (Doll, 1998). In a randomized clinical trial, patients are assigned at random to receive one treatment or another, usually a drug or a placebo. Because of random assignment, with an adequate number of subjects, it can be assumed that any differences in outcomes are due to the treatment, not to any extraneous factors. Replicated experiments of this kind can establish beyond any reasonable doubt the effectiveness (or lack thereof) of treatments intended for applied use (see Boruch, 1997).

EXPERIMENTS IN EDUCATION

In education, experiments are not uncommon, but they are usually brief, artificial experiments on topics of theoretical more than practical interest, often involving hapless college sophomores. Far more rare are experiments evaluating treatments of practical interest studied over a full school year or more. For example, there are many outstanding brief experiments published each year on the effects of various mnemonic teaching strategies. These have built a strong case for the effectiveness of mnemonic methods and provided a detailed understanding of the conditions under which they work best (see Levin & Levin, 1990). However, I am unaware of any experiment that has evaluated, for example, a year-long course making extensive use of mnemonic devices. The research on mnemonic strategies is directly useful to teachers, who can be encouraged to say, "When two vowels go walking, the first one does the talking," or present occasional mnemonics for remembering the order of planets out from the sun or trigonometric functions. Yet it is difficult to imagine that teaching and learning will make broad advances because teachers make occasional use of one or another mnemonic device. I write an educational psychology textbook (Slavin, 2003) that is full of research findings of this type, findings that are valuable in advancing theory and potentially valuable to teachers in understanding their craft. Yet the brief experiments, correlational studies, and descriptive studies that yield most of the information presented in my text or any other educational psychology text do not collectively add up to school reform. They are suggestions about how to think about daily teaching problems, not guides to the larger questions educators and policymakers must answer. Imagine that research in cardiology described heart function and carried out small-scale laboratory studies but never developed and tested an artificial heart valve. If this were the case, I would be an orphan. Imagine that agricultural research studied plant growth and diseases but never developed and tested new disease-resistant crops. Educational research has produced many rigorous and meaningful studies of basic principles of practice but very few rigorous studies of programs and practices that could serve as a solid base for policy and practice. Furthermore, there has been little respect for the studies of this kind that do exist. Because of this, policymakers have rarely seen the relevance of research to the decisions they have to make and therefore have provided minimal funding for research. This has led to a declining spiral, as inadequate investments in research lead to a dearth of the kind of large-scale, definitive research that policymakers would feel to be valuable, making these policymakers unwilling to invest in large-scale, definitive research.

SHIFTING POLICY PERSPECTIVES

The dramatic changes in federal education policies referred to earlier could potentially reverse this declining spiral. If the new funding flowing into research can produce some notable successes, we could have an ascending spiral: Rigorous research demonstrating positive effects of replicable programs on important student outcomes would lead to increased funding for such research, which would lead to more and better research and therefore more funding. More important, millions of children would benefit in the fairly near term.

Once we establish replicable paradigms for development, rigorous evaluation, replication, and dissemination, these mechanisms could be applied to any educational intervention or policy. Imagine if there were programs underway all the time to develop, evaluate, and disseminate new methods in every subject and every grade level, as well as programs on school-to-work transitions, special education, gifted children, dropout prevention, English language learners, race relations, drug abuse prevention, violence prevention, and so on. Every one of these areas lends itself to a development-evaluation-dissemination paradigm, as would many others. Over time, each area would experience the step-by-step, irreversible progress characteristic of medicine and agriculture because innovations would be held to strict standards of evaluation before being recommended for wide-scale use.

RESEARCH DESIGNS

The scientific revolution in education will take hold and produce its desired impacts only if research in fact begins to focus on replicable programs and practices central to education policy and teaching, and if it in fact employs research methods that meet the highest standards of rigor. This begs an important question: What kinds of research are necessary to produce findings of sufficient rigor to justify faith in the meaning of their outcomes?

OERI's director, Grover Whitehurst (2002), and other educational researchers (see, for example, Mosteller & Boruch, 2002) have argued that nothing less than randomized experiments will do for evaluations of educational interventions and policies. The strong emphasis on randomized experiments is welcome, but ironic. After many years of relative policy indifference to experiments of any kind, OERI is leaping over the rigorously matched experiment and demanding randomized experiments.

The difference in the value of randomized and well-matched experiments relates primarily to the problem of selection bias. In a matched experiment, it is always possible that observed differences are due not to treatments but to the fact that one set of schools or teachers was willing to implement a given treatment while another was not, or that a given set of students selected themselves or were selected into a given treatment while others were not.

When selection bias is a possibility at the student level, there are few if any alternatives to random assignment, because unmeasured (often unmeasurable) pre-existing differences are highly likely to be alternative explanations for study findings. For example, consider studies of after-school or summer school programs. If a researcher simply compared students attending such programs to those not attending who were similar in pretest scores or demographic factors, it is very likely that unmeasured factors such as student motivation, parents' support for education, and other consequential factors could explain any gains observed, because the more motivated children are more likely to show up. Similarly, studies comparing children assigned to gifted or special education programs to students with similar pretest scores are likely to miss key selection factors that were known to whoever assigned the students but not measured. If one child with an IQ of 130 is assigned to a gifted program and another with the same IQ is not, it is likely that the children differ in motivation, conscientiousness, or some other factor. In these kinds of situations, use of random assignment from within a selected pool is essential.

In contrast, there are situations in which it is teachers or schools that elect to implement a given treatment, but there is no selection bias that relates to the children. For example, a researcher might want to compare the achievement gains of children in classes using cooperative learning, or in schools using comprehensive reform models, to the gains made by demographically similar control groups starting at the same pretest levels. In such cases, random assignment of willing teachers or schools is still far preferable to matching, as matching leaves open the possibility that volunteer teachers or staffs are better than nonvolunteers. However, the likely bias is much less than in the case of student self-selection. Aggregate pretest scores in an entire school, for example, should indicate how effective the current staff has

been up to the present, so controlling for pretests in matched studies of existing schools or classes would control for much of the potential impact of having more willing teachers. For external validity, it is crucial to note that the findings of a well-matched experiment comparing volunteers to nonvolunteers apply only to schools or teachers who volunteer, but the potential for bias is moderate (after controlling for pretests and demographic factors).

The importance of this discussion lies in the fact that randomized experiments of interventions applying to entire classrooms can be extremely difficult and expensive to do and are sometimes impossible. My colleagues and I at Johns Hopkins University are working with a third-party evaluator, the University of Chicago's National Opinion Research Center, to do a randomized evaluation of Success for All, a comprehensive reform model. Recruiting schools for this study has been extremely difficult, even though we are offering substantial financial incentives to schools willing to be assigned at random to experimental or control groups. We initially offered schools $30,000 to participate, a total of $1.8 million just for incentives. Yet this was not sufficient; we ultimately had to offer the program at no cost to schools (but at a cost of about $70,000 per school to the study). For the same cost as that of doing this randomized study, we (and others) could have done two or three equally large-scale matched studies. It is at least arguable that replicated matched studies, done by different investigators in different places, might produce more valid and meaningful results than one definitive, once-in-a-lifetime randomized study.

Still, fully recognizing the difficulties of randomized experiments, I think they are nevertheless possible in most areas of policy-relevant program evaluation, and whenever they are possible, they should be used. Reviews of research in other fields have found that matched studies generally find stronger outcomes than randomized studies, although usually in the same direction (e.g., Fraker & Maynard, 1987; Friedlander & Robins, 1995; Ioannidis et al., 2001). Four randomized experiments we have planned or executed at Johns Hopkins University and the Success for All Foundation illustrate the potential and the pitfalls. One of these, mentioned earlier, involves randomly assigning 60 schools to Success for All or control conditions for a 3-year experiment. Initially, we offered $30,000 to each school, but we got hardly any takers. Schools were either unwilling to take a chance on being assigned to the control group for 3 years, or they could not afford the program costs beyond the $30,000 incentive. In spring 2002, we changed our offer. Schools willing to participate were randomly assigned to use Success for All either in grades K–2 or in grades 3–5, at no cost. Recruitment was still difficult, but under this arrangement we signed up adequate numbers of schools.

For another study proposed by my colleague Bette Chambers (but not funded), we recruited schools for a study of the Curiosity Corner preschool model. We offered schools the program for free, either in 2002–2003 or 2003–2004 (with random assignment to the two start dates). The 2003–2004 group would have served as the control group in 2002–2003. This delayed treatment control group design involving no cost to schools was easy for schools to accept, and we did not have serious recruiting problems.

In a study of an after-school tutoring program led by my colleague Toks Fashola, individual first graders whose parents agreed to have them participate were assigned at random to be tutored in spring 2002 or fall 2002. Again, the fall group served as a control group during the spring. Finally, Geoff Borman has done randomized evaluations of summer school programs in which individual children are randomly assigned to participate now or later (Borman, Boulay, Kaplan, Rachuba, & Hewes, 2001). In these cases, obtaining sufficient volunteers was not difficult.

These examples of a diverse set of research problems illustrate that, one way or another, it is usually possible to use random assignment to evaluate educational programs. There is no one formula for randomization, but with enough resources and cooperation from policymakers, random assignment is possible.

Beyond the benefits in terms of reducing selection bias, there is an important political reason to prefer randomized over matched studies at this point in history. Because of political develop-

ments in Washington, we have a once-in-a-lifetime opportunity to reverse the "awful reputation" that educational research has among policymakers (Kaestle, 1993; Lagemann, 2002). This is a time when it makes sense to concentrate resources and energies on a set of randomized experiments of impeccable quality and clear policy importance to demonstrate that such studies can be done. Over the longer run, I believe that a mix of randomized and rigorous matched experiments evaluating educational interventions would be healthier than a steady diet of randomized experiments, but right now we need to establish the highest possible standard of evidence, on a par with standards in other fields, to demonstrate what educational research can accomplish.

Of course, matched experiments, too, must be rigorous, planned in advance, and carefully designed to minimize selection bias. The hallmark of science is organized, disciplined inquiry that gives the null hypothesis every consideration. After the fact and pre-post experiments, for example, rarely meet this standard but are all too common in program evaluations.

NONEXPERIMENTAL RESEARCH

I should hasten to say that forms of research other than experiments, randomized or matched, can also be of great value. Correlational and descriptive research is essential in theory building and in suggesting variables worthy of inclusion in experiments. Our Success for All program, for example, owes a great deal to correlational and descriptive process-product studies of the 1970s and 1980s (see Slavin & Madden, 2001). As components of experiments, correlational and descriptive studies can also be essential in exploring variables that go beyond overall program impacts. In some policy contexts, experiments are impossible, and well-designed correlational or descriptive studies may be sufficient.

However, the experiment is the design of choice for studies that seek to make causal conclusions and particularly for evaluations of educational innovations. Educators and policymakers legitimately ask, "If we implement Program X instead of Program Y, or instead of our current program, what will be the likely outcomes for children?" For questions posed in this way, there are few alternatives to well-designed experiments.

RIGOROUSLY EVALUATED PROGRAMS AND PRACTICES VERSUS THOSE BASED ON SCIENTIFIC RESEARCH

If the scientific revolution in education is to achieve its potential to transform education policy and practice, it must focus on research that is genuinely of high quality and is appropriate to inform the decisions that educators and policymakers face. There is a key distinction that is easily lost in the current enthusiasm for science as a basis for practice. This is the distinction between programs and practices that are based on scientifically based research and those that have themselves been rigorously evaluated. In the No Child Left Behind legislation (U.S. Congress, 2001), the formulation, used 110 times, is "based on scientifically based research." The difficulty here is twofold. First, any program can find some research that supports the principles it incorporates. The legislation and guidance for No Child Left Behind and Reading First specify in some detail the specific reading research findings expected to be implemented under federal funding, but it is still possible for a broad range of programs to claim to be based on scientifically based reading research.

More important, the fact that a program is based on scientific research does not mean that it is in fact effective. For example, imagine an instructional program whose materials are thoroughly based on scientific research, but which is so difficult to implement that in practice teachers do a poor job of it, or which is so boring that students do not pay attention, or which provides so little or such poor professional development that teachers do not change their instructional practices. Before the Wright brothers, many inventors launched airplanes that were based on exactly the same scientifically based aviation research the brothers used at Kitty Hawk, but the other airplanes never got off the ground.

Given the current state of replicable research on programs in education, it would be difficult to require that federal funds be limited to programs that have been rigorously evaluated because there are so few such programs. However, programs that do have strong, rigorous evidence of effectiveness should be emphasized over those that are only based on valid principles, and there needs to be a strong effort to invest in development and evaluation of replicable programs in every area, so that eventually legislation can focus not on programs based on scientifically based research but on programs that have actually been successfully evaluated in rigorous experiments.

RESEARCH SYNTHESES

The evidence-based policy movement is by no means certain to succeed. Education has a long tradition of ignoring or even attacking rigorous research. Researchers themselves, even those who fundamentally agree on methodologies and basic principles, may disagree publicly about the findings of research. Individuals who oppose the entire concept of evidence-based reform will seize on these disagreements, which are a healthy and necessary part of the scientific process, as indications that even the experts disagree.

For these and many other reasons, it is essential that independent review commissions representing diverse viewpoints be frequently constituted to review the research and produce consensus on what works, in language that all educators can access. In the area of reading, it is impossible to overstate the policy impact of the National Reading Council (Snow, Burns, & Griffin, 1998) and National Reading Panel (1999) reports, which produced remarkable consensus on the state of the evidence. Consensus panels of this kind, with deep and talented staff support, should be in continual operation reviewing a broad range of policy-relevant questions so that practitioners and policymakers can cut through all the competing claims and isolated research findings to get to the big-picture findings that methodologically sophisticated researchers agree represent the evidence fairly and completely.

EVIDENCE IN THE AGE OF ACCOUNTABILITY

Evidence-based policies for education are important at any time, but they are especially important today, given the rise of accountability. State and national governments are asserting stronger control over local education, primarily by establishing consequences for schools based on gains or losses on state assessments. The accountability movement is hardly new; it has been the dominant policy focus in education since the early 1980s. Accountability systems are becoming more sophisticated and are reaching further into educational practice, but accountability is still a necessary but insufficient strategy for school reform. Most obviously, teachers and administrators need professional development, effective materials, and other supports closely aligned with state standards to help them move from where they are to where they need to be.

However, rewards and sanctions based on test score gains can be very inexact in fostering good practice. Year-to-year changes in an individual school are unreliable indicators of a school's quality (see Linn & Haug, 2002). Scores can fluctuate on a year-to-year basis for a hundred reasons that have nothing to do with program effectiveness. These include population changes, student mobility, changes in special education or bilingual policies, test preparation, and changes in promotion policies, as well as random factors. Also, it takes so long to report test scores that schools may be into the following school year still doing the wrong thing before they find out their test results.

For these and other reasons, it is essential that schools focus both on the evidence base for their programs and on the outcomes in their particular school. Hospitals might be held accountable for their success rates with various conditions, but they would never dream of implementing procedures discordant with rigorous, widely accepted research. Similarly, schools should be expected to use methods known to be effective in general and then to make certain that their particular implementation of those methods is of sufficient quality to ensure progress on the state assessments.

WILL EDUCATIONAL RESEARCH PRODUCE BREAKTHROUGHS?

In a recent op-ed piece in *Education Week*, James Gallagher (2002) argued that evidence-based policies are setting up false expectations among policymakers. He maintained that unlike medical research, educational research is unlikely to produce breakthroughs. He is perhaps right about this; education reform is not apt to invent exotic treatments that have the immediate impact that the Salk vaccine had on polio. However, the value of evidence-based policies does not depend on breakthroughs. Fields that invest in research and development often produce progressive, step-by-step improvements. Modern automobiles use the internal combustion engine, just like the Model T, but modern automobiles are far more efficient and effective. Physicians could remove ruptured appendices at the turn of the century, but these operations are far less risky now. In these and hundreds of other examples, it is the accumulation of small advances rather than breakthroughs that led to substantially improved practice. This is how evidence-based policies will probably improve education. Once we have dozens or hundreds of randomized or carefully matched experiments going on each year on all aspects of educational practice, we will begin to make steady, irreversible progress. Until then, we are merely riding the pendulum of educational fashion.

POTENTIAL IMPACT OF EVIDENCE-BASED POLICIES ON EDUCATIONAL RESEARCH

Up to now, I have written primarily about the potential impact of evidence-based policies on education policies and practice. I would now like to consider the potential impact on educational research. I believe that if evidence-based policies take hold, this will be enormously beneficial for all of educational research, not just research involving randomized or matched experiments. First, I am confident that when policymakers perceive that educational research and development is actually producing programs that are shown in rigorous experiments to improve student outcomes, they will fund research at far higher levels. This should not be a zero-sum game in which new funds for experiments are taken from the very limited funds now available for educational research (see Shavelson & Towne, 2002). Rather, I believe that making research relevant and important to policymakers will make them more, not less, willing to invest in all forms of disciplined inquiry in education, be it correlational, descriptive, ethnographic, or otherwise. The popularity of medical research depends totally on its ability to cure or prevent diseases, but because randomized experiments routinely identify effective treatments (and protect us from ineffective treatments), there is vast funding for basic research in medicine, including epidemiological, correlational, and descriptive studies. Researchers and developers will be able to argue convincingly that basic research is essential to tell us what kinds of educational programs are worth evaluating.

A climate favorable to evidence-based reform will be one in which individual researchers working on basic problems of teaching and learning will be encouraged and funded to take their findings from the laboratory or the small-scale experiment—or from the observation or interview protocol—to develop and then rigorously evaluate educational treatments. Education is an applied field. Research in education should ultimately have something to do with improving outcomes for children.

CONCLUSION

Evidence-based policies have great potential to transform the practice of education, as well as research in education. Evidence-based policies could finally set education on the path toward the kind of progressive improvement that most successful areas of our economy and society embarked on a century ago. With a robust research and development enterprise and government policies demanding solid evidence of effectiveness behind programs and practices in our schools, we could see genuine, generational progress instead of the usual pendulum swings of opinion and fashion.

This is an exciting time for educational research and reform. We have an unprecedented opportunity to make research matter and to then establish once and for all the importance of consistent and liberal support for high-quality research. Whatever their methodological or political orientations, educational researchers should support the movement toward evidence-based policies and

then set to work generating the evidence needed to create the schools our children deserve.

REFERENCES

Borman, G., Boulay, M., Kaplan, J., Rachuba, L., & Hewes, G. (2001). *Randomized Evaluation of a Multi-year Summer Program: Teach Baltimore.* Baltimore, MD: Johns Hopkins University, Center for Research on the Education of Students Placed at Risk.

Boruch, R. F. (1997). *Randomized Experiments for Planning and Evaluation: A Practical Guide.* Thousand Oaks, CA: Corwin.

Doll, R. (1998). "Controlled Trials: The 1948 Watershed." *British Medical Journal, 317*: 1217–1220.

Fraker, T., & Maynard, R. (1987). "The Adequacy of Comparison Group Designs for Evaluations of Employment-related Programs." *Journal of Human Resources, 22*(2): 194–227.

Friedlander, D., & Robins, P. K. (1995). "Evaluating Program Evaluations: New Evidence on Commonly Used Nonexperimental Methods." *American Economic Review, 85*(4): 923–937.

Gallagher, J. (2002). "What Next for OERI?" *Education Week, 21*(28): 52.

Herman, R. (1999). *An Educator's Guide to Schoolwide Reform.* Arlington, VA: Educational Research Service.

Ioannidis, J. P. A., et al. (2001). "Comparison of Evidence of Treatment Effects in Randomized and Nonrandomized Studies." *Journal of the American Medical Association, 286*(7): 821–830.

Kaestle, C. F. (1993). "The Awful Reputation of Educational Research." *Educational Researcher, 22*(1): 23, 26–31.

Lagemann, E. C. (2002, April). *An Elusive Science: The Troubling History of Education Research.* Paper presented at the annual meeting of the American Educational Research Association, New Orleans.

Levin, M. E., & Levin, J. R. (1990). "Scientific Mnemonics: Methods for Maximizing More than Memory." *American Educational Research Journal, 27*: 301–321.

Linn, R. L., & Haug, C. (2002). "Stability of School-building Accountability Scores and Gains." *Educational Evaluation and Policy Analysis, 24*(1): 29–36.

Mosteller, F., & Boruch, R. (Eds.). (2002). *Evidence Matters: Randomized Trials in Education Research.* Washington, DC: Brookings.

National Reading Panel. (1999). *Teaching Children to Read*. Washington, DC: U.S. Department of Education.

Rhine, W. R. (1981). *Making Schools More Effective: New Directions from Follow Through*. New York: Academic Press.

Shavelson, R. J., & Towne, L. (Eds.). (2002). *Scientific Research in Education*. Washington, DC: National Academy Press.

Slavin, R. E. (1989). "PET and the Pendulum: Faddism in Education and How to Stop It." *Phi Delta Kappan, 70*: 752–758.

Slavin, R. E. (1997). "Design Competitions: A Proposal for a New Federal Role in Educational Research and Development." *Educational Researcher, 26*(1): 22–28.

Slavin, R. E. (2003). *Educational Psychology: Theory into Practice* (7th ed.). Boston: Allyn & Bacon.

Slavin, R. E., & Madden, N. A. (Eds.). (2001). *One Million Children: Success for All*. Thousand Oaks, CA: Corwin.

Snow, C. E., Burns, S. M., & Griffin, P. (Eds.). (1998). *Preventing Reading Difficulties in Young Children*. Washington, DC: National Academy Press.

Southwest Educational Research Laboratory. (2002). *CSRD Database of Schools*. Retrieved from http://www.sedl.org/csrd/awards.html

U.S. Congress. (2001). *No Child Left Behind Act of 2001*. Washington, DC: Author.

U.S. Department of Education. (1999). *Guidance on the Comprehensive School Reform Program*. Washington, DC: Author.

U.S. Department of Education. (2002a). *2002 Application for New Grants: Preschool Curriculum Evaluation Research Grant Program* (CFDA No. 84.305J). Washington, DC: Author.

U.S. Department of Education. (2002b). *Strategic Plan, 2002–2007*. Washington, DC: Author.

U.S. Department of Education. (2002c). *Draft Guidance on the Comprehensive School Reform Program* (June 14, 2002 update). Washington, DC: Author.

Whitehurst, G. (2002). *Charting a New Course for the U.S. Office of Educational Research and Improvement*. Paper presented at the annual meeting of the American Educational Research Association, New Orleans.

DISCUSSION QUESTIONS

1. Do you believe that education is on the brink of a scientific revolution?
2. What are some of the promises and pitfalls of this scientific revolution?
3. What does the author believe is necessary to make this revolution a reality?
4. Do you believe that scientific breakthroughs in education are possible? What might be an example of such a breakthrough?
5. Would a scientific revolution in education make teaching more or less like the medical profession? Would this be a desirable outcome?

36

Challenges for Educators:
Lesbian, Gay, and Bisexual Families

JAMES T. SEARS

FOCUSING QUESTIONS

1. What are the major types of families in the United States today?
2. What seems to be the most influential factor in deciding whether to award custody or visitation rights when a gay, lesbian, or bisexual parent or couple is involved?
3. What are some of the difficulties that children with gay or lesbian parents might experience in gender development? Social development? The school classroom?
4. In what ways can accepting the values associated with lesbian or gay parenting benefit society?
5. How can educators help to dispel the myths and ignorance regarding children of lesbian and gay parents?
6. How can issues of homosexuality be integrated into the school curriculum?
7. Should issues of homosexuality be integrated into the school curriculum? Why? Why not?
8. In what ways can conversations between educators and lesbian, gay, and bisexual adults be helpful?

Kim and Carolyn, a Boston area lesbian couple, took in Earl, a Black deaf boy, who at the time was five years old. Kim is also deaf, although she can speak and lip-read. . . . Eventually Kim and Carolyn were formally approved as Earl's foster parents by Massachusetts social workers. Several years later the two women adopted Earl. . . . [At age 11] Earl is a child who is different. He is deaf in a hearing world; Black in a predominantly white community; and the son of [white and Asian] lesbians in a largely heterosexual culture. (Sands, 1988, pp. 46–47, 50)

Since I made the decision seven years ago to become a parent through anonymous donor insemination, the question that others have asked most frequently is, "But how are you going to explain this to your child?" . . . During breakfast today, in the middle of a discussion about Velcro closings

on shoes, Jonathon [her five year old son], asked why he has only a mom and some people have a mom and a dad. I explained that there are all kinds of families in the world and gave lots of examples of those he knows: some with, some without kids; some big, some small. We talked about the fact that from the time I was 15, I just had a dad and no mom. I explained that there are no set rules for who family members can be; rather, families are people who love and are there for one another. (Blumenthal, 1990/91, p. 45)

The seven-year-old daughter [Alicia] asked her father some questions about "Gene" (the lover), and the father answered them honestly, explaining that he loved Gene and he loved Mommy. The daughter did not seem concerned, but shortly afterward she asked her mother, "Do you still love Daddy?" Mother assured her that she did. "Do you love

Gene?" the daughter asked. "He's my friend," her mother answered, "but I love your father." (Matteson, 1987, p. 151)

Jennifer sits down at the kitchen table to eat her cereal and juice. "What will you be doing at school today?" asks Patsy, her mother. "Mrs. Thomkins says we will make Christmas trees today." Patsy's husband, Bill, pours another cup of coffee and says: "Well, I guess that means that we won't have to go and chop down a tree this year!" "Oh, no!" Jennifer exclaims, "We're going to make them out of paper. When are we going to get our tree?" "Well," Patsy's mother says, "When Pam's ship returns for Christmas next week. Until then, you and Bill can talk about where we should go this year for our tree." Jennifer finishes her meal, kisses her mother and Patsy's husband goodbye. "Oh, I almost forgot. Where's Bob?" Bob, Bill's lover of five years, sits in the living room reading the morning paper. "I'm out here, Jennifer. Give me a kiss before you go to school."—An Alabama family (circa 1991)

The traditional American family—to the degree that it ever existed—represents a minority of all households in the United States today (Kamerman & Hayes, 1982). There are three major types of American families: families of first marriage, single-parent families, and families of remarriage. Less than one in four students comes to school from a home occupied by both biological parents. Single-parent households account for about one-quarter of all American families; about one of every two African-American children (one of every four white children) lives with a lone parent (Glick, 1988). If current trends continue, six out of ten children will be part of a single family sometime before they become 18 years of age (Bozett & Hanson, 1991). These single households are generally the product of divorce or separation. Remarried families account for one in six households with nearly 6 million stepchildren (Glick, 1987).

In recent years, alternative family arrangements have emerged in which either one or both partners are a self-identified lesbian, gay man, or bisexual person (Alpert, 1988; Pollack & Vaughn, 1989; Schulenberg, 1985).[1] Children, like Jennifer, from these alternative marriages may be the product of a prior marriage in which the partner has custody or visiting privileges or the gay or

lesbian couple's decision, like Kim and Carolyn, to adopt (Jullion, 1985; Ricketts & Achtenberg, 1987).[2] Other children, like Alicia, may live in a biologically traditional family but have one or both parents who are openly bisexual (Matteson, 1985; 1987). Children, like Jonathon, may also come to school from households of a lesbian or bisexual woman who has elected to bear and raise the child following artificial insemination or the departure of the father (Pies, 1985; 1987). And, of course, the parents of many other children never choose to disclose their bisexuality or homosexuality to their family (Green & Clunis, 1989).

The publications on alternative families such as *Jenny Lives with Eric and Martin* (Bosche, 1983), *How Would You Feel If Your Dad Was Gay?* (Heron & Maran, 1990), and *Daddy's Roommate* (Wilhoite, 1990), as well as the controversy surrounding the New York City Public Schools' adoption of the Rainbow Curriculum and the subsequent dismissal of its superintendent, Frank Fernandez, may mean that few of our students will understand the true diversity among the families whose children attend their schools. Deleting lesbian, gay, and bisexual families from the school curriculum, however, does not remove them from the day-to-day realities of school life. If we are to truly serve all of our students, then educators must become more aware of the challenges facing lesbian, gay, and bisexual parents and their children.

CHALLENGES FACING LESBIAN, GAY, AND BISEXUAL PARENTS

How, the average person wants to know, can a lesbian possibly be a mother? If heterosexual intercourse is the usual prerequisite for maternity, how is it possible for women who by definition do not engage in heterosexual behavior to be mothers? If motherhood is a state which requires the expression of nurturance, altruism, and the sacrifice of sexual fulfillment, how can a lesbian, a being thought to be oversexed, narcissistic, and pleasure oriented, perform the maternal role? How can women who are "masculine," aggressive, and assumed to be confused about their gender be able to behave appropriately within its boundaries or to assume the quintessentially womanly task of motherhood? If lesbians are women whose lives are organized in terms of the relentless pursuit of clandestine pleasures, if lesbians are women who behave as quasi-men and who have been poorly socialized into their gender roles, then how can they expect to provide adequate models of feminine behavior to their children, to prepare them for their own sexual and parental careers? (Lewin & Lyons, 1982, p. 250)

Such questions pose challenges to women (and men) who are homosexual but choose parenting. While the assumptions underlying many of these questions are flawed (Sears, 1991a), the coupling of parenthood with homosexuality to form categories of lesbian mothers and gay fathers may appear contradictory. This contradiction, however, is of social not biological origin.

The difficulties confronted by acknowledged lesbian mothers or gay fathers are, in many ways, similar to those faced by single parents and divorced households, with the significant exception of the additional burden of wrestling with the social stigma associated with homosexuality. Two of the greatest challenges are securing or maintaining custody of their children and disclosing their homosexuality to their children.

Legal Barriers

In child custody decisions the judge has a wide leeway within common law to provide for the "best interest of the child" and not to interfere with existing custody arrangements unless there have been "material changes in circumstances" (Achtenberg, 1985; Basile, 1974; Payne, 1977/78). While heterosexual mothers have generally not lost custody of their children for unfitness, the sexual orientation of a parent has played a prominent role in both circumstances (Pagelow, 1980; Rivera, 1987).

In general, gay fathers seeking custody face the double burden of being male where the female is presumed more nurturant and of being homosexual where heterosexual is considered normal. Moreover, in those cases involving a son the court appears more concerned with issues of sexual development than those involving daughters (Miller, 1979b), and in custody disputes involving lesbian mothers, the woman loses 85 percent of those

cases that go to trial (Chesler, 1986). A disproportionate number of cases are between the mother and another relative (Hitchens, 1979/80), and in cases where lesbian mothers are provided custody, the courts have often demanded the absence of same-sex lovers in the household. One lesbian who won provisional custody of her five-year-old son lamented:

> That is unjust! They don't put those kinds of restrictions on a heterosexual mother . . . for 13 years I'm forbidden to set up a living relationship with a sexual partner of my choice. Sure, I don't have to be celibate—I can sneak out somewhere or I can send my son away—but I want to be free to set up my home with someone I love. It's much better for a child to have more than one parent figure—I can't possibly be available to answer all of my child's needs alone. (Pagelow, 1980, p. 194)

In deciding whether to award custody or even visiting privileges to a homosexual parent or to allow a lesbian or gay couple to adopt a child, judges often base their decisions on other unsubstantiated judicial fears such as "turning" the child into a homosexual, molesting the child, stigmatization of the child, and AIDS (Hitchens, 1979/80; Payne, 1977/78; Polikoff, 1987; Rivera, 1987). The willingness of the courts to entertain homosexuality as a factor for denying custody or restricting visiting rights has not escaped the attention of many lesbian mothers who, though themselves not a party to legal action, fear such a possibility (Kirkpatrick, Smith, & Roy, 1981).

Nonbiological parents and lesbians or gay men wishing to adopt also face significant legal hurdles. Six jurisdictions in the United States have ruled in favor of adoptions by same-sex parents (Alaska, Washington, Oregon, California, Minnesota, and the District of Columbia), and while only two states (Massachusetts and Florida) specifically prohibit gay men or lesbians from being foster or adoptive parents, most courts and agencies have allowed sodomy statutes (applicable in twenty-five states), prejudicial attitudes, or myths and stereotypes to affect their decision. In Minnesota, for example, one lesbian was denied visitation rights to a child she had raised with her former partner, and in Wisconsin the court refused to enforce a co-parenting contract signed by two former lovers. Even in states that have ruled in favor of adoptions, there remains bureaucratic and political resistance, and, if approved, joint adoptions by gay men or lesbians are unusual (Achtenberg, 1985; Ricketts & Achtenberg, 1987).

Only recently have educational associations, state departments of education, and school districts developed policies and programs regarding the discrimination and harassment of homosexual students or the inclusion of sexual orientation issues in the school curriculum; little attention has been given to children with a lesbian or gay parent. As I will discuss in the final section of this chapter, these policies and programs, however, can have a positive effect not only on the lesbian, gay, or bisexual student but also on the heterosexual student who comes from such an alternative family structure.

Disclosure to Children

Some, if not most, of our children from such families have not been told of their parent's sexual identity (Bozett, 1980; Miller, 1979a). In heterosexually coupled families with a gay, lesbian, or bisexual spouse, underlying tensions may create home problems (e.g., marital discord, emotional detachment from the child), which manifest themselves in a child's school behavior or academic achievement (Harris & Turner, 1985/86; Lewis, 1980; Matteson, 1987). In those families, for example, where gay fathers have not disclosed their sexual identity to their children, Miller (1979b) found "their fathering is of lower quality than the fathering of more overt respondents. . . . The guilt many of these men experienced over being homosexual manifested itself in over-indulgent behavior. . . . Data also indicate that respondents living with their wives tended to spend less time with their children" (p. 550). Educators who are aware of this social phenomenon can integrate this knowledge with their classroom assessment while respecting the confidentiality of the family.

Parents often fear the impact of such disclosure on their children. In deciding whether to disclose the parent's sexual identity, the most common parental fears are rejection from the child, inability of the child to understand, and

child rejection from peers (Shernoff, 1984; Wyers, 1984, 1987). The difficulties faced by the gay or bisexual partner in "coming out" to a child are well articulated by Matteson (1987) following his analysis of a nonclinical sample of forty-four spouses in mixed-orientation marriages:

> Since the beginning, I've been saying, "next year I'm leaving as soon as the children are bigger." Now that they are in college, I can't leave because they are my judges. They'd never forgive me for doing this all these years to their mother." (p. 145; quoted from Miller, 1978, p. 217)

The most common time for such disclosure is during a separation or a divorce or when the gay parent elects to enter into a domestic partnership (Bozett, 1981b; Miller, 1978). In the case of still-married bisexual spouses, somewhere between one-third to one-half of their school-age children have been informed (Coleman, 1985; Wolf, 1985). The mean age of gay parental self-disclosure or child discovery ranges from 8 to 11 years of age (Turner, Scadden, & Harris, 1985; Wyers, 1984). According to Bozett (1987b),

> The means by which the father discloses takes several forms. For example, with small children the father may disclose indirectly by taking children to a gay social event or by hugging another man in their presence. Both indirect and direct means may be used with older children in which the father also discusses his homosexuality with them. (p. 13)

Studies of gay parents and their children report different findings regarding the child's reaction (Bozett, 1980; Harris & Turner, 1985/86; Lewis, 1980; Miller, 1979b; Paul, 1986; Pennington, 1987; Turner, Scadden, & Harris, 1985; Wyers, 1987). In her clinical study of thirty-two children from twenty-eight lesbian-mother families, Pennington (1987) found that differing "children's reactions to mother 'coming out' generally range from 'Please, can't you change, you're ruining my life!' to 'I'm proud of my mom, and if other kids don't like it, then I don't want that kind of person to be my friend'" (p. 66). In his study of forty gay fathers, Miller (1979b), on the other hand, found all of their children to have reacted more positively than their fathers had anticipated. Furthermore, "children who showed the greatest acceptance were those who, prior to full disclosure, were gradually introduced by their parents to homosexuality through meeting gay family friends, reading about it, and discussing the topic informally with parents" (p. 549). In general, these and other studies (e.g., Gantz, 1983; Lamothe, 1989; Schulenberg, 1985) found the parent–child relationship was ultimately enhanced by such disclosure.

CHALLENGES FACED BY CHILDREN WITH LESBIAN, GAY, OR BISEXUAL PARENTS

Susan expected her family to be thrilled that she was finally "settling down" after a decade of working as a lawyer. Her mother's first reaction [to Susan's interest in having a baby], however, was "But you're not married!" After Susan explained that she was still lesbian and planned to raise the child with her lover, Susan's mother wondered, "But is it fair to the child? Everyone else will have a father; she'll feel different, she'll be treated badly." (Rohrbaugh, 1989, pp. 51–52)

In the past, concerns about children growing up in a homosexual household focused on the household as the potential problem. Children were believed to be at a higher risk of developing a gender-inappropriate identity or sex-typed behaviors, acquiring a homosexual orientation, or exhibiting behavioral or psychological problems. While these fears are unjustified, the difficulties of growing up in a lesbian, gay, or bisexual household are linked to the homophobia and heterosexism pervasive in our society and tolerated, if not magnified, in our public schools.

Impact of Parental Sexual Orientation on Children

As the discussion of gay parenting becomes more public, fears about a child living with a lesbian or gay parent have been expressed. One concern is that the child may become homosexual or experience sexual harassment from either the parent or parental friends. Though persons generally do not identify themselves as gay or lesbian until their late teens or early twenties (Rust, 1993; Sears, 1991a), there is no greater likelihood that a son

or daughter of a homosexual parent may declare a homosexual identity than those children from heterosexual households (Bozett, 1981a, 1981b; Gottman, 1990; Green, 1978, Miller, 1979b; Paul, 1986). Furthermore, there is no empirical evidence that such children living with lesbian or gay parents face any greater danger of sexual harassment or molestation than those living with heterosexual parents (Hotvedt & Mandel, 1982; Miller, 1979b).

Another concern is that children living in homosexual families may suffer in gender development or model "inappropriate" sex role behaviors. Here research studies present a mixed picture. While some studies have found that homosexual parents, like their heterosexual counterparts, encourage their child's use of sex-typed toys (Golombok, Spencer, & Rutter, 1983; Gottman, 1990; Harris & Turner, 1985/86; Kirkpatrick, Smith, & Roy, 1981; McGuire & Alexander, 1985; Turner, Scadden, & Harris, 1985), others have reported the opposite finding, including a greater emphasis on paternal nurturance or less preference for traditional sex-typed play (Hotvedt & Mandel, 1982; Scallen, 1981).

In general, studies comparing lesbian or gay men as parents with heterosexual single parents (Bigner & Jacobsen, 1989; Kirkpatrick, Smith, & Roy, 1981; Lewin & Lyons, 1982; Scallen, 1981) portray families that are either similar to the heterosexual norm or that excel in socially desirable ways (e.g., androgynous parenting behaviors, more child-centered fathers). Though the studies cited in this chapter varied in their methodology and samples, none found homosexuality to be incompatible with fatherhood or motherhood. Furthermore, these studies do not reveal parenting patterns that would be any less positive than those provided by a heterosexual parent (e.g., Bozett, 1985; Golombok, Spencer, & Rutter, 1983; Hoeffer, 1981; Robinson & Skeen, 1982).

In fact, those men who are most open about their homosexuality, compared with other homosexual fathers, display fatherhood traits that many professionals consider to be desirable. These fathers, for example, used corporal punishment less often, expressed a strong commitment to provide a nonsexist and egalitarian home environment, and were less authoritarian (Miller, 1979b). Similar findings were available for lesbian mothers. For example, in comparing black lesbian with black heterosexual mothers (Hill, 1981), the lesbians were found to be more tolerant and treated their male and female children in a more sex-equitable manner.

Those fathers and mothers who were the most publicly "out" were most likely to provide a supportive home environment. Ironically, given custody or visiting concerns as well as the general level of homophobia in society, those parents who are the most candid may be most vulnerable to denial of their parenting rights and visible targets for antigay harassment of themselves and their children.

Impact of Homophobia and Heterosexism on Children

The most commonly experienced problem or fear confronting children, most notably adolescents, from lesbian or gay households is rejection or harassment from peers or the fear that others would assume that they, too, were homosexual (Bigner & Bozett, 1990; Bozett, 1987a; Lewis, 1980; Paul, 1986; Wyers, 1987). An anecdote told to Pennington (1987) by a daughter of a lesbian mother illustrates the genuine acceptance of children *prior* to encountering stereotypes and harassment in school:

> When I was around five, my mom and Lois told me they were lesbians. I said good, and thought I want to be just like my mom. Well, when I reached about the fifth grade . . . I heard kids calling someone a faggot as a swear word, and I thought, "My God, they're talking about my mom." (p. 61)

Based on his study of sixteen children with a gay or bisexual father, Paul (1986), as well as others (e.g., Riddle & Arguelles, 1981), found that it was during adolescence that these children had the most difficult time coping with their father's sexuality. An excerpt from a case study, written by a family psychotherapist (Corley, 1990) who worked with the two lesbians, Jane and Marge, and their eight children—a family for more than

10 years—is illustrative. During the next three years of therapy, the family began their first open discussions about the special relationship between the two women and the feelings of their children. The therapist continues:

> Marge's two boys had difficult adjusting to do. . . . By now everyone at their school knew Joe and Tom had two mothers. Both of them had come to their school as the primary parent. The children started to tease them about having "lesbos" for parents. Both of the boys [in their early teens] were rather stout in nature so many fights erupted over the teasing they received. Since Joe and Tom were embarrassed over what the children at school were saying, they usually told the teachers and principal that there was no reason for the fights. When Jane and Marge would question them about the fights, they would equally clam up. . . . Because of the lack of intervention, the boys continued to get in trouble at school and started to act out in other ways. Although the boys were only average students, they always passed. Now they were bringing home failing marks. Since these were the first failing grades for either of them, Jane and Marge felt the situation would improve. Unfortunately, the grade situation only deteriorated. Several parent conferences were called at school. Although both women showed up at the conferences together, nothing was ever mentioned about the family unit or their relationship. It was not until the family came into therapy that the boys revealed they were having problems. (p. 80)

A prominent researcher in the study of children of gay fathers, Frederick Bozett (1980), relays a similar anecdote from a 14-year-old boy whose gay father had made several school visits: "All his jewelry was on. The teachers knew he was gay, and all the kids saw him and figured it out. It was obvious. They started calling me names like 'homoson.' It was awful. I couldn't stand it. I hate him for it. I really do" (p. 178).

According to Bozett (1987a), children generally use one of three "social control strategies" to deal with their parent's homosexuality. The first, *boundary control,* is evidenced in the child's control of the parent's behavior, the child's control of his or her own behavior vis-à-vis his or her gay parent, and the child's control of others' contact with the parent. Some of these controls are evidenced in an interview with two adolescent girls, both of whom have lesbian parents:

Margo: I try and hide stuff when people walk in, but probably most of my friends know.

Interviewer: Do they ever ask you directly?

Tania: My friends don't. My mother's girlfriend doesn't live with us. My mom keeps stuff out but I make a point of putting it away when someone is going to come over. . . .

Margo: I used to always walk between my mother and Cheryl. I used to make Cheryl walk at the curb and my mother inside and I'd walk right in the middle. . . . So it wouldn't be really obvious. But it probably was. . . . People say, "Why do they live together?" And you make up all these stories and they don't even fit together. . . . My mother tries to make up stories sometimes, but it doesn't work because they make no sense. "Oh my girlfriend, my brother's ex-wife's sister. . . ." I used to be real embarrassed. One of my girlfriends asked me once and I was really embarrassed. I was like "No! What are you talking about? Where did you get that idea from?" But it turned out that her mother was gay too. (Alpert, 1988, pp. 100–102)

The second controlling strategy, *nondisclosure,* is evidenced in the child's refusal to share about (and in some cases denial of) the parent's homosexuality. One lesbian woman, discussing the difficulties she faced in her daughter's denials, commented,

When I asked Noelle [now age 13] what she would say if anybody asked her about me she said she would deny it. I was very very hurt. I talked it over with Cathy (a lesbian and a close friend). She said her son . . . had got into a fight at school about her and had come home really upset. . . . She told him that she didn't expect him to fight her battles for her. . . . That was fine by her and that really helped me because I realized I should not expect Noelle to fight my battles either. . . . I actually did tell my children that if they want to deny it that's fine and I think that helped them because they were caught a bit between loyalties. (Lesbian Mothers Group, 1989, p. 126)

Some children, however, also employ nondisclosure to protect the parent who might be vulnerable

to a child custody challenge or to job discrimination (Paul, 1986).

The third controlling strategy, *disclosure,* is evidenced by a child's selective sharing of this personal information. In Miller's (1979b) study of gay fathers, one 17-year-old son stated, "I don't tell people if they're uptight types or unless I know them well. I've told my close friends and it's cool with them" (p. 548). In Gantz's (1983) study, a 13-year-old child of a household with two lesbians noted, "I've told one person. . . . We'd go do stuff like shoot pool and all that down in his basement. I just told him, you know, that they were gay. . . . I didn't know how he'd react. He said he'd keep it a secret, so that made me feel a little better" (p. 68). Another male respondent commented, "You have to be sure they won't tell somebody else. I was worried [about] people knowing [because] I was afraid of what they'd think of me; maybe it would be embarrassing" (Bozett, 1987a, p. 43).

Furthermore, according to Bozett (1987a), several factors influence the degree to which children employ one or more of these strategies. Those children who identify with the father because of their behavior, life-style, values, or beliefs are less likely to use any social control strategy, whereas children who view their father's homosexuality as "obtrusive," who are older, or who live with their father are more likely to employ these strategies.

Studies on children from gay families or homosexual mothers and fathers have been conducted within a Euro-American context. Only one study has examined minority homosexual parents (Hill, 1981), and there has been no research directed at minority children of a gay parent. Anecdotal writings by persons of color who are homosexual parents, however, convey some dissimilarities with their Anglo counterparts. For example, Lorde (1987) writes,

Black children of lesbian couples have an advantage because they learn, very early, that oppression comes in many different forms, none of which have anything to do with their own worth . . . I remember that for years, in the name-calling at school, boys shouted at Jonathan not—"Your mother's a lesbian"—but rather "Your mother's a nigger." (p. 222)

Research into the unique difficulties confronting lesbian or gay young adults who must cope with their emerging homosexual identity within the context of a nondominant culture underscores the difficulties of being a minority within a minority and suggests differences that minority children with gay or lesbian parents might confront (Johnson, 1981; Sears, 1991a). Morales (1990) explains:

> What does it mean to be an ethnic minority gay man or lesbian? For ethnic minority gays and lesbians, life is often living in three different communities: the gay/lesbian community, the ethnic minority community, and the predominantly heterosexual white mainstream society. Since these three social groups have norms, expectations, and styles, the minority lesbian or gay man must balance a set of often conflicting challenges and pressures. The multiminority status makes it difficult for a person to become integrated and assimilated. (p. 220)

This was evident in my study of young lesbian and gay African-American southerners (Sears, 1991a). Irwin, a working-class black man, for example, states, "When you're black in a black society and you're gay it's even harder. Blacks don't want it to be known because they don't want to mimic or imitate white people. They see it as a crutch and they don't want to have to deal with it" (p. 135). Malcolm comments, "If they are going to see you with a man at all, they would rather see you with another black man. . . . If they think you're gay and you're with a white man, they think that he's your sugar daddy or you're a snow queen" (p. 138). This is also evident in the anecdotal and autobiographical writings by people of color (e.g., Beam, 1986; Moraga & Anzaldua, 1981; Smith, 1983). A Chinese American (Lim-Hing, 1990/91), for example, writes about her family's reactions to her lesbianism:

> The implicit message my family gave me was not so much a condemnation as an embarrassed tolerance inextricably tied to a plea for secrecy. . . . At the end of my stay [with my father], he asked me if "they" would pick me up at Logan, although he knows Jacquelyn's name. My father's inability to accept my being a lesbian is related to his more traditional values: family first, make money and buy land, don't stand out. (p. 20)

A Puerto Rican (Vazquez, 1992) expresses his anger at racism encountered within the Anglo gay community: "I won't lay in my own bed with some Euro-American and do Racism 101. Nor do I want to sit down with the cute white boy I'm dating and deconstruct the statement 'I love sleeping with Puerto Ricans'" (p. 90).

Children from some minority families may have a particularly difficult time coping with the homosexuality of a parent or may choose to cope with the information in a culturally different manner than researchers such as Bozett have found. Whether it is a child "coming out" to his family, a parent disclosing her homosexual orientation to the children, or both revealing this information to their extended family, they do so within different cultural contexts, perhaps facing greater risks than their Euro-American counterparts. Morales (1990) writes that

> "Coming out" to the family tends to involve both the nuclear and extended family systems. Such a family collective is the major support system for the ethnic persons and is the source of great strength and pride. . . . For minority lesbians and gays coming out to the family not only jeopardizes the intra-family relationship, but also threatens their strong association with their ethnic community. As a result minority gays and lesbians may run the risk of feeling uprooted as an ethnic person. (p. 233)

Other difficulties faced by both Anglo and minority children of lesbian, gay, and bisexual parents may be the same as children from other families experiencing marital discord or integrating a new adult into the household (Hotvedt & Mandel, 1982; Miller, 1979b; Weeks, Derdeyn, & Langman, 1975). Like children of heterosexual divorces, adolescents generally experience the most difficult period of adjustment during the first year of separation. In one of the first studies of gay fathers and their children, Miller (1979b) found "problems of sexual acting out" in the biographies of forty-eight daughters and forty-two sons. Only

> two daughters reported premarital pregnancies and abortions; one admitted to engaging in some prostitution. Two interviewed offspring had problems in school, and one had had professional counseling for emotional difficulties. As studies of children of divorced heterosexual parents have revealed simi-

lar problems . . . these concerns may not result so much from the father's homosexuality as from family tensions surrounding marital instability, divorce, and residential relocation. Anger and bitterness toward parents are common to children with disrupted families, and respondents in this study were not immune to such feelings. (p. 547)

In another study matching separated or divorced lesbian mothers with heterosexual mothers and using a variety of questionnaires and attitude scales, as well as interviews for both parents and preadolescent children (ages 3 to 11), Hotvedt and Mandel (1982) concluded that there was "no evidence of gender identity conflict, poor peer relationships, or neglect" (p. 285). These findings were extended by Huggins (1989), who examined children's self-esteem through interviews and surveys of thirty-six adolescents whose head of household was lesbian. Compared with a matched-set of heterosexual single female parents, Huggins concluded that "the mother's sexual object choice does not appear to influence negatively the self-esteem of her adolescent children. . . . the assumption that children of lesbian mothers are socially stigmatized by their mothers' sexual choice is not borne out by this study" (p. 132).

While this study does not imply that these children experienced no difficulties because of the stigma of homosexuality, it does mean that "the development of self-esteem is primarily influenced by the interaction between children and their parents or primary caregivers" (Huggins, 1989, p. 132). For example, one study found that one out of two children of lesbian mothers experienced relationship problems with other people due to the stigma of their mother's sexual identity (Wyers, 1987), and another (Lewis, 1980) concluded that

Although the findings are similar to those . . . of children of divorce, the particular issue of acceptance of the "crisis" is dissimilar. . . . Children's initial reaction to divorce was denial of pain: follow-up one year later revealed more open acceptance of the hurt. One reason for this difference may be that children of divorce have community support for their pain; children of lesbians do not. (p. 199)

Of course, parenting by lesbians, gay men, and bisexuals presents society with alternative ap-

proaches to family life that can challenge oppressive sexist and heterosexist myths and stereotypes. Pollack (1989), though acknowledging the legal necessity for demonstrating the sameness between homosexual and heterosexual families, challenges the "underlying assumption that the lesbian mother should be judged on how well she compares to the heterosexual norm." For example, do we really believe that, as a society, we want to foster the continued sex-role education of children?

Pollack argues that, rather than accepting the values associated with the heterosexual family, lesbian and gay parenting affords opportunities to challenge these norms in society and in the upbringing of their children. The "possible benefits of being a child of a lesbian mother" include "the children of lesbians may become aware (perhaps more so than other children) of their responsibility for themselves and their choices" (p. 322). For example, one study (Harris & Turner, 1985/86) reported that lesbian mothers tended to use their homosexuality in a positive manner through assisting their children to accept their own sexuality, adopt empathetic and tolerant attitudes, and consider other points of view.

Central to the problems faced by children of lesbian and gay parents are the heterosexism and homophobia rampant in today's society. Homophobia—an irrational fear and hatred of homosexuals (Weinberg, 1972)—manifests itself in students' negative attitudes and feelings about homosexuality and in the institutionalization of sodomy statutes that deny rights of sexual expression among persons of the same gender, thus restricting the legal definition of marriage and family. Heterosexism—the presumption of superiority and exclusiveness of heterosexual relationships— is evidenced in the assumption that parents of all children are heterosexual or that a heterosexual adult will *prima facie* be a better parent than one who is homosexual.

As two leading researchers on gay parenting stated, "Much ignorance regarding homosexuality is due to the propagation of myths. It is important for educators in many disciplines and at all educational levels to dispel myths, impart facts, and promote values clarification" (Bigner & Bozett, 1990, p. 168). It is at this juncture that educators' concern for the student with a newly identified lesbian or gay parent is married to their concern for the gay or lesbian student and for the heterosexual student harboring intensely homophobic feelings and attitudes. Each of these students can benefit from honest discussion about homosexuality in the school (Sears, 1987, 1991b), the adoption and implementation of antiharassment guidelines (Sears, 1992d), the portrayal of the contributions and rich history of lesbians, gay men, and bisexuals (Sears, 1983), and the provision of gay-affirmative counseling services (Sears, 1989c).

Based on her interviews with children with lesbian mothers, Lewis (1980) concurred:

> The children of lesbians seem not to have peer support available to them, since most of these children have either pulled away from their friends altogether or maintained friends but with a sense of their own differentness. Children of lesbians have been taught the same stereotypical myths and prejudices against homosexuals as the rest of society. Better understanding is needed about available family support systems and other systems that should be provided. These might include peer supports as well as educational supports, for example, dissemination of information about homosexuality. (p. 202)

HOMOSEXUALITY AND THE SCHOOLS

Though some teachers, administrators, and guidance counselors are reluctant to discuss homosexuality in schools (Sears, 1992a, 1992b), every major professional educational association has adopted resolutions calling on schools to address this topic. Some school districts have adopted specific programs and policies, and a variety of recommendations have been made to integrate issues relating to homosexuality in the school curriculum. Educators who assume proactive roles not only benefit lesbian, gay, and bisexual students but are making inroads into the institutionalized homophobia and heterosexism that make school life more difficult for children from homosexual families.

Gay and Lesbian Students and Professional Standards

Professional educational associations have adopted policies affirming the worth and dignity of lesbians, gay men, and bisexuals and/or calling for an end to statutes, policies, and practices that effectively condone discrimination and harassment on the basis of sexual identity. Educators, school board members, and parents who have spearheaded these efforts acknowledge the simple social fact that being sexually different in a society of sexual sameness exacts a heavy psychological toll. Struggling to cope with their sexual identity, these students are more likely than other youth to attempt suicide, to abuse drugs or alcohol, and to experience academic problems (Gibson, 1989; Hetrick & Martin, 1987; Martin & Hetrick, 1988; Sears, 1989b; Teague, 1992; Zera, 1992). Other youth coping with their same-sex feelings may not display these symptoms but may excel in schoolwork, extracurricular activities, or sports as a means of hiding their sexual feelings from themselves or others (Sears, 1991a). Because of such hiding, however, their emotional and sexual development languishes (Martin, 1982).

Five states (Massachusetts, New Jersey, Wisconsin, Hawaii, and Minnesota) have adopted some type of antidiscrimination statutes. For example, Wisconsin's statute Section 118.13 reads, in part,

> No person may be denied admission to any public school or be denied participation in, be denied the benefits of or be discriminated against in any curricular, extracurricular, pupil services, recreational, or other program or activity because of the person's sex, race . . . marital or parental status, sexual orientation.

As part of the process of implementing its statute, the Wisconsin Department of Public Instruction issued a fifty-nine page booklet that noted that "the board shall adopt instructional and library media materials selection policies stating that instructional materials, texts, and library services reflect the cultural diversity and pluralist nature of American study" and cited lesbian and gay students as one underrepresented group.

Finally, many major educational organizations, such as the National Educational Association, American Federation of Teachers, and the Association for Supervision and Curriculum Development, have adopted statements affirming the rights of homosexual and bisexual students in K–12 schools and calling on their members to undertake proactive measures to combat the heterosexism and homophobia that are rampant in our nation's schools. For example, the American School Health Association issued a policy statement on gay and lesbian youth in schools, which stated, in part, that

> School personnel should discourage any sexually oriented, deprecating, harassing, and prejudicial statements injurious to students' self-esteem. Every school district should provide access to professional counseling, by specially trained personnel for students who may be concerned about sexual orientation.

School Policies and Programs

Since the late 1980s, the invisibility of homosexuality in education has lessened. Evidence of its being less invisible includes extensive sex education courses in this nation's schools (Haffner, 1990; Sears, 1992c), with some systems including units on homosexuality (Sears, 1991b); the first public funding of a school serving homosexual students, The Harvey Milk School, by the New York City public school system (Friends of Project 10, 1991; Rofes, 1989); the institution of the first gay-affirmative counseling service in a public high school, Project 10 within the Los Angeles Unified School District (Rofes, 1989); the election of the nation's first openly gay school board member in San Francisco; and the formation of the Lesbian and Gay Studies special interest group of the American Educational Research Association (Grayson, 1987).

Several school districts have adopted antiharassment guidelines. In 1987, the Cambridge (MA) public schools included in their policies the following statement:

> Harassment on the basis of an individual's sexual preference or orientation is prohibited. Words, action or other verbal, written, or physical conduct which ridicules, scorns, mocks, intimidates, or otherwise threatens an individual because of his/her sexual orientation/preference constitutes homophobic harassment when it has the purpose or effect of unreasonably interfering with the work performance or creating an intimidating, hostile, or offensive environment. (Peterkin, 1987)

More recently, in 1991, the St. Paul school board passed a human rights policy forbidding discrimination on the basis of "sexual or affectional orientation." Several large urban school districts (e.g., New York, Washington, DC, Cincinnati, Los Angeles, Des Moines, San Francisco) have implemented antigay and lesbian discrimination policies. Perhaps the most publicized effort to meet the needs of homosexual students has been the funding of a public alternative school for gay and lesbian youth in New York City and the development of counseling services expressly for this target population in Los Angeles. The Harvey Milk School, established in 1985 under the sponsorship of the Hetrick–Martin Institute, serves about forty students who are unable to function in the conventional school setting (Rofes, 1989). In Los Angeles, Project 10 at Fairfax High School has received international attention for the gay-affirmative services provided by its counseling staff. And, in 1993, the school district, under the auspices of Project 10, hosted the first conference for their high school gay youth at nearby Occidental College.

These policies and programs not only have a positive impact on the gay, lesbian, and bisexual student, but on heterosexual students, faculty, and staff, who often harbor homophobic feelings or heterosexist attitudes. Thus, these policies and programs can help to create a supportive school climate for heterosexual students who come from lesbian, gay, or bisexual households.

Curriculum and Staffing Recommendations

Elsewhere (Sears, 1987; Sears, 1991b; Sears, 1992b) I have discussed the importance of integrating issues of homosexuality into the school curriculum. Briefly, when the issue of homosexuality appears in the school curriculum, the most likely subjects to be targeted are science in the form of human physiology or health in the form of HIV/AIDS prevention (Sears, 1992c). In contrast, I believe, sexuality can serve as a transformative tool for thinking about the construction of one's sexual identities vis-à-vis the interrelationships among language, history, and society (Carlson, 1992; Macanghaill, 1991). As such, sexuality no longer becomes the province of sex educators teaching separate units within physical education or biology, but becomes a major strand woven throughout the curriculum (Sears, 1991b).

Educators have long argued that schools ought to be an embryonic environment for engaging young people in the art of democratic living and, in the process, moving society further along its democratic path (Dewey, 1916; Giroux, 1988; Rugg, 1939). In fact, however, the hidden curriculum of school fosters conformity and passivity, while seldom encouraging critical thinking, ethical behavior, and civic courage (Giroux, 1988; McLaren, 1991, 1993). Within this environment, controversial ideas and individual differences are seldom welcomed. The discussion of homosexuality, the treatment of lesbian, gay, and bisexual students, and the restrictive definition of family are some of the most glaring examples.

Specific strategies and materials that foster an awareness of homosexuality and homosexual persons already have been proposed or developed (e.g., Friends of Project 10, 1991; Goodman, 1983; Hubbard, 1989; Krysiak, 1987; Lipkin, 1992; Sears, 1983; Wilson, 1984). Educators have been admonished by scholars and activists alike to sit down and talk with bisexual, lesbian, and gay adults to learn first hand about the special problems they faced in school; the importance of lesbian and gay educators as role models for homosexual students has been stressed, as has the need for public school systems to follow the lead of communities such as Berkeley and Cambridge in adopting antislur policies and nonharassment guidelines (Griffin, 1992; Hetrick & Martin, 1987; Kissen, 1991; Martin & Hetrick, 1988; Peterkin, 1987; Rofes, 1989; Sears, 1987; Sears, 1993; Slater, 1988; Stover, 1992). In some schools, antihomophobia workshops with heterosexual students and educators have been conducted (Schneider & Tremble, 1986; Stewart, 1984). Professional educators as well as lesbian and gay activists ask, at the very least, for the construction of a nonjudgmental atmosphere in which homosexual-identified students can come to terms with their sexuality, the acquisition by school libraries of biographical books where students can discover the homosexuality of some famous people, and the integration of references to homosexual men and women as well as the topic of homosexuality into the high school curriculum (Jenkins, 1990; Sears, 1983, 1988b).

It should be noted that there is no legal justification for systematically barring discussion of homosexuality and the inclusion of the contributions of lesbian, gay, and bisexual artists, politicians, scientists, and athletes from the school curriculum. A United States Court of Appeals ruling that a state statute prohibiting educators and school staff from "advocating, soliciting, or promoting homosexual activity" was unconstitutional was let stand due to a deadlock Supreme Court vote (*National Gay Task Force* v. *Board of Education of the City of Oklahoma City,* 1984). Nevertheless, the integration of lesbian, gay, and bisexual topics or persons into the school curriculum appears too radical for many educators. Too few administrators refuse to acquiesce to a scissors and paste mentality of curriculum development in which only the most mundane, least controversial material survives the scrutiny of self-appointed moral vigilantes or the self-censorship of timid school officials (Sears, 1992d; Summerford, 1987; Tabbert, 1988).

In such an Orwellian school world, the curriculum is carefully crafted to omit (without the appearance of omission) the homoerotic imagery in the poetry of Walt Whitman, Sappho, and Langston Hughes or the visual arts of Donatello, Marsden Hartley, and Robert Mapplethorpe; the conflict between racial and sexual identities present in the literature of James Baldwin, Yukio Mishima, and Toni Morrison; or the conflict between the professional and personal lives of computer inventor Alan Turing, sports heroes David Kopay and Martina Navratilova, and political activists Eleanor Roosevelt and Susan B. Anthony. Just as sexuality is extracted from life and compartmentalized into units of sexuality education, so, too, are bisexuality and homosexuality exorcised from the body politic and tucked away in the curriculum closet.

In each of these areas, educators can play an important role in reducing homophobia and heterosexism. In the process, they can directly counter those litigants who petition courts to deny custody or visitation rights to lesbian or gay parents due to the fear of a "definite possibility of peer ridicule in the future" (Hitchens, 1979/80, p. 90).

SUMMARY OF RESEARCH

Studies on bisexual and homosexual parenting as well as on children of lesbians and gay men are far from complete. There are, however, some suggestive findings:

- Children are less accepting when a same-sex parent "comes out" than when a parent of the other gender discloses sexual identity.
- Children of a lesbian or gay parent are no more likely to define themselves as homosexual than children of heterosexual parents, nor are they any more likely to display atypical sex role preferences.
- Lesbian, gay, and bisexual parents often seek to provide children with a variety of gender role models.
- The earlier the disclosure to the child is, the fewer problems in the parent–child relationship.
- Children of a lesbian or gay parent follow typical developmental patterns of acquiring sex role concepts and sex-typed behaviors.
- Children of homosexual parents who have experienced marital turmoil face difficulties similar to those faced by children of divorce.
- Gay fathers may have a more difficult time disclosing their sexuality to their children than lesbian mothers, children of gay fathers are less likely to know of their parents' sexual identity, and the coming out process is more difficult for gay fathers with children at home.
- Sons are less accepting when learning their parent is gay than are daughters.
- As children enter adolescence, there is a greater likelihood that they will experience peer harassment about their parents' sexual identity and engage in a variety of self-protective mechanisms.
- Gay fathers are more likely to report their children experiencing difficulty with peer harassment because of the parent's homosexuality.

Recommendations for Educators

In several studies, researchers have noted the important role that educators can play in reducing the homophobia and heterosexism that create difficult environments for children of lesbian or gay families to learn in and for their parents to visit. Based on these and other writings (e.g., Casper & Wickens, 1992; Clay, 1990), educators should

- Redesign school paperwork in order to be inclusive. Replace words such as "mother" and "father" with "parent" or "parent 1, parent 2."
- When establishing associations such as parent–teacher organizations, develop assistance for single-parent families (e.g., child care) and create or identify a safe space for homosexual parents (e.g., support groups). Encouraging gay parents to share their family status with school officials is important. Based on his extensive research with children of gay fathers, Bozett (1987a) states that

  It is best for school officials to know about the father's homosexuality, especially if the father has child custody. Knowing about the family can alert school personnel to problems which may have the home situation as their genesis. Likewise, if the father is known about by school officials, both the father and his lover may participate in school affairs, attend school functions, or the lover may pick the child up at school all without the parents or the child having to make elaborate explanations. (p. 53)

- Represent family and cultural diversity in classroom materials and books, on bulletin boards, and in everyday teaching practices.
- Ensure that books depicting alternative family patterns are included in school libraries (see the following resource section for a few recommendations).
- Sensitize teachers and prepare guidance counselors to work with children as well as their gay parent as they confront issues ranging from the child's need for self-protection to the parent's need for respect for his or her sexual choice.
- Provide role models of gay or lesbian parents for students. Examples should reflect a multicultural emphasis, rather than reinforcing the stereotype of homosexuality existing only within the white community. Since some children in every school will identify themselves as lesbian or gay, it is important for them to have positive parenting role models should they elect to bear or foster children as adults.

- Inform parents of any sexual harassment or intimidation directed at their child.
- Modify the school's antislur and antiharassment policy to include sexual orientation and equally enforce violations against this policy.
- Interview potential teachers and counselors to determine their professional experiences and personal attitudes in working with several minorities.
- Revise hiring policies and procedures to enhance the likelihood of recruiting sexual minority faculty.
- Develop and publicize a counseling service for students who wish to discuss issues related to sexual identity.
- Hold a series of informal faculty meetings with gay and lesbian parents and faculty to identify needs and possible solutions.
- Meet with support services personnel (e.g., media specialists, counselors) to determine the adequacy of resource materials available for students and faculty about homosexuality and bisexuality.
- Review and revise accordingly student and faculty school-sanctioned activities that discriminate on the basis of sexual orientation (e.g., Junior ROTC, school dances, job-recruitment fairs).
- Review school textbooks for biased or misleading information about lesbians, gays, and bisexuals.
- Review the school curriculum to identify areas within *every* subject matter where relevant information (people, places, events) about lesbians, gay men, and bisexuals can be included.
- Engage teachers and administrators in formal activities that address the cognitive, affective, and behavioral dimensions of homophobia.
- Develop prejudice awareness among student leaders through after-school workshops.
- Invite former students and members of the community to address the student body on issues relating to homosexuality.

Resources for Educators

There is a wide selection of books, organizations, and journals appropriate for adults interested in lesbian and gay parents or their children. These include the following:

Alpert, H. (1988). *We Are Everywhere: Writings by and about Lesbian Parents.* Freedom, CA: Crossing Press.

Boys of Lesbian Mothers. 935 W. Broadway, Eugene, OR 97402.

Chain of Life. A newsletter for lesbian and gay adoptees. Box 8081, Berkeley, CA 94707.

Children of Gay/Lesbians. 8306 Wilshire Blvd., Suite 222, Beverly Hills, CA 90211.

Empathy: An Interdisciplinary Journal for Persons Working to End Oppression Based on Sexual Identities. Published twice a year (individuals $15, institutions $20), this 100+ page journal regularly includes essays on alternative family structures and issues relating to lesbian, gay, and bisexual youth. PO Box 5085, Columbia, SC 29250.

Gay and Lesbian Parents Coalition International. An advocacy and support group for lesbian and gay parents with a quarterly newsletter. PO Box 50360, Washington, DC 20091.

Gay Fathers (1981). *Some of Their Stories, Experience, and Advice.* Toronto: Author.

Gay Fathers Coalition, Box 50360, Washington, DC 20004.

Gay Parents Support Packet. National Gay Task Force, 80 Fifth Ave., Room 506, New York, NY 10011.

Jenkins, C. (1990, September 1). "Being Gay: Gay/lesbian Characters and Concerns in Young Adult Books." *Booklist,* 39–41.

Jullion, J. (1985). *Long Way Home: The Odyssey of a Lesbian Mother and Her Children.* Pittsburgh, PA: Cleis.

MacPike, L. (1989). *There's Something I've Been Meaning to Tell You.* Tallahassee, FL: Naiad Press.

Parents and Friends of Lesbians and Gays. PO Box 27605, Washington, DC 20038–7605.

Pollack, S., & Vaughn, S. (1987). *Politics of the Heart: A Lesbian Parenting Anthology.* Ithaca, NY: Firebrand.

Rafkin, L. (1990). *Different Mothers: Sons and Daughters of Lesbians Talk about Their Lives.* Pittsburgh, PA: Cleis.

Schulenburg, J. (1985). *Gay Parenting: A Complete Guide for Gay Men and Lesbians with Children.* Garden City, NY: Doubleday.

Wolf, V. (1989). "The Gay Family in Literature for Young People." *Children's Literature in Education, 20*(1): 51–58.

ENDNOTES

1. These real-world vignettes reflect the variety of lesbian, gay, and bisexual families. While the number of children of lesbian, gay, and bisexual parents is speculative, researchers cite a range of 6 to 14 million children (Bozett, 1987a; Rivera, 1987; Schulenberg, 1985). Empirical data, which are subject to sampling problems, suggest that approximately one in five lesbians and one in ten gay men have children (Bell & Weinberg, 1978; Jay & Young, 1979), with estimates of upward of 1.5 million lesbians living with their children (Hoeffer, 1981). Until recently, these children were the result of defunct heterosexual relationships or marriages in which a spouse's homosexuality remains undisclosed (Brown, 1976; Green, 1987; Miller, 1979a).

Studies on lesbian and gay parents and their families have been limited in terms of sample size and methodology. For example, some studies (e.g., Weeks, Derdeyn, & Langman, 1975) have been clinical case studies and others have relied on anecdotal evidence (e.g., Alpert, 1988; Brown, 1976; Mager, 1975); others have studied small (10 to 40) groups of homosexual parents identified through gay-related organizations (e.g., Scallen, 1981). Only a few studies have used larger samples with more sophisticated research designs (e.g., Bigner & Jacobsen, 1989; Hotvedt & Mandel, 1982). There have been no ethnographic, longitudinal, or nation-wide studies conducted. Furthermore, researchers generally have compared homosexual single parents with single heterosexual parents and, occasionally, homosexual parents living with a domestic partner with remarried heterosexual couples. Due to their incompatibility, no comparisons between homosexual parented households with the "traditional" two-parent heterosexual families have been made. Furthermore, few of these studies present statistical analyses, control for the presence of a male role model in the home, take into account the desire to appear socially acceptable, include a majority of adolescent subjects, or focus on bisexual parents (Gottman, 1990). Finally, only a handful of studies have directly interviewed, surveyed, or observed children raised by a father or mother who is homosexual (Bozett, 1980; 1987b; Green, 1978; Huggins, 1989; Paul, 1986). For a review of much of this literature, see Bozett (1989).

2. One tragedy of failures to challenge successfully state sodomy statutes in the courts and the legislature is the difficulty that lesbians, gay men, or bisexuals have in obtaining child custody or visiting privileges in divorce hearings or approval from adoption agencies even for children whose prospects for adoption are slim, such as an older child or an HIV-infected baby (Hitchens, 1979/80; Payne, 1977/1978; Ricketts & Achtenberg, 1987; Rivera, 1987).

REFERENCES

Achtenberg, R. (1985) *Sexual Orientation and the Law.* New York: Clark–Boardman.

Alpert, H. (1988). *We Are Everywhere: Writings by and about Lesbian Parents.* Freedom, CA: Crossing Press.

Basile, R. (1974). "Lesbian Mothers and Custody and Homosexual Parents." *Women's Rights Law Reporter, 2,* 3–25.

Beam, J. (Ed.) (1986). *In the Life: A Black Gay Anthology.* Boston: Alyson.

Bell, A., & Weinberg, M. (1978). *Homosexualities.* New York: Simon & Schuster.

Bigner, J., & Bozett, F. (1990). "Parenting by Gay Fathers." In F. Bozett & M. Sussman (Eds.), *Homosexuality and Family Relations* (pp. 155–175). New York: Haworth Press.

Bigner, J., & Jacobsen, R. (1989). "Parenting Behaviors of Homosexual and Heterosexual Fathers." In F. Bozett (Ed.), *Homosexuality and the Family* (pp. 173–186). New York: Haworth Press.

Blumenthal, A. (1990/1991). "Scrambled Eggs and Seed Daddies: Conversations with My Son." *Empathy, 2*(2): 45–48.

Bosche, S. (1983). *Jenny Lives with Eric and Martin.* London: Gay Men's Press.

Bozett, F. (1980). "Gay Fathers: How and Why Gay Fathers Disclose Their Homosexuality to Their Children." *Family Relations, 29:* 173–179.

Bozett, F. (1981a). "Gay Fathers: Evolution of the Gay-father Identity." *American Journal of Orthopsychiatry, 51:* 552–559.

Bozett, F. (1981b). "Gay Fathers: Identity Conflict Resolution through Integrative Sanctions." *Alternative Lifestyles, 4:* 90–107.

Bozett, F. (1985). "Gay Men as Fathers." In S. Hanson & F. Bozett (Eds.). *Dimensions of Fatherhood* (pp. 327– 352). Beverly Hills, CA: Sage.

Bozett, F. (1987a). "Children of Gay Fathers." In F. Bozett (Ed.), *Gay and Lesbian Parents* (pp. 39– 57). Westport, CT: Praeger.

Bozett, F. (1987b). "Gay Fathers." In F. Bozett (Ed.), *Gay and Lesbian Parents* (pp. 3–22). Westport, CT: Praeger.

Bozett, F. (1989). "Gay Fathers: A Review of the Literature." In F. Bozett (Ed.), *Homosexuality and the Family* (pp. 137–162). New York: Haworth Press.

Bozett, F., & Hanson, S. (1991). "Cultural Change and the Future of Fatherhood and Families." In F. Bozett & S. Hanson (Eds.), *Fatherhood and Families in Cultural Context* (pp. 263–274). New York: Springer.

Brown, H. (1976). "Married Homosexuals." In H. Brown (Ed.), *Familiar Faces, Hidden Lives* (pp. 108–130). New York: Harcourt Brace Jovanovich.

Carlson, D. (1992). "Ideological Conflict and Change in the Sexuality Curriculum." In J. Sears (Ed.), *Sexuality and the Curriculum* (pp. 34–57). New York: Teachers College Press.

Casper, V., & Wickens, E. (1992). "Gay and Lesbian Parents: Their Children in School." *Teachers College Record, 94* (1).

Chesler, P. (1986). *Mothers on Trial: The Battle for Children and Custody.* New York: McGraw-Hill.

Clay, J. (1990). "Working with Lesbian and Gay Parents and Their Children." *Young Children, 45*(3): 31–35.

Coleman, E. (1985). "Bisexual Women in Marriages." *Journal of Homosexuality, 11*, 87–100.

Corley, R. (1990). *The Final Closet.* N. Miami, FL: Editech Press.

Dewey, J. (1916). *Democracy and Education: An Introduction to the Philosophy of Education.* New York: Macmillan.

Friends of Project 10 (1991). *Project 10 Handbook: Addressing Lesbian and Gay Issues in Our Schools* (3rd edition). Los Angeles, CA: Author (ERIC Reproduction No. ED 337567).

Gantz, J. (1983). "The Weston/Roberts Family." In J. Gantz (Ed.), *Whose Child Cries: Children of Gay Parents Talk about Their Lives* (pp. 49–96). Rolling Hills Estate, CA: Jalmar Press.

Gibson, P. (1989). "Gay Male and Lesbian Youth Suicide." *Report of the Secretary's Task Force on Youth Suicide. Volume 3: Prevention and Interventions in Youth Suicide.* Washington, DC: U.S. Department of Health and Human Services.

Giroux, H. (1988). *Teachers as Intellectuals: Toward a Critical Pedagogy of Learning.* Boston: Bergin & Garvey.

Glick, P. (1987). *Remarried Families, Stepfamilies and Stepchildren.* Paper presented at the Wingspread Conference on the Remarried Family, Racine, Wisconsin.

Glick, P. (1988). "Fifty Years of Family Demography: A Record of Social Change." *Journal of Marriage and the Family, 50*(4): 861–873.

Golombok, S., Spencer, A., & Rutter, M. (1983). "Children in Lesbian and Single-parent Households: Psychosexual and Psychiatric Appraisal." *Journal of Child Psychology and Psychiatry, 24*: 551–572.

Goodman, J. (1983). "Out of the Closet by Paying the Price." *Interracial Books for Children, 9*(3/4): 13–15.

Gottman, J. (1990). "Children of Gay and Lesbian Parents." In F. Bozett & M. Sussman (Eds.), *Homosexuality and Family Relations* (pp. 177–196). New York: Haworth Press.

Grayson, D. (1987). "Emerging Equity Issues Related to Homosexuality in Education." *Peabody Journal of Education, 64*(4): 132–145.

Green, G. (1987, August 28). *Lesbian Mothers.* Paper presented at the Annual Convention of the American Psychological Association: ERIC Reproduction No. ED 297205.

Green, G., & Clunis, D. (1989). "Married Lesbians." In E. Rothblum & E. Cole (Eds.), *Lesbianism: Affirming Nontraditional Roles* (pp. 41–50). New York: Haworth Press.

Green, R. (1978). "Sexual Identity of 37 Children Raised by Homosexual or Transsexual Parents." *American Journal of Psychiatry, 135*(6): 692–697.

Griffin, P. (1992). "From Hiding Out to Coming Out: Empowering Lesbian and Gay Educators." In K. Harbeck (Ed.), *Homosexuality and Education.* New York: Haworth Press.

Haffner, D. (1990). *Sex Education 2000: A Call to Action.* New York: SIECUS.

Harris, M., & Turner, P. (1985/1986). "Gay and Lesbian Parents." *Journal of Homosexuality, 12*(2): 101–113.

Heron, A., & Maran, M. (1990). *How Would You Feel if Your Dad Was Gay?* Boston: Alyson.

Hetrick, E., & Martin, A. D. (1987). "Developmental Issues and Their Resolution for Gay and Lesbian Adolescents." *Journal of Homosexuality, 14*(1/2): 25–43.

Hill, M. (1981). *Effects of Conscious and Unconscious Factors on Child Reacting Attitudes of Lesbian Mothers.* Doctoral dissertation. Adelphia University. *Dissertation Abstracts International, 42*: 1608B.

Hitchens, D. (1979/1980). "Social Attitudes, Legal Standards, and Personal Trauma in Child Custody Cases." *Journal of Homosexuality, 5*(1/2): 89–95.

Hoeffer, B. (1981). "Children's Acquisition of Sex Role Behavior in Lesbian-mother Families." *American Journal of Orthopsychiatry, 51*(31): 536–544.

Hotvedt, M., & Mandel, J. (1982). "Children of Lesbian Mothers." In W. Paul, J. Weinrich, J. Gonsiorek, & M. Hotvedt (Eds.). *Homosexuality: Social, Psychological, and Biological Issues* (pp. 273–285). Beverly Hills, CA: Sage.

Hubbard, B. (1989). *Entering Adulthood: Living in Relationships. A Curriculum for Grades 9–12.* Santa Cruz, CA: Network Publications.

Huggins, S. (1989). "A Comparative Study of Self-esteem of Adolescent Children of Divorced Lesbian Mothers and Divorced Heterosexual Mothers." In F. Bozett (Ed.), *Homosexuality and the Family* (pp. 123–135). New York: Haworth Press.

Jay, K., & Young, A. (1979). *The Gay Report.* New York: Summit.

Jenkins, C. (1990, September 1). "Being Gay: Gay/lesbian Characters and Concerns in Young Adult Books." *Booklist,* 39–41.

Johnson, J. (1981). *Influence of Assimilation on the Psychosocial Adjustment of Black Homosexual Men.* Doctoral dissertation, California School of Professional Psychology, Berkeley, CA. *Dissertation Abstracts International* 42, 11, 4620B.

Jullion, J. (1985). *Long Way Home: The Odyssey of a Lesbian Mother and Her Children.* Pittsburgh, PA: Cleis.

Kamerman, S., & Hayes, C. (1982). "Families That Work." In S. Kamerman & C. Hayes (Eds.), *Children in a Changing World.* Washington, DC: National Academy Press.

Kirkpatrick, M., Smith, C., & Roy, R. (1981). "Lesbian Mothers and Their Children: A Comparative Study." *American Journal of Orthopsychiatry, 51*(3): 545–551.

Kissen, R. (1991). *Listening to Gay and Lesbian Teenagers.* Paper presented at the Annual Meeting of the National Council of Teachers of English, Seattle, WA. (ERIC Reproduction No. ED 344220.)

Krysiak, G. (1987). "Very Silent and Gay Minority." *School Counselor, 34*(4): 304–307.

Lamothe, D. (1989). *Previously Heterosexual Lesbian Mothers Who Have Come Out to an Adolescent Daughter: An Exploratory Study of the Coming Out Process.* Doctoral dissertation, Antioch University, Yellow Spring, OH. *Dissertation Abstracts International* 50, 5, 2157B.

Lesbian Mothers Group. (1989). "A Word Might Slip and That Would Be It: Lesbian Mothers and Their Children." In L. Holly (Ed.), *Girls and Sexuality: Teaching and Learning* (pp. 122–129). Milton Keynes, UK: Open University.

Lewin, E., & Lyons, T. (1982). "Everything in Its Place: The Coexistence of Lesbianism and Motherhood." In W. Paul, J. Weinrich, J. Gonsiorek, & M. Hotvedt (Eds.), *Homosexuality: Social, Psychological, and Biological Issues* (pp. 249–273). Beverly Hills, CA: Sage.

Lewis, K. (1980). "Children of Lesbians: Their Points of View." *Social Work, 25*(3): 198–203.

Lim-Hing, S. (1990/1991). "Dragon Ladies, Snow Queens, and Asian-American Dykes: Reflections on Race and Sexuality." *Empathy, 2*(2): 20–22.

Lipkin, A. (1992). "Project 10: Gay and Lesbian Students Find Acceptance in Their School Community." *Teaching Tolerance, 1*(2): 24–27.

Lorde, A. (1987). "Man Child: A Black Lesbian Feminist's Response." In S. Pollack & J. Vaughn (Eds.), *Politics of the Heart: A Lesbian Parenting Anthology* (pp. 220–226). Ithaca, NY: Firebrand.

Macanghaill, M. (1991). "Schooling, Sexuality and Male Power: Towards an Emancipatory Curriculum." *Gender and Education, 3*(3): 291–309.

Mager, D. (1975). "Faggot Father." In K. Jay & A. Young (Eds.), *After You're Out* (pp. 128–134). New York: Gage.

Martin, A. D. (1982). "Learning to Hide: The Socialization of the Gay Adolescent." In S. Feinstein & J. Looney (Eds.), *Adolescent Psychiatry: Developmental and Clinical Studies* (pp. 52–65). Chicago: University of Chicago Press.

Martin, A. D., & Hetrick, E. (1988). "The Stigmatization of Gay and Lesbian Adolescents." *Journal of Homosexuality, 15*(1–2): 163–185.

Matteson, D. (1985). "Bisexual Men in Marriages: Is a Positive Homosexual Identity and Stable Marriage Possible?" *Journal of Homosexuality, 11*: 149–173.

Matteson, D. (1987). "The Heterosexually Married Gay and Lesbian Parent." In F. Bozett (Ed.), *Gay and Lesbian Parents* (pp. 138–161). Westport, CT: Praeger.

McGuire, M., & Alexander, N. (1985). "Artificial Insemination of Single Women." *Fertility and Sterility, 43*: 182–184.

McLaren, P. (1991). "Critical Pedagogy: Constructing an Arch of Social Dreaming and a Doorway to Hope." *Journal of Education, 173*(1): 9–34.

McLaren, P. (1993). *Schooling as a Ritual Performance* (2nd ed.). London: Routledge.

Miller, B. (1978). "Adult Sexual Resocialization: Adjustments toward a Stigmatized Identity." *Alternative Lifestyles, 1*: 207–234.

Miller, B. (1979a). "Unpromised Paternity: The Lifestyles of Gay Fathers." In M. Levin (Ed.), *Gay Men: The Sociology of Male Homosexuality* (pp. 239–252). New York: Harper & Row.

Miller, B. (1979b). "Gay Fathers and Their Children." *Family Coordinator, 28*(4), 544–552.

Moraga, C., & Anzaldua, G. (Eds.). (1981). *This Bridge Called My Back: Writings by Radical Women of Color.* Watertown, MA: Persephone Press.

Morales, E. (1990). "Ethnic Minority Families and Minority Gays and Lesbians." In F. Bozett & M. Sussman (Eds.), *Homosexuality and Family Relations* (pp. 217–239). New York: Haworth Press.

National Gay Task Force v. *Board of Education of the City of Oklahoma City.* State of Oklahoma, 729 Fed.2d 1270 (1984). 33 FEP 1009 (1982).

Pagelow, M. (1980). "Heterosexual and Lesbian Single Mothers: A Comparison of Problems, Coping, and Solutions." *Journal of Homosexuality, 5*(3): 189–204.

Paul, J. (1986). "Growing Up with a Gay, Lesbian or Bisexual Parent: An Exploratory Study of Experiences and Perceptions." Doctoral dissertation, University of California, Berkeley. *Dissertation Abstracts International* 47, 7, 2756A.

Payne, A. (1977/1978). "Law and the Problem Patient: Custody and Parental Rights of Homosexual, Mentally Retarded, Mentally Ill, and Incarcerated Patients." *Journal of Family Law, 16*(4): 797–818.

Pennington, S. (1987). "Children of Lesbian Mothers." In F. Bozett (Ed.), *Gay and Lesbian Parents* (pp. 58–74). New York: Praeger.

Peterkin, R. (1987, June 11). Letter to Administrative Staff: Anti-harassment guidelines. Cambridge, MA.

Pies, C. (1985). *Considering Parenthood.* San Francisco: Spinster's Ink.

Pies, C. (1987). "Considering Parenthood: Psychosocial Issues for Gay Men and Lesbians Choosing Alternative Fertilization." In F. Bozett (Ed.), *Gay and Lesbian Parents* (pp. 165–174). Westport, CT: Praeger.

Polikoff, N. (1987). "Lesbian Mothers, Lesbian Families: Legal Obstacles, Legal Challenges." In S. Pollack & J. Vaughn (Eds.), *Politics of the Heart: A Lesbian Parenting Anthology* (pp. 325–332). Ithaca, NY: Firebrand.

Pollack, S. (1989). "Lesbian Mothers: A Lesbian-feminist Perspective on Research." In S. Pollack & J. Vaughn (Eds.), *Politics of the Heart: A Lesbian Parenting Anthology* (pp. 316–324). Ithaca, NY: Firebrand.

Pollack, S., & Vaughn, J. (Eds.) (1989). *Politics of the Heart: A Lesbian Parenting Anthology.* Ithaca, NY: Firebrand.

Ricketts, W., & Achtenberg, R. (1987). "The Adoptive and Foster Gay and Lesbian Parent." In F. Bozett (Ed.), *Gay and Lesbian Parents* (pp. 89–111). Westport, CT: Praeger.

Riddle, D., & Arguelles, M. (1981). "Children of Gay Parents: Homophobia's Victims." In I. Stuart & L. Abt (Eds.), *Children of Separation and Divorce.* New York: Van Nostrand Reinhold.

Rivera, R. (1987). "Legal Issues in Gay and Lesbian Parenting." In F. Bozett (Ed.), *Gay and Lesbian Parents* (pp. 199–227). Westport, CT: Praeger.

Robinson, B., & Skeen, P. (1982). "Sex-role Orientation of Gay Fathers versus Gay Nonfathers." *Perceptual and Motor Skills, 55*: 1055–1059.

Rofes, E. (1989). "Opening Up the Classroom Closet: Responding to the Educational Needs of Gay and Lesbian Youth." *Harvard Educational Review, 59*(4): 444–453.

Rohrbaugh, J. (1989). "Choosing Children: Psychological Issues in Lesbian Parenting." In E. Rothblum & E. Cole (Eds.), *Lesbianism: Affirming Nontraditional Roles* (pp. 51–64). New York: Haworth Press.

Rugg, H. (1939). *Democracy and the Curriculum: The Life and Progress of the American School.* New York: Appleton–Century.

Rust, P. (1993). "'Coming Out' in the Age of Social Constructionism: Sexual Identity Formation among Lesbian and Bisexual Women." *Gender and Society, 7*(1): 50–77.

Sands, A. (1988). "We Are Family." In H. Alpert (Ed.), *We Are Everywhere* (pp. 45–51). Freedom. CA: Crossing Press.

Scallen, R. (1981). *An Investigation of Paternal Attitudes and Behaviors in Homosexual and Heterosexual Fathers.* Doctoral dissertation. California School of Professional Psychology, Los Angeles,

CA. *Dissertation Abstracts International* 42, 9, 3809B.

Schneider, M., & Tremble, B. (1986). "Training Service Providers to Work with Gay or Lesbian Adolescents: A Workshop." *Journal of Counseling and Development, 65*(2): 98–99.

Schulenberg, J. (1985). *Gay Parenting.* Garden City, NY: Doubleday.

Sears, J. (1983). "Sexuality: Taking Off the Masks." *Changing Schools, 11*: 12–13.

Sears, J. (1987). "Peering into the Well of Loneliness: The Responsibility of Educators to Gay and Lesbian Youth." In Alex Molnar (Ed.), *Social Issues and Education: Challenge and Responsibility* (pp. 79–100). Alexandria, VA: Association for Supervision & Curriculum Development.

Sears, J. (1988b). "Growing Up Gay: Is Anyone There to Listen?" *American School Counselors Association Newsletter, 26*: 8–9.

Sears, J. (1989b). "The Impact of Gender and Race on Growing Up Lesbian and Gay in the South." *NWSA Journal, 1*(3): 422–457.

Sears, J. (1989c). "Counseling Sexual Minorities: An Interview with Virginia Uribe." *Empathy, 1*(2): 1, 8.

Sears, J. (1991a). *Growing Up Gay in the South: Race, Gender, and Journeys of the Spirit.* New York: Haworth Press.

Sears, J. (1991b). "Teaching for Diversity: Student Sexual Identities." *Educational Leadership, 49*: 54–57.

Sears, J. (1992a). "Educators, Homosexuality, and Homosexual Students: Are Personal Feelings Related to Professional Beliefs?" *Journal of Homosexuality, 29*–79.

Sears, J. (1992b). "The Impact of Culture and Ideology on the Construction of Gender and Sexual Identities: Developing a Critically-based Sexuality Curriculum." In J. Sears (Ed.), *Sexuality and the Curriculum: The Politics and Practices of Sexuality Education* (pp. 169–189). New York: Teachers College Press.

Sears, J. (1992c). "Dilemmas and Possibilities of Sexuality Education: Reproducing the Body Politic." In J. Sears (Ed.), *Sexuality and the Curriculum: The Politics and Practices of Sexuality Education* (pp. 19–50). New York: Teachers College Press.

Sears, J. (1992d). "Responding to the Sexual Diversity of Faculty and Students: An Agenda for Critically

Reflective Administrators." In C. Capper (Ed.), *The Social Context of Education: Administration in a Pluralist Society* (pp. 110–172). New York: State University of New York Press.

Sears, J. (1993). "Alston and Everetta: Too Risky for School?" In R. Donmoyer & R. Kos (Eds.). *At-risk Students* (pp. 153–172). New York: State University of New York Press.

Shernoff, M. (1984). "Family Therapy for Lesbian and Gay Clients." *Social Work, 29*(4): 393–396.

Slater, B. (1988). "Essential Issues in Working with Lesbian and Gay Male Youths." *Professional Psychology: Research and Practice, 19*(2): 226–235.

Smith, B. (Ed.) (1983). *Home Girls: A Black Feminist Anthology.* New York: Kitchen Table: Women of Color Press.

Stewart, J. (1984). "What Non-gay Therapists Need to Know to Work with Gay and Lesbian Clients." *Practice Digest, 7*(1), 28–32.

Stover, D. (1992). "The At-risk Kids Schools Ignore." *Executive Educator, 14*(3), 28–31.

Summerford, S. (1987). "The Public Library: Offensive by Design." *Public Libraries, 26*(2): 60–62.

Tabbert, B. (1988). "Battling over Books: Freedom and Responsibility Are Tested." *Emergency Librarian, 16*(1): 9–13.

Teague, J. (1992). "Issues Relating to the Treatment of Adolescent Lesbians and Homosexuals." *Journal of Mental Health Counseling, 14*(4): 422–439.

Turner, P., Scadden, L., & Harris, M. (1985, March). *Parenting in Gay and Lesbian Families.* Paper presented at the First Annual Future of Parenting Symposium, Chicago.

Vazquez, R. (1992). "(No Longer) Sleeping with the Enemy." *Empathy, 3*(1): 90–91.

Weeks, R., Derdeyn, A., & Langman, M. (1975). "Two Cases of Children of Homosexuals." *Child Psychiatry and Human Development, 6*(1): 26–32.

Weinberg, G. (1972). *Society and the Healthy Homosexual.* New York: St. Martin's Press.

Wilhoite, M. (1990). *Daddy's Roommate.* Boston: Alyson.

Wilson, D. (1984). "The Open Library." *English Journal, 43*(7): 60–63.

Wolf, T. (1985). "Marriages of Bisexual Men." *Journal of Homosexuality, 4*: 135–148.

Wyers, N. (1984). *Lesbian and Gay Spouses and Parents: Homosexuality in the Family.* Portland, OR: School of Social Work, Portland State University.

Wyers, N. (1987). "Homosexuality in the Family: Lesbian and Gay Spouses." *Social Work, 32*(2): 143–148.

Zera, D. (1992). "Coming of Age in a Heterosexist World: The Development of Gay and Lesbian Adolescents." *Adolescence, 27*(108): 849–854.

DISCUSSION QUESTIONS

1. Why does the sexual orientation of a parent play a prominent role in child custody cases?
2. According to research studies, what is the child's typical reaction to learning that a parent is gay or lesbian?
3. How do homophobia and heterosexism affect children of gay or lesbian parents?
4. What are some of the social control strategies that children use to deal with their parent's homosexuality?
5. Why should educators assume proactive roles on behalf of lesbian, gay, or bisexual students and families?
6. According to the author, how can discussions about sexuality be transformative?
7. How should preservice teacher education programs prepare future teachers to respond to issues faced by students of gay and lesbian parents?

37

Equity and Adequacy
in School Finance Today

ALLAN ODDEN

FOCUSING QUESTIONS

1. What are some of the equity and excellence obstacles for school reform?
2. What are some programs that have been initiated to overcome these obstacles?
3. What is the basic make-up of an adequately funded school? Why is this significant?
4. What are some of the obstacles that districts face in managing school aid?
5. What is the core need of an "adequate" education system? How can this be reached?

Standards-based education reform has been the focus of education policy for nearly 20 years, and it seems likely to remain so for years to come. Standards-based education reform seeks to educate more students to high levels of achievement, a goal that has elements of both equity and excellence built into it. Moreover, the goal is outcome-oriented and focuses on the results of the education system. The excellence part of the goal requires at least a doubling of the performance of our education system over the next decade or so. The equity part of the goal requires dramatically diminishing the "achievement gap" between low-income and minority students and all other students.

This education reform movement has already begun to change education finance, and it could easily change the governance of education as well. Long focused on fiscal equity, school finance is now shifting toward fiscal adequacy. And this shift represents a fundamental change: It means that school finance today encompasses not only fiscal inputs but also their connection to educational programs, teacher compensation, and student achievement.[1]

DON'T FORGET SCHOOL FINANCE INEQUITIES

Despite the shift to adequacy, those who make school finance policy must remain vigilant about fiscal disparities caused by the unequal distribution of the local property tax base. Although ameliorating these inequities was the focus of school finance reform for the last half of the 20th century and some progress was made,[2] unequal access to local education revenues is still a problem in most states.[3] During the 2000–2001 school year in Wisconsin, for example, the tax base behind the 10 percent of students in the districts with the lowest property wealth was just 18 percent of that for the 10 percent of students from districts with the highest property wealth. Fortunately, Wisconsin's school finance formula had been designed to offset most of those disparities by allowing school districts to access via state equalization aid the tax base that is about equal to that of the district at the 97th percentile, for spending up to $6,533 per pupil in the 2001 school year. The result is that Wisconsin's finance system meets most standards for fiscal equity.[4]

But unequal access to a local tax base for education is a fact in most other states. Although versions of state school finance equalization formulas function to offset the most egregious disparities caused by these local tax base inequalities, few are as successful as the Wisconsin system. Eliminating the bulk of such fiscal inequalities is probably necessary but not sufficient for creating an adequate school finance structure.

THE SHIFT TO ADEQUACY

During the 1990s, two key factors shifted the focus of school finance from equity to adequacy. The first was the question of whether differences in dollars spent per pupil produced substantive differences in educational opportunities or student learning. In other words, Does money matter? As states became the major funders of schools, policy makers raised this question with more intensity; they wanted evidence that different levels of fiscal resources produced important differences in educational opportunities and results. The second factor operating to shift the focus to adequacy was that the answer, in a standards-based environment, had to link dollars to results—that is, to student achievement.

Under standards-based education reform, the benchmark test of school finance policy is whether it provides sufficient—or adequate—revenues per pupil for districts and schools to deploy educational strategies that are successful in educating students to high standards of performance. Determining adequate revenue levels entails first identifying the costs of effective programs and strategies, then translating those costs into appropriate school finance structures, and finally ensuring that the resources are used in districts and schools to produce the desired results. Implementing this approach to school finance should also produce gains in fiscal equity because in most states it requires a "leveling up" of low-spending districts and schools. This new focus for

school finance was recommended by the National Research Council, in a report not accidentally entitled *Making Money Matter.*[5]

Reinforcing this shift in school finance policy, school finance litigation, which began with an equity focus, also shifted largely to a focus on adequacy.[6] Under an adequacy argument usually linked to the education clause in a state's constitution, the legal test is whether a state's school finance system provides adequate revenues for the average school to teach the average student to state-determined performance standards and whether adequate additional revenues are provided for the extra help students with special needs require to achieve at those same performance levels. The legal issue is not so much whether one district has more or less than another, but whether all districts in the state have revenues that are adequate for the programs and strategies they must deploy and for the teachers they must hire in order to educate students to specified levels of achievement.

As a result, unlike in the past, states can no longer allow districts to select their own spending levels. Under the adequacy framework, all districts and schools must spend at least at an adequate level. The structural implication of this requirement is that states must use a foundation type of funding formula. But the foundation—or required—expenditure level can no longer be "minimal," as it has been in many states in the past. The foundation expenditure level must be "adequate"—that is, high enough to enable each district and each school to provide a set of educational programs that are successful in educating students to the required performance standards.

DETERMINING ADEQUACY

Designing an adequate school finance system requires the state to identify both an adequate expenditure level for the typical student in the typical district and sufficient adjustments for different student needs. It also requires districts and schools to manage these resources so that students learn to the performance standards required by the state.

Four methods have been used to determine an adequate foundation expenditure level: (1) the successful district approach, (2) the cost function approach, (3) the professional judgment approach, and (4) the evidence-based approach.[7]

The *successful district approach*, which has been used in Illinois, Maryland, Mississippi, and Ohio, seeks to identify districts that have been successful in teaching students to meet proficiency standards. It then sets the adequacy level at the weighted average of the expenditures per pupil of those districts. Atypical districts are often eliminated from such analysis; these are usually the highest- and lowest-spending and highest- and lowest-wealth districts, as well as large urban districts. The result is that the districts identified are usually nonmetropolitan districts of average size that are relatively homogeneous demographically and that generally spend below the state average. The criticism of this approach is that the adequate expenditure level typically identified is difficult to relate to the needs of urban districts and small rural districts, even with adjustments for pupil needs and for geographic price differentials.

The *cost function approach* employs regression analysis with expenditure per pupil as the dependent variable and student and district characteristics, as well as desired performance levels, as the independent variables. The result produces an adequate expenditure per pupil for the average district. Then, for all other districts, that figure is adjusted to account for differences in pupil needs and educational prices, as well as the diseconomies of both large and small size. The expenditure level required generally rises or falls depending on the desired performance level. This kind of analysis usually produces an adjustment for city districts of two to three times the average expenditure level, which, when combined with the complex statistical analysis, makes its use problematic in a real political context.

No state currently uses this approach, though cost function research has been conducted for several states, including New York, Wisconsin, Texas, and Illinois.[8] This research showed that because of student and district needs, there was substantial variation in the average adequacy level, ranging from a low of 49 percent to a high of 460 percent of the average in Wisconsin and a low of 75 percent to a high of 158 percent of the average

in Texas. In both states, the figures for adequate expenditure in the large urban districts were at the highest levels.

Although both the successful district and cost function approaches link spending levels to performance levels, which is what policy makers want, neither indicates what educational strategies will produce those performance levels. The other two approaches remedy this shortcoming.

The *professional judgment approach*, called the *resource cost model* in the 1980s,[9] has been used most recently in Kansas, Maryland, Oregon, and Wyoming. This approach asks a group of educational experts to identify effective educational strategies for elementary, middle, and high schools and for special-needs students. The experts specify the ingredients required for each strategy, attach a price to each ingredient, and finally sum everything up to obtain a total expenditure per pupil. The approach can incorporate adjustments for both small and large schools, for a variety of students' special needs, and for geographic price variations so that the adequate expenditure level is sufficient for each region and type of school in a state.

A major advantage of this approach is that it identifies what is required to produce actual student performance. A disadvantage is that, other than through expert educational judgments, the strategies and ingredients have no clear link to actual performance levels. And expert judgments vary both within and across states, depending on how the process is conducted.[10]

The fourth approach to determining an adequate expenditure level is the *evidence-based approach* that I, together with Lawrence Picus at the University of Southern California, have developed. This approach identifies a set of ingredients that are required to deliver a high-quality, comprehensive, schoolwide instructional program. Then it determines an adequate expenditure level by assigning a price to each ingredient and aggregating to a total cost.[11] The evidence-based approach more directly identifies educational strategies that produce desired results, so it also helps guide schools in the most effective use of their dollars. This approach also uses the strategies and ingredients of comprehensive school design models, which themselves are compilations of research and best practices into schoolwide educational strategies.[12]

Initially, this model identified the following services and ingredients for adequately funding an elementary school of 500 students:

- One principal
- Two instructional facilitators, coaches, or mentors
- A preschool for 3- and 4-year-olds (at least for children from low-income backgrounds), with a teacher and an aide for every 15 students
- Teachers for a full-day kindergarten program
- Teachers to provide for class sizes of 15 students in grades K–3 and 25 in all other grades
- An additional number of teachers (20% of the total number) to provide for planning and preparation time and to teach art, music, physical education, and other noncore academic classes, with the requirement that a substantial portion of such time be used by regular classroom teachers for collaborative instructional improvement work
- Tutors (who are licensed teachers) for struggling students, at a rate of one tutor for every 20 percent of students from low-income backgrounds, with a minimum of one tutor for each school
- Sufficient funds for all severely disabled students
- An additional $2,000 per teacher for the training component of professional development
- About $250 per pupil for computer technologies, to cover purchase, upgrading, and repair
- One to five positions for a pupil support/family outreach strategy
- Other resources for materials, equipment, and supplies, for operation and maintenance, and for clerical support

This level of funding would allow schools to deploy just about every strategy research has shown to have a statistically significant impact on student learning and just about any comprehensive school reform model that exists.[13] It was used as the basis for the 1998 final state supreme court decree in the 25-year-old school finance litigation in New Jersey. A variation on this model has just been proposed for Wisconsin,[14] and this approach was the basis for a recent recommendation to the Kentucky State Board of Education.[15] It is also the method being used by the Joint Committee on Educational Adequacy, appointed after the Arkansas Supreme Court mandated the state to conduct a school finance adequacy study.

Both the professional judgment and evidence-based approaches build adequate funding from the school site up and need to be augmented with resources for the central office as well.

To date, no single approach to determining an adequate spending level is dominant across the country, and each approach produces different dollar amounts. Most analyses require substantial increases in education funding. Further, each study is conducted from the perspective of the state to determine what an adequate foundation expenditure level would be for each district.

Finally, the results of school finance adequacy studies can also be construed to provide the cost of implementing the federal No Child Left Behind (NCLB) legislation.[16] Though different in some details, NCLB essentially has the same objective as standards-based education reform—students achieving to high standards.

MANAGING DOLLARS IN DISTRICTS AND SCHOOLS

Whatever the adequate funding level turns out to be, it must be managed at the district and school levels to produce expected results. This imperative raises four issues related to uses of adequate education funding.

First, if states ensure that all districts have an "adequate" level of education funding, then districts cannot take increased state aid and use it for local tax relief; they must pass it on to schools so that each school has an adequate funding base. The use of increased state aid to fund local property tax relief has been a problem for many fiscally dependent urban school districts. In these districts, state aid hikes are often turned into property tax relief for city residents, or local education revenues are decreased instead of being used to bolster urban school programs. The adequacy case in New York City has explicitly raised this problem of school finance.

Second, districts must redesign professional development strategies and reallocate current professional development resources. Effective professional development is the key to transforming adequate resources into powerful and effective instructional programs. Research is showing that many large districts already spend between $4,000 and $8,000 per teacher on professional development that has little impact.[17] These dollars need to be reallocated and refocused on a small number of comprehensive professional development strategies that are structured to help teachers create the instructional practices needed to boost student performance to state proficiency levels.

Third, adequately funding each student at the school he or she attends means that districts must provide each student with a different level of funding, as varying student learning needs must be linked to the system's performance standards. So a student with a disability requires more funding than the typical student without a disability. Students from low-income homes or non–English-speaking backgrounds also require more funding, because their goal—to reach proficiency—is the same as that for all other students. School districts in Cincinnati, Houston, Milwaukee, San Francisco, Seattle, Verona (Wis.), and Washington, D.C., for example, have taken this approach by adopting "weighted-student formulas" for determining the funds provided to each school.

This funding approach ensures that dollars per pupil vary while outcome goals—achievement to specific performance standards—are held constant. Such a system can also be used in a choice or charter environment; that is, the students carry the same "adequate" level of funding to whatever public school they attend, because the goals for them are the same in each school. And to meet the adequacy standard, the level of funding overall and the adjustments for special needs have to be high enough to enable each student to meet the proficiency performance standard. This funding approach provides for both equity and adequacy of funding for each child.

Fourth, once schools receive adequate revenues, their challenge is to boost student achievement over time in order to educate students to rigorous performance standards. Since there is little, if any, hope that funding will rise by any significant amount, accomplishing the goals of standards-based education reform requires schools to use resources more productively by reallocating them to new and more effective education strategies.[18] Indeed, the Leandro school finance adequacy case in North Carolina requires that education dollars at the school site be used first to meet each student's needs and in the most effective way before any "non–research-based" uses of dollars are allowed. Though more money will probably be needed to boost student achievement to most state proficiency levels, using existing money more effectively will have to be the first step.

CHANGING TEACHER COMPENSATION

Finally, reallocating resources to more effective educational strategies and providing instruction that dramatically boosts student learning will require state-of-the-art knowledge and expertise on the part of teachers and administrators. Teachers will need more professional knowledge. They will need to know and be able to implement the best instructional strategies, fill various school leadership roles, and engage in school-based decision making. To recruit and retain teachers of such high quality, salary structures for teachers will probably need to change to more directly reward the acquisition and use of this high level of expertise. Most certainly, teacher salary levels will need to rise. State school finance systems will themselves be adequate only if they provide such sufficient salary dollars.[19]

The implications of school finance adequacy for teacher pay will ultimately require a new and explicit linkage between finance systems and pay levels; that is, a performance-based pay structure and higher teacher salary levels must be built into the school finance formula. Current finance systems do the best they can to compensate teachers. But across the country, evidence is growing that education is generally not getting its share of bright, able individuals. Furthermore, the situation is worse for teachers in such high-demand fields as mathematics, science, technology, and special education. Even more problematic, the least experienced and least effective teachers too often work in the toughest, neediest, high-poverty schools in urban and rural areas.

An adequate education system and an adequate finance system must therefore address the issues of teacher quality and teacher salaries. The legal imperatives of adequacy will mean that resources must be made sufficient to allow schools to recruit and pay for the talent they need to restructure themselves, to upgrade instruction, and to relentlessly teach all students to high performance standards. Adequacy will require that schools have sufficient funds to pay a wage that is truly competitive in the labor market, not only in the wealthiest school districts but also in poor urban and rural districts.

The shift in school finance from equity to adequacy requires an explicit connection between the funding provided to schools and the results produced in terms of student learning. The adequacy of education dollars will be measured by the degree to which students learn to the performance standards of the education system. This approach to school finance will improve fiscal equity, as the level of resources in many districts and schools will be raised to an adequate level; it will dramatically increase educational opportunities; and it should ultimately improve the equality of education results, as more and more students achieve at or above performance standards.

ENDNOTES

1. Helen Ladd and Janet Hansen, *Making Money Matter* (Washington, D.C.: National Academy Press, 1999).
2. Sheila Murray, William Evans, and Robert Schwab, "Education Finance Reform and the Distribution of Education Resources," *American Economic Review,* vol. 88, 1998, pp. 789–812.
3. Bruce J. Biddle and David C. Berliner, "Unequal School Funding in the United States," *Educational Leadership,* May 2002, pp. 48–59.
4. Allan Odden, "School Finance Change in the United States: Implications for Wisconsin," testimony before the Wisconsin Senate Education Finance Task Force,

Consortium for Policy Research in Education, Wisconsin Center for Education Research, University of Wisconsin, Madison, 2002.
5. Ladd and Hansen, *Making Money Matter.*
6. Paul Minorini and Stephen Sugarman, "Educational Adequacy and the Courts: The Promise and Problems of Moving to a New Paradigm," in Helen Ladd, Rosemary Chalk, and Janet Hansen, eds., *Equity and Adequacy in Education Finance: Issues and Perspectives* (Washington, D.C.: National Academy Press, 1999), pp. 175–208; and "School Finance Litigation in the Name of Educational Equity: Its Evolution, Impact, and Future," in Ladd, Chalk, and Hansen, pp. 34–71.
7. James W. Guthrie and Richard Rothstein, "Enabling 'Adequacy' to Achieve Reality: Translating Adequacy into State School Finance Distribution Arrangements," in Ladd, Chalk, and Hansen, pp. 209–59; and Allan Odden and Lawrence O. Picus, *School Finance: A Policy Perspective,* 3rd ed. (New York: McGraw-Hill, 2003).
8. Andrew Reschovsky and Jennifer Imazeki, "Achieving Educational Adequacy Through School Finance Reform," *Journal of Education Finance,* vol. 26, 2001, pp. 373–96.
9. Jay Chambers and Tomas Parrish, "State-Level Education Finance," in Herbert J. Walberg, ed., *Advanced in Educational Productivity* (Greenwich, Conn.: JAI Press, 1994), pp. 45–74.
10. John Augenblick, *Calculation of the Cost of an Adequate Education in Maryland in 1999–2000 Using Two Different Analytic Approaches* (Denver: Augenblick and Meyers, 2001); and James R. Smith, *Wyoming Education Finance: Proposed Revisions to the Cost-Based Block Grant (Submitted to the Wyoming State Legislature)* (Davis, Calif.: Management Analysis and Planning, Inc., January 2002).
11. I've provided some detail on evidence-based funding in two previous *Kappan* articles. See Allan Odden, "Costs of Sustaining Educational Change Through Comprehensive School Reform," *Phi Delta Kappan,* April 2000, pp. 433–38; and "The New School Finance," *Phi Delta Kappan,* September 2001, p. 88.
12. Allan Odden, *How to Rethink School Budgets to Support School Transformation,* Getting Better by Design Series, vol. 3 (Arlington, Va.: New American Schools, 1997); Allan Odden and Carolyn Busch, *Financing Schools for High Performance: Strategies for Improving the Use of Educational Resources* (San Francisco: Jossey-Bass, 1998); and Samuel Stringfield, Steven Ross, and Lana Smith, *Bold Plans for School*

Restructuring: The New American Schools Designs (Mahwah, N. J.: Erlbaum, 1996).

13. See, for example, Bari Anhalt Erlichson, Margaret Goertz, and Barbara J. Turnbull, *Implementing Whole-School Reform in New Jersey: Year One in the First Cohort Schools* (New Brunswick, N. J.: Department of Public Policy and Center for Government Services, Rutgers University, October 1999); and Bari Anhalt Erlichson and Margaret Goertz, *Implementing Whole-School Reform in New Jersey: Year Two* (New Brunswick, N. J.: Department of Public Policy and Center for Government Services, Rutgers University, January 2001).

14. Jack Norman, *Funding Our Future: An Adequacy Model for Wisconsin School Finance* (Milwaukee: Institute for Wisconsin's Future, 2002).

15. Allan Odden, Mark Fermanich, and Lawrence O. Picus, *A State-of-the-Art Approach to School Finance Adequacy in Kentucky* (Hollywood, Calif.: Lawrence O. Picus and Associates, 2003).

16. See William J. Mathis, "No Child Left Behind: Costs and Benefits," *Phi Delta Kappan,* May 2003, pp. 679–86.

17. Karen Hawley Miles et al., *An Analysis of Professional Development Spending in Four Districts Using a New Cost Framework* (Madison: Consortium for Policy Research in Education, Center for Education Research, University of Wisconsin, 2002).

18. Allan Odden and Sarah Archibald, *Reallocating Resources: How to Boost Student Achievement Without Asking for More* (Thousand Oaks, Calif.: Corwin Press, 2001).

19. Allan Odden and Carolyn Kelley, *Paying Teachers for What They Know and Do: New and Smarter Compensation Strategies to Improve Schools,* 2nd ed. (Thousand Oaks, Calif.: Corwin Press, 2002).

DISCUSSION QUESTIONS

1. What is the difference between education funding for equity and education funding for adequacy?
2. Has standards-based reform improved funding for education in your school or school district?
3. Would funding for adequacy be more or less fair than the current system in your school or school district?
4. Of the alternatives described by the author, which approach for determining adequacy of funding do you prefer?
5. How might schooling improve for teachers and students if funding were based on adequacy?

38

Dichotomizing Educational Reform

CARL D. GLICKMAN

FOCUSING QUESTIONS

1. What principles should guide education in the United States?
2. What are some examples of what the author calls ideological absolutes?
3. To what extent does ideological conflict contribute to pedagogical pain?
4. What does it mean to be an educated person in a democracy?
5. Is it possible to find common ground in the issues facing public education today?

I did not lightly take pen in hand (yes, I still use a pen) in writing this chapter. I have devoted my entire professional life to working with colleagues to create, establish, and sustain public schools that are driven by collaboration, personalization, and active and participatory student learning.[1] And I will continue to do so, as I personally believe such is the best way to prepare all students for the intellectual, social, and aesthetic life of a democracy.

Yet, even in the fervor of my beliefs, I still see other concepts of education that generate degrees of uncertainty in me. My memories of my own best teachers are revealing. Most taught in highly interactive ways, but one grand elder taught from behind a podium in a huge auditorium and engaged in little interaction with students. He was perhaps my greatest teacher. Such discrepancies don't change the strength of my own beliefs; they simply remind me that the viable possibilities of educating students well are broad indeed.

Ultimately, an American education must stand on a foundation that is wider than the beliefs of any one individual or any one group. It should encourage, respect, and support any conceptions—no matter how diametrically opposed to one's own—that are willing to be tested openly and freely. Furthermore, it should involve the willing and nondiscriminatory participation of all students, parents, and educators. That is what should

be at the core of an American education. But with the "winner take all" wars being fought today, I am seriously concerned about the future of our students and of our public schools and about the vitality of a better democracy.

IDEOLOGICAL ABSOLUTES

The either/or debates about standards versus no standards, intrinsic versus extrinsic motivation, core versus multicultural knowledge, direct instruction versus constructivist learning, and phonics versus whole language are symptomatic of ideologies that attempt to crush one another and leave only one solution standing. Whether the ideology is education anchored in traditional, behaviorist authority or progressive, inquiry-based learning, the stance toward the final outcome is the same. One group possesses the truth, and the other side is demonized as a pack of extremists: scary, evil persons. Articles and books present educators and the public with a forced choice that unfortunately disregards reality and endangers the very concept of an American education.[2]

Let me illustrate the incompleteness of ideological absolutes with one of today's most emotional issues, the relationship of race to socioeconomic achievement. One side of this debate argues that America is the land of opportunity, where freedom rings, where anyone—regardless of race, religion, gender, or class—can work hard and rise to a position of authority, success, and accomplishment. The other side argues that America is a hegemonic system, protecting the ruling class and extant privilege while keeping the poor, the dispossessed, and people of color stifled, oppressed, and marginalized. Well, which side of this debate is correct? The answer to that question has important implications for what our society needs to change in terms of practices, programs, and the targeting of resources. But the truth is that both contradictory realities have compelling evidence and must be used together to figure out what needs to be done next.

Consider the economic component of this debate. Seymour Martin Lipset compares the United States with other Western industrialized nations.[3] Since the post–Civil War era, America has been the wealthiest country, with a steady rise in living standards and unparalleled social and economic advances for the poor and working class. Yet the income of the poorest fifth of this nation continues to *decline* relative to that of other Americans.

The African American scholar Henry Louis Gates, Jr., takes on this same dichotomy in reference to race. He observes that, since 1967, the number of middle-class African American families has quadrupled. Since 1973 the top 100 African American businesses have moved from sales of $473 million to $11.7 billion. In 1970 "only one in ten blacks had attended college; today one in three has." He then goes on to discuss the continuous wrenching poverty of a third of African Americans today and concludes: "We need something we don't have: a way of speaking about black poverty that doesn't falsify the reality of black advancement, a way of speaking about black advancement that doesn't distort the enduring realities of black poverty. I'd venture that a lot depends on whether we get it."[4]

In truth, America has been one of the leading countries of opportunity for disenfranchised persons and, at the same time, a country of the greatest economic stratification between the luxury of the wealthiest and the wretched conditions of the poorest.[5] In essence, the beliefs of Ayn Rand and Pete Seeger are both correct. To speak only of one side and ignore the other is to create disbelief in

most ordinary citizens, who know firsthand of counterexamples to any single view. And this is what I believe to be the danger of ideological truth in education. Many educators in classrooms and schools feel that they have become pawns in the reformers' and policy makers' propaganda game that insists there is a single best way to change the system of American schools.

IDEOLOGY IN EDUCATION

The attacks by E. D. Hirsch, Jr., against progressive education and the equally strident attacks by others such as Alfie Kohn against traditional education are wonderful examples of this either/or ideological stance. Hirsch argues that a common core of knowledge is essential for all students, if they are to succeed in mainstream society. Without a common framework of spoken and written English, historical and cultural references, and direct instruction, marginalized and poor children are deprived of the education that wealthier children pick up automatically from their parents and peers. Thus there is the need to rid our schools of the overwhelming "permissive" practices of activity-based education and to use tests of common knowledge to ensure that all children are acquiring the "cultural capital" needed for success in later life. Kohn in turn speaks against standards, core knowledge, and tests and says that children, regardless of their circumstances, are innately curious and that teachers should explore the topics that intrigue them to open up new freedoms and possibilities. Each proponent has his version of "truth." Each sees little validity in any research supporting the methods that oppose his ideology. Again, the reality is that education is composed of many complexities that defeat any singular truth of how the world can and should work.

For example, might it be that both Hirsch and Kohn have valid perspectives? Focusing on core knowledge that students themselves might not choose but that gives them access to a society in which they might possibly change the current balance of power, wealth, and control seems quite reasonable. Using the curiosity of students to learn multiple histories and cultures and to explore a variety of intelligences in an intensely involving way also seems quite reasonable. It is important that schools be joyful and engaging places. Yet is all learning intrinsically or extrinsically motivated? Most would say it's both—we learn for the joy of it, but some of the most useful learning has taken place because others, not we ourselves, demanded that we do it, do it well, and do it until we got it right.

The polemics surrounding standards versus no standards do not account for complex realities. Are external standards bad or good? Might they be both? Might we have state standards and assessments for most (but not all) public schools in the same state? Some states have standards and assessments that have been well received by educators and the public—not seen as heavy-handed, intrusive, or unfair. Many states have standards and assessments that are volatile in makeup, format, pressure, and consequences.

The standards polarization—again, only one side can win—has come about because people have applied the term "standards" to all systems as if they were identical. However, Maine's standards are quite different from Virginia's. Elements of standards systems can be quite good, such as using disaggregated data to focus on the progress of all students, equalizing funding for poor students and communities, and targeting additional resources. Some states grant variances allowing schools and districts to develop their own assessments. And yes, there are cases in which it is good that standards can be used to close and reorganize schools that have done a disservice to students and parents. Standards systems can be demeaning and harmful—when they equate education with narrowly derived assessments and tests. They can also be tremendously positive in challenging schools and communities to leave no student behind.[6] We need to acknowledge simultaneous realities if we are to educate all students better than before.

PEDAGOGICAL PAIN

The "single-truth" wars have created much pain among teachers and school leaders who are swept into the battles. When whole language gained currency as "the" way to teach reading, teachers using phonics were lambasted, swept aside, and made to feel that they were evil, archaic, fascist practitioners of an indefensible method. Recently, the opposing force has "won" in states led by California and Texas. They have blamed whole language and invented spelling for declining literacy in America. Now teachers of whole language are made to feel abandoned and rejected as "feel-good," self-esteem–promoting contributors to the demise of basic skills.

These periodic surges and countersurges occur because one set of believers ignores any possible merits of the other side. Isn't it possible that many highly literate and culturally diverse people—people that you and I both know—were taught how to read mainly by decoding, phonics, and grammatical rules? Isn't it equally obvious that many highly literate and culturally diverse people have learned to read through literacy immersion, writing workshops, and experiential learning? Why is it so difficult to accept that an open mind about possibilities in education should be seen as a virtue rather than a liability?

Cooperative versus competitive learning is another such brawl. Cooperation is a key aspect of how one learns with and from others, and it undergirds much of community, civic, and business life. Research exists that demonstrates the power of structured team activities for academic and social development. Yet humans, as part of the animal kingdom, are also moved to learn by traits that have helped them to survive: dominance, power, and the need to test oneself against others. Cooperation and competition are not different versions of humanity; they are different dimensions of the same humanity. And thus there is evidence that both cooperation and competition bring out high performance in individuals.

The overarching debate about progressive, learner-centered schools versus teacher-centered, direct-instruction schools will be my last venture into the foolishness of single truths. This debate simplifies and silences the cultural and family values that Lisa Delpit so eloquently writes about in *Other People's Children.*[7] Asking students to conform to certain manners, expecting them to learn what adults determine is important for them, being didactic in instruction, and using "call and response" methods have resulted in great success for teachers and leaders such as Marva Collins, Jaime Escalante, and Lorraine Monroe and for a number of school programs.[8] Regardless of what one personally believes about the atmosphere of such classrooms and schools, students and parents in these settings see such didactic methods as expressions of teachers' love, care, and cultural solidarity.[9] The teachers are proud to demand that their students learn, and they go to almost any length to see that their students can compete with other students.

Yet progressive classrooms and schools that are activity- or project-centered and that cultivate imagination, problem solving, responsibility, and a variety of intellectual pursuits have, in the hands of the most dedicated teachers, also attained incredible success for students. Educators such as Eliot Wigginton, Deborah Meier, George Wood, Gloria Ladson-Billings, Sonia Nieto, and Jabari Mahiri have shown the power of inquiry-centered, progressive learning.

My point is *not* that all methods, techniques, curricula, and structures are of equal worth or that the attitude "anything goes" is acceptable. My point is that, when a group of students and parents choose to be with a group of educators dedicated to a particular philosophy and way of learning, the results for students can be awesome. No one group should have the presumption or power to tell another group that only its way is the right way. Instead, in accordance with publicly determined purposes and criteria, we should be seeking, testing, and developing research-based alternative conceptions and practices of successful education. Kenneth Wilson, a Nobel laureate in physics, remarked about the need to test a multitude of educational approaches through longitudinal research and self-correction to find out what works well, what can be adapted, and what should be discarded.[10] The idea is not to prove that one way is the only way but instead to allow for different conceptions of education to flourish in the marketplace of public education.

RELIGION IN AMERICA AND AN EDUCATED AMERICAN

Of all Western nations, America is the country with the highest percentage of citizens actively involved in religious and spiritual practices.[11] Why? Because it has no official state religion and no divine story behind its creation. Those countries that do have histories of such official state religion—a one way to believe for all—tend to have lower percentages of citizen involvement in religious practice. This example suggests why we must avoid a single governmental (local, state, or national) conception of education. The analogy with religion ends at a certain point, as the U.S. government needs to remain neutral and not use public funds to promote any particular set of religious beliefs. But government must use public funds to support a public education consistent with democratic ideals.[12] And the best way for doing so is to create a system of state schools that promote various publicly determined conceptions of an educated American.

Public education can be defined in several overlapping ways. Public education is funded by taxpayers, it is an education for the public, it is open and without cost to students and parents, it is compulsory, it is governed by public authority, it is nonprofit, and it always *should be* nondiscriminatory and nonrepressive of students and parents.[13] It is public because it serves a common good: the education of students to have choices of "life, liberty, and the pursuit of happiness" and to acknowledge those choices for others.

Within these definitions of public, American education is always an experiment—one hopes a thoughtful one—that must constantly test ways to further realize the hopes and aspirations of all the nation's people. Whenever one truth stamps out all others—whether it be through one system of tests, one approach to curriculum, one conception of knowledge, a single method of instruction, or a uniform structure for all public schools—democracy itself and education for a democracy are subverted.

In first proposing the need for common schools, Horace Mann wrote in the 1840s that public schools would be the great equalizers of human conditions, the balance wheel of the social machinery. Poverty would disappear and with it the discord between the haves and the have-nots; life for all people would be longer, better, and happier. The common school would be free, for poor and rich alike, as good as any private school, and nonsectarian. (The common school was not to be a school for common people but rather a school common to all people.) And the pedagogy of the common or free school would stress the "self-discipline of individuals, self-control, and self-governance." The issue for Mann was that the educated person was to have a free, deliberate choice between obedience and anarchy.[14]

Another view of the educated person in a democracy was shaped by the Lockean sympathies of early American thought. The educated person would be the one who renounced self-indulgence, practiced restraint, and saw the virtue of frugality and labor. In this view, one would work not for what one could accumulate but in order to focus the human mind and body.

Jefferson's concept of the educated person was the farmer—a person who lived apart from others; pursued his own curiosity about science, philosophy, and art after a long day of self-sustaining chores; and then determined those times that he should participate in neighborhood and community affairs. The farmer's life was a combination of aloneness, individuality, and self-learning with minimal but significant civic responsibility.

W. E. B. Du Bois, referring to the need for African American children to learn, saw public education as giving "our children the fairness of a start which will equip them with such an array of facts and such an attitude toward truth that they can have a real chance to judge what the world is and what its greater minds have thought it might be."[15]

Education might also be defined as making a good neighbor—one who cares for and respects others, who takes care of his or her own family needs, and who contributes to the welfare of others.[16] Such a person would possess a respect for other people and an understanding of life conditions locally, nationally, and internationally; the ability to communicate with diverse others; analytic and problem-solving skills; and the competence to choose what to do with one's own life in economic, social, recreational, and aesthetic pursuits. Does one need three years of high school or college-level preparatory mathematics to develop these attributes? Does one need to learn French? How about Chinese? What level of mastery does one need in the various disciplines? Is it better to study discrete subjects or an integrated curriculum with applications to the world outside of school? The question here is, What knowledge, skills, and understandings are needed to be a good neighbor and citizen?

In a high school curriculum controlled by college admission requirements, there are expected core courses, and good scores on the SAT or ACT have become essential measures of an educated American. Whether going to college or not, most students will not use most of what they are required to learn, whether mathematics or history or language or science. Is it still essential? Again, says who? Dare I ask the unspeakable: Can one be a good neighbor and a wise and productive citizen without going to college?

Is the purpose of public education to train a highly skilled work force to support American corporations? If so, the definition of a well-educated American as a good worker will place a great deal of emphasis on technology. But again, who should determine what is a well-educated person? For example, the Waldorf schools in America have children work with natural materials for the first three to five years of schooling.[17] Children work only with wood, clay, water, and paint, on long, painstaking projects for several years before the technological world becomes a source of their learning—no televisions, no phones, no computers in early childhood and primary classrooms. The prime emphasis is on imagination and work in an all-natural environment. Are these students educated less well than others? According to what criteria?

To be blunt, any single truth or concept of an educated American will be fraught with contradictions. The real danger of any one reform effort, such as a standards movement that relies on a single test, is the promotion of a single definition of the well-educated citizen as a college graduate who is technologically prepared to lead a successful economic life. The idea that an educated citizen might not want to make vast sums of money or work in a corporation but instead might seek success in quietness, resistance, or even detachment from corporate/college-controlled work, has eroded in America. Even to mention the idea that education is not mostly about jobs or money but about choosing how to live one's life among others is to be seen as a romantic, a throwback to another time.

My point is not to convince others of any one definition of a well-educated person but to share the need for varied conceptions of education, conceptions that must be in conformance with "public" criteria and equally based on data about student accomplishments and successes.

WHAT DO WE DO?

As a reformer who advocates the progressive tradition and assists schools in keeping it alive, I do not seek a common ground for public education—an eclectic "all things of equal merit" ground—but instead wish to move beyond that to a higher ground that incorporates complexity and competing conceptions. A higher ground where contradictory truths must be part and parcel of American democracy. We need an education system that supports multiple conceptions of an educated American, that subjects all such conceptions to the scrutiny of research and public accountability, and that fixes all actions of classrooms and schools within the boundaries of equity. American students and schools lose each time one "truth" gains currency and suppresses competing notions of public education.

So let me end by stating that, in my experience with schools, education reformers, policy makers, legislators, corporate persons, community activists, and citizens at large, I have found people of astonishingly good will and passionate intent who labor in the light of controversy about what our schools need or deserve. They are accused by their opponents of being self-indulgent conspirators with sinister motives, but most of them, or at least those that I know, are not. However, many of those who are most influential or powerful are singularly convinced that theirs is the true way to improve education and that all other ways are false, bad, and corrupt.

We need to realize that, most often, life does not contain single truths but instead is about predicaments, competing views, and apparent conflicts. The public school system must value and allow multiple conceptions of education that students, parents, and faculty members can choose from—some purebreds, some hybrids, and some yet to be known, but all devoted to students and their pursuit of the American Dream.

We must fight against any single model, structure, method, or system of education. We must expand the freedom of schools to test new

concepts of standards, assessments, and accountability. Ultimately, we must hold every school and district responsible for whether it has provided an education for all children that can be documented to increase choices of "life, liberty, and the pursuit of happiness." *That* is an American education.

ENDNOTES

1. Carl D. Glickman, *Revolutionizing America's Schools* (San Francisco: Jossey–Bass, 1998).

2. See E. D. Hirsch, Jr., *The Schools We Need and Why We Don't Have Them* (New York: Doubleday, 1996); Alfie Kohn, *The Schools Our Children Deserve* (Boston: Houghton Mifflin, 1999); Susan Ohanian, *One Size Fits Few: The Folly of Educational Standards* (Portsmouth, NH: Heinemann, 1999); and I. de Pommereau, "Tougher High School Standards Signal Greater Demands on Students," *Christian Science Monitor,* 16 June 1996, p. 12, 1-C.

3. Seymour Martin Lipset, *American Exceptionalism: A Double-Edged Sword* (New York: Norton, 1996).

4. Henry Louis Gates, Jr., and Cornel West, *The Future of the Race* (New York: Random House, 1996), pp. 19, 38.

5. Jim Myers, "Notes on the Murder of Thirty of My Neighbors," *Atlantic,* March 2000, pp. 72–88.

6. Chris Gallagher, "A Seat at the Table: Teachers Reclaiming Assessment Through Rethinking Accountability," *Phi Delta Kappan,* March 2000, pp. 502–7.

7. Lisa Delpit, *Other People's Children: Cultural Conflict in the Classroom* (New York: New Press, 1995).

8. See, for example, such schools as P.S. 161 in New York, KIPP Academies in Texas and New York, and the Frederick Douglass Middle School in New York.

9. Samuel Casey Carter, *No Excuses: Seven Principals of Low-Income Schools Who Set the Standards for High Achievement* (Washington, DC: Heritage Foundation, 1999); and Jacqueline Jordan Irvine, "Seeing with the Cultural Eye: Different Perspectives of African American Teachers and Researchers," *DeWitt Wallace–Reader's Digest Distinguished Lecture* presented at the annual meeting of the American Educational Research Association, New Orleans, April 2000.

10. Kenneth Wilson and Bennett Daviss, *Redesigning Education* (New York: Teachers College Press, 1994).

11. Lipset, op. cit.; and Warren A. Nord, *Religion and American Education: Rethinking a National Dilemma* (Chapel Hill: University of North Carolina Press, 1995).

12. John Dayton and Carl D. Glickman, "Curriculum Change and Implementation: Democratic Imperatives,"

Peabody Journal of Education, vol. 9, no. 4, 1994, pp. 62–86; Benjamin R. Barber, *An Aristocracy of Everyone: The Politics of Education and the Future of America* (New York: Ballantine, 1992); and Amy Gutmann, *Democratic Education* (Princeton, NJ: Princeton University Press, 1987).

13. Gutmann, op. cit.

14. Lawrence A. Cremin, *The Transformation of the School: Progressivism in American Education 1876–1957* (New York: Random House, 1964), pp. 3–11.

15. W. E. B. Du Bois, "The Freedom to Learn," in Philip S. Foner, ed., *W. E. B. Du Bois Speaks* (New York: Pathfinder, 1970), pp. 230–31.

16. George H. Wood, *A Time to Learn* (New York: Dutton, 1998).

17. Todd Oppenheimer, "Schooling the Imagination," *Atlantic,* September 1999, pp. 71–83.

DISCUSSION QUESTIONS

1. Does the United States live up to its reputation as the land of opportunity? Does public education live up to its reputation for providing a ladder to success for groups that are not part of the mainstream culture?

2. Are educational decisions made more often on the basis of good intentions, ideology, or results? Which is the criterion that is most appropriate for guiding practice?

3. What essential knowledge and skills should an educated person in a democracy possess?

4. Given the heated debates about education that are prevalent today, is it possible to make decisions about public education in a civil and responsible manner?

5. Would increasing the number of charter schools or the opportunities for school choice have the effect of undermining or reinforcing the principles of democracy?

39

A Wider Lens on the Black-White Achievement Gap

RICHARD ROTHSTEIN

FOCUSING QUESTIONS

1. How does social class impact learning? What are some of the at-home obstacles to learning? School obstacles? Societal obstacles?
2. How does race affect social-class learning differences?
3. What can schools do to limit the black-white achievement gap?
4. Why are untestable areas, such as noncognitive skills, important?
5. What are some programs that can help lessen a school's black-white achievement gap? What can a community do? What can a family do?

The 50th anniversary of the Supreme Court's school desegregation order in *Brown v. Board of Education* has intensified public awareness of the persistent gap in academic achievement between black students and white students. The black-white gap is made up partly of the difference between the achievement of all lower-class students and that of middle-class students, but there is an additional gap between black students and white students—even when the blacks and whites come from families with similar incomes.

The American public and its political leaders, along with professional educators, have frequently vowed to close these gaps. Americans believe in the ideal of equal opportunity, and they also believe that the best way to ensure that opportunity is to enable all children, regardless of their parents' social class, to leave school with skills that position them to compete fairly and productively in the nation's democratic governance and occupational structure. The fact that children's skills can so clearly be predicted by their race and family economic status is a direct challenge to our democratic ideals.

Policy makers almost universally conclude that these existing and persistent achievement gaps must be the result of wrongly designed school policies—either expectations that are too low, teachers who are insufficiently qualified, curricula that are badly designed, classes that are too large, school climates that are too undisciplined, leadership that is too unfocused, or a combination of these factors.

Americans have come to the conclusion that the achievement gap is the fault of "failing schools" because common sense seems to dictate that it could not be otherwise. After all, how much money a family has or the color of a child's skin should not influence how well that child learns to read. If teachers know how to teach reading—or math or any other subject—and if schools emphasize the importance of such tasks and permit no distractions, children should be able to learn these subjects, whatever their family income or skin color.

This commonsense perspective, however, is misleading and dangerous. It ignores how social-class characteristics in a stratified society such as ours may actually influence learning in school. It confuses social class, a concept that Americans have historically been loath to consider, with two of its characteristics: income and, in the United States, race. For it is true that income and skin color themselves don't influence academic achievement, but the collection of characteristics that define social-class differences inevitably influences that achievement.

SOCIAL CLASS AND ITS IMPACT ON LEARNING

Distinctly different child-rearing patterns are one mechanism through which social-class differences affect the academic performance of children. For example, parents of different social classes often have different ways of disciplining their children, different ways of communicating expectations, and even different ways of reading to their children. These differences do not express themselves consistently or apply to every family; rather, they influence the average tendencies of families from different social classes.

That there are personality and child-rearing differences, on average, between families in different social classes makes sense when you think about it. If upper-middle-class parents have jobs in which they are expected to collaborate with fellow employees, create new solutions to problems, or wonder how to improve their contributions, they are more likely to talk to their children in ways that differ from those of lower-class parents whose jobs simply require them to follow instructions without question. Children who are reared by parents who are professionals will, on average, have more inquisitive attitudes toward the material presented by their teachers than will children who are reared by working-class parents. As a result, no matter how competent the teacher, the academic achievement of lower-class children will, on average, almost inevitably be less than that of middle-class children. The probability of such reduced achievement increases as the characteristics of lower social class accumulate for particular families.

Many social and economic manifestations of social class also have important implications for learning. Health differences are among them.

On average, lower-class children have poorer vision than middle-class children, partly because of prenatal conditions and partly because of how their eyes are trained as infants. They have poorer oral hygiene, more lead poisoning, more asthma, poorer nutrition, less adequate pediatric care, more exposure to smoke, and a host of other problems. Each of these well-documented social-class differences is likely to have a palpable effect on academic achievement, and the combined influence of all of these differences is probably huge.

The growing unaffordability of adequate housing for low-income families is another social-class characteristic that has a demonstrable effect on average achievement. Children whose families have difficulty finding stable housing are more likely to be mobile, and student mobility is an important cause of low student achievement. Urban rents have risen faster than working-class incomes. Even families in which parents' employment is stable are more likely to move when they fall behind in rent payments. In some schools in minority neighborhoods, this need to move has boosted mobility rates to more than 100 percent: for every seat in the school, more than two children were enrolled at some time during the year.[1] It is hard to imagine how teachers, no matter how well trained, can be as effective for children who move in and out of their classrooms as they can be for children whose attendance is regular.

Differences in wealth between parents of different social classes are also likely to be important determinants of student achievement, but these differences are usually overlooked because most analysts focus only on annual income to indicate disadvantage. This practice makes it hard to understand, for example, why black students, on average, score lower than white students whose family incomes are the same. It is easier to understand this pattern when we recognize that children can have similar family incomes but be ranked differently in the social-class structure, even in economic terms. Black families with low income in any particular year are likely to have been poor for longer than white families with similar income in that year. White families are also likely to own far more assets that support their children's achievement than are black families at the same level of current income.

I use the term "lower class" here to describe the families of children whose achievement will, on average, be predictably lower than the achievement of middle-class children. American sociologists were once comfortable with this term, but it has fallen out of fashion. Instead, we tend to use such euphemisms as "disadvantaged" students, "at-risk" students, "inner-city" students, or students of "low socioeconomic status." None of these terms, however, can capture the central characteristic of lower-class families: a collection of occupational, psychological, personality, health, and economic traits that interact, predicting performance—not only in schools but in other institutions as well—that, on average, differs from the performance of children from families in higher social classes.

Much of the difference between the average performance of black children and that of white children can probably be traced to differences in their social-class characteristics. But there are also cultural characteristics that are likely to contribute a bit to the black-white achievement gap. These cultural characteristics may have identifiable origins in social and economic conditions—for example, black students may value education less than white students because a discriminatory labor market has not historically rewarded black workers for their education—but values can persist independently and outlast the economic circumstances that gave rise to them.

Some lower-class children do achieve at high levels, and many observers have falsely concluded from this that therefore all lower-class children should be able to succeed with appropriate instruction. One of the bars to our understanding of the achievement gap is that most Americans, even well-educated ones, are not expert in discussions of statistical distributions. The achievement gap is a phenomenon of averages, a difference between the average achievement level of lower-class children and the average achievement level of middle-class children. In human affairs, every average characteristic is a composite of many widely disparate characteristics.

For example, we know that lead poisoning has a demonstrable impact on young children's I.Q. scores. Children with high exposure to lead—from fumes or from ingesting paint or dust—have I.Q. scores that, on average, are several points lower than those of children who are not so exposed. But this does not mean that every child with lead poisoning has a lower I.Q. Some children with high lead levels in their blood have higher I.Q. scores than typical children with no lead exposure. When researchers say that lead poisoning seems to affect academic performance, they do not mean that every lead-exposed child performs less well. But the high performance of a few lead-exposed children does not disprove the conclusion that lead exposure is likely to harm academic achievement.

This kind of reasoning applies to each of the social-class characteristics that I discuss here, as well as to the many others that, because of lack of space or my own ignorance, I do not discuss. In each case, class differences in social or economic circumstances probably cause differences in the average academic performance of children from different social classes, but, in each case, some children with lower-class characteristics perform better than typical middle-class children.

SCHOOL REFORMS ALONE ARE NOT ENOUGH

The influence of social-class characteristics is probably so powerful that schools cannot overcome it, no matter how well trained their teachers and no matter how well designed their instructional programs and climates. But saying that a social-class achievement gap should be expected is not to make a logical statement. The fact that social-class differences are associated with, and probably cause, a big gap in academic performance does not mean that, in theory, excellent schools could not offset these differences. Indeed, today's policy makers and educators make many claims that higher standards, better teachers, more accountability, better discipline, or other effective practices can close the achievement gap.

The most prominent of these claims has been made by the Heritage Foundation (conservative) and the Education Trust (more liberal), by economists and statisticians who claim to have shown that better teachers do in fact close the gap, by prominent educators, and by social critics. Many (though not all) of the instructional practices promoted by these commentators are well designed, and these practices probably do succeed in delivering a better education to some lower-class children. But a careful examination of each claim that a particular school or practice has closed the race or social-class achievement gap shows that the claim is unfounded.

In some cases, a claim may fail because it reflects a statistical fluke—a school successful for only one year, in only one subject, or in only one grade—or because it reports success only on tests of the most basic skills. In other cases, a claim may fail because the successful schools identified have selective student bodies. Remember that the achievement gap is a phenomenon of averages—it compares the average achievement of lower- and middle-class students. In both social classes, some students perform well above or below the average performance of their social-class peers. If schools can select (or attract) a disproportionate share of lower-class students whose performance is above the average of their social class, those schools can appear to be quite successful. Many such schools are excellent and should be commended. But their successes provide no evidence that their instructional approaches would close the achievement gap if used with students who are average for their social-class groups.

LIMITATIONS OF THE CURRENT TESTING REGIME

Whether efforts to close the social-class achievement gap involve in-school reforms or socioeconomic reforms, it is difficult to know precisely how much any intervention will narrow the gap. We can't estimate the effect of various policies partly because we don't really know how big the achievement gap is overall or how big it is in particular schools or school systems.

This lack of knowledge about the size of the gap or the merits of any particular intervention might surprise many readers because so much attention is devoted these days to standardized test scores. It has been widely reported that, on average, if white students score at around the 50th percentile on a standardized math or reading test, black students typically score around the 23rd percentile. (In more technical statistical terms, black students score, on average, between 0.5 and 1.0 standard deviations below white students.)

But contrary to conventional belief, this may not be a good measure of the gap. Because of the high stakes attached to standardized tests in recent years, schools and teachers are under enormous pressure to raise students' test scores. The more pressure there has been, the less reliable these scores have become. In part, the tests themselves don't really measure the gap in the achievement of high standards because high standards (such as the production of good writing and the development of research skills and analysis) are expensive to test, and public officials are reluctant to spend the money. Instead, schools have tended to use inexpensive standardized tests that mostly, though not entirely, assess more basic skills. Gaps that show up on tests of basic skills may be quite different from the gaps that would show up on tests of higher standards of learning. And it is not the case that students acquire a hierarchy of skills sequentially. Thus truly narrowing the achievement gap would not require children to learn "the basics" first. Lower-class children cannot produce typical middle-class academic achievement unless they learn basic and more advanced skills simultaneously, with each reinforcing the other. This is, in fact, how middle-class children who come to school ready to learn acquire both basic and advanced skills.

The high stakes recently attached to standardized tests have given teachers incentives to revise the priorities of their instruction, especially for lower-class children, so that they devote greater time to drill on basic skills and less time to other, equally important (but untested) learning areas in which achievement gaps also appear. In a drive to raise test scores in math and reading, the curriculum has moved away not only from more advanced mathematical and literary skills, but also from social studies, literature, art, music, physical education, and other important subjects that are not tested for the purpose of judging school quality. We don't know how large the race or social-class achievement gaps are in these subjects, but there is no reason to believe that gaps in one domain are the same as the gaps in others or that the relationships between gaps in different domains will remain consistent at different ages and on different tests.

For example, educational researchers normally expect that gaps in reading will be greater than gaps in math, probably because social-class differences in parental support play a bigger role for reading than for math. Parents typically read to their very young children, and middle-class parents do so more and in more intellectually stimulating ways, but few parents do math problems with their young children. Yet, on at least one test of entering kindergartners, race and social-class gaps in math exceed those in reading.

THE IMPORTANCE OF NONCOGNITIVE SKILLS

We also don't know the extent of the social-class gaps in noncognitive skills—such character traits as perseverance, self-confidence, self-discipline, punctuality, the ability to communicate, social responsibility, and the ability to work with others and resolve conflicts. These are important goals of public education. In some respects, they may be more important than academic outcomes.

Employers, for example, consistently report that workers have more serious shortcomings in these noncognitive areas than in academic areas. Econometric studies show that noncognitive skills are a stronger predictor of future earnings than are standardized test scores. In public opinion surveys, Americans consistently say they want schools to produce good citizens and socially responsible adults first and people with high academic proficiency second. Yet we do a poor job—actually, no job at all—of assessing whether schools are generating such noncognitive outcomes. And so we also do a poor job of assessing whether schools are successfully narrowing the social-class gap in these traits or whether social and economic reform would be necessary here, too, to narrow the gap.

There is some evidence that the social-class gap in noncognitive skills should be a cause for concern. For very young children, measures of antisocial behavior mirror the gaps in academic test scores. Children of lower social classes exhibit more antisocial behavior than children of higher social classes, both in early childhood and in adolescence. It would be reasonable to expect that the same social and economic inequalities that seem likely to produce gaps in academic test scores also produce differences in noncognitive traits.

In some areas, however, it seems that the noncognitive gap may be smaller than the cognitive one. It particular, analyses of some affirmative action programs in higher education find that, when minority students with lower test scores than white students are admitted to colleges, the lower-scoring minority students may exhibit more leadership, devote more serious attention to their studies, and go on to make greater community contributions. This evidence reinforces the importance of measuring noncognitive student characteristics, something that few elementary or secondary schools attempt. Until we begin to measure these traits, we will have no insight into the extent of the noncognitive gaps between lower- and middle-class children.

MOVING FORWARD

Three tracks should be pursued vigorously and simultaneously if we are to make significant progress in narrowing the achievement gap. The first track is school improvement efforts that raise the quality of instruction in elementary and secondary schools. The second track is expanding the definition of schooling to include crucial out-of-school hours in which families and communities now are the sole influences. This means implementing comprehensive early childhood, after-school, and summer programs. And the third track is social and economic policies that will enable children to attend school more equally ready to learn. These policies include providing health services for lower-class children and their families, ensuring stable housing for working families with children, and narrowing the growing income inequalities in American society.

Many of the reforms in curriculum and school organization that are promoted by critics of education have merit and should be intensified. Repairing and upgrading the scandalously decrepit school facilities that serve some lower-class children, raising salaries to permit the recruitment of more qualified teachers for lower-class children, reducing class sizes for lower-class children (particularly in the early grades), insisting on higher academic standards that emphasize creativity and reasoning as well as basic skills, holding schools accountable for fairly measured performance, having a well-focused and disciplined school climate, doing more to encourage lower-class children to intensify their own ambitions—all of these measures and others can play a role in narrowing the achievement gap. These reforms are extensively covered in a wide range of books, articles, and public discussions of education, so I will not dwell on them here. Instead, my focus is the greater importance of reforming social and economic institutions if we truly want children to emerge from school with equal preparation.

Readers should not misinterpret this emphasis as implying that better schools are not important or that school improvement will not make a contribution to narrowing the achievement gap. Better school practices can no doubt narrow the gap. However, school reform is not enough.

In seeking to close the achievement gap for low-income and minority students, policy makers focus inordinate attention on the improvement of instruction because they apparently believe that social-class differences are immutable and that only schools can improve the destinies of lower-class children. This is a peculiarly American belief—that schools can be virtually the only instrument of social reform—but it is not based on evidence concerning the relative effectiveness of economic, social, and educational improvement efforts.

While many social-class characteristics are impervious to short-term change, many can easily be affected by public policies that narrow the social and economic gaps between lower- and middle-class children. These policies can probably have a more powerful impact on student achievement (and, in some cases, at less cost) than an exclusive focus on school reform. But we cannot say so for sure, because social scientists and educators have devoted no effort to studying the relative costs and benefits of nonschool versus school reforms. For example, establishing an optometric clinic in a school to improve the vision of low-income children could have a bigger impact on their test scores than spending the same money on instructional improvement.[2] Greater proportions of low-income than middle-class children are distracted by the discomfort of untreated dental cavities, and dental clinics can likewise be provided at costs comparable to what schools typically spend on less effective reforms. We can't be certain if

this is the case, however, because there have been no experiments to test the relative benefits of these alternative strategies. Of course, proposals to improve all facets of the health of lower-class children, not just their vision and oral health, should be evaluated for their academic impacts.

A full array of health services will be costly, but that cost cannot be avoided if we are truly to embrace the goal of raising the achievement of lower-class children. Some of these costs are not new, of course, and some can be recouped by school clinics by means of reimbursements from other underutilized government programs, such as Medicaid.

Other social reforms—for example, an increase in the number of Section 8 housing vouchers to increase the access of lower-class families to stable housing—also could have a significant educational impact.

Incomes have become more unequally distributed in the United States in the last generation, and this inequality contributes to the academic achievement gap. Proposals for a higher minimum wage or increases in the earned income tax credit, which are designed to help offset some of this inequality, should be considered education policies as well as economic ones, for they would be likely to result in higher academic performance by children whose families were more secure.

Although conventional opinion is that "failing" schools contribute mightily to the achievement gap, the evidence indicates that schools already do a great deal to combat it. Most of the social-class difference in average academic potential exists by the time children are 3 years old. This difference is exacerbated over the years that children spend in school, but during these years, the growth in the gap occurs mostly in the after-school hours and during the summertime, when children are not in classrooms.[3]

So, in addition to school improvement and broader reforms to narrow the social and economic inequalities that produce the gap in student achievement, investments should be made to expand the definition of schooling to cover those crucial out-of-school hours. Because the gap is already huge at 3 years old, the most important focus of this investment should probably be early childhood programs. The quality of the programs is as important as their existence. To narrow the gap, early childhood care, beginning with infants and toddlers, should be provided by adults who can offer the kind of intellectual environment that is typically experienced by middle-class infants and toddlers. This goal probably requires professional care givers and low child/adult ratios.

Providing after-school and summer experiences to lower-class children that are similar to those middle-class children take for granted would be likely to play an essential part in narrowing the achievement gap. But these experiences should not be restricted to remedial programs in which lower-class children get added drill in math and reading. Certainly, remedial instruction should be part of an adequate after-school and summer program—but only a part. The advantage that middle-class children gain after school and in the summer probably comes mostly from the self-confidence they acquire and the awareness they develop of the world outside their homes and immediate communities and from organized athletics, dance, drama, museum visits, recreational reading, and other activities that develop their inquisitiveness, creativity, self-discipline, and organizational skills. After-school and summer programs can be expected to have a chance of narrowing the achievement gap only by attempting to duplicate such experiences.

For nearly half a century, the association of social and economic disadvantage with a student achievement gap has been well known to economists, sociologists, and educators. However, most have avoided the obvious implications of this understanding: Raising the achievement of lower-class children requires the amelioration of the social and economic conditions of their lives, not just school reform. Perhaps we are now ready to reconsider this needlessly neglected opportunity.

ENDNOTES

1. David Kerbow, "Patterns of Urban Student Mobility and Local School Reform," *Journal of Education for Students Placed at Risk*, vol. 12, 1996, pp. 147–69; and James Bruno and Jo Ann Isken, "Inter- and Intraschool Site Student Transiency: Practical and Theoretical Implications for Instructional Continuity at Inner-City Schools," *Journal of Research and Development in Education*, vol. 29, 1996, pp. 239–52.

2. Paul Harris, "Learning-Related Visual Problems in Baltimore City: A Long-Term Program," *Journal of Optometric Vision Development*, vol. 33, 2002, pp. 75–115; and Marge Christensen Gould and Herman Gould, "A Clear Vision for Equity and Opportunity," *Phi Delta Kappan*, December 2003, pp. 324–29.

3. See Meredith Phillips, "Understanding Ethnic Differences in Academic Achievement: Empirical Lessons from National Data," in David W. Grissmer and J. Michael Ross, eds., *Analytic Issues in the Assessment of Student Achievement* (Washington, D.C.: U.S. Department of Education, NCES 2000–050, 2000), pp. 103–32, available at http://nces.ed.gov/pubs2000/2000osoa.pdf; Richard L. Allington and Anne McGill-Franzen, "The Impact of Summer Setback on the Reading Achievement Gap," *Phi Delta Kappan*, September 2003, pp. 68–75; and Doris Entwisle and Karl L. Alexander, "Summer Setback: Race, Poverty, School Composition, and Mathematics Achievement in the First Two Years of School," *American Sociological Review*, February 1992, pp. 72–84.

DISCUSSION QUESTIONS

1. Do social-class differences have a greater influence on student success than education?

2. Can education compensate for differences in social class? If so, how?

3. Do standardized tests provide an accurate indication of student achievement? Why or why not?

4. What kinds of noncognitive skills are necessary for success in life? Do schools do an adequate job of teaching these skills?

5. Should social services be more closely linked to the process of schooling? How would this change the nature of classrooms and schools?

40

Education, Equality, and Equity

ALLAN C. ORNSTEIN

FOCUSING QUESTIONS

1. What is the author's intent in comparing Johnny Cash with Darwin and Dewey?
2. How would you describe the conservative and liberal viewpoints toward class?
3. What evidence is available to show an increasing gap between the rich and the remaining American populace?
4. Why do works by liberal authors get assigned to education students more often than those by conservative authors?
5. Can a society promote both excellence and equality? Why? Why not?
6. What is a two-tier system of education? Do you believe such a system exists today? Why? Why not?

Given my advancing age, and the fact that time changes a person's thinking, in some sort of sneaky, wrenching way, I now realize my *education* heroes are not William McGuffey but Horace Mann, not William Harris but Henry Barnard, not John Dewey but George Counts, and not Charles Elliot or James Conant but Jane Addams and Michael Harrington.[1]

These people I mention were probably the most influential educators for their period and had an everlasting effect on teaching and schooling, yet most of you may not know who I'm talking about because these names do not appear on the *New York Times* best-seller lists or on MTV, nor do they get regularly listed on Amazon.com. Suffice it to say that educators are not considered famous or sexy—and thus not worth too much time or space in the media.

I realize I should also distinguish between the "good guys" and the "bad guys" as I interpret the world of equality and equity. Allow me, then, to take you back via a time tunnel. We will start with colonial America and in warp speed arrive in the twentieth century, say in one or two min-

utes of reading, depending on how well your brain cells work. My first anti-hero is Joseph Morgan, the self-proclaimed spokesman of the Lord who in 1732 argued that the poor should be "content with their station" and that the rich had a "miserable life . . . full of Fear and Care . . . whereas a man that have but food and Raiment with honest labour, is free from the fears and cares." My hero of this time period is the Quaker preacher John Woolman, who declared in 1754 the Christian virtue of "a just distribution of man's worldly goods, that excessive riches and abject poverty led to endless ills" in society.

One hundred years later, my anti-hero is Frances Bowen, the conservative Harvard philosopher who in 1859 declared great wealth as a moral right "following from Christianity and humanity." He recognized and accepted "the aggregation of immense wealth at one end of the scale, and the increasing amount of hopeless poverty at the other" so long as the wealthy did not "cease to bridge this interval between themselves and the poor by personal exercises of sympathy, . . . common brotherhood . . . and [giving] largely to public charities." For the same period, my hero is labor leader Thomas Skidmore of New York, who in 1829 maintained that education alone was bound to prove ineffective "in redressing the economic grievance of the working class," that the system of production and distribution had to be addressed otherwise the "American worker would be in the same desperate condition that darkened the existence of his fellow worker in England" and the rest of Europe.

At the turn of the twentieth century, the conservative anti-hero is E. L. Godkin, editor of the *Nation,* who maintained in 1896 that he knew of "no more mischievous person than man who, in free America, seeks to spread . . . the idea that they [the workers] are wronged and kept down by somebody; that somebody is to blame because they are not better lodged, better dressed, better educated." The liberal counterpart is Charles Francis Adams, a descendent of John Adams, who expressed in 1916 general disdain toward the new wealthy class and giants of industry, who he felt defined national destiny in terms of laissez-faire economics and self-interest and believed that the duty of government was to encourage expansion and protect big business. "Not one I have ever known would I care to meet again, either in the world or the next; nor is one of them associated in my mind with the ideas of humor, thought or humanity."

I have dredged up these people from the skeletons of American intellectual thought, knowing full well these names are not household names or those of superstars or super athletes—and thus not worth much time or space for the average reader, blogger, or Internet surfer. But, for those of us who appreciate the fine touches of history and social thought, their influence in their period is noteworthy, and they help show a consistent thread in the struggle for equality and equity.

CONSERVATIVE AND LIBERAL THOUGHTS CONCERNING CLASS

From my list of anti-heroes, it is safe to say I'm not a blue-blood or a Yankee fan, more like a Johnny Cash fan whose words describe the common man. I am especially not fond of Darwin,

although many of my colleagues treat him as a scientific rock star, sitting in some hall of fame—not in Cleveland but at Westminster Abbey, with Galileo, Bacon, Newton, and other gods in the pantheon of science. And, if allowed to make a giant leap, perhaps unfounded to those who sing praise of Adam Smith and Ayn Rand (conservative economists who see greed as good), Social Darwinism is nothing more than robber baronism and materialism packaged in social science diction. The students of Darwinism provide the inference that those in certain segments of society are not capable of being fully educated to reflect, problem solve, or engage in creative thought; they should work with their hands.

For those readers who are more apt to believe in the hereditarian conception of IQ, in predetermined progress, natural selection, and/or evolutionary sociology and economics (in simple terms, "the smartest rise to the top"), Darwin provides an English-honored, aristocratic explanation for history, human causation, and the design of all life. He is, to his fans, the greatest English thinker since Newton, fitting into both Victorian colonialization and U.S. Gilded Age capitalism—setting forth a doctrine of the strong celebrating the rightness of their power and status over the weak. The doctrine is antithetical to all the urban people brought up on the wrong side of the tracks playing hoops or listening to hip-hop and to all the folk people in rural America, playing their fiddles, banjos, and guitars on the porch and singing from the darkest hollows, "Don't forget me. I was someone. I mattered!" For Darwin, and his fans, these lower-end people don't count; they are either invisible or to be exploited in some form by those on top of the economic ladder.

Describing the Rich and the Poor

From the age of Gould, Rockefeller, and Vanderbilt right down to present-day CEOs such as Kozlowski (Tyco), Lay (Enron), and Ebbers (World Com), Darwinism,[2] interpreted by conservative thinkers, provides the materialistic conviction and macho image to individuals who bleed and plunder their companies of hundreds of millions of dollars in salaries, perks, and parties while the pay of smart, educated, and articulate teachers averages $47,000 (2003–2004 school year) and the average worker earns $35,000 a year.[3] More than 72 percent of the work force saw real wages (adjusted for inflation) slide since 1979, despite a 40 percent increase in worker productivity in the last twenty-five years. On the other hand, the average CEO of the Fortune 500 companies earns 525 times more than the average worker; in 1979, it was 40 times.[4] Indeed, there is a serious fog obscuring values and ethics when we begin to describe the differences between the American business class and the educator class, between the capitalistic class and the shrinking middle class, between the college educated and the non–college educated.

As far as places etched in time, I have lived among the business and capitalistic classes of Yankeeville for more than twenty-five years, first in Winnetka, Illinois, and now Manhasset, New York, where education spending tops $20,000 per student (more than twice their respective states' average spending) and the Brahmin class and my anti-hero class would feel comfortable and see Camelot. Nevertheless, I talk rather about ordinary people and the songs of Johnny Cash, the man in black who would not change colors until things got better for the plebian class or ordinary person, which he believed they never did. Let me say it in a different way with the hope you see the light, so you can see life the way Johnny saw it and the way Darwin (and the money class) could never see it because of their aristocratic lens and belief in testing and tracking in school, which filtered through their distrust and disdain toward the immigrant class. Their emphasis was on shrewdness and strength to explain their own rise to the top and why the poor and laboring class would remain in their station in life.

The titans of the Gilded Age were self-made men and, in general, self-culture and education were not part of their self-making. But the rise of obscure and ordinary men (and women) to great wealth is becoming a caricature of the past. Today, education counts even less in the "new law of the jungle," highlighted by corporate greed and get-rich schemes for fleecing the public. In an age of declining influence of meritoc-

racy, from a social standpoint it is family wealth and power that now provide much more opportunity to accumulate fortune. The vast majority, despite increased education,[5] are condemned at birth to become part of the new "struggling" working and middle classes—people who were called the "toiling class" in the Old World, "common folk" during the Jacksonian period of democracy, and the "silent majority" in the twentieth century.

It is Cash, not Darwin or Dewey, who provided a voice for the downtrodden, for all the lost souls and lost causes that might have found a place in the American dream of long ago[6]—but have no place in today's American dream. Despite increased education levels among Americans, there are more struggling Americans than ever before because the income gap between the top 20 percent (especially the top 5 and 1 percentiles) and the remaining populace has increased dramatically in the last twenty-five years or so, a fact that conventional economists have ignored.

For example, between 1979 and 2001, real family income in the bottom 20 percent increased 3 percent. The middle 20 percent increased 17 percent. But the top 20 percent gained 53 percent, and the top 5 percent increased 81 percent. The top 1 percent experienced a whopping increase of 201 percent. Put in actual dollars, the after-tax gains of the top 1 percent rose $576,400 in real dollars, while the middle fifth rose $5,500 and the bottom fifth rose $1,100.[7] It's no secret, then, that inequality is increasing as the gap between poor, working-, and middle-class people and the rich shows growing disparity; hence, the purchasing power of the lower and middle groups has declined. The net result is that education counts much less in terms of economic success than it did in the past; in short, it is no longer the "great equalizer" we grew up thinking it was.

Cash and Darwin came from totally different backgrounds and time periods. Yet their conclusions are somewhat similar: The strong survive and get ahead, and it has little to do with schooling. In light of post-modern America's obsession with education, it is remarkable how reluctant we are to admit that education has become less important in securing jobs, income, and, especially, wealth. Although it would be hard for the reader to render me as some sort of Republican, I am not comfortable with Marxism; and, I do believe that such a philosophy extracts the liberalism out of liberal arts and turns individuals into "idealots," or even worse—a mob. My ideas are more contextual, rooted in the ideas of a *social democrat* (apt terminology for describing Princeton economist Paul Krugman and Brandeis economist Robert Reich, also Secretary of Labor during the Clinton administration). That said, the current trend—whereby the income gap between the top 5 percent and the remaining population continues growing—reflects the makings of a dynasty or financial oligarchy.

But undoing centuries-old values of the American business class and upper class is a losing proposition. It was F. Scott Fitzgerald who some seventy-five years ago was able to capture the leisurely and extravagant life of the upper class in stories such as *This Side of Paradise,* "Flappers and Philosophers," and *The Great Gatsby:* "The rich are different from you and me." Lower-class and working-class youth knew this, feeling rejected by their middle-class and upper-class peers, and formed their own subculture—reminiscent of the movies *Grease* starring John Travolta and *Rebel Without a Cause* starring James Dean. The beat and hippie poet of the 1950s and 1960s, Alan Ginsberg, understood and noted in his book *Howl* that money was the driving force in American culture.

Greed and self-interest are good in Ayn Rand's world (*The Fountainhead,* 1943), as well as in Dinish D'Souza's world (*The Virtues of Prosperity,* 2000), where capitalism and corporations are designed to maximize profits. Capitalism is where self-interest and competition meet—and become a self-regulating mechanism—so that government regulations are supposedly unnecessary. In a free economy, according to a younger Alan Greenspan, government may step in "only after . . . fraud, . . . crime . . . or damage to the consumer,"[8] which basically puts the average person at the mercy of big business and assumes that people in power are naturally ethical. (Really?)

As with Darwin, gingerly, and later more precisely with Herbert Spencer, the mid-nineteenth century English philosopher and educator, the strong survive and the weak and poor are "unfit" —destined to decline and to remain in the deep hollows, invisible and without a political or economic voice. Indeed, there are no minimal safety nets for the slow runners and the uneducated in a corporate and business world. The American economy, rooted in railroad magnates like Vanderbilt, trading tycoons like Gould, oil barons like Rockefeller, and mass manufacturers like Ford, has been positioned to exploit first the vast landscape and then the workers. Safety nets, if any existed, were and still are for CEOs and other executives; they know when to jump ship and sell their stock since they control company financial and accounting or have inside information. They are provided with golden parachutes amounting to tens of millions of dollars, while workers often watch their stocks and pensions tumble during an economic downslide.

Conservative and Liberal Educators

Regardless of our political stripes, most of us admit that old-fashioned populists and liberals have their own blizzard of polemics and are often motivated by concern for the downtrodden. We know that liberal views vastly outnumber conservative views on college campuses. It is much easier to be politically correct than politically incorrect. In my field of study, which is education, I also have the gut feeling that neo-Marxists such as Michael Apple, Paulo Freire, and Henry Giroux get assigned five or six times more often than conservative thinkers such as William Bennett, Allan Bloom, and Diane Ravitch. How can it be that the smartest or most relevant educators are from the political left? Or, is it that many professors have their own liberal biases, and just prefer not to discuss the conservative viewpoint? What is this thing we call balance or neutrality? Which college professors, in rare instances of academic freedom triumphing over politics, never bother to check the cultural pulse related to gender, race, or ethnicity before offering their opinions? You can probably count the number on your toes.

Now, who are your heroes? Who among us reading this book want to discuss their education champions? Educators are not considered handsome or sexy, cool or charismatic. Biographies of educators are basically nonexistent, while our culture is obsessed with sports figures, actors, generals, CEOs, and politicians. Other than some subliminal association with John Dewey or Jean Piaget, few teachers have in-depth knowledge of any major education thinker or leader. Perhaps they are too tired at the end of the day? Maybe they have slipped into indifference, and just want to go home after work, have dinner, relax, watch the evening news, and then go to sleep. If we paid teachers more money, would they be motivated to read the education literature? Would they have education heroes? Probably not, although I have no crystal ball allowing me to answer with 100 percent confidence. Maybe I'm too harsh, expecting too much, and inviting teachers and other educators to say pretentious things about education people, hoping they quibble about nonexistent distinctions. The bottom line is that no educator has attained true celebrity status or has become a media superstar. I guess at the end of the day, the questions are: Do you still have professional dreams? Did you give it your best? Do you still enjoy teaching your students? Did you connect with them?

SPUTNIK AND THE POST-SPUTNIK ERA

Allow me to extend the analysis in terms of human capital. The phrase "post-industrial society," coined by Daniel Bell, describes the scientific-technological societies evolving in developed countries during the second half of the twentieth century. The singular feature of this new kind of society is the importance of *knowledge* as the source of production, innovation, capital, and policy formulation. Emerging from the older economic systems in both advanced and socialistic countries is a knowledge society based on education and on the preeminence of professionals, scientists, and technicians. In the United States during the 1950s and 1960s, Bell noted "this group outpaced all others in the rate of growth, which was twice that for clerical workers (the category that held the lead in the 1940s) and seven times more than the overall rate of work-

ers."[9] The stratified structure of this new society produced a highly trained research elite, bolstered by education credentials, and supported by a large managerial, scientific, and technical staff (all college-educated).

Talent, Testing, and Tracking

The basis of achievement, and the economic driving force in the post-industrial meritocracy, is education, whereas in the bourgeois society of the Old World it was inherited wealth. Merit and differential status, power, and income are awarded to highly educated and trained experts with credentials; they are seen as the decision makers and leaders who will inherit the power structure in business, government, science, and politics.[10] Thus the term "best and brightest," used to describe the Kennedy advisors, later described the intellectual and power elite of the new technological and information society in which we live.

The traditional view of meritocracy holds that most inequalities are not created by some central authority or discriminatory policy but arise out of the individual's innate or acquired skills, capabilities, education, and other resources. In a society based on unrestricted equality, where the government does not interfere, the individual with greater skills, capabilities, and/or education will be at an advantage. In some ways, however, the post–World War II period, bolstered by the Cold War and the need to beat the Soviets, led to a curriculum based on talent and ability, spearheaded by conservative or essentialist thinkers such as Arthur Bestor, James Conant, and Hyman Rickover. The political and social landscape produced a trend toward meritocracy of the intellectual elite and briefly aggravated inequalities from the mid-1940s to the 1980s. For example, Richard Herrnstein did not bother to check the social or cultural pulse before offering his blunt, often incendiary, opinions—for instance, as a society succeeds in equalizing opportunity, differences in outcome will emerge between groups based on IQ scores and talent. The more equal opportunity there is, the more it drives "the heritability component higher, making [it] progressively more important." Increasingly, new legislation will be introduced to solve problems "whose roots are both biological and social,"[11] but it is far more cogent to say that the problem is social. It's one thing to talk about smart or intelligent *individuals,* but it is totally different to talk about differentials in smartness or intelligence among *groups.* Herrnstein did not explicitly "slip into error . . . and explicitly draw the second conclusion,"[12] but the hint of biological factors as opposed to environmental factors was enough to draw intense criticism from his academic peers, especially from the political left and most educators.

In 1961, John Gardner, the former Secretary of Health, Education, and Welfare and founder of Common Cause, published a highly readable book, *Excellence: Can We Be Equal and Excellent Too?*, which captured the feasibility of higher standards and the need to balance excellence and equality. He was also concerned about the sorting out process based on ability, and he pointed out that "social hazards existed in rigorous selection" based on intelligence. The sorting out process, both in schools and society, he felt, was one of the "most delicate and difficult" processes we face as a democratic nation. It translates into Who goes to college? Who is going to manage society? Who is going to earn more money? In a stratified society—one based on a corrupt or tyrannical government, a religious order, or a hereditary aristocracy—there is no dilemma, for everyone knows their place. Given our democratic principles, we are easily able to distinguish "excellence and mediocrity in athletics but refuse to be similarly precise about differences in intelligence."[13] In our society, unlike most other societies, we are given multiple chances to succeed, but Gardner was still concerned that the search for talent and the importance of education in our high-tech and knowledge-based society would lead to increasing inequality between educated and uneducated individuals. However, Gardner was unable to judge the declining influence of education and the growing financial oligarchy based on inherited wealth, a trend which first became noticeable in the 1990s, given great wealth produced by an expanding gross national product, as well as by the super-sized salaries of modern sports gladiators and rock stars (education requirement—none).

In an expanding economy, the search for talent is relentless, and those with grades and desirable skills who attend the best colleges can expect to earn the most money—creating inequality based on merit, which coincides with the role of educators. Of course, those born to privilege and wealth always have had a better chance for a good education; thus the playing field for the lower strata has never been equal. A class war has always existed, but since the days of Thomas Jefferson it has been hoped that those who are talented and without money will find the way to go on to college. "Geniuses will be raked from the rubbish," wrote Jefferson.[14] Here one might argue that Jefferson was arguing in behalf of an elitist society, not necessarily an egalitarian society. But most of us who believe in the American dream are willing to accept elitism based on intellectual pursuits and merit, as opposed to elitism based on inherited wealth and privilege.

The problem is, we do not all begin equally at the starting gate, as evidenced by the tragic fact that "just 3 percent of students at the nation's top 146 colleges come from the families in the bottom socioeconomic quartile," that is, the bottom 25 percent.[15] And in a recent interview, former Harvard President Lawrence Summers, who is better known for his politically incorrect statements about female scientists, warned that "for the first time probably in the history of our country, the gap in life prospects between the children of the fortunate and the children of the less fortunate is rising."[16] Regardless of our so-called egalitarian views, those who start in the lower-income brackets have less social capital than those who start in the middle- or higher-income categories; moreover, those with less social capital come to school with fewer cognitive skills, and the gap worsens as students are passed from one grade level to the next. In addition, the parents with more social control are able to move into high-performing school districts, provide private tutoring for their children, and work the system through university alumni associations, professional networks, and social contracts—thus assisting their children's careers and ensuring the advantage of higher class.

Summers's concern is still a major reversal from the positions of a Harvard president of one hundred years ago, Charles Eliot, who believed in a stratified society and a curriculum that destined working-class and immigrant children into a vocational track and upper-class, Anglo-Saxon children into a college track. Nonetheless, in *Left Back,* Diane Ravitch, a conservative education historian, considered Eliot, along with William Harris, to be a liberal reformer intent on expanding public education at the turn of the twentieth century. What it all boils down to might be called *historical slant*—and laced between words and sentences are the thoughts and biases of any author, including myself as well as Ravitch.

It can be argued that stratification based on meritocracy is in its own way as unjust as any of the historic forms of aristocratic privilege. Of course, those who believe in democracy or in the capitalistic system see no problem in a society based on merit; it certainly beats the notion of hereditary privilege and power. Thus John Rawls, the Harvard philosopher, is somewhat quaint or idealistic in equating justice with absolute equality and arguing that if some citizens have more goods than others, it has been accomplished by the loss of freedom and economic hardship for those who have fewer goods. This is a zero-sum analysis: The more someone's income and earnings exceed the average, the less other people will get in the distribution of money.

Because of social and economic deprivation, and the resulting cognitive deficits, children of lower-class and minority groups start school at a disadvantage in terms of basic skills and are unable to compete successfully in a society based on educational credentials. Given a pessimistic interpretation of the American education system as an unchanging two-tier system, class war has been fought in schools since the days of the Great Awakening in New England, when the study of the classics seemed a useless luxury for lowly and ordinary people and in order to get accepted into college an applicant had to be well versed in Latin and the classics.

Class war is still apparent, today, on the playing fields of Dalton, New York, and Eaton, Massachusetts, as well as in the schoolyards in Harlem, New York, and Roxbury, Massachusetts. Without appropriate credentials, people are not needed by the economy; they may not be exploited as many liberals contend, but they are underpaid for their services—not necessarily discriminated against, but not in demand. An achievement-based society, based on standardized tests and academic credentials, freezes most lower-class groups (who start the race with major handicaps) at the lower end of the stratified social structure.

Equal Opportunity

It is not surprising that those who find it difficult to compete within this system condemn the selection procedures and seek other remedies and social policies. The rejection of measurements that register the consequences of poverty or deprivation has political and social implications and reinforces beliefs that certain groups are superior or inferior, or to put it in more generic terms: "We made it. Why can't they?" or "We didn't have much money when we started out, but we worked hard. Why can't they?" or "Our ancestors were discriminated against when they came to this country. They lived in segregated neighborhoods, too. But they didn't become crack addicted, give birth to illegitimate children, or wind up in prison." Whereas this kind of logic was once considered acceptable, in an age prior to multi-culturalism and pluralism, today such stale pieties result in close political and cultural scrutiny and criticism from the left. In a post-modern era, in which groupthink abounds, generalizations about any minority group, including disabled, overweight, and even elderly people (as well as traditional minorities), are forbidden.

For most educators, the phrase "equal opportunity" conceives school as a process involving the acquisition of skills and the inculcation of better work habits in order to increase the individual's productivity. Since income is related to productivity, the more education an individual has, the higher will be his or her income. Education also serves as a screening device to sort individuals into different jobs; the more talented and highly educated individuals obtain the better jobs. The resulting stratification, based on merit or performance, is acceptable in a democratic society. It was accepted by conservative educators such as William Harris and Charles Eliot at the turn of the twentieth century, by Arthur Bestor and James Conant at mid-century, and even by the liberal policy maker John Gardner in his book *Excellence*. The democratic system breaks down, however, when inherited wealth becomes entrenched through practices that even the conservative *Wall Street Journal* calls "lasting legacies" and "dynasty trusts"—permitting huge sums of money to be passed from one generation to the next while avoiding taxes,[17]—or when the gap between the wealthy and the unwealthy (with similar amounts of education) becomes increasingly more lopsided. Hence, the relationship between education and income diminish; what counts more is social class, rank, and family connections—what some of us refer to as "power and privilege."

In a modern technological society, additional years of schooling are supposed to signal greater skills and productivity—and higher income. This is true so long as salaries continue to outpace the costs of satisfying basic needs, such as healthcare and medicine, transportation, housing, and higher education. In 2001, the bottom 40 percent of all U.S. families received 12 percent of the total income, down from 17 percent in 1973, while the highest 20 percent received 50 percent and the top 5 percent received 22 percent. Between 1967 and 1998, the poorest 20 percent had an increase in real income of 4 percent, while the richest 5 percent had an increase of 59 percent; hence, 95 percent of the benefits of economic growth went to the richest 5 percent—resulting in widened gaps between the rich and poor.[18] But this story represents the tip of the iceberg.

SUPPLY AND DEMAND— AND THE AMERICAN DREAM

The changing American economy is beyond official measurement. For example, it counts workers as employed if they hold any job—whether they work 10 hours or 50 hours a week, temporary or permanent, earn $8 per hour or $80 per hour, especially if they get a 1099 IRS form at the end of the year. In 2003, nearly 10 million American workers earned the minimum wage, another 15 million workers earned less than $8 per hour,[19] and still another 6.4 million workers were em-

ployed part-time but wanted to and could not find full-time employment. When these three groups are added to the official unemployment rate of about 8.7 million (it varies annually), the total is more than 40 million workers.[20] From 1993 to 2003, the unemployment rate dropped slightly but compensation for semi- and unskilled American workers remained substantially the same because most new jobs were at the low end in sales and service.[21] (It was in the high-end job sectors that salaries increased beyond inflationary rates.) Even worse, official unemployment statistics do not count people who have given up looking for work after their unemployment benefits expire or who are forced into early retirement because of job displacement or trimming in a particular corporation or economic sector.[22] These "invisible," uncounted workers (and forced retirees) total another 8 to 12 million, depending on which survey one reads, whether corporate- or union-sponsored. If we assume 10 million as an average and if we add it to the 40 million, the number is now 50 million workers. In short, the official economic statistics mask the fact that millions of people, though not classified as poor, do not make a decent living and are not part of the American Dream; it is also doubtful if the children of these people have adequate nutrition for learning and proper dental care (pain inhibits learning). If we consider that the poverty index is too low, based on artificial and politically driven definitions, that it only considers the *minimum* costs for the *barest necessities* for medical care, food, rent, utilities, and transportation, and that it does not make adjustments for regional differences, then many more Americans are struggling and many more students than just those entitled to free lunch or Title I programs are economically deprived and educationally handicapped at the starting gate.

The Changing Marketplace

Ordinary people today have to work two or more jobs and families need two incomes to keep up with a 1967 standard of living, an era portrayed in David Reisman's *The Lonely Crowd*, William Whyte's *Organization Man*, and TV's popular show *Ozzie and Harriet*. Back then, it took a sociologist (like Reisman) or psychologist (like Dr. Benjamin Spock) to tell people what they were feeling. Now commentators like Lou Dobbs, Brian Williams, and Paula Zahn report to Americans about how we feel and how we struggle to make ends meet. Even worse, our jobs are being exported abroad (85% of our retail purchases are now manufactured overseas), which in turn compounds the imbalance of trade (cheap overseas labor entering as goods on the U.S. market) and in turn reduces job opportunities at home—unless your goal is to become a "hamburger helper" or Wal-Mart hostess (also called a "greeter") for less than $8 an hour. Moreover, the outsourcing of jobs is now affecting middle-class and white-collar employment as outsourced jobs increasingly include those in the knowledge, technological, and digital sectors of the economy. The question is, What jobs are left that the schools and colleges can prepare their students for? The bottom line is that to maintain our standard of living, the American working and middle classes now work more hours in a year than their counterparts in the world's thirteen other industrialized nations, and the United States is the only industrialized nation whose worker hours have increased since 1980. To be sure, the economy works for the rich, not the average or common person.

During the age of meritocracy, that is, coinciding with the period of Sputnik and the Cold War, education was considered the be-all, end-all panacea for improving social mobility. Most of us still operate under this assumption, not realizing that market conditions have changed. The economy is no longer expanding at the same postwar rate and college graduates have flooded the marketplace and are no longer in great demand. The outsourcing of professional and service jobs is commonplace, as is the theft of intellectual property by Asian manufacturers, especially the Chinese, who consistently engage in "reverse engineering"—taking a known product and working backwards to copy it and then paying foreign, especially American, patent holders nothing.

Salaries for college graduates remained high during the period of meritocracy, due to the fact that college graduates were in short supply relative to the number of professional and managerial

jobs. For example, in 1950, as many as 2.3 million students were enrolled in degree-granting institutions; 186,000 bachelor's degrees and 26,000 master's degrees were awarded. By 1998, there were some 14.6 million students enrolled in higher education institutions, with 1.2 million bachelor's and 430,000 master's degrees awarded.[23] In 1952, 7.9 percent of the workforce had college degrees, and there "were [some] 2.33 college-level jobs available" per college graduate. In 1969, 12.6 percent of the workforce had college degrees, and the ratio of college-level jobs to applicants was 1:0.9. By 1974, the college graduate portion of the workforce had risen to 15.5 percent, reducing the ratio of jobs to workers to 1:0.6."[24] Between 2001 and 2003, this supply-demand had turned upside down. More than 30 percent of the 21–25 age cohort had four or more years of college, and the ratio of jobs to college graduates was a fractional one—one job per 10 to 15 applicants—creating significant unemployment and underemployment for those starting their careers. (College graduates are now taxicab drivers, waiters and waitresses, airline servers, returning to college, etc.) Teaching as a second career is big business in many schools of education; preservice student counts are up as college graduates find themselves underemployed or unemployed, and switch to education.

Allow me to put the situation in personal terms. When I graduated from college, John F. Kennedy was president. That may seem like the Dark Ages for some of you—before plastic money, moon landings, and cell phones—but only 11 percent of my age cohort held a bachelor's degree. The economy was booming, and there was no such thing as an unemployed or underemployed college graduate. Economists say that the starting salary advantage of college graduates over wage earners was 17 percent (in 1961) and rose to a high of 24 percent in 1970. By 1974, it had plummeted to 10 percent, and it continued to hover below that figure until the mid-1980s,[25] when America was in the midst of a recession. Today, we call it an *economic slowdown,* a *dot-com bust,* or a *mild recession,* and the starting salary advantage of college graduates is again below 10 percent. Welcome once more to the wonderful world of college-educated waiters and taxicab drivers! Welcome to the world of a shrinking middle class, a world where education counts much less than it did in the age of meritocracy—when I graduated college.

Mounting Debt and Declining Mobility

What do all of these facts and figures mean? They hint that Americans are overeducated relative to job opportunities and that education is no longer the great panacea or a guarantee of the good life in America. Market factors other than education weigh in and influence job opportunities and economic outcomes. Even worse, ordinary students have had to borrow their way to a bachelor's or a graduate degree; in 2003 the median debt was $18,000 for a person graduating from college and $45,000 for a person completing graduate school,[26] meaning that more than 50 percent of such debt can be considered unmanageable. With short-term loans and plastic interest rates between 10 and 18 percent, the cumulative effect is that merely keeping one's head above water, rather than getting ahead, has become top priority for Americans between the ages of 21 and 34. Moreover, many of the so-called good jobs for college graduates are found in the big cities, where rents are the highest and young college graduates have to devote nearly half of their take home pay to rent. Pursuing the American Dream today, taking a shot at middle-class bliss, is not a "slam dunk" but requires serious capital up front or a safety net provided by parents; even then, there is no guarantee the investment will get you where you expect to go.

As Harvard law professor Elizabeth Warren puts it in her book *The Two Income Trap,* the next generation is starting its economic race 50 yards behind the starting line. Once you have accumulated debt, "the debt takes on a life of its own" and for years continues to take a bite out of your paycheck. Indeed, the middle class is not only shrinking, but it is also struggling. For example, the sky-rocketing of college tuition seems unchecked; tuition rose 47 percent at public four-year colleges and 42 percent at private four-year colleges in the last decade.[27] The good news is that if you study education and are willing to teach in the inner city, you might find a teacher education program that pays part or all of your tuition. And you can always join the military and have Uncle Sam pay for your college education. No wonder, then, that the rank-and-file of our teaching corps and our military is mostly members of the lower and working classes trying to get ahead and realize some segment of the economic pie, an American Dream that is evaporating for an increasing percentage of ordinary Americans. Of course, there is just enough truth left in the idea of the American Dream, of the self-made man or woman, to keep the masses sedated and believing in the system.

Interclass mobility is frozen more than we think, less fluid than the phrase "rags to riches" might suggest. As many as 85 percent of American families remain in the same class or have moved up or down one quintile three decades later. Putting this statistic a different way, some 61 percent of families in the lowest quintile in income in 1967 were in the same bottom level in 2002. In reverse, 59 percent of families in the highest fifth in income during the same 35-year period remained at the same level.[28] Statistically, first-generation immigrants have the best chance for upward mobility. Although they may no longer arrive with "rags," they usually start at the lowest or next-lowest point on the totem pole—and thus have more chance for improvement (a simple regression to the mean) than the average American. Through sweat and hard work, they are able to succeed in one generation—doing better than "American Americans" who have been embedded in the social system. The reason is that immigrants are rarely burdened by the culture of poverty that inflicts great social and psychological damage over generations; they are a self-selective group, highly motivated by the fact that they have uprooted themselves and come to a new land to start a new life. That said, American immigrants, as a group, have greater zeal and thus education has greater impact on them than on their American counterparts who know how to work the "freebie" system and/or who have various safety nets (Mom and Dad). If we exclude the immigrant population from our calculations, interclass mobility is either frozen or limited to one quintile upwards (or downwards) for 95 percent of American families—what I call our "struggling class."

To get into finger pointing about heredity or environment or about the influence of education on economic outcomes, or, in reverse, economic status on education, reflects our misconceptions about the nature of intelligence, talent, and merit. You can be very intelligent and talented in all sorts of ways but be handicapped by class (and race), or you can be relatively stupid and over your head at your job but be saved by the rank and privilege of class: CEOs, generals, and politicians are the best examples of the latter alternative, especially if their rise to the top had something to do with family connections or family fortunes. Some of us refer to the latter alternative as part of the "Peter Principle." I call it the "Idiot Principle" after John Hoover's book *How to Work for an Idiot*. His contention is that idiots inhabit levels of the workplace. Despite their education, they cause organizational waste and chaos and have a tendency to chew up and eliminate talented people.[29] Most of us are forced to work for idiots for portions of our careers. Just listen to teachers in the cafeteria or lounge describe their supervisors or principals; they tend to complain much more than they compliment these administrators.

Money and Morality

"Money, money money. Always sunny. In a rich man's world." These are the words of Abba, four (now retired) 1970s rock stars from Sweden who summed up life in a capitalist world. The four recently turned down $1 billion to reassemble as a group and perform 100 rock concerts around the world. One billion dollars split four ways would mean that each member of Abba would probably rank within the top 500 richest American households and perhaps the top 1000 households worldwide.

Abba's refusal of $1 billion seems unusual in a world driven by money, in which the overwhelming majority of us do have a price. It is worth noting that at issue here is not morality, rather it is ethics, which overlaps at one point with morality. The difference between ethics and morality is a philosophical quibble and depends on which sources you read and how you personally view the world. Right now, most of us would agree that there is a moral vacuum in our schools and so-

ciety, although conservative and liberal thinkers would differ over the causes and solutions.

Given the competitive nature of our society, there is a tendency to cheat—to wink at dishonesty—and to get ahead and win at all costs. Given high-stakes testing and the nature of grading in schools, which eventually affect who gets tracked into what program and who gets accepted into what college, there is a tendency among students to cheat. According to Nel Noddings, retired Stanford professor of education, "Many students deny that cheating is wrong" and teachers fail "to protect students who are committed to fair competition."[30] A 2001 study at Duke University indicates that about 75 percent of college students acknowledge some academic dishonesty. Why? These are typical responses to that question: "There are times when you need a little help." "Just about everyone is doing it." "You need to do it to keep the playing field even."[31]

We can blame the system and argue that it fosters a competitive culture that leads to winning at all costs. Or, we can blame society, which accepts the brutal law of survival of the smartest and most cunning. We can also blame parents for creating pressure to succeed, starting before their children enter school, when they begin lap reading and introduce their children to alphabet games in order to create super-smart toddlers on the road to Harvard or Yale.

The bottom line is that cheating reflects moral laxity, and competition reflects the desire to win—our heroes and stars compete and cheat, and the rest of us wink and nod. Athletes take drugs to enhance their performance because the result is higher salaries and more endorsements for more money. Politicians lie and are often caught with their fingers in the cookie jar or hiding stuffed shoeboxes in their closets and safe deposit boxes. Judges are bought, and their decisions are often based on politics, not the law. Legislators are often influenced more by lobbyists who represent big business, not by the people who elected them. The clergy steal children's innocence one moment, creating fear and guilt for the rest of those children's lives, and preach the gospel the next moment. Money managers are paid in full for investing retirees' pension plans, but the retirees are not always paid in full.[32] CEOs invent new accounting techniques to disguise losses, then proceed to cheat their employees and the general public out of billions of dollars while they become millions of dollars richer.

The goal should be to work for the common public good so that all of us can improve our quality of life, rather than to focus only on "money, money, money" at the expense or exploitation of those who run a slower race or are not as shrewd or as capable. What is evolving in American society, starting with preschools and continuing into the workplace, is a small group of people able to get an edge, play the system, and "screw" others in order to win the race.

Once upon a time, not long ago, when there was no plastic money, heart transplants, or satellite systems, when *Ozzie and Harriet* and *The Andy Griffith Show* dominated television air waves, when children showed respect for adult authority, cheating was a "no-no" and there was a moral code that guided behavior. Given the modern world we live in, with the Internet and instant communication, fast foods and fast cars, along with sex, drugs, and MTV, the youth of America have little connection with the past—what some kids might label as the "Stone Age" or what intellectuals writing about morality might refer to as the "pre–post modern age" or the "pre-Prozac era," or what Harvard professor David Reisman, in his book *The Lonely Crowd,* some fifty years ago dubbed the "inner-directed" society. We live in an age in which materialism, conspicuous consumption, and greed rule. This is an era in which deviancy—evidenced by new art and music and new models or heroes to emulate (such as Ludacris, Terrell Owens, Rod Strickland, Eminem, Madonna, Howard Stern, Cher, and Monica Lewinsky)—is considered normal or cutting edge, though traditional folks might say most of it is a little perverse, or at least stretching the boundaries of decency.

Can moral philosophy guide children (and adults) in their personal (or professional) lives? Educators are often uneasy about imposing certain values on students, and liberals are often worried that moral thinking leads to religious and faith-based thinking, which they feel should be kept out of the schools. The consequences of ignoring moral issues, under the guise of separation of church and state, are the growth of schooling alternatives and choices that meet the needs of people and the valuing of shrewdness and strength as more important than honesty and hard work.

Let us remember why our Founding Fathers risked their lives and signed the Declaration of Independence: for the natural rights of the people. But equality of political rights does not substitute for the decline in equal opportunity to share in the nation's wealth. Our ethics of wealth is simple: The son or daughter of a laborer can rise to become governor, Supreme Court judge, or president, and the son or grandson, daughter or granddaughter of a millionaire can descend to the working class. That kind of mobility is accepted in American folklore. But on a more realistic level, we now live in a society in which our moral compass has been distorted and even sidelined by money making, the common person has been beaten down by the money class, and the small businessman has been trounced by big business. This all leads to an increased struggling class. The muckrakers of the early twentieth century wrote about how the titans of industry and banking decided to bypass the laws of the land in order to get rich. Perhaps there was too much temptation; too many weak, bad men; too few strong, good ones. Nonetheless, at the turn of the twentieth century, popularists and muckrakers such as Henry Lloyd, in *Wealth Against Commonwealth,* Frank Norris, in *The Octopus* and *The Pit,* and John Dos Passos, in *The Big Money,* described the topsy-turvy Gilded Age, when the idea was to outsmart and outswindle your competitors before they did it to you and to raid the public treasury before someone else cut a deal with a politician and ran off with the loot.

Not much has changed today; in fact, since the narcissistic Gilded Age of the Reagan 1980s and Clinton 1990s, we can say that economic excesses and abuses are multiplying: People are now concerned about investing in Wall Street, and not Main Street; the rich are getting richer, and the nonrich are getting poorer relative to the rich (that is, income and wealth gaps are widening) and working more jobs and longer hours than the previous generation in order to survive and keep up their standard of living. Greed is still considered good. Wall Street buccaneers are still running wild, touting this stock or that stock, and scholars and money managers alike are writing books on how to invest and become the next millionaire. Whereas the populist agitation of the late nineteenth century and the muckraker reform movement of the early twentieth century were about the money class sucking the blood out of the agrarian and labor classes, now it can be said that the Ken Lays (Enron), Bernard Ebbers (World Com) and Jack Grubmans (Salomon Smith Barney) of the world have sucked the heart and soul out of the average person who had his or her retirement or pension money, job, or child's college tuition tied to some stock or mutual fund that went south or even disappeared from the charts. It's the heyday of the Gilded Age all over again, but with one more downside—the general public (more than 50 percent of Americans) is currently involved in Wall Street investing.

The Widening Gap between the Super-Rich and the Non-Rich

Apparently, the lessons about class differences and about money and morality are not the kind of lessons Americans want to learn. It's more comforting to our morale and spirit to believe in the American Dream, as well as to deny that this nation is becoming a financial oligarchy, where the top 1 percent (2.8 million people) received 13 percent of the national income in 2001. These individuals' after-tax income increased 201 percent between 1979 and 2000, while that of the middle fifth increased 15 percent, and that of the bottom fifth rose 9 percent.[33] The time has come to get real; the vast majority of Americans, about 90 to 95 percent of us, have become big economic losers in the last twenty years, the same period in which American education expenditures for grades K–12 increased from $86.9 billion to $324 billion (from $4554 per student to $7086 per student in 2000 dollars), college enrollment rates increased from 50.4 percent of high school graduates to 62.4 percent, and college enrollments (colleges and universities) increased from 8 million to 15 million students.[34]

In short, we have allowed the government to ignore income gaps between the super-rich and ordinary Americans, and by remaining indifferent, we are witnessing the decline of American democracy in favor of an oligarchy—big government allied with big business. Failure to understand that the past and the present differ in terms of class and opportunity could consign us to a terrible future. Our standard of living is likely to worsen as the income gap widens between the super-rich and rest of Americans—thus driving up the cost for basic items related to healthcare, housing, education, and so forth and reducing the quality of life for the vast majority of Americans. There is no good reason why a trip to the ballpark to see the "American pasttime," should cost a family of four sitting in the grandstands, 300 feet from home plate, eating some burgers and sodas, 40 to 50 percent of the weekly take-home pay of the average working person (making $35,000 a year).

Another factor may be in play. Fear of a tax that goes after the rich doesn't sit well with Americans generally. Americans don't seem to have problems with super-rich people who are self-made, even when they can pass their wealth to the next generation. We seem to be okay with people like Rockefeller, Kennedy, and Bush and don't think about what "side" deals were made and who was hurt to amass such fortunes. We merely refer to their descendants as part of the "lucky sperm club," not recognizing that inherited wealth under capitalism is not much different from the hereditary aristocracy of the Old World, exactly what our Founding Fathers despised and revolted against.

Now, if I've made you feel uncomfortable or second-best, if I have put a dent in or a damper on your idea of the American Dream, then I beg your indulgence. Education is no longer going to reduce inequality on a large scale in any marked or dramatic way; it is not the great equalizer that it was from the days of Horace Mann up through the Cold War and the age of meritocracy. But there is hope. There is still opportunity to devise income-sharing systems, to reduce the rewards of inherited wealth and even out the unfair chances of life. Christopher Jencks, in his 1971 book *Inequality,* was probably right in calling for income redistribution. Schools cannot equalize the social and cultural advantages that exist between classes. Americans have the vote and thus the ability to effect a peaceful change in the government and tax system that would reduce economic inequality, especially the extremely lopsided wealth of the top 1 to 5 percent of American households. However, up to 45 percent of qualified voters seem unable to find the voting booths during presidential elections, suggesting that our own indifference is slowly changing our land to *a foreign country*—a metaphoric equivalent of our vanishing democracy and its middle class, which is the backbone of that democracy.

In a period when meritocracy is waning, or is defined in vague ways that reflect not any objective criteria but a point of view, or when grade inflation makes it impossible to distinguish between A, B, and C students, the value of an education is reduced. Equality between occupations is nearly impossible in a society based on supply and demand, division of labor, and other market conditions. But when inherited wealth allows the same people, even incompetent people, to get most of the rewards, and then to multiply their wealth because assets and investments are taxed at a lower rate than is the income that ordinary people earn through their work, then the system becomes increasingly skewed. Not only is upward mobility hampered, but also the vitality of the society is at stake.

I do not like dividing the United States into the capitalist class and the working class, or the super-rich and the non-rich, because of the label that comes with this ideology, but fear of rampaging capitalism and inequality suggests that regulation is needed. I am not a fan of Eugene Debs, the railroad unionist from Terre Haute, Indiana, and the twentieth-century architect of American socialism, and therefore I am not advocating a boxing match with rival fighters (government versus business, the common folks versus the rich, red versus blue voters) in opposite corners. I'm appealing for the rights of small people to be heard and appreciated, as in the tradition reaching from Jefferson to FDR, JFK, and LBJ.

Sadly, most of us enrolled in Education 101 or History 101 fail to grasp that we are approaching a surreal dislocation or fundamental shift in our democratic idealism. There is a "point of view," and the key phrase here implies either a work of fiction or a serious point in our history: We are at the crossroads—not in terms of progressive education (that was Boyd Bode's dictum in 1938), but in terms of whether this nation, envisioned by its Founding Fathers as the new Athens and a country dearest to the Enlightenment, has lost or is about to lose its reason and humanism. Have we really become a foreign country in our own land? Are we a lost time, a lost generation, a lost people—strangers in our own land? Are we too short-sighted to recognize or just too plain selfish to admit that we are keeping down all the people who cannot successfully compete or who run a swift race in second place, or worse? Are we not undercutting the value of education and undervaluing our working- and middle-class populations? I leave you with the twin question: What is the value of an education, and what is happening to the middle class when a teacher can barely buy a bungalow, but some captain of industry or entertainment or sports figure lives a more luxurious life than the land barons of the aristocratic Old World that we Americans had hoped to break from in the democratic New World?

In a break with normal textbook practice, I have spent some time chatting with you, or what Lawrence Summers calls engaging in "plain talk." My voice has been quite personal, but I have avoided the trivia, such as my favorite ice cream flavor. I have tried to focus on the big picture, the ebb and flow of macroeconomic and education trends, rather than crowd the pages with figures so as to resemble a TV screen full of obscure sports stats or a CNN business report accompanied by a continuous scroll of NASDAQ stock prices. Having gone out of my way to avoid tiny pieces of information, I have touched on an important theme, the big picture involving class, inequality, and education.

Right now, the mobility ladder in our economic system is missing several steps; it needs major repair, and I doubt whether teachers or schools can fix the ladder while our society is manipulated by a few powerful, rich people. We are at the moment at which knowledgeable people and groups that comprise the leadership in business and government must hold up their bargain with American society for the common good. One of the obstacles to the full development of a democracy, noted by Thomas Jefferson and Horace

Mann, and later by John Gardner and Jonathan Kozol, is that we have not learned to support and make the most of bright and talented students who begin life in an impoverished situation, or even in a working-class environment.

Then, there is the flip side to the issue, involving a mental leap, an untidy subjective thought, and a sense of gloom and doom. Having once embraced the pervasive utopian American Dream, I now have doubts and believe it is dwindling for most of our children and grandchildren. Here at the end, I have memories of *Moby Dick,* which I read when I was a much younger man. The images have been transformed over time. I now feel an unsettling glimpse of Melville's whale circling around us, slowly gaining momentum in the deep bottomless water. "Our fate awaits us . . . and there is no escaping it," like Ahab's destiny. Now look toward the horizon, while you still can, and see the fault lines and cracks rippling on the water surface. (The metaphors here are the economic faults and social cracks of society.) Beyond the horizon is the declining sun—the long, cold night—and the whale is still circling and coming closer. We can hear and feel the unending anxieties of those who, if we continue to undercut and devaluate them, will, alas, become nothing but statistics.

ENDNOTES

1. Addams could be dubbed a "social democrat," although the term did not exist until the 1920s. Harrington was a social democrat and is best known for his book *The Other America,* which helped spark the War on Poverty.

2. Darwin conceived human nature as plastic, capable of adapting to the environment and improving it. The philosophical and economic interpretation of Darwin by conservative thinkers advocated the growth of full individuality. The smart person would adjust to changing needs and conditions, rising above the competition and crushing the little fellow. In a highly competitive social/economic system, students in school are groomed to succeed; moreover, they are sorted and tracked into programs based on their competitive natures and abilities. Some students are earmarked to go to Harvard, and others fall to the wayside and drop out of school or graduate as functional illiterates. The "sorting ma-

chine," what some people might refer to as an aspect of Social Darwinism, merely perpetuates prior class distinctions, because advantaged children have greater chances of going to Harvard from the start and disadvantaged children have greater chances of failing in school.

3. See Allan C. Ornstein, *Teaching and Schooling in America* (Boston: Allyn and Bacon, 2004).

4. "Nightly Business Report," April 23, 2004. Also see Jack Rasmus, *The War at Home: The Corporate Offensive in America from Reagan to Bush* (San Ramon, CA: Kyklos Productions, 2005).

5. In 1910 only 13.5 percent of persons age 25 and older had a high school diploma or higher degree, compared to 83.4 percent in 2000. See *Educational Digest 1971* (Washington, D.C.: U.S. Government Printing Office, 1972), Table 11, p. 9; *Education Digest 2000* (Washington, D.C.: U.S. Government Printing Office, 2001), Table 8, p. 17.

6. Elsewhere I have argued that Dewey was the most influential educator of the twentieth century.

7. "Income in the United States 2002," *Census Population Report* (September 2003), Tables A–3, A–4, pp. 25, 26–28.

8. "When Greed Was a Virtue and Regulation the Enemy." *New York Times,* July 21, 2002, sect. 4, p. 14.

9. Daniel Bell, *The Coming of Post-Industrial Society* (New York: Basic Books, 1973), p. 108.

10. C. Wright Mills, *The Power Elite* (New York: Oxford University Press, 1956); Max Weber, *Economy and Society* (New York: Bedminster Press, 1968).

11. Richard J. Herrnstein, *IQ with Meritocracy* (Boston: Little, Brown, 1971), pp. 45, 53.

12. Ibid., p. 54.

13. John W. Gardner, *Excellence: Can We Be Equal and Excellent Too?* Rev. Ed. (New York: W. W. Norton, 1984), pp. 82, 85.

14. Thomas Jefferson, *Notes on the State of Virginia* (originally published 1782) (Chapel Hill: University of North Carolina Press, 1955), p. 146.

15. William C. Symonds, "Leaving Harvard Greener," *Business Week,* January 24, 2005, p. 44.

16. Lawrence Summers, "Plain Talk from Larry Summers," *Business Week,* November 8, 2004, p. 73.

17. Rachel E. Silverman, "Looser Trust Laws Lure $100 Billion," *Wall Street Journal,* February 16, 2005, p. D1.

18. "Facts about Income That Every American Should Know." http://www.osjspm.org/101-income/htm; *The State of Working America 2002/2003* (Washington, D.C.: U.S. Government Printing Office, 2004).

19. Assuming a 40-hour work week, this amounts to $16,640 per year, which was below the poverty line ($18,850) for a family of four in 2004. See *Federal Register,* February 13, 2004, pp. 7336–7338.

20. "How Many People Are Unemployed in the U.S.?" *Pacific Views,* December 29, 2003. Originally published in the *Los Angeles Times.* Also see Rasmus, *The War at Home: The Corporate Offensive in America from Reagan to Bush.*

21. The number one American employer is Wal-Mart. The average salary for full-time employees is less than $7.00 an hour. One third are part-time employees—limited to less than 28 hours of work per week—and are not eligible for benefits. The rapid turnover—70 percent of employees leave within the first year—is due to a lack of recognition and inadequate pay. http://www.pbs.org/itvs/sorewars/stores3.html

22. As many as 48 percent of retirees are forced into early retirement. Of this group, 38 percent were for health reasons, 16 percent for job elimination, 10 percent for a buyout, and 7 percent for problems in the work environment. As many as 43 percent of retirees feel they are in a precarious position, and another 25 percent have serious concerns about their standard of living worsening. http://www.asec.org/rcs_key.htm

23. *Digest of Education Statistics 2000* (Washington, D.C.: U.S. Government Printing Office, 2001), Tables 172–173, pp. 201–202.

24. Richard B. Freeman, *The Over-Educated American* (New York: Academic Press, 1976), p. 18.

25. Richard B. Freeman and J. Herbert Holloman, "Declining Value of College Going," *Change* (September 1975), Table 1, p. 25; George L. Perry and James Tobin, *Economic Events, Ideas and Policies* (Washington, D.C.: Brookings Institution, 2000).

26. "Lou Dobbs Report," May 11, 2004; Brandan I. Koerner, "Generation Debt: The New Economics of Young" (March 17–23, 2004), pp. 1–8.

27. Elizabeth Warren and Amelia Warren Tyagi, *The Two Income Trap* (New York: Basic Books, 2003).

28. See Paul Krugman, "Democracy At Risk," *New York Times,* January 23, 2004; Krugman, "Jobs, Jobs, Jobs," *New York Times,* February 10, 2004; Krugman, "Promises, Promises," *New York Times,* March 9, 2004; and *The State of Working America* 2002–2003.

29. John Hoover, *How to Work for an Idiot: Survive and Thrive . . . Without Killing Your Boss* (New York: Career Press, 2004).

30. Nel Noddings, *The Challenge to Care in Schools* (New York: Teachers College Press, Columbia University, 1992), p. 101.

31. Glen C. Altschinler, "Battling the Cheats," *New York Times Education Life* (January 7, 2001), p. 15.

32. For example, in the years between 1999 and 2003, pension professionals who ran United's pension plan received $125 million in fees, but the plan lost $10.2 billion. Because of the federal government's pension insurance, the retirees will only lose $3.4 billion. Uncle Sam will foot the rest of the bill—meaning the U.S. taxpayers, you and me. See Mary W. Walsh, "How Wall Street Wrecked United's Pension," *New York Times,* July 31, 2005, sect. 3, pp. 1, 8.

33. http://www.osjspm.org/101, "CBPP Calculation, 1979–2000," *Congressional Budget Office* (Washington, D.C.: U.S. Government Printing Office, 2002); and "Income in the United States: 2002," Table A-3, pp. 25–26.

34. *Digest of Education Statistics 2000,* Tables 163, 170, 171–172; pp. 180–181, 192, 200–201.

DISCUSSION QUESTIONS

1. Does education still provide an avenue to the good life and a ladder for social mobility in the United States?

2. Are business values inherently inconsistent with those of education, or can the two be reconciled?

3. Do schools primarily sort students according to social class, or do they serve as an equalizer of differences?

4. In your experience, is the United States indeed becoming a nation of "haves" and "have-nots"?

5. Do educators have an obligation to address this emerging wealth gap? Is so, what can be done?

PRO-CON CHART 6

Should parental choice be a major consideration in determining where students attend school?

PRO	CON
1. The public school system is a monolithic structure that fosters middle-class conformity.	1. School choice will promote a dual-class educational system—schools for the rich and schools for the poor.
2. Public schooling perpetuates the existing power structure, including the subordinating effects of class, caste, and gender.	2. Parental choice will breed intolerance for diversity and will further religious, racial, and socioeconomic isolation.
3. The reduced quality of public education necessitates that parents be given options in order to locate better learning environments.	3. Transporting students out of neighborhoods is costly for school districts and is time-consuming for students.
4. Increasing choices means expanding educational opportunities for low-income and minority students.	4. Choice may not increase equity. In fact, it may lead to further segregation of low-income and minority students.
5. Competitive schools should stimulate statewide efforts to implement school reform.	5. Choice is not a solution for securing adequate funding, upgrading teachers' pedagogical skills, or reforming education.

CASE STUDY 6

School Board Debates Bilingual Education Program

"There can be no debate," demanded school board member Ricardo Del Rotberg. "Public education monies should be used for educating students in English only. Bilingual education is poor use of the community's tax dollars." Following this fiery opening statement, people in the gallery sat momentarily stunned. The entire community knew that this school year was sure to be contentious. No one doubted that the school board members were deeply divided over the issue of providing bilingual education to immigrant children.

After a long silence, board member Evita Ellmano moved toward the microphone. She reminded the board that the number of immigrant children attending district schools was increasing dramatically each year. She cited research showing that children who were given several years of instruction in their native language learned English faster and were successful academically. Ellmano also read results from the district's test scores, which demonstrated that students for whom English was not the dominant language lagged significantly behind other students academically. Del Rotberg retorted that it was his belief that multilingual education is an ill-founded practice that seeks to instill pride in students with low self-esteem. He also suggested that the school board lobby for legislation declaring English to be the nation's official language.

School board president Sarah Turner could no longer remain silent. She reminded board members that schools are obligated to help all students to live up to their fullest potential and to provide an education in their native language. Turner remarked that schools must embrace and value the traditions and cultures of all students. Moreover, she commented that bilingual education had become a target for people who opposed immigration. Finally, she stated that all teachers should be competent enough to teach their subject matter in at least one foreign language. Immediately, the teachers in the audience roared with protest. Turner pounded her gavel for nearly 8 minutes to restore order. Meanwhile, several security personnel came to the meeting room to encourage calmness.

Consider the following questions:

1. What information should be obtained to clarify the facts reflective of both positions?

2. What members of the community should become involved in discussions related to bilingual education programs?

3. Should teachers be expected to retool their pedagogical skills and learn to teach their subject matter in a foreign language? Why? Why not?

4. Are there programmatic alternatives to providing bilingual education to immigrant children?

5. Do schools have a responsibility in maintaining the ethnic culture of immigrant children?

CREDITS

Subject Index